THE volumes of the University of Michigan Studies and Publications are published by authority of the Board of Regents under the direction of the Executive Board of the Graduate School. The contributors are chiefly, but not exclusively, members of the faculties or graduates of the University. The expense is borne in part by gifts, in part by appropriations of the Board of Regents. A list of volumes already published or in preparation is given at the end of this volume. The other volumes in this Series are listed on page vi.

University of Michigan Publications

HISTORY AND POLITICAL SCIENCE

VOLUME VIII

THE LOW COUNTRIES AND THE HUNDRED YEARS' WAR, 1326–1347

THE LOW COUNTRIES AND THE HUNDRED YEARS' WAR, 1326-1347

BY

HENRY STEPHEN LUCAS

ANN ARBOR
UNIVERSITY OF MICHIGAN
1929

To

PROFESSOR HENRI PIRENNE

IN ADMIRATION OF HIS HISTORICAL SCHOLARSHIP

PREFACE

TWENTY-SEVEN years ago Professor Eugène Déprez gave to the world his important study on the opening of the Hundred Years' War. Tracing with minute detail the diplomatic relations between the courts of the Plantagenet and Valois monarchies between 1328 and 1342, he was the first historian to set forth in adequate fashion the political factors which produced a war that was to end only with the definitive expulsion of the English from Guienne in the middle of the fifteenth century. The conflict grew out of the fact that the Valois monarchy followed in the footsteps of the Capetian kings who had ever sought to concentrate in the person of the monarch all the functions of the state and thus inevitably created bitter feelings with the English court over Guienne. In his treatment of this theme, Professor Déprez limited himself to the relations between England and France and to the efforts of the popes who anxiously labored to prevent a desperate conflict between two of the major secular powers of Christendom. The connections of the princes of the Low Countries with this struggle were treated only incidentally and without any serious study of the sources.

Many writers have occupied themselves with the history of the various states of the Low Countries during this period, but nearly all of them have been concerned with topics of rather limited scope. General surveys were usually based upon inadequate study of the sources. Thus Professor James Mackinnon's *History of Edward III, 1327–1377,* treated the problem as it concerned the Low Countries without much study of the numerous sources printed in books and articles dealing with the history of such principalities as Flanders, Brabant, Hainault, Holland, Zeeland, Friesland, Guelders, Namur, Luxemburg, Tournai, Cambrai, Liège, and Utrecht. The lack of any such treatment has inspired me to attempt this study.

My purpose throughout these pages has ever been to let the argument proceed chiefly from the charters without much regard to opinions of earlier writers except when their views seemed to me fully justified in the light of the teaching of indisputably authentic sources. In this way I have been able to emancipate myself from a variety of misconceptions, which will be apparent to those acquainted with the literature of this subject. I have sought constantly to avoid ideas which others have taken directly or indirectly from Froissart who, except in so far as he drew upon John le Bel or may have received some information from his friend, John of Hainault, cannot be regarded as a trustworthy witness of the events recounted in these pages. In general only those statements of the chroniclers which appeared to have a very strong probability of truth when tested by authentic documents have been allowed to influence the argument. It is for this reason that Villani and Froissart, who have so often been accorded the highest confidence, have been abandoned for a number of less known but vastly more reliable chroniclers such as Hocsem, John le Bel, John Boendale, John Bernier (the Bourgeois of Valenciennes), and Willelmus Procurator, and the anonymous *Chronique de Tournai*, the *Chronicon Comitum Flandrensium*, the *Istore et Croniques de Flandres*, and the *Chronique Parisienne Anonyme*.

Much new material might have been secured from a protracted study at the Public Record Office in London. The task of examining that enormous collection of documents was obviously altogether too great, and I finally decided, for the present at least, to limit my search to the archives of the Continent, particularly the Archives Nationales in Paris, the Archives du Départment du Nord in Lille, which proved to be especially rich for my purposes, the Archives du Royaume at Brussels, and those in Mons, Ghent, and Bruges. The lamentable loss of the extraordinarily rich collections in Ypres and Arras during the late war has been a serious handicap in treating certain parts of the account which will probably never be known in detail. Some valuable data were found in the Rijksarchief in Zeeland at Middelburg and in the Rijksarchief at The Hague.

It was my original intention to begin this study with the relations of Edward I to the Low Countries; but as the vast mass of materials accumulated and the need of a protracted visit to the archives of England appeared more and more necessary, it was finally deemed best to publish the second half first. No better dividing point could be found than the significant events connected with the marriage of Edward III and Philippa of Hainault. The great dearth of literature in English dealing with the important rôle of the Low Countries during the Middle Ages has led me to attempt in the first chapter to give a general survey of some of the salient social, political, and economic factors in the history of the various principalities now included in Belgium, Luxemburg, and The Netherlands. This chapter, therefore, serves the dual function of a summary and an introduction, which may make it appear unduly long to some readers.

Regarding the spelling of place names, I have found it quite impossible to attain to strict uniformity. It is obvious that in French, German, and English names there is no difficulty at all; but in Flemish and Dutch names the problem is complicated by the fact that the English, French, and Germans have usually spelled them in various ways. When there is a well-established usage in English I have preferred not to follow local custom; hence such forms as Guelders, Hainault, Brussels, Antwerp, Ypres, Bruges, Ghent, and Flushing. In nearly all other cases I have followed local usage; but as this is difficult to determine in some instances, I may be open to the charge of being somewhat arbitrary. In all such cases the various spellings have been noted in the index. A similar criticism might be made in regard to names of people. Such forms as *van, de, le,* and *uten* have been spelled without capitals.

A number of important books and articles appeared too late to be of effective use in the final stages of revision. The third and fourth volumes of Professor Tout's very important study [1] of the administrative history of England did not come into my hands until after the manuscript had gone to press; they would have been especially valuable in determining the spelling of some of

[1] T. F. Tout, *Chapters in the Administrative History of Mediaeval England; the Wardrobe, the Chambers, and the Small Seals,* Vols. III and IV (London, 1928).

the English proper names. Although it appeared in 1927, Dr. Henri Laurent's article [2] on the political relations of the dukes of Brabant and the Valois monarchy was not accessible until the first chapters were already set up. I made no effort to change the references in the fourteenth chapter to the documents found in the Archives Nationales in Paris, of which excellent transcriptions were printed by him. Most unfortunate is the fact that all references to the chronicler Hocsem are to the now antiquated edition of Chapeaville's. It was impossible to secure a copy of the late Professor Godefroid Kurth's edition [3] in time to change the numerous citations. To these titles may be added the recent valuable articles from the hand of Dr. H. J. Smit on the origins of the commerce of the counties of Holland and Zeeland,[4] and Professor Pirenne on the general significance of the Low Countries in the economic history of medieval Europe.[5] Chotzen's interesting article about the activities of the Flemings before Calais in 1346 and 1347 [6] came into my hands only when the page proofs were ready to be returned to the printer.

My efforts and researches have been supported and encouraged by a large number of people. I wish to thank the Educational Foundation of the Commission for Relief in Belgium and the American Council of Learned Societies for their generous financial

[2] H. Laurent, "Les Conventions de Saint-Quentin (Juin, 1347). Contribution à l'Histoire de la première phase de la Guerre de Cent Ans dans les Pays-Bas," *BCRH*, XCI (1927), 89–180.

[3] G. Kurth, *La Chronique de Jean de Hocsem* (Bruxelles, 1927).

[4] H. J. Smit, "Handel en Scheepvaart in het Noordzeegebied gedurende de 13e Eeuw. Bijdrage tot de Kennis van de Opkomst van den Hollandschen en Zeeuwschen Handel," *Bijdragen voor Vaderlandsche Geschiedenis en Oudheidkunde*, 6th Ser., VII (1928), 161–204.

[5] H. Pirenne, "The Place of the Netherlands in the Economic History of Mediaeval Europe," *Economic History Review*, January, 1929, pp. 20–40.

[6] T. M. Chotzen, "De Vlamingen voor Calais (1346–1347)," *Revue Belge de Philologie et d'Histoire*, VII (1928), 1485–1492. Other articles might be added here: Coenen, "De laatste Dagen van het Graafschap Loon," *Limburg* VIII (1927); A. Hansay, "La Sigillographie des Comtes de Looz," *Verzamelde Opstellen uitgegeven door den Geschied- en Oudheidkundige Studiekring te Hasselt* (1928); H. A. Poelman, "De buitenlandsche Handel van Groningen in Verband met den Frieschen Handel gedurende de Twaalfde en Dertiende Eeuw," *Historische Opstellen opgedragen aan Prof. Dr. H. Brugmans, 1904–7 Maart–1929* (Amsterdam, 1929), pp. 9–21; H. J. Smit, "Amsterdams Handel met Engeland in de Middeleeuwen," *ibid.*, pp. 53–68.

aid. To Professor Henri Pirenne, who was especially kind to me during my sojourn as a student at the University of Ghent and took a lively interest in the main ideas of this study, I owe a debt for which my gratitude and acknowledgment are but a poor compensation. Particularly encouraging was the kindly advice given by Professor Peter J. Blok and Professor Albert Eekhof while I was a student at the University of Leiden. Among the archivists I am under great obligation to M. Max Bruchet of Lille who, with his assistant M. Flament, was quite eager to help me secure copies of documents. At Mons, M. Poncelet showed a similar interest. Professor Brugman at The Hague and the staffs of assistants at Middelburg, Ghent, and Bruges evinced the finest disposition to place everything at my disposal. Special thanks are due to M. Germain of Brussels for his ready assistance in reading partly decayed documents. Among Americans I especially wish to name Professor Earle W. Dow of the University of Michigan whose interest and kindly encouragement were ever a source of real inspiration. It was he who placed the manuscript before the committee appointed by the Dean of the Graduate School and urged them to accept it for publication. To these gentlemen I am greatly indebted for the honor of having this study appear under the auspices of the University of Michigan.

Since this study was executed largely on the west coast of America, far from the Low Countries, and without the benefit of a large library, I have been greatly dependent upon the co-operation of distant libraries and booksellers. The firm of Martinus Nijhoff at The Hague has helped me most effectively. The libraries of such universities as California, Stanford, Michigan, Minnesota, Chicago, and Harvard, as well as the Library of Congress, have shown a remarkable willingness to lend books which I could not possibly have purchased at the moment when I most needed them. In the revision of the manuscript I am under great obligation to my friend and colleague, Mr. Cecil Eden Quainton. For criticism and aid in revision and grammatical construction many thanks are due to the patient persistence of my wife. To Dr. Eugene S. McCartney I owe my sincerest gratitude for reading of proof and intelligent direction in the multitude of perplexing problems attending the printing of a book of this nature.

Finally, I feel that the careful work of the members of the staff of the Plimpton Press should not go unmentioned. The accuracy with which their part of the task was done greatly lessened the burden of seeing the volume through the press.

H. S. L.

Easter, 1929
University of Washington
Seattle, Washington

CONTENTS

MAP

THE LOW COUNTRIES AND ADJACENT PARTS AT THE
OPENING OF THE HUNDRED YEARS' WAR *At end of book*

ABBREVIATIONS

BCRH	Bulletin de la Commission Royale d'Histoire
BEC	Bibliothèque de l'École de Chartes
CCB	Collection de Chroniques Belges
CCR	Calendar of Close Rolls
CDI	Collection des Documents Inédits
CFR	Calendar of Fine Rolls
CPR	Calendar of Patent Rolls
Foedera	Rymer, Th., *Foedera, Conventiones, Literae, et Cujuscunque Generis Acta Publica*

THE LOW COUNTRIES AND THE HUNDRED YEARS' WAR, 1326–1347

CHAPTER I

THE LOW COUNTRIES IN 1325

i. Geography and Economics   ii. Political Divisions   iii. Political Relationships.

I. Geography and Economics

THE lands situated around the estuaries of the Schelde, the Meuse, and the Rhine, between the Aa on the west and the Ems on the east, were destined by the simple reason of their central position, to play a significant rôle in the history of western Europe. Ever since the close of the tenth century, which marks the definitive end of the worst welter of feudal anarchy, these lands, collectively called the Low Countries, have epitomized in a most striking manner the social and economic growth of Europe. The establishment of feudal institutions, which created a certain amount of order in the public life of the West Frankish kingdom after the complete disintegration of Carolingian governmental institutions, the creation of an effective state in the East Frankish kingdom under the Saxon dynasty of the tenth and eleventh centuries, and the steadying support of the church which was ever eager to mitigate the violence of a brutal feudalism were inevitably followed by a most significant revival of commerce and town life.

Such renewal of economic life tended to concentrate in Flanders, Brabant, and neighboring lands much of the trade of the long coast line of Europe from Gibraltar to Finland and North Cape. This enormous littoral, cut up by such extensive bodies of water as the Bay of Biscay, the English Channel, the Irish Sea, the North Sea, and the Baltic Sea, received the innumerable affluents which drain the vast plain of northern Europe, such as the Garonne, Loire, Seine, Schelde, Meuse, Rhine, Ems, Weser, Elbe, Oder, and Vistula, and, broken by countless capes, inlets,

1

harbors, and estuaries, was destined to become the avenue of a vast and varied commercial and industrial activity. In the extreme east it was connected by the Gulf of Finland and the Dwina with the Dnieper and the Volga which enabled the merchants of northwest Europe to tap the wealth of the Byzantine east and the little known lands of distant Asia.[1] Inevitably much of the world trade of this vast economic hinterland was bound to find its focal point in the Low Countries. Equidistant between lands of such climatic and geographic diversity as the Spanish peninsula and Scandinavia, Scotland and Italy, Greenland and Iceland and Kansai in China and the East Indies,[2] the Netherlandish towns naturally became an entrepôt for the sundry products of the most varied regions.

From Spain and Majorca came choice leathers, oil, quicksilver, iron, lard, tallow, hides, wool, silk, canvas, brooms, almonds, saffron, rice, figs, raisins, caraway, cumin, anise, licorice, wines, honey, wax, and dyestuffs for the prized scarlet cloths which made Flemish looms famous. These things, as well as dates, alum, sugar, also came from Morocco, Algeria, and Tunis. From Gascony, Guienne, and Brittany came wines, honey, wax, and especially salt. Normandy contributed grain, wine, cheese, nuts, lime, and herring. Many of these articles, grown in lands of the south temperate zone, were exchanged for the characteristic products of Scandinavian lands, such as charcoal, pitch, lumber, spars, ashes, grain, leather, furs, hides, cattle, horses, pork, bacon, tallow, hams, herring, and butter. From Greenland came the tusks of the walrus, prized as ivory.[3] Copper was brought from the numerous centers in the Harz region, rye from Pomerania and parts further east, enormous quantities of beer from Hamburg, and a busy traffic developed with such Baltic Sea ports

---

[1] P. Boissonnade, *Le Travail dans l'Europe Chrétienne* (*V^e–XVe Siècle*), pp. 196–235; K. Höhlbaum, " Die Gründung der Deutschen Kolonie an der Düna," *Hansische Geschichtsblätter*, I (1873), 21–65; H. Pirenne, *Medieval Cities, Their Origins, and the Revival of Trade*, pp. 47–55.

[2] P. Munck, *Pavelige Nuntiers Regnskabs- og Dagböger förte under Tiende- Opkraevningen i Norden, 1282–1334*, pp. 25, 28, 56. It required six years to go from Venice to Kansai (Hangchow) and to return. See E. Power, " Marco Polo," *Medieval People*, pp. 24–58, 181.

[3] K. Gjerset, *History of Iceland* (New York, 1924), pp. 79–80; *History of the Norwegian People*, I (New York, 1915), 200–204; P. Munck, *Det Norske Folks Historie*, 2d Division, Part I (Christiania, 1862), pp. 313–315.

as Lübeck, Stralsund, and Rostock. Other German goods were wines, pitch, ashes, lumber, grain, steel, and iron. Of the Slavic and other eastern European lands, whose trade in large measure passed through Wisby, Pernau, and Riga, Russia and Bulgaria sent furs and wax. Poland, Bohemia, and Hungary furnished wax, gold, silver, tin, and copper. The British Isles exported lead, coal (sea coal), grain, ale, cheese, hides, woolfells, and the all-important wool.[4]

The trade of Italy and other Mediterranean lands was also integrally bound up with this focal point of commercial activity. In earlier days Constantinople had enjoyed great prestige as the western distributing point of the trade with the Orient. It was the grand entrepôt through which the prized articles of luxury — the silks and cloths of gold from China and Tartary, the drugs and spices from the East Indies, and the choice products from the skilled hands of Arabian and Byzantine craftsmen — passed on their way to the Low Countries either by way of the Russian rivers or the growing towns of Italy. But energetic Italians, particularly Venetians, Genoese, and Pisans, had been able to filch this monopoly from the Byzantines during the crusades. These merchants developed connections with the Low Countries either by way of the Rhone, through Champagne, whose fairs early in the thirteenth century were the great commercial marts in the northwest of Europe, or along the Moselle and the Rhine rivers, or by way of the passes in the Alps. The decline of the fairs, however, accentuated apparently by the perennial struggle between Philip the Fair and the Flemings, made this overland connection undesirable as compared with the sea route, and soon the Venetians and Genoese began to send their galleys through the Strait of Gibraltar to the North Sea. The comparative safety of the route, its cheapness for articles of luxury, the stimulus of the severe famine in the lands around the North Sea in 1315 and 1316, and the very favorable treatment which they received at Bruges and Antwerp all contributed to develop a flourishing trade.[5]

---

[4] W. L. Warnkönig, *Histoire de la Flandre et de ses Institutions civiles et politiques jusqu'à l'Année 1305*, II (*Pièces Justificatives*), 512–516; R. Häpke, *Brügges Entwickelung zum mittelalterlichen Weltmarkt*.

[5] J. Finot, *Étude historique sur les Relations commerciales entre la Flandre et la République de Gênes au Moyen Âge* (Paris 1906), pp. 1–37;

This commercial hegemony of the Low Countries in the economic life of northwestern Europe was further assured by the fact that the chief industry of medieval times, the manufacture of cloth, also centered in these lands. Already under the Roman emperors the region inhabited by the Celtic Morini and Menapii was quite generally noted for its excellent cloths. But with the decline of the Roman Empire and the development of a purely agricultural and manorial type of economy, based almost entirely upon local production and local consumption, such manufacturing [6] almost wholly disappeared. This decline reached its lowest point during the ninth century.[7] Not until a modest measure of peace and order was secured by the feudal princes who consolidated their authority and developed a political organization could this industrial activity once more develop in Artois, Flanders, and Brabant.[8] The proximity of England with its rapidly growing production of wool, hides, and woolfells, furthered especially by the energy of the Cistercians, served to aliment the looms of the rising towns of Flanders and its neighbors. So vast was the amount of wool produced in that land of peasants

A. Schaube, " Die Anfänge der Venezianischen Galeerfahrten nach der Nordsee," *Historische Zeitschrift,* 101 (1908), 28–89; *Handelsgeschichte der Romanischen Völker des Mittelmeergebiets bis zum Ende der Kreuzzüge,* pp. 374–433.

[6] E. Meyer, " Die Sklaverei im Altertum," *Kleine Schriften zur Geschichtstheorien und zur wirtschaftlichten und politischen Geschichte des Altertums,* pp. 169–212, and " Die Wirtschaftliche Entwicklung des Altertums," *ibid.,* pp. 79–168; W. L. Westermann, " The Economic Basis of the Decline of Ancient Culture," *American Historical Review,* XX (1914–1915), 723–743.

[7] H. Pirenne, " Mahomet et Charlemagne," *Revue Belge de Philologie et d'Histoire,* I (1922), 77–86; Un Contraste Économique, *ibid.,* II (1923), 223–235; *Medieval Cities, Their Origins, and the Revival of Trade,* pp. 1–55.

[8] K. Bächtold, " Der Norddeutsche Handel im 12. und beginnenden 13. Jahrhundert," *Abhandlungen zur Mittleren und Neueren Geschichte,* Heft 21 (1910); B. Kuske, " Handel and Handelspolitik am Niederrheim vom 13. bis 16. Jahrhundert," *Hansische Geschichtsblätter,* XV (1909), 301–327; P. Meilink, *De Nederlandsche Steden tot het laatste Kwartaal der XIVe Eeuw,* pp. 34–101; J. G. Nanninga, *Het Handelsverkeer der Oosterlingen door Holland in de dertiende Eeuw;* H. A. Poelman, *Geschiedenis van den Handel van Noord-Nederland gedurende het Merovingische en Karolingische Tijdperk;* W. S. Unger, *De Levensmiddelenvoorziening der Hollandsche Steden in de Middeleeuwen;* H. Vanderlinden, *Les Gildes Marchandes dans les Pays-Bas au Moyen Âge;* B. van Rijswijk, *Geschiedenis van het Dordtsche Stapelrecht.*

and graziers that in 1297 it was estimated to be equal in value to one half of the land and to a fifth of the tax levied upon it.[9] At the opening of the Hundred Years' War the total annual growth of the wool was estimated variously between thirty and forty thousand sacks. The towns in the valley of the Meuse, of which Dinant was the chief, excelled in the manufacture of copper and brass articles. Although of less significance in the world of industry, they supplied a market probably as extensive as the looms of Flanders.[10]

These important economic developments inevitably brought in their wake significant social and political changes. The old manorial economy now underwent a remarkable revolution; the development of towns, analogous somewhat to the rise of the industrial city-states of ancient Hellas, marks the beginning of a new order in economics, politics, society, and culture. The change effected may be regarded as one of the most important of all social and economic transformations before the Industrial Revolution in the nineteenth century. The towns of Flanders and Brabant soon outdistanced the urban centers of other lands and rapidly assumed a new character. No longer did they serve merely as economic centers for the surrounding country; they became in a very real sense towns of world importance just as those of Italy had been since the crusades. Division of labor, production for a wide market, and the need of credit all required capital, and soon a class emerged which may truly be called capitalistic. Lombards and Cahorsins settled in such towns as Bruges, Ghent, Ypres, and Arras and began to share with the wealthy burghers the profits made possible through the operations of credit.[11] Just as in the years immediately following 1800 Belgium became a great industrial state, not even eclipsed in this respect by England,[12] Flanders and its neighbors had by the

[9] C. Bémont, *Chartes des Libertés Anglaises (1100–1305)*, p. 78: " Lana enim Anglie ascendit fere ad valorem medietatis totius terre, et vectigal quod inde solvitur ascendit ad quintam partem valoris totius terre."

[10] H. Pirenne, *Histoire de la Constitution de la Ville de Dinant*, pp. 90–110.

[11] G. Bigwood, "Les Financiers d'Arras. Contribution à l'Étude des Origines du Capitalisme Moderne," *Revue Belge de Philologie et d'Histoire*, III (1924), 465–508, 769–819; IV (1925), 109–119, 379–421.

[12] J. H. Clapham, *The Economic Development of France and Germany, 1815–1914* (Cambridge, 1923), pp. 57–58.

close of the thirteenth century definitely assumed the leadership of western Europe in the manufacture of cloth. The very liberal policy of such princes as John I, duke of Brabant (1261–1294), Guy de Dampierre, count of Flanders (1278–1305), and many others tended to attract English, Hanseatic, Italian, and Spanish merchants. Bruges became a market of world importance.[13] Other towns participated in this economic development; and nowhere in western Europe since the fall of Rome, and in northern Europe not even in Roman days, had there been such a concentration of population in so many towns dependent upon the markets of the world for the sale of their products and upon all the lands of Europe for their raw materials and their food-supplies, as in the region between Dordrecht, St. Omer, and Douai.

II. Political Divisions

The boundary line between the duchy of Lotharingia and the county of Flanders, parts of the empire and of the Capetian kingdom respectively, was the one which had been established by the Partition of Verdun in 843. It followed the estuary of the Schelde to about ten kilometers east of Terneuzen, crossed the country to Ghent, where it again joined the Schelde, which it did not leave until it reached Bouchain. Encircling the lands of the bishop of Cambrai, it bent eastward and separated the county of Hainault and the territories belonging to the bishop of Liège from those dependent on the king of France. The line thus cut athwart the country regardless of national considerations, and nothing could better illustrate the non-national character of the famous division effected at Verdun.[14] On either side of this boundary the political fortunes of the princes were closely bound up with the vicissitudes of the emperors and the Capetian kings. Because of the dissolution of the Carolingian monarchy in the tenth century and the impotence of the earlier Capetian kings, the county of Flanders remained practically independent until the reign of the masterly Philip Augustus (1180–1223) who began the successful policy of interference in the fortunes of the

[13] R. Häpke, *Brügges Entwicklung zum mittelalterlichen Weltmarkt.*
[14] See E. Parisot, *Le Royaume de Lorraine sous les Carolingiens (843–923)*, pp. 1–26, for a critical discussion of the Partition of Verdun.

counts. But on the other side of the boundary the country had been a dependency of the empire ever since the reign of Henry the Fowler (919–936) and his son Otto I (936–973). The failure of imperial policy, especially during the investiture conflict and after, became certain, however, when a number of powerful local families were able to carve out principalities of their own. Over these feudal states the emperors found it increasingly difficult to maintain an effective control. Thus at the very moment when the Capetians were extending their authority over Flanders exactly the opposite tendency manifested itself throughout the lands included in the duchy of Lotharingia. Besides the three ecclesiastical states of Cambrai, Liège, and Utrecht, upon which the emperor had originally relied through his control of the election and the investiture of the bishops to restrain the secular princes, a number of feudal states arose. These were the duchies of Brabant and Limburg, the counties of Hainault, Holland, and Zeeland, the seigniory of Friesland, the counties of Guelders, Namur, Loon (*Loos*), and Luxemburg. Although generally regarded more specifically as a part of Germany, the county of Juliers was often so closely identified with the states of the Low Countries that for the period covered by this study it may well be considered one of them.

The possessions of the counts of Flanders comprised since the Treaty of Athis-sur-Orge (June, 1305), which gave to the king of France some control over the castleries of Lille, Béthune, and Douai, the low and flat region between the Schelde and the North Sea. On the south it was bounded by the Schelde and the Ruppel, which separated it in part from the duchy of Brabant, by the county of Hainault, by the possessions of the bishop of Tournai on the left bank of the Schelde, and by the Lys and the Neuf Fosse which connects the Lys with the Aa. Most of the lands within these limits were held in fee of the French crown and were known as *Crown Flanders*. East of the imperial boundary there were a number of districts of various size known as Imperial Flanders, save Waasland (*Pays de Waes, Land van Waes*), which was really also a fief of the French crown, though tradition had it that it belonged to the empire. These lands were the county of Alost (*Aalst*) along the Dender, a tributary of the Schelde, the four districts (*Vier Ambachten, Quatre Métiers,*

Quatuor Officia) of Hulst, Bouchoute, Axel, and Assenede, situated between the estuary of the Schelde and Waasland, and the very small parcel called Over-Schelde (*Terre d'Outre-Escaut*), east of Ghent. Furthermore, the count of Flanders also held several allodial tracts, that of Dendermonde (*Land van Dendermonde,* or *Termonde*) on either side of the Schelde where the Ruppel joins it, Grammont (*Geraerdsbergen*) south of Alost, and Bornhem between the Ruppel and Dendermonde.[15]

What distinguished Flanders was its commerce and industry and the social organization developed thereby. In the early years of the weakness of the Capetian kings the counts extended their authority without restraint. By reason of the extent of their land, their control over churches and monastic foundations in the capacity of *advocati,* and their effective rule the counts were often led to describe their government as a *regnum,* or a *monarchia,* and one of them even went so far as to describe himself *post Deum princeps.* Imitating Carolingian models, the count's court was ambulant, passing from estate to estate, and living upon the count's own income. The innumerable payments in the earlier days when the government followed the example of Charlemagne's *capitulare de villis* were collected by officials known as notaries and by their assistants at points centrally situated. Such places became the centers of the castleries into which the country was divided, the chief points of military and political life.

This simple agrarian and seigniorial economy early underwent a rapid transformation. With the development of trade during the eleventh century, traders (*mercatores*) began to congregate at points centrally located for their activities and where they could secure protection. Hence arose the earliest towns such as Bruges, Ghent, St. Omer, Douai, Lille, Arras, and others. The *portus,* as such a place was called, embraced a motley population of varied origin living outside the normal social classifications of the day. The inhabitants, being neither slave nor serf nor noble and having new interests to protect, created a new society and a new organization — the town. The members of the group in the *portus,* whether wealthy merchants or humble craftsmen or laborers, were in the beginning quite homogeneous in their

[15] F. Lot, " La Frontière de la France et de l'Empire sur le Cours Supérieur de l'Escaut du IXe au XIIIe Siècle," *BEC,* LXXI (1910), 1–32.

needs and aims. Through the leadership of the guild of *mercatores* they secured boards of scabini to govern them in units
separate from those of the surrounding country. This freed them
from a law which poorly fitted the needs of a growing trade
center and in this way they received their new laws, regulated internal affairs, took adequate measures for defense, and provided
for police regulations within. But soon social cleavages developed
and wealth began to separate the merchants from the crafts; the
patricians became a closed group and tended to retain in their
hands the control of the government and usually adopted a
restrictive policy which proved irksome to the lower classes.

It is important to grasp that the towns of Flanders were as
a rule different from most medieval trade centers. Instead
of producing for a local town market and for the adjacent country, they began early to develop a great export trade. Favored
by a location uniquely advantageous for commerce, possessed
of superior technique, certain of a vast supply of the best wool
from England, and supported by the sympathetic policy of the
counts of Flanders, the towns soon found a market even more
extensive than Christendom itself for the numerous choice cloths
such as the scarlet, blue, green, brown, striped, and others that
were made on their looms. The *mercatores* waxed rich and the
crafts such as the weavers, dyers, fullers, and others connected
with the manufacture of cloth became very numerous and vastly
outnumbered the wealthy patricians and the bakers, butchers,
shoemakers, and others who produced for the local market.

The principles which operated in most medieval towns that
did not produce for an extensive market failed entirely in Flanders. Capital was necessary to pay the workers of the crafts, to
buy wool in great quantities from England, and to ship the cloth
to fairs and other distant markets. The entrepreneurs, more and
more limited to the wealthy patriciate as time went on, sold
these products in a world market subject only to slight restric-
tions and such as were generally imposed by competition. They
paid the masters for the cost of manufacture, who in turn paid
their assistants and hired workers. The latter were constrained
in large numbers to sell their labor in a highly restricted market
in towns where all industrial operations were rigidly controlled
by the scabini drawn entirely from the patriciate, which sought

to use its influence merely to buttress the interests of a jealous oligarchy. A proletariat arose under these conditions. It lived on a very scant margin of subsistence, sold its labor by the week, went to work and ceased operations with the sound of the bell in the belfry, drew a small amount of pay at the week's end, and lived in wretched hovels in abject misery and wretchedness which recall to one's mind the indescribable conditions which obtained in the early nineteenth century in England when the modern factory system was developing.

These violent social contrasts among the populace in the *portus* led to serious clashes during the thirteenth century. Profound dissatisfaction caused demands for reform. At Ghent in 1212 the bench of the thirteen scabini, which had hitherto acted in this capacity for life and which was charged with the general administration and the justice of the town, was named only for one year, and other towns speedily followed this example so that throughout all Flanders the lists of the scabini were henceforth changed annually. The purpose of this new regulation was nullified, however, by the practice of rotating the office among the prominent members of the patriciate. The thirteen scabini (*scepenen van der keur, échevins de la keure*) were assisted by thirteen councillors (*scepenenen van der ghedeele, échevins des parchons*). Another thirteen were held in reserve; they succeeded to the duties of the scabini in the next year and to those of the councillors in the one following.

This group perpetuated the old conditions; in fact they formed a college of thirty-nine which retained full control over each town. Violent outbursts were to be expected; there were desperate uprisings in Douai in 1245, known as the *Takehans*, at Ghent in 1275, at Douai again in 1280, at Bruges in the same year, and again on September 3, 1281, known as the *Groote Moerlemaye,* and at Ypres the *Cokerulle* in 1280. It is this social question, caused by the glaring inequalities among the populace in the *portus*, that played so significant a rôle in determining the position of Flanders in the political events of the time. When Philip the Fair (1285–1314) sought to extend his authority over Flanders, he found ready support among the patriciate ranged in determined opposition to the lower classes of the population who sought relief from their oppressors by securing the support of their count, Guy (1267–1305). It was the craftsmen who were responsible for the massacre of the French in Bruges (the *Matins of Bruges*) on May 17, 1302, and the bloody defeat of the chivalry of France at Courtrai on July 11. The count's resistance to the centralizing policy of the French crown was successfully carried out by the alliance with the crafts against the patricians who with the feudality tended to look to the crown for support.

During the thirteenth century the rapidly growing population in the Flemish towns became more and more dependent upon surrounding countries for food-supplies and the raw materials for their looms. The county was dotted, as it is today, with numerous towns such as Bruges, Sluis, Damme, Aardenburg, Oostburg, Eecloo, Ghent, Dendermonde, Courtrai, Oudenaarde, Alost, Grammont, Thourout, Dixmuide, Bergen, Poperingen, Ypres, Bourbourg, and many smaller places. Dependent upon the markets of the world, exactly as in the present day, the people of the towns in Flanders were often forced to choose between their political obligations and their economic interests and social needs. It is for this reason that the history of Flanders presents at this time a most interesting medley of feudal and industrial motives.[16]

Between the lower Meuse and the Schelde lay the duchy of Brabant. It was a region of gentle undulations; in the parts along these rivers there were lands at sea-level, while in the extreme south the hills often reached a height of a hundred and twenty feet. Of the six quarters into which the duchy was divided, the four largest were north of the linguistic boundary line which cuts across present-day Belgium from east to west, and were accordingly Germanic in speech, while the two small quarters were Walloon. In the twelfth century Brabant was essentially agrarian, and Brussels, Vilvoorde, and Louvain were mere centers of

---

[16] A. Blanchard, *La Flandre, Étude géographique de la Plaine Flamande en France, Belgique, et Hollande* (Paris, 1906); V. Fris, *Histoire de Gand*, pp. 15–80; F. Funck Brentano, *Les Origines de la Guerre de Cent Ans. Philippe le Bel en Flandre*, pp. 1–95; A. Giry, *Histoire de la Ville de Saint-Omer et de ses Institutions jusqu'au XIVe Siècle;* R. Häpke, *Brügges Entwicklung zum mittelalterlichen Weltmarkt;* H. Pirenne, *Histoire de Belgique,* I (3d ed.), 51–55, 98, 126, 171–234, 256–322, 368–427; *Belgian Democracy, Its Early History,* pp. 1–180; L. A. Warnkönig, *Histoire de la Flandre et de ses Institutions civiles et politiques jusqu'à l'Année 1305,* 5 Vols.

the prince's seignioral exploitation where his ambulant court held occasional sojourn. But far-reaching social transformations, exactly the same as those which had already so profoundly affected Flanders during the eleventh and twelfth centuries, were in store for this region.[17]

Owing to its position between the two great economic centers in the southern Low Countries, the Meuse and the Schelde rivers, it was only natural that the duchy of Brabant should, with the great revival of commerce and industry in western Europe, sooner or later become a connecting link between these two important highways. Its rivers, the Ruppel, Senne, Dyle, Gette, Demer, and the Nethe all converged upon the Schelde. Maastricht, a possession of the dukes since the beginning of the thirteenth century, bore a peculiar relation to the economic development of the duchy. Situated on the left bank of the Meuse, where the old Roman road from Boulogne and Rheims passed eastward toward Cologne, it early became important for the transit trade of goods from the Rhineland and Italy to the towns of Flanders and Brabant. In the western part of the duchy there grew up at strategic points suitable for commercial activities a number of centers such as Brussels and Vilvoorde on the Senne, Louvain and Mechelen on the Dyle, Diest and Aerschot on the Demer, Lier at the junction of the Great and Lesser Nethe, Herenthals on the Great Nethe, Leeuw (*Léau*), Tirlemont (*Tienen*), and Jodoigne on the Gette, and Antwerp at the head of the broad estuary of the Schelde.

The northern parts of the duchy were in contrast quite backward. The soil there was sandy, unfit for agriculture, and the population was therefore sparse. The numerous streams, the Donge, Dintle, Merk, and Dieze had no economic hinterland to attract merchants to their banks. Only the Dieze with its tributaries, the Dommel and the Aa, was of some importance. Here rose 's-Hertogenbosch (*Bois-le-Duc*) around the duke's castle. Towns such as Breda, St. Oedenrode, Helmond, Eindhoven, and Oosterwijk remained, in spite of their proximity to the Meuse, places of slight importance. Bergen-op-Zoom, where the dukes levied toll upon goods going to Antwerp, and

[17] For a map of Brabant, see J. Cuvelier, *Les Dénombrements de Foyers en Brabant* (*XIVᵉ–XVIᵉ Siècle*).

Steenbergen on the Vliet were more important. In the two Walloon quarters where the fertility of the soil favored agricultural development and where numerous Roman roads, branches of the great route to Cologne, stimulated commercial intercourse with Hainault, Namur, and Liège, a number of towns grew up. Boisy and Frasnes-lez-Grosselies had already in 1160 been granted town privileges. Other important centers came into being, such as Genappe on the upper reaches of the Dyle, Gembloux, Landen, Perwez, and Nivelles. But, like the towns in the northern part of the duchy, these likewise remained of rather local importance.[18]

The dukes of Brabant were a virile race. Their statecraft was patient and often unspectacular; laboriously they built up their patrimony. Situated in the very heart of the old duchy of Lotharingia, Brabant was the only state that bordered upon all the other important principalities in the Low Countries which included Flanders, Hainault, Namur, Liège, Guelders, Juliers, Holland, and Zeeland. Numerous conflicting titles and interests led to countless disputes, and it was ever necessary for the dukes to be circumspect in all their actions. Along the Meuse there were troubles with Guelders, Juliers, and Holland, and in the west with the count of Flanders over the seigniory of the Schelde. The bishops of Liège, whose power had been zealously advanced in earlier days by the emperors in order to extend imperial control over Lotharingia, still retained many vestiges of their old ascendancy. The right to enforce the Truce of God and the Peace of God, the famous *Judicium Pacis*, which in Flanders had been assumed by the counts, was still in the bishop's hands. There were also many enclaves, fiefs of the bishop, such as Mechelen, so strategically situated on the Senne and the Dyle, Heyst and Boisschot, Hougaerde, Bauvechain, and others.

The dukes were quite successful in spite of these limitations. On every hand they gradually extended their authority. Long known as dukes of Lotharingia, they were popularly called dukes of Brabant, although they were merely counts in Brabant and in Louvain. Soon this title was adopted in the official style. In the towns whose interests the dukes systematically fostered their authority was quite real. Profiting from the example of Flemish

[18] G. Smet, *Henri I, Duc de Brabant*, pp. 268–269.

towns, they allied themselves with the patriciate which was everywhere divided into seven *lignages* or groups of families each of whom had a seat on the bench of the scabini. Thus as the towns grew powerful because of the development of trade and industry, they became strong supporters of the ducal power and contributed to the duke's authority a solidarity which was so conspicuously lacking in the position of the count of Flanders. Hence the crafts were slow in securing political significance. Based upon the interests of the old feudality and the rising bourgeoisie, the ducal power revealed most vividly in its official acts the mingled industrial, commercial, and feudal elements over which it ruled. As economic considerations became more weighty the duke's prestige in the lands toward the Rhine and on the Schelde rose rapidly. Three thousand vassals, it is estimated, owed him military service.[19] The total population of Brabant in 1347 is placed at between three and four hundred thousand.[20] Feudal and economic motives inspired John I to strike a blow for the duchy of Limburg, which he snatched from the many contenders by the impressive victory at Woeringen on June 5, 1288. Brabançon patriotism, which thus sprang from the reciprocal support of prince, bourgeoisie, and feudality, and was based upon the new industrial and commercial economy, made the duke of Brabant a person ever to be taken into account.[21]

The narrow band of dunes along the coast of the North Sea from Vlieland to Zeeland on the south, flanked by patches of fertile sand and clay soil and a broad expanse of fens, stagnant pools, and sluggish rivers, formed the county of Holland. Removed from the busy centers in the Meuse and the Schelde valleys, it was distinctly behind Flanders and Brabant in commerce,

[19] L. Galesloot, *Le Livre des Feudataires de Jean III, Duc de Brabant* (Bruxelles, 1865). Cf. H. Pirenne, *Histoire de Belgique*, II (2d ed.), 13–14.

[20] J. Cuvelier, *Les Dénombrements de Foyers en Brabant (XIVᵉ–XVIᵉ Siècle)*, Introduction, p. xcii.

[21] P. Ernst, *Histoire du Limbourg suivie de celle des Comtes de Daelhem et de Fauquemont, des Annales de l'Abbaye de Rolduc*, Vols. IV and V; H. Pirenne, *Histoire de Belgique*, I (3d ed.), 66–81, 129–131, 202, 237–246, 322–323; and II (2d ed.), 47–50; N. Posthumus, *De Geschiedenis van de Leidsche Lakenindustrie*, I. *De Middeleeuwen*, 21–25; G. Smet, *Henri I. Duc de Brabant;* H. Vanderlinden, *Histoire de la Constitution de la Ville de Louvain au Moyen Âge;* A. Wauters, "Le Duc Jean Iᵉʳ et le Brabant sous le Règne de ce Prince (1267–1294)," *Mémoires couronnés et Autres Mémoires, Académie Royale de Belgique*, Vol. XIII (1862).

industry, and social development. It was a region where intercourse was mainly by water. The population was sparse except on the cultivable lands along the dunes and in the few villages on the coast where there was some fishing. Only by patient and laborious statecraft, attentive to petty details, could the counts of these unpromising lands build up an important principality.[22] Their earlier possessions lay in Kennemerland, between Haarlem and the small streams of the Rekere and the Zijpe. In 889 the emperor Arnulf, anxious to strengthen the coast against the Northmen, granted Gerulf, a count in Frisia, some villas and possessions between the Old Rhine, which flows through Rijnland, and the Rekere. By the famous charter of 922, granted by Charles the Simple, Dirk I received certain rights over the possessions of the abbey of Egmond. Their location has ever been in dispute, but it is certain that they extended along the fertile strip which skirted the dunes from Kennemerland southwards as far perhaps as Zuid Beveland. As this grant gave them only the *advocatia* over these monastic lands, the significance traditionally attributed to this charter that it was the foundation of the county of Holland is untenable.[23] Extensive possessions were added when in 985 the emperor Otto III (983–1002) granted to Dirk II lands in Maasland between the mouth of the Meuse and the Old Rhine and northward into West Friesland.

Protected by impenetrable bogs and shallow pools, the counts were able to increase their power in spite of the hostility of the bishops of Utrecht who, as representatives of the imperial policy in these regions, sought to subject them to the empire. In 1018 Dirk III (993–1039) extended his power along the mouth of the Old Meuse at Vlaardingen as far as the Merwede. Eastward along the Yssel of Holland and the Lek further encroachments followed at the expense of the bishops, who, as imperial princes, could find no means wherewith to stay his progress.[24] By 1149

---

[22] J. de Vries, *De Wikingen in de Lage Landen bij de Zee*, pp. 10–51; P. J. Blok, " Oud-Kennemerland," *Bijdragen voor Vaderlandsche Geschiedenis en Oudheidkunde*, 4th Ser., IV (1905), 335–392; J. Huizinga, " De Opkomst van Haarlem," *Bijdragen voor Vaderlandsche Geschiedenis en Oudheidkunde*, 4th Ser., IV (1905, 412–446, and Vol. V (1906), pp. 16–175.

[23] I. H. Gosses, *De Vorming van het Graafschap Holland*, pp. 1–45.

[24] H. A. Poelman, " De Verovering van het Merwede-gebiet door Graaf Dirk III," *Bijdragen voor Vaderlandsche Geschiedenis en Oudheidkunde*,

the counts were established at Heusden and were seeking to extend their authority over the West Friesians who occupied the lowlands so difficult of access east of the Rekere and the Zijpe. As yet the county nowhere touched the Zuider Zee from which it was separated by the seigniories of Waterland and of Amstelland which were dependent upon the bishop of Utrecht. But under Floris V (1256–1296) the final limits which the county was to have during the rest of the Middle Ages were attained. The Friesians were compelled to accept him as their lord, and the troubled state of the lands of the bishop enabled Count Floris to extend his feudal lordship over Waterland, Amstelland, Woerden, and the Gooi. Naarden was bought from the abbess of Elten.[25]

The counts of Holland gave abundant proof of their administrative sagacity. The county was divided into a number of districts, called *waterschappen*, which were charged with the problem of drainage, the construction of dykes and sluices, and many other matters. Their bailiffs were closely associated with the colleges of the officials (*heemraden*) in control of the *waterschappen* which were fully developed by the opening of the fourteenth century. That of Rijnland served as a model for others, such as Delftland, Schieland, Waterland, Kennemerland, and Woerden.[26] Clearing of land kept pace with progress in drainage.[27] The villas or *curtes* of the count, situated at focal points of the prince's manorial exploitation, such as Dordrecht, Haarlem, Delft, Schiedam, Leiden, Schoonhoven, Medemblik, and Amsterdam, which had begun its growth under the seigniors of Amstel, were places of but slight importance at first, but during the course of the thirteenth century began more and more to attract immigrants who speedily transformed them into emporia deriving their sustenance from the adjacent regions. The growth of trade, however, was quite slow; during the thirteenth century there was apparently little commercial intercourse with England,[28] nor

---

4th Ser., VIII (1910), 349–372; P. J. Blok, *Geschiedenis van het Nederlandsche Volk,* I, 97–98; I. H. Gosses and N. Japikse, *Handboek tot de Staatkundige Geschiedenis van Nederland,* pp. XLVIII–CIII.

[25] H. Obreen, *Floris V, Graaf van Holland en Zeeland.*

[26] R. Fruin, "Over de Opkomst van het Hoogheemraadschap van Rijnland," *Verspreide Geschriften,* VI, 176–235.

[27] I. H. Gosses, *De Vorming van het Graafschap Holland,* pp. 83–104.

[28] J. Noë, *De Handel van Noord–Nederland op Engeland in de dertiende*

was there any development of the cloth industry, except in Dordrecht.[29] From its position on the Merwede, a river formed by the junction of the Meuse and the Waal, it was able to profit by the trade of the Rhine.[30]

The commerce of the towns on the shores of the Baltic Sea in the twelfth century which passed westward under the protection of the islands off the Friesian coast by way of the Zuider Zee through Utrecht to Flanders began to shift its course. The constant turmoil in the lands of the bishop of Utrecht made this route unsafe and, prompted by the counts' energetic protection and privileges, the merchants and traders began to use the Y and other internal waterways of the county.[31] This appears to have been decisive in the growth of the towns of Holland. Privileges were granted to Dordrecht (1220), Schiedam (1275), Haarlem (1245), Delft (1246), Leiden (1266), 's-Gravezande (1246), Alkmaar (1254), Medemblik (1289), Amsterdam (1275), and Rotterdam (1299).[32]

The counts of Holland early sought to extend their dominion over the group of islands between the Old Meuse and the Zwin in Flanders. Voorne, Putten, Goeree, and Overflakkee were regarded as parts of the county of Holland and in 1300 Zeeland was said to lie between them and Cadzand. The county of Zee-

---

Eeuw; J. Ruinen, *De Oudste Handelsbetrekkingen van Holland en Zeeland met Engeland.*

[29] N. Posthumus, *De Geschiedenis van de Liedsche Lakenindustrie*, I. *De Middeleeuwen*, 4–13.

[30] B. van Rijswijk, *Geschiedenis van het Dordtsche Stapelrecht.*

[31] H. Brugmans, "De Binnenvaart door Holland in de dertiende Eeuw." *Mededeelingen der Koninglijke Akademie van Wetenschappen, Afdeeling Letterkunde,* Part 54, Ser. B, No. 5 (1922), and *Opkomst en Bloei van Amsterdam;* C. 't Hooft, *Het Ontstaan van Amsterdam;* J. G. Naninga, *Het Handelsverkeer der Oosterlingen door Holland in de dertiende Eeuw,* and "De Handelsweg door Holland in de dertiende Eeuw," *Bijdragen voor Vaderlandsche Geschiedenis en Oudheidkunde,* 6th Ser., II (1925), 94–108.

[32] P. J. Blok, *Geschiedenis eener Hollandsche Stad. Eene Hollandsche Stad in de Middeleeuwen,* pp. 1–79; H. Brugmans en C. H. Peters, *Oud-Nederlandsche Steden in haar Onstaan, Groei, en Ontwikkeling. Het Staatkundig en Maatschappelijk Leven der Nederlandsche Steden,* I, 39–47, 78–103; R. Fruin, "Naar Aanleiding der Vereeniging van Delftshaven en Rotterdam," *Verspreide Geschriften,* VI, 107–137; "Oudheid van Rotterdam," *ibid.,* pp. 1–85; "Het Oudste Keurboek van Rotterdam," *ibid.,* pp. 86–92.

land was divided into two parts by the Schelde River, or rather by the channel now known as the East Schelde. The eastern half (*Beoosten Schelde*) comprised Schouwen, Duiveland, and Tolen. Between it and the Wielingen and the Honte, at present the main channel of the Schelde, lay the five islands of the western half (*Bewesten Schelde*), Walcheren, Noord Beveland, Zuid Beveland, Borselen, and Wolfaartsdijk. Of the first half the counts of Holland were uncontested masters, but they waged a long feud with the counts of Flanders for the other half. The dispute was a tedious affair, and on February 23, 1167, it was agreed at Bruges that a joint control should be established and that the lands in question should be held of the counts of Flanders by the counts of Holland.[33] When Holland was drawn into the contest between the Avesnes and Dampierre dynasties, this arrangement came to an end, and not until March 6, 1323, was the matter definitely settled by the grant of full suzerainty to the count of Holland.[34]

These low-lying islands, flanked by a belt of sand dunes behind which lay stretches of fertile clay lands often submerged at high tide, had ever been buffeted by the fury of the sea. Numerous disasters mark the history of Zeeland before human ingenuity could put limits to the waters. Here too, as in Holland, a patient administrative watchfulness was amply rewarded. Reclamation was undertaken, polders were formed, and great dykes were constructed. On the rich clay lands agriculture flourished and villages throve. The numerous petty nobility were too weak to play any but a rôle of local importance, while the rest of the population was composed of freedmen.[35] Situated at the confluence of the Meuse and the Schelde, midway between Holland and the mouths of the Rhine on the north and Flanders and Brabant on the south, Zeeland saw the commerce of the Low Countries pass along its waters. Already in Roman days Walcheren had served as a bridgehead for military and commercial relations with

[33] H. Brosien, *Der Streit um Reichsflandern in der Zweiten Hälfte des dreizehnten Jahrhunderts* (Berlin, 1884); C. Sattler, *Die Flandrisch-Holländischen Verwicklungen unter Wilhelm von Holland, 1248–1256* (Göttingen, 1872).

[34] F. van Mieris, *Groot Charterboek*, II, 276.

[35] A. A. Beekman, *Nederland als Polderland. Geschiedenis en tegenwoordige Staat van de Lage Gronden voor Niet-Technici*, pp. 307–386.

Britain,[36] and with the revival of commerce this connection was once more bound to become very important. This affected the outlook of the population in matters of politics as, for example, the Anglophile attitude which some of the nobility evinced in opposition to the friendly policy of Counts Floris V (1256–1296) and John I (1296–1299) toward the Avesnes family and Philip the Fair.[37] Here too towns grew up; Middelburg became important for its commerce and manufacture of cloth,[38] and received privileges in 1217 and 1256. Similar charters were granted to Domburg and Westkapelle in 1223, Zierikzee in 1248, Veere probably later in the same century, Flushing in 1315, and Goes in 1342.[39]

The counts of Holland had long endeavored to extend their authority over the Friesians between the Lauwers and Kennermerland. After the decline of Roman power the Friesians had expanded along the lower Rhine westward as far as the Zwin and eastward beyond the Weser, but in the course of centuries the *Ducatus Frisiae*, as it was called in Carolingian days, was reduced on all sides by the encroachments of the sea, the rise of the counties of Holland and Zeeland, and by the loss of the region between the Lauwers and the Ems to the Saxon element around Groningen. In West Friesland between the Zijpe, the Rekere, and the Zuider Zee, the counts of Holland were successful after centuries of border feuds and raids. Floris V determined to avenge the death of his father William, king of the Romans, and began a systematic reduction of this region so difficult of access because of the treacherous bogs and lowlands. From Hoorn, Wijdenes, and Medemblik the count's influence went forth until in 1289 the entire region and even the island of Wieringen were definitely subjected to his sway.

[36] J. Holwerda, *Nederland's vroegste Geschiedenis* (Amsterdam, 1918), pp. 142–143. See M. P. Rooseboom, *The Scottish Staple in the Netherlands.*

[37] H. Obreen, *Floris V, Graaf van Holland en Zeeland;* M. S. Pols, " Graaf Jan I van Holland," *Bijdragen voor Vaderlandsche Geschiedenis en Oudheidkunde,* 3d Ser., X (1899), 1–60.

[38] N. Posthumus, *Geschiedenis der Leidsche Lakenindustrie,* I, *De Middeleeuwen,* 8–11, 15–21.

[39] J. ab Utrecht Dresselhuis, *De Aloude Gesteldheid der Provincie Zeeland* (Middelburg, 1836); H. Brugmans en C. Peters, *Oud-Nederlandsche Steden in haar Ontstaan, Groei, en Ontwikkeling, Het Staatkundig en Maatschappelijk Leven der Nederlandsche Steden,* I, 75–78.

Beyond the Zuider Zee, however, it was extremely difficult for the counts to exercise any consistent authority. Basing their claims apparently upon the grants of the emperors made early in the eleventh century but subsequently withdrawn in the interests of the bishop of Utrecht, they opposed the latter until Frederick Barbarossa in 1165 established a joint control which could of course never be effective and which after a century was, it appears, abandoned. It was impossible to control the country because the low clay lands and the high and low fens were cut up by innumerable streams, bogs, and meres which made the whole region well-nigh inaccessible. Here too the unrelenting sea wrought great havoc upon the weak coast; the expanse of waters between the sand dunes of Terschelling, Ameland, and Schiermonnikoog indicates the vast stretches that were carried away by the fury of the waves.

Thus protected by nature from the invader, the Friesians were destined to live an unrestrained and parochial life quite independent from that of their neighbors. There were only non-feudal nobles and freemen among the inhabitants. The three *pagi*, Oostergoo, Westergoo, and Zevenwolden, were divided into districts called *grietenijen*, each under a *grietman*, an official resembling a bailiff. The government of the communities was quite democratic; originally there had been meetings of heads of families in the villages and in the *grietenijen*, but the principle of representation gradually underwent important changes in the assemblies of the *pagi*. Popularly elected representatives from the *grietenijen* and the towns, appointees of the prelates, and a very few nobles appeared on these occasions. Friesian freedom and democracy easily and speedily degenerated into anarchy. The nobles were involved in blood feuds, and violent wars were common. Although they were exposed to great dangers because of their internal weakness, the inaccessibility of their land rendered the inhabitants comparatively safe from the encroachment of the counts of Holland.[40]

The region was of slight economic importance. Stavoren had enjoyed a lucrative commerce since the ninth century, simply because it lay on the route between Utrecht and the Rhine country

---

[40] For the government, see R. Fruin, *Geschiedenis der Staatsinstellingen in Nederland,* pp. 92–95.

and the Scandinavian north and German east.[41]   But Leeuwarden, Franeker, Bolsward, Dokkum, Sneek, and Ylst grew up as local staples and remained, in spite of some commercial development by 1300, of distinctly limited importance. Cattle raising — agriculture was almost impossible on the low clay lands — had been the chief source of wealth since the first century of our era. Reclamation was carried on in the absence of effective local government by the initiative of the Cistercian and Premonstratensian orders whose success in this respect was not surpassed in any other part of Europe.[42]

The county of Guelders was, next to that of Holland, the most important principality in the north. The emperors Henry II (1002–1024) and Henry III (1039–1056) had given to the two Flemish brothers who had established themselves at Wassenberg on the Meuse possessions which became the nuclei of the later counties of Cleves and Guelders. Gradually the counts of the latter line succeeded in absorbing other rights in the region including Roermond, Venloo, Guelders, and the county of Hoorne. In the same century they also acquired extensive rights in the fens and rich clay lands of the Betuwe, Bommelerwaard, Tielerwaard, Maas en Waal, which lay between the Waal, Rhine, and Meuse, and also in the Lijmers and Zevenaar. As *advocati* of St. Mary's in Utrecht they were soon recognized as counts in the sandy upland wastes of the Veluwe between the Yssel, Zuider Zee, and the lands of the bishop of Utrecht. In the following century the fens on the right bank of the Yssel and on both sides of the Berkel and the county of Zutfen passed to them through a matrimonial connection.[43]

These straggling possessions so diverse in character possessed no unity other than that impressed upon them by the counts whose political policies accordingly reveal a most varied orientation. There were numerous enclaves in Zutfen such as Lichten-

[41] K. Heeringa, *Het oude Staveren.*
[42] P. J. Blok, " Studien over Friesche Toestanden in de Middeleeuwen," *Bijdragen voor Vaderlandsche Geschiedenis en Oudheidkunde,* 3d Ser., VI (1892), 1–56.
[43] G. Müller, *Die Entwicklung der Landeshoheit in Geldern bis zur Mitte des 14. Jahrhunderts* (Marburg, 1889) ; C. Pijnacker Hordijk, " De oudste Graven van Wassenberg-Gelre," *Bijdragen voor Vaderlandsche Geschiedenis en Oudheidkunde,* 4th Ser., II (1902), 325–349.

voort, Borculo, Bronkhorst, and Bredevoort. Over these there were frequent clashes with the bishops of Münster which brought the counts into contact with the political problems of Westphalia.[44] With the bishops of Utrecht there were many questions both political and ecclesiastical which compelled the counts to seek a close understanding with the counts of Holland, whose wider political activities in turn also necessarily involved the counts of Guelders. On the southern border numerous differences with the dukes of Brabant in regard to Baardwijk, Heusden, Tiel, Zandwijk, Heerewaarden, Megen, Kempen, and Wassenberg might under favorable circumstances lead to violence.

The growing volume of commerce which had to pass over the streams of Guelders to its destination in the North Sea area also drew the counts into contact with distant lands. At suitable places along the Meuse, Waal, Rhine, Linge, Lek, Yssel, and Berkel urban centers engaged in commerce soon sprang up. After Dorestad had been ruined by the Northmen, Tiel became an enterprising entrepôt with an extensive commerce. Nijmegen, originally a royal *curtis*, possessed of a toll, and situated on the Waal, soon became important.[45] Zutfen on the Yssel and the Berkel was given privileges in 1190 which became the model for other towns of the county, such as Harderwijk and Elburg on the Zuider Zee, Arnhem on the Rhine, Roermond on the Meuse and Roer, Venloo on the Meuse, and many smaller places such as Wageningen, Gent, Heerewaarden, Culemborg, Maasbommel, and Zaltbommel.[46]

[44] H. G. Harkema, " De Betrekkingen van het Bisdom Munster tot de Nederlanden inzonderheid tot Gelderland, tot aan de Vrede van Kleef, 18 April, 1866," *Bijdragen en Mededeelingen, Gelre, Vereeningen tot Beoefening van Geldersche Geschiedenis, Oudheidkunde, en Recht,* VII (1904), 1–65.

[45] H. D. J. van Schevichaven, " Het Rijk van Nijmegen, zijne Dorpen en Heerlijkheden," *Bijdragen en Mededeelingen, Gelre, Veereeningen tot Beoefening van Geldersche Geschiedenis, Oudheidkunde, en Recht,* III (1900), 39–80; and " De Rijkstol te Nijmegen," *ibid.,* VIII (1905), 1–64.

[46] H. D. J. van Schevichaven, " Bijdrage tot de Geschiedenis van den Handel van Gelre voor 1400 en zijne Betrekking tot de Hanze," *Bijdragen en Mededeelingen, Gelre, Vereeniging tot Beoefening van Geldersche Geschiedenis, Oudheidkunde, en Recht,* XIII (1910), 1–148; H. Brugmans en C. Peters, *Oud-Nederlandsche Steden in haar Ontstaan, Groei, en Ontwikkeling. Het Staatkundig en Maatschappelijk Leven der Nederlandsche Steden,* I, 70–74.

Bounded by the Schelde on the west, the county of Hainault. was situated in the extreme point of the empire which projected into France. The county of Ostrevant between the Scarpe, Sensée, and the Schelde had long been associated with the counts of Hainault who owed homage for it to the Capetians.[47] The rolling uplands of fertile soil provided opportunity even under the Roman Empire for extensive agriculture, and a sturdy seigniorial régime existed. The chivalry of Hainault was especially renowned, as the reputation of John of Hainault and the chronicler Froissart sufficiently attest. As the rich deposits of coal were only slightly exploited until 1800 and no large towns existed as in Flanders or Brabant, the region was quite conservative in its outlook. Valenciennes on the Schelde was noted for commerce and the manufacture of cloth. Maubeuge on the Sambre was much less important, and other places such as Le Quesnoy, Avesnes, Mons, Binches, Bavay, Chimay, Bouchain, and Ath were either mainly local staples or simple strongholds of the prince. Accordingly, the absence of social problems made Hainault an essentially agrarian and powerful feudal state. Its strategic position rendered it very valuable for an invasion of Capetian territory from Flanders or Brabant.[48]

The county of Namur was of comparatively slight importance. Lying in the valleys of the Meuse and the Sambre, noted for its flourishing iron and copper industries and as the source of the desirable building stone so much in demand in Holland, Utrecht, Zeeland, and Brabant, this principality attained some industrial and commercial significance. Its chief town, Namur, which was built at the confluence of these rivers, exported latten ware in considerable quantities and had received already in 1121 a charter after a communal upheaval. In 1300 its population may be assumed to have been about eight thousand.[49] Surrounded by such powerful neighbors as the bishops of Liège, the dukes of Brabant, and the counts of Hainault, the counts of Namur could play only a relatively passive rôle.

The county of Luxemburg, situated between the Meuse and

[47] J. Viard, " L'Ostrevant. Enquête au Sujet de la Frontière Française sous Philippe VI de Valois," *BEC*, LXXXII (1921), 316–329.

[48] H. Pirenne, *Histoire de Belgique*, Vol. I (3d ed.), pp. 128–129, 202.

[49] J. Borgnet, *Cartulaire de la Commune de Namur*, I (Namur, 1871), 121.

Moselle rivers and removed from the great highways of commerce and intercourse, was, in contrast to Flanders, Brabant, Holland, and Guelders, very primitive in its social and political organization. The country, being hilly and even mountainous, intersected by the Semois, Sure, and Ourthe, provided but little opportunity for agriculture. The towns of Laroche, Houffalize, Echternach, Arlon, Ivoy, Montmédy, Orchimont, and Luxemburg were mere local staples and apparently devoid of industry. The population must, therefore, have presented an interesting contrast to those parts of the Low Countries which had been vitally transformed by industry and commerce. The counts of this relatively backward region were poor and after the battle of Woeringen (June 5, 1288) apparently doomed to play a rôle of purely local importance. But the proximity of Luxemburg to the boundary of the French kingdom enabled them to become allies of the Capetian kings and thus raised them out of their insignificance. When Count John acquired the crown of Bohemia by his marriage with Elizabeth, the daughter of King Wenceslaus of Bohemia, the county was bound to play a significant part in the history of the empire as an ally of the French monarchy.[50]

Utrecht, the largest diocese in the Low Countries, included the counties of Holland and Zeeland, the Quatuor Officia in Flanders, and everything in the present kingdom of the Netherlands north of the Meuse and the Waal and west of its present boundary, save that portion of the province of Gelderland known as the Achterhoek which belonged to the see of Münster, and a region in the north and east of the Lauwers, which belonged to the sees of Münster and Osnabrück. The lands directly dependent on the bishops were divided into three distinct districts.[51] The country around Utrecht, roughly coterminous with the present province of the same name, composed of the rich low fens and clay lands and the sandy heights west of the Eems, was the most valuable possession of the bishops. Through it flowed the Rhine and the Vechte, and the city of Utrecht was early a center of great commercial importance because of its trade with the Scan-

[50] E. Welvert, " Philippe le Bel et la Maison de Luxembourg," *BEC,* XLV (1884), 180–188.

[51] See the map of S. Muller Hzn., " Kaart van het Bisdom Utrecht in 1560," *Uitgave der Vereeniging tot Uitgaaf der Bronnen van het Oud-Vaderlandsche Recht* ('s-Gravenhage, 1919).

dinavian north and the Baltic shore. The eastern half of Overijsel was upland sand and sparsely inhabited, but in the west
along the Yssel there were rich clay lands and near the Zuider
Zee low fens. Along this route of commerce between Westphalia
and the Rhineland and the north, Deventer early became an
important place. Other towns were Zwolle and Kampen. North
of Overijsel were Drenthe and Vollenhove, a stretch of low and
high fens, waste heath, and other lands covered with forests.
These wild areas were of but slight value, the inhabitants were
few, and there were no towns or commerce. North of this backward region at the end of the Hondsrug, a heathery and sandy
elevation extending along the east frontier of Drenthe, at the
confluence of the Aa and the Hunze rivers which connected it
with the Fivel, was the prosperous town of Groningen. Originally
a market for the fertile lands around it, this town soon became an
important trading center having connections with England, Scandinavia, Wisby, and even Smolensk.[52]

The extent of these lands did not, however, give the bishops
any strength. Overijsel and Drenthe were separated from the
southern part of the bishop's possessions, known as the *Neder-
sticht,* by the sandy wastes of the Veluwe which the counts of
Guelders held in fee. This region was poor and the nobility in
the Yssel valley and in the Twente were uncontrollable. The
castellans in Koevorden regarded their position as a family
appanage. The towns of Deventer, Zwolle, Kampen, and even
the smaller places were practically free, like the open country.
In Utrecht the social problems of an industrial society materially
weakened the bishops, especially in their efforts to resist the encroachments of the counts of Holland who contested with them
the suzerainty over Oostergoo and Westergoo in Friesland and
successively took from them Amstelland, Waterland, and Woerden.

The diocese of Cambrai lay between the Schelde and the Dyle
and embraced most of Brabant at present included within the
kingdom of Belgium and parts of Flanders, Hainault, Namur,
and Ostrevant. Originally the see had been situated at Arras,

[52] J. B. Schepers, *Groningen als Hanzestad* (Groningen, 1891); S.
Gratema, " Het Ontstaan en de Ontwikkeling van het eigenlijke Stadsbe-
stuur te Groningen tot in het Begin der 15de Eeuw," *Bijdragen voor Vaderlandsche Geschiedenis en Oudheidkunde,* 3d Ser., VI (1892), 165–306.

but in 585 had been transferred to the old Roman town of Cameracum on the banks of the Schelde. Out of its possessions, repeatedly confirmed by the Saxon emperors who were so zealous to increase the power of the bishops and who gave them title and the authority of count, grew the Cambrésis. This was composed of the lands directly subject to the episcopal prince which lay on both sides of the Schelde and extended eastward as far as the Sambre.[53]

The position of the Cambrésis made this region especially susceptible to Capetian influences. The bishop of Cambrai was a suffragan of the see of Rheims. Situated in the western point of the empire in the Low Countries, surrounded by lands dependent on the king of France, the Cambrésis became a coveted prize for the Valois kings in their desire to encroach upon the lands of the old duchy of Lotharingia. Formerly the counts of Flanders had exercised much influence over the secular affairs of the bishop. Robert the Friesian (1071–1093) became his castellan and the counts were entitled to an annual payment (*gabellum*) by the church of Cambrai. But during the perennial contests between the two scions of the ruling Flemish house, the Dampierre and the Avesnes, the Capetians supported the latter in their sanguinary family feuds and were enabled to insinuate their way effectively into the Cambrésis by taking advantage of the ineffective rule of Rudolph of Hapsburg, Adolf of Nassau, and Albert of Austria. Bishops such as Enguerrand de Morigny (1306–1309) and Pierre de Lévis-Mirepoix (1309–1324) were named through royal influence. The emperor Henry VII was able to regain some of the ground lost, but Capetian influences remained powerful. The prestige of the resourceful William, count of Hainault, Holland, and Zeeland, was so great, however, that he could exercise much influence over the bishops during the two decades following the death of Philip the Fair.[54]

The diocese of Tournai, together with that of Thérouanne, embraced most of the territory of Flanders on the left bank of the Schelde. Thérouanne was but a small see and, since the city was situated in the kingdom of France, the bishops were much

[53] M. Reinecke, *Geschichte der Stadt Cambrai bis zur Erteilung der Lex Godefridi* (Marburg, 1896).

[54] H. Dubrulle, *Cambrai à la Fin du Moyen Âge (XIIIe–XVe Siècle)*, pp. 241–274.

influenced by the Capetian kings. The bishops of Tournai were lords of a small amount of territory, the Tournaisis, on the left bank of the Schelde between the Scarpe, Elnon, and the Espierre rivers. Although it lay on the west side of the imperial border and hence within the kingdom of the Capetians, the bishops long remained free from the domination of French kings. They early fell under the influence of the mighty counts of Flanders when they were in the heyday of their power. The counts and castellans of Tournai were vassals of the Flemish counts. But as the struggle between the Capetians and Flanders developed, the crown found it advantageous to use the see as a fulcrum of political influence against the Flemings. Since the days of Philip Augustus royal influence in the Tournaisis and in the town of Tournai increased. By the opening of the Hundred Years' War French ascendancy was unquestioned at this point.[55]

Between the dioceses of Utrecht and Cambrai lay that of the bishop of Liège. It included much of Brabant, Luxemburg, Limburg, Namur, and Hainault. In the earlier history of the diocese the emperors had, as in the case of Cambrai and Utrecht, endeavored to strengthen their own authority by making the bishops rich lords and powerful princes. In the see of Liège the lands controlled directly by the bishop and chapter never became a compact group. The Hesbaye and the lands around the city in the valley of the Meuse undoubtedly formed the core, but there were straggling parcels of episcopal territory, almost entirely detached from the main group of lands, in the valley of the Sambre and as far south as the banks of the Semois. North of the Hesbaye was the county of Loon which was held in fee of the bishop. The count of Hainault was an episcopal vassal. In industrial development the bishop's towns had not gone forward as had those of Brabant or Flanders. St. Trond, on the borders of the duchy and on the route between Cologne, Maastricht, and the towns of Brabant and Flanders, and Huy on the Meuse above Liège were noted for the manufacture of cloth. Dinant was famous for its latten ware, as the word *Dinanderie* sufficiently

[55] A. Cartelliere, *Philip II. August, König von Frankreich,* I, 266–268; H. Pirenne, *Histoire de Belgique,* I (3d ed.), 203, 218–219; H. van Werveke, *Het Bisdom Terwaan van den Oorsprong tot het Begin der veertiende Eeuw,* Recueil de Travaux publiés par la Faculté de Philosophie et Lettres de l'Université de Gand, fasc. 52 (1924).

attests. Wood was shipped to Holland and Flanders from the
Ardennes, and the fertile soil of the Hesbaye provided much corn.
The city of Liège derived its prosperity mostly from the presence
of the bishop's officials and because it was the chief center of the
episcopal establishment. But little trade came to it, for commercial activity on the Meuse above Maastricht was relatively
unimportant, save for the traffic in wood and in the building
stone which came from Namur. The smaller towns of Fexhe,
Jeneffe, Wihogne, Moha, Florennes, Walcourt, and others were
merely centers of local importance.

The bishops' power was seriously weakened by the fact that
everywhere the episcopal government had sought to retain its
authority in the face of the desires of the bourgeoisie of Liège,
Huy, and other towns. For this reason the towns were everywhere governed by two tribunals, the scabini, who represented
the episcopal authority and retained control of all justice, and
the councillors, or *jurati,* who managed the affairs of the townsmen. Everywhere the bourgeoisie was eager to extend its authority, and in many towns there was a state of chronic revolt. An
important remnant of the prestige once enjoyed by the see was
preserved by the *Judicium Pacis* which gave the bishops vast
power to enforce the Peace of God over the duchies of Brabant
and Limburg. After the battle of Woeringen (June 5, 1288), by
which John I of Brabant acquired definitive control over Limburg, the relations between the bishops and the dukes became
seriously strained. The former were ever determined to preserve
intact the patrimony of St. Lambert, while the latter desired
above all things to consolidate their authority within their lands.
This is the reason why the bishops since the middle of the thirteenth century looked to the kings of France for support. When
the fortunes of the Hohenstaufen rulers collapsed and the Interregnum in the empire followed, the Capetians were able to insinuate their way more effectively than ever into the local affairs of
the Low Countries. For them Liège was a valuable support of
their policy against the counts of Flanders and their aggressions
against the empire. Usually they were able to secure the election
of prelates favorable to their interests.[56]

[56] G. Kurth, *La Cité de Liège au Moyen Âge,* Vols. I and II; H.
Pirenne, *Histoire de Belgique,* I (3d ed.), 132–136, and II (2d ed.), 14–16;
Histoire de la Constitution de la Ville de Dinant au Moyen Âge.

III. Political Relationships

THREE phenomena of transcending importance in the political life of western Europe during the century before the opening of the Hundred Years' War have exercised a profound influence upon the principalities grouped around the mouths of the Schelde, the Meuse, and the Rhine. The first of these was the bankruptcy of the power of the Holy Roman Empire. Although patterned after the model of the Carolingian government when it was founded by Otto I (936–973), the promise of a brilliant career presented by the Saxon emperors was not to be realized. The long and bitter struggle which the emperors were obliged to wage with the church for the control of election and investiture, the antipathy of a feudality which never ceased to hope for complete freedom of action, the failure to establish in Germany, as was done by Capetian princes in France, the principle of hereditary succession, and the consequent impossibility of creating a crown domain so weakened the imperial authority, that, in spite of the efforts of the members of the Hohenstaufen house, unity was not to be attained. Only by giving free rein to centrifugal forces in Germany could Frederick II (1212–1250) maintain himself in Italy in his desperate encounter with the popes. With the death of Frederick II and his son Conrad IV in 1254, the defeat of his natural son Manfred in 1266 at the hands of Charles of Anjou on the field of Grandella, and of the pathetic Corradino at Tagliacozzo in 1268, the possibility of ever giving the empire the power which the princes of such states as France, England, and Naples possessed could never be realized. Henceforth the empire ceased to be a really effective force in European political life. Universalism in politics, the noble dream of medieval political theorists, foundered on the rocks of local and national sentiment.

A second factor was the centralized power of the Capetian kings of France whose gradual growth to absolutism was diametrically the opposite of the decline of imperial authority. Beginning with the reign of Louis the Fat (1108–1137), the members of this family successfully extended their domain and more and more concentrated public authority in their own hands. This policy was consistently maintained by Philip Augustus (1180–1223), Louis VIII (1223–1226), Louis IX (1226–1270), and was carried forward with startling thoroughness by Philip the Fair (1285–1314). Led by the exigencies of practical politics and the precepts of Roman law, the French crown ever sought to maintain its rights as suzerain and sovereign in its dealings with the papacy and the feudality. Success within was accompanied by expansion without. Not only was the county of Flanders drawn into closer relations with the crown; even the fiefs of the empire in the Low Countries and elsewhere along the western frontier increasingly felt the influence of the Capetians. The kingdom of Arles, united since 1032 with that of Germany, disintegrated with the decline of the effective authority of the emperors and finally broke up into a number of principalities which were practically independent. The most important of these were the Franche Comté, Provence, the Lyonnais, Dauphiné, and Savoy. The weakness of the empire during the period of the Interregnum (1254–1273) and the preoccupation of Rudolf of Hapsburg with the affairs of his house presented no obstacle to the insinuation of French influence in these lands as well as in Lorraine, Bar, and Burgundy.

The kings of England also exerted much influence upon the fortunes of Netherlandish princes. As feudal lords of Gascony they were vassals of the French crown and therefore were bound to resist the encroachments of their Capetian suzerains. Powerful because of an extensive authority the foundations of which had been laid by the genius of Norman and Angevin kings, they proved a serious obstacle to the success of the policy prosecuted by the Capetian kings. Because of their close economic relations with the Low Countries and the Rhineland they were usually able in moments of crisis to bring together a large number of Netherlandish and German allies to resist the kings of France. Because of these factors the principalities of the Low Countries, occupying a central position in the land mass of the continent of Europe, placed at a focal point with reference to the great drainage system and the lengthy coast line of western Europe, situated where the boundaries of the empire marched with those of the kingdom of France and opposite the island of England, were by reason of their varied economic, social, and political life bound to be vitally affected by the greater political factors in the life of the states of Europe.

The long and bitter contest waged between the Avesnes and the Dampierre branches of the ruling family of Hainault and Flanders greatly agitated the princes of the Low Countries. Count Baldwin, sixth of the line in Hainault and ninth in Flanders (1194–1202), left for the east on the fourth crusade in 1202 and was succeeded in the government by his daughter, Johanna of Constantinople (1202–1244). Her younger sister, Marguerite of Constantinople, early married Bouchard d'Avesnes, scion of the ancient seigniors of Avesnes, who, being a second or third son, was prepared for the church and became a subdeacon. The children of this concubinary union were of course illegitimate from the point of view of canon law and therefore, in accordance with customary law which made no concessions to bastardy, would surely be excluded from a share in the patrimony of Count Baldwin. This became an important matter when it was apparent that Countess Johanna would have no heirs of her body. In 1237 Gregory IX after due inquiry declared them illegitimate. The sons, Baldwin and John, appealed to Frederick II who in 1243 legitimated them.[57] But the quarrel became more and more acrid until in 1246 the matter was left to the arbitrament of Louis IX, king of France.

In July of that year St. Louis and Odo, bishop of Tusculum, gave their decision at Paris. John d'Avesnes was to receive Hainault and its dependencies, while Guillaume de Dampierre, a son by a second marriage, was to have Flanders upon the death of Marguerite.[58] The judgment did not please John who was not slow to take advantage of an important flaw in the arbitral decision. Certainly the rights of the emperor had been disregarded, and Baldwin protested the disposition of Waasland, which was regarded as an imperial fief, the county of Alost, the Quatuor Officia which included Hulst, Bouchoute, Axel, and Assenede, and

---

[57] See E. le Glay, *Histoire de Jeanne de Constantinople, Comtesse de Flandre et de Hainault* (Lille, 1841); and C. Duvivier, *La Querelle des d'Avesnes et des Dampierres,* I, 13–134.

[58] C. Duvivier, *La Querelle des d'Avesnes et des Dampierres,* II, 168–170. For the contest between the two claimants, see P. J. Blok, *Geschiedenis van het Nederlandsche Volk,* I, 149–153; H. Pirenne, *Histoire de Belgique,* I (3d ed.), 246–255.

Over-Schelde, east of Ghent. He also claimed the allodial possessions of Dendermonde, Grammont, and Bornhem, over which the French king had of course no authority. Finally, he demanded the part of the county of Zeeland west of the Schelde which was held by the counts of Holland in fee of the counts of Flanders. The decision at Paris was clearly an invasion of the rights of the emperor. To St. Louis it was a welcome opportunity to weaken a powerful feudatory, for he well understood the significance of Flanders. By separating Hainault from Flanders he materially weakened the resistance which the Flemish count might offer to his policy and thus acted in accordance with the traditional attitude of the Capetian kings toward the feudality of France.

In these circumstances it was quite inevitable that John d'Avesnes should draw close to the traditional enemy of the Flemish counts. Floris IV, count of Holland (1222–1234), had assumed the title of Count of Zeeland, but had in 1226 been obliged to retract, only to assume the title once more a few years later.[59] Count William (1234–1256) began to style himself Count of Zeeland in 1246.[60] Soon after the decision by St. Louis at Paris in July, John d'Avesnes married Aleida, sister of Count William. Shortly before this, on August 20, Henry II, duke of Brabant, whose sister Matilda had married Count Floris, and who therefore was uncle of William and Aleida, had joined this combination.[61] War broke out in 1247 in Waasland, and Rupelmonde was taken, but the contest became much more serious when Count William was elected emperor on October 3 by the papal party in opposition to Frederick II. William purposed to use his imperial position to advance his interests and those of his allies in the Low Countries. He invested John d'Avesnes

[59] For the question of the feudal title to Zeeland, see D. Berten, "Histoire du Lien Féodal entre la Flandre et la Zélande," *Annales de la Société d'Histoire et d'Archéologie de Gand,* X (1910), 73–163; C. Sattler, *Die Flandrische-Holländische Verwicklungen unter Wilhelm von Holland 1248–1256* (Göttingen, 1872).

[60] For William, count of Holland (1234–1256), see Th. Hasse, *König Wilhelm von Holland, 1247–1256* (Strassburg, 1885); O. Hintze, *Das Königtum Wilhelms von Holland* (Leipzig, 1885); A. Ulrich, *Geschichte des Römischen Königs Wilhelms von Holland, 1247–1256* (Hannover, 1882).

[61] C. Duvivier, *La Querelle des d'Avesnes et des Dampierres,* II, 120–171; P. C. van den Bergh, *Oorkondenboek van Holland en Zeeland,* I, 236.

with the county of Hainault contrary to the rights of Countess Marguerite who was the possessor and on April 27, 1248, declared the county of Namur, which had fallen into the power of St. Louis, forfeited, and bestowed it upon his brother-in-law.[62] On September 26, 1247, the bishop of Liège invested him with the county of Hainault.[63] Thus John d'Avesnes posed as the champion of the rights of the empire against the encroachments of the French king.

For the moment nothing was done to satisfy John d'Avesnes' claim to imperial Flanders. King William could not well continue his opposition to Countess Marguerite and at the same time seek to establish his authority in the empire. Accordingly, on July 7 he came to an agreement with her at Bruges whereby he promised to respect her rights in Zeeland west of the Schelde.[64] John d'Avesnes was not able to maintain the contest single-handed and now sought reconciliation with Marguerite. Already in June he was recognizing his mother as countess of Hainault, and soon began to style himself heir of Hainault.[65] In November John and Baldwin were in Paris and specifically approved St. Louis' decision of July, 1246. In January of the next year Marguerite promised to secure within forty days after her return to Flanders renunciation of the demand made by Guillaume de Dampierre before the king in compensation for the hostilities at Rupelmonde and for other matters. She also confirmed the king's decision regarding the rights of John to her properties as countess of Hainault. John and Baldwin on their part renounced in favor of their uterine brother their title to those islands of Zeeland known as *Bewesten Schelde,* and the Quatuor Officia, Alost, Grammont, and Waasland. They also declared that the castlery of Cambrai and the rights which the counts of Flanders had long enjoyed in the Cambrésis to collect incomes (the *gave, gavenne,* or *gabellum*) in return for the protection they granted the ecclesiastical possessions should belong to Flanders.[66] Finally, on

[62] C. Duvivier, *La Querelle des d'Avesnes et des Dampierres,* II, 187–191.

[63] *Ibid.,* p. 184.

[64] A. Wauters, *Table Chronologique,* III, 531–532.

[65] C. Duvivier, *La Querelle des d'Avesnes et des Dampierres,* II, 195–197, 199–200.

[66] *Ibid.,* pp. 205–208.

May 19, 1250, King William declared he would receive Countess Marguerite's son Guillaume as vassal for the imperial titles held by the count of Flanders.[67]

In the meanwhile John d'Avesnes had persevered in his efforts to secure a recognition of legitimacy from the church. In this he was successful; on November 25, 1249, the bishop of Châlons and the abbot of Liessies, after hearing much testimony, declared the brothers legitimate, which was made definite by a bull of Innocent IV issued on April 17, 1251.[68] But John was not mollified by this victory; he apparently proposed to use it to secure possession of the allodial lands and imperial fiefs of Flanders. In a tournament held at Trazegnies, the elder Dampierre was killed and the feud broke out anew. King William was dissatisfied with the treaty made by Henry III, duke of Brabant, between himself and Countess Marguerite in 1250.[69] His imperial position was strengthened when Frederick II died at the close of that year and when he married Elizabeth of Brunswick in January, 1252. This coincided with the renewal of the quarrel between John d'Avesnes and Countess Marguerite, and on July 11, in the presence of the princes of the empire among whom appeared the duke of Brabant and the bishop-elect of Liège, the emperor at Frankfurt declared that, inasmuch as Countess Marguerite had not performed homage for her imperial possessions and the county of Namur within a year and a day of his coronation at Aix-la-Chapelle, these titles were vacant, and forthwith gave them to John d'Avesnes.[70]

In the bitter war which followed Marguerite and her sons were forced to look to France for help. On July 4, 1253, their troops were defeated by the Hollanders at Westkapelle on the island of Walcheren, and in the meantime her subjects in Hainault showed a decided preference for John d'Avesnes. Marguerite now turned to the twenty-six-year-old Charles of Anjou, brother of Louis IX, and in the autumn surrendered to him her titles to Hainault. John found it hard to resist him and was forced to abandon Le Quesnoy, Mons, Ath, Beaumont, Maubeuge, Bouchain, and Ber-

---

[67] C. Duvivier, *La Querelle des d'Avesnes et des Dampierres*, II, p. 257.

[68] *Ibid.*, pp. 253–254, 262–263.

[69] O. Hintze, *Das Königtum Wilhelms von Holland*, pp. 102–108.

[70] C. Duvivier, *La Querelle des d'Avesnes et des Dampierres*, I, 282–288.

laimont. He appealed to the bishop-elect of Liège. King William also appeared to aid him and at a meeting at Mechelen in February they confirmed his titles.[71] In July William appeared at Le Quesnoy and on the 26th succeeded in arranging a truce which was repeatedly extended until September, 1256. On the 24th was rendered the important *Dit de Péronne*. Charles of Anjou was to abandon his title to the county of Hainault in return for 16,000*l*. Tournois. The decision of July, 1246, was to remain in force in all its clauses except that the fiefs, Crèvecoeur, Arleux, Bouchain, and Ostrevant, were to be given to the count of Flanders and all quarrels were to be abandoned. John and Baldwin renounced all claim upon the county of Namur. They could do no more than accept this unfavorable decision, for their brother-in-law, King William, had died on January 28 fighting the Friesians of West Friesland.[72] The imperial throne was vacant, the period of the Interregnum had begun, and no help could be sought in that quarter. On October 21 peace was arranged at Brussels by the intercession of Henry III, duke of Brabant. The status of the county of Zeeland west of the Schelde was to remain exactly as it had been settled by the treaty of 1167 and that of 1246 at Bruges. Both parties ratified the disposition of Hainault and Flanders, and Count Floris V, son of King William, was to take as his wife Beatrice, daughter of Guy de Dampierre, heir apparent of Countess Marguerite.[73]

John d'Avesnes could not rest peaceably after being deprived of Crèvecoeur, Arleux, Bouchain, and Ostrevant, not to mention imperial Flanders and the fact that Hainault had been sadly ravaged by hostile troops, especially those of Charles of Anjou. He turned to Richard of Cornwall and furthered his election which took place at Frankfurt on January 13, 1257. So successful was he that on October 29 the citizens of Cambrai were enjoined to render homage to him as imperial vicar.[74] Seeing the close understanding between the Avesnes brothers and Richard of Cornwall, Marguerite and the Dampierres were uneasy and evinced a willingness to revise the excessively rigorous terms of

[71] *Ibid.,* pp. 360–363.
[72] *Ibid.,* pp. 413–427.
[73] A. Wauters, *Table Chronologique*, V, 134–135.
[74] C. Duvivier, *La Querelle des d'Avesnes et des Dampierres,* II, 477–478.

the decision of Péronne. On November 22 Guy de Dampierre renounced his claims upon the county of Ostrevant and Bouchain and recognized the feudal rights of Hainault over Namur together with Poilvache, Durbuy, and Laroche.[75]

It is instructive to note that in all his efforts to vindicate his rights John d'Avesnes had been forced to look to the empire for assistance. The Dampierres for their part looked to their suzerains, the kings of France, who sustained them in their possession of Flanders. The empire was too feeble to resist successfully the invasions of Capetian influence which, because of its support of the Dampierre family, had insinuated its way more and more into the courts of Low Country princes. The matrimonial unions of the children of Guy de Dampierre were especially important in this connection. Beatrice was the wife of Floris V, count of Holland; Marie was married to William, count of Juliers, and Marguerite to John I, duke of Brabant; and a second Marguerite was married first to Alexander, a son of Alexander, king of Scotland, and later to Reginald I, count of Guelders and Zutfen.[76] Guy's son, John, was bishop of Liège from 1282 to 1292, and from this date onward French influence was solidly established at this point which had ever been a center of imperial influence, as was seen in the recent struggles of the Avesnes against the Dampierres.[77]

Meanwhile the waning authority of the emperor during the Interregnum (1254–1273) and the reign of Rudolf of Hapsburg (1273–1291) gave the duke of Brabant an opportunity to achieve everything but *de jure* independence. In 1280 the last male member of the ducal house of Limburg died, and two years later Rudolf bestowed the duchy upon Ermengarde, the wife of Reginald I, count of Guelders and Zutfen. Other claimants appeared, the cadet branch of the Limburg dukes being represented by the seignior of Valkenburg, the count of Luxemburg, and the count of Berg. John I, duke of Brabant (1261–1294), could not afford to let the duchy, important because of its situation on the highway of commerce between the Rhine and Schelde valleys and

[75] *Ibid.*, pp. 479–494.

[76] L. Vanderkindere, *La Formation Territoriale des Principautés Belges*, Vol. I, Tableau V.

[77] E. Poncelet, "La Guerre dite 'de la Vache de Ciney,'" *BCRH*, 5th Ser., III (1893), 275–395.

possessed of important strategic places such as Limburg, 's-Hertogenrade (*Rode* or *Rolduc*), Sprimont, and Hervé, pass into other
hands. He bought the rights which the counts of Berg claimed
and prepared to assert his claims against the count of Guelders.
The archbishop of Cologne, loath to see any extension of Brabançon influence eastward, allied with the counts of Guelders and
Luxemburg.[78] Duke John secured the support of his brother-in-
law, the bishop of Liège, the counts of Juliers and of Cleves, the
burghers of Cologne, and also Count Floris of Holland who had
some unsettled quarrels with Count Reginald.[79] The defeat of
all his enemies on June 5, 1288, at Woeringen made the imperial
will completely nugatory; and the intercession of Philip the Fair
who established peace at Paris on October 15, 1289, between the
warring princes appeared a great triumph of Capetian diplomacy
in the ancient duchy of Lotharingia.[80]

In 1290 relations between John d'Avesnes and Philip the Fair
became acute. John's father had died in 1257 and bequeathed
to him the memory of intense hatred for the Dampierre family.
His active hostility to Count Guy began in 1271 when Countess
Marguerite surrendered imperial Flanders to her son, and on her
death in 1278 Rudolf of Hapsburg granted him the investiture.[81]
John could get no help from the empire; and from the French
king, who supported Count Guy, he could expect only hostility.
When the burghers of Valenciennes arose against him in September, 1290, because of his efforts to centralize his government,[82]
they appealed to Philip, who, ever eager to maintain his titles, demanded of Count John the performance of his feudal obligations
for Ostrevant, which had apparently never before been exacted,
and sent some troops into the country. John was helpless, and

[78] S. P. Ernst, *Histoire du Limbourg*, IV, 377–570; K. Stallaert,
Geschiedenis van Hertog Jan den Eersten van Braband en zijn Tijkvak
(Brussel, 1859).

[79] H. Pirenne, *Histoire de Belgique*, I (3d ed.), 240–246; P. J. Blok,
Geschiedenis van het Nederlanche Volk, I, 188–190.

[80] S. P. Ernst, *Histoire du Limbourg*, VI (*Codex Diplomaticus Valken-
burgensis*), 382–397.

[81] C. Duvivier, *La Querelle des d'Avesnes et des Dampierres*, I, 319.

[82] For the relations of Count John and Valenciennes, see A. Wauters,
"Le Hainaut pendant la Guerre du Comte Jean d'Avesnes contre la
Ville de Valenciennes (1290–1297)," *BCRH*, 4th Ser., II (1875), 295–342.
See also S. A. Waller Zeper, *Jan van Henegouwen, Heer van Beaumont*,
Ch. I.

yielded on September 16. Supported by Rudolf of Hapsburg, John reopened his struggle with the burghers in 1291. He now appealed to Guy, count of Flanders, who had among his numerous allies the duke of Brabant, who really intended to remain neutral, and the counts of Luxemburg, Loon, and Namur. Adolf of Nassau, elected emperor in August, 1292, supported Count John. At this moment Philip the Fair assumed some unheard-of authority in connection with the acquisition of the fiefs Alain and Warchin by the commune of Tournai, and even began to advance some claim to Valenciennes which, he contended, was a part of Ostrevant. The burghers accepted Philip's suzerainty on August 29, and the king at once entrusted Count Guy with the protection of his rights. The old feud flared up once more, war broke out, Flemish soldiers appeared in Hainault and took Le Quesnoy, and Philip the Fair sent his brother Charles of Valois to St. Quentin.

Count John could effect nothing in the face of this opposition and surrendered himself to Charles of Valois. The king imprisoned him at Montlhéry, but on October 6 freed him, whereupon a truce was made with Count Guy on October 14 which was to last until June 24 of the next year during which time the duke of Brabant should have control over Valenciennes. In December John went to Paris and on February 15 was forced to accept the king's terms. He was to raze the gates of his castle at Bouchain, pay the monastic establishments of Ostrevant 40,000*l*. Tournois as indemnity, and send his officials who had collected his assessments upon them to Paris where they were to be punished by imprisonment in the Châtelet. All his castellans and the nobility of Hainault were to promise to support Philip should their count refuse obedience to his authority in Ostrevant. But John was soon to be freed from the king's demands, for when the quarrel between Philip the Fair and Edward I, king of England, about their relations as lord and vassal became increasingly bitter and was aggravated by the destruction of the French fleet by the English at Brest on May 15, 1293, a new arrangement of alliances in the Low Countries was necessary.[83]

Philip, whose motives in his differences with Hainault, Flan-

[83] K. Vickers, *England in the Later Middle Ages*, pp. 44–46.

ders, and England were based upon the same reasons — the extension of his power — now alienated the Flemish count by interfering in the internal affairs of the county. He took advantage of the discord between the patricians of the towns and the count. The scabini of Ghent appealed to the king, who sent an officer to assume protection over the town. This was a serious invasion of the established rights of the count, who now entered into negotiations with Edward I. Adolf of Nassau, resenting the aggressions of French kings upon the imperial frontier, joined them. An extensive chain of alliances was forged which included Edward, Adolf, Guy, count of Flanders, Floris, count of Holland, Reginald, count of Guelders, Walram, seignior of Valkenburg, John, seignior of Cuyk, Siegfried, archbishop of Cologne, and numerous princes whose lands were situated upon or near the imperial border. The attitude of John I, duke of Brabant, in this crisis is very illuminating. Although Philip the Fair had negotiated peace between him and his vanquished foes in 1289, he was far from being a subservient satellite of Capetian ambitions. Situated at the center of the southern Low Countries, the duchy of Brabant demanded a policy of aloofness from the quarrels of its neighbors. Only when the interests of his bourgeoisie were involved, as in the case of the duchy of Limburg, would the duke take the offensive. Thus he might be concerned in the struggle between John, count of Hainault, and Guy, count of Flanders, but he would never allow himself to be drawn into the conflict. In 1290 his son had married Marguerite, Edward's daughter.[84] He now allied himself with England and became a most prominent agent of his father-in-law who in August assigned to him 22,000*l*. sterling, which was to be used to further alliances against Philip with princes in Savoy and in Burgundy. His attitude is revealed by the Brabançon chronicler Lodewijk van Velthem, who states that the duke declared that he would draw a greater sum from these negotiations than the total annual income from his lands.[85]

[84] *Foedera*, I, 734.
[85] Lodewijk van Velthem, *Spieghel Historiael*, p. 190:
        " Dus mochte wel gevallen daer
        Dat ick'er an winnen soude voorwaer
        Meer goets in perlementen
        Dan myn lant een iaer soude renten."

Count Guy's alliance with Edward was definitely closed by the treaty made at Lier in Brabant on August 31. But while his relations with England were satisfactory, Adolf of Nassau was inclined to support Floris, count of Holland, who desired to secure the part of Zeeland west of the Schelde, notwithstanding the fact that both Floris and Guy were allies of Edward. During the first months of 1295 there were hostilities at Sluis in spite of Edward's efforts to appease the enemies. Meanwhile Philip the Fair decided to draw close to John, count of Hainault, in order to secure his help against the count of Flanders. And at the close of March Adolf moved to secure for Count John that old bone of contention, the lands of imperial Flanders. All efforts at settlement failed, and the old dynastic antagonisms flared up with unabated fierceness. The count of Hainault drew close to Count Floris, and the latter, when in Paris on January 9, 1296, became an ally of Philip. He was to receive an annual pension of 4,000*l*. Tournois and a cash sum of 25,000*l*. Tournois. Philip now abandoned the burghers of Valenciennes and withdrew his protection on March 25. On April 1 Count Guy incorporated Valenciennes as a Flemish county and active hostilities began. But the intimate relations between the Avesnes and the count of Holland of forty years ago were not to be revived, for some of the nobles of Holland, who were sympathetic toward England and disliked the French alliance, conspired against Floris and slew him in June. His youthful son, John, who was staying in England, had married Edward's daughter, Elizabeth. He succeeded Floris in the government and adopted a policy entirely friendly toward England.[86]

[86] For all these relations, see A. Bergengrün, *Die politische Beziehungen Deutschlands zu Frankreich während der Regierung Adolfs von Nassau* (Strassburg, 1884); H. Brosien, *Der Streit um Reichsflandern in der zweiten Hälfte des dreizehnten Jahrhunderts* (Berlin, 1884); C. Hentze, *England, Frankreich, und König Adolf von Nassau, 1294–1298;* K. Franke, " Beiträge zur Geschichte Johanns II von Hennegau-Holland," *Westdeutsche Zeitschrift für Geschichte und Kunst Ergänzungsheft* V (1889); F. Funck-Brentano, *Philippe le Bel en Flandre,* pp. 198–206; F. Kern, *Die Anfänge der Fanzösischen Ausdehnungspolitik bis zum Jahr 1308,* pp. 173–189; H. Obreen, *Floris V, Graaf von Holland en Zeeland, Heer van Friesland, 1256–1296,* pp. 152–161; H. Pirenne, *Histoire de Belgique,* Vol. I (3d ed.), pp. 394–402; M. Pols, " Graaf Jan I van Holland," *Bijdragen voor Vaderlandsche Geschiedenis en Oudheidkunde,* 3d Ser., X (1899), 1–60 (second pagination).

The *rapprochement* of the count of Hainault and Philip the Fair ended in an offensive and defensive alliance concluded at Pont-Sainte-Maxence at the close of May, 1297. It was to be binding upon the heirs of each and to be renewable every ten years. The king was to be allowed to place garrisons in Hainault and the count was to aid the king with a thousand troops in Flanders, Hainault, and as far west as the Seine. In June all unsettled questions relating to Valenciennes were adjudicated in the count's favor, the homage for Ostrevant was limited, and the count was given the *advocatia* over the monasteries in that county.[87] Thus in the summer of 1297 the count of Holland was inactive, the duke of Brabant was not inclined to move, the English king was late in sailing to Flanders because of the opposition of his barons to foreign service, and when Philip with his army, supported by the levies of the count of Hainault, approached Flanders, Count Guy was practically isolated. Edward arrived too late to accomplish anything; Lille had fallen into Philip's hands, the Flemish troops had been defeated at Veurne, and all Flanders was at the mercy of the French king. A truce was arranged between Edward and Philip at St. Baafs Vijve (*Vive St. Bavon*) on October 9, which was repeatedly extended until decision was rendered by Boniface VIII on June 27, 1298, and accepted by Edward on June 19, 1299, at Montreuil-sur-Mer. It said nothing about relations between the count of Flanders and the king of France.

Flanders now lay open to French troops. Charles of Valois, the king's brother, reduced all resistance and Count Guy became a prisoner in Philip's hands. The emperor Albert of Hapsburg, who had succeeded Adolf of Nassau on July 27, 1287, invested Count Guy with the imperial fiefs of Flanders and sought the coöperation of the English king against Philip the Fair, but, because of the treaty of Montreuil-sur-Mer and the hostile bearing of Boniface VIII, was led to seek an understanding with Philip in 1299, which was accomplished after long discussions in a meeting between the two princes in December near Vaucouleurs. John, count of Holland, died on November 10, and Albert claimed that the fief had thereby become vacant. John II, count of Hainault, as son of John d'Avesnes and Aleida,

[87] L. Devillers, *Monuments*, III, 552–557.

sister of William, count of Holland, claimed both Holland and Zeeland. John was able to ingratiate himself with the magnates of Holland and even with those of Zeeland who preferred friendship with England. All efforts to dislodge him failed. He was of course greatly helped by the impotency of the Flemings who were chafing under the unsympathetic rule of Philip's governor, Jacques de Châtillon.

This situation was brusquely changed. The craftsmen of the Flemish towns lived in violent hatred of the patricians whom they called the *Leliaarts* or the champions of the *fleur de lis*. They therefore supported the count and were called *Clauwaarts*, or the men of the lion's claw, in allusion to the heraldic device on the coat of arms of Flanders. On May 17 and 18 occurred the famous Matins of Bruges which rendered Peter de Koninck immortal in the history of the Low Countries, and on July 11 the levies from the towns met the chivalry of France on the fields below Courtrai at Groeninghe and totally defeated them. The French were now expelled from Flanders and a decisive defeat was inflicted upon the whole policy of expansion so vigorously prosecuted by Philip the Fair. A mighty patriotism now moved the craftsmen who turned their arms against Philip's ally in the north of Flanders. Zeeland west of the Schelde fell into their hands, Zierikzee was invested in 1304, Holland was invaded and as far as Kennemerland the county fell into the hands of the Flemings. The duke of Brabant advanced as their ally and took everything south of the Merwede. The appearance of Witte van Haemstede, a natural son of Count Floris, on the dunes near Haarlem in May delivered the county from the Flemings. The defeat of the besiegers at Zierikzee on the waters of the Gouwe by the Genoese commander, Grimaldi, who was in French service, and by Count John's son at the close of July definitely turned back the tide of Flemish aggression. This was followed by the indecisive battle at Mons-en-Pévèle on August 18 and by a truce in September.[88]

The negotiations which followed led to the Treaty of Athis-sur-Orge in June, 1305. The Flemings were forced to pay 420,-000*l*. Tournois, agree to a large number of humiliating clauses which vastly tightened the king's authority over Flanders,

[88] J. Herent, *La Bataille de Mons-en-Pévèle* (*18 Août, 1304*).

and leave in the king's hands the castleries of Lille, Douai, and
Béthune, the stronghold of Cassel, and the town of Courtrai.
These terms were exceptionally severe; and in the eyes of the
craftsmen who had won a glorious battle on the field of Groeninghe it was unjust. But the military situation after the battle
at Mons-en-Pévèle and the defeat on the Gouwe near Zierikzee
really warranted nothing better. To continue the contest might
invite the count of Hainault and Holland to seize some of the
lands for which his family had struggled so long. John II had died
on September 11, 1304, and was succeeded by William, third of
the line in Holland and first in Hainault (1304–1337). Since
May, 1303, there had been negotiations about his marriage with
Jeanne, daughter of Charles of Valois and niece of Philip the Fair.
This union was effected in May, 1305, at Longpont, thus binding
the Avesnes and Capetians still more firmly in allegiance. A continuance of the common policy between the two houses was inevitable, for Count Robert III (1305–1322), who had succeeded
Count Guy, adopted a policy of evasion in which the crafts of the
towns patriotically supported him.

The terms of the Treaty of Athis-sur-Orge had brought a stop
to hostilities between Flanders and Hainault, but did not affect
the relations between Flanders and Holland and Zeeland. On
August 2, 1305, an agreement was reached by the duke of Brabant, Count Robert, and Count William about Guy, the bishop
of Utrecht and brother of Count John II, who had been involved
in the conflicts at the time of the succession in Holland and Zeeland and had been taken prisoner.[89] A commission was named
in 1306 to arrange a settlement of all differences between the
parties which did not, however, accomplish much. In April,
1307, peace was established by Count William with the count
of Namur and the duke of Brabant; the count of Namur rendered homage as vassal of Count William, while the duke surrendered all title as overlord of South Holland.[90] A defensive
alliance was made by them whereby the count of Namur promised not to interfere in any future hostilities between Count
William and Count Guy. In this way William was enabled

[89] L. Devillers, "Notice sur un Cartulaire de la Trésorerie des Comtes
de Hainaut," *BCRH*, 3d Ser., XII, 428–430.
[90] F. van Mieris, *Groot Charterboek*, II, 63.

to occupy Zeeland west of the Schelde without much effective opposition.[91] The armed truce continued until 1310, when Count Robert determined to settle accounts with his hereditary enemy. The armies of Flanders and Count William stood facing each other at Trimpont on the Dender. But hostilities were avoided by an agreement to submit all the disputed points to arbitration. The appointed parties met on July 30 and decided that pronouncement should be made at Tournai in August. The decision of the 17th was wholly unacceptable to Count William, for all of imperial Flanders was adjudged to Count Robert, and William was bound to surrender his claims to the lordship of Zeeland west of the Schelde. Lessines and Flobecq were declared to be parts of the old barony of Oudenaarde and hence a fief of the county of Flanders and subject to the count's right as overlord. The incomes from ecclesiastical property in the Cambrésis, payable to the protector of the church of Cambrai, were likewise adjudged to the count of Flanders. Crèvecoeur, Arleux, and the castlery of Cambrai were declared to belong to William of Flanders, seignior of Crèvecoeur.[92]

The failure of this attempt to arbitrate the disputed points threatened a renewal of war, but Philip the Fair was able to secure a truce which was finally extended until the day of St. John the Baptist in 1312. Count William sought the powerful aid of his ally to secure a satisfactory settlement of his claims. A conference at Tournai in September, 1311, failed; Count Robert was cited to appear before the Parlement in Paris in February, 1312, and yielded. At Pontoise in June Philip was accepted as judge in the questions in dispute and a decision was to be made by All Saints' Day, while the truce was to remain in force until Christmas, 1314. But nothing was accomplished, and Count Robert definitely broke with his suzerain in the summer of 1314. The inevitable answer to this was a renewal of the old alliance between the Avesnes and the Capetians, which was effected in October.[93] On November 29 Philip died, and was succeeded by Louis X (1314–1316). Summoned to do homage, Count Robert

[91] L. Devillers, *Monuments*, I, 68.
[92] S. A. Waller Zeper, *Jan van Henegouwen, Heer van Beaumont*, pp. 30–43.
[93] L. Devillers, *Monuments*, Vol. III, p. 37–39.

temporized, and finally, on June 23, 1315, his fiefs were declared forfeited. Before this, however, on February 16, a new alliance had been made. Count William was to invade Flanders from the side of Zeeland with 50,000 men-at-arms.[94]

The campaign of 1315 is interesting because it illustrates the extensive influence of the French king in the Low Countries. Closely allied with the count of Hainault, Holland, and Zeeland, with the bishop of Liège, Adolph de la Marck, whose election he had brought about in 1313 through his influence at the curia, and with John, count of Luxemburg and king of Bohemia, King Louis sought to secure the support of the duke of Brabant. John II had died in 1313 and his son, the sagacious John III who had married Marie, daughter of Louis, count of Evreux, son of Philip III, was called upon to pursue the policy of aloofness which had become traditional with the ducal house. Louis was collecting a fleet at Calais with which he hoped to cut off the Flemings from the sea. On the waters of the Schelde Count William would of course harass them. The king also called upon Edward II of England to lend him the aid of the English fleet and not allow any foodstuffs or warlike equipment go to Flanders.[95] The Flemings were thus hemmed in on every side except the east. If the duke of Brabant would coöperate with Louis and Count William, they would be completely surrounded. Louis relied upon the treaty of 1304 whereby Duke John II had become a liege vassal of Philip the Fair,[96] but the youthful duke revealed a remarkable astuteness in refusing to become a passive instrument in the hands of the French king. Nor did Edward II show any alacrity to assist Louis; a polite excuse accompanied the offer on September 18 to send but a small number of his ships. The Flemish had been ordered on the first to leave the realm by October 24 and the admiral, John de Sturmy, was notified to get ready to aid the French fleet.[97] But by this time any assistance that Edward might have given was too late. On August 1 the French stood facing the Flemings at Bondue near Lille, unable to advance because of the torrential rains which had begun in April.[98] Louis

---

[94] *Ibid.*, pp. 678–679.   [95] *Foedera*, Vol. II (1), pp. 69, 87.

[96] J. F. Willems, *Codex Diplomaticus*, I, 719–720.

[97] *Foedera*, II (1), 87.

[98] Le Muisit, p. 87, de Nangis, I, 422–423.

retreated, leaving his war materials behind him, and when Count William heard of this he too drew back.

The reign of Count Robert is important in the history of the Low Countries because it conserved for the Flemings the fruit of victory won at Groeninghe by their craftsmen in 1302. The extraordinarily severe clauses of the Treaty of Athis-sur-Orge could not be enforced, and in January, 1308, Philip the Fair had agreed to accept a cash payment of 200,000*l*. Tournois in lieu of one half of the 20,000*l*. Tournois income in land which the Flemings were to provide him in the county of Réthel and other acceptable parts. Four years later was arranged the famous *Transport de Flandre*, whereby the remaining 10,000*l*. were to be supplied by assessing this amount, which the Flemish towns were bound to pay, upon the count who in turn should surrender to the king all right to his incomes from the castleries of Lille, Douai, and Béthune. In 1316 the clauses were again modified, and the Flemings were required to pay 200,000*l*. Tournois instead of the 400,000*l*. demanded in 1305. Count Robert succeeded most fortunately in his policy of evasion, thanks to the difficulties with which Philip V (1316–1322) had to contend. Whereupon threatened with invasion by the French king and troubled with the dissensions between his sons, Louis and Robert, he decided to make peace with his suzerain. On May 5, 1320, he appeared in Paris, performed homage for his fiefs, sanctioned the status of Lille, Douai, and Béthune, and arranged the marriage of the king's daughter Marguerite and his grandson, Louis de Crécy.[99]

On September 17, 1322, the eighty-two-year-old Count Robert died, and the new count, Louis, succeeded him. The youth had been educated in France, was ignorant of the hereditary feud between his house and that of the Avesnes, quite unsympathetic to the interests of the Flemings, and was to prove himself entirely devoted to his suzerain. Charles IV, who had succeeded his brother Philip V in 1322, was therefore enabled to effect an accord between him and Count William on March 23, 1323. Louis abandoned all title to Zeeland west of the Schelde, but William yielded his position in regard to imperial Flanders and

[99] See H. Vanderlinden, "Les Relations politiques de la Flandre avec la France au XIVe Siècle," *BCRH*, 5th Ser., III (1893), 469–542; F. Funck Brentano, *Philippe le Bel en Flandre*, pp. 498–508, 516–519.

the incomes from the ecclesiastical property of the church of Cambrai. William also promised to yield his claim to Crève- coeur and Arleux if they should be given to John of Flanders, second son of William, seignior of Crèvecoeur, a stipulation which was to become important at a later date.[100] This treaty was to have an important bearing upon Count William's policy. The struggle with Count Guy of Flanders had forced him to draw close to the Capetian house. Now that all questions with Flan- ders had been solved, what would be his attitude toward the French king? All differences with the French monarchy had by no means been settled in the days following the *rapprochement* of his father, John II, with Philip the Fair. The differences about Fismy and Solesmes in Ostrevant had been the subject of long litigation. In 1323 Count William sought settlement in this matter,[101] but nothing was accomplished. Charles IV was pacifi- cally inclined, however, and it was not until the accession of Philip VI in 1328 that the new enmity between the Avesnes and Capetian houses began.

Meanwhile, Count William's prestige among his neighbors had risen vastly. At the opening of 1314 he had mediated between Adolph de la Marck, bishop of Liège, and his opponents.[102] In the imperial election of that year he played an important rôle. The party which opposed the candidacy of Frederick of Austria and supported Lewis the Bavarian was especially powerful in the Low Countries, for it comprised Gerhard, count of Juliers, Reg- inald, count of Guelders, Thierry, count of Cleves, the count of Loon, John, king of Bohemia and count of Luxemburg, and also Count William.[103] Lewis the Bavarian's chief opponent in the Rhineland was Henry of Virneburg, archbishop of Cologne, who was forced to accept peace at Bacherach in June, 1317. The peace was to be enforced by Count William whose title in this capacity was *advocatus provincialis Terrae Inferioris*. For sev-

---

[100] F. van Mieris, *Groot Charterboek,* II, 275–276.

[101] A. Hulshof, "Oorkonden in de Archives Nationales te Parijs aan- gaande de Betrekkingen der Hollandsche Graven uit het Henegouwsche en het Beiersche Huis tot Frankrijk," *Bijdragen en Mededeelingen van het Historisch Genootschap,* XXXII (1911), 310.

[102] Hocsemius, p. 365.

[103] *Ibid.,* pp. 368–369; L. Devillers, *Monuments,* III, 41–42; T. Lacom- blet, *Urkundenbuch für die Geschichte des Niederrheins,* III, 103.

eral years he and his brother John of Hainault had to devote their attention to these affairs which brought them into very close contact with Rhenish and imperial matters.[104]   William's daughters, Margaret and Johanna, were betrothed to Lewis the Bavarian and William, heir apparent of the county of Juliers. The marriage of both took place at Cologne in 1324.[105]

Count William was forced to pay a good deal of attention to the activity of the duke of Brabant.   John III disliked the mortgaging of Mechelen by the bishop of Liège to Count William in 1313.[106]   On March 10, 1316, Floris Berthout, seignior of Mechelen, sold to William his ancestral possessions for an annual income of 2,300*l.* Tournois from land to be held in fee of the count.[107]   This aroused the duke's ire, for the sale planted Count William's power in the very heart of Brabant.   The matter came to an end in 1318 when Adolph de la Marck redeemed the mortgage.[108]   Before this, on May 25, William had returned the titles which he had secured from Floris Berthout.[109]   There also were tedious disputes with the duke about boundary rights.   In 1317 occurred the quarrel and fighting between the duke and Otto, seignior of Buren, who had married a natural sister of the count. William interfered and brought about the arbitral decision made at Turnhout on October 21.[110]   In 1318 the involved relations of the seigniory of Heusden led to difficulty which produced a rupture.   On March 8 the matter was left to the arbitration of Gerhard, count of Juliers, which was rendered at Nidekken on September 25, 1320.   The duke was declared to have a legitimate title to Heusden.[111]

In 1318 the feud between the duke and Reginald, seignior of

---

[104] S. A. Waller Zeper, *Jan van Henegouwen, Heer van Beaumont,* pp. 24–82.

[105] Willelmus Procurator, p. 145.

[106] Hocsemius, p. 364; L. Devillers, *Monuments,* III, 656–657; J. David, *Geschiedenis van de Stad en de Heerlykheid van Mechelen, Bylagen,* No. XV.

[107] L. Devillers, *Monuments,* III, 58–62.

[108] S. Bormans et E. Schoolmeesters, *Cartulaire de l'Église Saint-Lambert à Liège,* II, 179–180.

[109] L. Devillers, *Monuments,* III, 80–83.

[110] Boendale, *Brabantsche Yeesten,* I, 446–448; F. van Mieris, *Groot Charterboek,* II, 190.

[111] Boendale, *Brabantsche Yeesten,* I, 462–464; F. van Mieris, *Groot Charterboek,* II, 193–219.

Valkenburg, broke out. John made it a cardinal point in his policy to maintain the peace between the Meuse and the Rhine. Reginald began to lay heavy impositions upon the burghers of Maastricht, who had important trade connections with Cologne and used the route which passed near the castle of Reginald at Valkenburg. A large army was gathered in the duchy and laid siege to the castle of Sittard on August 1. The attacks of the duke's militia from the towns were so energetic that capitulation followed on the 10th, whereupon John annexed the castle and its dependent territories to his domains.[112] But Reginald could not submit and, when the war was at the point of breaking out again, some nobles of Brabant appealed to Count William. He decided that Reginald should retire into honorable captivity in Louvain.[113] But it was impossible to arrive at a decision, for relations between the two became worse. There were raids and violence of all kinds, and the duke even extended his control in Reginald's lands. A document was drawn up by Count William on October 15, 1321, which set forth all his futile efforts to maintain the peace.[114]

The quarrel between Reginald, count of Guelders, and his son Reginald had also become acute and led to intervention by Count William. The younger Reginald objected to his father's luxury and extravagance, and sought support among the merchants and the Flemish party which had secured ascendancy in the affairs of Guelders after the defeat at Woeringen. Count William was very much interested in these matters, for his policy toward Utrecht needed the coöperation of the count of Guelders and also because his relations with the Flemings were not yet settled. In 1318 he sought to calm the differences between father and son which, however, failed of any lasting result, and war broke out. William sent an army into the Bommelerwaard. Duke John also sent a force to Amerzoden and Hedel to support Count Reginald. Finally, on October 13, Count William and the younger Reginald met at Ter Horst near Rhenen and it was decided to refer their differences to the arbitration

---

[112] Boendale, *Brabantsche Yeesten*, I, 451–458; Hocsemius, p. 376; E. Dynter, *Chronicon Ducum Brabantiae*, II, 498.

[113] F. van Mieris, *Groot Charterboek*, II, 266–267.

[114] *Ibid.,* pp. 267–268.

of John of Hainault and Henry of Flanders, count of Lodi. On November 10, 1319, at Woudrichem Count William secured the unequivocal promise of young Reginald's friendship.[115] Trouble about Heusden became once more acute, but was settled by an arbitral decision pronounced at Mechelen on January 12, 1321.[116]

Count William's interest in the political activities of the duke is explained by the position of the duchy of Brabant. It separated Zeeland and Holland from Hainault, a fact which made the duke's friendship a necessity. For these reasons William labored sincerely to settle all outstanding boundary questions with him. His connections with the count of Guelders made him interested in the disputes between him and the duke of Brabant. The situation between the Meuse and the Schelde, which was kept unsettled by the turbulency of the seignior of Valkenburg, dictated his efforts as mediator. On October 21, 1322, the two made an arrangement at Mechelen whereby John's oldest daughter, Johanna, was betrothed to William, eldest son and heir of the count of Holland. As they were but children, the formal betrothal was postponed until they should become of age. Should either of them die before that time the oldest child of each parent was to succeed to the obligations. William promised that his son would inherit all his possessions of Hainault, Holland, Zeeland, and Friesland, and that he in his own lifetime would make him count of Zeeland, a title which he was to receive as soon as he had married Johanna. As for Mechelen, William promised to transfer to his heir such claims as he still had. Johanna was to have as her marriage portion 8,000*l*. Tournois a year, and, should she become heiress of Brabant, this amount was to be increased to 10,000*l*. John promised that, should he have no male heir, Johanna would inherit Brabant, Limburg, and the duchy of Lotharingia. Should there be no male heir at the time of the marriage, the son-in-law was to receive 33,000*l*. Tournois in land annually. If he did have a male heir at that date, he was to be given 44,000*l*. Among those to affix their seals to this document were John, king of Bohemia, Reginald, count of Guelders, John, count of Namur, Gerhard, count of Juliers, Arnold, count of Loon,

---

[115] F. van Mieris, *Groot Charterboek*, II, pp. 227–228; S. A. Waller Zeper, *Jan van Henegouwen, Heer van Beaumont*, pp. 76–80.

[116] F. van Mieris, *Groot Charterboek*, II, 273–274.

Godefroid, seignior of Heinsberg, John of Hainault, and the leading towns of Brabant, Hainault, Holland, and Zeeland.[117] As Johanna and William were second cousins, and hence within the prohibited degrees, the pope, John XXII, granted his dispensation on January 27, 1323.[118]

Thus in 1325 the count of Hainault, Holland, and Zeeland had acquired a unique position among the princes of the Low Countries. The alliance with the duke of Brabant and the treaty with the count of Flanders seemed to have settled his most difficult problems. The count of Guelders was friendly to him and bound to pursue a policy toward the bishop of Utrecht in harmony with his own. The count of Juliers' heir was his son-in-law and was likely to prove an important ally in his efforts to maintain the peace between Guelders, Brabant, and other princes between the Meuse and the Rhine. Especially important was his position for the Capetian policy in the Low Countries and its relations with England and Germany. For nearly three decades the French kings had been in alliance with Count John II and Count William. With the accession of Louis de Crécy in 1322, and the settlement of the old feud between Flanders and Hainault, Holland, and Zeeland, the reason for this alliance disappeared. Whether Count William would remain a faithful supporter of the French monarchy depended upon circumstances, which between 1328 and 1336 so antagonized him toward Philip VI as to cause him to use his immense influence in the Low Countries and in Germany to inflict the greatest possible damage upon the French crown.

[117] L. Devillers, *Monuments,* III, 746–752.
[118] G. Brom, *Bullarium Trajectense,* I, 290–291.

CHAPTER II

THE MARRIAGE OF EDWARD III AND PHILIPPA OF HAINAULT (1326–1328)

i. Queen Isabella's Sojourn in the Low Countries (1326) ii. The Negotiations for the Papal Dispensation (1327) iii. The Feud between John, Duke of Brabant, and Reginald, Seignior of Valkenburg (Summer, 1327) iv. The Marriage of Philippa of Hainault and Edward III (Autumn, 1327 — Winter, 1328) v. The Valois Succession (Spring, 1328) vi. The Valkenburg Feud (1328)

I. Queen Isabella's Sojourn in the Low Countries (1326)

AFTER the scandalous relations of Queen Isabella of England with her paramour Roger Mortimer had stirred her husband Edward II, king of England, to action and rendered her continued sojourn in Paris impolitic for her brother Charles IV, king of France, who found it impossible to aid the aggrieved queen, she was constrained to look elsewhere for assistance.[1] During the final illness of Charles of Valois in December, 1325,[2] his daughter Jeanne, wife of William, count of Hainault, Holland, and Zeeland, had visited Paris, and it was apparently on this occasion that Queen Isabella's handsome and likeable son,[3] Prince Edward, first became acquainted with Philippa of Hainault, the countess' daughter.[4] The meeting of the queen and her cousin may well have had something to do with her determination to seek aid in Hainault. John of Hainault, seignior of Beaumont, younger brother of Count William, who was universally esteemed for his probity and regarded as a perfect knight, would, it was

---

[1] Edward left England on September 12, 1325, to join his mother who had gone to Paris before him in March. See *CCR* (1323–7), p. 507; *Foedera*, II(1), 609. For the king's efforts to get her to return, see K. H. Vickers, *England in the Later Middle Ages*, p. 132.

[2] *Chronique Parisienne Anonyme*, p. 101; Hocsemius, p. 385; Baker, p. 36. Cf. L. Petit, *Charles de Valois (1270–1326)*, pp. 219–220.

[3] Baker, p. 20.

[4] H. J. Smit, *Rekeningen der Graven en Gravinnen uit het Hene-*

hoped, lend his assistance.[5] Froissart's statement that the queen was guided in these steps by the advice of Robert of Artois need not therefore be accepted, especially as that prince's friendship for Edward III, which really sprang from a bitter hostility to Philip VI after his accession to the throne of France in 1328, did not begin until 1332.[6]

Relations between William, count of Hainault, Holland, and Zeeland, and Edward II of England, were at this moment seriously strained. Count William had agreed to compensate English sailors for damages inflicted by merchants of Zeeland,[7] but had failed to keep his promise, and in the autumn of 1325 renewed outrages had provoked further complaints.[8] A conference had been arranged to meet in London on January 14, 1326, but the

---

gouwsche Huis, I, 147–151 and 169. The following table will serve to make these relations clear:

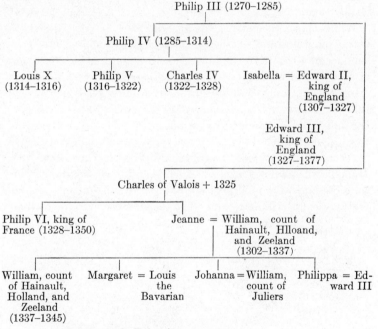

Philip III (1270–1285)

Philip IV (1285–1314)

Louis X (1314–1316)   Philip V (1316–1322)   Charles IV (1322–1328)   Isabella = Edward II, king of England (1307–1327)

Edward III, king of England (1327–1377)

Charles of Valois + 1325

Philip VI, king of France (1328–1350)   Jeanne = William, count of Hainault, Hlloand, and Zeeland (1302–1337)

William, count of Hainault, Holland, and Zeeland (1337–1345)   Margaret = Louis the Bavarian   Johanna = William, count of Juliers   Philippa = Edward III

[5] *Bourgeois de Valenciennes,* p. 141.
[6] Froissart, I, 226–227.
[7] *CPR* (1324–7), pp. 140–141.
[8] *Foedera,* II(1), 609; *CCR* (1323–7), pp. 527–528.

count's men did not appear. In spite of Edward's futile anxiety to preserve peace [9] other outrages followed — this time at the hands of English sailors off Dover, who in retaliation seized a ship from Zierikzee and killed its owner, Hanekin den Loper, and seventeen others. Count William at once appealed to Edward through Richard de Béthune, mayor of the staple,[10] and on December 12 authorized Hanekin's kin to make proper reprisals and recover 40*l.* Tournois under supervision of the scabini and bailiff of Zierikzee.[11] Attacks and confiscation followed, and on June 1, 1326, Edward dispatched John de Florencia, a member of his household, to confer with Count William.[12] On May 20 Edward had already ordered the bailiffs of Sandwich and John de Sturmy, admiral of his fleet north of the Thames, to seize all ships from Zeeland,[13] and on the 31st he explained his reasons and expressed surprise at the count's order to seize the ships of his subjects, and promised safe keeping of all prizes taken until settlement should be duly made.[14]

While Queen Isabella's consort was thus in great difficulties with Count William, she herself arrived in Hainault in the early summer of 1326.[15] In the Low Countries many believed that she was the wronged party,[16] and her sojourn met with success at every turn. Count William's brother, John of Hainault, lent his fullest support.[17] The count and countess received Isabella most cordially and apparently made no effort to hide their hostility toward the English king. The chronicler of Egmond is silent as to Count William's part in arranging the hostile expedition which Isabella was planning to send against her husband, King Edward, but contemporary observers are practically unanimous, and correctly so, in ascribing to him a chief rôle in the events which now

---

[9] *CCR* (1323–7), pp. 505–506.

[10] *Ibid.,* pp. 540–541; *Foedera,* II (1), 614.

[11] F. van Mieris, *Groot Charterboek,* II, 371.

[12] *CPR* (1324–7), p. 273.

[13] *CCR* (1323–7), p. 568.

[14] *Ibid.,* p. 569.

[15] *Istore et Croniques,* I, 334.

[16] *Chronicon Comitum Flandrensium,* pp. 200–201: "Nam ipsa regina Judith, fortitudine induta manuque Domini roborata, praecinxit se virtute. . . ."

[17] Willelmus Procurator, p. 173; S. A. Waller Zeper, *Jan van Henegouwen, Heer van Beaumont,* p. 87.

took place.[18] On August 25 the marriage contract between Prince Edward and Philippa was drawn up and sealed wholly without conference with the English king and his council and apparently against their wishes.[19] Prince Edward swore on the Holy Gospels to provide Philippa with a proper dowry and to marry her within two years from date under forfeiture of 10,000*l.* sterling. Mortimer and Kent, who accompanied Queen Isabella, each guaranteed these conditions in special documents and promised, in the event of failure to carry out these terms within the time specified, to send four knights to stay in Valenciennes within one month before the expiration of the final date and to remain there at the disposal of the count until the contract should be carried out.[20]

In the meantime plans for the invasion were vigorously prosecuted. Count William had on July 24 ordered his bailiffs, receivers, and officials of his household to collect at Flushing, Middelburg, and Westkapelle a hundred and forty boats and to have them ready for the enterprise between Dordrecht and Rotterdam by September 5. They were instructed to coöperate with Mortimer and the queen's attendants and to secure the ships at the least possible expense exactly as if they were acting in the count's behalf. The collectors of tolls were ordered to make no charge for provisions. The count promised to reimburse owners of the boats for all losses, and the queen and Prince Edward on August 3 pledged 1,500*l.* Tournois.[21] On the 30th [22] the queen, after passing through Brabant,[23] arrived at Dordrecht from Hainault. For a brief space there was much activity at Dordrecht, Rotterdam, The Hague, and Brielle, in which Count William, Countess Jeanne, Philippa, William, burgrave of Voorne, and his wife, John of Hainault, the seignior of Bousies, and others of the force

---

[18] See, for example, Villani, col. 606; Murimuth, p. 46; Hocsemius, p. 385, and Avesbury, p. 281, who speaks of an alliance.

[19] *Auctor Bridlingtoniensis*, p. 85; *Melsa*, II, 350; Baker, p. 20; Avesbury, p. 281; Willelmus Procurator, p. 173; *Istore et Croniques*, I, 334. It should be noted that in 1320 and 1321 there had been negotiations between Edward and Count William for the marriage of Edward and the latter's eldest daughter, Margaret. See *Foedera*, II (1), 437, 446.

[20] Kervyn, *Oeuvres de Froissart*, II (notes), 502–504; J. de St. Genois, *Monumens Anciens*, I, ccxvii; P. L. Muller, *Regesta Hannonensia*, p. 153.

[21] F. van Mieris, *Groot Charterboek*, II, 393–394, 396. Cf. *Istore et Croniques*, I, 334.

[22] According to Willelmus Procurator, p. 173, on September 8.

[23] Isabella passed through Diest. See *Foedera*, II (2), 226.

which was to aid in the venture,[24] took an active part. Something like seven hundred men-at-arms had been brought together by John of Hainault, largely, it would seem, from the chivalry of Hainault.[25] Thereupon followed the invasion of England under the command of John of Hainault, which unseated Edward II and placed the government in the hands of Queen Isabella and Edward, her son.[26]

II. The Negotiations for the Papal Dispensation (1327)

Three problems now confronted the new régime in England: the homage to be rendered to the French king for Gascony, involving interminable questions between lord and vassal; [27] the hostility of the Scots, who sought to take advantage of the recent troubles in England; and a papal dispensation necessary for the marriage of Edward and Philippa because they were second cousins and therefore within the prohibited degrees of blood relationship.

In the negotiations which now followed, John of Hainault, as popular at the English court as elsewhere, played an important part. When the coronation took place on February 1, 1327, he dubbed Edward knight,[28] and on the 22d he was granted full powers along with William Ayreminne, bishop of Norwich, John de Stratford, bishop of Winchester, John de Bretagne, earl of Richmond, and Hugh de Audley, to negotiate for peace and settlement of the numerous outstanding questions between the English and French crowns.[29] The English court adopted a conciliatory attitude, for on the 4th King Edward ordered the restoration of the sequestrated possessions of numerous alien French

[24] H. J. Smit, *Rekeningen der Graven en Gravinnen uit het Henegouwsche Huis,* I, 260–263.

[25] *Istore et Croniques,* I, 334; Boendale, *Van den derden Eduwaert,* p. 307; *Bourgeois de Valenciennes,* pp. 144–145; Villani, col. 606.

[26] *Istore et Croniques,* I, 334–335; Hocsemius, p. 385; *Chronicon Comitum Flandrensium,* pp. 200–201. For the expedition, see S. A. Waller Zeper, *Jan van Henegouwen, Heer van Beaumont,* Chapter V.

[27] E. Déprez, *Les Préliminaires de la Guerre de Cent Ans,* pp. 27–37.

[28] *Bourgeois de Valenciennes,* p. 143; *Chronicon Comitum Flandrensium,* p. 201; Baker, p. 34. Cf. *Foedera,* II (2), 685.

[29] *Foedera,* II (2), 69; I. Lubimenko, *Jean de Bretagne, Comte de Richmond, sa Vie et son Activité en Angleterre, en Écosse, et en France (1266–1334),* p. 118.

priories in England.[30]   Before the close of the month John of
Hainault hurried back to the continent to take part in a tournament at Condé in Hainault,[31] where he would meet many of his
relatives and friends with whom he would naturally discuss matters of political import.   Forthwith he departed for Roquemadour in southern France to satisfy a vow made when he undertook the dangerous campaign in behalf of Queen Isabella against
Edward II.[32]   On his return from this mission he met the English
deputies, who had set out for France on March 9.[33]   It looked
as if the mission would be successful, for Charles IV desired peace,
and the pope, eager to avoid hostilities, had on September 28 of
the preceding year asked the archbishops of Sens and of Rheims
and their clergy to pray for peace,[34] while the English envoys,
prompted by the wishes of King Edward's court to be unencumbered in its dealings with the pope and the Scots, were willing to
yield most points.   Accordingly at Paris on March 31 the French
deputies accepted an agreement which [35] Edward ratified on
April 11, when he also ordered his steward in Gascony to return
to King Charles the lands taken from him in the recent disturbances.[36]

As to the negotiations with the curia in Avignon, little was done
for the moment.   Not until the close of March, when negotiations
with Charles IV had favorably advanced, were Adam de Orleton,
bishop of Hereford, and Bartholomew de Burghersh, constable of
Dover Castle and warden of the Cinque Ports, sent to Avignon
to petition for a dispensation.[37]   John XXII was expecting the
mission, for Edward and Isabella had delegated John of Hainault
to prepare the way for them at the curia, and discussions concern-

---

[30] *CCR* (1327–30), pp. 18–19.

[31] Le Bel, I, 33–35; *Bourgeois de Valenciennes,* p. 146.

[32] Willelmus Procurator, p. 181.

[33] L. Mirot et E. Déprez, "Les Ambassades Anglaises pendant la
Guerre de Cent Ans," *BEC,* LIX (1898), 555. See *CPR* (1327–30), pp.
30, 31.

[34] A. Fayen, *Lettres de Jean XXII (1316–1334),* No. 1841.

[35] *Foedera,* II (2), 700–701.

[36] *Ibid.,* p. 703; *CPR* (1327–30), p. 66.

[37] L. Mirot et E. Déprez, "Les Ambassades Anglaises pendant la
Guerre de Cent Ans," *BEC,* LIX (1898), 556. See *CPR* (1327–30), pp. 59,
60, 61, 62, 143, for letters of protection, etc., dated March 24.   Cf. also
Annales Paulini, p. 333.

ing this matter had evidently been held when John of Hainault had returned to the Low Countries from Roquemadour by way of Avignon. But his zealous solicitations failed to move the pope,[38] and this was without doubt the reason why he appeared in Zeeland at the close of April to confer with his brother, Count William.[39]

What were the motives of the curia in refusing the dispensation? John XXII was trying to carry out the high claims of Boniface VIII as arbiter of Christendom. The contested imperial election of 1314 in Germany had been followed by civil dissensions, and not until Lewis the Bavarian had defeated Frederick the Fair of Austria at Mühldorf in September, 1322, did any danger threaten papal power in Italy. But when in March, 1323, the emperor, Lewis the Bavarian, sent troops into Lombardy to aid the Ghibelline Galeazzo Visconti against the attacks of papal troops upon Milan and appointed Berthold von Neiffen imperial vicar, the old struggle between *regnum* and *sacerdotium* had blazed forth anew. The pope now sought to destroy Lewis' power in Germany, while the Bavarian granted hospitality to Marsiglio of Padua, whose political doctrines in the *Defensor Pacis* scandalized the high papal party, and supported the Franciscan faction of Michael de Cesena in its struggle for the uncomfortable dogma of apostolic poverty. The request for the dispensation proved most inopportune for the pope because at this moment Lewis the Bavarian stood ready at Trent to invade Italy and measure arms with the Guelf adherents of the papacy.[40]

The political importance of Count William in reference to this situation made the dispensation a very delicate matter. Of his daughters, Margaret had in 1324 become the wife of Lewis the Bavarian,[41] and Johanna was the wife of William, son and heir

[38] Willelmus Procurator, pp. 181–182.

[39] Count William was at Zierikzee on April 16, 19, and 20, after which he spent a week at Geertruidenberg. See F. van Mieris, *Groot Charterboek,* II, 423–428. Willelmus Procurator, p. 182, dates the arrival of John of Hainault in Zeeland " circa finem maiji."

[40] A. Chroust, *Die Romfahrt Ludwigs des Bayers (1327–1329),* pp. 62–74; W. Altmann, *Der Römerzug Ludwigs des Baiern. Ein Beitrag zur Geschichte des Kampfes zwischen Papsttum und Kaisertum,* pp. 21–26.

[41] Willelmus Procurator, p. 144; *Bourgeois de Valenciennes,* pp. 126, 139, 160.

apparent of Gerhard, count of Juliers,[42] whose influence in the Rhineland was a vital matter for the curia because his lands were situated in the archbishopric of Cologne and his house had long coveted the archiepiscopal dignity for one of its own members.[43] The aged and infirm archbishop, Henry of Virneburg, was not expected to live long, and the vital question of a successor was therefore certain to come up soon.[44] To deny Gerhard's desires might, since he was already so closely identified with Lewis the Bavarian's interests, convert him into an active enemy of the pope. Count Gerhard had already shown some zeal in supporting the papal cause; he had sent a knight to Lombardy to support the Guelf party,[45] and in March, 1328, the pope repaid the favor by providing his nephew, Henry of Juliers,[46] with a deanery and a canonry in the episcopal church of Halberstadt, in spite of the fact that he had already been similarly favored in the churches of Münster, Cologne, and Bonn.[47] The count now boldly asked for the reservation of the see and suggested a personal visit to the curia. But on May 9 the pope, realizing that the count's successor was a brother-in-law of Lewis the Bavarian and that this additional power would therefore be likely to strengthen his enemies, refused to entertain such a request before the death of the occupant, stating politely, and apparently with a hint of possible favor, that the matter of a successor would be discussed with his brethren in the curia, and thanked him for the services of the knight.[48] It is apparent that Count Gerhard had sent the knight

---

[42] Willelmus Procurator, p. 145.

[43] K. Kunze, *Die Politische Stellung der Niederrheinischen Fürsten in den Jahren 1314–1334,* pp. 26–30.

[44] W. Preger, "Die Verträge Ludwigs des Baiern mit Friedrich dem Schönen in den Jahren 1325 und 1326 mit J. H. Reinkens auszügen aus Urkunden des Vatikanischen Archivs von 1325–1334," *Abhandlungen der historischen Classe der Bayerischen Akademie,* XXII (1886), 202.

[45] *Ibid.,* p. 200.

[46] For the identity of this person, see K. Hoffman, *Die Haltung des Erzbistums Kölns in den Kirchenpolitischen Kämpfen Ludwigs des Bayern,* p. 33 (note 1).

[47] G. Schmidt, "Päpstliche Urkunden und Regesten aus den Jahren 1295–1352, die Gebiete der Heutigen Provinz Sachsen und deren Umland Betreffend," *Geschichtsquellen der Provinz Sachsen und angrenzender Gebiete,* XXI (1886), 173, 177, 190.

[48] W. Preger, "Die Verträge Ludwigs des Baiern mit Friederich dem Schönen in den Jahren 1325–1326 mit J. H. Reinkens Auszügen aus Urkun-

only to win favor with the curia,[49] and that he did not wish to break with Count William in whose circle the youthful heir apparent of Juliers was constantly appearing.[50]

The pope could not count on the support of those bishops in the Low Countries in whose dioceses lay the lands of William, count of Hainault, Holland, and Zeeland, and those of his friends, for they were too much under his influence to do anything for the church in this crisis. Gui d'Arvernia, bishop of Cambrai, was Count William's close friend and finally made an agreement with him on May 25, 1327, by which bishop, chapter, and church promised to pay to Count William 500*l.* Tournois at once, 1,000*l.* at Christmas, and a similar sum on each succeeding Day of St. John the Baptist, in return for which William was to protect to the best of his power both spirituality and temporalities of the church of Cambrai against all parties save the king of France and the king of the Romans.[51]

Over the bishop of Utrecht the count's power was still more striking. That prelate was, as ever, in financial straits and was now constrained to mortgage on March 16, 1326, to Zweder van Abcoude his castle and its appurtenances at Ter Horst, and half the justice and tolls at Rhenen for 4,000*l.* black Tournois. Count William promised the bishop his full support in carrying out this contract.[52] Before this, Count William's natural brother, Simon, had been appointed marshal in the episcopal possessions west of the Yssel [53] and the bishop had borrowed 650*l.* from William van Duivenvoorde, Count William's chamberlain.[54] In spite of opposition in the episcopal curia [55] 3,700*l.* was borrowed on October

---

den des Vatikanischen Archivs von 1325–1334," *Abhandlungen der historischen Classe der Bayerischen Akademie,* XVII (1886), 223.

[49] For the policy of Juliers before and after 1324, see K. Hoffmann, *Die Haltung des Erzbistums Kölns in den kirchenpolitischen Kämpfen Ludwigs des Bayern,* pp. 27–34.

[50] H. J. Smit, *Rekeningen der Graven en Gravinnen uit het Henegouwsche Huis,* I, 158, 160, 168, 169.

[51] P. L. Muller, *Regesta Hannonensia,* p. 209; L. Devillers, *Monuments,* III, 767–768 and 771–772. Cf. H. Dubrulle, *Cambrai à la Fin du Moyen Âge (XIIIe–XVIe Siècle),* pp. 276–277.

[52] S. Muller Fz., *De Registers en Rekeningen van het Bisdom Utrecht,* I, 22–24, 26–27.

[53] *Ibid.,* pp. 33–35. At the same time he ordered his bailiffs of Amstelland and Woerden to lend him the necessary support.

[54] *Ibid.,* p. 35.   [55] Willelmus Procurator, p. 205.

7, 1327, and the castle of Vredeland, valued at 200*l.* annually, was offered as a pledge. The bishop then appointed John van Outshoorne marshal over his lands west of the Yssel and the count ordered " all his friends in the bishopric of Utrecht, his bailiffs, and subjects " to support him in maintaining the rights of the bishop as often as he might request their aid.[56] To silence all possible objections William declared that he would be ready to relinquish Vredeland as soon as the pledge should be redeemed.[57] On October 10, 1327, both parties agreed to carry out the terms made on the 7th and solemnly swore to support each other in their respective rights.[58]

With Reginald, count of Guelders, William's influence had long made itself vitally felt; in fact both were following a common policy toward the see of Utrecht. Hence when on April 11, 1325, the bishop formed a defensive alliance with John, count of Bentheim, William and Reginald were both excluded from its terms.[59] And when the men of Oostringen in East Friesland sought compensation for goods taken from some merchants of Jever by subjects of Count William, they requested on July 26, 1327, the good offices of Count Reginald.[60] Shortly before this Count Reginald had borrowed from Gerhard, count of Juliers, 12,000*l.* black Tournois and offered as pledge his castle at Montfoort and its dependencies.[61]

Thus because of his close relations with the bishops of Cambrai and Utrecht, with the counts of Guelders and Juliers in the north, and John, duke of Brabant and Limburg, in the south,[62] Count William's position was important for the interests of the papacy in all these parts and in the Rhineland as far south as the Moselle. And his connection with Lewis the Bavarian and the royal family of France made him a personage of European significance. This, it is interesting to note, was also the testimony of con-

---

[56] S. Muller Fz., *De Registers en Rekeningen van het Bisdom Utrecht,* I, 96–100; *Chronicon Tielense,* p. 334.

[57] F. van Mieris, *Groot Charterboek,* II, 446.

[58] S. Muller Fz., *De Registers en Rekeningen van het Bisdom Utrecht,* I, 100.

[59] *Ibid.,* pp. 39–41.

[60] I. A. Nijhoff, *Gedenkwaardigheden uit de Geschiedenis van Gelderland,* I, 213–214.

[61] *Ibid.,* pp. 208–211.

[62] Cf. *infra,* pp. 76–78.

temporaries. Marino Sanudo, who was so active in promoting a crusade to recover the Holy Land, repeatedly urged the pope in 1326 and 1327 to make peace with Lewis the Bavarian, and suggested Count William as arbiter. Because of his moderation and wisdom and because of his numerous family connections, this person appeared to him and others especially fit to labor for the repose of Christendom.[63]

The reasons for the pope's reluctance to grant the dispensation for the marriage of Philippa and Edward are thus sufficiently apparent. He feared that the union might forge a strong link of interest between Lewis the Bavarian and the English court. It might place all the industrial and commercial power in the Low Countries, where the most powerful, the Flemings, had been for several years in full revolt against their suzerain, the king of France, at the side of the excommunicate king of the Romans. John XXII had shown hostility towards the Flemings in no uncertain manner,[64] for on April 6 he had ordered the archbishop of Rheims, the bishop of Senlis, and the abbot of St. Denis to excommunicate them and place them under the interdict.[65] Furthermore, the perennial disputes between English kings and their suzerains, the kings of France, in regard to Gascony might, notwithstanding the settlement of March 31, 1327, flare up anew at any moment and the marriage could then conceivably become an important factor in forming a vast European coalition which would be directed against France and the papacy. In fact, at this very moment Charles IV was making warlike preparations on the borders of Gascony.[66] These were certainly no idle considerations, and Pope John might well labor zealously to establish peace between France and England. The news of the treaty pleased him and on May 1 he thanked the bishops of Norwich and Winchester for their efforts and urged them to labor for the full execution of its provisions.[67]

[63] Marino Sanudo, *Epistolae*, J. Bongarsius, *Gesta Dei per Francos*, II, 304–310, 312.

[64] *Chronicon Comitum Flandrensium*, p. 179: " Homo benignus qui non armis, sed papalibus litteris visus est Flandriam impugnare."

[65] A. Fayen, *Lettres de Jean XXII (1316–1334)*, No. 1942; L. Gilliodts van Severen, *Inventaire des Archives de la Ville de Bruges*, I, 384–387.

[66] M. Jusselin, " Comment la France se Préparait à la Guerre de Cent Ans," *BEC*, LXXIII (1912), 213, 220, 221.

[67] W. H. Bliss, *Calendar of Entries in the Papal Registers*, II, 484.

During the first three months of 1327 Lewis the Bavarian was at Innsbruck and Trent in consultation with the Visconti and a large number of the Ghibelline enemies of the pope. In January he wrote to the duke of Brabant that the meeting, which had been fixed for February 9, had been postponed for one month and that the duke, William, count of Hainault, Holland, and Zeeland, and Baldwin, archbishop of Trier, were to appear before him at Nuremburg, where he intended to issue some decrees and make plans for the projected invasion of Lombardy.[68] The cautious duke of Brabant preferred to stay at home, and William, count of Hainault, Holland, and Zeeland, who had repeatedly urged his imperial son-in-law to carry the contest into Italy, now also failed to appear.[69] On March 13 earnest solicitations were again sent to Count William [70] and again on April 10 from Como [71] similar missives were despatched begging him to hasten to the aid of his son-in-law. The bishop of Utrecht [72] and also Reginald, count of Guelders,[73] were ordered to appear before the emperor not later than May. But these princes could not be induced to move when Count William, so vitally interested in the dispensation, thought it wisest not to respond even after the third summons. Nevertheless, Lewis the Bavarian was determined to have succor from the Low Countries and sent a messenger, who appeared in Utrecht on May 31, to summon the bishop orally to discharge his duty toward the empire. The prelate hesitated and even questioned the validity of the Bavarian's title,[74] probably because of Count William's wavering policy and

[68] J. F. Boehmer, " Briefe Ludwigs des Baiern," *Fontes Rerum Germanicarum.* I, 193–194; J. F. Boehmer, *Regesten Kaiser Ludwigs des Baiern und seiner Zeit,* p. 319.

[69] On March 13 the Bavarian wrote: " memor quod ad hoc nos semper sollicitasti quodque nobis in Italiam obsequi promisisti," see Willelmus Procurator, p. 187. He again wrote in similar vein on April 10: " memores etiam multarum instantiarum et persuasionum tuarum, quibus frequenter conatus es, nos ad progressus subscriptos pro viribus inclinare. . . ." See F. van Mieris, *Groot Charterboek,* II, 422. See also the letter of June 20 in Willelmus Procurator, pp. 192–193.

[70] Willelmus Procurator, pp. 184–187.

[71] F. van Mieris, *Groot Charterboek,* II, 422.

[72] S. Muller Fz., *De Registers en Rekeningen van het Bisdom Utrecht,* I, 130–132.

[73] J. F. Boehmer, " Briefe Ludwigs des Baiern," *Fontes Rerum Germanicarum,* I, 196.

[74] Willelmus Procurator, pp. 198–199.

the papal excommunication which had been published on April 22 in the dioceses of Liège and Utrecht and throughout the province of Cologne.[75] To oppose the pope under these circumstances would be folly, and Count William accordingly hesitated for a moment and at last prudently decided to abandon the emperor, his son-in-law.

The pope's anxiety was also stimulated, it appears, by the participation of Count William's brother, John of Hainault, in the Stanhope Park campaign of 1327 against the Scots. It had been arranged before John's departure from London in February that he should return with a force of men-at-arms by about May 6.[76] The chivalry of the Cambrésis, Hainault, Flanders, Brabant, and Liège were eager to serve under one whose prestige had vastly risen because of his successful expedition in behalf of Queen Isabella and Edward against Edward II. Among those to flock to his standard was John le Bel, canon of St. Lambert in Liège, who was to become the historian of the campaign. Beyond the Meuse, Thierry of Heinsberg and William of Juliers planned to come with five hundred men whom they had collected at their own expense. And William's relations with his father, Count Gerhard, who had shown himself considerate of the pope's political feelings, were said to be anything but cordial at this moment.[77] The situation appeared delicate enough, for the people in the lower Rhine region were by no means eager for the papal cause. On April 5, for example, Pope John had to urge the apparently wavering townsmen of Cologne to remain steadfast.[78] Toward the end of May seven hundred and eighty men-at-arms, not including the contingent from beyond the Meuse, set out for England, crossed the Channel from Wissant to Dover, and, passing through Canterbury, finally arrived at York.[79] Every effort had been made to give them a hospitable reception, since the sher-

[75] A. Fayen, *Lettres de Jean XXII (1316–1334)*, No. 1951; G. Brom, *Bullarium Trajectense*, Vol. I, No. 716.

[76] *Rotuli Scotiae*, I, 210–211; *CPR* (1327–30), p. 108.

[77] Le Bel, I, 39–41.

[78] W. Preger, "Die Verträge Ludwigs des Baiern mit Friedrich dem Schönen in den Jahren 1325 und 1326 mit J. H. Reinkens Auszügen aus Urkunden des Vatikanischen Archivs von 1325–1334," *Abhandlungen der historischen Classe der Bayerischen Akademie,* Vol. XVII (1886), Nos. 327, 362.

[79] *Bourgeois de Valenciennes*, p. 144; le Bel, I, 41.

iffs and members of the royal household had been expressly commanded to provide all comforts and necessaries for the journey.[80] The campaign was over on August 9 but added nothing to John of Hainault's laurels.[81] On the 20th Edward granted him 4,000*l.* sterling as compensation, directed carriages to be provided, and ordered John de Insula to conduct the entire contingent back to Dover.[82]

Thus by midsummer Count William, who had in the meantime allowed the collection of money for papal purposes from the clergy in his own dominions,[83] clearly revealed his decision to follow his own local interests rather than to support his imperial son-in-law in Italy. Nevertheless, the pope was fully determined to grant the dispensation only when he could be certain of the consequences, and so still persisted in his refusal. Hugo de Engolisma, archdeacon of Canterbury, kept the curia informed of the state of opinion in England through his envoy Aitius de Clerencio. This person was detained by Pope John to await the English envoys, the bishop of Hereford, Bartholomew de Burghersh, and Hugh de Astele. To the urgent requests of Edward and Isabella the pope replied on June 30, and, begging to be excused, sent oral instructions for Edward's fuller information.[84] What these must have been is revealed in Edward's reply of August 15, in which he lamented the fact that certain grave insinuations had been made in the curia against Count William and prejudicial to the marriage.[85] Similar response was given in Avignon by Count William's agents, the abbot of Vicogne, and Michael de Linea, seignior of Pontoit, who supported the bishop and his party. Finally, on July 14, John declared that the request could not be granted for the moment and directed the English party to explain orally the situation to Count William when on their way to

[80] *Rotuli Scotiae*, I, 210–211; *Foedera*, II (2), 706.

[81] Le Bel, I, 42–77; S. A. Waller Zeper, *Jan van Henegouwen, Heer van Beaumont*, pp. 98–107; J. H. Ramsay, *The Genesis of Lancaster*, I, 189–194.

[82] *Foedera*, II (2), 713.

[83] Willelmus Procurator, pp. 192–193.

[84] W. H. Bliss, *Calendar of Entries in the Papal Registers*, II, 484.

[85] *Foedera*, II (2), 712–713: " Verum, pater sanctissime, etsi turbemur in intimis ex hiis, quae vobis de praefato comite non absque suspitione sinistra sunt relata, nec credamus ea ex malivolentia, set potius ex levitate quadam vel forsan fabricatione aemulorum, prodiisse, cum nec promissa in litteris, quae sibi ascribuntur, in opere sint completa. . . ."

England.[86]   On August 4 they were at Le Quesnoy in Hainault [87] where they were entertained by the countess, Jeanne.

The pope's opposition might well react to his own disadvantage. Shortly after John's pronouncement of June 30 Count William returned from Brabant and appeared at Katwijk at the close of the third week in July before his subjects to discuss the question of going to the support of Lewis the Bavarian. The people and also the nobility were favorable, and his eldest son, William, was accepted to act as regent during his absence.[88] It was said that Reginald, count of Guelders, and Gerhard, count of Juliers, stood ready to join Count William.[89] The truth of this is difficult to establish; for Guelders it is quite possible, but in the case of Juliers, who was eagerly courting the favor of the curia, improbable.[90] At any rate Count William had definitely decided to threaten the pope with an expedition to Italy, where Lewis the Bavarian had already received the crown of Lombardy at the hands of the Ghibellines.

This hostile activity apparently caused the pope to consider the advisability of moderation. Negotiations were still in progress, and on August 15 Edward addressed the pope in reassuring tone. Protesting vigorously against the papal view of Count William's activities, he pointed out that nothing had as yet happened to justify the rumor which had been circulated, undoubtedly referring to his failure to support Lewis the Bavarian in Italy. Furthermore, he promised to ask the count to conform in every way to the wishes of the pope and stated that John of Hainault, now ready to return to the continent from the campaign against the Scots, would use his influence with Count William so that no evil should come from the proposed marriage.[91]

[86] A. Fayen, *Lettres de Jean XXII* (*1316–1334*), No. 2002; G. Brom, *Bullarium Trajectense*, Vol. I, No. 719.

[87] J. H. Smit, *Rekeningen der Graven en Gravinnen uit het Henegouwsche Huis,* I, 284. William was at Mons on August 10. Cf. F. van Mieris, *Groot Charterboek,* II, 431–435.

[88] Willelmus Procurator, pp. 200–201. He was in The Hague on July 21, 22, and 24. See F. van Mieris, *Groot Charterboek,* II, 431–435.

[89] Willelmus Procurator, p. 199; Beka, p. 113, who confuses this with Count William's proposal to visit the curia at Avignon in 1330.

[90] W. Preger, " Die Verträge Ludwigs der Baiern mit Friedrich dem Schönen in den Jahren 1325 und 1326 mit J. H. Reinkens Auszügen aus Vatikanischen Archivs von 1325–1334," *Abhandlungen der historischen Classe der Bayerischen Akademie,* Vol. XVII (1886), Nos. 356, 357, 362, 375.

[91] *Foedera,* II (2), 712–713.

A long threatened outbreak of hostilities between John, duke of Brabant, and Reginald, seignior of Valkenburg, now occurred and at once diverted Count William's attention, delaying his expedition for several months at least. Nor could the counts of Juliers and Guelders, also vitally concerned in the matter of Valkenburg, do anything to aid the emperor.[92] The danger of Count William's open opposition to the pope was thus averted, and the representatives of King Edward and William finally overcame the pope's reluctance. The abbot of Vicogne and the seignior de Pontoit promised on August 29 that their lord the count would obey the pope even against Lewis the Bavarian.[93] On the following day the coveted dispensation was granted.[94] The pope also reconfirmed the privilege of November 12, 1320, whereby six clerks of the count's appointment might draw the fruits of their benefices even though absent.[95] On September 3 he replied in full to statements made by the envoys. He accepted the excuses made, promised to regard Count William as a devoted son of the church, urged the Countess Jeanne to labor for her husband's loyalty toward mother church, and promised that the relics of her uncle, St. Louis, bishop of Toulouse, who had been canonized in 1317, would be sent to her with despatch.[96]

III. The Feud Between John, Duke of Brabant, and Reginald, Seignior of Valkenburg (Summer, 1327)

The feud between John, duke of Brabant, and Reginald, seignior of Valkenburg, had not only prevented William, count of Hainault, Holland, and Zeeland, from going to the support of Lewis the Bavarian, but also had given the duke, who above everything else preferred to protect his local interests, a good

---

[92] Hocsemius, pp. 497–499; Boendale, *Brabantsche Yeesten,* I, 470–471, 477.

[93] P. L. Muller, *Regesta Hannonensia,* p. 164.

[94] A. Fayen, *Lettres de Jean XXII (1316–1334),* No. 2020; G. Brom, *Bullarium Trajectense,* Vol. I, No. 727; W. H. Bliss, *Calendar of Entries in the Papal Registers,* II, 265. John of Hainault arrived in Hainault in September where he received the news of the dispensation. See Willelmus Procurator, pp. 202–203, and H. J. Smit, *Rekeningen der Graven en Gravinnen uit het Henegouwsche Huis,* I, 417–418.

[95] A. Fayen, *Lettres de Jean XXII (1316–1334),* No. 2019.

[96] *Ibid.,* No. 2027; G. Brom, *Bullarium Trajectense,* Vol. I, Nos. 727, 728.

reason for not appearing in Lombardy. On November 26 Reginald had been freed from prison, where he had been incarcerated by the duke, at the intervention of William, count of Hainault, Holland, and Zeeland, Reginald, count of Guelders, and Adolph, bishop of Liège, on the promise that he would return to Genappe by August 1, 1326, under penalty of forfeiting 20,000*l.* black Tournois and would render proper compensation in case of any violence against the duke's subjects.[97] Reginald failed to appear and apparently at the close of June began to plunder the duke's merchants. By August 1 as many as eighteen villages in Limburg were said to have been laid in ashes. The men of Maastricht, subjects of the duke of Brabant, were singled out as special objects of Reginald's revenge. An attempt was even made to seize the duke while he was passing through a forest. John now threatened to settle once for all with his troublesome neighbor, and his subjects, noble as well as bourgeois, were eager for military action.[98]

The seignior of Valkenburg now turned for aid to John, king of Bohemia and count of Luxemburg, the lifelong enemy of the duke of Brabant.[99] Among the forces collected to resist the Brabanters were Conrad, seignior of Schleiden, and Conrad, count of Tomburg, and the *advocatus* of Cologne, sent without doubt, in the interests of the archbishop of Cologne, who viewed the duke's expansion east of the Meuse with grave apprehension.[100] William, count of Hainault, Holland, and Zeeland, visited Duke John in Brabant about July 11 when on his return from France to Holland, and sought to assuage his anger, but in vain,[101] for the duke crossed the Meuse toward the close of July [102] at the head of an enthusiastic communal militia and laid siege to the town and stronghold of Valkenburg.[103]

Craftsmen had been drawn from the towns of Brabant to construct machines and a person especially skilled in building engines, who had been present at the siege of Volmarstein on the

[97] L. Devillers, *Monuments,* III, 205–206 (note).
[98] Willelmus Procurator, p. 201; Boendale, *Brabantsche Yeesten,* I, 470.
[99] Willelmus Procurator, p. 201.
[100] Boendale, *Brabantsche Yeesten,* I, 470.
[101] Willelmus Procurator, p. 201.
[102] Hocsemius, p. 399; *Chronicon Tielense,* p. 320.
[103] Boendale, *Brabantsche Yeesten,* I, 471–472.

Ruhr in 1324,[104] took charge of four hundred men and pressed the operations with vigor.[105] The place had been strongly fortified and surrounded by a wall and a moat through which the waters of the Geule ran. Part of the stronghold was on high ground and its reduction was no easy matter. The castle had been well provisioned, Reginald had friends within to defend it, and, as the king of Bohemia was expected to succor them speedily, the defenders were optimistic. But the king of Bohemia was a shaking reed and failed to appear. Assaults were in vain. Finally, the duke's men constructed a dam across the Geule on the banks of which the stronghold was situated and turned the waters through the town. The lower parts were soon submerged and the people betook themselves to the higher spots near the castle on the left bank only to find the doors closed before them.[106]

Powerless to relieve his ally, the king of Bohemia sent two knights to confer with the duke of Brabant. They announced that the king of Bohemia would soon come in person to raise the siege, a futile thing as the duke knew only too well, for it was clear to all that this spendthrift knight-errant had never sufficient funds to pay even his ordinary debts. As the duke refused to move, appeal was made to the count of Juliers and a reconciliation was finally effected at 's-Hertogenrade. The siege was to end and the walls and gates of the stronghold were to be razed. An agreement was also made with the king of Bohemia, who had now arrived on the scene of action and swore to support his cousin at all times. The duke of Brabant agreed to abide by the decision of arbiters who were to be appointed by the king of Bohemia to render a decision at an early date.[107]

The Brabanters returned home on October 1. The king of Bohemia accompanied the duke to Brussels and was entertained most sumptuously. He even became the godfather of the duke's second child and the reconciliation appeared complete.[108] This seemed still further confirmed when on January 4, 1328, he surrendered for a sum of money all claim upon any share of the

---

[104] Willelmus Procurator, p. 151; Levold de Northof, p. 100.
[105] Willelmus Procurator, pp. 201–202.
[106] Boendale, *Brabantsche Yeesten,* I, 472–479.
[107] *Ibid.,* pp. 476–478.
[108] *Ibid.,* p. 479.

duke's possessions.[109]   Three days later Duke John yielded his
rights to homage which the king owed him for Arlon and Rode,
a privilege which was also extended to those of his successors who
should be kings and to the first three generations without such
title upon the condition that these fiefs should never be alienated
without the consent of the duke or his heirs.[110]

IV. The Marriage of Philippa of Hainault and Edward III
(Autumn, 1327 — Winter, 1328)

Since May 15 Roger of Northburgh, bishop of Coventry and
Lichfield, had held himself in readiness to cross the Channel
to Hainault to complete the final arrangements for the marriage
of Edward and Philippa.[111]   The delay in securing the dispensation had kept him waiting until October when on the 8th he was
reappointed to contract the marriage for King Edward and settle
the matter of the dowry.   Count William himself was expected to
cross to England with Philippa and everything was put in readiness for their reception.[112]   The bishop departed at once [113] and
found the court in Hainault in great excitement, for the marriage
of a count's daughter with a king was no ordinary event in the
annals of the house of Avesnes.   The countess and Philippa were
in Valenciennes toward the end of October.   Important figures
among the Hainault nobility, the ladies of Werchen, of Gom-
mengnies, and of Fontenelles, the seignior of Bousies, and many
others were ready on the 25th to greet the bishop and his company, who arrived in the evening.[114]   Count William put in his
appearance on the following day, and they forthwith proceeded

---

[109] F. J. Boehmer, *Regesten Kaiser Ludwigs des Baiern und seiner
Zeit*, p. 297.   This was apparently a formal conclusion of promises made at
Rolduc during the preceding summer.

[110] J. F. Willems, *Codex Diplomaticus*, I, 776–777; E. Dynter, *Chronicon Ducum Brabantiae*, II, 548 and 782; C. Butkens *Trophées tant Sacrés
que Profanes du Duché de Brabant*, I (*Preuves*), 162.   For a vidimus by
the duke, see F. J. Boehmer, *Regesten Kaiser Ludwigs des Baiern und
seiner Zeit*, p. 296.

[111] *CPR* (1327–30), p. 266.

[112] *Foedera*, II(2), 718; *CPR* (1327–30), pp. 177, 179.

[113] F. Devon, *Issues of the Exchequer: Henry III to Henry IV*, p. 140.

[114] H. J. Smit, *Rekeningen der Graven en Gravinnen uit het Henegouwsche Huis*, I, 373, 376.

to business and drew up a document on the 28th, the count, John of Hainault, seignior of Beaumont, and Walter, seignior of Bousies, acting as witnesses.[115]

A season of brilliant festivities now opened in the count's castle at Valenciennes. Among the distinguished guests were John, king of Bohemia, who was ever eager to witness such brilliant ceremonies, Gerhard, count of Juliers, John, count of Namur, the count of Arnsberg, Adolph, count of Berg, William, heir apparent of Juliers, and his brother Walram, destined to become archbishop of Cologne, William, burgrave of Voorne, the bishops of Cambrai, Tournai, and Arras, and, not least of these, John of Hainault himself, all of whom came after St. Nicholas' Day to grace the final ceremonies.[116] There had been, it seems, an unforeseen delay, for on October 29 John de Hoby, the bishop's clerk, hastened to England for some instructions, and was not back in Valenciennes until December 8, where he found all these notables.[117] On November 28 Edward had ordered Bartholomew de Burghersh, constable of Dover Castle, and William de Clinton to conduct Count William and Philippa to England.[118] The departure was now hastened and on December 16 Philippa started on her journey, accompanied by Walter de Manny, who later was to find a splendid career in England,[119] and others such as Jean de Bernier, member of the count's council, provost of Valenciennes and grand bailiff and receiver of Hainault,[120] Gerard, seignior of Pottes, and William van Duivenvoorde, the count's chamberlain.[121] At Wissant they took passage and landed at Dover.[122] As Count William had stayed in Hainault,[123] the direction of the escort had been fittingly entrusted to John of Hainault

[115] *Archives de l'État,* Mons, *Trésor des Chartes,* October 28, 1327.

[116] H. J. Smit, *Rekeningen der Graven en Gravinnen uit het Henegouwsche Huis,* I, 375–376, 396.

[117] F. Devon, *Issues of the Exchequer: Henry III to Henry IV,* pp. 140–141.

[118] *Foedera,* II (2), 724.

[119] Le Bel, I, 81.

[120] *Bourgeois de Valenciennes,* pp. 49, 59.

[121] H. J. Smit, *Rekeningen der Graven en Gravinnen uit het Henegouwsche Huis,* I, 376; *Froissart,* I, 76–77.

[122] Willelmus Procurator, p. 205; Froissart, I, 76.

[123] He was at Binche on December 21. See F. van Mieris, *Groot Charterboek,* II, 449.

and Adolph, count of Berg.[124]   They were soon met by the bishops of Norwich and Hereford,[125] arrived in London on the 22d,[126] and were enthusiastically received by the public [127] and clergy who came out in procession.   On the 24th a gift of choice victuals, said to have been worth three hundred marks, was presented to Philippa.   The mayor and a goodly company of burghers then escorted her to Holborn on the 27th [128] whence she proceeded on her way northward.[129]

At York preparation for the final ceremonies had been started on the 18th when King Edward instructed Nicholas de Hugate, canon of St. Peter's,[130] to superintend preparations in the archiepiscopal palace.[131]   On January 23, 1328, Count William arrived with Roger, the bishop of Coventry and Lichfield,[132] for whom the final solemnization, which took place on the 25th,[133] apparently had to wait.   In May, in accordance with his former promise to Count William, Edward agreed to settle on Philippa 15,000*l.* black Tournois.[134]   Liberal rewards were granted as follows: to Jean de Bernier, land in fee simple in England or Ponthieu of an annual value of 100*l.* Tournois,[135] and to van Duivenvoorde and

---

[124] H. J. Smit, *Rekeningen der Graven en Gravinnen uit het Henegouwsche Huis,* I, 376; Froissart, I, 76, 285.

[125] *Annales Paulini,* p. 338.   Froissart, I, 285, states that they were Reginald de Cobham and the earl of Warwick.

[126] *Annales Paulini,* p. 339.   Knighton, I, 446, states that it was on the 24th.   See *French Chronicle of London,* p. 61; le Bel, I, 80; *Auctor Bridlingtoniensis,* p. 99.

[127] Knighton, I, 446.

[128] *Annales Paulini,* p. 339.   The account by le Bel, I, 80, is erroneous.

[129] Froissart, I, 286, tells how John of Hainault left her in tears at Eltham.

[130] *CCR* (1327–30), p. 316.

[131] F. Devon, *Issues of the Exchequer: Henry III to Henry IV,* p. 140. On December 6 Robert de Wodehouse, the king's keeper of the wardrobe, borrowed from Richard and William de la Pole 1,200*l.* sterling.   See *CPR* (1327–30), p. 191.

[132] F. Devon, *Issues of the Exchequer: Henry III to Henry IV,* pp. 140–141.

[133] Knighton, I, 446–447; Froissart, I, 287; Walsingham, *Historia Anglicana,* p. 192; *Annales de Bermundeseia,* p. 472; *Auctor Bridlingtoniensis,* p. 99; *Annales Paulini,* p. 339 (where it is dated January 30); Murimuth, p. 57; Walsingham, *Ypodigma,* VII, 268; Melsa, II, 357; *French Chronicle of London,* p. 61; *Scalacronica,* p. 155.

[134] *Foedera,* II (2), 743; *CPR* (1327–30), p. 270.

[135] *CPR* (1327–30), p. 270; *Bourgeois de Valenciennes,* p. 59 (20*l.* sterling equal 100*l.* Tournois of Hainault).

the seignior of Pottes each, 20*l*. sterling annually out of the customs receipts of Yarmouth.[136]   Thus was finally concluded this marriage which greatly raised the prestige of Count William. With pardonable pride might the chronicler of Egmond exult that the count of Hainault, Holland, and Zeeland could now call the kings of both England and Germany his sons-in-law.[137]

V. THE VALOIS SUCCESSION (SPRING, 1328)

CHARLES IV, king of France, became ill at Christmas, 1327, and died on the first of the following February,[138] leaving no son to succeed him.   But the queen was *enceinte,* and until the birth of the child a regent would have to be appointed.   To this honor no person was better entitled than the nearest male heir through direct male descent, Philip of Valois, the son of Charles of Valois, younger brother of Philip the Fair, and hence the brother-in-law of William, count of Hainault, Holland, and Zeeland.   The latter was on this account quite prominent among the leading personages at the court [139] and was, it is said, influential in naming Philip regent.[140]

In his anxiety over Lewis the Bavarian's progress in Italy the pope now turned to Philip.   It had long been a tradition to look to France for aid in the struggle against the *imperium* and Philip in 1320 had led an army into Italy as lieutenant of the papal vicar general, Robert, king of Naples.[141]   In the warfare between Lewis the Bavarian and Frederick of Austria, the latter's brother, Duke Leopold, had drawn close to Charles IV, and at Bar-sur-Aube on July 27, 1324, had promised him the imperial crown.[142]   The inert king, however, abandoned the project upon the reconciliation of

[136] *CPR* (1327–30), pp. 270, 421, 454.

[137] Willelmus Procurator, p. 205.

[138] *Chronique Parisienne Anonyme,* pp. 113, 114; Willelmus Procurator, p. 208; Hocsemius, p. 391.

[139] Launcelot, "Mémoire pour servir à l'Histoire de Robert d'Artois," *Mémoires de Littérature tiréz des Registres de l'Académie Royale des Inscriptions et Belles Lettres,* X (1736), 618.

[140] *Bourgeois de Valenciennes,* p. 147; de Nangis, II, 84; Villani, col. 607; *Chronicon Comitum Flandrensium,* p. 202.

[141] A. Chroust, *Die Romfahrt Ludwigs des Bayers (1327–1329),* pp. 20–22.   See Willelmus Procurator, pp. 260.

[142] F. J. Boehmer, *Regesten Kaiser Ludwigs des Baiern und Seiner Zeit,* p. 252.

the Bavarian with Frederick of Austria at Trausnitz in the spring
of 1325 and the death of Leopold in February, 1326.[143] But John
XXII was undaunted, and requested Charles IV on February 2,
1326, to send a person of high estate to Languedoc, who with five
hundred men-at-arms should sustain the Guelf cause. But it was
in vain, for on April 5 he had to repeat his request.[144]

Lewis the Bavarian and his wife Margaret had been crowned at
Rome on January 17, 1328,[145] and the pope replied on the 21st
with an order that a crusade should be preached against him in
all churches, promising the same spiritual rewards that came
from expeditions to the Holy Land.[146] Supporters of the Guelf
cause now flocked around the pope, all spiritual weapons in the
papal armory were brought into use, and a new election was
forthwith ordered.[147] But the regent, Philip of Valois, could ill
afford to embark upon any chimerical enterprise in Italy at a
moment when the crown might fall upon him as heir presumptive
of the Capetian line. The many knotty problems connected
with the English homage for Gascony were bound to come up
and the Flemings would have to be dealt with. Since the Treaty
of Arques of April 19, 1326,[148] the free farmers of the Flemish
coast and the men of the towns of Bruges and Ypres had risen
in revolt and ejected their count, Louis of Nevers. Charles IV
was on the point of taking determined measures to repress them
when he fell ill and died,[149] and the violent attack in a sermon
against Lewis the Bavarian by Peter de Rosiers, abbot of Fé-
camp, in Paris on February 17, apparently before the king and the
court, naturally failed to arouse any response.[150] Philip was
keenly enough interested in imperial concerns [151] and noted with

[143] E. Werunsky, *Geschichte Kaiser Karls IV und Seiner Zeit,* I, 21;
W. Friedensburg, *Ludwig IV der Baier und Friedrich von Oesterreich
von dem Vertrag zu Trausnitz bis zur Zusammenkunft in Innsbruck,
1325–1326.*
[144] S. Riezler, *Vatikanische Akten,* No. 623.
[145] F. van Mieris, *Groot Charterboek,* II, 450.
[146] J. Ficker, *Urkunden zur Geschichte des Römerzuges Kaiser Ludwigs
des Baiers,* Documents Nos. 108, 109, 110.
[147] W. Altmann, *Der Römerzug Ludwigs des Baiern,* pp. 79–87.
[148] T. de Limburg Stirum, *Codex Diplomaticus Flandriae,* II, 385–398.
[149] *Chronicon Comitum Flandrensium,* p. 202.
[150] *Vita Karoli,* p. 232; E. Werunsky, *Geschichte Kaiser Karls IV und
Seiner Zeit,* I, 20.
[151] Cf. *infra,* pp. 116–117, 168–171.

care Lewis' career, of which the pope kept him informed,[152] but the interests of the crown forced him to refuse the overtures of Huego, the papal nuncio, who offered him the Lombard crown to be held in fee of the papacy.[153] The mysterious presence of Lombard knights in Count William's household on Easter of this year may possibly have been due to an effort to exert pressure upon Philip through his sister and brother-in-law.[154]

Count William of Hainault, Holland, and Zeeland had his own difficulties of long standing with the Capetians, and evidently thought the moment opportune to secure a definitive settlement. In 1301 Philip the Fair had proclaimed himself *advocatus* of the monastery and lands at Solesmes and Fismy, situated in the Cambrésis, and therefore within the bounds of the empire.[155] Question had repeatedly been raised regarding their ownership and ever failed of settlement.[156] Accordingly in the Louvre at Paris Count William performed homage for Ostrevant on February 13, and it was agreed that an inquest by four men, two to be appointed by each party, should determine exactly what lands belonged to the French crown.[157] Philip at once directed the bishop of Laon and Bouchard de Montmorency to proceed to Ostrevant *hastivement et sans délai*, and, when Bouchard was relieved of this burden, William Flote was substituted on April 24.[158] In the meantime differences had risen regarding the justice of the Scarpe between the town of Douai and its castellan and the seignior of Lalaing, supported by his suzerain, Count William.

[152] S. Riezler, *Vatikanische Akten,* No. 1198.

[153] W. Felten, *Die Bulle "Ne Pretereat" und die Reconciliations Verhandlungen Ludwigs des Bayers mit dem Papste Johann XXII,* I, 35; A. Lehleiter, *Die Politik König Johanns von Böhmen in den Jahren 1330–1334,* pp. 37–39.

[154] H. J. Smit, *De Rekeningen der Graven en Gravinnen uit het Henegouwsche Huis,* I, 384.

[155] F. Kern, *Die Anfänge der Französischen Ausdehnungspolitik bis zum Jahr 1308,* pp. 247–248; H. Dubrulle, *Cambrai à la Fin du Moyen Âge (XIIIe–XVIe Siècle),* p. 258.

[156] A. Hulshoff, "Oorkonden in de Archives Nationales te Parijs aangaande de Betrekkingen der Hollandsche Graven uit het Henegouwsche en het Beiersche Huis tot Frankrijk," *Bijdragen en Mededeelingen van het Historisch Genootschap gevestigd te Utrecht,* XXXII (1911), 310; J. Viard, "L'Ostrevant. Enquête au Sujet de la Frontière Française sous Philippe de Valois," *BEC,* LXXXII (1921), 316–329.

[157] L. Devillers, *Monuments,* III, 185.

[158] *Ibid.,* pp. 186–189, 191–193.

Philip apparently revealed his desire for an accommodation by ordering on April 28 the bailiffs of Lille, Douai, Tournai, and Hainault to investigate the claims by inquest.[159]   And in June he granted to his nephew William, heir of Hainault, Holland, and Zeeland, his possessions at Blaton in Hainault, which he had held before his accession to the throne and which had originally been a grant of Count William's.[160]   While awaiting the birth of the queen's child, King Edward of England also determined to assert his rights which had suffered from the aggressions of the Capetians and, on March 28, declared his intention of recovering them.[161]   An attempt upon France might accordingly be made by him through Gascony.   When the child arrived on April 1, it proved to be a girl,[162] and the question of the succession now threatened to become acute.   Because of his connection with the English king and the emperor, his ascendancy in the Low Countries, and the intimate bond with the Valois family, Count William's position now became a matter of vital importance to his brother-in-law.[163]

VI. The Valkenburg Feud (1328)

The old feud between Brabant and Valkenburg now threatened to break out again.   John, king of Bohemia, did not wish to favor John, duke of Brabant, and, in spite of the latter's insistence, kept deferring his decision from time to time.   In violation of the agreement made at 's-Hertogenrade, the walls and gates of Valkenburg castle had not been razed and work had even been done to strengthen them.[164]   The quarrel became so serious that William, count of Hainault, Holland, and Zeeland, felt obliged to assuage their bitter hatred and in March went to Mechelen to discuss the matter with the king and the duke in the presence of other princes.   Nothing, however, was accomplished as Reginald of Valkenburg stubbornly refused to appear and sent messengers armed with letters.   The well-meaning efforts of

---

[159] L. Devillers, *Monuments,* III, pp. 194–195.
[160] *Ibid.,* p. 195. See also pp. 206–208.
[161] *Foedera,* II (2), 736.
[162] *Grandes Chroniques,* V, 306.
[163] See Willelmus Procurator, p. 208, for an expression of his enhanced prestige.
[164] Boendale, *Brabantsche Yeesten,* I, 479–480.

Count William and his friends thus appeared futile.[165] Between April 10 and 14 there were renewed discussions in Louvain [166] and a truce to last until June 24 was finally accepted.[167] But an outbreak was inevitable. A quarrel developed between the town of Valkenburg and the seignior of Heinsberg and his accomplices. By stratagem the latter managed to enter the gates on an early morning. Some of the inhabitants found safety in the castle and others perished in the fire or by the sword, whereupon the marauders returned home.[168] A settled state of hostility now developed on the border of Limburg and Valkenburg. In July Reginald sent his lieutenant, the seignior of Schleiden, to harry Limburg with fire and sword, and a great quantity of booty and sheep was taken. Duke John was enraged with his royal cousin who by his procrastination was no doubt in part to blame for the situation.[169]

These events inevitably led to a closer understanding between John, duke of Brabant, and Count William who was so intimate with the counts of Juliers and Guelders, both of whom were also vitally concerned with the fate of Valkenburg. Accordingly, on August 6 a defensive agreement was arranged whereby each promised to support the honor and integrity of the other, protect his burghers, and extend his aid under all circumstances. Military assistance was to be sent by each at his own expense in the territories which lay between Aubenton, Bohain, and Douai on the south and west, and Bonn, Nijmegen, and Arnhem on the north and east. Beyond these limits each was bound to furnish at the expense of the party needing them six hundred men-at-arms for the duration of the hostilities. No new war was to be undertaken without the advice of the other unless for purely local reasons, nor was any alliance to be made contrary to the interests of the other party, and, if in case of conflict between the vassals

[165] Willelmus Procurator, p. 211.

[166] Count William was at Zïerikzee on the 8th and at Geertruidenberg on the 10th. See F. van Mieris, *Groot Charterboek*, II, 453, 455. The scabini of Ghent sent two of their number to meet him in Louvain and they were gone from the 9th to the 14th. See J. Vuylsteke, *Gentsche Stads- en Baljuwsrekeningen, 1280–1336*, II, 596.

[167] Willelmus Procurator, p. 211.

[168] *Ibid.*, pp. 211–212; *Chronicon Tielense*, p. 320.

[169] Willelmus Procurator, p. 217; Boendale, *Brabantsche Yeesten*, I, 480.

and friends of both, arbitration should be refused, the terms of the alliance were not to be applicable. Possible border disputes were to be settled by the arbitrament of four men, two to be chosen by each side. And finally, in order to maintain amity each promised never to acquire in any manner the episcopal rights in Mechelen so long as the alliance should endure.[170] Thereupon Count William agreed not to interfere with any attempt to punish Valkenburg nor aid the latter in any way,[171] and the duke renounced all right to any military aid in the expedition beyond the Meuse.[172] Peace was thus guaranteed, the duke secured freedom from hostility from the counts of Guelders and Juliers, and Count William was now at liberty to aid in reducing the Flemings. Duke John was pleased with the security thus obtained, and proof of his friendship for William may be seen in the solemn disavowal made by him when the seignior of Putten was suspected of having some treasonable plan with Otto, seignior of Cuyk, one of the duke's most trusted vassals, to harm William's interests in Holland and Utrecht.[173]

[170] L. Devillers, *Monuments,* III, 198–203, 204.
[171] F. van Mieris, *Groot Charterboek,* II, 467.
[172] L. Devillers, *Monuments,* III, 205.
[173] F. van Mieris, *Groot Charterboek,* II, 468.

CHAPTER III

THE POLITICAL POSITION OF WILLIAM, COUNT OF HAINAULT, HOLLAND, AND ZEELAND (1328–1332)

i. Edward III, the French Crown, and the Flemings (1328)   ii. The Battle of Cassel (August 23, 1328)   iii. The Valkenburg Feud (1329)   iv. William, Count of Hainault, Holland, and Zeeland, the Empire, and the Papacy (1328–1330)   v. The Marriage of Reginald, Count of Guelders, and Eleanor Plantagenet (1331–1332)

I. EDWARD III, THE FRENCH CROWN, AND THE FLEMINGS (1328)

FROM the beginning of his regency Philip of Valois had been forced to pay attention to the Flemings. Deputies were sent by the loyal scabini of Ghent, with whom William, count of Hainault, Holland, and Zeeland, and John of Hainault were in close contact,[1] to the regent at Compiègne between March 9 and 27.[2] Later, when at Amiens, the king submitted his differences with the rebels to arbitration, and appointed Andrew de Florence, treasurer of Rheims, Robert de Bertrand, marshal of France, and Thomas de Marfontaine, a knight, to discuss these questions with the delegates of Bruges and Ypres and their supporters. Philip's men, accompanied by Louis, count of Flanders, John, count of Namur, and two of the scabini of Ghent, appeared at the appointed time at Thérouanne where the meeting was to be held.[3] But the rebels did not put in an appearance, and after waiting two days the representatives returned.[4] Perhaps they were counting upon the support of Edward III who, after the succession of Philip of Valois on April 2,[5] claimed the throne inasmuch as he was the nearest heir. On May 16 he despatched Adam de

---

[1] J. Vuylsteke, *Gentsche Stads- en Baljuwsrekeningen, 1280–1336*, II, 594, 596.

[2] *Ibid.*, p. 596.

[3] *Ibid.*, p. 597.

[4] *Archives Nationales*, Paris, J. 569, No. 1.

[5] Hocsemius, p. 391, *Chronique Parisienne Anonyme*, p. 116; *Chronicon Comitum Flandrensium*, p. 202.

Orleton, bishop of Worcester, and Roger de Northburgh, bishop of Coventry and Lichfield, to France to protest against Philip's elevation, present his claims, and demand satisfaction.[6]   No attention, however, was paid to them, and the coronation took place at Rheims on May 29 [7] amid a great throng of notables, among whom were a number from the Low Countries, such as William, count of Hainault, Holland, and Zeeland, Countess Jeanne, and her household,[8] John of Hainault,[9] John, king of Bohemia,[10] Louis, count of Flanders,[11] and others.

During the ceremonies there were rumors of Edward's intention to aid the Flemings.[12]   Perhaps the rebels had broken off negotiations with the king in anticipation of a war between the two claimants of the French crown.   French and English seamen were already at blows in the Channel, and on June 28 Edward ordered his sheriffs to make reprisals.[13] Since the preceding year he had been zealous to cultivate the best relations with Bruges and Ypres; wrongs had been redressed and compensation for losses had been rendered with alacrity.[14]   On May 11, five weeks after Philip's succession to the throne, when it was fully evident that the French would not hearken to his claims, he sent John de Chidiok, a knight, as special envoy to Bruges to state orally his desires [15] to William de Deken, the soul of the Flemish rebellion.[16] The tenor of these conversations may be surmised from the in-

[6] *Foedera,* II (2), 743.

[7] P. Varin, *Archives Administratives de la Ville de Reims,* II (1), 202; *Bourgeois de Valenciennes,* p. 148; le Bel, I, 92; *Chronicon Comitum Flandrensium,* p. 202; le Muisit, p. 98; de Nangis, II, 91.

[8] H. J. Smit, *Rekeningen der Graven en Gravinnen uit het Henegouwsche Huis,* I, 396, 473.

[9] *Ibid.,* pp. 386–387.

[10] *Ibid.,* pp. 388–389; Froissart, I, 296–297; *Königsaaler Geschichts-Quellen,* p. 455. He had to borrow 195*l.* from John of Hainault to pay his expenses. See F. van Mieris, *Groot Charterboek,* II, 459.

[11] Ghent contributed 1,000*l.* toward his expenses. See J. Vuylsteke, *Gentsche Stads- en Baljuwsrekeningen, 1280–1336,* II, 586. The bishop of Liège was absent because of the rebellion of his subjects. See Hocsemius, p. 397.

[12] *Grandes Chroniques,* V, 309; de Nangis, II, 90; Willelmus Procurator, pp. 219–220.

[13] *Foedera,* II (2), 745; *CCR* (1327–30), pp. 306, 320–321.

[14] *CPR* (1327–30), pp. 64, 65, 83, 91, 155, 227, 291.

[15] *Foedera,* II (2), 742; *CCR* (1327–30), p. 386.

[16] For William de Deken, see E. Varenberg, "Guillaume de Deken," *Biographie Nationale,* Vol. V, col. 78–81.

structions of June 9 given to Chidiok and Reginald de Cobham, a knight, for the duke of Brabant and the towns of Brabant and Flanders, with whom they were to work for an alliance and discuss all necessary details.[17] But the duke's gaze was fixed upon the situation beyond the Meuse, and these proposals were without result so far as he was concerned. Cobham returned to England by August 6,[18] and on the 22d Edward empowered him and John de Hildesle, canon of Chichester, to treat for alliances, and make arrangements for the payment of troops and loss of horses, with John, duke of Brabant, Reginald, count of Guelders, Thierry, count of Loon, Henry de Bautreshem, a Brabançon nobleman, and other important personages.[19]

These negotiations occupied the envoys until Christmas,[20] but were everywhere futile save in Flanders. The craftsmen of Bruges and Ypres, supported by the free peasantry of the coast, were resolved to have nothing to do with their count or with the king of France. The activities of William de Deken in this connection are particularly significant. Since the Treaty of Arques, of April 19, 1326, he had made several trips to England and on some of these occasions at least had made representations to Edward that he ought of right to be king of France. These visits must accordingly have taken place either during the regency or most likely immediately after Philip's accession. He even went so far as to offer Edward the lordship of Flanders,[21] and at home fomented rebellion everywhere, induced the Flemings to refuse the coinage of the king of France as legal tender, and was guilty

[17] *Foedera,* II(2), 744.

[18] *CCR* (1327–30), pp. 307, 320, 338.

[19] *Foedera,* II(2), 749; *CCR* (1327–30), p. 353.

[20] L. Mirot et E. Déprez, " Les Ambassades Anglaises pendant la Guerre de Cent Ans," *BEC,* LIX (1898), 556. See *CCR* (1327–30), pp. 338, 353.

[21] See H. Stein, " Les Conséquences de la Bataille de Cassel pour la Ville de Bruges et la Mort de Guillaume de Deken, son ancien Bourgmestre (1328)," *BCRH,* 68(1899), 656: " Item, que plusieurs fois puis la darrenière pais (i.e. Arques) ledit Guillaume a esté en Engleterre pour traictier avec le Roy d'Angleterre qu'il feust leurs sires en Flandres et avecques ce qu'il feust Roys de France.

" Respont que il n'i fu onques puis qu'il fu prins à Calais, mais avant il y avoit bien esté pour traictier des dommages qui avoient esté fais entre les Anglois et les Flamens, et dit que il ne scet que les Flamenz envoiassent onques en Engleterre pour faire alliances." These are the words in the report drawn up at the inquest in Paris.

of many treasonable actions.[22]   These were all denied by him when he subsequently faced trial at Paris, but there can be no question of their accuracy.   A delegation of important personages was actually sent by the rebels to Edward III for exactly this purpose, as the chronicler of Egmond states; [23] in fact, the matter was an open secret in the circles in which William, count of Hainault, Holland, and Zeeland, moved, for as father-in-law of the English king he was undoubtedly approached by the Flemings for aid.[24]   At any rate, the report was current among them that he and Edward purposed to support the rebellion.[25]   And this is further substantiated by the fact that Edward on August 7 gave to John de Chidiok letters directed to the chief abettors of sedition and rebellion in Bruges, the burgomasters William de Deken and John Schinkel, and Peter van Sonnebeke, clerk of the scabini.[26]

It is impossible to determine precisely how much influence the representations of the Flemish envoys may have exercised upon Edward who naturally enough was chagrined that the French should so lightly disregard his pretended rights.   Any attempt by Edward upon France could be expected only through Aquitaine or through the Low Countries where a rebellion was raging which was obviously viewed with grave apprehension by Philip.   To

[22] H. Stein, *op. cit.,* p. 655.

[23] Willelmus Procurator, p. 219.   He states that it was composed of "twelve" members.   This may be a paleographical error for "three," as Professor Pirenne has shown.   See H. Pirenne, "La première Tentative faite pour Reconnaître Édouard III d'Angleterre comme Roi de France," *Annales de la Société d'Histoire et d'Archéologie de Gand,* V (1902), 9 (note 3).

[24] Willelmus Procurator, pp. 219–220.

[25] See the testimony of Lamsin de Lene in N. de Pauw, "L'Enquête de Bruges après la Bataille de Cassel, Documents inédits publiés," *BCRH,* 68 (1899), 699: ". . . k'il venoit en le parroche de Ysendike sour l'âtre prêchier, et prêçoit às gens communalement k'il se tenroient bien et fort aveuc le ville de Bruges encontre le roy de France et contre Monsingneur de Flandres, et encontre tous chiaus ki vauroient grever le ville de Bruges, et dist k'il fust bien seurs ke li ville de Bruges, et tout le paijs de Flandres de luer alliés aroient en brief tans soucours dou roy d'Engleterre et dou conte de Hollande et de Zélande, et k'il se vauroient déporter aveuc eaus comme frères; et tout chou fu fait et prêchiet en préjudice Monsingneur de Flandres, pour Monsingneur de Flandres déshiriter et le roy de France comme souverain; et sont des plusseurs persones pourtrait de ce et de mult des autres mals."

[26] *Foedera,* II (2), 747.

league with these rebels offered some prospect of success, and that
Edward thought of this is proved by his efforts to secure as allies
at precisely this moment John, duke of Brabant, Thierry, count
of Loon, and Reginald, count of Guelders. It is also obvious
that he hoped for aid from his father-in-law, Count William.
Thus the English court followed the traditional path as marked
out by John Lackland and Edward I in their struggles with
Philip Augustus and Philip the Fair. It is under these circumstances quite possible that William de Deken's suggestions influenced Edward and his advisers to strike at Philip by aiding the
Flemings. It is also instructive to note in passing, as Professor
Pirenne has pointed out, that this idea was later borrowed by
Jacob van Artevelde when in 1340 Edward was solemnly ac-
cepted in Flanders as the legitimate king of France.[27]

Several factors, however, prevented a general conflict at this
moment. The duke of Brabant was faced with the problem of
Valkenburg, in which the counts of Juliers and Guelders were
vitally interested, and doggedly refused to be drawn away. There
was a revolt among the crafts of Liège. They had been inspired
to rise, it appears, by the spectacle of an apparently successful
rebellion in Flanders.[28] This, of course, interested all those princes
who would not ally with any revolutionary element in the Low
Countries to support Edward against King Philip. Aside from his
friendship for his brother-in-law, the king of France, this was
certainly a powerful motive with Count William in wishing to
suppress a movement which sought to subvert the authority of a
legitimate prince. The chronicler of Egmond states that for a
moment he entertained some desire to support Edward as it
would exalt his own daughter.[29] While this may be really little
more than a patriotic reflection of the chronicler, it is interesting
to note that the archbishop of Canterbury was at William's
court during these days. Nothing, however, is known of the
purpose of his visit.[30]

---

[27] H. Pirenne, " La première Tentative faite pour Reconnaître Édouard
III d'Angleterre comme Roi de France," *Annales de la Société et d'Archéologie de Gand,* V (1902), 5–11.

[28] G. Kurth, *La Cité de Liège au Moyen Âge,* II, 31–34.

[29] Willelmus Procurator, pp. 219–220.

[30] H. J. Smit, *Rekeningen der Graven en Gravinnen uit het Henegouwsche Huis,* I, 394.

The Flemings, whose hopes had been unduly raised, were thus deserted at the supreme moment. Edward was not ready to fight; he never seriously entertained the thought, it would seem. The Close and Patent Rolls reveal no effort to collect troops in any number during these months. On June 28 reprisals for damages inflicted by Norman seamen were authorized,[31] on August 3 men-at-arms were forbidden to leave the realm,[32] and on the 30th the officials of Guernsey were empowered to force the bishops in Normandy to discharge their feudal obligations in Guernsey, Jersey, Alderney, and Sark.[33] But the serious difficulties at home, where the party of Isabella and Mortimer met with determined opposition during these months,[34] made any active support of the Flemings unthinkable, and Edward contented himself with diplomatic efforts in the Low Countries and also in the south of France. The problem was thus opportunely simplified for Count William. On July 22 he appeared at Geertruidenberg [35] before the nobility and officials of Holland and Zeeland to discuss the " horrible wickedness " of the Flemings and placed before them the proposition of aiding Philip. To this they agreed, and on August 10 the levies of Holland and Zeeland began to hurry southward to Hainault [36] to join the royal forces which were being collected at Arras.

II. The Battle of Cassel (August 23, 1328)

At the time of the coronation at Rheims the Flemish situation had thus assumed a most serious aspect. Many a French notable had poignant memories of the frightful disaster at Courtrai in 1302. Louis, count of Flanders, pressed his suzerain to aid in putting down the rebels with expedition.[37] Orders were issued for

---

[31] *Foedera,* II (2), 745.
[32] *Ibid.,* p. 746.
[33] *Ibid.,* p. 750.
[34] J. H. Ramsay, *Genesis of Lancaster,* I, 202–203.
[35] F. van Mieris, *Groot Charterboek,* II, 460–461.
[36] Willelmus Procurator, pp. 201–202.
[37] *Chronicon Comitum Flandrensium,* p. 203. According to Froissart, I, 296–297, who embellished the scene with his art, Philip's decision was made at the instigation of Count Louis' dramatic actions. Cf. also *Grandes Chroniques,* V, 309–310; de Nangis, II, 90–91; *Istore et Croniques,* I, 342.

the levies to meet at Arras on July 31.[38]   There was much activity
in preparation for the campaign,[39] and the king left Paris about
July 24 and was at Arras by August 6.[40]   The royal army moved
northward, crossed the Lys and the Neuf Fosse near Aire on Saturday morning, August 20, moved toward the eminence of Cassel
by way of Blaringhem, and halted at the monastery of Woestine.[41]   The levies from Hainault, Holland, and Zeeland had
by this time joined the king's forces.   The household accounts
of Countess Jeanne contain numerous references to matters connected with the movements of the men-at-arms.   On August
18 William, count of Juliers, and his following were entertained at Le Quesnoy.[42]   His brother, Godefroid, also came,
and Count William put in his appearance at Valenciennes on
the 14th.[43]

Philip had been careful to strengthen the garrisons at St. Omer,
Lille, and Tournai.[44]   A party of Count Louis' forces stationed
at Biervliet under Hector Vilain overran the countryside as far
as Bruges, and Count Louis and John, count of Namur, left
Ghent with the communal militia to join the king.[45]   To oppose
these invaders the Flemings took up a position on the top of the
hill of Cassel so that their tents could be descried by the royal
troops at Woestine.[46]   Philip now began systematic destruction.
Homesteads and villages were set afire on every hand in order to
draw the Flemings from their strong position, but the king waited
in vain for three whole days.[47]   On the 22d he moved his forces to
the Peene, a rivulet only a league from the enemy, and continued

---

[38] *Grandes Chroniques,* V, 310; *Chronicon Comitum Flandrensium,*
p. 204; *Istore et Chroniques,* I, 342.

[39] For the activities of Philip, see J. Viard, " La Guerre de Flandres
(1328)," *BEC,* LXXXIII (1922), 362–382; P. J. E. de Smyttere, *La Bataille
du Val de Cassel en 1328* (Lille, 1883).

[40] J. Viard, " Itinéraire de Philippe de Valois," *BEC,* LXXXIV (1913),
90.

[41] *Chronicon Comitum Flandrensium,* p. 204; *Istore et Croniques,* I,
343–344; *Grandes Chroniques,* V, 312.

[42] H. J. Smit, *Rekeningen der Graven en Gravinnen uit het Henegouwsche Huis,* I, 368–369, 444, 473.

[43] *Ibid.,* p. 394.

[44] *Istore et Croniques,* I, 342; *Grandes Chroniques,* V, 311–312.

[45] *Chronicon Comitum Flandrensium,* p. 204; *de Budt,* p. 322.

[46] *Grandes Chroniques,* V, 314; *Istore et Croniques,* I, 344.

[47] *Chronicon Comitum Flandrensium,* pp. 204–205; *de Budt,* p. 322;
Grandes Chroniques, V, 311.

plundering, but the Flemings still refused to stir.[48] His troops
were composed of nine divisions in all besides a rear guard commanded by Robert of Artois. That of Count William was the
eighth and to it had been added the levies of John, king of Bohemia, commanded by John of Hainault.[49] The entire force was
arranged in three groups in circular form at the foot of the hill
with the king's command at the south, Count William's in the
middle and, it would seem, somewhat nearer the hill,[50] and a third
body, of which we hear little, at the extreme north.[51] The king
sent troops to ride around the hill and cut off the enemy from their
country and their source of food, which at once became scarce.[52]
In the early morning of the 23d some of the royal troops began
to skirmish with the Flemings in the vain hope of drawing them
to the foot. In accordance with the decisions of a council held
at this moment, Robert of Cassel, uncle of Louis, count of Flanders, was despatched toward Bergen to lay the entire countryside in ashes. But the farmers and craftsmen stubbornly refused
to be drawn down to the plain where they would be at a disadvantage.[53]

The Flemings had formed the plan to deliver a surprise attack during the night.[54] With bitter hatred they had watched
Philip's approach, and, feeling safe in the presence of chivalry
because of their positions, they proceeded to taunt the king, perhaps in the hope of inducing him to attack at once. They raised
a banner on which was inscribed the legend:

> " Quant ce coq ci chanté ara
> Le roi trouvé ça entrera." [55]

A more insulting term than *rex inventus*, which was aimed at his
illegitimate title, could scarcely be imagined.[56] But the king

[48] *Istore et Croniques*, I, 344; de Budt, p. 322; *Grandes Chroniques*, V,
314-315.   [49] *Grandes Chroniques*, V, 313-314; de Budt, p. 322.

[50] Willelmus Procurator, p. 222.

[51] *Grandes Chroniques*, V, 315; *Bourgeois de Valenciennes*, p. 150;
Froissart, I, 85, 299.   [52] *Chronicon Comitum Flandrensium*, p. 205.

[53] *Grandes Chroniques*, V, 315; *Istore et Croniques*, I, 344; de Budt,
p. 322. Robert arrived in the army on the 22d.

[54] *Chronicon Comitum Flandrensium*, p. 205; de Budt, p. 322.

[55] *Grandes Chroniques*, V, 311. For other versions, see *Chronique
Parisienne Anonyme*, p. 118; de Nangis, II, 94-95; de Budt, p. 322.

[56] De Nangis, II, 95: " Unde et subsannantes regi, dicebant eum et voca-
bant regem inventum."

stayed at the foot of the hill and thus during the whole day there
was a lull. The knights in his following, wearied by the heat of
the day, became heedless and were off their guard.[57] Philip himself had retired to his tent after dinner, as was his custom.[58]
Nicholas Zannekin, who commanded the contingent from Nieuwpoort, perceived the opportunity and urged the Flemings to attack
at once.[59] Exasperated at the sight of their homes which had been
burning around them for several days, they agreed, and arranged
themselves in three groups [60] each of which was to attack the
royal division before it. Rapidly and noiselessly they de-
scended,[61] armed with scythes and clubs and, "thick as the
rain," bore down upon the enemy in a most unexpected manner.[62]
The first to see them broke and fled in the direction of St. Omer.[63]
Zannekin's wing preceded the others and fell first upon the contingent from Tournai which had taken a position in the king's
section nearest that of Count William,[64] unperceived by the
rest.[65] The Flemings were already near the rear where the victual
vendors were stationed and hard by the royal tents [66] before the
trumpets began to sound a general alarm and before the knights
could begin to hasten to the defense so sorely needed. At this
very critical juncture Count William, who had seen the enemy
rush down the hillside,[67] and whose troops were not entirely off
their guard, hurried to deliver the first effectual resistance. With

[57] *Grandes Chroniques*, V, 315–316.

[58] De Nangis, II, 96.

[59] *Chronicon Comitum Flandrensium*, p. 205; de Budt, p. 323.

[60] *Bourgeois de Valenciennes*, p. 150; *Istore et Croniques,* I, 344; Froissart, I, 85, 299.

[61] *Bourgeois de Valenciennes,* p. 150; *Grandes Chroniques*, V, 316;
Istore et Croniques; I, 244; *Chronicon Comitum Flandrensium*, p. 205, de
Budt, p. 323, and de Nangis, II, 97, state that there was much clamor.

[62] *Chronique Parisienne Anonyme*, p. 118; *Bourgeois de Valenciennes,*
p. 150.

[63] *Grandes Chroniques*, V, 316.

[64] Le Muisit, pp. 99–100.

[65] *Chronique Parisienne Anonyme*, p. 118.

[66] *Bourgeois de Valenciennes*, p. 150; *Grandes Chroniques,* V, 316;
de Nangis, II, 97; *Chronique Parisienne Anonyme*, p. 119.

[67] This would be the case if at the moment of attack Count William was
with his men. This is implied by the *Chronique Parisienne Anonyme*,
p. 119, the *Bourgeois de Valenciennes*, p. 151, and the *Istore et Croniques,*
I, 244. With less probability the *Grandes Chroniques*, V, 316, the *Chronicon Comitum Flandrensium*, p. 205, and de Budt, p. 323, state that he was
in the king's tent.

John of Hainault, Robert of Cassel, who had just returned from his expedition,[68] and others at his side, he fell upon Zannekin's right flank from the north, and, as he came up around the contour of the hill, upon his rear, thus surrounding the Flemings and cutting off all possibility of retreat.[69]

Zannekin's men stood their ground well and resisted with vigor. They wrought fearful execution among the horses of the knights with their scythes and clubs and formed themselves in a circle to present a solid front.[70] Count William's men dismounted and, with the cry of *Hainault!* in answer to that of the French *Montjoie St. Denis!* with levelled lance and shield in place, pressed upon the Flemings. A desperate struggle ensued in which Count William set a splendid example of heroism for his men. He was roughly handled, his legs and feet were wounded by scythe cuts, and at a critical moment he had to be saved by his men.[71] But only a ruse could break the solid front. Suddenly the knights opened their ranks towards the hill and the craftsmen and peasants, hoping to escape the death trap, sought to flee. Their front was broken and soon resistance was at an end.[72] Desperate also was the fighting on the count's left where the second Flemish contingent had attacked some time after Zannekin's men had come in contact with the French, but these too were finally dispersed with much effort.[73] Of the third division we hear nothing. When evening came Philip had climbed the top of the hill and burned Cassel, and the banner of Hainault waved in the breeze beside that of France.[74]

Thus Count William rendered an inestimable service to his brother-in-law. Perhaps more than to any other factor the victory was due to his watchfulness and timely action. This was

[68] According to the *Grandes Chroniques,* V, 316, he led this force.

[69] *Bourgeois de Valenciennes,* p. 151; *Chronique Parisienne Anonyme,* p. 118; Willelmus Procurator, p. 223; de Nangis, II, 98–99.

[70] *Chronicon Comitum Flandrensium,* p. 205; de Budt, p. 323.

[71] *Bourgeois de Valenciennes,* p. 151; *Istore et Croniques,* I, 345–346; *Grandes Chroniques,* V, 317–318.

[72] De Budt, p. 323.

[73] Willelmus Procurator, p. 223. This is what the *Bourgeois de Valenciennes,* p. 151, means where he states " car il avoit bien des deus pars des Flamens sur sa bataille."

[74] *Bourgeois de Valenciennes,* pp. 151–152; *Chronicon Comitum Flandrensium,* p. 206.

the opinion of contemporary chroniclers [75] and of Count William himself, for his son William in 1340 referred to his father's invaluable services on this occasion as proof of Philip's dastardly ingratitude.[76] And in September was completed the success over the popular revolutionary movements in the Low Countries which were so dangerous to France because in any attempt of Edward to secure the crown or resist encroachments in Gascony the support of the craftsmen might become a most significant factor. With an unerring instinct of self-preservation, Reginald, count of Guelders, Adolph, count of Marck, Adolph, count of Berg, William, count of Juliers, Otto, seignior of Cuyk, and many Brabanters flocked to the support of Adolph de la Marck, bishop of Liège, against the rebels of Liège, Huy, and other places, and defeated them on September 25 at Hoesselt.[77] Nor had John, duke of Brabant, any sympathy with the fugitive William de Deken, who had fled to Antwerp ostensibly for business, but, as was later charged, really to raise up enemies against Philip. The duke surrendered him whereupon he was brought to Paris, placed on trial, and, in spite of a spirited legal defense, executed in a most horrible manner.[78]

Count William accompanied Philip into Flanders where order was rapidly restored and rested with him at Lille.[79] On August 26 he arrived at Le Quesnoy,[80] after which he was at a tournament in Haarlem, and then proceeded toward France, apparently in the interests of peace. There he tarried until about the middle of March, 1329.[81] Philip, who was pressing Edward to perform

[75] Hocsemius, p. 395, states, "... simul cum eo (i.e. Philip) castra metatus est in vallibus de Casleto, Flandrensibus in montibus congregatis, qui descendentes quandam Regis aciem invaserunt, quae vix ad castra fugienda regia est saluata, Rege tunc in supremo periculo existente nisi Wilhelmus Comes Hannoniae succurrisset eidem, qui cum sua cohorte circumdando Flamingos fortiter impugnavit." Cf. also *Chronicon Tielense*, p. 321; Willelmus Procurator, pp. 222–223.

[76] Kervyn, *Oeuvres de Froissart*, XVIII, 137.

[77] Hocsemius, p. 413; Levold de Northof, p. 168; Willelmus Procurator, pp. 225–226. Cf. G. Kurth, *La Cité de Liège au Moyen Âge*, II, 34.

[78] H. Stein, "Les Conséquences de la Bataille de Cassel pour la Ville de Bruges et la Mort de Guillaume de Deken, son ancien Bourgmestre (1328)," *BCRH,* 68 (1899), 656, 658.

[79] Willelmus Procurator, p. 225.

[80] H. J. Smit, *Rekeningen der Graven en Gravinnen uit het Henegouwsche Huis*, I, 444, 473.

[81] Willelmus Procurator, p. 229.

homage for Gascony, soon adopted a threatening tone and sent Peter Roger, bishop of Arras, and the seignoir of Craon, to take over the lands in question and dispatched formal summons to Edward.[82]   Count William now hastened to Zeeland toward April,[83] whence he dispatched envoys to Edward. He thereupon hurried to Aquitaine in order to avoid an outbreak of hostilities.[84] On April 14 Edward explained to Philip that the delay was due to no fault of his own and proposed homage in person and sent Thomas de Orleton, bishop of Hereford, and Bartholomew de Burghersh to make arrangements for the ceremony [85] which was performed at Amiens on June 6. Thither went the Countess Jeanne with a train of six hundred horses, the count of Juliers and his brother-in-law, the count of Sayn, the countess of Namur, the bishop of Cambrai,[86] John of Hainault,[87] Louis, count of Flanders,[88] and many others to grace the brilliant spectacle.[89]

III. The Valkenburg Feud (1328–1329)

EVER since the treaty of September, 1328, John, king of Bohemia, had repeatedly refused the insistent demands of John, duke of Brabant, for a decision in his quarrel with Reginald of Valkenburg. Finally, a conference was arranged to be held at Nivelles. After a heated altercation both parties separated in high anger, took to their mounts, and rode off. The king then sent a messenger to renounce his allegiance and all promises, a formality which the duke forthwith returned.[90]

The chronicler of Egmond has given us many details of the

---

[82] *Grandes Chroniques,* V, 323–325; de Nangis, II, 106.

[83] He was at Geertruidenberg on April 2. See F. van Mieris, *Groot Charterboek,* II, 454.

[84] Willelmus Procurator, pp. 231–235.

[85] *Foedera,* II (2), 760.

[86] H. J. Smit, *Rekeningen der Graven en Gravinnen uit het Henegouwsche Huis,* I, 464, 470.

[87] Froissart, I, 306–307, J. Waller Zeper, *Jan van Henegouwen, Heer van Beaumont,* p. 390.

[88] J. Vuylsteke, *Gentsche Stads- en Baljuwsrekeningen, 1280–1336,* II, 654, 655.

[89] *Istore et Croniques,* I, 347; *Bourgeois de Valenciennes,* p. 153.

[90] Boendale, *Brabantsche Yeesten,* I, 380–482. The renewal of hostilities was sufficient to prevent the king's going to aid Alfonso IV, the king of Aragon, against the Moors. See H. Finke, *Acta Aragonensia,* III, 545.

wretched situation beyond the Meuse which are highly colored by his hostility toward the duke of Brabant and difficult to use because of his confused chronology. He accuses the duke of stirring to rebellion by means of gifts some of Reginald's subjects and of finding two knights ready to accept his advances. Reginald waged war upon one of them, destroyed his property, began to invest his stronghold and only at the urgent solicitation of William, count of Juliers, could he be induced to withdraw. But he soon advanced upon Maastricht, attacked the burghers, killed some of them, and returned with booty and prisoners. Later, when a tournament was to be held in Cologne, a natural brother of Duke John sought to apprehend Reginald when on the way to the city, but was thwarted by him, for he evidently had the sympathy of the officials of Cologne. There was a mêlée; a number were killed and others were taken prisoner and were surrendered to the burghers for custody. A plot was formed in Reginald's own castles to destroy the master in return for bribes of Duke John, but was divulged by loyal retainers. The traitors were promptly punished upon Reginald's return. A stronghold in which the duke's adherents had sought refuge was attacked and taken and some of the defenders were killed, among whom was a near relative of the duke to whom his head was forthwith presented. Reginald next swooped upon the cattle of the duke's subjects in Limburg and made away with them. The men of Maastricht beheaded one of his subjects whereupon three of the burghers were caught, their hands cut off, two totally blinded, and the third suffered to keep one eye, so as to be able to lead the others to their homes. Some Brabanters who especially hated Reginald made an attempt to seize him, but were dispersed, and those who were caught, among whom was the seignior of Petersheim, perished in the halter.[91]

These events stirred the duke to the point of explosion. No choice remained but to cross the Meuse once more. The winter of 1328–1329 was a cold one and Duke John waited until Ash Wednesday when he again took up his position before Valkenburg. But Reginald had stocked it well with provisions and wisely absented himself. Seeing the great strength of the fortifications, Duke John resorted to the unheroic but certain method of starv-

[91] Willelmus Procurator, pp. 233–237.

ing the defenders.[92]   After nine weeks, on May 11, long before
provisions had given out, they surrendered at the instigation of
the count of Virneburg.[93]

William, count of Hainault, Holland, and Zeeland, maintained a neutral attitude during these quarrels and sought to
bring about an accord.   In March he appeared in Brabant.   It
appears that discussions were held regarding the proposed marriage of his daughter Isabella to John, eldest son and heir; of
the duke of Brabant.   The differences which had already arisen
regarding the treaty of 1322 by which William, heir of Hainault,
Holland, and Zeeland, was betrothed to Johanna, the duke's
eldest daughter, were apparently not discussed.[94]   These negotiations finally led to a definite betrothal on October 25 of Isabella
and John [95] and were followed on the 28th by a contract containing the terms of marriage.[96]   At the same time efforts which
may have been due to Count William were made to assuage the
asperity of the enemies.   At Easter, John of Diest, the bishop
of Utrecht, sent some parties apparently to intercede for peace;
a chaplain went to Valenciennes, where the count was staying,
and to Henry, seignior of Vianen, to treat in behalf of some
prisoners retained at Louvain, and his marshal was sent to Reginald of Valkenburg.[97]   These efforts, however, were quite inef-
fectual.

John, king of Bohemia, in his fantastic way, supported his
friend Reginald.   He was off to Prussia to wage war upon the
heathen, but sent letters in his behalf.   Philip VI also wrote to the
duke urging him to make peace.[98]   When King John returned
about July 1,[99] learning of Reginald's desperate plight, he was
greatly angered and threatened to raise a large army in Germany

[92] Boendale, *Brabantsche Yeesten,* I, 482–484.
[93] *Ibid.,* I, 485; Willelmus Procurator, p. 238; Outremeuse, VI, 455.
[94] Willelmus Procurator, p. 232.
[95] Contained in a vidimus dated 1333.   See P. L. Muller, *Regesta Hannonensia,* p. 181.
[96] J. de St. Genois, *Monumens Anciens,* I, 219; C. Butkens, *Trophées tant Sacrés que Profanes du Duché de Brabant,* I (*Preuves*), 139.
[97] S. Muller Fz., *De Registers en Rekeningen van het Bisdom van Utrecht, 1325–1336,* I, 324.
[98] Willelmus Procurator, p. 236.
[99] He was at Frankfurt in June.   See J. F. Boehmer, *Die Urkunden Kaiser Ludwigs, Additamentum Primum,* p. 248.

against the duke of Brabant. On July 11 he was in conference with William, count of Hainault, Holland, and Zeeland, at Aix-la-Chapelle, but was speedily off to support the candidacy of his uncle Baldwin, archbishop of Trier, for the see of Mainz. Finally, Count William secured an arrangement. But when it was suggested that a sum of 8,000*l.* should be paid to Reginald and the castle restored to him, Duke John refused. The chronicler of Egmond states that this brought the anger of other princes upon him,[100] but it may be assumed with certainty that the duke felt willing to reject this proposal because of his understanding with Count William who was so intimate with the count of Juliers, his son-in-law.[101] Duke John remained obdurate during the winter of 1329–1330, in spite of the efforts of Count William who afterwards made a trip to Limburg and was in Brabant on St. Valentine's day. Later, when a quarrel which had broken out between Edward, count of Bar, and John, king of Bohemia, was settled, the errant king proposed to lead his troops against the duke of Brabant. But Count William again interposed his influence, thus averting a possible crisis.[102]

IV. William, Count of Hainault, Holland, and Zeeland, the Empire, and the Papacy (1328–1330)

By 1328 William, count of Hainault, Holland, and Zeeland, occupied a unique position in the political life of Christendom. In the Low Countries he enjoyed an unquestioned ascendancy because of his connections with Reginald, count of Guelders, William, count of Juliers, John, duke of Brabant, Louis, count of Flanders, and the bishops of Utrecht and Cambrai. The three major forces in western Europe were still more intimately bound to him: the king of England, Edward III, was his son-in-law, the king of France, Philip VI, his brother-in-law, and the em-

---

[100] Willelmus Procurator, pp. 242–243.

[101] On August 6 Count William settled upon his daughter Johanna, countess of Juliers, an annual income of 1,000*l.* Tournois from certain lands in Holland as had been promised by treaty. See F. van Mieris, *Groot Charterboek*, II, 484, and also L. Devillers, *Description analytique de Cartulaires et de Chartriers du Hainault*, II, 31.

[102] Willelmus Procurator, pp. 246, 248, 250–251; H. Finke, *Acta Aragonensia*, II, 545–546.

peror, Lewis the Bavarian, also his son-in-law. This was truly
an extraordinary situation for a prince of his rank and resources.
An observer of the quality of Marino Sanudo thought that
through his connections with both France and the empire a unanimous agreement regarding a crusade might be secured in Europe.
On February 15, 1328, he wrote to the archbishop of Capua,
chancellor of the kingdom of Jerusalem and of the king of Sicily,
that this was an opinion held by many persons.[103] On April 10,
1330, he repeated substantially the same ideas in a letter to Bertrand, bishop of Ostia and Velletre and legate of the Holy See.[104]

Jeanne, countess of Hainault, Holland, and Zeeland, exercised
considerable influence in connection with her husband's many
affiliations. She was a woman of strong maternal feeling and
never lost interest in the welfare of her children and near relatives. Her household became a center of much activity and
there was constant intercourse with the courts in England and
France as well as in Germany. In Philippa's own household
numerous subjects of Hainault had found service [105] and the ties
between her and her mother appear to have been particularly
intimate. Later, during the earlier years of the Hundred Years'
War, the countess grieved sincerely over the hostility between
her close relatives, and her appeals had some influence in arranging a number of truces. In the autumn of 1329 she hurried to the
side of her daughter Johanna, countess of Juliers, to comfort
her in her illness.[106] In the following year, at the close of April,
Johanna and her husband, William, announced the birth of a
child.[107] In June, 1331, there was again anxiety for Johanna's
health.[108] On May 12, 1330, the empress Margaret announced
the birth of her son, Lewis,[109] and four weeks later came news of

[103] Marino Sanudo, " Epistolae," J. Bongarsius, *Gesta Dei per Francos,*
II, 314: " . . . homo est qui propinquus est utriusque partis, et est sapiens
et probus, ut vestra dominatio bene novit, et ut est publica vox et fama."

[104] F. Kunstmann, " Studien über Marino Sanudo den Aelteren mit
einem Anhange seiner Ungedruckten Briefe," *Abhandlungen der historischen Classe der Bayerischen Akademie,* VII(1853), 874.

[105] For Nicasius of Hainault, her usher, see *CPR* (1334–8), p. 337, and
others Kervyn, *Oeuvres de Froissart,* II (notes), 513–514.

[106] Willelmus Procurator, p. 244.

[107] *Foedera,* II(2), 792.

[108] H. J. Smit, *Rekeningen der Graven en Gravinnen uit het Henegouwsche Huis,* I, 522–523.

[109] Willelmus Procurator, pp. 248, 252–253; K. A. Muffat, " Feststellung

the birth of Edward, the Black Prince, son of Philippa. And, in the autumn of 1331 when the latter was again *enceinte,* the countess planned a visit to her daughter as she was about to retire to the royal manor of Clarendon. In September a stately group, among whom were William, count of Juliers, William, burgrave of Voorne, and others, accompanied by forty horses, embarked at Wissant in ships provided by the warden of the Cinque Ports.[110] Before this, from September, 1330, to the following May, Jeanne had made a protracted visit at the court of her brother, Philip VI, at Senlis, the Louvre in Paris, and St. Germain-en-Laye.[111] And in the spring of 1332 Philippa and Johanna again announced the arrival of two more grandchildren.[112]

Pope John XXII pursued Lewis the Bavarian with implacable hostility and hoped for aid from Philip VI.[113] But in spite of his appeals and favors, the king would not be moved to abandon his local problems for the more remote advantages to be secured in the empire by actively opposing the emperor.[114] There still were questions unsettled with King Edward, whose homage performed at Amiens in 1328 was not liege homage, and possibly the situation in the Low Countries was not quite as satisfactory as he could wish despite the victory at Cassel and Count William's friendly policy. He sought to increase his influence in these parts through papal favor. Thus he asked the pope for an appointment to the see of Mainz, which had already been reserved, however, for a connection of John, king of Bohemia.[115] Later he asked for the translation of Baldwin of Trier to this see, which was also refused.[116] And in the spring of 1329, he requested Cologne for Henry of Namur. But the pope on March 17 de-

---

der Geburtsdaten von Kaiser Ludwigs des Bayern Sohnen," *Abhundlungen der historischen Classe der Bayerischen Akademie,* XXIV(1893), 889–898.

[110] Willelmus Procurator, p. 262; *Foedera,* II(2), 823; *CCR* (1330–3), pp. 262, 380.

[111] H. J. Smit, *Rekeningen der Graven en Gravinnen uit het Henegouwsche Huis,* I, 481–489.   [112] *Ibid.,* pp. 563, 557.

[113] A. Fayen, *Lettres de Jean XXII (1316–1334),* No. 2238.

[114] *Ibid.,* Nos. 2191, 2196, 2221, 2222, 2258; de Nangis, II, 95, 121.

[115] W. Preger, "Die Verträge Ludwigs des Baiern mit Friedrich dem Schönen in den Jahren 1325 und 1326 mit J. H. Reinkens Auszügen aus Urkunden des Vatikanischen Archivs von 1325–1334," *Abhandlungen der historischen Classe der Bayerischen Akademie,* XVII(1886), No. 449.

[116] *Ibid.,* No. 457.

clined, stating that a " fit person was ready," that is, as was to be revealed in a few years, Walram, brother of William, count of Juliers.[117]   Nevertheless, relations between king and pope remained cordial, as the appointment to a number of livings in the Low Countries amply attests.[118]   In the Rhineland, however, Philip's influence was in the ascendant, for on December 22, 1328, William, count of Juliers, agreed to aid him against all parties, save the emperor and the duke of Brabant, for an annual sum of 600*l.* Tournois.   Just before this the archbishop and William, count of Juliers, had buried their past differences and agreed to submit all new difficulties to arbitration.[119]

Early in 1330 William, count of Hainault, Holland, and Zeeland, determined to bring about a reconciliation between the two heads of Christendom.   The reported death of the antipope Nicholas V seemed to present a favorable opportunity.   After discussing the matter at length with his brother-in-law, he decided to go to Avignon in spite of his rheumatism, and letters were at once exchanged regarding the proposed reconciliation.[120]   The expedition appears to have been prepared with Philip's cooperation, and Count William set out from Paris about March 18, accompanied by the king's brother, Charles, count of Alençon, and about eight hundred men-at-arms.[121]   But the pope was determined to persevere in his hostility and refused the count's advances.[122]   It was reported that he feared for his safety when Lewis the Bavarian's father-in-law came at the head of so large a following.[123]   The papal palace was hastily put into condition for defense,[124] and at Clermont-Ferrand deputies appeared be-

[117] W. Preger, *op. cit.*, No. 470; A. Fayen, *Lettres de Jean XXII (1316–1334)*, No. 2402.

[118] A. Fayen, *Lettres de Jean XXII (1316–1334)*, Nos. 2369, 2383, 2411, 2456, 2489, 2512.

[119] T. J. Lacomblet, *Urkundenbuch für die Geschichte des Niederrheins*, II, 197.

[120] Willelmus Procurator, pp. 248–249.

[121] K. Müller, *Der Kampf Ludwigs des Baiern mit der römischen Curie*, pp. 275 (note), 375–376, erroneously states that this occurred in 1332.

[122] Willelmus Procurator, p. 250.

[123] See John's letter of September 26, 1330, to Countess Jeanne setting forth his reasons in A. Fayen, *Lettres de Jean XXII (1316–1334)*, No. 2848, and G. Brom, *Bullarium Trajectense*, Vol. I, No. 850.

[124] Villani, col. 698.

fore the count to announce the pope's displeasure.[125]   The bridges were ordered broken down to intercept his progress and troops were made ready to oppose him on the river bank.   Unable to advance, he returned to Paris in high anger because his well-meant endeavors had thus been so lightly set at naught and again conferred with Philip, who was no less incensed and who informed the pope of his own state of feelings as well as Count William's.[126]

At Paris Count William found the English envoys, Adam de Orleton, bishop of Worcester, Henry, earl of Lancaster, John Wawayn, canon of Hereford, and John de Shoreditch, professor of civil law, who had been appointed on January 27 and April 10 to negotiate a treaty with Philip.   But whether he exerted much influence in the quarrel at this time is not possible to ascertain; perhaps the bitterness of it rendered peace unlikely despite any influence he might have.   The negotiations finally came to a conclusion on May 8 in the royal Bois de Vincennes when a formal statement was drawn up.[127]

On May 12 Count William returned to Holland and forthwith proceeded to Speier where he met the emperor, Lewis the Bavarian, on June 3.[128]   Here a series of discussions took place, but what was said regarding the pope is not known.   A close sympathy was apparent between the two; documents were issued whereby all imperial rights, save homage, in Holland, Zeeland, and Friesland were surrendered, the *grietmannen* and consuls of Westergoo and Oostergoo were enjoined to accept Count William as their lawful seignior, and full powers were bestowed upon him to settle the boundaries of the empire in Ostrevant.[129]   Pope John now feared that he had overshot the mark, and two knights, agents of the curia, presented themselves before William in Speier, but were refused audience.[130]   The countess' sensibilities were likewise wounded.   With her own hand she addressed three letters to the Holy Father, complaining of the treatment given her

---

[125] De Nangis, II, 195.
[126] Willelmus Procurator, p. 251; *Grandes Chroniques,* V, 337.
[127] E. Déprez, *Les Préliminaires de la Guerre de Cent Ans,* pp. 46–58; CPR (1327–30), pp. 482, 511; *Foedera,* II (2), 777, 785, 781–792.
[128] Willelmus Procurator, p. 251.
[129] L. Devillers, *Monuments,* III, 224–227.
[130] Willelmus Procurator, pp. 251–252.

husband. In his reply of September 26, the pope protested that the number of the count's followers, the uncertainty regarding his intentions, and the difficulties which he himself had with some of his feudatories at Avignon had rendered Count William an object of suspicion. He had not repulsed him; had his letter been read with diligence the count might have learned that if the objections were removed his appeal would have been favorably considered.[131] But the wound was not healed thereby. Count William appeared in Brussels at the opening of the next year and agreed on February 8 with John, duke of Brabant, upon the financial clauses of the marriage of Johanna of Brabant to the count's heir apparent, William.[132] A tournament, which was to have been held at Bruges but was transferred to Brussels, graced the event. Among those present was John of Hainault who was on his way with five hundred men to war with the Moslem of Spain, and although his route lay directly through Avignon, he did not, as was noticed by the chronicler of Egmond, pass that way, probably to show his resentment of the treatment accorded his brother in the previous year.[133]

V. The Marriage of Reginald, Count of Guelders, and Eleanor Plantagenet (1331–1332)

The negotiations between Philip and Edward, which came to a close at Vincennes on May 8, 1330, were without result and thus the perennial differences between the sovereigns again threatened to break out in open war. Finally the English king was cited to appear before the Parlement of Paris on July 28, 1331.[134] In the face of possible difficulties Edward again turned to the Low Countries for allies. On October 7 he empowered William Fitz-Waryn, a knight, Hugh Elys, dean of Wolverhampton, and John de Hildesle, canon of Chichester, to arrange an alliance with

---

[131] A. Fayen, *Lettres de Jean XXII (1316–1334)*, No. 2848.

[132] F. van Mieris, *Groot Charterboek*, II, 492–493.

[133] Willelmus Procurator, pp. 259–260; W. Preger, " Die Verträge Ludwigs des Baiern mit Friedrich dem Schönen in den Jahren 1325 und 1326 mit J. H. Reinkens Auszügen aus Urkunden des Vatikanischen Archivs von 1325–1334," *Abhandlungen der historischen Classe der Bayerischen Akademie*, XVII (1886), Nos. 559, 580, 637.

[134] E. Déprez, *Les Préliminaires de la Guerre de Cent Ans,* pp. 63–64.

John, duke of Brabant, and Louis, count of Flanders,[135] and, on the 11th, also with Reginald, count of Guelders, Thierry, count of Loon, and other nobles.[136] But diplomatic efforts were made once more to avert a breach. On November 7, John de Hildesle and John de Shoreditch were named proctors with power to discuss with Philip the points in dispute and especially the question of homage for Aquitaine.[137] They were required to appear before the king a fortnight after St. Andrew's Day, for Edward had been cited a second time. On January 16, 1331, William de Ayreminne, bishop of Winchester, Adam de Orleton, bishop of Worcester, William, count of Hainault, Holland, and Zeeland, Henry de Percy and Hugh de Audley, knights, and John de Shoreditch were given full powers to treat with Philip.[138] A treaty was arranged on March 9 and ratified by Edward on the 30th.[139]

40286

Negotiations for alliances apparently met with slight, if any, result save in the case of Reginald, count of Guelders. With him William, count of Hainault, Holland, and Zeeland, had long lived in intimate political and other relations. He had favored the burghers of Harderwijk,[140] had arbitrated successfully Reginald's quarrel with the burgrave of Voorne [141] and aided by the count of Juliers, settled differences with Cologne,[142] and finally, on July 22, 1331, had come to a decision with him regarding their respective spheres of influence in the lands of the diocese of Utrecht whereby Reginald had bound himself not to secure possessions west of the Yssel and William east of that river.[143] Reginald's wife, Sophia Berthout of Mechelen, had died on May 3, 1329,[144] and, at about the time of Hildesle's activities, the proposition of his marriage with Eleanor, sister of Edward

---

[135] *Foedera,* II(2), 799.
[136] *CPR* (1330–4), pp. 9, 16.
[137] *Ibid.,* p. 38.
[138] *Ibid.,* p. 48.
[139] *Ibid.,* pp. 90–95. Count William went to France after the marriage of his son, William, at Brussels. See Willelmus Procurator, p. 261.
[140] F. van Mieris, *Groot Charterboek,* II, 485, 469.
[141] Ibid., p. 505; P. L. Muller, *Regesta Hannonensia,* pp. 237, 238.
[142] L. Ennen und G. Eckertz, *Quellen zur Geschichte der Stat Köln,* IV, 193.
[143] F. van Mieris, *Groot Charterboek,* II, 518. See *ibid.,* pp. 508–518.
[144] Willelmus Procurator, pp. 237–238; *Chronicon Tielense,* pp. 323–324.

III, was apparently broached.[145]   She had been considered in the
negotiations of 1329 and 1330 for peace with Philip VI as a bride
for Peter, eldest son of the king of Aragon.[146]

Count William may have seen in this marriage a guarantee of
the arrangements between himself and Count Reginald in regard
to Utrecht and additional solidarity of interests in the lands
between Cologne, the Ems, and Flanders. The matter concerned
a number of parties, but he was on excellent terms with them
all. Thus on June 8 the emperor, Lewis the Bavarian, declared
that the heir, whether son or daughter, should inherit the imperial
rights in Nijmegen, held in fee by the counts of Guelders ever
since the days of the Roman King William, and also the tolls
at Lobith on the Rhine.[147] On September 28 the bishop of Utrecht
guaranteed the proposed arrangements in regard to Eleanor's
income from the Veluwe, a fief of the see of Utrecht held by the
count of Guelders of the duke of Brabant, who in turn held it
of the bishop. He also agreed to the proposal to disinherit
the three daughters of Count Reginald's first marriage in favor
of the children that might be born of the new union.[148]   On
October 3 Count Reginald thereupon empowered Otto, seignior
of Cuyk, Ricoldus, archdeacon and provost of St. Peter's of
Utrecht, and Jacob Mierlaer, a knight, to conclude the negotiations at Edward's court.[149]

They arrived at Westminster, and on the 20th the king named
John de Stratford, bishop of Winchester, William de Ayreminne,
bishop of Norwich, Galfridus le Scrope and William de Herle,
knights, to treat with them.[150]   The definitive contract was
drawn up on the same day. Reginald promised to settle upon
Eleanor an income of 16,000*l.* small Tournois annually, 14,000
from the count's possessions in the Veluwe, and 2,000 from
those in Elst, Gent, and Angeren. John, duke of Brabant,
because of his interests in the Veluwe, and William, count of
Hainault, Holland, and Zeeland, as the intimate friend of Count

[145] *Foedera,* II (2), 766, 777, 794, 822.
[146] *CPR* (1330–4), p. 7.
[147] I. A. Nijhoff, *Gedenkwaardigheden uit de Geschiedenis van Gelderland,* I, 264.
[148] *Ibid.,* pp. 264–266.
[149] *Foedera,* II (2), 832.
[150] *Ibid.,* p. 826.

Reginald, were requested to guarantee Eleanor's usufruct. If this sum, which was to be available in two months after the marriage, should not be forthcoming or should fail at any moment, Reginald promised to provide the deficit. The children of Eleanor were to inherit all the rights of Guelders save 10,000*l.* small Tournois, which were reserved as provision for the children of Sophia Berthout.[151] Edward promised a dowry of 10,000*l.* sterling, 5,000 payable in the first week of May at Sluis in Flanders, and 5,000 at Bruges on June 24, 1333. He was also to pay the expense of getting her ready and sending her to Sluis where she was to be received by Reginald, at whose expense she was to proceed to Guelders.[152] The envoys returned to the Low Countries, and on February 12, 1332, Edward ratified the agreement.[153]

Preparations were forthwith begun in the royal household.[154] On April 18 officials were ordered to provide suitable transportation for Eleanor and her jewels. Ships were collected [155] and ordered to be ready on May 1 in sufficient number to provide for the passage of a train of five hundred horses.[156] Safe-conduct was issued at this time to many individuals who were to accompany Eleanor, such as Richard Tong, Hugh de Audley, Thomas de Roscelyn, Adam, bishop of Worcester, Roger de Broynton, archdeacon of Gloucester, William, abbot of Langdon, William de Clinton, and members of her household such as Constantine de Mortuo Maris, a steward, William la Zouche and his wife, Eleanor, Amice de Echingham, and others, among whom were a number of parsons and a leech.[157] The voyage was apparently without incident and the marriage was celebrated at Nijmegen in due time and with great splendor.[158]

---

[151] I. A. Nijhoff, *Gedenkwaardigheden uit de Geschiedenis van Gelderland*, I, 266–270. For the promise of Duke John and Count William, see *ibid.*, pp. 271–272. These documents were of course carried with the envoys to Westminster, and their essential parts were included in the contract of October 20.

[152] *Foedera*, II (2), 834–835.

[153] *Ibid.*, p. 832.

[154] F. Devon, *Issues of the Exchequer: Henry III to Henry IV*, p. 142.

[155] *CPR* (1330–4), pp. 274, 553.

[156] *CCR* (1330–3), p. 559.

[157] *CPR* (1330–4), pp. 274–279; *CFR* (1327–32), p. 308.

[158] Willelmus Procurator, pp. 267–268; *Chronicon Tielense*, p. 324; Knighton, I, 461; *Grandes Chroniques*, V, 347.

CHAPTER IV

THE POLITICAL POSITION OF JOHN III, DUKE OF BRABANT AND LIMBURG (1328–1333)

i. John, Duke of Brabant, and his Neighbors (1328–1332)   ii. Philip VI, King of France, and the Low Countries (1328–1331)   iii. The First Attack upon the Duke of Brabant (Winter and Spring, 1332)   iv. The Negotiations at Compiègne (June, 1332)   v. The Political Activities of William, Count of Hainault, Holland, and Zeeland (1332–1333)   vi. The Proposed Diocese for Brabant and Limburg (1332–1333)

I. John, Duke of Brabant, and His Neighbors (1328–1332)

THANKS to the able policy of Duke John III, Brabant enjoyed great prestige among its many neighbors. Conscious of the great strength which a central position and a loyal bourgeoisie gave him, the duke had quietly stayed at home, content in jealously watching over his interests rather than seeking advantages farther away. He well understood what dangers lurked in the lands of the counts of Guelders and Juliers and other neighbors beyond the Meuse. These had viewed with grave misgivings the annexation of Sittart and Valkenburg, so that William, count of Hainault, Holland, and Zeeland, had long found it imperative to labor for peace between the Meuse and the Rhine. Was not the duke's policy a patent reversion to that of his grandfather John I which determined, after the battle of Woeringen (June 5, 1288), the union of Limburg with Brabant? All the old claims of the dukes of Limburg were now pressed much more vigorously than ever; the dukes of Brabant were actively assuming the guardianship over the peace between the Meuse and the Rhine, and their power had accordingly increased too uncomfortably in those parts for the counts of Guelders and Juliers, the archbishop of Cologne, and a host of lesser feudatories.

Along the north and east boundaries of Brabant there were many knotty problems arising from the uncertain and therefore often debatable obligations concerning petty seigniories. That of Heusden, for example, situated where the Meuse leaves its old bed and bends northward to join the Waal and form the Merwede, was especially obnoxious. The part north of the Old Meuse was held in fee by its seignior of the counts of Cleves; the part south of the river was held of the counts of Guelders. The counts of Holland as *advocati* of the abbots of St. Trond had long possessed extensive rights at many points in the seigniory north of the old course and it was their policy to extend these as much as possible.[1] They were eager to round out their possessions between the Waal and the Meuse and were in a fair way to absorb completely the seigniory of Altena [2] situated between Heusden and the Merwede. This was purchased by them from the count of Cleves in 1332.[3] Count Floris V of Holland (1256–1296) had managed to force his pretensions upon the seigniors of Heusden who unwillingly performed homage for the northern part of their possessions in 1290.[4] But the dukes of Brabant cherished the same ambition, and John II had levied war upon the seignior of Heusden. A clash followed, and, when in 1318 the matter was left to the arbitral decision of Gerhard, count of Juliers, Duke John succeeded in presenting an apparently better claim.[5] Three years later he again defeated Count William in a controversy touching the justice of Drongelen, a fief of the seigniory of Heusden.[6]

More numerous were the actual and potential differences with the count of Guelders. The dukes had long exercised, subject to the suzerainty of the bishops of Utrecht, some shadowy rights over the Veluwe, which the counts held from them in fee.[7] Also their part of the seigniory of Heusden, embracing the villages of Oud Heusden, Heusden, Vlijmen, Hedikhuizen, and Engelen,

---

[1] I. H. Gosses, *De Vorming van het Graafschap Holland*, pp. 104–105.

[2] For these seigniories, see J. C. Ramaer, " Geographische Geschiedenis van Holland bezuiden de Lek en Nieuwe Maas in de Middeleeuwen," *Verhandelingen der Koninglijke Akademie van Wetenschappen, Afdeeling Letterkunde*, New Ser., II (1900), 224–235.

[3] F. van Mieris, *Groot Charterboek*, II, 536.

[4] L. Ph. C. van den Bergh, *Oorkondenboek van Holland en Zeeland*, II, 311.

[5] F. van Mieris, *Groot Charterboek*, II, 218–220.

[6] *Ibid.*, p. 295.

[7] L. Vanderkindere, *La Formation Territoriale des Principautés Belges au Moyen Âge*, II, 308–309.

was the subject of persistent litigation.[8] There were also conflicting claims about Baardwijk near Heusden,[9] Meerhout,[10] Megen,
Herpen, Genderen, Boxtel, Mervelt on the Meuse,[11] Geldrop on
the Aa, and at Tiel, Zandwijk, and Heerewaarden on the Waal.[12]
There was some difficulty in regard to an obscure sale of the
advocatiae of Herkenchon and Merwede,[13] titles very difficult to
trace, and the counts could not forget that after the battle of
Woeringen the duke of Brabant had filched some rights from the
seigniors of Heinsberg in Wassenberg.[14] Tiel on the Waal was
held by the duke, but was vehemently claimed by the count of
Guelders whose chief desire in his attack upon Brabant was to
regain possession of it. And as the duke had been so successful
in his dealings with William, count of Hainault, Holland, and
Zeeland, and had added to his possessions in these parts through
the surrender by Otto, seignior of Cuyk, in 1323 of his allodial
possessions at Cuyk [15] and of those at Grave in 1328 [16] to be
held henceforth in fee, the count of Guelders became apprehensive and eager to put limits to the duke's expansion.[17]

The count of Juliers was likewise restive; his interests clashed
with those of the duke at many vital points. The count was
subadvocatus of Aix-la-Chapelle, a place of considerable strategic importance for the overland commercial connection between
Cologne and the towns of Brabant and Flanders; but he found
that his power here was subordinate to that of the duke who
called himself *superior advocatus*.[18] It was Duke John's policy
to foster the best of relations with the burghers of this place,

---

[8] E. Dynter, *Chronicon Ducum Brabantiae,* II, 577–578.

[9] *Ibid.,* p. 578.

[10] *Ibid.,* p. 577, where it is spelled " Meerbont." It is located in the
Kempen. See L. Galesloot, *Le Livre des Feudataires de Jean III, index,*
sub Meerhout.

[11] E. Dynter, *Chronicon Ducum Brabantiae,* II, 577.

[12] *Ibid.,* pp. 578–579. For these places, see A. Verkooren, *Inventaire,*
Brabant, I, 261–264.

[13] E. Dynter, *Chronicon Ducum Brabantiae,* II, 576.

[14] Boendale, *Brabantsche Yeesten,* I, 490–491.

[15] F. van Meris, *Groot Charterboek,* II, 319.   [16] *Ibid.,* p. 460.

[17] In 1333 he demanded that the duke should not attempt to secure any
more territory in either Guelders or Juliers. See L. Devillers, *Monuments,*
III, 302.

[18] C. Butkens, *Trophées tant Sacrés que Profanes du Duché de Brabant,*
I (*Preuves*), 156.

who must have been pleased with the solid advantages which came from a friendly attitude shown by their powerful neighbor. They were obliged to furnish a contingent of fifty men-at-arms for the duke's forces which was apparently done quite willingly, as can be inferred from the duke's considerate treatment of the burghers in respect to this obligation.[19] In 1321 he granted them full freedom with exemption from tolls to visit Limburg and especially Galoppe and Maastricht.[20] As *superior advocatus* he also arbitrated on November 9 of the same year a dispute between them and the men of Walhorn.[21] Over the abbey of Burtscheid, east of Aix-la-Chapelle, he enjoyed similar authority.[22] The count of Juliers naturally viewed this extension of Brabançon influence with alarm and was in no mood to abandon meekly his claims upon certain properties in Limburg near Rolduc [23] and Lewenick.[24]

Nor could the archbishop of Cologne view with indifference these significant facts, especially when after the death of Henry of Virneburg in January, 1332, Walram, brother of William, count of Juliers, was elevated to the archiepiscopal dignity. The old enmity between the duke and the archbishop was thus increased by this dynastic tie.[25] Hardly less eager was John, king of Bohemia, to be avenged for the loss of Limburg,[26] and the dispossessed Reginald, seignior of Valkenburg, would naturally look to these disgruntled neighbors for aid in recovering his titles.

[19] S. P. Ernst, *Histoire du Limbourg*, V, 32–33.

[20] C. Quix, *Codex Diplomaticus Aquensis*, II, 202.

[21] *Ibid.*, pp. 199³200; E. Dynter, *Chronicon Ducum Brabantiae*, II, 534, 672.

[22] C. Quix, *Geschichte der Ehemaligen Reichs-Abtei Burtscheid von Ihrer Gründung im 7ten. Jahrhundert bis 1400* (Aachen, 1834), pp. 130–131; E. Dynter, *Chronicon Ducum Brabantiae*, II, 551–552 (wrongly dated 1318).

[23] See S. A. Waller Zeper, *Jan van Henegouwen, Heer van Beaumont* (*Bijlage II*), p. 448. See also E. Butkens, *Trophées tant Sacrés que Profanes du Duché de Brabant*, I (*Preuves*), 158.

[24] L. Devillers, *Monuments*, III, 302.

[25] Wilhelmus Procurator, p. 266. He was appointed on January 27, 1332. See W. Preger, "Die Verträge Ludwigs des Baiern mit Friedrich dem Schönen in dem Jahren 1325 und 1326 mit J. H. Reinkens Auszügen aus Urkunden des Vatikanischen Archivs von 1325–1334," *Abhandlungen der historischen Classe der Bayerischen Akademie*, XVIII (1886), No. 500, and S. Riezler, *Vatikanische Akten*, Nos. 526, 530.

[26] *Königsaaler Geschichte-Quellen*, p. 500.

The duke of Brabant also had many disputes with his neighbors west of the Meuse. Those with the counts of Namur were especially persistent. In 1321 Duke John had bought from Baldwin of Aiseau his rights at Aiseau and debate soon ensued concerning the limits of the jurisdiction of the count of Namur.[27] There was trouble about the castle at Sanson, possessions at Hollogne-sur-Geer, Boneffe, and other titles.[28] In 1328 claim to the *advocatia* of Argenteau was in dispute.[29] For a moment it seemed as if this problem and other questions concerning some property at Bohaing and elsewhere, which had just become the subject of dispute, were about to be solved. On June 28 arbitration was agreed upon; the duke named Simon, abbot of Heylissem, and John de Grambays, castellan of Genappe, and the count appointed Henry, abbot of Grand-Pré, and Colin Leurent, a burgher of Namur, to settle the matter.[30] It appears, however, that nothing was accomplished, and in the following year there were other difficulties occasioned by the conduct of some of the duke's subjects in the count's jurisdiction.[31]

The count of Loon, vassal of the bishop of Liège, whose lands were almost surrounded by those of the duke, had little liberty of action in the presence of this powerful neighbor and cannot have failed to sympathize with any attempt to check by force his rapid expansion. Nor was Adolph de la Marck, bishop of Liège, a friend of the duke, in spite of the fact that he had not interfered with the latter in his attack upon the seignior of Valkenburg. Reginald had been shortsighted enough to offend the bishop's subjects which thus made it impossible for him to secure aid from that quarter.[32] Situated between Limburg and Brabant, and striving to retain effective control over his diocesan and special jurisdictions, the bishop of Liège viewed with uneasiness the duke's rapid success. Since 1328 the latter appears to have planned to abolish the annoying *Judicium Pacis* and to create an independent diocese for his lands.[33] Quarrels regarding titles and

---

[27] A. Verkooren, *Inventaire, Brabant*, I, 195–196.

[28] J. Dumont *Corps Universel Diplomatique*, II (2), 139.

[29] J. de St. Genois, *Monumens Anciens*, I, DCCCCLXXXLX.

[30] C. Piot, *Inventaire des Chartes des Comtes de Namur*, p. 140.

[31] J. de St. Genois, *Monumens Anciens*, I, DCCCCLXXXXLL.

[32] Boendale, *Brabantsche Yeesten*, I, 457; Levold de Northof, p. 376; Hocsemius, p. 376.

[33] G. Kurth, *La Cité de Liège au Moyen Âge*, II, 54–55.

other rights were always possible as, for example, those of Hervé in Limburg held by the abbey of St. Denis of Liège subject to the annual payment of twenty measures of corn to the duke as *advocatus*.[34] On one occasion the latter seized some treasure which had been deposited by a Lombard for safe-keeping in the church of St. Servaas in Maastricht. The guard had been slain, and the cantor forthwith excommunicated the duke, but the quarrel was speedily mended.[35]

There were some difficulties at 's-Hertogenbosch and at Tirlemont,[36] but a more serious situation developed when in 1331 Duke John began to encroach upon St. Trond, a town on the confines of Brabant, but within the lands of the bishop of Liège and desirable for the connection with Maastricht, Valkenburg, Limburg, and the Rhine.[37] The town had grown up around the monastery of the same name over which the dukes exercised rights as *advocati*.[38] A squire of the neighborhood was taken and beheaded and his home burned. The bailiff of Tirlemont, an official of the duke, seized a large quantity of cloth belonging to the merchants of St. Trond who had stored it in a church for safety whither they had fled for protection. Some of the townsmen appear to have been maltreated, and a number were killed and imprisoned.

A delegation of two knights, two canons from St. Lambert of Liège of whom Hocsem was one, and two burghers from each of the towns in the land of Liège was sent to bring the duke before the bishop's court of law. At Rotselaer they found John on October 9 celebrating the nuptials of a natural daughter. A day was set for a conference at Brussels as the duke did not happen to have his councillors with him. The envoys presented themselves at the appointed time and were entertained sumptuously, but the duke showed himself obdurate in regard to St. Trond. He declared his willingness to treat with the bishop of Liège, but would under no circumstances grant the burghers of St. Trond

[34] A. Miraeus et F. Foppens, *Opera Diplomatica,* III, 159–160.
[35] Outremeuse, VI, 486.
[36] J. F. Willems, *Codex Diplomaticus,* I, 772.
[37] E. Fairon, " Un Projet du Démembrement du Diocèse de Liège Proposé par les Brabançons en 1332," *BCRH,* 78 (1909), 194; Outremeuse, VI, 485.
[38] C. Leclere, *Les Avoués de St. Trond,* p. 28.

a truce. The envoys were not able to press the matter as winter
was at hand and, when they learned that the duke did not intend
to proceed against the men of St. Trond at once, they agreed to
discuss the matter at some future date.[39]

The conflicting claims upon the seigniory and the justice on
the course (*stroom*) of the Schelde was an ever-potential source
of disputes with Louis, count of Flanders, his powerful neighbor
on the west. Duke John was not the man to yield in a matter of
primary concern for his towns. In 1331 the question had again
been discussed, and the litigants finally agreed to leave the matter
to the decision of four arbiters, Josse van Hemsrode, and Blok van
Steenlant, representing the count, and Raoul Pipenpoy, and one
other whose name is not given, representing the duke. These men
were to meet at Enghien on September 8.[40] On June 19 Louis directed his commissioners to proceed to the spot where the conflict
had developed, make diligent enquiry, call before themselves all
those implicated, and settle such irregularities as they might discover.[41] Both parties would, of course, always be guilty of encroachment on this most important artery of commerce so long as
the delimitation of authority, which included the justice up
stream as far as Eyckenvliet, the rights on it before Antwerp, the
right of pursuit of any who refused to pay the tolls even into the
lands of the count, and similar matters remained undefined.[42]
Nothing more is heard of these negotiations, but there must have
been some approach to a settlement inasmuch as Count Louis observed a benevolent neutrality toward his neighbor when he was
assailed by his many jealous enemies in the spring of 1332.[43]

II. Philip VI, King of France, and the Low Countries
(1328–1331)

The political prestige of the French king, Philip VI, was materially greater in 1331 than it had been at the moment of his cor-

[39] Hocsemius, p. 407; *Gesta Abbatum Sancti Trudonis*, pp. 421–422;
E. Fairon, " Un Projet du Démembrement Diocèse de Liège Proposé par
les Brabançons en 1332," *BCRH*, 78 (1909), 194.

[40] *Archives du Département du Nord,* Lille, B 264 (6.294).

[41] *Ibid.,* B 264 (6.8296).

[42] Cf. *ibid.,* B 264 (6.823); B 264 (14.478); B 264 (14.83 *bis*).

[43] Hocsemius, p. 412.

onation in 1328. The Flemings had been constrained to return to their lawful allegiance after their defeat at Cassel. Edward had performed homage, and although its terms were not entirely satisfactory, had apparently desisted for the moment from pressing his claim upon the French crown. These matters had kept Philip fully occupied so that he had not been able to adopt any decided policy toward Lewis the Bavarian and the empire. But in 1331 there was a clearly discernible tendency on the part of Philip to draw close to John, king of Bohemia. The reason for this was the desire of the former to have validated his purposed aggressions against the empire in the Low Countries, Arles, and elsewhere, and of the latter to secure the imperial dignity for himself in order to extend the Luxemburg *Hausmacht* in Germany and shatter that of the Wittelsbach family.

In all these schemes it would be necessary for King Philip to take notice of the position and influence of his brother-in-law, William, count of Hainault, Holland, and Zeeland. As in 1327 and 1328, so now would Count William's prestige be of central significance. According to the royal historiographical tradition,[44] Philip viewed his ascendancy in the Low Countries and his influence in Germany and England with alarm. Philip realized that his own difficulties with King Edward in Gascony might at any moment bring about a serious conflict. William's many connections might then easily become the basis of an alliance against France, the proportions of which neither Philip Augustus nor Philip the Fair had ever seen. He was of course acquainted with Edward's attempt to secure alliances with the rebellious Flemings and others in 1328 and again in 1330 with the duke of Brabant and the counts of Flanders, Loon, Namur, and Guelders, exactly at the moment when his own relations with Edward were seriously strained. In September and October, 1331, the abbot of Langdon visited Brabant, Germany, and Hainault in the interests of the English king.[45] These sinister activities had been followed by the betrothal of Edward's sister Eleanor to Reginald, count of Guelders, in which Count William appeared

[44] *Grandes Chroniques,* V, 34; *Istore et Croniques,* I, 349–350; *Chronographia,* II, 15–16.
[45] L. Mirot and E. Déprez, "Les Ambassades Anglaises pendant la Guerre de Cent Ans," *BEC,* LIX (1898), 559.

especially interested.[46]   John of Hainault, whose friendship was
prized in every quarter, received an annual pension of a thousand
marks from the English treasury.   That Philip was vitally
interested in what happened in the Low Countries is revealed with
special clearness by his policy toward the commune of Tournai.
During 1328 and 1329 he had not taken any determined stand
in the matter of the royal rights in the city, but his officials again
became active in 1330 and during the next four years Philip
definitively consolidated his rights.   From that time onward
Tournai appears as a possession of the Valois monarchy.[47]   Because of his great interests in the region north of the Meuse in the
old duchy of Lotharingia it was only natural for Philip, once his
suspicion or fears had been aroused, to ascribe the growth of
English influence in those parts to Count William's numerous
dynastic and political relations.

It is difficult to determine exactly when the enmity between
the brothers-in-law developed; that it was gradual is the most
satisfactory supposition.   Count William may well have been
dissatisfied with Philip's policies which seemed to overlook entirely his own interests.   He had aided him in the days of the
regency, had been instrumental in securing for him the succession
to the crown, had helped materially in the battle at Cassel, and
had labored with some effect to smooth out the tangled relations
between him and Edward III.   On the other hand, Philip had
done nothing to settle the debate concerning Ostrevant, Solesmes,
and Fismy.[48]   Philip, it appears, took no notice of the fact that
the political problems of the house of Avesnes had entirely
changed with the definitive settlement of its hereditary disputes
with Flanders by Count William and Louis, count of Flanders,
in 1323, and could not understand that his brother-in-law no
longer had need of the support of the French king in order to
render his own position in the Low Countries secure.   Accordingly,

---

[46] See *Foedera*, II (2), 826, for Edward's letter in October, 1331, concerning the progress of the negotiations.

[47] *CCR* (1333-7), pp. 37–38, 77–78, 200, 265, 345.   A. d'Herbomez, " Les
Constitutions de Tournay sous Philippe de Valois," *Nouvelle Revue
Historique de Droit Français et Étranger*, XXX (1906), 351–381, 453–476;
" Notes et Documents pour Servir à l'Histoire des Rois Fils de Philippe le
Bel," *BEC*, LIX, 520–523, 689–710.

[48] The matter was again under consideration in January, 1332.   See
L. Devillers, *Monuments*, II, 264–265.

when it became apparent that Philip intended to use his influence to extend the prestige of the Valois monarchy, Count William had no choice but to draw closer to England and to the empire.

The position of the count of Juliers was still of pivotal importance. Ever since his participation in the Stanhope Park campaign in 1327 [49] Count William had drawn a pension of six hundred marks annually from the English treasury.[50] At the same time he was a vassal of Philip who, however, did not try to secure the reservation to the see of Cologne for Count William's brother, Walram of Juliers, but supported the candidacy of his henchman, Adolph de la Marck, bishop of Liège.[51] This candidacy was intimately bound up with the count's visit to Avignon under pretence of a crusade against the Mohammedans in Spain when, on January 30, 1332, he promised to be ever faithful to the church, never to aid his brother-in-law, Lewis the Bavarian, and guaranteed that Walram would similarly bind himself before Easter.[52] Count William's policy was thus dictated largely by local interests; in any struggle between Edward and Philip he would most likely be guided by them and by his family connections.

The position of Namur appeared favorable to Philip's schemes. The count was an uncle of Louis, count of Flanders, and had loyally aided his nephew by supporting the remnant of his authority at Ghent when the rest of Flanders was in the hands of rebels. Later, upon the count's death, Philip was called upon to arbitrate the dispute between the countess, Marie of Artois, and her son John II, which was settled on February 17, 1332.[53]

Philip now determined to secure the friendship or support of John, duke of Brabant. The strategical position of that prince made an understanding with him highly desirable. Lying between Flanders on the west and Liège on the east, whose princes were both decidedly under Philip's influence, Brabant might

---

[49] *Foedera*, II (2) 759, 771, 793, 800, 822, 827, 829; *CCR* (1330–3), pp. 5, 38, 73, 108, 109, 204, 265, 357, 371–372, 413, 462, 512; *CPR* (1330–4), p. 228.

[50] *CCR* (1333–7), pp. 58–59, 159.

[51] A. Fayen, *Lettres de Jean XXII* (*1316–1334*), No. 3176.

[52] P. K. Eubel, "Der vom Grafen Wilhelm von Jülich am 30 Januar, 1332, dem Papste Johann XXII geleistete Treueid," *Historisches Jahrbuch*, XIX (1898), 568–570.

[53] C. Piot, *Inventaire des Chartes de Comtes de Namur*, pp. 132, 144.

unite these two lands with Namur and form a solid block of French prestige in the Low Countries. And because the duchy with its towns and industry was sufficiently like Flanders to have similar social and political problems, the duke, who ever jealously restrained the aspirations of the crafts, might possibly be counted upon to aid in checking any future democratic movement of the Flemings against their suzerain. But, as was the case with the Flemish craftsmen, the economic ties with England made him little inclined to turn a deaf ear to Edward's insinuations.

King Edward's agents had for some years been busy strengthening English influence in Brabant. On September 28, 1328, William de Monte Acuto and Bartholomew de Burghersh were empowered to approach Otto, seignior of Cuyk, son of John of Cuyk, a former pensioner of Edward I, and an influential figure in the household of the duke of Brabant, and secure him as a member of the royal council.[54] An agreement was made whereby Otto was to receive the 1,000*l.* sterling in arrears which had been suspended after the overthrow of Edward II, and, in addition, 250*l.* annually thereafter.[55] But Duke John was not visibly moved by Edward's wishes. On the other hand, when Philip suggested, apparently after 1329, that his dispute with Reginald of Valkenburg should be left to his arbitrament, he refused.[56] For years William, count of Hainault, Holland, and Zeeland, had labored to secure the political friendship of Duke John in order to insure his own interests; in the same way Philip would now seek an understanding with him in order to advance his own power in the Low Countries.

An opportunity soon presented itself. The county of Artois had in 1302 been given to Mahaut, daughter of Robert II, rather than to his grandson, Robert, who was in his minority. The youth was not satisfied with this arrangement, which was dictated by local custom and, as soon as he became of age, appealed to the peers of France, but in vain. The accession of his brother-in-law Philip, for which he is said to have shown great zeal,[57]

---

[54] *Foedera,* II (2), 773; *CRR* (1327–30), p. 445; *CCR* (1330–3), p. 40.
[55] *CCR* (1330–3), pp. 354, 495; *CCR* (1333–7), pp. 5, 31, 69, 217.
[56] Willelmus Procurator, p. 236.
[57] *Chronique Parisienne Anonyme,* pp. 158–159; le Bel, I, 95.

gave him renewed hope. At Cassel he played a useful rôle.[58] In 1329 when Edward performed homage at Amiens Robert secured the services of William de Breuil, a jurist of reputation. Documents were forged with the help of several accomplices and the matter was again brought before the peers. When this failed, Robert is said to have brought about the death of Mahaut at the end of November by the use of poison, and on January 21, 1330, also that of her daughter Jeanne.[59] Meanwhile he had sought to strengthen himself in Artois when Philip sent his governor to care for the lands of the county.[60] Presently the forgery was confessed by one of the culprits, Jeanne de Duvion, but Robert nevertheless stoutly maintained the genuineness of the documents and was finally cited to appear before the peers on September 29, 1331.[61]

Fearing for his personal safety, Robert fled France, left his wife and children at Philip's mercy, and betook himself to his kinsman John, duke of Brabant,[62] who received him with kindness in Brussels and allowed him to take into his service the *advocatus* of Huy as his valet. He assigned to him Louvain as residence [63] where he tarried until the summer of 1332. When Robert failed to appear at Michaelmas and again on St. Andrew's Day, a third summons was served. Robert replied by letters dated Brussels, February 13, 1332, by which he empowered Henry, dean of Ste. Gudule of Brussels, Thibaut de Mieux, a canon of Cambrai, John de Brussels, a lawyer, and Jean Coppelet to present his excuses for not appearing on Tuesday, the 18th. He had been cited to present himself on the 17th, but, notwithstanding his disobedience and the discovery of some new evidence of his complicity, the

[58] *Chronique Parisienne Anonyme,* p. 120.

[59] H. Moranvillé, " Guillaume du Breuil et Robert d'Artois," *BEC,* XLVIII (1887), 641–650. See also A. Coville, " Les Prèmiers Valois. La Guerre de Cent Ans (1328 à 1422)," E. Lavisse, *Histoire de France,* IV (Part I), 6–8.

[60] C. Hirschauer, *Les États d'Artois de leurs Origines à l'Occupation Française,* 1340–1640, I, 10–11.

[61] Lancelot, " Mémoires pour Servir à l'Histoire de Robert d'Artois," *Mémoires de Littérature tiréz des Registres de l'Académie Royale des Inscriptions et Belles Lettres,* X (1736), 614.

[62] *Grandes Chroniques,* V, 345; *Chronographia,* II, 15; de Nangis, II, 126–127; Lescot, p. 26; Hocsemius, p. 408; Boendale, *Van den derden Eduwaert,* p. 349; Froissart, I, 101, 308.

[63] Outremeuse, VI, 486–487. At Argenteau, according to le Bel, I, 92.

king agreed to a fourth citation and commanded him to appear on April 9.[64]

Philip could ill afford to have an enemy of such a character as Robert in Brabant where he could in perfect liberty weave plots against his safety. Messengers were sent to summon him, but to no avail.[65] After the third citation it was reported that Robert was in touch with Flemish malcontents [66] who had been driven to desperation by the savage policy of revenge adopted by the king and count. In 1331 there was a revolt led by one Monac.[67] This must have moved Philip to violent wrath and he again requested the duke not to extend hospitality to the fugitive,[68] which caused John to marvel, inasmuch as he was a vassal not of Philip but of the emperor. In haughty accents he informed the king that since this was so and since some of his lands were allodial, he was responsible for them to God alone and could not therefore entertain his request.[69]

John, king of Bohemia, was greatly pleased to hear of the strained relations which now so suddenly developed between Philip and his own mortal enemy, the duke of Brabant. Ever since the victory of Mühldorf in September, 1322, King John had followed a policy of aggrandizement for his house. He sought to win advantage as a third powerful party in the antagonisms of the two major forces in the empire, Lewis the Bavarian, ever eager to rob the pope of all secular support in Germany, and the Hapsburgs who desired the imperial crown. His diplomatic skill in the summer of 1330 enabled him to secure the favor of both. His agreement with Otto, duke of Austria, at Landau in May of that year seemed to dissipate the Hapsburg fear of an attack from Lewis the Bavarian, and his arbitration between the two at

[64] Lancelot, " Mémoires pour Servir à l'Histoire de Robert d'Artois," *Mémoires de Littérature tiréz des Registres de l'Académie Royale des Inscriptions et Belles Lettres,* X (1736), 615–617.

[65] De Nangis, II, 217; Boendale, *Van den derden Eduwaert,* p. 350.

[66] Lancelot, " Mémoires pour Servir à l'Histoire de Robert d'Artois." *Mémoires de Littérature tiréz des Registres de l'Académie Royale des Inscriptions et Belles Lettres,* X (1736), 617–618.

[67] *Chronicon Comitum Flandresium,* p. 222. For the reaction, see H. Pirenne, *Le Soulèvement de la Flandre Maritime,* pp. XXXII–XXXVII.

[68] Hocsemius, p. 408; Boendale, *Brabantsche Yeesten,* I, 494, and *Van den derden Eduwaert,* p. 350; cf. Outremeuse, VI, 489.

[69] Boendale, *Brabantsche Yeesten,* I, 494–495, *and Van den derden Eduwaert,* p. 350.

Hagenau on August 6 satisfied Lewis the Bavarian's desire for security from papal attacks in this quarter and granted some territorial compensation to Otto, who now agreed to aid the emperor in restoring his power in Italy.[70] This obligation John now assumed for a consideration of 10,000 marks. Thereupon on September 16 followed the marriage of his second son John and Marguerite, daughter of Henry, duke of Carinthia and count of Tyrol. The Hapsburgs viewed with uneasiness the possibility of Luxemburg power establishing itself south of Austria. They therefore secretly agreed with the suspicious Lewis the Bavarian at Augsburg on November 26 that they should eventually succeed to the duchy of Carinthia, promising to the Wittelsbach house in return the county of Tyrol. Then followed in 1331 and 1332 the remarkable growth of the Bohemian king's power in Lombardy when the dominion of more than twenty towns was granted to him by the *signorie*.[71]

Title to supreme authority could of course not be granted by the seigniories of these Italian towns and was contested by the pope and the emperor. With the former King John came to an agreement at Piumaccio; with the latter at Regensburg in July and August, 1331. Lewis the Bavarian was recognized as lord of all his possessions in Italy, save Parma, Modena, and Reggio, which had, it appears, been granted by the pope to Philip VI as early as 1328 in the vain hope of securing French help to combat the victorious career of the Bavarian.[72] King John had other interests for his *Hausmacht* in the empire besides his titles in Italy, and why should he not now turn for aid to France, the traditional supporter of Luxemburg schemes? Philip showed himself eager to draw still closer the ties already intimate between the two houses.[73] The Luxemburger could lend the Valois cause

[70] F. von Weech, *Kaiser Ludwig der Baier und König Johann von Böhmen mit Urkundlichen Beilagen,* pp. 20–41; E. Werunsky, *Geschichte Kaiser Karls IV und seiner Zeit,* I, 31–37.

[71] L. Pöppelmann, "Johann von Böhmen in Italien, 1330–1333. Ein Beitrag zur Geschichte des XIV Jahrhunderts," *Archiv für Oesterreichische Geschichte,* XXXV (1865), 249–259.

[72] A. Lehleiter, *Die Politik König Johans von Böhmen in den Jahren 1330–1334,* pp. 30–39.

[73] Charles, son of King John, had been at the French court from 1322 to 1330 and received as wife Blanca, daughter of Charles of Valois, and hence was Philip's brother-in-law. See *Vita Caroli,* pp. 233–235; *Königsaaler Geschichts-Quellen,* p. 501.

substantial aid in the Low Countries by the side of the count of Flanders and the bishop of Liège as well as in the Franche Comté and the kingdom of Arles.

Apprised, it would seem, by the bishop of Liège of the situation in the Low Countries,[74] King John hastily returned on December 6 to Prague from the borders of Moravia, where he had been fighting the Hungarians. By lavish promises he induced the nobles to proceed against the Austrians and Hungarians in his absence, and on the 13th at night, quietly, and accompanied by only ten men, hastened forth to Paris where he hoped to be on Christmas Eve. On the 14th he arrived at the monastery of Tepel, and on the 15th at Neuburg in Bavaria. To spectators he seemed not to ride but fairly to fly, and to act as a servant obeying orders rather than as a lord giving commands.[75]

The king was in Paris on January 2,[76] and soon thereafter at Fontainebleau [77] an agreement was made whereby John promised to validate any encroachment by Philip upon the empire in case the imperial crown should come into the possession of himself or other members of his house, aid him in any strife with a vassal of the empire should the emperor seek to protect such a party and to aid the French cause in the Champagne, Vermandois, and the Amiénois with a force of four hundred men-at-arms, and elsewhere with three hundred, even if he should become Roman king. In addition to these terms a contract of marriage was now drawn up. John's daughter Gutta, or Bonna, as she was called in France, was to marry John, duke of Normandy, Philip's heir apparent, and bring with her a dowry of 120,000 florins payable in six years.[78] And at Vincennes on February 8, the Bohemian king was named Philip's lieutenant in Gascony.[79]

[74] E. Fairon, "Un Projet de Démembrement du Diocèse de Liège Proposé par les Brabançons," *BCRH*, 78 (1904), 184.

[75] *Königsaaler Geschichts-Quellen*, pp. 488–489; *Boendale, Brabantsche Yeesten*, I, 492, 495.

[76] *Vita Caroli*, p. 237.

[77] The king was at Fontainebleau on January 6 and 11. See J. Viard, "Itinéraire de Philippe VI de Valois," *BEC*, LXXXIV (1913), 10.

[78] F. J. Boehmer, *Regesten Kaiser Ludwig des Baiern und seiner Zeit. Additamentum Primum,* p. 298.

[79] P. A. Lenz, "Jean l'Aveugle, Roi de Bohème, Comte de Luxembourg, Marquis d'Arlon," *Nouvelle Archives Historiques,* II (1840), 259 (note 5). The date, however, should manifestly be 1332 instead of 1331. See W. Felten, *Die Bulle "Ne Pretereat,"* II, 154 (note 114).

Thus was cemented the old friendship of the French reigning house with the Luxemburgs. While their *Hausmacht* in the Low Countries was slight and Luxemburg itself was of but little consequence, King John might nevertheless become the center of friendly influence for the Valois house, especially as he was on intimate terms with nearly all the princes of these parts. The military convention reveals Philip's anxiety in regard to the Low Countries; with the aid of the count of Flanders, the king of Bohemia, the duke of Brabant, and the bishop of Liège he hoped to make himself secure in this quarter.

III. THE FIRST ATTACK UPON THE DUKE OF BRABANT (WINTER AND SPRING, 1332)

THE envy and hatred of well-nigh every neighbor toward the duke of Brabant could now be satisfied. With the express approval of Philip a coalition was now formed.[80] It appears that the king desired to remain free from direct participation, and apparently no formal agreement was drawn up. The count of Eu, constable of France, joined the league to avenge the slight offered his master, and even the duke's cousin, Edward, count of Bar, went with him.[81] In the alliance were William, count of Juliers, Reginald, count of Guelders, John, count of Namur,[82] Reginald, seignior of Valkenburg, the bishop of Liège, and the archbishop of Cologne.[83] William, count of Hainault, Holland, and Zeeland, remained neutral, notwithstanding the attitude of the duke who had shown himself little inclined to carry out the terms of the marriage contract of 1328.[83a]

It would have been rash for Count William to join in the attack

[80] Hocsemius, p. 408: "... annuente rege Francorum." This took place on February 2, according to Outremeuse, VI, 487–490, but his statements have slight, if any, authority.

[81] Hocsemius, p. 408.

[82] In March, 1332, Guy, brother of Count John, had become a vassal of John, king of Bohemia. See Piot, *Inventaire des Chartes de Comtes de Namur*, p. 157.

[83] *Vita Caroli*, p. 247; le Bel, I, 99; Boendale, *Brabantsche Yeesten*, I, 496–497; Levold de Northof, p. 401; *Königsaaler Geschichts-Quellen*, pp. 499–500; *Grandes Chroniques*, I, 346; *Chronographia*, II, 16; *Gesta Abbatum Sancti Trudonis*, p. 422.

[83a] L. Devillers, *Monuments*, III, 298–303. See F. van Mieris, *Groot Charterboek*, II, 541–542.

upon the duke of Brabant and risk the results of so much patient labor. That he was fully acquainted with all the intrigues and even with Philip's deeper motives is certain. If he bore any feeling of dissatisfaction toward him, it remained covert, for with John of Hainault and Louis, count of Flanders, he had appeared at Paris on October 6 when Jeanne de Duvion was burned to death in the Place-aux-Porceaux,[84] and again on April 9, when Robert of Artois was finally condemned.[85] John of Hainault, however, did join the coalition, partly perhaps to express Count William's feelings toward the duke.[86] Thus the frontier of Brabant, save where it marched with Flanders, Hainault, Holland, and Zeeland, was open to attack.

The confederates congregated at Fexhe-le-haut-Clocher, northeast of Liège, about April 23.[87] As some of them had to come from various quarters, a preliminary meeting had apparently been arranged. Edward, the count of Bar, and Walram, archbishop of Cologne, were absent.[88] A conference was first held with the towns of Liège after which began the burning of the adjacent lands and villages in Brabant.[89] Duke John had been apprized betimes of the impending danger and had mobilized his forces which were strengthened by the arrival of some knights from Flanders.[90] He immediately fortified Leeuw, as an attack from the direction of St. Trond was feared, but, when a small detachment of his troops had been routed at Hannut, he led his forces toward the monastery of Heylissem, where he entrenched himself in an inaccessible spot behind the Gette so that the enemy could scarcely attack him as he quietly watched on the defensive.[91]

[84] *Chronique Parisienne Anonyme,* pp. 147–148.

[85] Lancelot, " Mémoire pour Servir à l'Histoire de Robert d'Artois," *Mémoires de Littérature tiréz des Registres de l'Académie Royale des Inscriptions et Belles Lettres,* X (1736), 618; *Grandes Chroniques,* V, 349.

[86] S. A. Walter Zeper, *Jan van Henegouwen, Heer van Beaumont,* p. 124. Cf. Outremeuse, VI, 488.

[87] Hocsemius, p. 409.

[88] *Ibid.;* K. Hoffmann, *Die Haltung des Erzbistums Kölns in den Kirchenpolitischen Kämpfen Ludwigs des Baiern,* p. 54 (note 5).

[89] *Gesta Abbatum Sancti Trudonis,* p. 422; Hocsemius, p. 409; Outremeuse, VI, 490.

[90] Boendale, *Brabantsche Yeesten,* I, 498.

[91] *Ibid.,* Hocsemius, p. 408; Willelmus Procurator, p. 267; Outremeuse, VI, 492; Levold de Northof, p. 401. The duke was here made a knight.

The king of Bohemia now proposed a temporary cessation of hostilities. The motive for this is unknown, unless it was to secure reënforcements with which the allies would be better able to meet the strength of the duke.[92] As peace had been restored in the bishop's city, its militia could now be employed for this purpose. On *Quasimodo* Sunday (April 26), after an absence of seven years, Bishop Adolph de la Marck, accompanied by his allies, again entered Liège.[93] The commune was eager to fight the hereditary enemy of the *patria* and redress the many wrongs received at his hands and readily responded to the bishop's appeal. On May 4 the leaders once more returned to the Hesbaye, accompanied by the count of Bar. Two days later the militia marched out under the standard of St. Lambert, led by the *advocatus* of Hesbaye. Everybody was now ready to resume the attack on the following day when the fortnight agreed upon would come to an end.[94] But the allied powers did not care to attack the duke who was " better entrenched there than in twelve castles." [95] Encamped on Brabançon soil for eight days, they plundered and burned the whole countryside east of the Gette.[96] Finally the rain began to fall in torrents, the roads became impassable, victualling was extremely difficult, and the horses were exhausted with the cold. The duke himself could not have retreated even if he had wanted to.[97]

Fighting thus ceased; and the struggle was transferred to the field of diplomacy. Chagrined that King Philip by this most unexpected action against the duke of Brabant might perhaps seriously delay the crusade upon which the curia had set its heart, the pope wrote to him and to the queen begging them to seek earnestly some basis of accord.[98] But Philip had already sent to Brabant, William, archbishop of Sens, and John, bishop of Thérouanne, to induce the duke and his council to come to

---

[92] Hocsemius, p. 409.

[93] G. Kurth, *La Cité de Liège au Moyen Âge,* II, 43.

[94] Hocsemius, p. 409.

[95] Outremeuse, VI, 494; Willelmus Procurator, p. 267. See also *Gesta Abbatum Sancti Trudonis,* p. 422.

[96] *Gesta Abbatum Sancti Trudonis,* p. 422; Hocsemius, p. 409; Willelmus Procurator, p. 267.

[97] Boendale, *Brabantsche Yeesten,* I, 498.

[98] A. Fayen, *Lettres de Jean XXII (1316–1334),* Nos. 1321, 1322.

France and submit the disputes to his arbitration.[99]   Count William of Hainault, Holland, and Zeeland now also interposed his good offices and coöperated with the efforts of his brother-in-law.[100]   Just as the duke was planning an attack, William, afflicted with rheumatic pains which became worse with age so that he had to be carried in a litter, arrived from Zeeland and presented himself before him.[101]

Although a neutral in the struggle and enjoying excellent prestige among all the confederates with whom he was on very friendly terms, Count William nevertheless found it difficult at first to secure a hearing.   He at once went to their camp at St. Trond.   But the plundering did not cease, and the duke invited his adversaries to a contest on the frontiers of Brabant, which was refused.   Duke John's position was a strong one, and the confederates soon came to a realization that they could accomplish little more than to lay waste his lands.[102]   For two days Count William passed back and forth while the plundering was in progress.   Once he was mistaken as an enemy by the troops from Antwerp, but was saved by one of the duke's bailiffs.[103]   On the next day, May 11, the terms of a truce were drawn up at Heylissem: hostilities were to stop until a fortnight after St. John the Baptist's Day and all questions were to be left to the arbitrament of King Philip at Compiègne.[104]

On May 13 the confederates began to evacuate Brabant, but not before concluding on May 11 an alliance which was to govern their further relations with the duke.   In case the duke renewed hostilities with any one of the allies, no separate peace

[99] Boendale, *Brabantsche Yeesten,* I, 502.

[100] Hocsemius, p. 409; Levold de Northof, p. 401.

[101] Willelmus Procurator, pp. 266–267; Boendale, *Brabantsche Yeesten,* I, 499.

[102] Boendale, *Brabantsche Yeesten,* I, 499–500.

[103] *Ibid.,* pp. 502–503.   See *Gesta Abbatum Sancti Trudonis,* p. 422.

[104] Willelmus Procurator, p. 267.   Cf. Boendale, *Brabantsche Yeesten,* I, 504.   The document is printed in J. F. Willems, *Codex Diplomaticus,* I, 788.   Bishop Adolph, however, was opposed to the truce, according to Hocsemius, p. 409.   The document is dated May 11, but apparently was not accepted by the allies until the 13th.   According to Hocsemius, p. 409, the militia of Liège left the city on May 6 and plundered for eight days. Counting May 6 as the first, the forays must have continued until the 13th, or at least until the moment when the leaders began to leave Brabant. The document was thus probably drawn up in the duke's camp at Heylissem, but had to wait two days for the seals of the other parties.

was to be accepted and the others were to come to his rescue. Special provisions were inserted to provide for any prisoners that might be taken. All castles and strongholds seized were to belong to the coalition until they should be disposed of, and illness could not serve as a valid excuse for failure to coöperate.[105] Thus the coalition continued to exist; the confederates were ready for any eventuality, even for war, at any moment after July 9.

IV. The Negotiations at Compiègne (June, 1332)

The scene of further activities now shifted to France. Thither William, count of Juliers, Reginald, count of Guelders, and Walram, archbishop of Cologne, betook themselves toward the close of May, apparently to come to an understanding with King Philip in regard to the duke of Brabant before negotiations should begin. At Senlis they met Philip, who was on his way toward Compiègne,[106] and made a formal agreement with him. They promised to aid him and his son John against Robert of Artois, John, duke of Brabant, and all others who might wish to aid the fugitive, and help the king against his enemies whether in France or elsewhere. Each was to provide a thousand men at Philip's expense, should the latter be forced to dislodge Robert from Brabant.[107] John of Hainault had apparently gone to France before them, for when there on the 23d he loaned 480 gold florins to the ever penurious king of Bohemia.[108] At Senlis he acted as intermediary and pledged his possessions in France as guarantee that the counts and the archbishop would carry out their agreements.[109]

[105] I. A. Nijhoff, *Gedenkwaardigheden uit de Geschiedenis van Gelderland,* I, 277–279. On June 4 John XXII wrote to the king of Sicily of his relief. See A. Fayen, *Lettres de Jean XXII (1316–1334),* No. 3231.

[106] Philip was at Senlis on May 28. See J. Viard, "Itinéraire de Jules Viard," *BEC,* LXXIV (1913), 107.

[107] I. A. Nijhoff, *Gedenkwaardigheden uit de Geschiedenis van Gelderland,* I, 280–283, and H. Schrohe, "Kleinere Beiträge," *Mitteilungen des Instituts für Oesterreichische Geschichtsforchung,* XXVI (1905), 483–485.

[108] F. J. Boehmer, *Regesten Kaiser Ludwigs des Baiern und seiner Zeit, Additamentum Tertium,* p. 400. He had to borrow 2,512 Florentine florins from John of Hainault on July 15 and 2,000*l.* on July 13. See *ibid.,* and F. van Mieris, *Groot Charterboek,* II, 530.

[109] See the *vidimus* of June 24 in F. van Mieris, *Groot Charterboek,* II, 528.

Presently the other allied princes and interested parties came together at Royallieu, a monastery near Compiègne.   There were the king's brother-in-law, William, count of Hainault, Holland, and Zeeland, Baldwin, archbishop of Trier, and a great crowd of nobles from France and Germany, drawn thither by the prospect of brilliant entertainment and tournament.[110]   John, duke of Brabant, arrived betimes in gleaming array,[111] and from the outset Philip, king of Navarre, and Charles, count d'Estampes, treated him with marked consideration.   The king and the duke were together much of the time and discussed the bases of an accord and alliance.[112]   Finally, on June 30, Duke John,[113] Raoul, count of Eu,[114] and others declared their willingness to submit their differences to Philip's arbitration under the guarantee that the spiritual and secular princes should each forfeit 100,000 silver marks in case they failed to accept the decision.   The date of the final pronouncement could also be postponed, if necessary, to June 24 or even until the following Christmas.[115]

Philip thereupon declared a state of peace on June 21.   Prisoners were to be liberated without ransom, obligations contracted by any party in the war were to be cancelled, alliances were to cease and all relations between vassals and lords were to be reëstablished.   For the rest the king reserved decision in accordance with the documents drawn up on the preceding day.[116]   On the 23d he considered the case of his friend Adolph, bishop of Liège, who had drawn up a long complaint in fifty-five articles dealing with the duke's aggressions.   Philip ordered John to make fitting restitution to the burghers of St. Trond for all losses he had inflicted upon them.[117]   The bishop's spiritual jurisdiction over

[110] *Chronique Parisienne Anonyme,* p. 49; Levold de Northof, p. 401; Boendale, *Brabantsche Yeesten,* I, 506; *Chronographia,* II, 16; *Grandes Chroniques,* V, 346.

[111] Boendale, *Brabantsche Yeesten,* I, 505.

[112] *Ibid.,* p. 507; *Grandes Chroniques,* V, 346.

[113] L. P. Gachard, "Les Archives Royales de Dusseldorf," *BRCH,* 4th Ser., IX.(1881), 276.   For Philip's promise, see J. Dumont, *Corps Universel Diplomatique,* I(2), 133–134.

[114] J. Dumont, *Corps Universel Diplomatique,* I(2), 133.

[115] *Archives Nationales,* Paris, J. 524a, no. 30[1].

[116] *Archives Nationales,* Paris, J. 524, no. 30[7] and J 568[4].

[117] According to Outremeuse VI, 500, he was to give them 12,000 florins.

Brabant was to be obeyed and the interdict which Adolph had pronounced in the previous year, apparently in connection with the duke's actions at St. Trond, was to be lifted.[118]   In another document, which, like the preceding one, appears to have been lost, Philip ordered John to pay Reginald, seignior of Valkenburg, 30,000 florins and to return to him his lands within three weeks.[119]   The remaining points were to be reserved for further investigation until May, 1333, and, should decision then still be impossible, until the following Christmas.[120]

Hard upon these events followed the betrothal of Philip's daughter Marie to John, the duke's heir apparent.[121]   Philip, it is stated, induced the duke of Brabant to break the treaty arrangements of 1329 because a connection with Count William's daughter Isabella would be less honorable.[122]   But the real motives with John were without doubt other than this; he hoped for more favorable consideration of his rights from Philip in the pending decisions and was also thinking of Philip's possible aid at the curia in securing an independent diocese for Brabant and Limburg. The king promised a dowry of 130,000*l.* small Tournois, payable in three equal instalments at the close of each of the first three years after the marriage, and John was to assign to his son the duchy of Limburg as an appanage and 10,000*l.* Tournois in land to be located preferably in the Walloon section of Brabant, and to promise that, in the event of his son's death before the marriage should take place, his second son Henry should marry Marie.[123]   In the interests of peace and the cause of the crusade, the pope readily granted the necessary dispensation.[124]

As part of this remarkable *volte-face,* the duke of Brabant agreed to a new political and military accommodation. Duke John and his son were to perform liege homage in consideration of 100*l.* small Tournois annually, for which he promised aid in person with two hundred men-at-arms against all of Philip's

[118] Hocsemius, p. 409.

[119] Outremeuse, VI, 500.

[120] Hocsemius, pp. 409–410 (paged as 402).

[121] H. J. Smit, *Rekeningen der Graven en Gravinnen uit het Henegouwsche Huis,* I, 564.

[122] *Chronographia,* II, 16; *Grandes Chroniques,* V, 346.

[123] A. Verkooren, *Inventaire, Brabant,* I, 243–244.

[124] S. Riezler, *Vatikanische Akten,* No. 556; A. Fairon, *Les Lettres de Jean XXII (1316–1334),* No. 3259.

enemies save the emperor, and, should this aid be required more than once in a year, all expenses were to be paid by the king. Furthermore, no subject of the duke's should ever aid the king's enemies, none of whom were to be received in Brabant or Limburg.[125]   Philip promised that he would never conclude a separate truce and would always stand ready to give aid and comfort in case the duke incurred the hostility of anyone on account of this agreement.[126]   Robert of Artois was now quite defenseless and had to flee. The harmony between John and Philip is further revealed when in October the latter renounced all claim upon the jewels left by Robert in his hurried departure from Brussels.[127] As earnest of his good intentions, Duke John also sent his son to Paris in accordance with Philip's wish.[128]

V. The Political Activities of William, Count of Hainault, Holland, and Zeeland (1332–1333)

Philip had won a noteworthy diplomatic victory in the Low Countries; the alliance with the duke of Brabant, secured by a matrimonial connection, might, with the aid of Louis, count of Flanders, John, king of Bohemia, and Bishop Adolph de la Marck, provide a solid support of French policy in the Low Countries, which would be useful in any serious clash with Edward III. And to these advantages perhaps might be added the alliance with the counts of Juliers and Guelders and the archbishop of Cologne.

It was, however, a question whether the feelings of Count William, the king's brother-in-law, who ever afterwards regarded the repudiation of the treaty arrangements with the duke of Brabant in 1329 as a mortal insult and gross betrayal of brotherly confidence, could be thus lightly set at naught.[129] From the very beginning of the negotiations the enemies of the duke were also suspicious of Philip's friendliness toward him, and, when the royal decision of June 21 was announced, made their dissatisfaction

---

[125] A. Verkooren, *Inventaire Brabant*, I, 243–244.

[126] *Archives Nationales,* Paris, J. 524, no. 30³.

[127] A. Wauters, "Analectes de Diplomatique." *BCRH,* 4th Ser., X (1882), 97.

[128] Boendale, *Brabantsche Yeesten,* I, 507.

[129] *Grandes Chroniques,* IV, 346; *Chronographia,* II, 15–16, 32.

known.[130]   Before leaving Compiègne they bound themselves on June 24 to continue their defensive alliance against the duke. They feared his revenge and, in order to avoid any divisions among themselves, promised never to seize arms against each other. All grievances were to be submitted to the arbitration of some member of the alliance. In such a crisis they were all to meet, within eight days after arbitration should be requested, at Binche in Hainault for all problems arising in the *Romain pais*, and at Aix-la-Chapelle for the *Thiois pais*, where they were to sojourn until a decision could be reached.[131]

Countess Jeanne was visiting her brother Philip during these days at the Bois de Vincennes.[132]   When on the 28th she heard of the new matrimonial arrangements of the duke, she sent the master of her pantry posthaste to carry the news to her husband.[133]   A decided change in sentiment toward his brother-in-law now took place in William's mind, but he was careful, it would seem, not to betray any serious resentment; at any rate it did not obviously influence his immediate actions. He made preparations to be present at the marriage which was to take place at Paris on September 29, an act which courtesy required. His old malady, rheumatism, prevented him, however; but his son William was determined to go, and money was borrowed from the Lombards at Valenciennes and horses and equipment were collected. At the last moment the youth's illness made his departure impossible.[134]   At Melun on July 28 had been concluded the marriage, delayed since the previous spring, of Bonna to John, duke of Normandy.[135]   The king of Bohemia came rushing from Prague, which he visited only eight days,[136] to witness the final celebra-

---

[130] Hocsemius, p. 402.

[131] I. A. Nijhoff, *Gedenkwaardigheden uit de Geschiedenis van Gelderland*, I, 284–287.

[132] H. J. Smit, *De Rekeningen der Graven en Gravinnen uit het Henegouwsche Huis*, I, 572–580, 584.

[133] *Ibid.*, p. 564: " Ce jour, à Baudouin le panetier pour aller en Haynnau à monseigneur porter novelles pour marriage le fil de duc de Brabant et dame Marie de France: 40s. Parisis.   Item, 1 cheval liewet par 6 jours à Noyon: 12s. Parisis; pour le despens dou sien qu'il i laissa, parmi miel; 13s.; messages et gourles: 4s."

[134] The seignior of Bousies, however, did go.   See *ibid.*, pp. 635–636.

[135] *Chronique Parisienne Anonyme*, p. 150; de Nangis, II, 133; *Grandes Chroniques*, V, 350; Lescot, p. 29.

[136] *Königsaaler Geschichts-Quellen*, p. 492.

tion of his son Charles' marriage, which was also to occur on September 29. A great number of notables came, the king of Navarre, the dukes of Burgundy, Lorraine, Brittany, and Bourbon, the counts of Evreux, Bar, and Clermont, besides the duke of Brabant, the count of Juliers, and John of Hainault. There was much rejoicing, feasting, and jousting, and the knighting of the duke of Normandy was followed by the nuptials.[137]

Count William revealed his resentment toward the duke of Brabant when on February 10, 1333, he agreed to join the alliance arranged on June 24 at Compiègne. He however expressly retained the right to treat independently with the duke in regard to the marriage of Duke John's daughter Johanna and William.[138] His position among his neighbors was a strong one, as is attested by his harmonious relations with the counts of Guelders and Juliers. An assignment of an income of 700*l.* from the wood at Mormal, which had been made to the count of Juliers in satisfaction of the unpaid part of Johanna's marriage portion, was now changed into a cash payment. Count William promised to pay him 6,000*l.* Tournois out of the money which Reginald, count of Guelders, still owed him for relinquishing his claim upon some rights in Mechelen and an additional sum of 1,000*l.* at Easter.[139] On March 1 the terms of the marriage of Gerard, heir apparent of Juliers, and Marguerite, eldest daughter of Count Reginald, were drawn up. She was to have the old Berthout possessions in Mechelen, except Schinne and Teveren, 2,000*l.* Tournois annually from lands in Guelders adjacent to Juliers, and the seigniory of Heymbach. As guarantors in behalf of Reginald, there appeared the archbishop of Cologne, the bishop of Liège, the king of Bohemia, the counts of Flanders, Loon, Namur, Cleves, Berg, Marck, Sayn, and Lodi, John of Hainault, Otto, seignior of Cuyk, the nobility of Guelders, representatives of the towns of Roermond, Guelders, Nijmegen, and Arnhem, besides Count William.[140] On the 20th Reginald promised to indemnify Count

[137] *Chronique Parisienne Anonyme*, p. 151; *Grandes Chroniques*, V, 346–350; *Chronographia*, II, 16; de Nangis, II, 133–134.

[138] I. A. Nijhoff, *Gedenkwaardigheden uit de Geschiedenis van Gelderland*, I, 287–288.

[139] L. Devillers, *Monuments*, III, 294–296; F. van Mieris, *Groot Charterboek*, II, 538.

[140] I. A. Nijhoff, *Gedenkwaardigheden uit de Geschiedenis van Gelderland*, I, 300–305.

William for the 84,000*l.* advanced by him as a guarantee to the count of Juliers.[141]

On April 11, two weeks before the end of the term within which decision was to be rendered, Philip appointed John, bishop of Arras, and Hugh Quieret commissioners to settle the differences between Brabant and the allies,[142] and postponed final settlement until Christmas.[143] Five days later the deputies appeared at Mechelen where Reginald, count of Guelders, and Louis, count of Flanders, the former in behalf of the allies and the latter for Duke John of Brabant, rendered a decision in their presence. The pronouncements on June 23, 1332, regarding the relations of the duke and the bishop of Liège, as secular and ecclesiastical princes, were to be put into operation without delay. Other debated points were to be settled by the Sunday before Pentecost, and, if this should prove impossible, on Pentecost Sunday at Cambrai, also before the royal deputies.

Relations of the duke of Brabant and his neighbors on his eastern borders were now also considered. Normal conditions were restored in the lands held in fee of the duke by the count of Juliers. John's claim to the village of Lewenich was examined. The count of Juliers refused to admit it, and consequently the duke was ordered to produce documents to substantiate his demands. The warfare levied upon Conrad, seignior of Schleiden, and the seignior of Sceveman was to cease for two years. Finally, the duke was forbidden to acquire any new towns, castles, or lands within the possessions of the counts of Guelders and Juliers. All other undecided questions were to be considered at the session in Cambrai.

In the matter of the marriage between Johanna of Brabant and William, heir apparent of Hainault, Holland, and Zeeland, it was decreed that, in view of the " grave consequences which it involved," Johanna should be allowed to go to her husband not later than October 1, that the dowry should be assigned within fifteen days, and when this should be complied with, young Wil-

---

[141] L. Devillers, *Monuments,* III, 341–342.

[142] *Archives Nationales,* Paris, J. 424ᵃ, No. 30¹². See J. de Saint Genois, *Monumens Anciens,* II, DCCCCXXII–DCCCCXXIII; I. A. Nijhoff, *Gedenkwaardigheden uit de Geschiedenis van Gelderland,* I, 314–317, where the document is contained in another of October 8, 1333.

[143] *Archives Nationales,* Paris, J 524ᵃ, No. 30²².

liam should be free to go to see her as often as he might wish.
Count William was loud in his complaints of the duke's persistent
refusal to allow Johanna the necessary freedom, and especially
of his faithlessness in the betrothal of his daughter Isabella
to the heir apparent of Brabant. In compensation he was
awarded 35,000*l. regales* payable within two years. All the old
agreements, save the clauses referring to the marriage of Johanna
and William, were declared void.[144]

The bishop of Arras and Hugh Quieret had in the meantime
conducted their negotiations at Mechelen and Brussels and finally
decided that the duke of Brabant and his council should appear
at Cambrai on May 14. On the 22d it was decreed that the
spiritual jurisdiction — the *Judicium Pacis* — of the bishop of
Liège should remain unaltered. John de Raucourt and Thierry
de Haneffe, knights, and John de Cadzand, a canon of St. Paul's
in Liège and of the church of Courtrai, were named to investigate
and assess by the following Christmas all damages which the duke
had inflicted upon the friars and canons of St. Servaas in Maastricht. The duke's subjects who had been taken prisoner at Perwez and held for ransom for the creditors of the bishop of Liège
and the king of Bohemia, contrary to Philip's pronouncement at
Compiègne, were to be surrendered into the royal hand.[145] These
provisions were extended by a document of June 12 drawn up by
John, bishop of Thérouanne, the abbot of St. Nicaise of Rheims,
the archdeacon of Tournai, and Michael de Raucourt, who appear
to have supplemented the activities of the bishop of Arras and
Hugh Quieret. The duke's order that no one should heed the
jurisdiction of the bishop of Liège was rescinded, and John was
ordered to give notice to his officials to that effect. Further provision was made for regulating the subjects of each in the other's
domain and documents were drawn up concerning rights and alleged titles, the bishop's claim to 's-Hertogenrade, prisoners, fines,
and other matters.[146]

[144] L. Devillers, *Monuments,* III, 298–303; F. van Mieris, *Groot Charterboek,* II, 591–542; A. Hulshof, " Oorkonden aangaande de Betrekkingen
der Geldersche Vorsten tot Frankrijk," *Werken uitgegeven door de
Vereeniging Gelre,* VIII (1912), 17–22.

[145] Outremeuse, VI, 512–518.

[146] *Ibid.,* pp. 508–511; A. Wauters, *Table Chronologique,* IX, 431, assigns this document to 1332 which is clearly impossible.

The long dispute between the counts of Flanders and Hainault regarding Flobecq and Lessines now also came to an end. In the episcopal palace at Cambrai on May 22, before a large number of witnesses, including the counts of Juliers, Guelders, and Lodi, John of Hainault, and others, Count William and Count Louis for themselves and their heirs vowed eternal friendship. The lands were given to William to be held as fiefs of Flanders, on the condition that they should never be fortified, for a cash payment of 30,000*l.* Parisian. Louis was to do homage for 1,000*l.* Tournois annually, secured by incomes from lands at Blaton and Fismy, and promised not to interfere in possible hostilities between Count William and the duke of Brabant.[147] Final disposition of all these matters was now hastened.[148]

The provisions concerning the marriage of Johanna of Brabant and William, heir apparent of Hainault, were carried out in June. In accordance with the agreement reached at Mechelen between the counts of Flanders and Guelders, Count William appointed as his deputies the seigniors of Ligny, Voorne, and Arkel, and Henry d'Antoing to carry out the assignment of lands for Johanna,[149] which were the same as those provided in the treaty of January 8, 1331 — 8,000*l.* Tournois from certain lands in North Holland, West Friesland, Kennemerland, and the manor of Mont-Aubert.[150] On June 21 at Tervuren Duke John promised to accept these terms,[151] and soon thereafter the household accounts of young William contain references to visits paid to his bride. Thus he was in Brussels, Tervuren, and Mechelen from July 17 to 21 and in August visited Nivelles, and Tervuren again on the 15th and the 16th.[152]

[147] L. Devillers, *Monuments,* III, 308–312.
[148] *Ibid.,* pp. 312–314, 324–326, 332, 333–335, 336–337, 337–339.
[149] *Ibid.,* pp. 298–299 (note).
[150] F. van Mieris, *Groot Charterboek,* II, 492–493.
[151] L. Devillers, *Monuments,* III, 300 (footnote); J. de Saint Genois, *Monumens Anciens,* II, ccxx, 219.
[152] H. J. Smit, *De Rekeningen der Graven en Gravinnen uit het Henegouwsche Huis,* I, 642, 666–667.

VI. The Proposed Diocese for Brabant and Limburg
(1332–1333)

After the conference at Compiègne and the fealty sworn to Philip VI, John, duke of Brabant, deemed the moment auspicious to secure what he most earnestly desired — the creation of an independent bishopric for all his territories with a cathedral at Louvain. Since this concerned the two dioceses of Cambrai and Liège, the matter required strong influence at the curia and he counted upon Philip's aid.[153] Accordingly, about September 1, 1332, Duke John sent a formal request to the pope. His envoys, John Mayor of Meerbeke and Henry Coke of Brussels, were well supplied with funds intended apparently for purposes of bribery.[154] But the pope, John XXII, was ever jealous of the rights and position of the church and could not readily acquiesce in this division, which could serve only political motives. On the 12th he informed the duke of their arrival, promised to consider the matter in due course,[155] stated that the bishops involved would have to be consulted, and promised a reply by about St. Martin's Day.[156] A digest of John's arguments was transmitted to the bishop of Cambrai on the 13th,[157] but nothing was heard from him or his chapter in regard to the matter. From Liège, however, where relations with Brabant were anything but amicable, a lively refutation was received.

The reasons advanced in the duke's request were as follows: (1) certain places in Brabant under the control of the bishop of Cambrai were three times as far removed from Cambrai as from Liège and should be included in a new bishopric which would be able to take better care of them; (2) as a result of the ecclesiastical division of Brabant there was no uniformity in the observance of fast days or the celebration of festivals; (3) the extent of the

[153] Outremeuse, VI, 506–507.

[154] Hocsemius, p. 410 (paged as 402); Outremeuse, VI, 507.

[155] A. Fayen, *Lettres de Jean XXII (1316–1334)*, No. 3281; E. Fairon, "Un Projet de Démembrement du Diocèse de Liège Proposé par les Brabançons en 1332–1336," *BCRH*, 78 (1909), 168.

[156] A. Fayen, *Lettres de Jean XXII (1316–1334)*, No. 3282.

[157] Hocsemius, p. 410 (paged as 402); E. Fairon, "Un Projet de Démembrement du Diocèse de Liège Proposé par les Brabançons de 1332–1336," *BCRH*, 78 (1909), 173–185.

territory of each diocese was too great to be cared for adequately
by the bishops; (4) the clergy of the parts involved as well as
the parishioners were eager for such a new diocese; (5) neither
bishop had any temporal power within the duchy of Brabant; (6)
the exercise of spiritual jurisdiction by the bishops of Cambrai
and Liège had repeatedly caused the peace to be violated; and
(7) the erection of a new diocese could not hurt the position of
either see and would in general be advantageous for all the people concerned.

The duke's statements were answered for the chapter of St.
Lambert by the pen of the erudite and well-informed man of affairs, the chronicler Hocsem.[158] Point for point it was a crushing
rebuttal: (1) if the duke's first statement were true, it would be
wiser to add those places so far distant from Cambrai to the
diocese of Liège. Some localities in the diocese of Liège were even
nearer Cambrai than Liège, as Chimay and Fontaine-l'Évêque,
both of which, however, were not in Brabant. But, as a matter of
fact, all places in the duchy of Brabant and in the diocese Liège, as,
for example, Nivelles, were nearer Liège than Cambrai; (2) as for
the lack of unity in the observation of fasts and feasts, this was the
condition throughout Christendom and was in no way the result of
existing diocesan divisions nor could it be remedied by creating a
new diocese; (3) to erect an episcopal see at Brussels or Louvain or
Limburg would create a diocese more extensive than that of
either Cambrai or Liège, which the duke pretended were too large
to be cared for efficaciously; (4) the duke did not tell the truth
when he stated that the clergy wanted a new bishopric, and the
writer added the incident of 's-Hertogenbosch as proof; (5) the
bishop of Liège did have temporal power within the duke's borders. In some villages such as Hougaerde, Tourines, and Bauvechain, he had the *merum et mixtum imperium*. More than twenty
villages of Brabant had borrowed their constitutions from the city
of Liège and had appealed doubtful cases to its scabini, and all
the inhabitants of the duchies of Brabant and of Limburg in his
diocese were subject to the bishop's jurisdiction in the three cases
of *vis, raptus,* and *spolium;* (6) the duke himself was the in-
stigator whenever the peace had been disturbed, as, for example,

---

[158] E. Fairon, *ibid.*, pp. 163–167, seems to have proved that it is from
the pen of the Liège *scholasticus*.

in the matter of St. Trond which started the late war; (7) a new diocese would injure the power of both bishoprics. Rather, their power should be extended so that they could better enforce the peace in face of the disturber, and thus promote the welfare of the people of both dioceses. The erection of such a new diocese was furthermore an absurdity. It would be cut into two parts by a strip of land extending northward along the Meuse as far as Maastricht over which the bishop of Liège had at the moment both temporal and spiritual power.

Duke John's maneuver could hardly be successful. Pope John XXII was not influenced by the wishes of secular princes to a very great extent, and Philip cared little to press the case which would compromise him with the bishop of Liège and the chapter of St. Lambert and even sent representatives to the curia to advise against the change.[159] And, furthermore, the duke's violence in the case of the friars and canons of St. Servaas at Maastricht and on other occasions had greatly diminished the force of his arguments. Hence on December 19 the pope declared the proposal impossible to entertain.[160]

---

[159] See Hocsemius, p. 410 (paged as 402): "Contra quos (ambassiatores) mittit episcopus et ecclesia cum literis regis, qui multum propter sua grata servitia fauebat episcopo. . . ."

[160] A. Fayen, *Lettres de Jean XXII (1316–1334)*, No. 3368. On June 2, 1333, the pope favored the two deputies. See *ibid.*, Nos. 3430, 3432.

CHAPTER V

THE INTERVENTION OF PHILIP VI IN THE LOW COUNTRIES: THE TREATY OF AMIENS (1333–1334)

i. The Contest for Mechelen and the Schelde (1333) ii. The Anglo-Scotch Crisis (1332–1334) iii. The Second Attack upon the Duke of Brabant (Winter, 1334) iv. The Papal Intervention (February-March, 1334) v. The Treaty of Amiens (August, 1334)

I. THE CONTEST FOR MECHELEN AND THE SCHELDE (1333)

LOUIS, count of Flanders, had shown a benevolent friendship [1] toward the duke of Brabant during the crisis after Easter in 1332.[2] Accordingly, the negotiations between them regarding the jurisdiction over the course (*stroom*) of the Schelde came to an amicable conclusion early in 1333. On St. Valentine's Day, Duke John and Louis were at Alost in the latter's castle in order to perform the final ceremonies. In the presence of important nobles, ecclesiastics, and men-at-law, chosen to bear witness for each party, they performed reciprocal homage, swore fealty, and promised to support each other against all parties except the kings of France and Germany. For this, the duke agreed to give each year a stag and a wild boar, and the count a falcon. Thereupon the terms of the alliance were read, and both swore with their hands touching the canon and gospels to preserve inviolate all points of the treaty. Each was to protect the honor and subjects of the other, and lend military aid in person with as many as a thousand men-at-arms within three weeks after request should be made. Neither was to conclude a separate truce or peace or contract any obligations prejudicial to these provisions. In case of imprisonment the other would be bound to secure his liberation, and two men were to be appointed by each to arbitrate all serious differences that might come up between them.[3] Within three weeks a notary named by Count

[1] Hocsemius, p. 414 (paged as 406).
[2] Boendale, *Brabantsche Yeesten,* I, 498.
[3] *Archives du Département du Nord,* Lille, Nos. B264 (6.573) and B264 (1.574). These documents are not dated and bear no seals, but seem to refer to these agreements.

Louis was to receive from the duke a document containing the terms of the agreement touching the Schelde. The two princes now kissed the canon and the witnesses all solemnly swore to maintain intact this agreement.[4] This reconciliation was apparent rather than real, for Duke John did not intend to abate a jot of his claims to the seigniory of the Schelde. Three weeks passed, no document was produced, and the reiterated requests of Count Louis availed naught. And the duke was even guilty of fresh aggressions.[5]

These difficulties synchronized with another quarrel between Duke John and the men of Ghent. Some of the burghers were held in confinement by the duke, and on February 1 two of the scabini were sent to secure their freedom.[6] The prisoners were John van Halen and his son Simon, members of the wealthy Lombard family of Mirabello already long established in Ghent. Their properties in Duke John's dominions had been sequestrated,[7] and the matter of their treatment had been brought up when the duke and Count Louis were at Alost,[8] but the latter apparently did not want to jeopardize the political settlement by demanding satisfaction. From February 17 to 20 two scabini, William van Vaernewijc and Wasselin van Lens, interviewed Count Louis at Bruges, and the matter was further discussed in the meeting of the deputies from the three towns of Flanders at Bruges between March 1 and 4, and again at Courtrai between the 5th and the 7th. On the 19th the scabini of Ghent sent William van Vaernewijc to the duke of Brabant to intercede for the prisoners.[9] On the 23d Count Louis even appointed Simon van Halen his representative with general powers to treat with the duke,[10] and an accord was finally arrived at, but during the negotiations John van Halen died.[11]

---

[4] Kervyn, *Oeuvres de Froissart,* XX, 411–412.

[5] *Archives du Département du Nord,* Lille, *Cartulaire de Liège et de Malines,* B1571, pièce 76.

[6] J. Vuylsteke, *Gentsche Stads- en Baljuwsrekeningen, 1280–1336,* II, 836.

[7] Kervyn, *Oeuvres de Froissart,* XXI, 486–487.

[8] J. Vuylsteke, *Gentsche Stads- en Baljuwsrekeningen, 1280–1336,* II, 836.

[9] *Ibid.,* pp. 836, 837, 844.

[10] J. de St. Genois, *Inventaire Analytique des Chartes des Comtes de Flandre,* p. 469.

[11] *Archives du Département du Nord,* Lille, *Cartulaire de Liège et de Malines,* B1571, pièce 76; Kervyn, *Oeuvres de Froissart,* XXI, 485.

No indication of hostility in Louis' conduct toward Duke John can be noticed, at least not for a few months. During the negotiations conducted at Mechelen on April 16 he appeared in behalf of the duke to treat with Reginald, count of Guelders, who was spokesman for the allies against the duke of Brabant. Count Louis even agreed to advance at once to William, count of Hainault, Holland, and Zeeland, the 35,000*l*. Tournois which Duke John was required to pay two years later.[12] Among the clauses in the treaty of alliance arranged at Cambrai on May 22 there was one in which Louis expressly excluded the duke.[13] But the count's patience was nearly exhausted. It was at this moment that the bishop of Liège became exceedingly dissatisfied with the decrees of the French commissioners and took no pains to hide his feelings. The idea of selling the episcopal rights in Mechelen was now suggested, and Count Louis, influenced by the advice of his councillor, William d'Auxonne, at once showed himself eager to acquire them.[14] On May 22 Louis authorized John de Cadzand to negotiate the sale, and a convention was drawn up on June 12 by him and the bishop of Liège whereby the transfer was arranged subject to the approval of the chapter of St. Lambert. Count Louis agreed to pay 100,000 French *regales* on the condition that he and his heirs should hold the seigniory as a fief of the chapter and never alienate it. He was to do homage for these rights and also for Grammont and Bornhem, which the chapter had not been able to free from the duke's encroachments, and over which rights of lordship had not been exercised for a long time.[15]

This precipitate action betrayed an inimical desire to hurt the duke of Brabant at a most vital point. The proposal was of course speedily made known to him, and his relations with Count Louis, already unpleasant, were at once stretched to the breaking point. Duke John now refused to pay the count the 35,000*l*. Tournois as prescribed in the treaty of May 22.[16] He regarded

---

[12] L. Devillers, *Monuments,* III, 298–303.   [13] *Ibid.,* pp. 308–311.
[14] Hocsemius, p. 410 (paged as 402), 412; *Chronicon Comitum Flandrensium,* p. 210.
[15] *Archives du Département du Nord,* Lille, *Cartulaire de Liège et de Malines,* G6605, G6606. See Hocsemius, pp. 410, 412.
[16] *Archives du Département du Nord,* Lille, *Cartulaire de Liège et de Malines,* B1571, pièce 76.

the transfer of Mechelen as a serious challenge to his entire political policy. Since it was wholly surrounded by his own territories, it seemed that this town and its dependent parts must needs ultimately belong to him. Situated on both banks of the Dyle and near the Ruppel, it commanded access for many towns in Brabant to the greater centers of commerce. The counts of Flanders might seek to throttle the progress of Antwerp, sever its connection with its economic hinterland, and even divert some of its ever-growing volume of trade to their own towns. The duke had long staged a bitter contest with Reginald, seignior of Valkenburg, and some of his neighbors in behalf of his own bourgeoisie for whom an unrestricted contact with the Rhine was indispensable. With equal zeal he watched over his rights on the course (*stroom*) of the Schelde.

This policy becomes impressive when viewed in the light of the duke's wider economic connections, especially with England. The staple of English wool and woolfells at Bruges had been abolished on May 1, 1326, by the Ordinance of Kenilworth. Henceforth at a number of designated towns in England, Wales, and Ireland denizens were to bring their wares and expose them for sale for a fortnight, and aliens were to purchase as much as they might want. The remaining articles might then be disposed of anywhere else.[17] In the Parliament of Northampton, Edward III continued his father's legislation, but certain individuals arbitrarily sought to constrain all English merchants in the Low Countries to bring their wool and woolfells to Bruges where they extorted much unlawful gain. Eager to have the wool come directly into his own lands and to be freed from the Bruges staple, Duke John complained to Edward. On January 27, 1332, commissions of oyer and terminer were issued to conduct an inquest;[18] but only after repeated efforts could the abuse be brought to an end.[19] Relations with England in this respect were quite friendly.[20] In recognition of services rendered to Isabella when she passed through Brabant, the town of Diest was granted special privileges on December 12, 1329,[21] and in March, 1332, at the

[17] *CPR* (1324–7), p. 269; *CPR* (1327–30), pp. 98–99.
[18] *CPR* (1330–4), p. 283.
[19] *CCR* (1330–3), pp. 466–467, 498, 519.
[20] *Foedera,* II (2), 772.   [21] *Ibid.,* p. 776.

duke's special request, the merchants of Louvain were taken into the king's protection.[22] In 1333 he invited, under guarantee of the fullest security, English merchants to trade in Antwerp and urged John de Preston, the mayor of London, to exert his influence with them in his behalf. Soon thereafter, on October 1, the magistrates of Antwerp also urged John de Preston and others to avail themselves of the advantages of this port.[23]

At this time the duke also sought settlement of the debts which his father John II had contracted with English merchants. Perhaps he hoped to create a better understanding with English merchants, especially now that the fixed staple in Flanders no longer existed. At any rate, negotiations were opened by the duke in the autumn of 1331, and it was decreed in the Westminster Parliament of Michaelmas that the creditors should present themselves before the king and council on May 29, 1332, when deputies from the duke would be present to listen to their envoys.[24] But since the war with his neighbors in the following spring engaged all his attention, it was not possible to attend to this matter and the meeting was repeatedly postponed to Michaelmas, to a fortnight after Easter, 1333, to a fortnight after Michaelmas, and, finally, again to Easter, 1334.[25] This persistent appreciation of the needs of his towns and the tenacious policy of furthering their interests wherever he could, made it impossible for Duke John to witness the transfer of Mechelen with indifference.

After prolonged discussion the sale of the seigniory of Mechelen was approved on July 28.[26] During August the formal preliminaries of the transfer were effected. On the 10th Count Louis promised for himself and his heirs to perform homage for Mechelen, Grammont, and Bornhem,[27] and empowered John d'Espierre, a clerk of Tournai, to receive the oaths of ratification from the

---

[22] *Ibid.*, p. 812.

[23] *Calendar of Letter Books, City of London, Letter Book E,* pp. 286–287.

[24] *Rotuli Parliamentorum,* II, 63, No. 20.

[25] *Foedera,* II (2), 827, 833, 839, 857, 871.

[26] S. Bormans et E. Schoolmeesters, *Cartulaire de l'Église Saint Lambert de Liège,* III, 417–420. The correct date is July. See *Archives du Département du Nord,* Lille, No. B264 (6.636).

[27] *Archives du Département du Nord,* Lille, *Cartulaire de Liège et de Malines,* G6647.

representatives of the bishop and chapter of Liège. On the 21st a *vidimus*, attested by a notary, was drawn up declaring that this had been duly performed and also that it had been agreed that Count Louis should pay as soon as possible 50,000*l*. Tournois to the bishop's deputies and the remaining 50,000*l*. under specific guarantees. The representatives again met on the 23d to swear on the Gospels that they would carry out all promises and that all the documents touching the titles of Mechelen would thereupon be surrendered to the count.[28] On the 25th Hocsem handed these over to the count's men.[29] Louis at once began payment. On September 7 the bishop and chapter gave him a receipt for the first instalment of 18,000*l*.,[30] and on the 30th another, declaring that in all 80,000*l*. had been paid.[31] The remainder was guaranteed by the deposit of jewels and precious stones with Bishop Adolph.[32]

On October 2 the bishop informed the nobles, vassals, and the bourgeoisie of Mechelen of the sale, and ordered them to obey the count of Flanders as their new lord.[33] On the 16th Louis performed homage for his new fiefs in the Benedictine monastery of St. Adrian at Grammont,[34] and the bishop again ordered his subjects to accept him.[35] At the same time the count ordered Gilles de Vremde and Thierry de Belsele, his bailiffs of the county of Alost and of Bruges, to take over in his name the newly acquired possessions and their government.[36] This order was at once executed, for a number of the scabini of Ghent, who had gone to

---

[28] J. de St. Genois, *Inventaire Analytique des Chartes des Comtes de Flandre*, p. 470. The charter printed by J. David, *Geschiedenis van de Stad en de Heerlykheid van Mechelen, Bylagen*, pp. 492–504, and dated May 28 by him appears to have been drawn up at this time.

[29] *Archives du Département du Nord*, Lille, *Cartulaire de Liège et de Malines*, G6652.

[30] S. Bormans et E. Schoolmeesters, *Cartulaire de l'Église de Saint Lambert de Liège*, III, 425–426.

[31] *Archives du Département du Nord*, Lille, No. B264 (6.663).

[32] *Ibid.*, No. B264 (6.675).

[33] *Ibid.*, No. B264 (6.667). See M. G. de Louvrex, *Recueil contenant les Édits et Règlements Faits pour le Pays de Liège et Comté de Looz*, I, 164.

[34] *Archives du Département du Nord*, Lille, No. B264 (6.684). Cf. Outremeuse, VI, 521.

[35] *Archives du Département du Nord*, Lille, No. B264 (6.680), and *Cinquième Cartulaire de Flandre*, No. 153.

[36] *Archives du Département du Nord*, Lille, No. B264 (6.681).

Grammont to be present with the delegates of the other towns of Flanders, went to Mechelen after the ceremony, and returned on the 22d.[37]

The burghers of Mechelen, quite as much as Duke John himself, regarded the transaction with thorough disfavor. They might now be employed as a political weapon by Count Louis in his struggles with the duke of Brabant. While they undoubtedly desired above all things to preserve their independence, their geographical position clearly compelled them to live at peace with the powerful neighbor whose lands surrounded them on all sides. There was a powerful party in Mechelen favorable to the duke, and this element, which apparently had the support of nearly all the burghers, now vigorously opposed the alienation of the seigniory.[38] They preferred the distant and not very effectual control of the bishop and chapter to the near-by supervision of the count. They soon came to an understanding with Duke John [39] who promised to protect their rights and privileges and especially their connection with the church of St. Lambert.[40] This dated back to 1307 when Gilles Berthout and Theobald de Bar, bishop of Liège, had agreed that the episcopal rights in Mechelen should never be alienated.[41]

The men of Mechelen at once resisted the deputies of the count, who on the 21st ordered the arrest and confiscation of all their property that could be found in his jurisdiction. On November 3 he appointed John van Heile, bailiff of the waters of Muiden and of Sluis, and two others to take charge of the fleet which was being sent up the Dyle to operate against them.[42] Louis defied the duke and rigorously enforced the blockade on the *stroom* of the Dyle and on the Schelde and would not allow any food or any ar-

---

[37] J. Vuylsteke, *Gentsche Stads- en Baljuwsrekeningen, 1280–1336,* II, 895.   [38] Boendale, *Brabantsche Yeesten,* I, 509, 511–512.

[39] Hocsemius, p. 414 (paged as 406): "Dux vero, cui displicebat iste contractus . . . post multa verborum subterfugia secum Mechliniensibus foederavit, quod comes sentiens diffidavit eundem." Cf. also Levold de Northof, p. 402.

[40] Boendale, *Brabantsche Yeesten,* I, 509.

[41] A. Fayen, *Lettres de Jean XXII (1316–1334),* No. 3501; J. David, *Geschiedenis van de Stad en de Heerlykheid van Mechelen, Bylagen,* pp. 482–487.

[42] *Archives du Département du Nord,* Lille, *Cinquième Cartulaire de Flandre,* Nos. 381 *ter,* 636, 637.

ticles of commerce to leave Brabant.[43] Virulent discussions followed; John claimed that the bishop had no right to alienate property of which he could enjoy only the usufruct. But Louis proposed to keep these properties [44] and at once prepared for war.[45]

The duke's passions became still more inflamed when Count Louis secured the rights of the Berthout family who had long been *advocati* in Mechelen. These titles had been made over to Sophia, only child of Floris Berthout, on January 24, 1310.[46] Subsequently she became the wife of Reginald, son of the count of Guelders, but she died on May 3, 1329.[47] Two years later Floris himself died,[48] and the rights of the family thus passed to Sophia's daughter, Marguerite. Count Reginald was at this moment exercising the right of guardianship over his daughter's possessions. During November it became certain that the enemies of the duke would renew the war, and toward the close of the month they met in Hainault with Count Louis and Count William to arrange plans. Then was suggested the sale of the *advocatia* to Count Louis who would thus secure a full control of Mechelen.

At Le Quesnoy on December 1 the terms of the new transaction were drawn up by Count Louis, Count Reginald, and William, count of Juliers, who was interested because his son Gerard was engaged to marry Marguerite. The price was 60,000*l.* Tournois of which 10,000 were to be paid at Bruges or Ghent on February 2, 10,000 on June 24, 20,000 at Christmas, and the remainder on June 24, 1335. As guarantors were named Adolph, bishop of Liège, William, count of Hainault, Holland, and Zeeland, John of Hainault, and Gerard of Voorne, burgrave of Zeeland. Thus passed the *advocatia* of Mechelen with its dependent parts, Hevere, Muyssen, Hombeest, Hefne, Leest, Nieuwland, and Neckerspoel into Count Louis' hands.[49] On December 6 at Valen-

---

[43] *Archives due Departement du Nord*, Lille, *Cinquième Cartulaire de Flandre*, No. 2; Hocsemius, p. 414 (paged as 406).

[44] Boendale, *Brabantsche Yeesten*, I, 508–509, 512. Cf. *Grandes Chroniques*, V, 355.   [45] Hocsemius, p. 414 (paged as 406).

[46] F. vanden Branden de Reeth, " La Famille des Berthouts," *Mémoires Couronnés et Mémoires des Savants Étrangers*, XVII (1845), 172.

[47] Willelmus Procurator, p. 237.

[48] J. David, *Geschiedenis van de Stad en de Heerlykheid van Mechelen*, *Bylagen*, p. 439.

[49] *Archives du Département du Nord*, Lille, No. B265 (6.705). For payments, see *ibid.*, Nos. B264 (6.788), B264 (6.759).

ciennes these four men affixed their seals to the document.[50] On the 2d Count Reginald ordered the men of Mechelen to obey Count Louis,[51] and at Oschen on the 15th a series of documents was drawn up whereby Marguerite ratified the sale in the presence of notaries,[52] authorized Count Louis to take possession and ordered her subjects to accept him as their lord.[53] Five days later all the parties to the sale appeared before the bishop of Liège and solemnly confirmed the transfer.[54] It is needless to add that the duke of Brabant, who had been overlord of the *advocatia* since 1310, would not tolerate this action.

II. The Anglo-Scotch Crisis (1332–1334)

HOSTILITIES between England and Scotland, quiescent since the Treaty of Northampton, the "Shameful Peace" of May 4, 1328, again broke out in 1332. In spite of the marriage of his sister, Joan, to David, son of Robert Bruce, Edward had received Edward Balliol in England and even allowed him to prepare a party of the "Disinherited" and to sail from the Humber in July. The battle of Dupplin Moor on August 12 won for the latter a temporary control over Scotland, and Edward recognized Balliol as king and vassal by the Treaty of Roxburgh on November 23.[55]

This produced a dangerous crisis in the political relations of Western Europe. The enmity between the Plantagenet and Valois houses, inflamed over the difficulties in Gascony, might now at any moment range England against a united Scotland and France, and raise the question of the political affiliations of the various Low Country princes. It might affect the quarrel be-

[50] *Ibid.,* No. B264 (6.711).
[51] *Ibid.,* No. B264 (6.707).
[52] *Ibid.,* Nos. B264 (6.718); B264 (6.722).
[53] *Ibid.,* Nos. B264 (6.715); B264 (6.716).
[54] *Ibid.,* Nos. B264 (6.720); B264 (6.721). On April 10, 1334, Marguerite promised at the demand of Josse de Wastine, clerk and notary for Count Louis, that she would not in the least oppose his securing possession of her rights, and that she would repeat, should it be desired, this renunciation when she should become of age. See J. de St. Genois, *Inventaire Analytique des Chartes des Comtes de Flandre,* pp. 473–474, 523–524.
[55] E. Mackinnon. *The History of Edward the Third (1327–1377),* pp. 48–57.

tween the emperor and Pope John XXII and set at naught the efforts of the latter to smother the differences of rival princes in a united effort to recover the Holy Land.[56]

Balliol was supported in Perth by a fleet of English ships on the Tay and was besieged by a force of Scots under the earl of Dunbar and Sir Archibald Douglas. John Crabbe, a noted Flemish pirate, came into the Firth with ten Flemish ships [57] and sought to burn the English craft in an effort to get to the town. In the struggle the Flemings were totally routed and Crabbe escaped only with great difficulty.[58]

King Edward was thus committed to the support of Balliol, and planned the conquest of Berwick in the spring of 1333. He especially desired to secure the neutrality of Flanders. On April 27 he wrote to Count Louis and the magistrates of Bruges, Ghent, and Ypres from Newcastle, requesting their coöperation in stopping the aid which Flemish subjects were furnishing the Scots by sea.[59] The count's messengers who, it appears, were dispatched at once upon the receipt of these letters [60] merely complained of the outrages of which Edward's subjects were claimed to be guilty. The king replied from Tweedmouth on June 5 and announced the sending of envoys empowered to discuss the grievances as well as the aid rendered to his enemies. He begged Louis to overlook in the meantime any violent actions of which his subjects might be guilty and promised that they would be promptly rectified.[61]

On June 7 the envoys, John de Hildesle, canon of Chichester and baron of the Exchequer, William de la Pole, a merchant of Hull, and Robert de Kellesley were sent with instructions to discuss the aid given to the Scots by land and sea, the attack of

[56] E. Déprez, *Les Préliminaires de la Guerre de Cent Ans,* pp. 99.

[57] *Exchequer Rolls, Scotland,* I, cxlii. According to the *Grandes Chroniques,* I, 354, ten ships laden with victuals and filled with men-at-arms were at Philip's investigation sent to carry aid to the Scots. They were, however, forced to seek refuge from a storm in Sluis.

[58] *Auctor Bridlingtoniensis,* pp. 107–108; *Melsa,* II, 365; *Scalacronica,* p. 161; Knighton, I, 464–465. For the career of John Crabbe, see *Calendar of Documents relating to Scotland Preserved in Her Majesty's Public Record Office, London,* III, 79, 126, 190, 196, 204, 229, 237, 239, 274–275.

[59] *Foedera,* II (2), 860; *Rotuli Scotiae,* I, 233–234.

[60] J. Vuylsteke, *Gentsche Stads- en Baljuwsrekeningen, 1280–1336,* II, 845.

[61] *Foedera,* II (2), 862; *CCR* (1333–7), pp. 52, 118.

Flemish sailors upon some English ships off the coast of Flanders when their goods were taken and crews killed, and the damage inflicted by English sailors ' upon Flemings.[62] But negotiations could not proceed apace. Suspicions were rife and, to aid the Scots with supplies, Philip VI got ready a fleet of ten ships at Sluis, which were, however, unable to leave the harbor because of adverse winds.[63]

Quarrels between the Flemings and the English soon became more acute. Fearing for their safety, many of the count's subjects who had formerly traded in Scotland now ceased to frequent their customary places in England. Edward was especially eager to retain the friendship of the Flemings and on August 16 ordered all his sheriffs to proclaim wherever desirable that all merchants of any country should be free to carry on their affairs in the customary manner and that nothing would be taken from them against their will.[64] Nevertheless, some did suffer. The king's officials at Hartlepool seized the goods of some merchants of Bruges because they suspected that their wool and hides were intended for the Scots,[65] and at Lincoln Hugh Chamberlayn, a merchant of Flanders, was held because of some " malevolence and hatred entertained toward the king." [66]

After some discussions [67] the English envoys were successful. It was agreed that all goods and persons arrested in either Flanders or England were to be liberated at once and that all merchants were to have full freedom to trade. On September 8 at Letham Edward notified his sheriffs that by All Saints' Day two representatives of the king and two of the count and delegates of the towns of Bruges, Ghent, and Ypres would appear at York to hear all complaints of violence which had been committed since the day he had performed homage at Amiens in 1329.[68] They were ordered to make the necessary notarial depositions, and at

---

[62] *Foedera,* II (2), 862.

[63] *Grandes Chroniques,* V, 354; Lescot, p. 33.

[64] *Foedera,* II (2), 868.

[65] *CCR* (1333–7), p. 77; *Calendar of Documents relating to Scotland Preserved in Her Majesty's Public Record Office, London,* III, 197–198.

[66] *CCR* (1333–7), pp. 138–139, 156.

[67] J. Vuylsteke, *Gentsche Stads- en Baljuwsrekeningen, 1280–1336,* II, 840. The scabini, William Yoons, H. de Grutere, and P. vander Mersch, represented Ghent from July 24 to 27 in the negotiations at Bruges.

[68] *Foedera,* II (2), 869.

once proceed to Bruges to do the same in Flanders in order that final satisfaction might be rendered by the Feast of the Purification on February 2.[69] All parties with grievances were to be present on November 2.[70]

Representatives of the Flemish towns met with Count Louis at Courtrai from October 5 to 6 to confer in regard to the treaty.[71] But the Flemish envoys apparently failed to appear at the expected time, for it was not until November 8 that Edward appointed Thomas de Brayton and Simon de Stanes his representatives to receive the complaints of his subjects.[72] Soon thereafter they met Paulinus de la Mote, canon of St. Donatian of Bruges, and John van Harlebeke, a burgher of Bruges, and many indentures were apparently drawn up. Question was raised regarding losses sustained before the time of the king's homage at Amiens, but, as the instructions did not cover these points, these matters had to be deferred. On January 7, 1334, Edward empowered Robert de Scarburgh, baron of the Exchequer, to take the place of Thomas de Boynton and with Simon de Stanes to receive depositions of all harm inflicted before the homage rendered at Amiens.[73] These negotiations made some progress and arrangements were effected for hearing the claims before Mid-Lent.

On February 5 the king appointed Simon de Stanes, Robert de Kellesley, citizen of London, and William Fox [74] proctors and ordered them to be at Bruges by February 10.[75] Success apparently attended these efforts, although nothing is said in the document regarding the compensations promised for the outrages which had been the occasion for the indentures. It was agreed that merchants of Flanders and England should be free to trade in each country until August 5 and under the safe-conduct of the king or the count. As the latter was now at war with the duke of Brabant and sought to inflict as much damage as possible

---

[69] *CCR* (1333–7), pp. 77, 147, 172–173, 213.

[70] Foedera, II (2), 871.

[71] J. Vuylsteke, *Gentsche Stads- en Baljuwsrekeningen, 1280–1336,* II, 894–895.

[72] *Foedera,* II (2), 872.

[73] *Ibid.,* p. 875; *CPR* (1330–4), p. 479; *CCR* (1333–7), p. 189.

[74] E. Déprez et L. Mirot, " Les Ambassades Anglaises pendant la Guerre de Cent Ans," *BEC,* LIX (1898), 561.

[75] *Foedera,* II (2), 875. Stanes left on February 8, see *ibid.,* pp. 606–607; *CCR* (1333–7), p. 220.

upon the trade of his subjects, even the English merchants sojourning at the moment in the duke's jurisdiction were not to be protected. Edward was anxious to arrive at an understanding in view of the crisis in his relations with the king of France, and therefore sacrificed the interests of a few of his subjects and on April 5 made proclamation of this treaty to all his sheriffs.[76]

III. The Second Attack upon the Duke of Brabant (Winter, 1334)

The crisis precipitated by the sale of Mechelen made further efforts of the French envoys quite useless. The bishop of Thérouanne and his associates realized the gravity of the matter and on June 13, apparently in response to the duke's protests, decreed that the sale of Mechelen did not harm the rights of the bishop of Liège in the least and that it should be considered valid.[77] The pronouncements of the bishop of Arras and Hugh Quieret on July 2 at Cambrai which commanded the liberation of some prisoners taken at Perwez and elsewhere, who had been kept in confinement because of hatred toward the duke, could now be of no avail.[78] The situation seemed to be getting beyond Philip's control. Although on April 11 at Buxy-St. Lieffart he had solemnly declared the alliance of the bishop of Liège, the king of Bohemia, and the counts of Guelders and Juliers null and void. he thought it necessary to remind these parties on October 8 that they should not attack the duke.[79]

The efforts to create better relations between John, the count of Namur, and the duke of Brabant had indeed made some progress, but apparently without Philip's efforts. On November 18 each party agreed to name two members of the other's council to settle all future difficulties. The count of Namur agreed to hold in fee of the duke the castle at Hollogne-sur-Geer, the allodial possessions at Boneffe, the 200*l.* income from land which his father had received from the duke, and to yield to John title

---

[76] *Foedera,* II (2), 884–885.
[77] Outremeuse, VI, 509.
[78] *Archives Nationales,* Paris, J524ª, no. 30¹⁰.
[79] I. A. Nijhoff, *Gedenkwaardigheden uit de Geschiedenis van Gelderland,* I, 314–317.

to the castle at Sanson on condition that he could place his men therein in time of war. He also performed homage for the titles at Ramillies and other places, and for the marshes and waste lands (*werichaux*) near the castle of Gauthier de Juppleu, at Neuville-sur-Mehaigne. On the 20th the duke confirmed this agreement at Brussels when also were chosen as arbiters of future differences, by the count from the duke's council, John van Heelbeke and John de Raucourt, and by the duke from the count's council Warnier, seignior of Done, and Gauthier de Juppleu.[80] But when relations between Duke John and the confederates became strained to the breaking point before the end of the same month, the count of Namur was suspected of having hostile designs, for on the 27th Otto, seignior of Cuyk, Arnold, seignior of Stein, John de Raucourt, John van Heelbeke, and Herman van Oss received a formal assurance from the count that he would remain faithful to the alliance newly made with the duke.[81] Yet when the struggle broke out, Count John was to be found in the ranks of the duke's enemies. Small wonder that as Christmas drew near observers felt that Philip's policy had practically failed.[82]

William, count of Hainault, Holland, and Zeeland, had in the meantime persevered in a policy which would ultimately enhance his prestige among all his neighbors. He had not taken any extreme action against Duke John. When Philip's daughter Marie suddenly died on September 22,[83] the question of Isabella's marriage with the heir apparent of Brabant could again be considered. And toward Philip he had not yet, it would appear, openly shown any resentment. Thus when Philip took the cross at Paris on the Pré-aux-Clercs on October 2, he was present with the dukes of Brabant, Burgundy, and Bourbon, Philip, king of Navarre, and many other lay as well as spiritual figures.[84] But the duke of Brabant was bitter toward the bishop and

---

[80] C. Piot, *Inventaire des Chartes des Comtes de Namur*, pp. 163–164. See J. de St. Genois, *Monumens Anciens*, II, DCCCCLXXV, DCCCCLXXXXIX.

[81] C. Piot, *Inventaire des Chartes des Comtes de Namur*, p. 164.

[82] Hocsemius, p. 410 (paged as 402).

[83] *Ibid.*, p. 412; C. Butkens, *Trophées tant Sacrés que Profanes du Duché de Brabant*, I, 444–445; *Chronique Parisienne Anonyme*, p. 154.

[84] *Grandes Chroniques*, V, 350–351; de Nangis, II, 134; Lescot, p. 30; *Chronique Parisienne Anonyme*, p. 154.

chapter of Liège, balked as he was in his hopes for a separate diocese and disillusioned in the prospect of help from France,[85] and now even refused to carry out the clauses of the treaty sealed at Mechelen on April 16. So when October 1 came, he did not permit his daughter Johanna to go to her husband, William, son of William, count of Hainault, Holland, and Zeeland,[86] nor would he pay, as he had agreed, the 35,000l. Tournois which had been awarded to the count of Flanders. But he did allow William to see her in Brabant, for the accounts of the youth's household state that on October 31 William arrived at Geertruidenberg from The Hague and spent eight days thereafter with the duke at Breda and Brussels whence he departed with Thierry de Walcourt and Simon de Besuten with about thirty-three horses toward Braine into Hainault.[87] The violation of his plighted word at once brought into action against the duke the league formed at Perwez, to which the elder William had secretly adhered on February 10, 1333.[88]

On November 30 the confederates came together at Le Quesnoy, as was mentioned above, where Count William, still ailing with his old disease, now took a leading part in the attack upon the duke. A document was drawn up in which they all agreed to substantially the same points as were contained in the treaty of June 11 at Perwez, save that such castles or towns as might be taken from the duke should be held not by a committee for the allies as a whole but by the captor. Apparently each was planning to seize what he claimed to be his. The count of Flanders as well as Count William was now also reckoned among the confederates.[89] He promised to reimburse the counts of Guelders and Juliers for all losses that might come from supporting him in the struggle for Mechelen.[90] And on December 4 these parties and also the bishop of Liège, the archbishop of

---

[85] Hocsemius, p. 412.

[86] L. Devillers, *Monuments,* III, 299–300.

[87] J. Finot, *Inventaire Sommaire des Archives Départementales Antérieures à 1790,* VII, 155–156.

[88] *Grandes Chroniques,* V, 355; Lescot, p. 34; *Chronique Parisienne Anonyme,* p. 155; *Chronicon Tielense,* p. 326.

[89] I. A. Nijhoff, *Gedenkwaardigheden uit de Geschiedenis van Gelderland,* I, 322–328; Kervyn, *Oeuvres de Froissart,* XX, 345–355.

[90] F. van Mieris, *Groot Charterboek,* II, 555.

Cologne, and the king of Bohemia asked the pope to sanction the transfer.[91]

Count Louis' complaints against the duke were especially bitter. Besides the numerous confiscated properties of John van Halen scattered throughout the duke's dominions and the very harsh treatment accorded to him and his son Simon,[92] Duke John had refused to grant the letters which he had promised at Alost in regard to the Schelde and to repay the 35,000*l.* Tournois. He supported the burghers of Mechelen and refused justice to his vassal Gerard, seignior of Liedekerke, in regard to the barony of Breda of which he had long been deprived.[93] Count Louis agreed to attack Brabant from the west and keep the Brabanters occupied, while the others would thus have time to assail the duke's possessions along the Meuse.[94] The allies desired all possible help against their redoubtable enemy and requested the influential William van Duivenvoorde, seignior of Oosterhout, a vassal of the duke, to support them under a guarantee of full indemnity for all harm that might come from his desertion.[95] Finally, before Epiphany in 1334, when the confederates again met, they sent a declaration of hostilities to the duke from Valenciennes [96] and on the 5th drew up another document embodying substantially the same arrangements as that of November 5.[97]

A blockade was at once instituted, Brabant was now assailed from every quarter, and not " as much as an egg could find its way into the duke's lands." [98] Count Louis zealously proceeded against the persons and property of the duke's subjects and friends. Safe-conduct was specifically withheld from them

---

[91] *Archives du Département du Nord*, Lille, No. B264 (6.709).

[92] Kervyn, *Oeuvres de Froissart*, XXI, 485–487.

[93] *Archives du Département du Nord*, Lille, *Cartulaire de Liège et de Malines*, B1571, pièce 76.

[94] Boendale, *Brabantsche Yeesten*, I, 511; Hocsemius, p. 415 (paged as 406).

[95] *Archives du Département du Nord*, Lille, *Cinquième Cartulaire de Flandre*, pièce 164.

[96] Boendale, *Brabantsche Yeesten*, I, 513; Hocsemius, p. 415 (paged as 406). For Count Louis' letter of defiance, see Kervyn, *Oeuvres de Froissart*, XXI, 207.

[97] T. Lacomblet, *Urkundenbuch für die Geschichte des Niederrheins* III, 214–218; J. Wolters, *Codex Diplomaticus Lossensis*, p. 240.

[98] Boendale, *Brabantsche Yeesten*, I, 513–514.

during the great fair at Ypres.[99]   In fact, all trade with Brabant
and Mechelen was prohibited.[100]   Goods were seized,[101] the men
of Mechelen were imprisoned whenever possible,[102] and some
burghers of St. Trond, suspected of connections with the duke,
were also arrested.[103]   John's appeal to the dean of the chapter of
Cologne on January 14 to induce the archbishop to interfere
could of course not be successful.[104]   Of all the enemies leagued
against him in 1332 only Edward, count of Bar, was friendly and
came to his aid.[105]   But the duke had the full support of his
bourgeoisie who were eager to aid their prince to protect their
interests.   On December 21 he took into his protection the burghers of Maastricht who were subject both to himself and the
bishop of Liège [106] and favors were granted to Louvain, Brussels,
and Diest in return for military aid.[107]

The poet Boendale compared the duke's predicament to that
of a chicken caught in a trap from which it could not escape.[108]
The danger for the *patria Brabantinensis* was so great that it
powerfully moved the imagination of succeeding generations and
gave birth to the martial *Wapenlied* of John III.   The taunt of
the count of Guelders that the duke would now feel the teeth
of the enemy and fail in the contest sprang from the pent-up
wrath nourished by the memory of a long series of aggressions by
the dukes of Brabant beyond the Meuse and concretely represents

[99] *Archives du Département du Nord,* Lille, *Cinquième Cartulaire de
Flandre,* No. 691.
[100] *Ibid.,* Nos. 691, 696, 698.
[101] *Ibid.,* No. 175.
[102] *Ibid.,* Nos. 636, 637.
[103] *Ibid.,* No. 191.
[104] T. Lacomblet, *Urkundenbuch für die Geschichte des Niederrheins,*
III, 214. Cf. K. Kunze, *Die Politische Stellung der Niederrheinischen
Fürsten,* p. 76.
[105] J. F. Willems, " Wapenlied van Jan den IIIe, Hertog van Braband,"
Belgisch Museum, III (1837), 295.
[106] J. Habets, " Codex Diplomaticus Mosae-Trajectensis," *Publications
de la Société Historique et Archéologique dans le Duché de Limburg,*
V (1868), 70–71.
[107] J. F. Willems, *Codex Diplomaticus,* p. 792; *Luyster ende Glorie van
Brabant,* I, 95; C. Stallaert, " Inventaire Analytique des Chartes Concernant les Seigneurs et la Ville de Diest," *BCRH,* 4th Ser., III (1875),
217; *Inventaire Chronologique des Chartes et Autres Documents sur
Parchemin appartenant aux Archives de la Ville de Louvain, 1164–1793,* p.
41.
[108] Boendale, *Brabantsche Yeesten,* I, 513.

the situation. To the boast that all these wrongs would now be redressed the duke replied with a haughtiness which only a sure knowledge of his great strength could give him: " I am the Duke of Brabant and my kith and kin, save the Count of Bar, have all deserted me and now visit me with their hatred. Your overweening pride and threats are not worthy; but if you rashly seek to hew through my shield then choose a day for the contest and take what lot may be given you. Do you think to reverse the fate of Woeringen? I will maintain my rights even as did my grandfather!" [109]

The first attack came from the side of Flanders, as had been planned. On January 17 Count Louis appointed Henry of Flanders, count of Lodi, supreme commander of his forces, and other troops were ordered to come to his aid.[110]   As early as February 2 the militia of Ghent was stationed at Alost.[111]   A hasty raid was conducted into Brabançon territory near Malderen and Lippeloo, but the plunderers hastily withdrew to Dendermonde. Duke John at once led out a force from Assche and laid waste with fire and sword the countryside from Alost up to the gates of Dendermonde, an exploit which particularly pleased Boendale. The Flemings retaliated by a raid upon the monastery of Af-flighem. The place had been duly warned; the monks fled to Brussels, but the burghers failed to take the proper precautions for defense. The duke sought to aid them, but in vain, and at the close of January the monastery was sacked. Later the Flemings came to tear down the church which had been used by the Brabanters to observe the activities in the market place of Alost.[112]   A number of Flemings — Boendale states that there were at least 20,000 — sallied forth from Alost and Dendermonde and unexpectedly attacked Assche which was defended by only a few men-at-arms. They were forced to retreat, leaving behind them William van Kranendonck and a few others. The

[109] J. F. Willems, " Wapenlied van Jan den IIIe, Hertog van Braband," *Belgisch Museum*, III (1837), 291–296.

[110] *Archives du Département du Nord*, Lille, *Cinquième Cartulaire de Flandre*, Nos. 377, 379, 387, 393.

[111] J. Vuylsteke, *Gentsche Stads- en Baljuwsrekeningen, 1280–1336*, II, 918–922. The expedition cost the town 17,600*l*. 19*s*. 4*d*. See pp. 897–898 for the weekly payments.

[112] Boendale, *Brabantsche Yeesten*, I, 515–517; Hocsemius, p. 415 (paged as 407); *Gesta Abbatum Sancti Trudonis*, p. 422.

enemy burned the town, but retreated when the duke's men came
pouring out of Brussels and other places toward Assche. But
these could accomplish little, for the enemy sought safety behind the gates of Alost and Dendermonde.[113]

Encouraged by their successes at Assche and Afflighem, and
reinforced by some nobles who joined them early in March,[114]
the Flemings began to plunder farther into the duchy. But the
Brabanters ever held themselves on the defensive, and the Flemings allowed themselves to be drawn far from home. The duke
sent forces from Brussels and Vilvoorde where the count of Bar's
men were stationed. The Flemings, marching toward Brussels
from Ninove, fell into an ambush and were attacked in the rear.
When the count of Bar came up with three hundred men, they
scattered like frightened sparrows and sought safety in the canals,
hedges, barns, or sheepfolds, while most of them fled to Flanders.
At least a hundred were taken and imprisoned in Louvain and
Tervuren — " pleasant guests for the duke " are the words of
Boendale.[115] This proved to be the end of the Flemish effort;
there was not enough time to rally before Philip and the papal
envoys managed to arrange a truce.

The bishop of Liège, Adolph de la Marck, had in the meantime
also begun the attack. Toward the end of January his brother,
Conrad, led a band from St. Trond and seized Landen, which
had been fortified by the duke and entrusted to the bailiff of Tirlemont. Although he had a hundred men under him, he failed to
appear when the attack was delivered.[116] Reginald, count of
Guelders, at the opening of hostilities had invested Tiel on the
Waal, and the burghers were, it appears, quite reluctant to op-

[113] Boendale, *Brabantsche Yeesten*, I, 521–522. The contingent from
Ghent numbered about 750 men. See J. Vuylsteke, *Gentsche Stads- en
Baljuwsrekeningen, 1280–1336*, II, 918–922. Hocsemius, p. 415 (paged as
407), refers to Assche as " Alke," which undoubtedly is a paleographical
error.

[114] *Archives du Département du Nord*, Lille, *Cinquième Cartulaire de
Flandre*, pièce 129.

[115] Boendale, *Brabantsche Yeesten*, I 528–529; Hocsemius, p. 415 (paged
as 407); *Chronique Parisienne Anonyme*, p. 155. The ambush was laid
near Ten Hellekene, see A. Henne and A. Wauters, *Histoire de Bruxelles*,
I, 100–101.

[116] *Gesta Abbatum Sancti Trudonis*, p. 422; Hocsemius, p 417 (paged
as 407); Boendale, *Brabantsche Yeesten*, I, 518–519.

pose him. There was much disagreement within the walls which finally resulted in its surrender on January 21.[117] William, count of Hainault, Holland, and Zeeland, took some prisoners at Heusden.[118] The king of Bohemia plundered Limburg while on his way to aid the counts of Guelders and Juliers and forced Hervé, Villers-aux-Tours, Anthisnes, and other defenseless places to yield to his will.[119]

William, count of Juliers, had begun the siege of the castle at Ringberghe, to which he claimed some title [120] and next took up his position before 's-Hertogenrade. Count Reginald now attacked Sittard, and John of Hainault, John, king of Bohemia, and the archbishop of Cologne joined him. The castle had been carefully victualled and men of reputation placed in command.[121] But the duke was prevented by the Flemings from coming to its relief at once and a desultory attempt by loyal bands from Limburg and Dolhain was easily beaten off. In spite of unfavorable weather in January and February, the defenders were forced in view of imminent starvation to agree to a truce on March 1 upon the condition that, should the duke come within a fortnight, the fate of the stronghold should be decided by open combat.[122]

IV. THE PAPAL INTERVENTION (FEBRUARY–MARCH, 1334)

THE renewal of strife in the Low Countries was most inopportune for the plans of Pope John XXII. King Philip had taken the cross in October, 1333, and Edward professed a willingness to do the same. The pope earnestly hoped that a united effort to deliver the sepulcher would now be possible. But Philip's interests in the Low Countries and Edward's persistence in looking after his interests in Aquitaine and the problem in Scotland se-

---

[117] *Chronicon Tielense*, p. 327; Boendale, *Brabantsche Yeesten*, I, 519–520.

[118] P. L. Muller, *Regesta Hannonensia*, p. 223.

[119] Outremeuse, VI, 524–527.

[120] Kervyn, *Oeuvres de Froissart*, XX, 428; S. A. Waller Zeper, *Jan van Henegouwen, Heer van Beaumont, Bijlage II*, p. 448.

[121] Levold de Northof, p. 401; Boendale, *Brabantsche Yeesten*, I, 530–531; Kervyn, *Oeuvres de Froissart*, XX, 423–429.

[122] *Brabantsche Yeesten*, pp. 531–532; Hocsemius, p. 415 (paged as 407); *Gesta Abbatum Sancti Trudonis*, p. 422.

riously endangered this prospect.[123]   For the moment, accordingly, the matter of Mechelen loomed large and proved difficult to settle. Should it remain in the hands of Count Louis, it would be a perennial source of discord; if the duke should keep it, there would be actual war. Furthermore, Philip could not offend his vassal, Count Louis, by giving it to the duke. The return to the *status quo ante* was the only logical solution: it suited the policies of both John XXII and Philip VI.

Meanwhile the pope sought to quiet the passions of the contestants. The corporation of Mechelen had lodged a protest with the curia against the violation of the contract between Floris Berthout and Theobald, bishop of Liège, and on October 29 the pope made known his disapproval to Adolph de la Marck. On December 5 he expressed great uneasiness to Count Louis and requested that envoys be sent to inform him fully about the transaction so that a settlement could be effected. In similar vein he wrote to the bishop and to the magistrates of Mechelen. By this time Duke John had also lodged his protests with the curia through his representatives, Henry Coke and the seignior of Crainhem, to which the pope replied on December 8.[124] Four days before this the confederates asked him to approve the sale.[125] Thus all parties concerned virtually appealed to the pope's arbitration.

Although the allied princes were winning a few advantages beyond the Meuse, a decided victory was out of the question. The Flemish efforts were over by the close of March and a deadlock ensued which bade fair to last until the fate of 's-Hertogenrade should be settled. Philip had already sent the archbishop of Auch and the abbot of St. Nicaise to work for a truce. They met the confederates on February 22 at Aix-la-Chapelle, but failed to secure any tangible results. The allied leaders presented a list of grievances and declared that, if the duke should be willing to redress them, they would meet his envoys on the borders at St. Trond on March 6, when Count Louis of Flanders could also be present.[126] At about this time Philip sent a small force with his

---

[123] E. Déprez, *Les Préliminaires de la Guerre de Cent Ans,* pp. 99–101.
[124] A. Fayen, *Lettres de Jean XXII (1316–1334),* Nos. 3501, 3518–3521.
[125] *Archives du Département du Nord,* Lille, No. B264 (6.709).
[126] Hocsemius, p. 415 (paged as 407).

brother, Charles, count of Alençon, Charles, count of Estampes, and Philip, king of Navarre, to support Duke John in a diplomatic way. They were denied passage through Hainault by Count William, but Duke John marched with a powerful force to meet them, according to the account of the poet Boendale. This was enough, and William allowed them to pass when the Brabanters appeared at Nivelles.[127]

Duke John now hastened to the relief of 's-Hertogenrade. On March 8 he crossed the Meuse at Maastricht and the next day appeared before the beleaguered castle. There was consternation in the camp of the allies; the king of Bohemia was loud in his complaints of Count Louis' failure to keep the duke occupied west of the Meuse. John spent the night in the open, in rain and mud near Gulpen, and as the entire countryside was deserted and stripped of all provisions, his troops were in great discomfort. On the morning of the 9th he immediately dispatched two knights to invite the enemy to march out and give battle. But they were expecting reinforcements from Liège and Cologne and did not care to meet the duke's strong force in open combat and declined the offer. John of Hainault held that the duke had played his part as befitted a knight and rebuked his colleagues for not keeping their part of the agreement.[128] No choice remained but to settle down to a regular siege, a thing which had apparently not been anticipated by the duke. He was far from home and could find neither food for his famished men nor shelter from the torrential spring rains. And treason was also at work at Sittard. The town and castle had been entrusted to the faithful seignior of Stein, but, when the latter was in conference with the duke on the 8th, the garrison and townsmen who were sympathetic to the Valkenburg house and feared the consequences of an investment by Reginald, count of Guelders, declared for the enemy.[129]

Other factors of a more serious nature now made it advisable to retreat at once. Duke John had sought to raise against Adolph,

---

[127] Hocsemius; Boendale, *Brabantsche Yeesten*, I, 353; *Chronique Parisienne Anonyme*, p. 155. According to the *Grandes Chroniques*, V, 355, these French nobles went to the duke's support.

[128] Boendale, *Brabantsche Yeesten*, I, 533–541; Levold de Northof, p. 401; Hocsemius, p. 415 (paged as 407). See S. A. Waller Zeper, *Jan van Henegouwen, Heer van Beaumont*, p. 135.

[129] E. Dynter, *Chronicon Ducum Brabantiae*, II, 570.

bishop of Liège, some of the bourgeoisie of the *Pays de Liège* and especially those of the town of Huy. He had spent much money and with some degree of assurance expected that the militia of the city of Liège and the towns would prevent the bishop from marching against him.[130] But the latter remained master of the domestic situation and was soon ready to move toward Maastricht and cut off the duke's connections with Brabant.[131] Even Thierry, count of Loon, who had allowed John to cross his territory without resistance on the way to 's-Hertogenrade, adopted a hostile attitude, joined the bishop, and began to tear down the bridges along the route over which the duke would have to return home. In great wrath he tarried before 's-Hertogenrade all day of the 9th, ready to give battle in spite of the hunger of his troops, and kept vigil in the incessant rain until the following morning. Then he ordered retreat and on the same day crossed the Meuse at Maastricht before the bishop, who was delayed by the duke's bribery of the men of Huy, could intercept him. The men of Maastricht were sympathetic and allowed him to pass even though his troops were armed. On the 11th John burned and plundered in Loon and was soon back in Brabant.[132]

The proposed conference at St. Trond took place on Sunday, March 13, but only the French and Flemish envoys appeared. Count Louis had on the 10th ordered Lambert, abbot of Dunes, Gerard de Grandpré, seignior of Roussy, Louis de Marcke, bailiff of Ypres, and John de Cadzand to represent him.[133] Meanwhile Philip de Melduno, archdeacon of Meldune, a kin of the duke, arrived with new instructions from Philip. He was received at Nivelles by the duke's men and conducted to Brussels, where the representatives of the towns and nobility of Brabant were in session. Accompanied by the abbot of St. Nicaise, the archbishop of Auch, and others, he proceeded to Maastricht where the allied leaders were trying to punish the burghers for conniving at the escape of the duke. The latter was safe in Brabant and unassailable, no further gains could be expected, and the moment for

---

[130] E. Hocsemius, p. 415 (paged as 407)–416; Levold de Northof, p. 401.

[131] Outremeuse, VI, 522–523, 529–530; Boendale, *Brabantsche Yeesten,* I, 538; Hocsemius, p. 416.

[132] Boendale, *Brabantsche Yeesten,* I, 537, 541–543; Hocsemius, p. 416.

[133] *Archives du Département du Nord,* Lille, *Cinquième Cartulaire de Flandre,* Nos. 2, 3.

negotiation had apparently come. Philip's envoys at once settled the differences between the bishop and the burghers and then took up the discussion of a truce to which Adolph at first was strenuously opposed, but was finally induced to yield.[134]   In St. Peter's of Maastricht on the 16th the terms were drawn up. All hostilities west of the Meuse were to cease on the 22d — and east of the Meuse on the 23d until the morning of May 19; the allies were to present themselves in person or by proxy at Cambrai on April 17 to treat for a definitive settlement in coöperation with the envoys of King Philip; and the situation at the castle Ringberghe, which was still being besieged by William, count of Juliers, was to remain as it was.[135]   Thereupon the French party proceeded to Brussels whence on the 21st they requested Count Louis to observe the truce.[136]

John XXII was also bending every effort for peace. On February 4 a letter from King Philip was read in the curia. It suggested that, in view of the grave danger to the success of the projected crusade, the princes should be exhorted to accept peace, and, as a preliminary step, be released from their oaths. But it was a question whether this should be done because persons concerned had not requested it, and a division was at once created among the cardinals. One was so outspoken as to recall to the pope how he had failed against Lewis the Bavarian, who had managed to retain the support of fourteen bishops and their dioceses, and warned him not to undertake something that might prove too much for him to accomplish.

Nevertheless it was decided to send nuncios to Flanders and Brabant with powers of granting absolution, supported with the threat of the usual ecclesiastical censures. On March 1 bulls were issued for John Artaudi, bishop of Marseilles, who was charged to proceed with great caution,[137] and Duke John and

---

[134] Levold de Northof, p. 401; Hocsemius, pp. 416–417; Boendale, *Brabantsche Yeesten,* I, 545–546; Outremeuse, VI, 532.

[135] *Archives du Département du Nord,* Lille, *Cinquième Cartulaire de Flandre,* Nos. 127, 129; S. A. Waller Zeper, *Jan van Henegouwen, Heer van Beaumont, Bijlage II,* pp. 447–449. See also Hocsemius, p. 417; le Muisit, p. 108.

[136] *Archives du Département du Nord,* Lille, *Cinquième Cartulaire de Flandre,* No. 124.

[137] Hocsemius, pp. 416–417; E. Fayen, *Lettres de Jean XXII (1316–1334),* No. 3553.

Count Louis were besought to look with favor upon his efforts. A special letter to the latter set forth the attitude of the curia. Repeating the pope's position already made known in a letter of January 29, it held that the sale was illegal, and, inasmuch as the duke and the scabini of Mechelen had declared their desire to have the papal decision in this matter, advised him to yield his position in the general interests of Christendom.[138] On the 5th the allied leaders, the representatives of Philip VI, the bishops of Münster, Paderborn, and Utrecht, and Duke John were apprised officially of the mission, and letters were issued commending the nuncios to all ecclesiastical parties who were requested to pay them ten gold florins daily for their support. On the 17th the oaths which had sealed the confederation were relaxed and all alliances were annulled, and John, bishop of Amiens, William, bishop of Noyon, and the abbot of St. Cornelius at Compiègne were urgently requested to support the endeavors of the nuncios.[139]

It was difficult to arrange a compromise. John, king of Bohemia, and Bishop Adolph revealed their reluctance when in a conference at Huy on March 22 the princes agreed to have a preliminary discussion at Mons to which they invited Count Louis,[140] who appeared with the representatives of the three towns [141] at the appointed place, apparently on April 13, whence they proceeded to Noyon to meet the king who had found it impossible to come to Cambrai.[142] For more than a fortnight the French envoys labored with Duke John and his enemies, but in vain, and, seeing that nothing could be accomplished before the expiration of the truce, Philip extended the term to St. John the Baptist's Day.[143] The burden of negotiating the disputed points other than those regarding Mechelen had been assigned to John, bishop of Thérouanne, the abbot of St. Nicaise of Rheims, the arch-

[138] E. Fayen, *Lettres de Jean XXII (1316–1334)*, Nos. 3534, 3554–3556.
[139] *Ibid.*, Nos. 3557–3559, 3562–3563.
[140] *Archives du Département du Nord*, Lille, *Cinquième Cartulaire de Flandre*, No. 998; S. A. Waller Zeper, *Jan van Henegouwen, Heer van Beaumont, Bijlage* II, pp. 448–449.
[141] J. Vuylsteke, *Gentsche Stads- en Baljuwsrekeningen, 1280–1336*, II, 899.
[142] Hocsemius, p. 417; J. Viard, "Itinéraire de Philippe VI de Valois," *BEC*, LXXIV (1913), 114.
[143] A. Verkooren, *Inventaire, Brabant*, I, 259.

deacon of Tournai, Matthew de Trie, Philip's marshal, Ferri de Pequigny, Guy Turpin, and Michael de Raucourt. Just when this move was made cannot be ascertained, but the abbot was in the Low Countries as early as February 22, and steps can hardly have been taken before the truce was agreed upon.[144] They met the allied leaders in conference at Mons on June 12, when it was decided to continue negotiations at Cambrai before the close of the truce.[145]

But they did make some pronouncement concerning the relations of Brabant and the see of Liège. John was required to retract his order that none of his subjects should respond to the spiritual jurisdiction of the bishop and to issue letters to his officials to this effect; to deposit 200*l.* large Tournois in Philip's hands for the prisoners taken at Perwez who were still imprisoned; to grant the Franciscans of Maastricht certain documents which he had hitherto refused to do; and with the bishop to present the documents regarding the disputed liberties of certain churches to be adjudicated by Philip in the approaching conference in Cambrai. The question of indemnities was to be settled by an inquest of four men, two lay and two clerical, one of each to be appointed by the duke and the bishop, who were to present their decision at the conference in Cambrai. In regard to Mechelen the deputies would do nothing but state that the sale could not be revoked and that no harm had been done to the bishop, chapter, or the see of Liège by its alienation.[146]

The obstinacy of the bishop and his chapter caused much worry in the curia at Avignon and in Philip's council. The nuncios, who did not leave Avignon until March 8 because of opposition in the curia, were soon in contact with the French king. On June 1 John XXII urged the magistrates of Mechelen to coöperate with their efforts, and was naturally greatly relieved when Philip extended the truce to St. John the Baptist's Day. But progress was impossible and the letters of June 12 from the nuncios seemed to announce a deadlock. However, John ordered them on the 22d to persevere and return only if it became utterly impossible to

---

144 Hocsemius, p. 417; F. van Mieris, *Groot Charterboek,* II, 566.
145 A. Verkooren, *Inventaire, Brabant,* I, 257–258.
146 Outremeuse, VI, 508–511, where the document is dated 1333. M. G. de Louvrex, *Recueil des Ordonnances,* I, 168–169, assigns it to 1323.

do anything. On grounds of the great expense involved Philip proposed that the task entrusted to the mission be given to the bishops of Noyon, Tournai, and Thérouanne. But as this carried with it power of pronouncing ecclesiastical censures, the pope refused.[147] Some progress, however, was made. Count Louis was in Paris from June 22 to July 5 with the representatives of Bruges, Ghent, and Ypres,[148] and yielded to Philip's threats to cancel the contract with the church of Liège.[149] On June 26 the king suggested that constraint be put upon the bishop and the chapter, which the curia was loath to allow as it aimed to win by persuasion. In his reply John XXII stated that he had written in this tenor to the bishop on the 25th and to the chapter and Count Louis on the 27th, and at once ordered the nuncios not to pronounce the interdict except at his command.[150]

On the 20th the pope sent instructions to govern the nuncios in their dealings with the duke of Brabant. They were to arrange a general compensation whereby the chapter would not be harmed nor incur the ducal displeasure. Should an amicable accommodation be impossible, they were to resort to process of law, and, if any legal flaws should be found, which the pope believed to exist, they were to declare the transfer null and void by virtue of their apostolic authority. As a last measure they were to bring the matter before the curia. So difficult was their task that the pope deemed it advisable to bring all possible pressure upon the reluctant parties. On August 18 he instructed the bishops of Cambrai and Utrecht to order Adolph de la Marck and his chapter under pain of excommunication not to use the money accruing from the sale of Mechelen and urged the bishops to take it into their custody until the final decision.[151] These efforts were of no avail, for secular interests were to have their way.

The coalition was in the meantime showing clear signs of dissolution. William, count of Hainault, Holland, and Zeeland, had

---

[147] A. Fayen, *Lettres de Jean XXII (1316–1334)*, Nos. 3565, 3577, 3581, 3595, 3601.

[148] J. Vuylsteke, *Gentsche Stads- en Baljuwsrekeningen, 1280–1336*, II, 901.

[149] Levold de Northof, p. 402. It is possible, however, that Louis did not yield until the meeting at Amiens.

[150] A. Fayen, *Lettres de Jean XXII (1316–1334)*, Nos. 2602–3605.

[151] *Ibid.*, Nos. 3615, 3623, 3635.

not made it too uncomfortable for Duke John, and a reconcilia-tion with him was soon in order. Complaints regarding some boundary difficulties were submitted to the arbitration of parties appointed by each, apparently in accordance with the treaty of 1328. They went to the places in dispute at Hal and Wautier-Braine, and discovered that the duke's claims were correct, and William on May 22 acquiesced in their findings.[152] In June it was agreed that, should peace crown the activities of the French deputies, the marriage of Isabella and Duke John's heir apparent John should be carried out, and, in case of the youth's early death his brother Henry should incur the obligation.[153] Soon after this the duke also agreed that the question of the moneys de-manded by Count William should be left to the decision of John van Heelbeke and William van Duivenvoorde, and that the docu-ments drawn up in connection with the old contract of 1329 should be renewed, inasmuch as they had been repudiated. Further-more, the numerous differences in connection with the seigniory of Heusden were either settled outright or left to arbitration.[154] On May 4 Thierry, count of Cleves, had sold to Count William his rights in the town and dependent parts of Heusden. This was but half of Thierry's patrimony in the seigniory, since the other half remained in the hands of his brother, John of Linne, dean of the chapter of Cologne. The whole was held as a fief of the count by the seigniors of Altena.[155] On June 5 the documents touching these rights, save what had been sold to Count William, were given to Duke John who promised to return them upon re-payment of 15,000*l.* black Tournois.[156]

This friendliness displayed between Count William and Duke John apparently disquieted the king of Bohemia and especially Count Louis, who feared renewed difficulties on the Schelde and perhaps actual war over Mechelen which at this moment he was

[152] F. van Mieris, *Groot Charterboek*, II, 563; A. Verkooren, *Inven-taire, Brabant*, I, 256–257; C. Butkens, *Trophées tant Sacrés que Profanes du Duché de Brabant*, I (*Preuves*), 174.

[153] J. F. Willems, *Codex Diplomaticus*, I, 793–794; A. Verkooren, *In-ventaire, Brabant*, I, 259; P. L. Muller, *Regesta Hannonensia*, p. 224; E. Dynter, *Chronicon Ducum Brabantiae*, II, 509.

[154] *Rijks Archief*, The Hague, *Heusden* (June 4, 1334).

[155] F. van Mieris, *Groot Charterboek*, II, 562–563.

[156] P. L. Muller, *Regesta Hannonensia*, p. 224; E. Dynter, *Chronicon Ducum Brabantiae*, II, 509.

zealous to retain. At Mons on June 9 they drew up the terms of an alliance whereby King John promised to succor Count Louis with a hundred men against either the duke or Mechelen.[157] William, count of Juliers, agreed on the 11th to support Louis,[158] and with the count of Guelders pledged 150,000 florins which the impecunious king of Bohemia owed the count of Flanders.[159] But even though the counts of Juliers and Guelders were apparently closely associated with the malcontent King John, William, count of Hainault, Holland, and Zeeland, still retained control over the situation. Difficulties in Utrecht between William van Duivenvoorde and the burghers of Oudewater and other matters demanded the coöperation of Reginald with Count William,[160] and the count of Juliers for his part remained friendly toward his father-in-law.[161] On July 17 at Cambrai the *rapprochement* of Count William and the duke was carried further when the seigniory of Heusden and the entire justice of Drongelen were definitely recognized as belonging to the duchy of Brabant, out of the income of which the duke was to pay the count a hundred pounds annually.[162]

V. The Treaty of Amiens (August, 1334)

Meanwhile Philip proceeded to Cambrai and Amiens, where he hoped to settle the numerous points in dispute. It was a striking event in the history of the Low Countries. Never before had the Capetians been able to intervene so vitally in the political problems of the lands which formerly belonged to the duchy of Lotharingia. At Cambrai Philip annulled all alliances and ordered the allied princes to observe the peace with the duke. Prisoners were to be freed and all civil, commercial, and political relations reëstablished as they were before the war, although homage was to be performed anew.[163]

---

[157] *Archives du Département du Nord,* Lille, No. B264 (823).

[158] *Codex Diplomaticus Neerlandicus,* 2d Ser., I, 31.

[159] I. A. Nijhof, *Gedenkwaardigheden uit de Geschiedenis van Gelderland,* I, 330–331.

[160] P. L. Muller, *Regesta Hannonensia,* pp. 222–224; F. van Mieris, *Groot Charterboek,* II, 560, 564–565.

[161] L. Devillers, *Monuments,* III, 355.

[162] E. Dynter, *Chronicon Ducum Brabantiae,* II, 509.

[163] *Ibid.,* pp. 573–576.

Many questions between Reginald, count of Guelders, and John, duke of Brabant, were also settled at this time.[164] The title to the *advocatiae* of Herkenchon and of the Merwede, claimed as fiefs by Reginald to be held of him by the duke, was referred to four men, two to be named by each party. These were also to investigate the disputes concerning Tiel and Heusden. An inquest was to decide by November 2 the difficulties regarding Diegheden. The duke was ordered to bring to the assembly at Amiens within three weeks the original documents upon which he based his claim to Herpen, Megen, Meerhout, Genderen,[165] and the justice of Boxtel which its seigniors held in fee of the counts of Guelders. An inquest by four men, two from each side, was to investigate the knotty and intricate claims touching Heusden before All Saints' Day and a presiding party was to be named at Amiens who would tender decision with them before Christmas. A similar inquest was ordered for Baardwijk. The titles to Tiel, Zandwijk, and Heerewaarden were to be exchanged for that of the seigniory of Heusden and its dependent parts as the inquest might determine before All Saints' Day. A principal (*souverain*) was to be named who would render final decision by February 2. All letters in any way touching the alliances of earlier dukes of Brabant with the counts of Guelders were to be brought to Amiens by Duke John. The disputes concerning lands at 's-Hertogenrade and Heinsberg were to be submitted to eight men from Bach near 's-Hertogenrade and investigated by October 1. John of Valkenburg, second son of Reginald, seignior of Valkenburg, who had died in 1332, was to receive Herpen and its seigniory. Count Reginald was to have returned to him by Christmas his share (a third) of the 20,000*l*. Tournois advanced in behalf of Reginald of Valkenburg when he broke faith by refusing to return to Genappe by August 1, 1326. The burghers of the towns of Brabant were to regain their rights in Guelders.

[164] E. Dynter, *Chronicon Ducum Brabantiae,* II, pp. 576–581; F. van Mieris, *Groot Charterboek,* II, 566–568, where this document is contained in the decision of August 3 at Cambrai; C. Butkens, *Trophées tant Sacrés que Profanes du Duché de Brabant,* I (*Preuves*), 160–161, where it is dated August 25.

[165] It is, perhaps, impossible to discover what the *advocatiae* of Herkenches and Merwede really were. The identity of Diegheden (Drongelen?), Herpen (Herpe?), "à la Grève," and Gerdoren (Genderen?) is uncertain.

These terms were to be further strengthened by the betrothal of Duke John's second daughter Marie to Reginald, the count's heir. Of the dowry of 64,000*l*. Tournois one half was to be paid at once in accordance with the stipulations of King Philip, William, count of Hainault, Holland, and Zeeland, and John, king of Bohemia. Reginald promised to settle upon his daughter-in-law 12,000*l*. annually from the incomes of Zutfen, the Veluwe, and the tolls of Lobith. Philip offered to get the necessary dispensation.[166]

At Amiens negotiations were opened early in August, and Philip was on hand before the 9th.[167] The matter of Mechelen was considered at once, and on the 18th the archbishop of Rouen, the bishops of Arras and Thérouanne, and a knight declared that it would be necessary for the nuncios to absolve Count Louis from his oath never to separate Mechelen from Flanders.[168] On the same day Louis assented, and the king promised that these rights would never come into the duke's hands, but would be returned to the chapter of St. Lambert. The rights of Marguerite of Guelders were likewise to be restored and on the 21st Louis was formally absolved.[169]

Relations between Brabant and Guelders were further defined. On the 25th Duke John accepted the transactions made at Cambrai and on the 26th Philip made further pronouncement. The old documents upon which the duke rested his claims against the count were annulled; the latter was to do homage by the following Christmas for all fiefs held of the duke and questions relating to the dowry were further regulated.[170] Other agreements were made between the count of Juliers and the duke of Brabant, some of which have been lost, it appears, and which were strengthened by the betrothal of the duke's youngest son Godefroid to Johanna, daughter of Count William.[171] The differences between

[166] E. Dynter, *Chronicon Ducum Brabantiae*, II, 573–581. Cf. *Chronicon Tielense*, pp. 327–328.

[167] For the delegation from Ghent with Count Louis, see J. Vuylsteke, *Gentsche Stads- en Baljuwsrekeningen, 1280–1336*, II, 901, 960; for Philip's itinerary, J. Viard, "Itinéraire de Philippe VI de Valois," *BEC*, LXXIV (1913), 114–115. See also Hocsemius, p. 417.

[168] J. Albanes, *Gallia Christiana Novissima, Marseilles*, col. 276.

[169] *Archives du Département du Nord*, Lille, No. B264 (6.867); J. B. Sollerius, *Acta Sancti Rumoldi*, p. 183; Hocsemius, p. 418.

[170] E. Dynter, *Chronicon Ducum Brabantiae*, II, 582–586.

[171] A. Verkooren, *Inventaire, Brabant*, I, 271–272. Count William for-

the count of Namur and the duke of Brabant were left to arbiters who were to meet on October 1, and, in case of disagreement, were to be assisted by Ferri de Pequigny, the representative of Philip.[172] Meanwhile, the agreements of November 18, 1333, were to remain in force.[173]

Philip next announced the terms which should henceforth regulate the relations of the dukes of Brabant with the see of Liège. Four arbiters were to settle the numerous questions concerning the bishop's possessions within the borders of Brabant; the bishop was to retain all his spiritual and secular jurisdictions such as the *Judicium Pacis* and the *quarantaines* and the duke was not to tax the properties of the clergy. The arbiters were also to investigate certain declarations made at Cambrai why the rights of Mechelen should not be returned to Liège. John was to retain all his old rights in Maastricht and the damages inflicted by his men were to be investigated by the close of September. Episcopal claim to Simpleveld, Eysden, and other places was to be further studied and, finally, the duke was to be allowed to present claim for all losses caused by the bishop before the outbreak of war.[174]

In regard to Valkenburg it was decreed that the duke should return all its rights to the heirs of Reginald, who had died in 1332, but that it should be held as a fief of the duke of Brabant and his heirs.[175] Thierry, seignior of Heinsberg, who had succeeded his father Reginald in 1332, was to receive the seigniory of Wassenberg and its dependencies for the duration of his life, at the close of which the duke might secure it by purchase.[176]

---

mally accepted Philip's decision on September 30. See *ibid.*, pp. 280 and 282–283.

[172] C. Piot, *Inventaire des Chartes des Comtes de Namur*, p. 166.

[173] A. Verkooren, *Inventaire, Brabant*, I, 276.

[174] *Ibid.*, pp. 272–275. Cf. J. F. Willems, *Codex Diplomaticus*, I, 798–799.

[175] Hocsemius, p. 417. On October 23 Thierry, seignior of Valkenberg and Montjoy, received these lands in fee. See M. Jansen, *Inventaire van het oud Archief der Gemeente Sittard, 1243–1609*, II, 14–15; T. Lacomblet, *Urkundenbuch für die Geschichte des Niederrheins*, III, 234. Reginald had appealed in 1333 to the emperor. See Winkelmann, *Acta Imperii*, p. 347.

[176] E. Dynter, *Chronicon Ducum Brabantiae*, II, 589–590; A. Ver-

John, king of Bohemia, was to cease his feuds with the duke of
Brabant for the duchy of Limburg and received 160,000 *regales*,[177] which of course was quickly absorbed by his numerous
creditors — it " disappeared like smoke." [178] The archbishop of
Cologne was awarded 35,000 *regales*, the bishop of Liège, 30,000,
the count of Juliers, 30,000, the count of Guelders, 60,000, and the
count of Loon, 18,000.[179] These provisions were undoubtedly
made at Amiens although no document can be found specifying
these matters.[180]

The status of the barony of Breda also came up for settlement.
Its seignior had died in 1324 leaving one half of his possessions to
his daughter Adelise who later married Gerard, seignior of Rasseghem, Lens, and Liedekerke. The other half had been granted
to two younger daughters. Gerard was in sore need of money and
sold the town of Breda with its dependencies on February 14,
1326, to Duke John to be held of him in fee.[181] No mention of
his sisters-in-law was made, nor were they informed of the transaction, and trouble developed. Nor was Adelise satisfied. Louis,
count of Flanders, for some reason regarded the status of these
properties disadvantageous to the seignior of Breda, who was also
his vassal, and complained to King Philip in 1335. The legality
of the protests would seem nil as Gerard was his vassal only for

---

kooren, *Inventaire, Brabant,* I, 265–266. For the duke's connections with
Wassenberg, see *ibid.,* 135, 137, 140, 230–232, 242–243, 377.

[177] *Königsaaler Geschichts-Quellen,* p. 508.

[178] According to the *Königsaaler Geschichts-Quellen,* p. 508, he received 150,000 *regales.* See also Hocsemius, p. 417; Outremeuse, VI,
544–545. See for payments by the duke, J. F. Boehmer, *Die Urkunden
Kaiser Ludwigs des Baiern, und seiner Zeit, Additamentum Primum,* p. 300.

[179] E. Dynter, *Chronicon Ducum Brabantiae,* II, 582.

[180] Hocsemius, p. 417; Outremeuse, VI, 544–545 where the document
is dated at Paris "l'an MCCC et XXXV, le jour del Epyphanie." The
date cannot be regarded as trustworthy, for it would seem that the king
at Paris would date a document according to the Easter and not the
Christmas style which was in vogue in the diocese of Liège. The correct
date is perhaps August 30, 1334, for on that day the duke paid to the bishop
in accordance with Philip's decision, 30,000 Florentine florins. See
A. Verkooren, *Inventaire, Brabant,* I, 275. For many such documents
dated after August 30, see *ibid.,* pp. 277, 279–280, 282, 284, 285–287, 292–
293, 296, 297–304. Since a large number of these are dated before January
5, 1335, it would seem that the document must be assigned to 1334.

[181] T. E. van Goor, *Beschrijving der Stadt en Lande van Breda,* pp. 13,
448–450.

Liedekerke. But the question was referred to Philip who on August 30 ordered that the purchase money should be returned and the illegal transaction cancelled.[182]

Relations between Reginald, count of Guelders, and the bishop of Münster were also regulated. On September 5 the former promised not to disturb the episcopal rights within his lands.[183] It is impossible to determine exactly what passed between these two hereditary enemies during the wars with Brabant. The long dispute about the seigniory of Bredevoort, of which the bishop was overlord, began when it was transferred to Count Otto II in 1246. But a scion of the old possessors was in control of it at the opening of the century and sold it to the bishop in 1316. When Reginald I was declared insane, his son, later Count Reginald II, opened a struggle in 1322 for the prized enclave. The intervention of the counts of Juliers and of Berg in 1323 led to a truce which was soon broken. The bishop was seized and held for ransom and upon his release in 1324 led a raid into Guelders and plundered the country. Each party marshaled its supporters; Reginald could boast of the aid of John, king of Bohemia, the bishops of Liège and Utrecht, the counts of Holland, Flanders, Artois, Juliers, and Berg, and at Coesfeld they met the allies of the bishop of Münster, the counts of Lippe, Waldeck, Sayn, the bishop of Osnabrück, and other Germans. A truce was arranged whereby Bredevoort was given to Guelders who was, however, dissatisfied, and the war was reopened. Finally, on June 28, 1326, it was agreed that Guelders was to retain Bredevoort but surrender the seigniory of Bermentvelde and hold in pawn the justice of Winterswijk, Aalten, and Dinxperloo which the bishop might, however, redeem.[184] There apparently were differences in 1329 and 1330,[185] and it may very well be that the bishop on this account displayed sympathy toward the duke of Brabant during the crises of 1332 and 1334.

[182] T. E. van Goor, *op. cit.,* pp. 454–456; H. Pirenne, *Le Soulèvement de ia Flandre Maritime (1323–1328),* pp. 190–191.

[183] A. Verkooren, *Inventaire, Brabant,* I, pp. 278–280.

[184] H. G. Harkema, " De Betrekkingen van het Bisdom Munster tot de Nederlanden, inzonderheid tot Gelderland tot aan den Vrede van Kleef, 18 April, 1666," *Werken uitgegeven door de Vereeniging Gelre,* VII (1909), 3–8, 55–59.

[185] A. van Slichtenhorst, *XIV Boeken van de Geldersse Geschiedenissen* (Arnhem, 1654), pp. 120–121.

CHAPTER VI

THE ANGLO–SCOTCH CRISIS (1335–1337)

i. The Political Prestige of William, Count of Hainault, Holland, and Zeeland (1334 — Summer, 1336) ii. The Flight of Robert of Artois to England (Spring, 1334–1337) iii. The Scotch Campaign (1335) iv. The Rupture between King Edward III and Louis, Count of Flanders (1335 — October, 1336) v. The Diplomatic Activities of William, Count of Juliers (1335–1336) vi. Edward's Negotiations in the Low Countries (Summer, 1336 — Spring, 1337) vii. The Social and Economic Crisis in Flanders (Spring, 1337)

I. The Political Prestige of William, Count of Hainault, Holland, and Zeeland (1334 — Summer, 1336)

THE events of 1334 which culminated in the Treaty of Amiens in August were of prime importance locally and of some significance in the wider field of European politics. The pope had been annoyed because the attack upon the duke of Brabant happened at a moment when plans for a crusade against the Turks seemed nearly ready. Marino Sanudo expressed considerable relief in a letter to Louis, duke of Bourbon, on October 22, 1334, when he learned that this impediment had been removed.[1]

John, duke of Brabant, could in a way count himself fortunate because of the terms of the arrangements made at Amiens. Although he was required to pay great sums, he did not lose any really significant territory. He had lost Tiel, Heerewaarden, and Zantwijk, but secured undisputed possession of Heusden. Definitive recognition of his rights in the duchy of Limburg was given him by his rival John, king of Bohemia and count of Luxemburg. The lands of the seignior of Valkenburg, so vital for the protection of his interests east of the Meuse, were henceforth to be held in fee of him and his successors. These were to be the last significant gains in the annals of the duchy.

[1] K. Kunstmann, "Studien über Marino Sanudo den aelteren mit einen Anhange seiner Ungedruckten Briefe," *Abhandlungen der Historischen Classe der Bayerischen Akademie,* VII (1853), 809.

Philip VI, on the contrary, had overshot his mark. Never before had a French king disposed so freely of the local issues in the Low Countries. Philip soon sent Ferri de Pequigny as his lieutenant to take charge of Mechelen, which was to remain in his possession until a decision could be reached.[2] In this way he would be able to exert a vast influence in these parts of the empire. The ostensible purpose in áll these transactions had ever been to establish peace in Europe so that Christendom might gird itself for an attack upon the infidel. But there were individuals suspicious of Philip's motives, and Hocsem, the acute *scholasticus* of Liège, guessed that he cherished some design upon the empire.[3] Other observers also seemed to have similar thoughts.

It was in this connection that the covert resentment of William, count of Hainault, Holland, and Zeeland, toward his brother-in-law became of crucial significance. He had independently of Philip's efforts drawn close to the duke of Brabant after the truce had been made at Maastricht. The repudiated matrimonial alliance was once more agreed upon and on August 30, 1334, was given its final form.[4] The dowry was fixed: the duke was to invest his son John with the title of all his possessions except Limburg as soon as he and Isabella were old enough to marry, while he himself would retain the full usufruct. Should the heir apparent die, Henry, the second son, was to succeed to these obligations.[5] On September 5 Duke John solemnly promised to observe all of Philip's pronouncements, and Count William was now able to bring the princes in the Low Countries who were most immediately under his influence to a common understanding. The archbishop of Cologne, Reginald, count of Guelders, Count William and his son William, titular count of Zeeland, and John, duke of Brabant, made a treaty of amity and defense regarding commerce and delivery of war materials to any one of

---

[2] Boendale, *Brabantsche Yeesten,* I, 550; Hocsemius, p. 418.

[3] Hocsemius, p. 410 (paged as 402): " . . . qua pactione nescitur, nisi quod dicebatur illos velle secum ducere pro recuperatione terrae sanctae, quia crucem fecit postmodum praedicare; ego vero ex his quae praemisi credo quod illis mediantibus aliquid circa imperium agere intendebat."

[4] Notwithstanding the statement of Boendale, *Brabantsche Yeesten,* I, 541, that this too was part of the king's decision.

[5] J. F. Willems, *Codex Diplomaticus,* I, 794–797.

their number who should be involved in war. Provision for reconciliation was made in case of differences among themselves. The alliance was to be enforced against all parties except the emperor, the king of France, and the duke of Normandy. Duke John of Brabant was grateful to the count of Bar and included him in this list.[6]

It is a noteworthy fact that the princes more immediately under the influence of the king of France — Louis, count of Flanders, Adolph, bishop of Liège, and John, king of Bohemia — did not join the alliance formed by the initiative of Count William. In this connection, the situation in the empire and in Italy is interesting. Robert, king of Naples, had been displeased with the career of the king of Bohemia in northern Italy. He also disliked the prospect of an increase of French power in the Mediterranean, which seemed certain if the agreement should be fulfilled between Lewis the Bavarian and John of Bohemia, whereby the former would resign his imperial office to Henry of Bavaria, who had in turn promised to mortgage to Philip VI numerous titles in the kingdoms of Arles and Vienne under conditions practically impossible to redeem. He himself had rights in the counties of Provence and Forcalquier. This is the motive behind the memoir which he sent about the middle of 1334 to John XXII.[7] The pope had made enemies in championing the unpopular view regarding the beatific vision. The Spiritual Franciscans opposed him and in the curia Cardinal Orsini ranged himself with them and Robert of Naples. A letter was sent to Lewis the Bavarian, charging the pope with heresy and urging him to convoke a general council before which he could lay his own troubles with the pontiff. It also urged a close understanding between Lewis the Bavarian, Robert of Naples, and the enemies of the papal policies in northern Italy. Influenced undoubtedly in part by these representations, Lewis the Bavarian formally announced in July, 1334, that he never had entertained any intention of abdicating.[8] Thus the Bohemian king was again ranged against the Bavarian,

[6] I. A. Nijhoff, *Gedenkwaardigheden uit de Geschiedenis van Gelderland*, I, 333–336.

[7] K. Müller, *Der Kampf Ludwigs des Baiern mit der Römischen Curie*, I (*Anhang*), 393–405.

[8] P. Fournier, *Le Royaume d'Arles et de Vienne (1138–1378)*, pp. 401–405.

and Philip was thwarted in his far-reaching schemes to secure many titles in Arles and Vienne which had so long been coveted by his predecessors.

The bonds between the kings of France and Bohemia, already intimate, were now drawn even closer. King John was in Vincennes in October when he sold to Philip his rights to the city, county, and seigniory of Lucca for 180,000 small Florentine florins.[9] King John was now a widower; he was in great need of money to finance his extensive schemes,[10] and King Philip undoubtedly evolved plans of satisfying his financial needs by an advantageous marriage which would weld the Luxemburger inseparably to the interests of the Valois house. The choice fell upon Beatrice, daughter of Louis, the count of Bourbon.

Beatrice received as her marriage portion an annual sum of 4,000*l*. Tournois from the castle, town, and barony of Creil in the county of Clermont, and, in addition, 1,000*l*. Tournois from the duchy of Bourbonnais upon the death of her father. For these rights John and Beatrice were required to perform homage to the count of Clermont and the duke of Bourbon. King John promised his bride an income of 6,000*l*. Tournois from the castle, town, burgraviate, and provostship of Arlon and Marcoville, the town and provostship of St. Mard, the castle and burgraviate of Bouillon, and the castle and town of Doynvillers. The county of Luxemburg, the county of Laroche, the margraviate of Arlon, the seigniories of Durburg and Poilvache, and John's possessions in Hainault were to pass to the male issue of this marriage.[11] This connection was purely political in its aims and the Bohemians were not at all pleased with the prospect of being used still further for their king's political adventures.[12] But the pope on January 9, 1335, gave his dispensation [13] and the marriage ceremony was soon celebrated with great display. Still further went the ramifications of the Valois-Luxemburg political schemes when King John's daughter Anna, successively engaged

---

[9] J. Dumont, *Corps Diplomatique*, I (2), 148.

[10] Johannis Victoriensis, p. 144.

[11] J. Bertholet, *Histoire Ecclésiastique et Civile du Duché de Luxemburg*, VI (*Preuves*), No. XXVI; A. Huillard Bréholles, *Inventaire des Titres de la Maison Ducale de Bourbon*, I, 319, 362, 373, 385, 395, 409.

[12] *Königsaaler Geschichts-Quellen*, pp. 520, 523.

[13] S. Riezler, *Vatikanische Akten*, No. 578.

to Ladislav of Hungary, Otto of Austria, and Lewis, son of Lewis the Bavarian, was finally married to Otto of Austria in the following February.[14]

During these months the duke of Brabant found it advantageous to draw even closer to William, count of Hainault, Holland, and Zeeland. The obligations imposed upon the duke at Amiens entailed a burdensome taxation which led to difficulties in the course of which Count William proved a trusted friend and adviser. The heavy demands upon the subjects of Brabant gave them renewed opportunity to reassert old privileges and claim new ones. Since the famous French and Walloon Charters had been granted in 1314, and in spite of the provision in the latter requiring a strict account of all money collected by ducal officials,[15] malversations and abuses in collection had remained rampant. Duke John's promise of September 28, 1332, made to secure money after the first attack by the allies, provided for an annual investigation of the acts of all his officials. But this apparently was without result and soon thereafter the duke was forced to reconfirm the Charter of Cortenberghe and consent to its immediate execution.[16]

This was delayed, however, by the speedy reopening of the struggle with his neighbors. In May, 1334, at Pont-l'Évêque John ordered Henry Berthout, seignior of Duffel, and Arnold, seignior of Crainhem, with four knights, and one representative from each of the towns of Louvain, Brussels, and Antwerp to try all officials, who were suspected of extortions during the general inquest, which, it appears, had not yet been concluded.[17] But there was no progress and complaints continued. On October 4, the duke commissioned four knights, two representatives from Louvain, two from Brussels, and one each from Antwerp, Tirlemont, 's-Hertogenbosch, and Nivelles to proceed with the judgment and punishment of the culpable officials, under the express guarantee that he and his heirs would protect them from any en-

---

[14] *Konigsaaler Geschichts-Quellen,* p. 518.

[15] J. B. Ansems, *Den Luyster ende Glorie van het Hertogdom van Brabant,* Part I, pp. 77–81.

[16] *Ibid.,* pp. 93, 95–97.

[17] J. F. Willems, *Codex Diplomaticus,* I, 792–793; A. Verkooren, *Inventaire, Brabant,* I, 256.

mity they might incur.[18]   Ten days later some changes were
made when the duke consented to the appointment of a commission of six men, two from his council, two from Louvain, and
two from Brussels to receive the contributions which had been
demanded in order to pay the obligations imposed at Amiens
and to make the prescribed payments.[19]   The inquest seems to
have begun almost at once, for a statement of February 1, 1335,
mentions it in the past tense,[20] and on August 2 the duke issued a
statement that the inquest and trial had come to an end.   Baldwin de Wilde was convicted and the judges declared his lands
confiscated.[21]

A large number of documents in the Royal Archives in Brussels
abundantly proves the sincerity and patriotism of the nobles and
bourgeoisie of Brabant.[22]   They had staunchly supported the duke
in his attack upon the seignior of Valkenburg and now for the
same reason consented to heavy taxation.   Not so, however, the
clergy; many of the abbots and abbesses of various opulent monastic establishments in Brabant refused to contribute their share
and complained of what they called the duke's unjust exactions.
So determined were they to uphold the clergy's independence of
the secular power that they appealed to Pope Benedict XII [23]
who on June 30, 1335, issued a bull to the archbishop of Cologne
and the bishops of Cambrai and Laon recounting the alleged aggression [24] and appointing them to investigate the cause of the
complaint.   Nothing was apparently accomplished until May,

[18] C. Piot, " Une Enquête sur la Conduite des Fonctionnaires sous le
Règne de Jean III, Duc de Brabant," *BCRH*, 4th Ser., IX (1881), 54.   The
towns issued a similar decree, see *ibid.*, pp. 60–63, and A. Verkooren,
Inventaire, Brabant, I, 287–289.

[19] C. Piot, " Une Enquête sur la Conduite des Fonctionnaires sous le
Règne de Jean III, Duc de Brabant," *BCRH*, 4th Ser., IX (1881), 54–57;
J. F. Willems, *Codex Diplomaticus,* I, 800; J. B. Ansems, *Den Luyster ende
Glorie van het Hertogdom van Brabant,* Part I, pp. 98–101.

[20] C. Piot, " Une Enquête sur la Conduite des Fonctionnaires sous le
Règne de Jean III, Duc de Brabant," *BCRH*, 4th Ser., IX (1881), 67.

[21] J. F. Willems, *Codex Diplomaticus,* I, 801–802.

[22] A. Verkooren, *Inventaire, Brabant,* I, 290–305.

[23] E. Schoolmeesters, " Recueil des Lettres Adressées, pendant le XIVᵉ
Siècle, aux Papes et aux Cardinaux pour les Affaires de la Principauté de
Liège," *Analectes pour Servir à l'Histoire ecclésiastique de la Belgique,*
XV (1878), 20–21.   The document is not dated.

[24] A. Henne and A. Wauters, *Histoire de Bruxelles,* I, p. 102.

1336, when a recital of the duke's actions was addressed to the pope, who on the 31st begged John to stay his course.[25]

The matter was finally referred to the arbitration of William, count of Hainault, Holland, and Zeeland, who had not ceased to manifest a lively interest in the affairs of Brabant. On November 14, 1334, the duke associated Thierry de Walcourt, marshal of Hainault, with the men appointed to make an inquest of the ducal functionaries,[26] and on the 27th Count William promised to aid in preserving order and government in Brabant in accordance with the privileges granted by the dukes.[27] A year later, October 24, 1335, William decreed that the terms of the charter granted on October 30, 1312, by John II should remain in force.[28] Of the *corvées*, the extraordinary ones should be paid in time of military necessity, but the ordinary ones only periodically.[29] Furthermore, the 1,600 days of these *corvées* still due to the duke were to be paid, and finally, on October 24, 1336, the clergy of Brabant were ordered to contribute 30,000 Florentine florins toward paying the debts incurred in the recent wars.[30]

While Count William was thus intimately concerned with the financial and political problems of Brabant, his friendship with Louis, count of Flanders, continued unabated, as is shown by the latter's coöperation in the transfer to him of the fiefs Flobecq and Lessines by William de Montagne, seignior of Dossemer, negotiations for which had begun early in 1335. In March Count Louis' bailiff of Alost was ordered to arrange the transfer; in November the claims of Gerard, seignior of Grandpré, and his wife, Marguerite de Dossemer, were bought and the final formalities were completed on May 1, 1336.[31] Meanwhile the 35,-

---

[25] For the duke's actions at Parc near Louvain, see A. Fierens, *Lettres de Benoît XII (1334–1342). Textes et Analyses*, No. 176.

[26] F. van Mieris, *Groot Charterboek*, II, 570; L. Devillers, *Monuments*, III, 392–395.

[27] C. Piot, "Une Enquête sur la Conduite des Fonctionnaires sous le Règne de Jean III, Duc de Brabant," *BCRH*, 4th Ser., IX (1881), 59.

[28] *Placcaeten, Ordonnantien, Lant-Charters, Privilegien, ende Instructien* . . . , III, 161–163. E. Dynter, *Chronicon Ducum Brabantiae*, II, 600–605.

[29] Placcaeten, *Ordonnantien, Lant-Charters, Privilegien, ende Instructien* . . . , III, 160; A. Verkooren, *Inventaire, Brabant*, I, 307–308.

[30] A. Verkooren, *Inventaire, Brabant*, I, 309–310.

[31] L. Devillers, *Monuments*, III, 431–434, 442–448.

000 gold *regales* which Count William was to receive from Duke John and to pay Count Louis, in accordance with the terms of the Treaty of Cambrai in 1333, were paid in December, 1335.[32]

These harmonious relations prepared the way for a general understanding between the count of Flanders and the duke of Brabant through the efforts of Count William whose nobles in March, 1336, requested of Louis a conference which was to settle the matters in dispute. The three parties came together at Dendermonde on March 31 to settle the status of Mechelen. Philip had not been able to secure an arrangement; the chapter of St. Lambert was thoroughly dissatisfied with the procedure at Amiens and refused to ask the pope to revoke the oaths made at the moment of the sale [33] and had kept the purchase money paid by Count Louis. The canons voted to use this amount in an attempt to enforce the claims of the bishop of Liège upon the county of Loon in the contest with Thierry of Heinsberg who had taken possession of the county in January upon the death of Count Louis.[34]   Louis, count of Flanders, cannot have been pleased with the suspense and Duke John had no reasons whatever to be satisfied with Philip's policy, for the king had also failed in settling the debate concerning Aiseau with the count of Namur. On December 17, 1334, Philip declared that, inasmuch as his representative, Ferri de Pequigny, and made no progress, he commanded him to return to France, and announced that the disputants would henceforth be directly subject to him in this matter, while the revenues of Aiseau were to be administered by himself.[35]

Without reference to his suzerain's wishes or to those of the pope, Count Louis agreed to a settlement with the duke of the vexatious dispute concerning Mechelen. One half of it was to be held by each and his heirs who were to hold it from the other in fee. The annual appointment of the *scultetus* and *advocatus* was to be made by the count and duke alternately. A receiver was to be named, but in such manner that when the duke appointed the *scultetus* and *advocatus* the count would name him

---

[32] A. Verkooren, *Inventaire, Brabant,* I, pp. 304–305.

[33] See letter of Benedict XII to Philip VI on December 4, 1335, in G. Daumet, *Benoît XII (1334–1342). Lettres Closes, Patentes, et Curiales se rapportant à la France,* No. 125.

[34] Hocsemius, p. 430.

[35] C. Piot, *Inventaires des Chartes des Comtes de Namur,* p. 166.

and vice versa. Neither was to coin money or erect fortresses in Mechelen without the consent of the other. Joint efforts were to be made in case the town should refuse obedience to either party.

The seigniory of the Schelde, which extended upstream as far as that river was navigable, was to remain in the count's possession, save at Antwerp where for both high and low justice the scabini were to give him annually a pair of gold spurs. All customary rights enjoyed by merchants and fishers, and also those in force at fords, were to remain as before. Clauses dealing with tolls, the pursuit of criminals, flotsam and jetsam, and the seigniory of the Ruppel upstream to Eyckenvliet were also added. Each party was bound to protect the land and subjects of the other, and made the usual arrangements for arbitration.[36] It is impossible to find any agreement made at this time regarding the financial settlement which it would seem this new arrangement about Mechelen necessitated. But eleven years later Count Louis renounced his rights to the seigniory and *advocatia* in return for **86,500** *regales* which was approximately half the purchase price of these titles secured by his father.[37] As nothing was said in 1347 about the payment for the half of these rights which the duke now received, it appears that satisfaction in some form was given.

These arrangements were followed by a treaty of alliance between Count William, Count Louis, and Duke John on April 1. They agreed to work for the peace, protection, and general welfare of each other's lands and subjects. Commerce was to be safeguarded. At the request of any one of the contracting parties the other two were to appear with **10,000** foot and **500** horse. In case of serious difficulties or questions touching the interests of the neighbors, the representatives of the lands concerned were to meet at certain specified places near the border. In especially grave cases, three men chosen from each of the towns of Brabant, of Hainault, Holland, and Zeeland, and of Flanders were to be associated with these three representatives.[38]

[36] J. David, *Geschiedenis van de Stad en Heerlykheid van Mechelen, Bylagen,* No. XVIII, pp. 501–505; F. J. Willems, *Codex Diplomaticus,* II, 441–454.

[37] *Archives Nationales,* Paris, No. J523, no. 14 *bis.*

[38] L. P. C. van den Bergh, *Gedenkstukken tot Opheldering der Nederlandsche Geschiedenis,* I, 134–158.

II. The Flight of Robert of Artois to England
(Spring, 1334–1337)

THE numerous connections of Edward III in the Low Countries, the splendid example of chivalry and courtesy at his court,[39]
and the growing prestige of his father-in-law, Count William,
greatly enhanced English influence in these parts. When the report of important victories over the Scots at Berwick and at Halidon Hill in 1333 was circulated, many an admirer and friend became zealous to serve under him.[40] Among such was Robert of
Artois who no doubt reasoned that Edward as enemy of the Scots
must needs also be hostile to his own mortal enemy, King Philip
of France.

Constrained to leave Brabant when the duke came to an understanding with Philip, this prince covertly passed from castle
to castle in the south of the duchy, without doubt at the connivance of the duke.[41] He tarried with the seignior of Boxtel
for a time, asked the *advocatus* of Huy for someone to guide him
in those parts where he was a stranger, and took into his service
the former's chaplain, the Trinitarian Henry de Sagebran, to
whom he assigned an annual pension of a hundred and twenty
florins until a suitable prebend should be found. The friar, however, refused at this moment to go into France in Robert's service,
and the matter was accordingly entrusted to a canon named Em-
reit. Since Robert was weary from his wanderings, the *advocatus* assigned him his relative's castle at Argenteau.[42] Forced
to leave at the end of three months by some remarks, said to be
of a slanderous nature, he proceeded, at the advice of the *advocatus*, by night to Sartir, a half league from Huy and in the
territory of the bishop of Liège, took refuge in the castle of his

[39] Le Bel, I, 105; J. H. Ramsay, *Genesis of Lancaster and the three
Reigns of Edward I, Edward II, and Edward III*, I, 224–225.

[40] Le Bel, I, 114.

[41] Launcelot, " Mémoires pour Servir à l'Histoire de Robert d'Artois,"
*Mémoires de Littérature tiréz des Registres de l'Académie Royale des
Inscriptions et Belles Lettres*, X (1736), 622; le Bel, I, 98.

[42] Launcelot, " Mémoires pour Servir à l'Histoire de Robert d'Artois,"
*Mémoires de Littérature tiréz des Registres de l'Académie Royale des
Inscriptions et Belles Lettres*, X (1736), 622. According to le Bel, I, 92, it
was at the connivance of the duke. Cf. Froissart, I, 101.

valet Berthelot, and begged his nephew John II, count of Namur, for admission into his territory. Sanson was assigned him as a temporary residence, and upon the count's return Robert secretly moved into his castle in Namur.[43]

Robert's machinations in Namur greatly aroused the fury of Philip VI. Efforts in June, 1336, to kill the latter by some magical writings in red and black naturally failed. Thereupon he hired assassins to go to Paris to perform the deed and put out of the way also the duke of Burgundy, now possessor of Artois, the chancellor Peter Forget, the marshal le Trie, and the count of Bar, all of whom were bitterly opposed to him. Accompanied by friar Henry, the assassins passed through Cambrai where they were informed that they might find the count of Bar at a feast at Rheims. Thither they went, but learned that their plans had become known to the king, who had been apprised of them, it was said, by the *advocatus* of Huy, and they forthwith retraced their steps to Namur.

In September Robert made a secret trip into France with a few companions and returned in a fortnight after a visit with his wife.[44] He talked volubly about his being a favorite among the people of Paris, of the king's indebtedness to him for his crown, and of how basely he had been requited, and said that his friends in Paris were willing to lend him a vast sum, apparently to undo the king.[45] In October he sought to kill the king and queen by piercing to the heart the baptized waxen images that had been made of them.[46] These efforts were soon known to Philip as they were fully divulged when his officials seized friar Henry and John Aimery, a priest who had gone to France on some dark mission in Robert's behalf. They made a full confession on January 31, 1334.[47] Suspicion fell upon Robert's wife; it was said that she

[43] Hocsemius, p. 407.

[44] Launcelot, " Mémoires pour Servir à l'Histoire de Robert d'Artois," *Mémoires de Littérature tiréz des Registres de l'Académie Royale des Inscriptions et Belles Lettres,* X (1736), 622–627; *Chronique Parisienne Anonyme,* pp. 157–158.

[45] *Chronique Parisienne Anonyme,* pp. 157–159.

[46] Launcelot, " Mémoires pour Servir à l'Histoire de Robert d'Artois," *Mémoires de Littérature tiréz des Registres de l'Académie Royale des Inscriptions et Belles Lettres,* X (1736), 627–629.

[47] *Chronique Parisienne Anonyme,* pp. 156–157. These events are here assigned to the weeks after Easter.

and her sons also had tried to kill the king and queen by means of magic, and they too were placed in confinement.[48] With fierce brutality the king now proceeded against the fugitive. He sent envoys to Namur who, accompanied by men of the bishop of Liège, appeared before the count's bailiffs. But the officers were loath to give him up and pretended that they knew nothing of his whereabouts. They offered to search for him, but the bishop distrusted them and placed them in prison for a time. Meanwhile the fugitive disappeared.[49]

In the meantime the war against the duke of Brabant had broken out in full fury and the situation may well have seemed serious to Robert, who was entirely homeless and friendless when the truce was arranged in March. The count of Flanders was loyal to his suzerain and hostile to Robert who had connived with the Flemish malcontents. William, count of Hainault, Holland, and Zeeland, outwardly at least friendly to Philip, was unsafe, as also were the counts of Guelders, Juliers, and Loon, and the archbishop of Cologne. The bishop of Liège, who was an active partisan of Philip, and the duke of Brabant, now engaged in a desperate struggle with his allied enemies, were not to be relied upon. In great secrecy, therefore, during the spring of 1334 he fled, disguised as a merchant, to the court of Edward III and was honorably received.[50]

The question of the date of Robert's flight can be decided only in a circumstantial way. French tradition later represented this as having taken place as early as March, 1334.[51] John le Bel states that when the count of Namur and his brothers went to Edward's aid against the Scots in the spring of 1335 they were chiefly influenced in this by their hope of seeing their uncle, " for

---

[48] *Grandes Chroniques*, V, 356; *Chronographia*, II, 35–36; J. Viard, *Les Journaux du Trésor de Philippe VI*, pp. 139, 473.

[49] Hocsemius, p. 408 (paged as 402): "Deinde rex Franciae legatos mittit cum episcopo Leodiensi ad Namurcenses, requirendo quatenus dominum Robertum traderent, et locum tenentes comitis, qui tunc absens erat, alioquin ipsos rex et Leodiensis episcopus diffidabant: qui negantes ipsum ibi fore, patientiam praestant ipsum ubilibet perquirendi; locum tenentes vero captivitatem episcopi usque ad certum terminum intraverunt; et deinceps, quo Robertus, devenerit, ignoretur."

[50] Le Bel, I, 99–100, 107–108; Boendale, *Van den derden Eduwaert*, p. 350.

[51] *Grandes Chroniques*, V, 357; *Istore et Croniques*, I, 352, 354.

they knew full well that he was in splendid station in the entourage of Edward." [52] Considering the situation in the Low Countries in the spring of 1334, it would seem most convincing to place the flight at about Easter of that year.

What influence, if any, did Robert of Artois exert upon the growing hostility between Edward III and Philip VI? In the Low Countries it was the belief of contemporary observers that it was considerable. This view, expressed by John le Bel and the Bourgeois of Valenciennes,[53] is more fully emphasized in the chronicles embodying the tradition of the Valois court according to which Robert actively labored to aggravate the hostility by urging warlike measures.[54] Of the English chronicles, however, Avesbury, Murimuth, Hemingburgh, Melsa, Baker,[55] the *Chronicle of Lanercost,* and the later *Chronicon Angliae,* are totally silent on this point. On the other hand, little of a documentary nature is available which can elucidate the extent of his influence. In 1335 he was apparently close to Edward [56] and in the next year accompanied him on the expedition against the Scots.[57] But positive proof of his evil endeavor is furnished by a letter of November 22, 1336, which the pope, Benedict XII, wrote to Edward in which he complained that his friendship for the fugitive greatly interfered with the peace of France and England, for Philip could not consider proposals without suspicion so long as Robert stayed at his court.[58]

Not until 1337 is there any record of much financial support given to Robert by the English king. On April 23, Edward as-

[52] Le Bel, I, 114–115.

[53] *Ibid.,* pp. 99–100, 120; Outremeuse, VI, 595; *Bourgeois de Valenciennes,* pp. 156–157.

[54] *Istore et Croniques,* I, 352, 354; *Grandes Chroniques,* V, p. 367; de Nangis, II, 157, 182, 196, where William, count of Hainault, Holland, and Zeeland, is accused of the same thing.

[55] Baker, p. 70 (*sub* 1340): "Ad regem nempe confugit, petens auxilium contra tirannum Francorum, qui possessiones patrum suorum in Artosia et Brabancia detinuit iniuste; unde rex eius homagio auxilium spopondit et prebuit eidem."

[56] Le Bel, I, 114–115.

[57] *CPR* (1334–8), pp. 322, 327. Order to John de Pulteney, citizen of London, to pay him 500 marks.

[58] G. Daumet, *Benoît XII* (*1334–1342*). *Lettres Closes, Patentes et Curiales se rapportant à la France,* No. 242; W. H. Bliss, *Calendar of Entries in the Papal Registers,* II, 561–562.

signed him the castles of Guildford, Wallingford, and Somerton, and on May 5 an annual pension of 1,200 marks.[59]   According to John le Bel [60] he received the earldom of Richmond. This, however, was in the possession of John de Bretagne, who died in 1334, and who had granted it on November 7, 1333, to his niece, Marie of St. Pol, wife of the earl of Pembroke, for life in return for an annual sum of 1,000*l.* sterling.[60a] The titles in question did not pass into Robert's hands at all. In 1341 the earldom was given to John, count of Montfort, whose candidature for the Breton inheritance Edward then championed.[60b] While the evidence from English sources is thus quite scanty, it is nevertheless certain, especially in view of Pope Benedict's letter of November 22, 1336, that Robert's presence did embitter Philip who dispatched several letters to Edward, as he stated to the pope on December 26, in which he cited him to appear and answer for his conduct.[61]

The famous *Vow of the Heron* purports to set forth a dramatic occasion which opened the war between Edward and Philip. It describes a meeting in London in September, 1338, when Robert taunted Edward for not pressing his claims upon the throne of France. There were present the queen, the earls of Salisbury, Derby, and Suffolk, Walter de Manny, John of Valkenburg, and John of Hainault, all of whom answered the dramatic challenge with the most fearful oaths.[62] It would be futile to point out the gross anachronisms in this poem which should be regarded merely as an interesting example of the strange blending of chivalrous vows with characteristic ascetic and erotic *motifs* so very common at that time.[63] The historical elements have but slight, if

[59] *Foedera,* II(2), 967, 969; Kervyn, *Oeuvres de Froissart,* II, 523, and XX, 179–182; Baker, p. 170.

[60] Le Bel, I, 99–100.

[60a] *Rymer,* II(2), 873; *CPR* (1330–4), p. 484; I. Lubimenko, *Jean de Bretagne, Comte de Richmond. Sa Vie et son Activité en Angleterre, en Écosse, et en France (1266–1334),* p. 134; *Dictionary of National Biography,* II, pp. 288–290.   [60b] *Foedera,* II(2), 1176.

[61] E. Déprez, *Les Préliminaires de la Guerre de Cent Ans (Pièces Justificatives),* No. VI.

[62] For text, see T. Wright, *Political Poems and Songs Relating to English History, Composed during the Period from the Accession of Edward III to that of Richard III,* I, 1–25, and " Les Voeux du Héron," *Société des Bibliophiles de Mons,* III (1839).

[63] On this point, see J. Huizinga, *Herfsttij der Middeleeuwen,* pp. 139–140.

any, value.[64] From internal evidence it is clear that the poem was written after 1339 or 1340. It probably appeared in the chivalrous circles of Hainault which were of course fully acquainted with the story of Robert's bitterness toward Philip. The tradition that Robert's enmity was the chief cause of the war grew up among a chivalry which would characteristically ascribe great consequences to such personal differences. This story was popularized by Froissart who thus created the traditional view [65] which has come down to the present day through such writers as Fabyan and Holinshed.[66]

III. The Scotch Campaign (1335)

THE crisis in the relations of King Edward and the Scots in the summer of 1335, when the truce which had been arranged in April of that year terminated on June 24, was a serious matter for the relations of England and France and the repose of Christendom in which of course the Low Countries would be intimately concerned.[67] Even before the expiration of the truce both parties were preparing for the struggle. The pope, already disquieted perhaps by the presence of Robert of Artois in England, was greatly alarmed by the attitude of princes in Germany,[68] especially, it appears, when he heard of the preparations of some princes in the Low Countries to go to Edward's aid. On July 31 he communicated his fears to Philip and to Queen Philippa, begged that peace be preserved, and sent Hugh, bishop of St. Paul-Trois-Châteaux, and Roland d'Asti, a canon of Laon, to labor for peace.[69]

[64] See E. Déprez, *Les Préliminaires de la Guerre de Cent Ans*, p. 225, who correctly rejected it as apocryphal, although G. Monod refused to go so far. See *Revue Historique*, LXXX (1902), 100. See also T. Wright, *Political Poems and Songs Relating to English History, Composed during the Period from the Accession of Edward III to that of Richard III, Introduction*, I, XV. [65] Froissart, I, 119.

[66] R. Fabyan, *The New Chronicles of England and France*, ed. by H. Ellis (London, 1811), pp. 444, 491; R. Holinshed, *Chronicles of Scotland and Ireland*, II (London, 1807), 605.

[67] *Foedera*, II (2), pp. 910, 911. See Baker, p. 57; Fordun, p. 358.

[68] S. Reizler, *Vatikanische Akten*, No. 1729.

[69] G. Daumet, *Benoît XII (1334–1342). Lettres Closes, Patentes et Curiales se rapportant à la France*, Nos. 89, 90; S. Riezler, *Vatikansche Akten*, p. 591; H. Bliss, *Registers of Entries in the Papal Registers*, II, 560.

Guy, count of Namur, and his brother Philip went to England to join Edward by way of Wissant, Dover, and London, and finally arrived at Newcastle where on the first night they were " lodged in an ancient town known in the days of the Round Table of King Arthur as the ' Castle of Maidens.' " [70]   When at Carlisle on July 11, Edward had ordered his sheriffs to aid them with carriages, ships, and other necessaries for their journey. William, count of Juliers, Edward's brother-in-law, also came with a hundred men-at-arms. [71]   Herman Blankaerd, provost of the cathedral of Aix-la-Chapelle, was with him. [72]   On June 12 Edward had requested his officials at Kingston-upon-Hull to get ready at that place a ship loaded with victuals for them and for others who might come from parts subject to the count of Juliers, [73] and on July 1 issued a safe-conduct to last until All Saints' Day. [74] The count's marshal, Theodoric Schinmann, arrived alone, and on June 15 was granted safe-conduct until Michaelmas. He was hurrying northward to meet his master who was coming by water, [75] and arrived in Edward's presence at Carlisle on July 12. [76] Two days later Edward showed his appreciation by extending his special protection to the merchants of the count's dominions who traded in England. [77]

Less important personages also came to aid Edward. Among them was the yeoman John de Thrandeston from Cologne, who was later to prove an invaluable envoy for Edward in the negotiations with the princes of the Low Countries. He was retained by the royal command from June 20 until September 11, contrary to the express wishes of the magistrates of the corporation of Cologne. [78] On August 8 seven individuals from Burgundy were given safe-conduct until September 29. [79] Henry de Montfaucon, count of Mömpelgard, was also given letters of protection on the

[70] Le Bel, II, 115.

[71] *Rotuli Scotiae*, I, 362; *Melsa*, II, 374–375; *Lanercost*, p. 281.

[72] *Foedera*, II (2), 927.   [74] *Ibid.*, p. 358; Foedera, II (2), 912.

[73] *Rotuli Scotiae*, I, 354.   [75] *Foedera*, II (2), 910.

[76] *Lanercost*, p. 281. The chronicles refer to Juliers as " Guelders," a confusion which apparently arose from the similarity of " Juliacensis " and " Gelrensis."   [77] *CPR* (1334–8), p. 153.

[78] *Ibid.* He had been in England in 1331 in the company of Thomas Roscelyn. See *CCR* (1330–3), p. 288.

[79] *CPR* (1334–8), p. 161. They are Louis, John, and Erold Dagymont, Henry de Wallehayng, Walter de Houeffe, John de Los, and Godfrey de Hardewemont. See *CCR* (1333–7), p. 518.

30th.[80] At the same moment, William, count of Hainault, Holland, and Zeeland, had a diplomatic agent in England.[81] When one considers the powerful influence of the latter in the Low Countries and that of the count of Juliers in the Rhineland, where he exercised more influence perhaps than any other secular prince, one need not wonder at the pope's solicitude.[82]

The campaign which followed was of slight consequence. Edward divided his forces into two divisions; one under his own command which was accompanied by the count of Juliers advanced through Annandale toward Stirling,[83] and the other, led by Edward Balliol, proceeded from Berwick through Clydesdale toward Perth, where both forces were to meet. In a third division, which was conducted by some English guides and soldiers, came the men of the count of Namur. As they were approaching Edinburgh they found themselves quite suddenly surrounded at Boroughmuir by a force of Scots headed by the Regent Moray, Douglas, and Ramsey.[84] Forced to seek refuge in the dilapidated castle at Edinburgh, the breaches of which they filled with the bodies of their slain horses, they were hard pressed. They sought to slake their thirst by licking the dew; their provisions were soon exhausted, and, overcome with the cold, they were compelled to surrender on July 20.[85] Moray wanted to please Philip VI, from whose presence he had recently returned, and deemed it politic to conduct the count of Namur and his forces, including the Englishmen, back to Berwick.[86] But on his return he was seized at Roxburgh by Edward's follower, William de Preston.[87]

[80] *Foedera*, II(2), 921. For him see E. Clerc, *Essai sur l'Histoire de la Franche-Comté*, II, 46.

[81] *CCR* (1333–7), p. 526. See William's concessions to English merchants on October 11 in P. L. Muller, *Regesta Hannonensia*, p. 234.

[82] S. Riezler, *Vatikanische Akten*, No. 919.

[83] *Lanercost*, p. 281; *Melsa*, II, 374–375.

[84] *Auctor Bridlingtoniensis*, 123; *Melsa*, II, p. 375.

[85] *Lanercost*, p. 282; *Melsa*, II, 375; *Scalacronica*, II, 319; Wyntoun, II, 419–420; Fordun, I, 359; *Liber Pluscardensis*, I, 278–279; *Grandes Chroniques*, V, 363; Lescot, p. 39; de Nangis, II, 148–150; le Bel, II, 114–117.

[86] Guy of Namur, Raoul, seignior d'Aubigny, and his uncle William advanced a sum of 4,000*l.* as ransom for the English. See C. E. Niffle-Anciaux, "Guy II de Namur," *Annales de la Société Archéologique de Namur*, XVIII(1889), 317; *Scalacronica*, p. 165; Wyntoun, II, 420. The men of Namur were allowed to go without ransom. Only one was retained, William, the seignior of Grochee. See *CPR* (1334–5), p. 500.

[87] *Auctor Bridlingtoniensis*, p. 123; *Lanercost*, p. 288; Fordun, I, 358;

From Berwick the count of Namur with his household and followers, accompanied by Queen Philippa,[88] went by sea to Perth, where he was cordially received by the king who presented the count's brother Philip with choice and costly gifts on August 3.[89] The more important followers were rewarded on the 20th. Forty marks were given to the seignior of Karendon, twenty to the seignior of Walcourt, ten to the seignior of Licherolles, gold and silver articles valued at more than twelve marks to Thierry of Walcourt, and forty shillings to a clerk, John de Bovyne. The approaching marriage of Blanche of Namur, sister of Count Guy, to Magnus, king of Norway, gave Edward another opportunity to show his good will in a concrete way. On the 20th he took her and her fleet, which the count had been assembling at Sluis and neighboring ports to conduct her to Norway, under his special protection and ordered his admirals, sheriffs, and other officials to lend all possible aid. In recognition of Count Guy's services, two days later he granted to him and his heirs two hundred marks annually in fee on condition of service with as many as two hundred men-at-arms at the royal expense against all save the duke of Brabant and the counts of Hainault, Flanders, and Guelders. Order was issued to the treasurers on the 27th to pay two hundred marks, the first instalment of Guy's pension, and three days later at York, when preparations were made for return to the Low Countries, an additional sum of 12*l.* 7*s.* 9*d.* to cover his expenses.[90]

The count of Juliers was shown every possible courtesy. Edward ordered the treasurer on September 19 to pay him fifty pounds for the expenses of his household [91] and four days later instructed his officials to aid him on his return voyage.[92] But important diplomatic matters were under consideration and the count tarried in England while his household returned to the Low Countries.[93]

Grandes Chroniques, V, 363; Lescot, p. 39; *Liber Pluscardensis*, I, 279; F. Devon, *Issues of the Exchequer: Henry III and Henry IV*, p. 142.

[88] *Scalacronica*, p. 165.   [90] *Ibid.*, pp. 919–921.

[89] *Foedera*, II (2), 916.   [91] *Ibid.*, p. 922; *CPR* (1334–8), p. 166.

[92] *CPR* (1334–8), p. 188. On September 18 William of Juliers appointed Tidemannus Mayemburgh attorney to receive his pension. Cf. *CCR* (1333–7), p. 441.

[93] *Foedera*, II (2), 926.

The truce which Edward had made with the Scots at Perth on August 18 was, as everybody knew, not to last long. The pope, eager to avert a rupture between Edward and Philip, sought to induce the English and Scots to cease their hostilities. At the solicitation of the papal envoys, the bishop of St. Paul-Trois-Châteaux, and Roland d'Asti, with whom Philip's agents appeared, Edward on November 1 appointed William de Montague, Robert de Ufford, and Ralph de Neville to negotiate with the Regent Moray. A truce was arranged, to expire on November 26, which was repeatedly extended to December 3, Christmas, January 25, 1336, January 31, April 14, and finally to June 9, when hostilities were reopened.[94] During all this time there was little faith between Edward and Philip, and the latter's apparent support of the Scots in retaliation against Edward's attitude regarding Aquitaine seemed to forecast a serious quarrel.

The situation in the empire, where in April, 1335, Henry, duke of Carinthia, had died and the Hapsburgs, supported by the Wittelsbachs, were arrayed against the Luxemburg party in a struggle over the heritage, now became important.[95] Edward seemed to think that an alliance with Otto, duke of Austria, might be useful, since, in a struggle with Philip, John of Bohemia as head of the Luxemburg faction might throw his support to France. Accordingly, on July 18 he empowered John de Shoreditch and William Trussel to treat with him for a matrimonial connection between the duke's son and his own daughter, Johanna.[96] These agents did not return until the close of October.[97] Meanwhile there were discussions of the political situation, and it was decided that the count of Juliers with Shoreditch and Trussel should broach the subject of alliances with Walram, archbishop of Cologne, Reginald, count of Guelders, and John, duke of Brabant.[98] The instructions of July 18 were reissued, this time to Shoreditch and William FitzWaryn.[99] The

[94] *Ibid.*, pp. 925, 926, 928, 930–931, 933, 938; Avesbury, pp. 298, 300; Murimuth, pp. 76–77.

[95] F. von Krones, *Handbuch der Geschichte Oesterreichs von den Ältesten bis zur neuesten Zeit,* II, 125–126; E. Werunsky, *Geschichte Kaiser Karls IV und seiner Zeit,* I, 121–122.

[96] *Foedera,* II (2), 915.

[97] *CCR* (1333–7), pp. 437, 446.

[98] See letters of December 18, *Foedera,* II (2), 928.

[99] *Ibid.*, p. 929.

count of Juliers was then ready to depart. On December 12, Edward presented to him 206*l.* 13*s.* 4*d.*; to Herman Blankaerd, provost of Aix-la-Chapelle, 100 marks; and to Matthew Stumble and a companion, 20*l.* At the moment of departure they each received an enameled and gilded silver cup and other costly gifts; two palfreys were given to the count and countess.[100]   William de Clinton, constable of Dover Castle and warden of the Cinque Ports, was ordered to provide ships for the passage from Dover to Wissant.[101]

IV. The Rupture between King Edward III and Louis, Count of Flanders (1335 — October, 1336)

The better relations between Edward, king of England, and the Flemings which followed the arrangements of March 23, 1334,[102] provided but a brief respite. Difficulties over matters of trade soon arose, and in March of the following year Simon de Stanes was sent to Flanders as representative of the king.[103] Later Blok de Steenlant and delegates from Bruges, Ghent, and Ypres agreed with John de Hildesle, now baron of the Exchequer, and William de la Pole, king's merchant from Hull,[104] that all questions in dispute should be settled by proctors appointed by Edward and Count Louis by Pentecost.[105] On May 16 William was appointed [106] with John de Causton, William Fox,[107] and William de Preston to meet the Flemings [108] at Bruges.[109]

The delegates agreed to a truce which was to begin on June 15 and last until Christmas of 1336. Each prince was to guarantee that the subjects of the other could come in full freedom to buy,

---

[100] See letters of December 18, *Foedera,* II (2), pp. 927–928.

[101] *CCR* (1333–7), p. 535.

[102] *Foedera,* II (2), 884–885.

[103] *CCR* (1333–7), 473.

[104] *Foedera,* II (2), 907.

[105] *CPR* (1334–8), 103.

[106] *CCR* (1337–7), 416–417, 419.

[107] L. Mirot, et E. Déprez, "Les Ambassades Anglaises pendant la Guerre de Cent Ans," *BEC,* LIX (1898), 562; *Foedera,* II (2), 907. On May 22 the king ordered William de Preston to hasten to Flanders. Cf. *CCR* (1333–7), pp. 486–487.

[108] *Foedera,* II (2), 908.

[109] J. Vuylsteke, *Gentsche Stads- en Baljuwsrekeningen, 1280–1336,* II. 966–967.

sell, or trade in the land of the other.[110] Specific points in the indentures drawn up by the deputies on both sides were not easily adjusted and William Fox finally crossed the North Sea and agreed with the count's representatives to settle the matter by a fortnight after Easter, 1336. Edward approved the treaty at Carlisle on July 10, and on August 16 commanded his sheriffs and officials to proclaim the terms at all ports.[111] To Count Louis and the three towns he indicated his intention of carrying out the terms in good faith and suggested that " if any injury should be inflicted by his subjects, the treaty would not be dissolved on that account, that speedy remedy would be applied, and prayed that the Flemings would act in the same manner." [112]

But relations between Flanders and England were intimately bound up with the larger problem of the relations between Edward and Philip. The Scots were known to have the sympathy of the French king, and in March, 1336, rumor had it that they were making alliances with foreigners — no doubt the French — and Edward on the 15th ordered his lieges to arrest ships of forty tons burden.[113] On March 7 Philip declared Robert of Artois an enemy of the realm [114] and complained of Edward's friendship for the fugitive.[115] On February 16 all men in England between the ages of sixteen and sixty were ordered by the sheriffs to hold themselves in readiness for the defense of the realm.

Edward's attention was so engrossed that when the date for the negotiations with the Flemings drew near he found it impossible to give the matter thought and on March 20 begged Count Louis and his towns to postpone the meeting until June 24.[116] The outlook for peace was very gloomy and Philip was loath to go on the crusade in view of Edward's hostility, so on March 13 the

---

[110] *Foedera,* II (2), 918; *CPR* (1334–8), p. 197.

[111] *CPR* (1334–8), pp. 164, 197.

[112] *Foedera,* II (2), 918. For a subsequent proclamation on October 10, see *CCR* (1333–7), p. 510.

[113] *CCR* (1333–7), p. 658.

[114] *Recueil Général des Anciennes Lois Françaises dépuis l'An 420 jusqu'à la Révolution de 1789,* IV, 428.

[115] G. Daumet, *Benoît XII (1334–1342). Lettres Closes, Patentes et Curiales se rapportant à la France,* No. 242; H. Bliss, *Calendar of Entries in the Papal Registers,* II, 561–562.

[116] *Foedera,* II (2), 931, 935. He did, however, send William Fox and John de Percebrigg on March 25. See *CCR* (1333–7), p. 600.

pope reluctantly consented to a postponement.[117]   Edward was seeking to strengthen himself in Spain.   On June 14, 1335, he had sent Bernard, seignior of Albret, William FitzWaryn, and Gerard du Puy to the court of Alfonso, king of Castile, to propose a marriage between the latter's son Pedro and Edward's eldest daughter Isabella and to suggest closer relations.   Alfonso, however, evaded the proposal of a matrimonial alliance, but expressed himself eager for closer friendship, for which Edward thanked him on March 3, 1336, and urged him to send envoys for the negotiations.   Later, on June 3, Gilles de Ispannia was sent to Alfonso, king of Portugal and Algarve, to discuss matters of interest to Edward.[118]

Besides diplomatic efforts, Edward turned to his people for aid in the impending breach with Philip.   The clergy, barons, knights of the shire, and the burgesses were summoned to Westminster in March and consented to raise a tenth and a fifteenth.[119]   But the real sinews of war were to be provided by the manipulation of the wool of the realm, and in order to secure a monopoly of it Edward consulted the merchants who finally met at Northampton toward the close of June.[120]   They agreed to the king's suggestions not to permit any export of wool, hides, or woolfells.   On August 12 the officials of London and fifteen other towns were instructed to surrender their cocket seals to the mayor and four lawful men in each.[121]

On September 23 a group of the more important merchants met at Nottingham apparently along with Parliament.   A subsidy of forty shillings payable by denizens and sixty shillings by foreigners was granted and also a second tenth and fifteenth.[122]   Upon the strength of the earlier acts of the Parliament, Paul de Monte Florum and Lawrence Fastolf, canons of Lincoln and

---

[117] S. Riezler, *Vatikansche Akten*, No. 1782.

[118] *Foedera*, II (2), 909, 932; *CCR* (1333–7), pp. 649, 678.

[119] *Report on the Dignity of a Peer*, IV, 454; Murimuth, p. 77.

[120] *Report on the Dignity of a Peer*, IV, 458–460; *CCR* (1333–7), pp. 674, 677.   A meeting had been planned to be held at Oxford on the morrow of Trinity Sunday.   Cf. also *Lanercost*, p. 288; Knighton, I, 476; *Melsa*, III, 379; Baker, pp. 58–59; Murimuth, p. 81.

[121] *CCR* (1333–7), p. 700; *Foedera*, II (2), 943–944.

[122] *CPR* (1334–8), p. 322; Knighton, I, 477; *Scalacronica*, p. 102; *Lanercost*, p. 289; F. R. Barnes, "The Taxation on Wool, 1327–1348," *Finance and Trade under Edward III by Members of the History School*, pp. 143–144.

London, were empowered on July 15 to raise for the king's needs
various sums amounting to 200,000*l*.[123] Meanwhile difficulties between the men of the Cinque Ports and those of Calais and Wissant began to imperil the Straits of Dover for sailors, and on
June 12 Edward thought it necessary to take strong measures.[124]
English sailors had trouble in Normandy and it was difficult to
secure redress.[125] The priors of alien monasteries were forbidden
to take wealth out of the realm [126] and on August 20 the seneschal
of Gascony, Oliver de Ingham, was ordered to send ships to intercept subjects trading with the Scots.[127] The admirals of the
fleets were commanded on August 5 to remain at sea and intercept the galleys which were reported to be on the way to succor
the Scots, and on November 27 the keepers of Devon were ordered to be vigilant in preventing hostile incursions.[128]

Edward's monopoly of the wool of his realm is explained chiefly
by his desire to have sufficient resources to carry on the struggle
and to prevent the wool from going out to aid his enemy. It also
was of great diplomatic importance in his efforts to secure allies
in the Low Countries, as the next few years were to prove. Louis,
count of Flanders, since the division of Mechelen between himself and John, duke of Brabant, had thought of means to legitimatize this arrangement. Philip had suggested to Benedict in
March, 1336, that the sale should be confirmed or else revoked.
But the pope felt that such confirmation could not take place
without a hearing from the canons of St. Lambert and the count
of Flanders. To cancel the sale would require a preliminary
study of the terms of the contract made at the time of the transaction and neither party had given him any chance to study its
legality. Thus he wrote on April 5 and suggested that for the
moment Mechelen should remain in the hands of Philip.[129]

Count Louis was in Avignon on May 9 and 10 ostensibly to con-

[123] *CPR* (1334–8), p. 260.

[124] *Ibid.*, p. 395; *CCR* (1333–7), pp. 43–45. See *Foedera*, II (2), 943.

[125] *CCR* (1333–7), p. 53.

[126] *Ibid.*, pp. 683–684.

[127] *Foedera*, II (2), 944.

[128] *CCR* (1333–7), pp. 693, 697, 723.

[129] G. Daumet, *Benoît XII (1334–1342). Lettres Closes, Patentes et
Curiales se rapportant à la France*, No. 155; S. Riezler, *Vatikansche Akten*,
No. 1787; A. Fierens, *Lettres de Benoît XII (1334–1342)*, No. 270.

gratulate the pope on his election, but really to explain his position in regard to Mechelen and his relations with the duke of Brabant, and to secure the papal approval of the transaction of March 31 at Dendermonde. On the 10th these matters were discussed in secret council, but the pope insisted that the question could not be considered because the other parties interested in Mechelen — the chapter, the corporation of Mechelen, Philip, and the duke of Brabant — were all absent. He also urged him not to press the matter and to remember Philip's service to Flanders as, for example, at Cassel in 1328. The repose of Christendom demanded that no trouble should be stirred up in the Low Countries, and Count Louis agreed.[130] Thereupon the latter in July joined Philip who had likewise visited Avignon and afterwards had endeavored to establish peace in Burgundy, where Duke Eudes had much difficulty with his vassals.[131]

While Count Louis was thus on friendly terms with his suzerain, his relations with Edward became strained, and sooner or later he would be forced to make a choice. Edward, it is said, requested an alliance which Louis, ever faithful to Philip, refused.[132] While no proof can be found that such an offer was actually made at this time, it is by no means improbable. The order from Perth on August 12 laying a stringent embargo upon the export of wool, hides, and woolfells may thus have had a diplomatic as well as an economic motive. Louis apparently took Philip's side in the controversy and his sympathy for him was seemingly reflected in the seizure and confiscation of the goods of Richard de Barkendale of York by the scabini of Ghent and of the ship of William Reyngeld of Orwell which was taken as a prize to Sluis.[133] Edward, however, showed no hostility and labored to

[130] J. de St. Genois, " Relation des Voyages de Louis de Nevers à Avignon," *Messager des Siences et des Arts Historiques* (1846), pp. 73–77; A. Fierens, *Lettres de Benoît XII (1334–1342)*, No. 288; G. Daumet, *Benoît XII (1334–1342). Lettres Closes, Patentes, et Curiales, se rapportant à la France*, No. 178. Louis' chancellor, Guillaume d'Auxonne, was with him. See le Muisit, p. 108 (*sub* 1335).

[131] De Nangis, II, 151–153; Lescot, pp. 40–41; *Grandes Chroniques*, V, 364–365; E. Petit, *Histoire des Ducs de Bourgogne*, VII, 145–146, and his *Pièces Justificatives* in the same volume, p. 153; N. de Pauw en J. Vuylsteke, *Rekeningen der Stad Gent*, I, 67.

[132] *Chronographia*, II, 42.

[133] *CCR* (1333–7), pp. 327–328; *CCR* (1337–9), pp. 43–45, 74.

secure redress as he had announced in the previous year. The men of Hellevoetsluis in the county of Holland, erroneously thought by Edward's officials to be in Flanders, were given special protection out of consideration for Guy, count of Namur, who was closely related to Count Louis, provided that they would not trade with the Scots.[134] Guy was also besought on October 6 to intercede for Jordan de Staunford, a sergeant of William Tonnok, who was king's mariner from Newcastle. The former had been incarcerated by the scabini at Sluis when he had ventured to show opposition to some " injuries offered the king and his subjects." Edward asked Guy to bring the matter before Count Louis and secure at least tender treatment.[135]

Open rupture developed by October. The arrest of Barkendale and Reyngeld was not an isolated matter, for English goods were quite generally seized and merchants remanded to jail.[136] Edward retaliated forthwith and on October 5 ordered the sheriffs, the warden of the Cinque Ports, and the admirals to proceed against the count's subjects in the same manner, whether on land or on sea, and to submit from time to time indentures of goods taken. On the 18th he expostulated with Count Louis and his towns, Bruges, Ghent, and Ypres. He dwelt upon their old friendship, saying that English merchants had resorted to Flanders in accordance with the guarantees of the treaty of March of the previous year, which was to hold until next Christmas; he complained that customary time to allow them to withdraw their goods had not been granted; he asked that his subjects and their property be released at once [137] and on the 21st sent John de Rypon and Stephen de la Garde, merchants from Beverley, to Flanders.[138]

V. The Diplomatic Activities of William, Count of Juliers
(1335–1336)

Edward's ambassadors, John de Shoreditch and William Fitz-Waryn, had left England on January 2, 1336, and had gone to

---

[134] *CPR* (1334–8), p. 164. [135] *Foedera,* II (2), 923.

[136] *CCR* (1333–7), pp. 327–328; N. de Pauw en J. Vuylsteke, *Rekeningen der Stad Gent,* I, 57; *Melsa,* II, 379.

[137] *Foedera,* II (2), 948.

[138] *CPR* (1334–8), p. 326.

Germany, where they were active until May in securing an alliance with the Hapsburg dukes.[139]   Count William of Juliers' relations to these efforts cannot be traced — even his credentials cannot be found — but we are warranted in believing that he played a major part, for on July 1 Edward speaks of the treaty with Duke Albert as having been effected by him.[140]

For the peace of Christendom and for Philip in particular the situation in Germany was disquieting.   The struggle of the Wittelsbachs and Hapsburgs with John, king of Bohemia, concerning the heritage of Henry, duke of Carinthia, had been temporarily quieted by the truce of Regensburg on September 16, 1335, between Lewis the Bavarian and King John.[141]   But the interim, which was to end on June 24, 1336, was employed by the energetic Luxemburgs to secure alliances with the kings of Poland and Hungary at Vizegrad in November.   In January Prince Charles, son of John, king of Bohemia, went to Tyrol to assume the government and the defense of the county against the enemies of the Luxemburgs.   And in March John himself at the head of a powerful army appeared in Austria along the borders of Bohemia and Moravia and began systematic plundering.[142]

Thus many of the princes of Germany might conceivably be drawn into various camps.   With Lewis the Bavarian would then be ranged Baldwin, archbishop of Trier, whose attitude was doubtful, and all those closely related to English interests in the Low Countries, chief of whom were William, count of Hainault, Holland, and Zeeland, who was the father-in-law of both Edward and Lewis the Bavarian, and William, count of Juliers, the brother-in-law of both, who was at this very moment active in Edward's behalf.   For a moment Philip may well have been uneasy because of the alliance of Louis, count of Flanders, with William, count of Hainault, Holland, and Zeeland, and John, duke

---

[139] L. Mirot and E. Déprez, " Les Ambassades Anglaises pendant la Guerre de Cent Ans," *BEC*, LIX (1898), 562–563. For their expenses, see *CCR* (1333–7), p. 590.

[140] *CCR* (1333–7), p. 688.

[141] F. von Weech, *Kaiser Ludwig der Baier und König Johann von Böhmen, Beilage V*, pp. 119–122.

[142] T. Lindner, *Deutsche Geschichte unter den Hapsburgern und Luxemburgern (1273–1437)*, I, 428–432; E. Werunsky, *Geschichte Kaiser Karls IV und seiner Zeit;* I, 141–163; G. Sievers, *Die Politischen Beziehungen Kaiser Ludwigs des Baiern zu Frankreich in den Jahren 1314–1337*, pp. 121–148.

of Brabant, and because of the arrangements regarding Mechelen which were made wholly without any reference to his wishes. There were also difficulties in Burgundy, and on every hand great tension developed in an atmosphere already heavily charged with suspicion and intrigue. A letter from the hand of someone reported to be well acquainted with opinion in France and sympathetic toward Edward mentioned over a thousand magnates and princes hostile toward Philip, among whom were the count of Guelders, the dukes of Austria, the emperor Lewis, and Count Henry of Mömpelgard, who had in 1335 visited England.[143] This analysis is by no means fanciful, for the pope in a letter to Philip on May 13 expressed substantially the same ideas.[144]

Lewis the Bavarian was careful to contradict such opinions, as he was anxious for a reconciliation with the pope, and, at the close of August, wrote that the alliance between King Edward and the Hapsburgs had no political significance whatever.[145] But it was of course patent that this understanding appreciably strengthened the parties opposed to the French interests and seemed to bring a cataclysm nearer. Queen Philippa appears to have aided in the negotiations, for as sister-in-law of both William, count of Juliers, and the emperor, and mother of Johanna, the proposed bride of Otto of Hapsburg, she could naturally exert some influence. In her correspondence she used the customary imperial titles in referring to Lewis, for which the pope on September 5 absolved her from all blame punishable by excommunication.[146]

Meanwhile William, count of Juliers, had been closely associated with Lewis the Bavarian and the Hapsburgs against the Luxemburg forces.[147] To him was entrusted the command of the

[143] Kervyn, *Oeuvres de Froissart,* XVII, 41. Reginald, count of Guelders, is here called " Comes Talariae."

[144] F. Daumet, *Benoît XII (1334–1342). Lettres Closes, Patentes, et Curiales, se rapportant à la France,* No. 178: " Rursus contentis in secunda littera faciente mentionem de Ludovico de Bavaria consideranter attentis, nuncios ejusdem Ludovici existentes pro negocio suo in curia vocari fecimus coram nobis et eis exposito per nos a fide dignis noviter audivisse ipsum Ludovicum quasdam confederationes et ligas cum nonnullis potentibus de Alamannia et partibus aliis tractasse vel inisse, que tibi fili dilectissime regnoque tuo esse periculose numium poterant ac nocive. . . ."

[145] S. Riezler, *Vatikanische Akten,* No. 1831.

[146] *Ibid.,* No. 1829.   [147] Johannis Victoriensis, p. 422.

troops which William, count of Hainault, Holland, and Zeeland, dispatched to aid his son-in-law.[148]   And that his services were duly appreciated is proved by the privilege granted him to wear the Hapsburg decoration on his helmet,[149] by the promotion of the county of Juliers to the dignity of a margraviate on August 21,[150] and by the confirmation on the 16th of his claims to Berg and other coveted rights.[151]   Proof of Reginald of Guelders' hostility to Philip is clearly established by the letter of July 23 from Frankfurt whereby Lewis authorized him to proceed against Philip " who calls himself king of France," to defend the border of the empire against his encroachments, and if necessary to mortgage the parcels in question.[152]   In April Edward had sent Thomas de Kenilworth to Germany,[153] and on June 5 another agent, each charged to present orally his views before the duke of Austria.   The treaty, which has never been printed, was thereupon drawn up, and, although not fully satisfactory in every respect, was gladly accepted by Edward who instructed a special envoy on July 1 to discuss the points contained therein.[154]

VI. Edward's Negotiations in the Low Countries (Summer, 1336 — Spring, 1337)

To French chroniclers the intimacy between Edward, the Hapsburgs, and the emperor during the summer of 1336 appeared equivalent to an Anglo-imperial alliance.[155]   In spite of the fact that William, count of Hainault, Holland, and Zeeland, and his intimate friends and allies, John, duke of Brabant, and Reginald, count of Guelders, were undoubtedly interested in the negotiations between England and the empire, little can be ascertained of the activities of these princes.   Yet the instructions of December

---

[148] L. Devillers, *Monuments,* III, 450.

[149] Johannis Victoriensis, p. 422.

[150] T. Lacomblet, *Urkundenbuch für die Geschichte des Niederrheins,* III, 248–249.

[151] *Ibid.,* p. 248.

[152] *Ibid.,* p. 247.

[153] L. Mirot et E. Déprez, " Les Ambassades Anglaises pendant la Guerre de Cent Ans," *BEC,* LIX (1898), 562–563.

[154] *CCR* (1333–7), pp. 679, 688.

[155] De Nangis, II, 154; Lescot, p. 43, and also the Italian Villani, col. 793.

15 and 16, 1335, to John de Shoreditch and FitzWaryn suggested an alliance with them and there were undoubtedly some discussions.[156] The return of these envoys on May 16 and 24 respectively [157] acquainted Edward fully with the temper of his friends in Germany and the Low Countries, but he was apparently not ready to act until the failure of the negotiations with Philip in July and the meeting of the merchants and the other estates of the realm at Nottingham in September.

John de Thrandeston of Cologne, still in Edward's service and now a member of the royal household, received at Nottingham from the king, who was in consultation with his council, instructions and letters for William, count of Hainault, Holland, and Zeeland, William, margrave of Juliers, Reginald, count of Guelders, and other personages. Leaving the royal presence on September 13 he passed by way of Dover and Wissant to the continent and went directly to Cologne, where he tarried from the 28th to October 5 to await the arrival of William, margrave of Juliers. He next proceeded to Nijmegen in Guelders where he spent six days in conference, apparently with Count Reginald, and then two days at Stockhem on the Meuse below Maastricht, where he awaited the arrival of Reginald, William, and other princes, and their response which he received on the 20th. Charged to go to Valenciennes, he waited twelve days at the court of Count William in order to receive the report of the deliberations of the latter with John, duke of Brabant.[158]

It is evident that in all these negotiations Edward's father-in-law played the chief part. Count William had not yet digested his anger toward his brother-in-law Philip who showed so little appreciation for the services rendered during his regency, at the battle of Cassel, and during the negotiations at Compiègne in 1332. To these grievances had been added others which goaded his spirit to fury. No progress had been made in settling their respective rights in Ostrevant in 1332 and 1333.[159] On November 23, 1334, Philip had ordered his officials to do nothing

[156] *Foedera,* II (2), 955.

[157] L. Mirot et E. Déprez, " Les Ambassades Anglaises pendant la Guerre de Cent Ans," *BEC,* LIX (1898), 562–563.

[158] Kervyn, *Oeuvres de Froissart,* XVIII, 153–155.

[159] Philip's last letter that can be found dealing with this matter is dated December 31, 1331. See L. Devillers, *Monuments,* III, 264–265.

in the debated lands contrary to William's rights.[160]   The latter vigorously protested Philip's claims to the disputed lands, and it is evident that there was much ill feeling on the subject.

Philip yielded so far as to promise in September, 1335, that he would not allow anyone but the count and countess of Hainault to acquire possession of these lands for their son William, count of Ostrevant.[161]   But Philip had also begun negotiations to acquire from Engergier, seignior of Amboise and of Néelle, his possessions at Crèvecoeur, Arleux, St. Supplet, Rumilly, and in the castlery of Cambrai.   This would of course considerably augment his influence on the borders of the Low Countries within the imperial boundaries under the spiritual jurisdiction of the bishop of Cambrai.   In this matter Philip followed the example set by his predecessors when they secured effective control over the Tournaisis.   William also had claims to these titles, and the emperor, his father-in-law, could readily be moved to protest against this invasion of the empire.   And Lewis the Bavarian did instruct Godefroid, abbot of Vicogne, to appear before the bishop of Cambrai and order him under pain of imperial indignation not to suffer the transfer of these lands.   This was done on September 18, 1335.[162]

But all protest was in vain.   On June 21, 1336, Philip ordered his officials to investigate with the count's men whether the contested parts of Ostrevant lay within the imperial border.[163]   These orders, which were repeated in December,[164] were as devoid of result as all the previous ones had been since 1328.   And on February 28, 1337, Philip finally secured definitive possession of the titles of Engergier.[165]   This was too much for William to endure, and from that moment he used his influence to bring into existence the great coalition against Philip.[166]   Although

[160] *Archives du Département du Nord,* Lille, B1220 (6.900).

[161] *Ibid.,* B1220 (7.013).

[162] *Ibid.,* B1055 (7.015).

[163] *Ibid.,* B1220 (7.099).

[164] *Ibid.,* B1055 (7.137).

[165] H. Dubrulle, *Cambrai à la Fin du Moyen Âge (XIIIᵉ–XVIᵉ Siècle),* *Pièces Justificatives,* No. 40.   See, for the date, A. Wauters, *Table Chronologique,* IX, 605.

[166] For William's attitude, see the testimony of Boendale, *Van den derden Eduwaert,* pp. 332–333, and especially the *Bourgeois de Valenciennes,* pp. 74–75, and Kervyn, *Oeuvres de Froissart,* XVIII, 137.

bed-ridden with his old malady, he gave remarkable proof of his singular ability and influence in directing the intrigues of Edward's agents. He suggested to Thrandeston that Philip, count of Namur, and his mother, who probably resented Philip's savagery toward Robert of Artois, the bishop of Liège and Reginald de Ghore, his councillor, and a number of influential personages in Flanders might be secured for Edward's plans, in addition to William, margrave of Juliers, and Reginald, count of Guelders. Crossing the Strait of Dover again at Wissant, Thrandeston finally arrived at York on November 16 and was immediately closeted with Edward and his councillors.[167]

Meanwhile other diplomatic efforts had been made. At the advice of his council, Edward had sent Arnold de Tyle on October 3 to confer with Count William at Valenciennes as well as with John, duke of Brabant, and parties in Germany.[168] Much money was spent by others as well as by Arnold de Tyle and John de Thrandeston, for considerable sums were borrowed from time to time to further the " secret affairs " of the king.[169] The Scots were reported to be receiving assistance from subjects of Holland, Zeeland, and Guelders, and on November 3 letters were addressed to Count William and Count Reginald requesting that this should be stopped.[170] At York plans were formed by the chancellor and the council for Thrandeston's second journey. He was given letters at Bothwell on December 4 empowering him to treat with Count William at Valenciennes, William, margrave of Juliers, the count of Namur and his mother, the bishop of Liège, Reginald de Ghore,[171] and a number of important personages in Flanders,[172] wholly in accordance with the recent suggestions of Count William.

---

[167] Kervyn, *Oeuvres de Froissart,* XVIII, 153–155.

[168] *CCR* (1333–7), p. 611; *CCR* (1337–9), p. 43. He spent 200*l.*

[169] See the order of July 6, 1336, to reimburse Paul de Monte Florum for 1,500*l.* advanced to the king and council, *CCR* (1333–7), pp. 596–597; to John de Pulteney, 200*l.* on July 8, *ibid.,* p. 601; to the Bardi, 3,000 marks on October 3, *CPR* (1334–8), p. 322.

[170] Also to the king of Norway, *Foedera,* II(2), 949–950.

[171] *Ibid.,* p. 952.

[172] From Thrandeston's itinerary we learn who these were: " . . . et en Fflaundres à mounsire Seyer Courtroysin, à monsire Ricwyn Standard, à monsire Godeschall de la More et monsire Ector Vileyn, qui à cel eure estoyent menours et governours de Fflaunders. . . ." See Kervyn, *Oeuvres de Froissart,* XVIII, 155. For letters to Standard, see *CRR* (1333–7), p. 730.

Setting out from York on October 5, he crossed from Lynn to Middelburg, where he arrived on the 16th. He then went to Antwerp, where he tarried some days, and to Le Quesnoy, where he received advice from Count William before approaching the bishop of Liège, his lord, with whom he had ever lived on good terms. Upon receipt of the bishop's response he directed his steps to Nijmegen in Guelders and then to Nidekken, the ancestral home of the margrave of Juliers. After receiving the advice of both of these men, he hurried to confer with the count of Namur.[173]

The duke of Brabant, zealous promoter of the interests of his bourgeoisie, saw his opportunity at once. The Flemish cloth industry was languishing and the embargo of August 12 had well-nigh cut off all importation of wool. Why should the weavers of Brabant not profit from this situation? On the other hand the pressure of Edward's allies, the counts of Guelders, and of Hainault, Holland, and Zeeland, and the margrave of Juliers, whose territories surrounded his own, was persistent. Duke John accordingly drew the logical conclusion from the situation created by English diplomacy and once more revealed the whole opportunist tendency of his government. Immediately after the conferences with Thrandeston he requested that the wool staple should be established in his lands. On December 3 Edward replied that, in view of their family connections and especially their generally friendly relations, he would gladly accede to his request, provided that English merchants should be entirely free in going to and from the staple and that no wool should in any way be allowed to reach Flanders. Some merchants of the realm were to be sent to Brabant to discuss plans with the duke and his towns and arrange the necessary details.[174]

Meanwhile steps were taken to carry on the negotiations initiated by Thrandeston. John de Montgomery, a knight, and John Wawayn, canon of Darlington, skilled in civil and canon law, were given extensive powers, on December 15. They were to state orally Edward's intimate desires and treat with the archbishop of Cologne, the bishop of Liège, the count of Guelders,

---

[173] Kervyn, *Oeuvres de Froissart*, XVIII, 155–156.

[174] *Foedera*, II (2), 952. On September 24 Edward had granted the merchants of Louvain safe-conduct for one year. *CCR* (1334–8), p. 317.

and William, count of Hainault, Holland and Zeeland.[175] On the following day the king expressed his ideas more fully in a document to his father-in-law, who was now appointed his proctor to contract alliances even where special mandate might be required,[176] to treat concerning all points which would inevitably come up in making plans, and to levy troops.[177] The margrave of Juliers was likewise given similar powers to be executed in conjunction with Montgomery and Wawayn.[178] Protection and safe-conduct were granted them,[179] and means were found to pay their expenses.[180]

With the efforts of Wawayn and Montgomery, Thrandeston appears to have had nothing to do. From Namur he returned to Nijmegen where he tarried four days and conferred with Reginald of Guelders and William of Juliers and their councils. On January 18 he proceeded to Antwerp and crossed from Middelburg to Yarmouth, then proceeded by way of Oxford to London and soon received other credentials from the king and his council.[181] He was recommended to the count of Marck and to the burgomasters and scabini of Brussels, Louvain, and Mechelen.[182] On February 21 he received his credentials to Count Reginald, Count William of Hainault, and the countess of Namur, sailed from Yarmouth to Middelburg, and arrived at Antwerp on the 28th.[183] He betook himself at once to Nijmegen where for four days he vainly awaited Reginald's arrival. Directed by the latter to come to him at Mechelen, he spent two days in that place. At Antwerp he met Montgomery and Wawayn, and returned with them to Mechelen, where they had further discussions.[184] From the 15th to the 23d Thrandeston was busy in Flanders, whence he went to Wissant for the passage to Dover on the 29th. With him were John of Valkenburg of the council of the count of Guelders, Tyleman von Müllenark, and Claes Stuyck of Dor-

[175] *Foedera,* II(2), 954–955.

[176] *CPR* (1334–8), p. 348. [177] *Foedera,* II(2), 955.

[178] *Ibid.,* p. 955; *CPR* (1334–8), p. 347. Wawayn was retained on December 14 as member of the council. See *CPR* (1334–8) p. 341.

[179] *CPR* (1334–8), p. 341. [180] *CCR* (1333–7), p. 640.

[181] Kervyn, *Oeuvres de Froissart,* XVIII, 156.

[182] *Foedera,* II(2), 959.

[183] Kervyn, *Oeuvres de Froissart,* XVIII, 157. On February 20 the king ordered 73*l.* to be paid the Bardi for divers jewels bought for Thrandeston's use, apparently as douceurs. See *CCR* (1337–9), pp. 3–4.

[184] Kervyn, *Oeuvres de Froissart,* XVIII, 157–158.

drecht, a notary of the council of William, count of Hainault, Holland, and Zeeland. These men were all sumptuously entertained and amply compensated.[185]   At about the same time also came a yeoman representing the duke of Brabant.[186]

VII. THE SOCIAL AND ECONOMIC CRISIS IN FLANDERS (SPRING, 1337)

THE rupture of Count Louis with England meant serious social problems in the towns of Flanders. The importation of wool, hides, and woolfells had ceased altogether, save for the negligible amount which might chance to be smuggled past the customs.[187] The proclamation of December 15, 1336, forbidding the export of corn and food-stuffs to foreign parts [188] was carefully enforced, and licenses were issued to parties wishing to take victuals, wheat, ale, and similar articles to such places on condition that they should provide security that they would not fall into the hands of the enemy.[189]   Later, on April 15, ox-hides, feathers, rabbit skins, and cheese were also forbidden to be taken to Flanders.[190] The pressure was soon felt in the great centers of population such as Bruges, Ghent, and Ypres. The scabini of these towns were apprehensive of the future, and representatives of the three towns met at Bruges at the request of Count Louis to discuss the crisis with England in the week of St. Martin's Day, in the fortnight following, from December 1 to 3,[191] and again on the 15th.[192]

[185] On April 18, 1337, Edward assigned to John de Pulteney 71*l.* 13*s.* 8*d.* paid by him to purchase " four palfreys bought for the use of the Lord of Faukmont and certain clerks who came to the king as envoys from the Count of Hainault . . . and given to them by the king." See *CPR* (1334–8), p. 416.

[186] The duke sent a yeoman for whom two cups and an ewer, valued at 12*l.* 6*s.* 8*d.*, were given. See *CCR* (1337–9), p. 54.

[187] See the royal commission to conduct inquests of such alleged cases in Suffolk, February 13, 1337. *CPR* (1334–8), pp. 281–282.

[188] *Foedera,* II (2), 954–955.

[189] *CPR* (1334–8), pp. 315, 333, 337, 340, 351.   [190] *Ibid.,* p. 435.

[191] N. de Pauw and J. Vuylsteke, *Rekeningen der Stad Gent,* I, 53–54; " . . . ten parlemente datter geleit was omme doccoison vande orlogen van Yngelant. . . ."

[192] *Ibid.,* p. 55: " . . . te Brucge ten parlemente, daer mijn heere van Vlaenderen ontboden adde al sine steden in Vlaendren, omme sorlogen wille dat rees tusscen Vrankerike en Ingelant. . . ."

Food-stuffs became scarce and very costly.[193] Flemish shipping disappeared from the sea, Flemings languished in English prisons, and their property was everywhere confiscated.[194] Piracy developed in the Channel and the North Sea,[195] and Sluis became a convenient place to dispose of prizes.[196] Edward even endeavored to turn Spanish merchants from Flanders and began negotiations with Alfonso XI of Castile early in 1337 in order to prevent any food-stuffs, merchandise, or military material from entering the country.[197] There was some prospect of success, for Alfonso proposed to send a mission to discuss the bases of an accord before Easter.[198]

Coupled with these measures was the desire to stop all intercourse between the Scots and the Flemings. On February 6, 1337, Edward ordered his admiral, John de Roos, to collect ships at Orwell, prepare them for war, and take measures to end the help given by foreigners to the Scots and the damages inflicted upon English ships on the seas. Information was received that some ships were loaded with victuals and warlike equipment destined for Aberdeen, and John de Wesenham was enjoined to take ships from Lynn and neighboring parts to attack them upon the Flemish coasts.[199] The Scots meanwhile persisted in treating the Flemings with great consideration and paid for the loss of their ships destroyed in the attempt in 1332 to wipe out the English fleet in the Tay when they attacked Perth.[200]

The threat of starvation became alarming; actual want increased, and it is not strange that there should be violence. In Ghent, where the weavers were especially agitated, stern measures were taken by executing some of them as examples.[201] The scabini sought to avoid upheavals by posting from January 9 to 13 as watchmen forty-eight members of the guilds and twenty-six

---

[193] *Chronicon Comitum Flandrensium*, p. 120; *Chronographia*, II, 42.
[194] *CCR* (1337-9), p. 42.
[195] Hocsemius, p. 432.   [196] *CCR* (1337-9), pp. 24-25, 45.
[197] *CCR* (1333-7), pp. 697-698; *Foedera*, II (2), 961.
[198] *Foedera*, II (2), 961. See also G. Daumet, *Étude sur l'Alliance de la France et de la Castile au XIVe et au XVe Siècles*, p. 6.
[199] *Rotuli Scotiae*, I, 482, 485.
[200] *Rotuli Scaccarii Regum Scotorum*, I, 450-451.
[201] N. de Pauw en J. Vuylsteke, *Rekeningen der Stad Gent*, I, 88: "Item van der ghere costen die omme ghinghen doemen de wever onthoefde."

others under the direction of John van Wiendeke, dean of the fullers, and Jacob Deynoot and Claes de Keyser, receivers. On the nights of January 13 and 14 eighteen were posted.[202] During these days of excitement a demand was made to enforce the industrial privileges of the town, and on the 12th the bailiff, acting under the count's orders, and two of the scabini, Jacob Deynoot and John van Wiendeke, accompanied by representatives from the fullers, weavers, and other crafts, rode out on Sunday, the 12th, with sixty-six horses. For three days they viewed throughout the parishes the manufacturing of cloth contrary to the privileges of the town, and took measures to prevent the erection of necessary equipment.[203] On February 3 sixty police guards (*scerewetters*) from the guilds began to guard the scabini, and on the 16th thirty of them were detailed to patrol the outlying streets until the 19th. During the succeeding month (February 19–March 19) thirty men were posted under the command of a captain (*conincstavele*) except for three nights when one of the scabini took his place.[204]

At Bruges the situation must have been very much the same. Beginning with January 23 thirty-six guards (*scerewetters*) were appointed to patrol the streets.[205] Fuller information, unfortunately, cannot be gleaned from the laconic accounts of that town, while for Ypres no data whatever can be found. Everything seemed to point to a sure and swift approach of a violent social upheaval. Driven by starvation, the craftsmen fled the towns and roamed far and wide, begging their bread in droves at Tournai and even in some other towns of France.[206] On March 21 [207] three scabini, Claes uten Hove, John de Raven, and Lievin de Amman, and the dean of the fullers, John van Wiendeke, assisted by Philip van Calkine and Jacob Deynoot, distributed 4,000*l.* in loans to the fullers and an equal sum to the other guilds.[208] These measures were temporarily successful and quieted the craftsmen. From March 19 to May 14 a smaller force was needed to keep the peace and only ten guards were stationed under the command of the bailiff's aid.[209]

[202] N. de Pauw en J. Vuylsteke, *op. cit.*, p. 93.
[203] *Ibid.*, pp. 57–58.   [204] *Ibid.*, pp. 93–99.
[205] *Ms. Rekeningen, 1336–1337,* Bruges, folio 50, recto.
[206] *Chronicon Comitum Flandrensium,* p. 210; Hocsemius, p. 432.
[207] N. de Pauw en J. Vuylsteke, *Rekeningen der Stad Gent,* I, 88.
[208] *Ibid.*, pp. 24–33.   [209] *Ibid.*, pp. 95–96.

Meanwhile, Edward's restrictive policy took on a severer aspect. The clergy, barons, and representatives of the shires and boroughs were convoked at Westminster early in March.[210] Six of the king's trusted servants were elevated to the peerage: Henry, son of the earl of Lancaster, as earl of Derby; William de Bohun as earl of Northampton; William de Montague as earl of Salisbury; Hugh de Audley as earl of Gloucester; Robert de Ufford as earl of Suffolk; and William de Clinton as earl of Huntingdon, all of whom were destined to play important parts in the diplomatic intrigues which from this moment Edward was to carry on in the Low Countries with redoubled vigor.[211]

The exportation of wool was again forbidden and no cloth of foreign manufacture was to be bought or imported after Michaelmas.[212] These measures, together with renewed invitations to foreign weavers to settle in England and the permission of English craftsmen to make cloth of any length they might wish, have usually been regarded as evidence of the royal wish to foster native industry and to break the Flemish monopoly.[213] But Edward was interested rather in the diplomatic effect of this policy and it is clearly erroneous to see in his efforts an early example of royal protection.[214] Meanwhile John de Thrandeston actively labored in his behalf. Count Louis and the delegates of the Flemish towns conferred with the duke of Brabant and his towns at Rupelmonde on February 27.[215] The general economic crisis in both lands was undoubtedly an important topic of conversation. Thrandeston was with the count of Guelders at Mechelen early in March, and on the 15th proceeded to Ghent, and was active until the 21st at Bruges, Ypres, and Wynendael,[216] where he no doubt sought the presence of Count Louis. At Male the latter met the deputies of the towns and on the following day, the 21st, Thrandeston proceeded to Wissant.[217]

---

[210] *CCR* (1333–7), pp. 736–737.

[211] Murimuth, p. 81; Baker, pp. 58–59; Knighton, I, 476; *Melsa*, II, 379; *Chronicon Angliae*, p. 5.

[212] *Statutes of the Realm*, I, 280–288; Murimuth, p. 79; Baker, p. 59.

[213] See, for example, W. Cunningham, *The Growth of English Industry and Commerce during the Early and Middle Ages* (3d ed.), I, 305–306.

[214] See G. Unwin, *Trade and Finance under Edward III, Introduction*, pp. xviii–xix.

[215] N. de Pauw en J. Vuylsteke, *Rekeningen der Stad Gent*, I, 58.

[216] Kervyn, *Oeuvres de Froissart*, XVIII, 158.

[217] N. de Pauw en J. Vuylsteke, *Rekeningen der Stad Gent*, I, 59.

CHAPTER VII

FRENCH AND ENGLISH DIPLOMACY IN THE LOW COUNTRIES (1337–1338)

i. English Negotiations at Valenciennes (Spring, 1337) ii. English Negotiations with John, Duke of Brabant (Spring and Summer, 1337) iii. King Edward's Negotiations with Lewis the Bavarian (Summer, 1337) iv. The Crisis in Flanders (Spring, 1337) v. King Philip's Diplomacy in the Low Countries (Summer, 1337 — Autumn, 1338) vi. Edward's Invasion of France postponed until June, 1338

I. English Negotiations at Valenciennes (Spring, 1337)

JOHN de Thrandeston was given credentials a fourth time by the king and his council, and on April 13 left London. Travelling again by way of Dover to Wissant, he arrived at Valenciennes on the 21st and informed Count William of the speedy coming of a group of plenipotentiaries, Henry de Burghersh, bishop of Lincoln, William de Montague, earl of Salisbury, and William de Clinton, earl of Huntington, to negotiate the definitive alliances. Here he tarried until their arrival, for he had been instructed to place himself at their disposal.[1]

Letters were at once issued to the members of the proposed embassy. They were empowered to treat with Louis, count of Flanders, and his towns, Bruges, Ghent, Ypres, and others concerning all matters which had occasioned the recent rupture, to negotiate a treaty of friendship, to labor for an alliance, and to make provision for suitable remuneration. Similar instructions also were issued on April 15 to Reginald de Cobham, William Trussel, and Nicholas de la Beche, who were expected to act as assistants to the more important members of the embassy. The bishop and his associates were also to treat with the allies and their friends concerning the staple of wool and all points touching the time and manner of holding it, a matter which of course concerned the duke of Brabant most, but which could also be

---

[1] Kervyn, *Oeuvres de Froissart*, XVIII, 158.

204

employed advantageously in the negotiations with the towns
of Flanders. It was hoped, though too sanguinely, that a matrimonial arrangement might be effected between Count Louis'
first-born son Louis and Edward's daughter Johanna, and the
envoys were given extensive powers on April 19 to settle all matters. Finally, full power was conferred to treat at their discretion for alliances and settle such questions as compensation and
military aid. Because of their acquaintance with the practical
situation among the princes of the Low Countries, John de Montgomery and John Wawayn were to be associated with them.[2]
Relations between Philip and Edward were strained to the limit,
and the instructions of the 18th to the envoys to secure an accommodation with France in the matter of Aquitaine [3] can hardly
have been expected to be successful.

This extraordinary diplomatic mission, well supplied with
money and handsomely accoutred,[4] attended by a numerous train
of bannerets, knights, horses, etc., crossed the Strait from Dover
to Wissant toward the close of April.[5] At Valenciennes a busy
scene of intrigue began in the fortnight after Easter, for William,
count of Hainault, Holland, and Zeeland, had arranged through
the activities of Thrandeston, Montgomery, Wawayn, and William, margrave of Juliers, that a large number of the magnates
of the Low Countries should come there to meet the fully accredited envoys of the English king.[6] There was much feasting
and lavish display, and money was spent freely.[7] The margrave

[2] *Foedera*, II (2), 967. Cf. *CCR* (1337–9), p. 127.

[3] *Foedera*, II (2), 966; Hemingburgh, II, 313; *Bourgeois de Valenciennes*, pp. 157–158.

[4] *CCR* (1337–9), p. 63. Edward requested the Bardi to pay the bishop
of Lincoln and the earls 2,000*l*. Cf. *ibid.*, p. 86. For an assignment of
370*l*. 17*s*. 2*d*. advanced to Salisbury by John de Pulteney, see *CPR* (1334–8),
p. 416.

[5] For safe-conduct for the bishop, April 24, see *Foedera*, II (2), 966;
for Salisbury, Huntingdon, Nicholas de la Beche, and Trussel, see *CPR*
(1334–8), pp. 412, 428. Salisbury left London on the 18th. See his itinerary as given in the account rendered to the Exchequer printed by W.
Stechele, " England und der Niederrhein bei Beginn der Regierung Eduards
III (1327–1377)," Anlage III," *Westdeutsche Zeitschrift für Geschichte und
Kunst*, XXVII (1908), 471.

[6] *Chronographia*, II, 32; Froissart, I, 372. Easter fell on April 20 and
the first treaty concluded at Valenciennes is dated May 24. See *Foedera*,
II (2), 969, 973, for the document issued in Hainault.

[7] Boendale, *Van den derden Eduwaert*, pp. 311–312.

of Juliers was present as representative of the emperor; his brother Walram, archbishop of Cologne, was with him, also William, titular count of Zeeland, Thierry, seignior of Valkenburg, Reginald, count of Guelders, Adolph, count of Marck, Everhard, count of Limburg, Thierry, count of Loon, John of Hainault, and Adolph, count of Berg, who was said to represent the duke of Brabant.[8]

In the negotiations which now followed Count William and Count Reginald took the initiative with the bishop of Lincoln and the earls. The relations between Edward and Philip, including the matter of Robert of Artois, were discussed at length. The sojourn of the latter at the English court and his alleged influence in embittering the relations between Philip and Edward were important matters for a number of Low Country princes as well as for Edward, because at Senlis in May, 1332, Count Reginald, Walram, archbishop of Cologne, William, then count, now margrave of Juliers, and John of Hainault had promised to aid Philip against Robert of Artois and any one who should wish to support him.[9] An official document was drawn up; Robert of Artois, it was stated, had come to England protesting his innocence, complaining of extreme mistreatment, and begging protection. He had asked for a safe-conduct to appear before Philip and the peers. Seeing his desire to appear in response to summons, Edward had received him out of pity and had granted his request, provided that he attempt nothing against Philip. It was now proposed that Robert should be allowed to appear with the fullest guarantee of personal safety and with the express privilege of returning to England. Should he fail to clear himself of the accusations, Edward would then expel him from the realm. Furthermore, Philip was to be requested to abandon the Scots and to discuss the bases of a peace.[10]

During these discussions Countess Jeanne was able to bring her influence to bear upon all parties. Solicitous for her numerous and close relatives and saddened by the prospect of the fratricidal struggle, she eagerly urged further negotiations with Philip. The fact that the latter was her brother may well have

[8] Le Bel, I, 126; *Istore et Croniques,* I, 360.
[9] Cf. *supra,* p. 121.
[10] Kervyn, *Oeuvres de Froissart,* XVIII, 30–33.

induced the negotiators at Valenciennes to hearken to her and to allow her to proceed to Paris. On May 17 a sworn declaration was drawn up wherein she and Reginald guaranteed that Robert would come to France under Philip's safe-conduct and stand trial before his peers within one month after Pentecost.[11] Accompanied by John of Hainault, whose affability would strongly recommend him for such a mission, she set out for Paris. But they met with a chilly reception; no one could be induced to take any interest in their case, and it was only after a good deal of persuasion that Philip would even consent to meet them. Irritated by the busy going to and fro of English agents in the Low Countries, especially in Hainault, and quite naturally failing to understand Count William's policy as mediator, Philip is said to have exclaimed, " You, John of Hainault, and your brother, the count of Hainault, wish to drive me from my realm. God forbid! Never will you be able to do this! " After brief deliberation he rejected his sister's appeal without ceremony, and the latter, for once at least greatly angered with her brother, left Paris and hurried back to Valenciennes. But Philip was not blind to John of Hainault's many good qualities and, if Froissart may be believed, sent him after his departure a beautiful prize falcon as a mark of personal esteem.[12]

Meanwhile Thrandeston had busied himself in the service of the English emissaries. He negotiated with many seigniors in Flanders, Brabant, Namur, and Liège, seeking to smooth the way for the numerous conventions which were being planned.[13] With an extraordinary rapidity which attests to the success of his and the other agents' activities in the winter months, a series of agreements was now concluded with various parties at Valenciennes. On May 12 Henry de Jodoigne, professor of civil law, canon in the church of Cambrai, and an important personage, since he was a notary public residing at Cambrai which was falling into the hands of Philip VI, promised Edward his support for a life annuity of 100 gold florins.[14] Adolph, count of Berg, also had done likewise shortly before and had promised to serve

---

[11] L. Devillers, *Monuments*, III, 465–466.
[12] *Bourgeois de Valenciennes*, p. 159; Froissart, I, 373.
[13] Kervyn, *Oeuvres de Froissart*, XVIII, 158–159.
[14] *Foedera*, II (2), 969–970.

with a hundred men against all the king's enemies save the emperor and Adolph de la Marck, bishop of Liège. That Reginald, count of Guelders, who was no doubt very instrumental in these negotiations possessed Edward's fullest confidence is apparent from the statement that, should the stipends for the soldiers in his judgment not be sufficient, he could increase them at his discretion.[15] Lesser persons were not passed by. On May 15 a number of petty and unimportant magnates were bound by oath of homage.[16] On the 24th the count of Marck, to whom Reginald had already promised 3,000 small florins annually for the services of a hundred men, also made his contract. Others were Henry de Gemenaith, Ernest von Müllenark, William van Duivenvoorde,[17] Everhard, count of Limburg,[18] and finally, on the 28th, Herman Blankaerd, dean of the church of Aix-la-Chapelle and provost of Werden.[19]

More important were the agreements to which the margrave of Juliers and the counts of Guelders and Hainault affixed their seals. The alliance of May 24 aimed to defend the imperial frontier against the aggressions of King Philip. Should he levy war upon any one of these parties, each would raise and maintain at Edward's expense for one year a thousand men-at-arms. If, however, the French should prove too powerful, an additional thousand might be raised, also at his expense. The rate for each soldier was to be fifteen Florentine florins per month, which became the regular compensation subsequently promised to most parties by the English agents. The levy of the second thousand was, however, to be kept in the field only until the arrival of Edward, which was tentatively set for September 17. Perceiving that his own days were numbered and being anxious for revenge upon his brother-in-law Philip, William, count of Hainault, Holland, and Zeeland, caused the English envoys to make the same terms with his son William, titular count of Zeeland, who was promised Arleux, Crèvecoeur, and St. Supplet in

---

[15] *Foedera*, II (2), pp. 970, 971, where he is referred to as *Comes de Marlia*.   [16] *Ibid.*, p. 970.

[17] *Ibid.*, p. 971. The identity of Henry de Gemenaith and Ernest von Müllenark is uncertain, and "Winandus de Dunzenchoyven" is undoubtedly meant for William van Duivenvoorde.

[18] *Ibid.*, p. 972.

[19] *Ibid.*, p. 973.

perpetual possession as soon as he or Edward's allies should capture them. The king also promised to compensate his father-in-law for the inevitable confiscation of his properties in France by Philip, by assigning him on the same day, May 24, an annual income of 6,000*l.* Tournois.[20] The margrave of Juliers was now handsomely rewarded for his zeal in Edward's behalf. On the 27th he received 5,000*l.* sterling and was guaranteed proper compensation in case the properties of his mother-in-law Jeanne, countess of Hainault, Holland, and Zeeland, should be confiscated.[21]

Thus the diplomatic efforts of the past nine months came to a successful conclusion. The margrave of Juliers, the counts of Guelders, Hainault, Holland, and Zeeland, and many others were definitely committed to support Edward in a war with Philip which now appeared inevitable as the royal order to confiscate Aquitaine had gone forth on May 24.[22] Edward was endeavoring in the meanwhile to secure the aid of the nobility and towns of Gascony [23] and was carrying on negotiations with Alfonso, king of Castile, the marshal of the king of Sicily,[24] the count of Geneva, and numerous other princes in the south of the continent.[25] Ruprecht, count of the Rhenish Palatinate, and Lewis, the elector of Brandenburg, son of Lewis the Bavarian, also entered his services.[26]

Philip was thus surrounded on every side by a fringe of hostile territory, the strategic point of which from a military, political, and economic point of view undoubtedly lay in the Low Countries. Here there were, however, a number of principalities whose support was desirable if not vital for Edward — Brabant, Flanders, to a less extent Liège, and Luxemburg whose count, John, king of Bohemia, was closely associated with the policies of Philip and in the empire bound to oppose Lewis the Bavarian at every point. It is now necessary to turn our attention to these parties.

---

[20] *Ibid.,* pp. 970–972.
[21] *Ibid.,* p. 973.
[22] E. Déprez, *Les Préliminaires de la Guerre de Cent Ans* (*1328–1342*), p. 154, and note 1; *Chronique Parisienne Anonyme,* pp. 170–171.
[23] *Foedera,* II (2), 975–979.
[24] *Ibid.,* p. 977.
[25] *Ibid.,* p. 980.
[26] *Ibid.,* pp. 979–980.

II. English Negotiations with John, Duke of Brabant (Spring and Summer, 1337)

John, duke of Brabant, had warily absented himself from the gathering at Valenciennes and preferred, it is said, to be represented by Adolph, count of Berg.[27] Yet he was in close contact with the English envoys through his representatives, William de Boys and William de Petersheim. And in Brabant he had had numerous conferences with John de Thrandeston and his associates and other agents of the English court such as Trussel, Shoreditch, Wawayn, and Montgomery. They had undoubtedly suggested an alliance against their mutual enemies for a period of six years during which time English wool was to be sold only at Antwerp. The duke was to serve at the king's expense with 500 men, and, should he need help, receive from Edward the service of 200 knights and 1,000 archers, and, in case of confiscation of his incomes in France, an adequate compensation.[28]

The bishop of Lincoln and his party confidently anticipated the duke's support. Was he not Edward's cousin and was not his daughter Johanna the wife of William, son of William, count of Hainault? For two years and more the latter had used his good offices to prepare an understanding between John and the clergy of Brabant when the monks refused to contribute their quotas of the assessments made necessary by the treaties sealed at Amiens. Since that time a treaty had been made with Count William and Count Louis of Flanders providing for common protection and an agreement was made with the latter through William's coöperation concerning Mechelen. Since Louis was clearly determined to adhere to the cause of Philip, the duke might well reflect upon the advantages which an English alliance would give him. His feelings toward Count William, furthermore, were quite cordial. They had on April 6 agreed to issue a coin which would circulate as legal tender in each other's domains.[29] John

---

[27] *Chronographia,* II, 32.

[28] The document is not dated, but must apparently be assigned to the early part of 1337. See Kervyn, *Oeuvres de Froissart,* XVIII, 38–39.

[29] F. van Mieris, *Groot Charterboek,* II, 305, where it is assigned to 1336. Cf. R. Chalon, *Récherches sur les Monnaies des Comtes de Hainault,* pp. 186–187.

also borrowed a sum of money from the Lombards at Ath for
which Count William, John of Hainault, and Reginald, count of
Guelders, acted as guarantors on May 11, at the very moment
when the negotiations at Valenciennes were in full progress.[30]

Political, economic, and diplomatic considerations dictated for
the duke a policy of aloofness. The burdensome debts imposed
by Philip at Amiens were still unpaid.[31] Furthermore, the duchy
occupied a central position. To the east were the lands of the
bishop of Liège, known friend and guardian of French influence
in those parts. With him and the chapter of St. Lambert the
duke had a great number of serious differences. On January 21,
1336, the county of Loon, a fief of the bishop, had fallen vacant.
Thierry de Heinsberg, son of Matilda, the daughter of Arnold VI
(1280–1323), claimed it, notwithstanding the law that title was
transmissible only through males.[32] Relations between Count
Louis IV (1323-1336) and his nephew Thierry had for some time
been quite close. Thus in 1335 Louis had mortgaged his possessions at Stockhem, Maaseyck, and Bree to Thierry and finally
also made him his heir. Thierry had married a lady of the
lineage of the counts of Marck and was a brother-in-law of
Adolph, bishop of Liège, who in spite of his own legal rights [33] was
reluctant to proceed against his sister and her husband.

Thierry was thus unopposed, so took possession and appealed
to the emperor, Lewis the Bavarian, who granted him the investiture in April. But the chapter was determined not to allow
its rights to be thus flagrantly neglected and urged the bishop to
proceed against the pretender. The canons allowed Adolph to
appropriate 4,000 florins out of the proceeds of the sale of Mechelen and induced him to convoke the magnates and towns of the

[30] L. Devillers, *Monuments,* III, 463–464. On August 10 he promised
Count William, son of the late count, to reimburse him fully for his pledge
made on March 18. Cf. L. Devillers, *Cartulaire,* I, 4–5. See a similar
promise of May 12 to the count of Guelders, in I. A. Nijhoff, *Gedenkwaardigheden uit de Geschiedenis van Gelderland,* I, 358.

[31] He had not yet paid Adolph, bishop of Liège, in full as was required by the decision at Amiens. See S. Bormans et E. Schoolmeesters,
Cartulaire de l'Église Saint-Lambert à Liège, III, 540.

[32] Hocsemius, pp. 429–430; Levold de Northof, p. 402; Outremeuse,
VI, 581.

[33] S. Bormans et E. Schoolmeesters, *Cartulaire de l'Église Saint-
Lambert à Liège,* III, 478.

Pays de Liège. These met in the middle of April, the request of the chapter was accepted, the standards were raised, and the army was called out. Some subjects of Loon who disliked to see their lands burned called upon Reginald, count of Guelders, to intervene, with the intention of handing the county over to the chapter. In the negotiations which followed it was agreed that the bishop should receive the possessions and name a lieutenant. But none, it appears, would accept the office when appointed and the chapter again saw the coveted titles slip from its hands.[34] Meanwhile the chapter turned to Benedict XII and in the middle of March sent Anthony de Bugella to the curia with a statement of the rights of the bishop.[35] Peter, cardinal of St. Praxed, was named to investigate the conflicting claims and cited Thierry to appear on October 1. A number of cardinals wrote to Adolph and induced him to take action, and the bishop on August 4 actually commanded the levies to be ready a fortnight later. But Adolph was able to put the chapter and the cardinals off from time to time, and in February, 1337, was absent on a visit to his relatives in Westphalia.[36] The rights of the duke of Brabant were not infringed by the chapter, but he could hardly view with equanimity the addition of so much territory — about half as large as the *Pays de Liège* itself — to the possessions of the bishop and chapter. It would endanger his vital connections with Maastricht, Limburg, Valkenburg, and the Rhineland.

In August, 1337, a serious quarrel broke out between the duke of Brabant and the chapter. The church of St. Denis of Liège had long exercised the *merum et mixtum imperium* in Melin, and some rights to certain titles in the parish of Hervé. For two years the duke's officials, by threatening to impose bodily penalties and forfeiture of goods, had successfully resisted the collection of these tithes which had occasioned the church of St. Denis, to which they belonged, according to their claim, a loss of 3,000 florins. The produce remained in the fields where it rotted or was destroyed by cattle. At Melin Reginald of Argenteau, Duke

[34] S. Bormans et E. Schoolmeesters, *op. cit.,* p. 497; Hocsemius, p. 430.

[35] E. Schoolmeesters, " Recueil des Lettres Adressées pendant le XIVe Siècle, aux Papes et aux Cardinaux pour les Affaires de la Principauté de Liège," *Analectes pour Servir à l'Histoire ecclésiastique de la Belgique,* XV (1878), 18–20.

[36] Hocsemius, pp. 430–434.

John's seneschal of Limburg, seized the scabini at the command of his master, loaded them with chains, and confined them in prison for a brief space. This did not make them tractable; they balked and refused to render justice or cultivate the lands which they held from St. Denis. The duke wrathfully ordered a raid which was executed during the night. The inhabitants were robbed and plundered; some were imprisoned or grievously maltreated,[37] and two were even beheaded.[38]

On July 16, 1337, the chapter of the cathedral and collegiate churches of Liège begged the pope to aid the chapter of St. Denis whose rights were constantly being infringed by John's seneschal of Limburg. The appeal, however, had no effect, and on August 10 Adolph de La Marck ordered the priests of that part of his diocese which had jurisdiction over the subjects of the duke to put Limburg under the interdict and publish the ban of excommunication against Reginald of Argenteau, Hadier, and the *mayeur* of Hervé, for their violence.[39] But Duke John still nursed the wound of his defeated effort to secure a separate diocese for his lands and did not propose to yield tamely; he seized three of the bishop's subjects who had proclaimed the bans and summarily beheaded them.

In anticipation of difficulty which Duke John had correctly expected, the bishop called his estates to Liège to assemble on August 12 and appealed to them for aid. All the duke's lands in the diocese were now laid under interdict and a peremptory demand was made upon him for proper restitution. John in reply seized the goods of the clergy, a measure which naturally provoked great commotion.[40] The duke had been especially embittered by Adolph's persistent refusal to recognize the change in the status of Mechelen effected on March 31 of the previous year. On June 11 Adolph had protested to the corporation of Mechelen and sent a canon and his official to dissuade them from their present course.[41] It was apparently at this time that the

[37] A. Fierens, *Lettres de Benoît XII* (*1334–1342*), Nos. 453, 454.

[38] Hocsemius, p. 438.

[39] S. Bormans, "Notices des Cartulaires de la Collégiale de Saint-Denis," *BCRH*, 3d Ser., XIV (1872), 108–109.

[40] Hocsemius, p. 438.

[41] J. B. Sollerius, *Acta Sancti Rumoldi*, p. 183; J. David, *Geschiedenis van de Stad en de Heerlykheid van Mechelen, Bylagen,* pp. 511–512.

duke made another effort at the curia to abolish the obnoxious *Judicium Pacis*, but the papal proctor who was to investigate the case failed, if in fact he was ever appointed, to approve the representations which John's envoys made.[42]

Duke John was obliged to play a waiting game with the count of Flanders because of their joint domination over Mechelen. Philip VI sought to maintain his influence in these parts through the bishop of Liège and the count of Flanders, and accordingly the duchy of Brabant situated between them might at any moment be made the keystone of a powerful alliance which could conceivably nullify much of Edward's efforts in an offensive attack upon France. Conversely, the duke could unite the forces of Edward's scattered allies, the counts of Hainault, Holland, and Zeeland, and Guelders, the margrave of Juliers, and the towns of Flanders which might decide to join the enemy of France, and thus render Philip's support in the Low Countries impotent. This pivotal position dictated the duke's political policy, which consisted in procrastination and bargaining for whatever he might gain for his subjects.

Duke John determined to wring the utmost concession from Edward. First of all he stipulated that English wool should again come to Brabant to relieve the serious situation among the crafts. On May 24 Edward took under his protection the merchants of Brabant who would henceforth come into England to purchase wool and other necessaries. Beginning June 24 the merchants and buyers of wool from the duke's towns such as Louvain, Brussels, Antwerp, 's-Hertogenbosch, Mechelen, Tirlemont, Leeuw, Nivelles, Diest, Herenthals, Lier, Vilvoorde, Maastricht, Jodoigne, Grave, Breda, Bergen-op-Zoom, and Aerschot, as well as other places possessing any franchise, were to be free to secure the precious commodity. The amount of it was to be carefully controlled, for from each town two burghers were to be sent armed with letters from the duke who were to swear on the Gospels how much wool each needed for the ensuing half year. The amount could then be purchased and transported to Brabant, provided it would not find its way to Flanders. In the event of protracted hostilities between England and France, which was

[42] R. W. Nitzsch, "Heinrich IV und der Gottes und Landfrieden," *Forschungen zur Deutschen Geschichte*, XXI (1881), 295.

deemed quite likely, these terms could be extended for one or more periods of a half-year each.[43]

It was a splendid opportunity to drive an advantageous bargain. The duke demanded satisfaction for some outstanding claim of 10,000*l*. sterling. Seeking to humor him, no doubt, Edward agreed on June 8 to leave the case to the arbitration of the earl of Salisbury and Otto, seignior of Cuyk, who promised to render their decision before All Saints' Day.[44] On July 1 Edward promised 60,000*l*. sterling to be paid in Antwerp or some other town in Brabant. Of this sum 15,000*l*. were to be paid by August 1, at the following Christmas 5,000*l*., and the remaining 40,000*l*. in three instalments of 13,333*l*. 6*s*. 8*d*. at each Christmas thereafter. The exact reasons for this extraordinary gift are not set forth in the document, but it was no doubt intended as an inducement to Duke John.[45]

Meanwhile, the bishop of Lincoln and his company had arrived in Brussels from Hainault. There at the ducal court they met William van Duivenvoorde,[46] a pensioner of their royal master and vassal of the duke. They were nobly entertained and, according to John le Bel, it was on this occasion that John promised Edward his unconditional support.[47] The terms were enumerated in a document drawn up in the royal presence at Stamford on July 13. As soon as Edward should arrive in the Low Countries and advance upon the borders of France, the duke would raise and equip a force of 1,200 men-at-arms at Edward's expense. The earl of Huntingdon and Otto, seignior of Cuyk, pensioner of Edward as well as vassal of Brabant, were to appraise the value of the horses, excepting those of the baggage-trains, which might be lost during the expedition. Settlement was to be rendered within one month after declaration of such loss had been served by the duke's marshal or lieutenant. In case the duke or any of his subjects were captured, Edward promised to secure their restoration either by ransom or exchange.

[43] *Foedera*, II (2), 971–972.
[44] *Ibid.*, p. 974: " . . . Jehans . . . Duc de Lothr., de Brabant, et de Lembourgh, nous demande, et veult avoir de nous, pur certaine cause, la somme de dis mille livres d'estrelins."
[45] *Ibid.*, p. 981.
[46] *Ibid.*, p. 973.
[47] Le Bel, I, 125.

Furthermore, the duke might also, " if the welfare of the empire needed it," levy an extra thousand horse subject to the same terms as had been arranged with the counts of Hainault and Guelders.[48] On paper, at least, the duke of Brabant was now fully committed to Edward's support.

III. King Edward's Negotiations with Lewis the Bavarian (Summer, 1337)

HAVING thus arrived at an understanding with all the important parties in the Low Countries save Flanders and Liège, the bishop of Lincoln and the earls of Salisbury and Huntingdon betook themselves at the middle of June to Frankfurt [49] where the emperor was sojourning. Resentful of Philip's encroachment upon his imperial rights in the Low Countries and elsewhere and angry because of the treatment accorded to his father-in-law, Lewis the Bavarian was now wholly inclined to listen to English proposals. During the spring he had been kept informed by the English envoys and by those of his father-in-law, Claes Stuyck of Dordrecht and William de Gruuthuse, of the negotiations between Edward and Philip and especially of the propositions for the return of Robert of Artois.[50] For a fortnight many projects were discussed. Lewis was to provide 2,000 men-at-arms for the defense of the frontier in the Low Countries by November 30.[51] There was also some talk of securing the succession to the imperial crown for Edward.[52] Lewis even appears to have made an oral promise to name the English king his vicar,[53] a title which was intended to enhance greatly [54] Edward's prestige among the

[48] *Foedera*, II (2), 985.
[49] Hocsemius, p. 434; Kervyn, *Oeuvres de Froissart*, XVIII, 159.
[50] Kervyn, *Oeuvres de Froissart*, XVIII, 33.
[51] *Foedera*, II (2), 980.
[52] *Ibid.*, p. 984.
[53] See the statement of the earls of Salisbury and Huntingdon on July 20 in J. A. Nijhoff, *Gedenkwaardigheden uit de Geschiedenis van Gelderland*, I, 361: ". . . dominus Ludowicus . . . dominum nostrum regem Angliae, in gwerra, quam idem dominus imperator pro recuperatione jurium imperii, domino Phylippo de Valesio, pro rege Franciae se gerenti, movere intendit, suum constituerit, fecerit et creavit vicarium generalem. . . ." Cf. also *ibid.*, pp. 369–370.
[54] See Lewis' letter on July 12 to Count William, in *Foedera*, II (2), 984.

princes along the lower Rhine and to give him a certain appearance of legal authority in dealing with vassals of the empire.

At this time Ruprecht, count of the Rhenish Palatinate and a close relative of the emperor, also joined the enemies of Philip. He had accompanied the margrave of Juliers on his mission to Avignon and Paris in the spring of 1336,[55] and constantly showed a tendency to draw close to the party of English sympathizers. On May 25 he agreed to marry Marie, a daughter of Reginald, count of Guelders.[56] On June 30 he promised to provide one hundred and fifty men-at-arms in Edward's struggle to defend his rights, for which he was to receive 15,000 gold Florentine florins at Dordrecht on September 29 and, in addition, compensation for all loss of arms and horses within three months after appraisal should be made by the count's marshals. The margrave of Juliers' intimacy with all parties is revealed by the fact that in case of disagreement in regard to the terms of the treaty he and the bishop of Salisbury were to arrange an equitable settlement. A supplementary agreement promised Ruprecht a further sum of 16,000 florins payable at Dordrecht on September 29.[57] Later, on July 10, he was promised an additional 2,700 florins to use in counteracting the activities of French agents and their sympathizers in the empire.[58] On June 30 Markwart von Randegg, provost of Bamberg and a trusted councillor of Lewis the Bavarian, bound himself to serve Edward for a life annuity of one hundred and fifty florins and, should his services as envoy be required, as was apparently expected, he was to receive in addition two florins a day.[59]

Early in July the English envoys departed from Frankfurt,[60] but the margrave of Juliers and the count of Guelders tarried with the emperor who on July 7 appointed them his vicars gen-

[55] S. Riezler, *Vatikanische Akten*, No. 1877; J. Schwalm, " Reise nach Italien im Herbst, 1898," *Neues Archiv der Gesellschaft für aeltere Deutsche Geschichtskunde*, XXVII (1900), 724–726.

[56] I. A. Nijhoff, *Gedenkwaardigheden uit de Geschiedenis van Gelderland*, I, 357–358.

[57] *Foedera*, II (2), 979–980.

[58] *Ibid.*, p. 983.

[59] *Ibid.*, p. 980.

[60] They were still at Frankfurt on July 3 when they assigned to Claes Stuc, or Nicholas Stuyck, of Dordrecht, clerk of Count William's council, an annuity of 200 Florentine florins. See *ibid.*, p. 982.

eral for the diocese of Cambrai with full powers of a judicial and administrative nature and at the same time ordered the magistrates and burghers of Cambrai to obey them.[61] At this moment the envoys were again in Brussels where they secured the support of several petty magnates, Walram de Stein, Lambert d'Oupey, Philip de Kenteny, Craye de Hofstad, each with four helmets, and Ruprecht, count of Virneburg, with as many as thirty helmets. On the 10th they were at Cologne [62] and three days later at Roermond. John de Quatremars promised to aid with a party of ten men.[63] They made eager efforts to win as many supporters as possible, " by persuasion, blandishments, the promise of ample pecuniary reward, and by threats." [64]

The English agents next appeared at Gorinchem in Holland where on the 19th they gave the margrave of Juliers full powers to secure four hundred helmets in the region between Cologne, Lorraine, and Luxemburg, from every possible source.[65] During these days of busy traveling from place to place more definite arrangements had been made with Thierry, count of Loon, who bound himself to serve with two hundred men for an annual pension of 1,200 Florentine florins. Thierry, seignior of Valkenburg and Mountjoy, promised a hundred helmets for a like sum.[66] His attitude is especially interesting, for, aside from being the trusted councillor of the count of Guelders, he had married Matilda, daughter of Gerard, seignior of Voorne and burgrave of Zeeland, who had recently died and whose fiefs he had received from Count William.[67]

The English envoys had reappeared in the Low Countries as the bishop of Lincoln was expected to return to England.[68] The earls of Salisbury and Huntingdon were left to continue the work so well carried forward, and, having no doubt received instructions

---

[61] I. A. Nijhoff, *Gedenkwaardigheden uit de Geschiedenis van Gelderland,* I, 359–360.

[62] *Foedera,* II (2), 983.

[63] *Ibid.,* p. 985.

[64] See the letter of the archbishop of Cologne to Benedict XII, September 5, 1337, in S. Riezler, *Vatikanische Akten,* No. 1910.

[65] *Foedera,* II (2), 986.   [66] *Ibid.,* p. 992.

[67] F. van Mieris, *Groot Charterboek,* II, 596–597. Thierry had bound himself to serve his suzerain with a hundred and fifty men. See *ibid.,* pp. 597–598; J. Wolters, *Codex Diplomaticus Lossensis,* p. 210.

[68] Cf. *infra.* p. 233.

and financial resources from John de Woume,[69] returned to the emperor at Frankfurt where final arrangements were now made. On July 23 Lewis the Bavarian promised that he would serve Edward with 2,000 helmets for two months, beginning about October 1, for which he was to receive at Dordrecht 300,000 gold Florentine florins in three equal instalments on September 29, 1337, and February 2 and September 29, 1338. In this document Edward was called his vicar general.[70] The margrave of Juliers and count of Guelders, to whom the earls had given mandate to treat with the emperor, promised to increase the regular compensation of fifteen florins monthly for each man-at-arms to twenty, should this be deemed necessary at the expiration of the first two months of service.[71] Lewis, elector of Brandenburg, agreed to appear with a hundred helmets within one month's notice from his father, Lewis the Bavarian.[72] The emperor at once issued orders to his subjects along the lower Rhine to prepare for the coming campaign.[73]

IV. THE CRISIS IN FLANDERS (SPRING, 1337)

THE prevailing lack of food-stuffs and raw materials such as wool, woolfells, and hides became so serious in the towns of Flanders in April and May, 1337, that increased agitation is clearly discernible. Furthermore, the king had forbidden the use of foreign cloth in England and on May 3 had invited weavers and other craftsmen to settle in his realm.[74] This seemed to be aimed against the Flemish cloth monopoly and designed to stimulate the already rapidly developing English woollen industries and may have helped to increase the general depression.[75] The

[69] Kervyn, *Oeuvres de Froissart,* XVIII, 52.

[70] S. Riezler, "Urkunden zur Baierischen und Deutsche Geschichten aus den Jahren (1256–1343)," *Forschungen zur Deutschen Geschichte,* XX (1880), 270–271.

[71] J. Schwalm, "Reiseberichte, 1894–1896. Mit Beilagen," *Neues Archiv der Gesellschaft für aeltere Deutsche Geschichtskunde,* XXIII (1898), 345.   [72] *Foedera,* II (2), 996.

[73] For the order of the bishop of Liège, see Hocsemius, p. 438.

[74] *Foedera,* II (2), 696.

[75] On this point see H. Heaton, *The Woollen Industries of Yorkshire,* pp. 13, 20–21; E. Lipson, *The History of English Woollen and Worsted Industries,* pp. 12–13.

uneasiness among the crafts can well be illustrated from the accounts of the scabini of Ghent. Between April 16 and May 14 only a small number of watchmen were needed. The ten men who had kept watch from March 19 to April 16 were retained for the same duties until May 14. Extra guards were posted only on three nights when seven, four, and three men were added. On the 14th more were needed and two of the scabini and the bailiff's lieutenant had, besides the ten sergeants (*serianten*), fifty, seventy-two, and twelve watchmen on the next three nights. On the fourth and fifth they had twenty-six.[76]

Seventy men-at-arms were kept posted from May 20 until June 13 when a hundred were employed until the 23d. On the 14th fifty were appointed to patrol the streets of the crafts in order to supplement the endeavors of the hundred who had begun to watch the previous day, all under the command of two of the regular scabini, one of the councillors, and the bailiff's lieutenant.[77] On the 20th there appears to have been especial danger. The town was in great excitement when John van Everghem with sixty-seven men, eleven captains, and fifty-five soldiers (*selscutters*) operated for one night. On the 21st he led forth ten soldiers and twenty-two others with John uten Hove and went to Gavere by ship in order to enforce the town's rights in connection with the fisheries.[78]

Under these circumstances it was inevitable that there should be much consultation among the towns regarding the dire needs of the crafts who might at any moment break forth in violent upheaval. At Thielt representatives of the three towns met in the middle of May to discuss the seriousness of the situation.[79] On the 19th Ghent sent a deputation of the scabini, John uten Hove, a receiver's clerk, and ten representatives from its five parishes with thirty-five horses to Bruges to confer with the other towns.[80] It was apparently on this occasion that an appeal to

[76] N. de Pauw en J. Vuylsteke, *Rekeningen der Stad Gent,* I, 95 (note 3).

[77] *Ibid.,* p. 96 and notes.

[78] *Ibid.,* p. 97 and notes.

[79] *Ibid.,* p. 61: " . . . omme raet te ebbene up de bederven van den lande. . . ."

[80] *Ibid.,* p. 61: " . . . die voeren te Brucgheward smaendages naer alf meye ten parlemente, dar alt tlant was omme grote bederven van minen heere ende vanden lande. . . ."

Philip was decided upon. For the representatives returned on the 22d, and on the following day the scabini despatched two of their colleagues, John Spelliard and Everdey de Grutere, and three others, Tonis Bette, Lievin Bevelant, and Peter Zoetard, to lay the matter before the king and the countess of Flanders then tarrying in Paris.[81] Other meetings were held at Bruges on May 28 and 29 and on June 23 and 24, and at Oudenaarde from June 26 to 28.[82] The situation was decidedly threatening and certain rumors of unrest now began to be recorded in the accounts of Ghent. At Houthem there appears to have been an incipient upheaval and everything necessary was done to prevent an outbreak.[83]

Three courses were open to the Flemings. The first, upon which they were at present embarked, was to fulfill their feudal obligations toward their lawful suzerain Philip. But this policy had brought upon the country its present plight. The second was to break with him and support the English. This was impossible for the present as Count Louis was determined to remain loyal, and not until he and his Francophile supporters had definitively departed from the country at the opening of 1340 was this step to be taken. The third course was a policy of neutrality which aimed to steer between the two extremes. While remaining true to their suzerain, they might yet seek to come to an understanding with Edward regarding the importation of wool and foodstuffs. The Flemings, of course, knew of the negotiations between the duke of Brabant and the English envoys for the establishment of the wool staple at Antwerp. It would be necessary to treat also with him and with Count William of Hainault who was at this moment the focal point of English intrigue. This indeed appears to have been the topic of discussion among the representatives from Brabant, Hainault, and the towns of Flanders in the meeting at Male whither Ghent on April 18 had sent

[81] *Ibid.,* pp. 61–62: " . . . die voeren te Parijsward, 23 dage in mey an onsen heere den coninc, ende ane miere vrouwen van Vlaendren die daer was, omme raet ende ulpe hoe men ter neringhen soude moghen commen."

[82] *Ibid.,* pp. 62–63.

[83] *Ibid.,* p. 63: " Item scepenen Jan Speellard ende Jan van Pontraven, die voeren tHouthem in sente Pieters avonde omme daer te verhoeden datter ghene onruste gesciede. . . ."

two scabini, William van Vaernewijc and Lievin Abelin, one member from each of the five parishes, and John uten Hove.[84]

It cannot surprise anyone that in this troubled society there should be people exerting all their influence to secure a better appreciation of a policy friendly toward England. John de Thrandeston, who had orders to place himself at the disposal of the English envoys at the court of Count William in Valenciennes soon after his arrival there, was in contact with the situation in the Flemish towns which he solicitously visited.[85] Other agents undoubtedly were also passing from town to town covertly dropping suggestions calculated to rouse opposition to Philip.[86] Thrandeston appears to have been the chief of these, and, sufficiently armed with credentials, was the one who at this moment zealously labored with Count Louis and the towns of Bruges, Ghent, and Ypres for an economic, political, and matrimonial arrangement.[87]

Doubtless he came in contact with Sohier de Courtrai, an influential seignior and burgher of Ghent and pensioner of Philip.[88] He was accused of being in correspondence with the English representatives,[89] of actively furthering their intrigues,[90] and of receiving money from them with which to corrupt influential Flemings.[91] In his zeal for an arrangement with the English king he gave expression to thoughts which bordered upon treason.[92] Did Jacob van Artevelde at this time evince any decided bias for an English understanding? According to John le Bel and Froissart,[93] whom historians have usually accepted, he did. It

[84] *Ibid.*, pp. 59–60: " . . . die voeren some in goeden vridage, ende zome in paeschavonde te Malen ten parlemente daer de goede lieden waren vanden steden om dacort te sprekene van Vlaendren ende van Brabant ende van Henegouwe. . . ."

[85] Kervyn, *Oeuvres de Froissart,* XVIII, 158.

[86] *Grandes Chroniques,* V, 370.

[87] Kervyn, *Oeuvres de Froissart,* XVIII, 158.

[88] J. Viard, *Les Journaux du Trésor de Philippe VI,* pp. 879, 904.

[89] Le Muisit, p. 110.

[90] Le Bel, I, 132–133. Cf. Froissart, I, 129–131, 396–397. According to le Bel, I, 131–134, the bishop of Lincoln also visited Flanders, but there is no documentary evidence for this.

[91] *Grandes Chroniques,* V, 370; de Budt, p. 325.

[92] *Chronographia,* II, 42; de Budt, p. 325. See the words of Edward to his son on May 8, 1338, in *Foedera,* II (2), 1035.

[93] Le Bel, I, 132–134; Froissart, I, 129–131.

is by no means impossible that he did confer with Edward's emissaries. But this cannot be proved from trustworthy documents. And even if he did, Sohier de Courtrai was undoubtedly the chief agitator at this moment.

V. King Philip's Diplomacy in the Low Countries
(Summer, 1337 — Autumn, 1338)

With evident anxiety King Philip saw the storm clouds gathering on all sides. More than ever he looked to the Scots to provide a diversion by attacking Edward. He treated with their representatives when at Lyons at about Easter and promised to aid them to the limit of his power. There was an extravagant rumor that in the ports of Normandy there were 2,300 vessels and thirty galleys with 21,000 mariners, a force which was deemed irresistible. Warlike equipment was being collected, men-at-arms were hastening to his aid from such parts as Flanders, Brabant, and Germany, and even a day and place were assigned, as rumor had it, for the Scots to join the French, and their combined forces were said to number 40,000 men.[94]

Philip took measures for defense at all points in Aquitaine, on the Channel, and especially on the side of the Low Countries whence to all appearances the first blow would come, for Edward had arranged with his allies to be on the borders of the Cambrésis in August or September. On May 9 he had his bailiff in Vermandois make public proclamation ordering his subjects to be ready to join him by Pentecost. On the 23d the barons and nobles were commanded to present themselves before the king at Amiens by July 7. On July 11 the bailiff of Vermandois was instructed to visit the castles and strongholds of his jurisdiction, repair them, and provide them with troops, victuals, and other things needed for their support. Later, the royal army was ordered to be at Amiens on August 1.[95]

While no direct information has come to us regarding Philip's

[94] Kervyn, *Oeuvres de Froissart*, IV, 39–40.

[95] P. Varin, *Archives Administratives de la Ville de Rheims*, II (2), 782–783, 786–787; J. Viard, " Les Ressources Extraordinaires de la Royauté sous Philippe VI de Valois," *Revue des Questions Historiques*, Vol. XLIV (1888), p. 178; J. Viard, *Documents Parisiens de Philippe VI de Valois*, I, 291.

reception of the delegation from Ghent, it can safely be assumed
that he could not be moved to favorable action by the misery in
the towns. He did not intend that Flanders should in any way
play a rôle detrimental to himself in the impending struggle.
While Edward realized that without Flanders his chances for success in any campaign against France were less promising, Philip
would surely seek to avoid a repetition of what happened in the
days of Philip Augustus and Philip the Fair, regardless of what
misery might be engendered thereby. He accordingly sought to
put a stop to English intrigue in Flanders by inflicting exemplary
punishment upon one who was accused of having exchanged letters with the English envoys and of being seduced by them by
plentiful gifts of money. He ordered the count to seize Sohier de
Courtrai, the ringleader of all those who urged an understanding
with the king of England.[96] This step was taken at Bruges on
July 6 when Count Louis met the representatives of the towns to
discuss ways and means to aid the crafts.[97] Among the envoys
from Ghent was Sohier de Courtrai. He was charged with treasonable intercourse with the envoys of the English king and, in spite
of his denial of all guilt and the protests of his colleagues, was
at once placed in prison.[98]

This was a maneuver not calculated to assuage the troubled
guilds, because an understanding with Edward was for the time
being impossible and English wool would apparently never come
to Flanders. The magistrates of Ghent were greatly angered and
they held that the arrest was in violation of their liberties.[99] Immediately informed of the event,[100] they forthwith dispatched two
of the scabini to confer with their companions at Bruges, demanded
that Sohier de Courtrai be handed over to them for punishment,
and followed the count to Ypres, persisting in their pressing

[96] *Grandes Chroniques,* V, 370. Le Muisit, p. 110.

[97] N. de Pauw en J. Vuylsteke, *Rekeningen der Stad Gent,* I, 63:
" . . . te Brucghe ten parlemete daer lant was omme raet ende wech te
vindene over de neringhe, ende daer wart mijn heere de Courtrosijn up
ghehouden. . . ."

[98] *Chronographia,* II, 43; de Budt, p. 325; *Grandes Chroniques,* V, 370;
N. de Pauw en J. Vuylsteke, *Rekeningen der Stad Gent,* I, 63–64.

[99] *Chronographia,* II, 43; *Grandes Chroniques,* V, 370.

[100] N. de Pauw en J. Vuylsteke, *Rekeningen der Stad Gent,* I, 79:
" Item 1 bode die quam van Br. smandages daer naer (i.e. on July 7) met
lrn. tote scepenen, 20s."

plea.[101]   On the 10th a delegation of two scabini and eight representatives from the parishes went to Bruges to continue the demand and followed the count to Ypres and Courtrai.[102]   Appeal was made to the duke of Brabant to join in the plea, but even his requests, if he made any, were without avail.[103]   The scabinus, Everdey de Grutere, and Gilles vanden Houtte were sent to Paris on July 11 to seek Philip's intervention, but they too met with no success.[104]   From the 14th to the 22d a delegation dogged Louis' steps at Bruges, Ypres, and Courtrai, while on the 15th a messenger was sent to beg William, count of Hainault, Holland, and Zeeland, and his brother, John of Hainault, to interpose their good offices.[105]

Philip made some concessions.   At Moncel-lez-Pons-Sainte-Maxence on August 15 he cancelled the 80,000*l.* Parisian which the towns still owed for the previous two years under the Treaty of Arques, reduced by a half the amount due on May 1, and granted a delay for the rest.   He also surrendered a claim to 10,000*l.* still due for 1310, 1311, and 1312, which represented an assignment upon properties in the castleries of Lille and Douai made in accordance with the agreements amending the Treaty of Athis-sur-Orge.   Furthermore, Flanders was to have the monopoly of all wool grown in France, provided an investigation should reveal the inhabitants to be wholly devoted to the king.[106]   These measures of course could not alleviate the cause of the trouble — the embargo upon English wool — as the annual growth of French wool was negligible in comparison with the English.

On the 16th of August an alliance was formed between Louis and Philip, whereby the former promised to comport himself as

---

[101] *Ibid.,* pp. 63–64: "... ende worden naer gesent te Brucge scepenen Clais uten Hove ende Willem de Groote, omme te sprekene metgaders haren gesellen scepenen die daer waren, minen here van Vlaendren omme de deliveranche vanden Courtrosijn, ende daer omme volgeden sij nerenstelike minen heere al tYpre. . . ."   Cf. *Chronographia,* II, 43.

[102] *Ibid.,* p. 64.   This effort cost 160*l.*

[103] On August 10, 1337.   See *ibid.*

[104] They were out twenty-four days, *ibid.*   They returned on August 3 and on the following day sent another delegation to Philip at Compiègne, *ibid.,* p. 66.

[105] *Ibid.,* p. 65.   On the 23d another appeal was made to the duke of Brabant and again on July 31, *ibid.,* p. 66.

[106] Kervyn, *Histoire de Flandre,* III, 173–174.

a loyal vassal and pledged the aid of Crown Flanders and even Imperial Flanders against all enemies of France. Philip swore to protect Louis against all enemies, especially the emperor, and never to make peace with the latter or with Edward or their accomplices without including him in its terms.[107] In other ways Philip was careful to show his favor; he sanctioned the arrangements between Louis and Eudes, duke of Burgundy and count of Artois, by which some lands were held in fee in Artois;[108] and later, on August 22, at St. Cloud approved the grant of 200*l.* annually by Louis and the countess to Peter des Essars, *maître des comptes.*[109]

Meanwhile, the royal representatives, Andrew de Florence, the bishop of Tournai, Hugh Quieret, Peter de Cugnières, Nicholas Béhuchet, and Peter des Essars,[110] who had been dispatched to Flanders to investigate the loyalty of the Flemings, appeared at Ypres. On the 27th a delegation of two scabini, their clerk, John uten Hove, and three others left Ghent, and with the deputies of Bruges and Ypres presented themselves before them. On the 29th the royal representatives declared themselves fully satisfied with their loyalty and solemnly renewed the royal concessions made at Moncel-lez-Pons-Sainte-Maxence.[111] To the scabini of Bruges special favor was shown. As early as May they had appealed to the king for the right to deepen and widen a portion of the town moat in order to secure a plentiful supply of fresh water which was seriously needed to maintain the brewing activities of the town. The bishop and his associates had been directed to proceed to the spot and investigate the validity of their statements. This was done and a document was issued, also

---

[107] Kervyn, *Oeuvres de Froissart,* XVIII, 45–47. The *Chronicon Comitum Flandrensium,* p. 210, however, states that Count Louis was opposed to Philip's request that the Flemings aid him against the English.

[108] E. Petit, *Histoire des Ducs de Bourgogne, VIII (Pièces Justificatives),* 368–369.

[109] J. Viard, *Documents Inédits Parisiens du Règne de Philippe VI de Valois;* I, 308–310.

[110] For the personnel, see L. Gilliodts van Severen, *Archives de la Ville de Bruges,* I, 482; I. L. A. Diegerick, *Inventaire des Archives de Ypres,* II, 99–100.

[111] Kervyn, *Histoire de Flandre,* III, 174 (note), quoting from the *Ruwenboek* in the archives of Bruges. See N. de Pauw en J. Vuylsteke, *Rekeningen der Stad Gent,* I, 169.

on the 29th at Ypres, granting the right to make the improve-
ments between the St. Catherine and Coolkerke gates.[112]

Thus supported by Count Louis and part of the patriciate in
the great towns, Flanders seemed quite solidly committed to uphold Philip's interests in the Low Countries. Efforts were made
on the Zwin to lend aid to the Scots during these months. The
bishop of Glasgow visited Flanders and appears to have been
busy in securing warlike equipment for them.[113] Hostile craft
were fitted out during the early part of the year, and, on February 6, Edward ordered John de Roos, admiral of his fleet north of
the Thames, to impress ships on the North Sea and collect them
at Orwell with the intention of opposing those bringing aid to the
Scots. On March 10 John de Wesenham was commanded to take
two ships from Lynn to attack the Flemish craft on the coasts
of Scotland which were said to have come from the Zwin laden
with warlike materials and victuals.[114] The Scotch government
did its best to cultivate the friendship of the Flemings; an item
in the Exchequer Rolls of Scotland of this year mentions the payment to some Flemish merchants of 300*l.* 4*s.* 9*d.* for the damage
inflicted by John Crabbe's ships in the Firth of Tay in 1332 in
connection with the hostilities at Perth and Berwick.[115] A vain
effort was made to detach Reginald, count of Guelders, from the
alliance with Edward. The Scotch king, Bruce, who had married
Joan, a sister of Countess Eleanor, sent Archibald de Cragbarry
to the Low Countries, but he could accomplish practically nothing.[116]

The duchy of Brabant remained aloof from Philip. The violent
antagonism between the duke and the bishop of Liège was quite
sufficient to prevent the former from ranging himself in the camp

[112] L. Gilliodts van Severen, *Inventaire de la Ville de Bruges,* I, 480–
481.

[113] Hemingburgh, II, 314; *Lanercost,* p. 291; Knighton, II, 2; *Melsa,*
II, 378 (*sub* 1335). See also *Kervyn, Oeuvres de Froissart,* XVIII, 39–40

[114] *Rotuli Scotiae,* II, 482–485.

[115] See *Rotuli Scaccarii Regum Scotorum,* I, 450–451: " Et in solucione
facta computanti, pro dampnis et gravaminibus illatis quibusdam merca-
toribus Flandriae, quorum naves, de mandato speciali comitis Marchie et
Andreae de Moravia, tunc custodum de Berwyco, in acquam de Tey misse,
periclitabantur, per literas ipsorum dominorum ostensas super compotum
cccixl*b.* iiij*s.*"

[116] See *ibid.,* p. 450: " Et in solucione facta Archibaldo de Cragbarry,

of Philip's supporters. The dire industrial condition of Flanders was the duke's opportunity, and during the whole of 1337 he revealed an unmistakable leaning toward Edward. Under these circumstances Adolph de la Marck would never consent to support Edward and his personal enemy the duke against his traditional friend, the king of France. In vain did the English agents send him costly gifts and seek to lure him to their side.[117]

Equally futile were the efforts of John de Woume who in September of this year sought to act as intermediary between the two enemies when negotiations were opened.[118] Since the duke of Brabant was clearly inclined toward an English alliance, Bishop Adolph promised on July 29 to send five hundred men as far west as Compiègne to aid Philip against Edward and the emperor in return for a cash payment of 15,000*l.* Parisian and wages for himself and his followers.[119] His allegiance was thus definitely settled when orders came from the emperor at the beginning of August to prepare for an invasion of France. But few of the clergy knew at first how irresolute Louis was. Some of the canons of Liège were frightened, " but in vain," as the *scholasticus* Hocsem, whose observations are usually sound, states in his chronicle.[120]

With patent anxiety Philip also watched the storm gathering in the empire. All sorts of rumors, caused by the insidious intrigues of English envoys, were rife. In August the pope was suspected by Philip of some readiness to absolve the margrave of

---

transeunti in negociis domini regis ad comitem de Gelre, iiii*lb.*" For the possible date, see *ibid.,* p. cxlvii.

[117] Le Bel, I, 127; Froissart, I, 126. Nevertheless Edward did not give up hope of winning some support at Liège. On October 4 he granted to Renardus de Ghore, canon of St. Lambert's, an annual pension of six hundred Florentine florins. See *Foedera,* II (2), 1000.

[118] Kervyn, *Oeuvres de Froissart,* XVIII, 51: " . . . d'Angvers vers Loveyn II jours (Sept. 16–18) et de là à Brusseles I jour à un tretys que le duk avoit ovesque l'evesque de Leges et là demourai, II jours."

[119] *Ibid.,* pp. 42–45; le Bel, I, 127; J. Schwalm, " Reiseberichte, 1894–1896. Mit Beilagen," *Neues Archiv der Gesellschaft für aeltere Deutsche Geschichtskunde,* XXVII (1897), 346–349. Adolph and Engelbert de la Marck were receiving pensions and gifts from Philip in 1338 and 1339, and also in 1337, it would seem. See J. Viard, *Les Journaux de Philippe VI,* pp. 878, 884, 903–904, 906, 926.

[120] Hocsemius, p. 438.

Juliers and the count of Guelders from their oaths of vassalage to the French crown. This of course touched the support which they were bound to give him against Robert of Artois, and any such absolution would naturally be deemed prejudicial to the French king's safety. There was also vague talk of some papal effort to settle the unsatisfactory arrangement of Mechelen; but Benedict in a letter of October 3 took great pains to remove all suspicion of any partisan sympathy.[121] And the situation became worse as the autumn wore on. There was much talk about hostile feeling in Germany. Edward's eventual succession to the kingship of the Romans was much discussed, as also the proposal of naming him vicar for life in lower Germany whence he would be able to strike effectively at France. It was said that great wealth was being collected to secure the adherence of all princes and that all Germany in fact was in Edward's camp. It was even rumored that plans were being laid to punish such German princes as might seek to aid France.[122]

The king of Bohemia was bound to support Philip. The English agents, it is said, even made no effort to secure his allegiance, knowing full well his family connections with the Valois house.[123] King John was in Prague when he heard of the presence of the bishop of Lincoln and the earls of Salisbury and of Huntingdon at Frankfurt. He fairly flew over the country, and in three days was with the emperor. But in the few days he spent with him he was quite unable to deter him from allying with Edward.[124] Thereupon he proceeded to France and on August 6 agreed to aid Philip with five hundred men-at-arms at the latter's expense. He was to receive 30,000*l*. Parisian with which to equip and maintain his troops.[125]

But there were also some other parties in the empire who would not yield to English blandishments. Walram, archbishop of Cologne, although a brother of the margrave of Juliers, was fully de-

[121] S. Riezler, *Vatikanische Akten,* No. 1885; W. H. Bliss, *Calendar of Entries in the Papal Registers,* II, 564; A. Fierens, *Lettres de Benoit XII (1334–1342),* No. 430.

[122] W. H. Bliss, *Calendar of Entries in the Papal Registers,* II, 565–566. See also Kervyn, *Oeuvres de Froissart,* XVIII, 41.

[123] Le Bel, I, 127.

[124] Königsaaler, *Geschichts-Quellen,* p. 531.

[125] *Archives Nationales,* Paris, J. 432. No. 11.

termined in accordance with his oath of 1332 to adhere to the papal policy of exalted aloofness from the secular antagonisms of the princes of Christendom. During the summer he steadily resisted the pressure of Edward's allies and refused to join the many-headed coalition.[126] It was hoped that his influence would be sufficient to insure a friendly attitude on the part of the burghers of Cologne. From Vincennes on October 2 Philip dispatched Thomas de Septem Fontanis and John de Dintavilla with letters to the magistrates of the city to protest the statements of Edward and the emperor to the effect that he had invaded the rights of the empire in the Low Countries and, in spite of many efforts and representations, had refused persistently to withdraw. He denied these charges and declared that he merely sought his just rights. On the 23d the magistrates of Cologne made reply in friendly language, declaring their belief that Philip was the legitimate king of France and desiring to see no harm come to him.[127] A number of minor figures also were to be found among his supporters: Henry, count of Vaudémont,[128] Nicholas of Salm, and Godefroid, count of Linange.[129] Curiously enough, the seignior of Quatremars, already bound to serve Edward, saw an excellent opportunity to enrich himself by promising also to support Philip.[130] More important than these petty figures was Henry, duke of Lower Bavaria, a bitter enemy of Lewis the Bavarian. At the suggestion of his father-in-law, John, king of Bohemia, he promised on November 9 to serve Philip in return for 56,000 small florins.[131] King John remained the chief hope of the French king in Germany during the next year. At the opening of 1338

126 S. Riezler, *Vatikanische Akten,* No. 1910.

127 See the appendix in Lescot, pp. 211–213.

128 *Ibid.,* p. 221. J. Viard, *Les Journaux de Philippe VI,* p. 883.

129 Cf. appendix in Lescot, p. 221 (notes).

130 J. Viard, " La France sous Philippe VI," *Revue des Questions Historiques,* LIX (1895), 351 (note); J. Viard, *Les Journaux de Philippe VI,* pp. 883–905. For Arnulf de Shene, see *ibid.,* p. 878, and the bishop of Metz, p. 882.

131 H. Schrohe, " Kleine Beiträge zu den Regesten der Könige Rudolf bis Karl IV," *Mitteilungen des Instituts für Oesterreichische Geschichtsforschung,* XXVI (1905), 485–486; J. Schwalm, " Reise nach Italien im Herbst, 1898," *Neues Archiv der Gesellschaft für aeltere Deutsche Geschichtskunde,* XXV (1899), 761–762; F. von Weech, *Kaiser Ludwig der Baier und König Johann von Böhmen,* p. 68.

this royal busybody was with Philip's representatives in Flanders and was designated the king's lieutenant in Languedoc.[132]

Philip also sought to detach Reginald, count of Guelders, from his enemy. John de Dintavilla and Thomas de Septem Fontanis were ordered to proceed to his presence, when on their mission to Cologne, and present Philip's demand drawn up at Vincennes on October 6. Reginald was required in view of a former understanding, apparently that of Senlis in 1332, to come to his aid at Amiens with the specified number of men-at-arms by a fortnight after All Saints' Day. They found the count at Montfoort where a notarial instrument was drawn up on the 28th. John de Dintavilla recited Edward's connection with Robert of Artois and called upon him to protect Philip's rights. Reginald, however, sought to put him off, stated that he purposed to carry out his plighted word, and declared that he wished to be true to Philip in spite of the fact that his wife was a sister of Edward, but that, since he did not have his councillors with him, immediate response was out of the question.[133]

That Philip had little faith that Count Reginald would act in accordance with his plighted word is abundantly proved by his effort to cultivate the friendship of the Friesians.[134] Reginald's interests in the lands of the bishop of Utrecht east of the Yssel were paramount and in the north he was bound to come in conflict with the Friesians who were determined to resist his encroachments. At the close of August in 1336 he appeared with a strong force at Vollenhove and was victorious in a clash with them.[135] Living under the perpetual shadow of the power of the counts of Holland and of Guelders, the Friesians readily listened to Philip's letter of October 7 in which he referred to the apocryphal priv-

[132] N. de Pauw en J. Vuylsteke, *Rekeningen der Stad Gent,* I, 180. His title was "locumtenens domini regis Franciae in partibus occitanis. . . ." See *Recueil Général des Anciennes Lois Françaises dépuis l'An 420 jusqu'à la Révolution de 1789,* IV, 446–447.

[133] A. Hulshof, "Oorkonden aangaande de Betrekkingen der Gelderschen Vorsten tot Frankrijk," *Werken uitgegeven door de Vereeniging Gelre,* IX (1912), 222–227. For Thomas' pension, see J. Viard, *Les Journaux de Philippe VI,* pp. 881–882.

[134] F. Kern, "Frankreich und die Friesen. Analekten zur Geschichte des 13 und 14 Jahrhunderts," *Mitteilungen des Instituts für Oesterreichische Geschichtsforschung,* XXXI (1910), 82–87.

[135] *Chronicon Tielense,* pp. 329–330.

ileges and other favors of Charlemagne, "his predecessor," and asked their coöperation against Count Reginald, the emperor, and the king of England. This letter was brought to the Cistercian abbot, Wibrand of Klaarkamp, by John Richer, a professor of law, and Baldwin, a monk of Klaarkamp, who had attended the *studium* in Paris. The people of Westergoo assembled and on November 8 and 13 promised to regard Philip's enemies, the count of Guelders and his accomplices, as their own. This decision was further extended when delegates from all the districts of Friesland solemnly ratified it on March 18 of the ensuing year.[136]

It is interesting to note that in all these negotiations no effort was made by Philip to arouse the Friesians against the count of Hainault, Holland, and Zeeland who had long carried on a feud with them and was really a much more serious enemy of their liberties than Reginald. Edward's father-in-law had finally died on June 7,[137] and the youthful heir William soon showed dangerous signs of friendship for Philip. When Edward's visit to the Low Countries at the close of August was postponed and his forces failed to appear on the borders of the Cambrésis, Count William was compelled to do homage to Philip for Ostrevant. To refuse would have been folly, for Philip's forces had been ordered to collect at Amiens on August 1. On November 17 he discharged his feudal duties and Philip, probably to reassure the young count of his good will and wean him from the English party, appointed the bishop of Arras and Peter de Cugnières to investigate the vexatious question of Solesmes and Fismy, and ordered his officials to make only the accustomed levies in Ostrevant.[138] To incite the Friesians against him at this stage might drive William definitely into the ranks of Philip's enemies.

Although Philip's position in the Low Countries was serious, it was far from hopeless. For the time being he could rely upon the count of Flanders and a part of the Flemish patriciate to keep that region faithful. The bishop of Liège and John, king

[136] F. Kern, "Frankreich und die Friesen. Analekten zur Geschichte des 13 und 14 Jahrhunderts," *Mitteilungen des Instituts für Oesterreichische Geschichtsforschung,* XXXI (1910), 82–87.

[137] *Bourgeois de Valenciennes,* p. 160; *Chronique Parisienne Anonyme,* p. 170; *Chronicon Tielense,* pp. 329–331.

[138] L. Devillers, *Cartulaire,* I, 9–10.

of Bohemia, were allies of unshakable loyalty. The church of Tournai had been taken under his protection in August, 1335, and the loyalty of the scabini of Tournai was entirely trustworthy.[139] The archbishop of Cologne was determined to remain neutral. On the other hand, the duke of Brabant was wholly uncertain, while the effort to keep the count of Guelders and the margrave of Juliers faithful by threatening the former in his vital interests in Friesland and by insisting that both should fulfill their sworn obligations toward him was bound to fail. Philip had treated his brother-in-law William, count of Hainault, Holland, and Zeeland, with scant consideration and thereby had driven him into active opposition. With tact and skilful diplomacy he could possibly prevent his youthful successor from joining Edward.

VI. Edward's Invasion of France Postponed until June, 1338

IN AUGUST Henry de Burghersh, the bishop of Lincoln, was ready to proceed to England and orally report to Edward the condition of affairs in the Low Countries and in the empire. But the passage between Wissant and Dover was swarming with hostile ships sent out by King Philip who was anxious to intercept the bishop's return.[140] Edward had taken steps to meet the danger and on June 27 ordered Nicholas Usomaris, the vice-admiral of the fleet of Aquitaine, to collect as many ships as possible and sail along the French coast to destroy them. John de Roos, admiral of the fleet north of the Thames, had been directed on the 20th to proceed to Dordrecht with forty ships where they were expected to be waiting on the 30th in order to escort the bishop and his company.[141]

At the same time the king dispatched John de Woume, a merchant of York,[142] with letters for the bishop, the earls, and the count of Guelders. Setting out from Stamford, he sailed from

---

[139] *Archives du Département du Nord*, Lille, No. B729. For favors granted to the scabini of Tournai in April, 1334, see J. Viard, *Documents Parisiens du Règne de Philippe VI de Valois*, I, 193–194.

[140] G. de la Roncière, *Histoire de la Marine Française*, I, 396; de Nangis, II, 156.

[141] *Foedera*, II (2), 974, 977; cf. *CPR* (1334–8), pp. 456–457.

[142] *CCR* (1333–7), pp. 110–111, 366, 732; *CPR* (1334–8), p. 416.

Yarmouth and arrived at Brielle on July 10, whence he hastened to Nijmegen where he delivered his documents three days later. Thereafter he was at the service of the ambassadors and allies in the Low Countries and was employed in many financial and diplomatic negotiations. On July 16 he was at Bruges where he received 2,000 marks which he delivered at Dordrecht on the 22d and he immediately repeated this journey for the same purpose and was again back at Dordrecht and Schiedam on the 31st. On August 2 he departed for Brussels to pay a sum which was due on August 15 and September 8 to parties who had entered Edward's services. Retracing his steps without halting at Brussels, he arrived at Schiedam on the 10th. On his way he had picked up certain information that French galleys had appeared in the North Sea and were hovering off the coast to intercept the passage of the returning envoys. This news at once evoked efforts to frustrate possible attacks. In Holland sailors were engaged with ships to defend the narrow waters around the islands and possibly to divert the attention of the French from the bishop and his company, and John de Woume was hurriedly sent to Antwerp to secure a loan of 1,000 marks for some troops.[143]

Meanwhile the bishop of Lincoln and his attendants sailed. They apparently took advantage of a storm to elude the watchfulness of the enemy and crossed over directly from the mouth of the Meuse to England. During the tempest some of the English company and their horses were forced to land in Holland. When John de Woume returned from Antwerp he tarried at Dordrecht from August 23 to 28 and cared for them, paying their expenses, and securing a place for them to stay at Geertruidenberg. Others appear to have landed off Voorne and to have wrought some violence upon the subjects of Brielle which Edward promptly sought to rectify by apology and promise to investigate.[144] The French galleys nevertheless continued their efforts by raiding and hovering off the Schelde mouths, thus making it impossible for de Woume to cross to England from

---

[143] He received his safe-conduct on June 28. Cf. *CPR* (1334–8), p. 465. For the itinerary, see Kervyn, *Oeuvres de Froissart*, XVIII, 52; Froissart, I, 134.

[144] *CCR* (1337–9), p. 269. The order is dated September 3.

Middelburg on September 1 and a week later from either that place or from Veere.[145]

Hardly had John de Roos sailed past the coast of Zeeland and the Schelde mouth when he fell in with a ship named *La Cogge de Flanders*. It conveyed John Steward, bishop of Glasgow, who, as was noted above, had been active in Flanders in behalf of his countrymen. With him were a large company of Scotch magnates including David de la Haye, Hugh Gifford, John de la More, William Baly, Alexander Fygas, and William Muffet. They were carrying a large amount of money, weapons of war, and many diplomatic documents.[146] A fight ensued in which many of the Scots were killed and the bishop was so wounded that he died before the ship could reach port at Sandwich whither it was taken as a prize for the king.[147]

Meanwhile, the bishop of Lincoln landed safely at Dover and on August 7 arrived in London.[148] Edward greeted him with approval and on the 26th solemnly ratified the conventions made at Valenciennes, Binche, Frankfurt, Cologne, Roermond, Brussels, and Gorinchem,[149] and presented him with a gift of 1,000 marks. To the emperor he expressed his entire satisfaction with the terms of the alliance and promised that he himself and his heirs would be ever ready to labor for the recovery of the rights of the empire at any time when called upon and further bound himself not to make a separate truce or peace with Philip.[150]

Warlike preparations were now in full swing on every hand as Edward was planning to be in the Low Countries by September 17. The alien priories and benefices held by subjects of Philip were sequestrated on July 1;[151] Welsh troops were collected,

[145] Kervyn, *Oeuvres de Froissart,* XVIII, 52.

[146] Hemingburgh, II, 314, states that there were 250 in all; *Lanercost,* p. 291; Knighton, II, 2; *Melsa,* II, 378 (*sub* 1335), where the number of Scots and Flemings is given as 160.

[147] *CCR* (1337–9), pp. 93, 171–2, 331–332, 334. C. Eubel, *Hierarchia Catholica,* I, 275, however, states that the bishop died on February 17, 1337.

[148] W. Stechele, "England und der Niederrhein bei Beginn der Regierung König Eduards III (1327–1337)," *Westdeutsche Zeitschrift für Geschichte und Kunst,* XXVII (1908), *Anlage III,* 472–473; Froissart, I, 134–135.

[149] *Foedera,* II (2), 991–992.

[150] *Ibid.,* pp. 991–995.

[151] *Ibid.,* p. 982; Knighton, II, 2; *CCR* (1337–9), p. 151; *CPR* (1334–8), pp. 479, 487, 488.

equipped, and ordered to be at Canterbury on September 30; exportation of precious metals was forbidden; Walter de Manny and Bartholomew de Burghersh were appointed admirals of the fleets north and west of the Thames respectively and were ordered to put out to sea;[152] and the king carefully manipulated the clergy and laity for the coming crisis to secure a grant in the meeting to take place at Westminster on September 26.[153]

But particularly striking was the gigantic monopoly of wool which the council arranged at London on July 26 with the more important merchants of the realm, chief of whom were William de la Pole of Hull and Reginald de Conductu of London. They were to purchase wool at a rate fixed by a schedule which ranged from five to twelve marks a sack for the better quality, while the inferior product was to be bought freely. The growers were to receive from the merchants promises to pay one half within six months and the balance at the end of the year. When the wool was collected at the ports the king was to transport it under convoy to the Low Countries as would be determined by the council. Not until the 30,000 sacks had been disposed of was any other wool to leave England. Hence high prices were to be maintained and the royal portion — one half the net proceeds — would be very great. The total sum, including the customs, was estimated at 200,000*l.* and it was provided that the merchants were to advance from time to time amounts equalling this sum as the wool was sold. As security they were to control the customs until they should be fully compensated.[154]

The widening breach between Edward and Philip thus threatened a great war in which most of the princes of Christendom would be concerned. The pope was naturally eager to avert a rupture, but in vain.[155] He still sought to act in his customary rôle as pacifier and had sent the archbishops of Sens and Rouen in June to both kings to urge peace.[156] Frightened by fresh war-

---

[152] *Foedera,* II (2), 986–987.

[153] J. F. Willard, "Edward III's Negotiations for a Grant in 1337," *English Historical Review,* XXI (1906), 727–731. Cf. *CCR* (1337–9) pp. 241–241–255.

[154] *CCR* (1337–9), pp. 148–150. For an account of this monopoly, see G. Unwin, *The Estates of Merchants in Finance and Trade under Edward III,* pp. 190–195.

[155] Baker, p. 60; *Chronographia,* II, 55.

[156] W. H. Bliss, *Calendar of Entries in the Papal Registers,* II, 563.

like activities in England, he sent Peter de Burgundionis, papal chaplain and auditor, on June 24 to confer with the king, and on July 20 ordered Edward, who had asked for license to form a confederation with Lewis the Bavarian, to have no dealings with the heretic. He begged him to recall how his grandfather had failed to profit from similar alliances with German princes. Philip was amenable to the papal desires and on September 24 agreed to cease operations in Gascony and attacks elsewhere upon Edward until Christmas. The pope now urged the nuncios who had gained this success to cross at once over to England " that the spark may not become a flame." [157] But there was no danger of immediate hostilities, for Edward even before their arrival had postponed his expedition to the Low Countries. On September 24 — one week after the day when he had promised to be in the Cambrésis — he ordered all officials who were collecting troops to dismiss those that were ready.[158]

The real reason for the change in the royal plans was the failure of the merchants to collect the wool as had been contracted for in London on July 27. The growers were reluctant to part with their wool at a fixed low price.[159] The ships which had been collected in the Thames and the various ports to transport the king and the wool to the Low Countries were forced to lie idle. The shipmasters were confronted with unusual expenses and some were even constrained by threat of starvation to sell their ships. The idleness of so many vessels seriously interfered with the trade in unrestricted articles and naturally occasioned great dissatisfaction among all classes concerned with shipping and trade. In the country the growers resorted to all manner of evasion. As had been expected by the king and council, some concealed their wool from the collectors.[160] In Southampton, for example, none could be found, and there was armed resistance. On October 25 the king ordered the sheriff to go to places where wool was known to be stored and make confiscations to the amount of 500 sacks.[161] If necessary he was to use the *posse com-*

---

[157] *Ibid.*, pp. 563–565; *Chronographia*, II, 55–56.

[158] *Foedera*, II (2), p. 997; Villani, col. 808–809.

[159] Murimuth, p. 80; Knighton, II, 1.

[160] *Annales Paulini*, p. 366; Murimuth, p. 80.

[161] *CPR* (1334–8), pp. 480–481. This was the entire quota expected from Southampton.

itatus to put down the rebels and imprison them as such. The collectors were armed with wide powers and the exercise of them naturally provoked discontent, as is revealed by the order of October 7 to the sheriffs " that all who have to complain of injuries inflicted on them by the takers of wool " should be at London on December 1 when their complaints could be heard.[162]

Among the higher officials there also was abuse. The chancellor, the bishop of Hereford, had secured exemption from the collectors, but allowed other merchants to store their wool in his hostel under pretense that it belonged to him. Opposition, whether active or passive, appears to have been quite general and on October 10 the king ordered his clerk, John de Charneles, whom he had appointed to supervise the sale of wool beyond the seas, to scrutinize diligently all the wool that was ready in order to prevent smuggling. The impatient king ordered the merchants at this time to send " with all speed " the wool contracted for to London by December 1.[163] But at the most only about 10,000 sacks, a third of the amount originally contracted for, reached the Low Countries before the close of the year.[164] Edward accordingly could not readily meet all his obligations and was constrained to postpone his departure from day to day.[165] The demands of his allies were insistent and his prestige threatened to be seriously undermined. It is apparently for this reason, in part at least, that Reginald, count of Guelders, was expected in England on a hurried visit to discuss with his brother-in-law the situation in the Low Countries.[166]

Since the prospect of collecting the wool vanished as the month of October wore on, the king was more and more inclined to hearken to the admonitions of the pope. Early in the month Benedict had urged his nuncios, Peter, cardinal priest of St. Praxed, and Bertrand, cardinal deacon of St. Mary's in Aquiro,

[162] *CCR* (1337–9), pp. 270–271.

[163] *Ibid.*, pp. 184, 188, 268–270.

[164] *Ibid.*, p. 228.

[165] According to the *Scalacronica*, p. 297, Salisbury is said to have felt that the alliance was not advantageous because of the greed of the German princes, including of course those of the Low Countries.

[166] *Foedera*, II (2), 996; *CCR* (1337–9), p. 183. See E. Déprez, *Les Préliminaires de la Guerre de Cent Ans,* p. 152, and *CPR* (1334–8), pp. 508, 553, for Edward's efforts to pay. It is not certain whether Reginald actually went to England.

to proceed forthwith to England because he believed that Edward could be more easily dissuaded from beginning the campaign before he should cross over to the continent than he would be if surrounded by his numerous relatives and friends in Germany and the Low Countries.[167] On the 7th, in anticipation of their arrival, Edward appointed the bishop of Lincoln, the earls of Northampton and Suffolk, and John Darcy to discuss the matter with them,[168] and granted the nuncios audience.[169] On October 7 Edward called upon Philip " who calls himself King of France " to surrender the crown,[170] and John, duke of Brabant, William, margrave of Juliers, Reginald, count of Guelders, and William, count of Hainault, Holland, and Zeeland, were named proctors with full sovereign powers to look after Edward's rights in France where the magnates, lay and ecclesiastical, were commanded to hearken to them.[171]

This was, as Professor Déprez properly calls it, but a *coup de théâtre*, and clearly revealed the king's financial inability. In response to the appeals of the nuncios Edward consented on December 24 to postpone all hostile activities until March 1 pending the decision of the clergy, barons, and commons, who had been summoned on the 20th to appear at Westminster on February 3.[172] The royal finances were not such as to permit a campaign in the late winter, and accordingly on February 24 Edward promised the cardinals that the attack would be delayed until June 24.[173]

[167] W. H. Bliss, *Calendar of Entries in the Papal Registers,* II, 565.
[168] *Foedera,* II(2), 1002; *Chronographia,* II, 56.
[169] *Annales Paulini,* p. 367; Murimuth, p. 81. See also *CFR* (1337–47), p. 82; *CCR* (1337–9), p. 230; *CPR* (1338–40), pp. 1, 86.
[170] E. Déprez, *Les Préliminaires de la Guerre de Cent Ans,* pp. 171–172.
[171] *Foedera,* II(2), 1001.
[172] *Ibid.,* p. 1007; Murimuth, p. 81.
[173] *Foedera,* II(2), 1014.

CHAPTER VIII

THE RISE OF VAN ARTEVELDE AND THE NEUTRALITY OF FLANDERS (1337–1338)

i. The Delivery of English Wool at Dordrecht (Autumn–Winter, 1337) ii. Edward's Diplomacy in the Low Countries (Autumn, 1337—Spring, 1338) iii. The Emergence of van Artevelde (December, 1337) iv. The Neutrality of Flanders (Winter–Summer, 1338) v. Edward's Arrival in Brabant (July, 1338)

I. The Delivery of English Wool at Dordrecht
(Autumn–Winter, 1337)

EDWARD was determined to press his advantage over Philip and in the autumn of 1337 turned his attention to many important matters such as the financial obligations to be discharged, old alliances to be strengthened, and new ones to be made.[1] Since August the personnel of a new embassy had been prepared; on October 3 Henry de Burghersh, bishop of Lincoln, the earls of Suffolk and Northampton, and John Darcy, steward of the royal household, and a numerous following [2] were instructed to treat for alliances and the location of the staple, to make arrangements with the emperor, and, finally, to negotiate with Louis, count of Flanders, for the marriage of Edward's daughter Johanna and the count's heir apparent Louis and prepare the terms for the reconciliation between the king and Bruges, Ghent, and Ypres.[3]

Purveyance for the fleet which was to carry the wool that had been accumulated was actively furthered. Corn, ale, and other food-stuffs were ordered to be collected for its use in Holland and Zeeland.[4] Stephen le Blount, purveyor and receiver of victuals

---

[1] Villani, col. 808.

[2] *CCR* (1334–8), pp. 505, 517, 527, 530–537, 540–541.

[3] *Foedera,* II (2), 997–999.

[4] For the activities of John de Wesenham, Thomas de Melchbourn of Lynn, and John Costyn of Holland, see *CPR* (1334–8), pp. 539, 542–543, 553; *CFR* (1327–37), pp. 41–42; *CCR* (1337–9), p. 199.

for the fleet, was ordered to hasten revictualling of those ships which were without food-supplies.[5] Finally, the fleet of four hundred and forty vessels [6] commanded by the admiral, Walter de Manny,[7] was ready and soon after All Saints' Day sailed forth toward the mouths of the Schelde. On board were the bishop of Lincoln and the other envoys, accompanied by many men-at-arms, archers, and others.[8] But only about a third of the total levy of wool, or about 10,000 sacks, was carried.[9]

The collection of so great a number of ships caused much uneasiness among the French who feared a descent upon their coasts, and they sent the king of Navarre and the count of Alençon with troops to Boulogne.[10] There were also some French ships at Calais, and John de Woume, who suspected them of planning to intercept the fleet, sent a spy in the middle of October to ascertain their intentions.[11] Soon thereafter he betook himself to the island of Walcheren in the mouth of the Schelde and was at Middelburg and Flushing from October 27 to November 6 on which date he crossed over the Honte to Cadzand and to Damme.[12] The count of Flanders had placed a garrison on Cadzand which was strategically situated at the approaches to Bruges. In this force there were Durere, seignior of Halluin, John de Neetkerke, John Rode, Arnold de Brugdam, and Guy, a bastard brother of the count, who was their commander.[13] In anticipation of the fleet's arrival the scabini of Ghent had on November 8 sent out toward Sluis, which was situated on the Zwin, a hundred men-at-arms (*selscutters*), six hundred and

---

[5] *CCR* (1337–9), pp. 197–199.

[6] *Auctor Bridlingtoniensis*, p. 135; *Melsa*, II 383; and Villani, col. 808, 809, and le Muisit, p. 112, who state that the number was three hundred.

[7] *Foedera*, II (2), 1005.

[8] Murimuth, p. 80; *Melsa*, II, 384; *Lanercost*, p. 294; Walsingham, I, 222; *Chronique Normande*, p. 39; Froissart, I, 135; Villani, col. 809.

[9] According to the *Auctor Bridlingtoniensis*, p. 133, half the wool of the realm; to *Lanercost*, p. 295, 14,000 sacks, to Murimuth, p. 80, the total levy, to Villani, col. 809, 12,000 sacks. The correct number is 10,000. See *CCR* (1337–9), p. 228; Knighton, II, 2.

[10] *Grandes Chroniques*, V, 369–370.

[11] Kervyn, *Oeuvres de Froissart*, XVIII, 55.

[12] *Ibid.*, p. 52. " Dremue " is apparently a paleographical misreading for " Damme."

[13] De Budt, p. 326; le Muisit, p. 112; *Chronographia*, II, 44–45; *Grandes Chroniques*, V, 371; Froissart, I, 132.

thirty-six sergeants (*serianten*) and sixty-one captains, together with all manner of warlike equipment such as wagons, boats, tents, and victuals.[14] Similar expeditions were also sent out by the scabini of Ypres [15] and Bruges.[16]

Walter de Manny decided to attack the count's forces on Cadzand in the Schelde in order to execute vengeance upon the inhabitants for some wrongs inflicted upon a number of Englishmen who at some previous time had gone ashore on this island in order to secure a supply of fresh water.[17] Perhaps the real motive was to cover the passage of the ships laden with wool for Zeeland and Holland. The English admiral appeared on the Zwin near Sluis [18] and his design [19] to attack was apparent to the garrison who held themselves in readiness on the shore to meet the English. Here the skill of the archers was at once manifest. As the assailants approached they poured a deadly fire upon the Flemings and wrought such execution that they were speedily forced to flee. Having effected a landing, the English proceeded to attack a church where a desperate struggle ensued. The structure was set afire when the defenders refused to surrender, and all the inmates were burned to death.[20] Thereupon the whole island was harried and a large number of the inhabitants were put to the sword.[21] The flames of the burning hamlets could be descried from the walls of Bruges.[22] The archers had given an intimation of their future rôle [23] at Crécy and Poitiers.[24]

[14] N. de Pauw en J. Vuylsteke, *Rekeningen der Stad Gent*, I, 228–229.

[15] N. de Pauw, *Ypre jeghen Poperinghe*, pp. 268–269.

[16] *Ms. Rekeningen*, Bruges, *1336–1337*, folios 115 recto and 125 verso. See also *Grandes Chroniques*, V, 371; *Chronographia*, II, p. 45.

[17] Murimuth, pp. 80–81; Baker, p. 60; Walsingham, I, 222.

[18] *Lanercost*, p. 295; *Villani*, col. 809.

[19] *Bourgeois de Valenciennes*, p. 162; Walsingham, I, 222.

[20] *Lanercost*, p. 295; *Chronographia*, II, 44–45; Froissart, I, 409; Walsingham, I, 222; *Auctor Bridlingtoniensis*, p. 133.

[21] According to the *Bourgeois de Valenciennes*, p. 162, 11,000; to le Muisit, p. 112, 500; to Walsingham, I, 222, 3,000. See also de Budt, p. 326, and *Chronique Parisienne Anonyme*, p. 172.

[22] *Chronographia*, II, 45.

[23] J. E. Morris, "The Archers of Crécy," *English Historical Review*, XII (1897), 427–436.

[24] For other references to this battle, see Murimuth, pp. 80–81; *French Chronicle of London*, p. 71 (*sub* 1338); *Melsa*, II, 383–384; *Grandes Chroniques*, V, 371; *Istore et Croniques*, II, 362–363, 411; *Breve Chronicon Flandrie*, p. 6; Lescot, p. 146; *Scalacronica*, p. 168.

The English embarked at once and proceeded toward Holland, to the evident relief of the towns in Flanders who withdrew their militia.[25]   Meanwhile John de Woume came aboard and undoubtedly apprised the bishop and the earls of the situation among the allies.[26]   Whether the fleet convoyed the ships to Dordrecht cannot be ascertained.   When on their return to England, they fell in with a number of French craft carrying wine from France, and seized them.[27]   The wool arrived safely,[28] and within a fortnight Walter de Manny was back in Orwell [29] and with him as hostage was Guy of Flanders, who had been taken in the course of the fighting on Cadzand.[30]

Edward intended that Dordrecht should be the great center for the distribution of wool.   This undoubtedly is the motive for the safe-conduct granted on October 1 to the merchants of the dominions of Count William in return for similar favors requested by the king for English merchants of wool and other commodities.[31]   Detailed arrangements at Dordrecht were made by John de Woume.[32]   A regular organization was formed to manage all the business.   John de Charneles [33] had been appointed on August 26 to act as receiver of all wools, to supervise the sale, and render account of all moneys taken from this and other sources.[34]   Master John Wawayn, the king's trusted servant, was to act as comptroller upon whose authorization alone could Charneles issue payments.[35]   These men made conscientious use of their wide powers while in the Low Countries, for we learn that Charneles arrested a shipment of 2,100 woolfells and detained them upon suspicion that customs and subsidy had not been duly paid.[36]

[25] N. de Pauw en J. Vuylsteke, *Rekeningen der Stad Gent*, I, 229.   A part of the force had not yet arrived when the news came.

[26] Kervyn, *Oeuvres de Froissart*, XVIII, 58.

[27] *Chronique Parisienne Anonyme*, p. 172; *Lanercost*, pp. 294–295.

[28] Villani, col. 809; Froissart, I, 134; *Bourgeois de Valenciennes*, p. 163, who states that the wool went to Antwerp.

[29] *Foedera*, II (2), 1005.

[30] Murimuth, pp. 80–81; de Nangis, II, 159.   Cf. also *Foedera*, II (2), 1123.

[31] *CPR* (1334–8), p. 535.

[32] Kervyn, *Oeuvres de Froissart*, XVIII, 55.

[33] *CPR* (1334–8), pp. 521, 527, 529.

[34] *CFR* (1337–47), p. 38; *CCR* (1337–9), p. 188.

[35] *CPR* (1334–8), p. 542; *CCR* (1337–9), pp. 228, 230.

[36] *CCR* (1337–9), pp. 345–346.

Regarding the price at which the wool was actually sold, it is not possible to say much. The monopoly no doubt took into consideration the actual price of the wool on the market in the Low Countries. It had been proposed that the merchants should advance to the king 200,000*l.* as his share of the profits, which was to be one half of the total. Accordingly, the 30,000 sacks were expected to sell at a profit of about 14*l.* each. This, it should be noted, is exactly the figure quoted by the chronicler Knighton.[37] After deducting the customs and the subsidy of 20*s.* per sack, the profit would appear to be enormous, as some writers have thought.[38] But there is really no reason to question these figures. It should be remembered that in England the wool which had not been exported in considerable quantities since the summer of 1336, was very cheap, as is evident from the schedule of low prices drawn up for the various counties,[39] and that in Flanders and Brabant, where little wool had been received since the embargo of August, 1336,[40] it must have soared to fabulous prices.

Edward's expectations of abundant financial resources were, however, bound to be shattered. By the close of the year there were further shipments amounting to about 1,500 sacks.[41] The collection of wool did not progress more favorably during these months so that really but little more than a third of the total number of sacks originally expected ever reached Dordrecht. It is partly for this reason that Edward summoned the clergy, barons, and commons to Westminster for a meeting on February 3 [42] when the king was granted one half of the wool of the realm, estimated at 20,000 sacks. On March 10 all further export was stringently forbidden until after the royal share had been collected.[43] Hence but little wool can have reached the staple at Dordrecht other than the 11,500 sacks that had passed the seas by January, 1338.

Most of the wool collected at Dordrecht remained unsold. The

[37] Knighton, II, 1–2.
[38] G. Unwin, "The Estates of the Merchants (1336–1365)," *Trade and Finance under Edward III,* p. 190.
[39] *CCR* (1337–9), p. 149; *Melsa,* II, 378.
[40] Hocsemius, p. 432.
[41] *CCR* (1337–9), p. 228.
[42] *Foedera,* II(2), 1007; *Report on the Dignity of a Peer,* IV, 480–489.
[43] *Foedera,* II(2), 1022; *CCR* (1337–9), p. 393.

reason for this is difficult to ascertain. Since the merchants were to have full control over the sale, it has been conjectured that they sought to increase their profits by withholding it still longer from the markets.[44] It is, however, known that as soon as van Artevelde was in power efforts were made to secure wool from the supplies at Dordrecht for the Flemish industries and that on February 11 a representation from Ghent arrived there to secure a consignment of wool.[45] There is also an order of January 5 to the bishop of Lincoln and John de Charneles commanding them to deliver to the Bardi fifteen hundred sacks for debts contracted by the king with that society.[46] Nor can diplomatic exigencies explain why such a large part of the wool remained unsold. The king could easily enough have forced the sale of the wool as he subsequently did. It becomes the more inexplicable when one considers the delicate diplomatic situation in the Low Countries where the hearty coöperation of the various princes, and especially of the Duke of Brabant, could only be secured by the prompt delivery of the wool for which they had contracted and the payment of their wages for prosecuting Edward's schemes.

II. Edward's Diplomacy in the Low Countries Autumn, 1337 — Spring, 1338)

At the opening of 1338 King Edward could not meet his financial obligations and his diplomatic prestige suffered accordingly. His brother-in-law Reginald, count of Guelders, had not been paid the 100,000 gold florins due him at Michaelmas, in spite of the fact that he had incurred heavy expenses in the negotiations of the past year in behalf of Edward's rights. On November 30 the bishop of Lincoln and his colleagues besought him to wait for payment until the following Lent when this amount and the instalment then due would be fully paid at Dordrecht or Nijmegen.[47] Particularly dangerous was the apparent friend-

---

[44] S. B. Terry, *The Financing of the Hundred Years' War, 1337–1360*, pp. 18, 21.

[45] N. de Pauw en J. Vuylsteke, *Rekeningen der Stad Gent*, I, 177, 179.

[46] *CCR* (1337–9), p. 228.

[47] I. A. Nijhoff, *Gedenkwaardigheden uit de Geschiedenis van Gelderland*, I, 367–368.

ship of William, count of Hainault, Holland, and Zeeland, for his uncle King Philip which was revealed by the agreement made with him in regard to his succession in the county of Ostrevant. The position of John, duke of Brabant, remained as uncertain as ever.

A meeting was held at Mechelen early in December when the English envoys and John de Woume [48] met Reginald, count of Guelders, John, duke of Brabant,[49] William, count of Hainault, Holland, and Zeeland, and others, among whom perhaps also appeared William, margrave of Juliers. The alliances against Philip were undoubtedly discussed, for on the 12th Count William declared his intention to obey the order of the emperor, or of King Edward, should he be German king or imperial vicar, and assist him in recovering from Philip the rights of the empire in the Low Countries, and solemnly reaffirmed the promises made by his father in the preceding spring at Valenciennes. Witnesses for Count William were John of Hainault, William van Duivenvoorde, the seigniors of Havrech and Boulant, Henry de Jodoigne, and Claes Stuyck.[50]

On this occasion the matter of Robert of Artois was again brought up. As Philip was pressing the count of Guelders and the margrave of Juliers to fulfil their obligations assumed at Senlis in 1332, the bishop of Lincoln and the earls of Suffolk and Northampton now drew up a document which was apparently intended to release from these demands the chief supporters of English policy in the Low Countries. On December 5 the envoys declared that when Robert and his secretaries and friends in England had heard of the discussions about him at Valenciennes and of the obligations of the count of Guelders and of the margrave of Juliers toward Philip regarding him, they forthwith departed from England. They stated that it was not known where he was at that moment and that he was no longer kept or supported

48 He was at Mechelen apparently from December 4 to 12. See Kervyn, *Oeuvres de Froissart,* XVIII, 53–54.

49 He was at Mechelen on December 11. See J. E. Willems, *Codex Diplomaticus,* I, 800.

50 J. Schwalm, " Reise nach Holland, Belgien, Nord Frankreich, und dem Niederrhein im Sommer, 1894," *Neues Archiv der Gesellschaft für Aeltere Deutsche Geschichtskunde,* XX (1895), 431–432; I. A. Nijhoff, *Gedenkwaardigheden uit de Geschiedenis van Gelderland,* I, 369–370.

by the king.[51]   The truth of these assertions may well have been
doubted or disbelieved by Edward's allies especially as Reginald,
count of Guelders, himself had visited England during the previous months.

During the last months of the year Edward's representatives
treated Count William with studied consideration.   Protection
and safe-conduct were freely granted to the merchants of
Hainault, Holland, Zeeland, and Friesland who wanted to trade
in England,[52] a favor which William also accorded to English subjects.[53]   Those whose goods had been seized in England were to
have them restored at once by Edward's order of January 3.[54]
Trade in articles not forbidden, such as spices, honey, corn, and
ale, was encouraged and licenses were freely granted.[55]   A Zee-
lander, whose property had been seized when the order to seques-
trate all possessions of French religious houses in England had
gone forth, was given full satisfaction.[56]

Because of his financial failures, Edward's dealings with the
duke of Brabant were particularly unfortunate.   The duke's
commerce was shown every possible consideration.   The Almain
merchants, Godekin de Revele and Hildebrand Sudermann,
originally from Cologne and Dortmund, but whose chief business
was now centered in Antwerp, were allowed extensive rights to
deal in everything except wool in Brabant and other parts
friendly to the king.[57]   Licenses were issued freely to merchants
of Brabant,[58] who were encouraged to trade actively not only
with Holland and Zeeland, but also with Brabant.[59]   The sole
restriction was that their merchandise should not reach lands hos-

[51] I. A. Nijhoff, *Gedenkwaardigheden uit de Geschiedenis van Gelderland,* I, 368–369.
[52] *CPR* (1334–8), pp. 517, 525, 535–537.
[53] P. L. Muller, *Regesta Hannonensia,* p. 249.
[54] *CCR* (1337–9), pp. 229–230.
[55] *Ibid.,* pp. 85–86; *CPR* (1334–8), pp. 453, 535–537, 542, 546; *CPR*
(1338–40), pp. 20–46.
[56] *CCR* (1337–9), p. 167.
[57] J. Hansen, "Der Englische Staatskredit unter König Eduard
III (1327–1377) und die Hansischen Kaufleute," *Hansische Geschichtsblätter,* XVI (1910), 373.   For Sudermann, see J. Haerynx, *Jan Boendale,* p. 41.
Cf. also *CPR* (1334–8), p. 538.
[58] *CCR* (1337–9), pp. 350–351.
[59] *Ibid.,* pp. 85–86, 546, 571, 643–644; *CPR* (1334–8), pp. 463, 520, 554,
556, 571, 581; *CPR* (1338–40), pp. 5, 19, 25, 68–69.

tile to the king, particularly Flanders, and a careful control was
exercised by requiring bonds which would be cancelled upon
presentation of proof that the goods in question had reached the
lands of the king's friends.[60]   Unfortunately, however, the slow-
ness with which Edward fulfilled his contract of May 24, 1337,
whereby the merchants of Brabant were allowed to import a
quantity of wool to be agreed upon by the representatives from
the various towns [61] seriously impaired his prestige.   When the
merchants' monopoly went into effect in July, 1337, they had
already secured 2,200 sacks, apparently in accordance with the
terms of this agreement.[62]   But the collectors of wool for the
monopoly acted in obedience to their orders and often arrested
such wool as had been actually collected by the duke's men.
This caused much confusion and delay.[63]   Inasmuch as little
wool was actually sold at Dordrecht before May, 1338, and the
amount allotted to the merchants of Brabant was not received
before that month,[64] the duke could have scant reason to display
much zeal in Edward's cause.

Superficially, at least, it appeared that the duke of Brabant was
steering into the wake of English diplomatic intrigue.   Thierry,
count of Loon, was eager for his support against the chapter of
St. Lambert and at Louvain on December 19 promised the duke
and his heirs free passage in going to and returning from his lands
beyond the Meuse whenever they should have occasion to visit
them whether armed or unarmed, and even bound himself to protect the duke in the exercise of this privilege.   Each bound himself to provide a stated number of troops to defend his lands
which included the duchies of Lotharingia, Brabant, and Limburg, the county of Loon, and the ancestral domains of Thierry
of Heinsberg.   In case war should be begun by the bishop of
Liège upon either of them, they would unite against him and
make no separate peace or truce.   As earnest of their faithful

---

[60] Cf., for example, *CPR* (1334–8), p. 579; *CCR* (1533–7), pp. 643–644.

[61] *Foedera*, II (2), 971–972.

[62] *CPR* (1338–40), pp. 43, 45; *CCR* (1337–9), p. 364; *CFR* (1337–47),
pp. 72–73.

[63] For orders of de-arrest, see *CCR* (1337–9), pp. 181, 306, 314–315,
400–401.

[64] *CFR* (1337–47), pp. 72–73; *CCR* (1337–9), p. 364; *CPR* (1338–40),
pp. 42, 45.

intentions, each named two parties to whom all differences in the future were to be referred for settlement. As witnesses there appeared, besides the nobility of Brabant and of Loon, William, count of Hainault, Holland, and Zeeland, Reginald, count of Guelders, William, margrave of Juliers, and John of Hainault — figures closely associated with Edward's intrigues in the Low Countries.[65]

But Duke John could not unreservedly join either Edward or Philip. His difficulties with Liège and his interests in Mechelen could not very well make him eager to support the latter. Situated between Liège and Flanders, his lands were exposed to the hostile acts of Philip's friends and supporters. On the other hand, the economic situation among his bourgeoisie made at least apparent friendship with the English party necessary. Edward's abettors were powerful, and, should an attack upon France be made, any rejection of proffers by his allies might prove disastrous. Thus at this time no cordial adherence to any party was possible, and the duke persevered in a policy of watchful waiting which could gain him no serious enemies and might ultimately pay handsomely.

For these reasons Duke John really evinced slight enthusiasm in supporting Edward's agents in securing an alliance with the Flemings. Although he had been named lieutenant of the king, his name is mentioned but once in the constant negotiations between the English agents and the scabini of Ghent.[66] In spite of the fact that these parleys took place on the soil of Brabant Reginald, count of Guelders, assumed the chief rôle.[67] Possibly the duke believed that the *rapprochement* between Edward and the Flemish towns would be detrimental to the interests of his own towns.

On the other hand the duke sought to remain on friendly terms with Philip and thus avoid the consequences which might come from joining either side.[68] According to John le Bel he feared

[65] A. Verkooren, *Inventaire, Brabant,* I, 321–322; E. Dynter, *Chronicon Ducum Brabantiae,* II, 593.

[66] N. de Pauw en J. Vuylsteke, *Rekeningen der Stad Gent,* I, 176.

[67] *Ibid.,* pp. 177–183.

[68] Le Bel, I, 136: "Ainsy vouloit le dit duc de Brabant nager entre deux yauues. Il vouloit faire croire au roy de France que jà ne luy seroit contraire, et luy fist entendre moult longuement combien que tout le pays veist bien le contraire evidanment."

that the king, who had opposed him in 1332, might become dangerous should Edward fail to come to the Low Countries or should his expedition meet with some disaster. He therefore sent Leon de Crainhem,[69] a knight and member of his council, and some others from time to time to France to make proper explanations. He asked Philip how he could act otherwise; since Edward was his kinsman, he could not well keep the English envoys from his dominions especially as they were paying their own expenses. This, he claimed, was the extent of his wrongdoing and Philip perforce agreed with him.[70] The king may have been sincere in this, for, although John had readily enough consented to use his influence with Count Louis in the autumn of 1337 for the release of Sohier de Courtrai, he had, it appears, done nothing to aid the movement among the Flemings which aimed at friendship with England.[71] Furthermore, the duke and Arnulf, seignior of Liedekerke, a member of his household, still remained pensioners of Philip and received annual sums from the royal treasury.[72]

Philip was especially alarmed because of the attitude of the Flemings, and hence was careful to treat the duke with the greatest consideration. His uneasiness is revealed by his belief in a wild rumor that the princes in the Low Countries were planning to poison him, the queen, the duke of Normandy, and the members of his council. The rumor had its origin in the gossip of someone who had come from the Low Countries. When arrested by the king, he mentioned as being guilty in particular the count of Guelders and the margrave of Juliers, who, it should be remembered in this connection, had for some time been vassals of Philip. Reginald and William at once sought to prove

[69] Le Bel, I, 135–136, where he is called Louis. According to Kervyn, *Oeuvres de Froissart,* XXI, 53, and XVII, 59, 67, his name is Leon. Froissart, I, 133, following le Bel, calls him Louis. For members of the family, cf. A. Verkooren, *Inventaire, Brabant,* Vol. I, index, *sub voce.* That he is Leon de Crainhem would seem certain from the fact that on November 18, 1339, a person by this name became a vassal of Philip in return for 300*l.* Tournois. See *Archives Nationales,* Paris, J. 624, No. 31.

[70] Le Bel, I, 135–136. The editor assigns this to 1340, but the chronicler, pp. 136–137, regards this as happening before the winter prior to Edward's arrival in Antwerp in July, 1338. Froissart, I, 135–136, places it before the affair at Cadzand.

[71] N. de Pauw en J. Vuylsteke, *Rekeningen der Stad Gent,* I, 169, 171–172.

[72] J. Viard, *Les Journaux de Philippe VI,* pp. 873, 901.

their innocence, and at a meeting in Brussels on February 4, 1338, John, duke of Brabant, William, count of Hainault, Holland, and Zeeland, Adolph, count of Berg, Thierry, count of Loon, Thierry, seignior of Valkenburg, William, seignior of Altena, and Otto, seignior of Cuyk, all solemnly swore that the accused parties were not guilty. A document was drawn up by Peter Bel, Philip's deputy, and dispatched to Paris.[73]

The bishop of Lincoln and the other English envoys were eager to do everything possible to cultivate the duke's friendship. The quota of wool assigned to each town of Brabant now appeared to be ready for delivery and the magistrates promised to fulfil the terms of the agreement made between the duke and Edward and under no circumstances to permit the wool to leave Brabant.[74] But Duke John expressed alarm and was reluctant to coöperate with the envoys. He feared the consequences of his promise to aid Edward with 1,200 men-at-arms. The bishop, the earls of Northampton and Suffolk, and John Darcy accordingly promised at Nijmegen on February 1 that Edward would never reveal to any man this agreement so long as the war between him and France should last, and that the king would restore the document at the close of hostilities. Besides this it was stipulated that none of Edward's party should cross the duke's territory without paying their expenses. All questions concerning the sum of money which Edward was bound to pay under the treaties of the previous year were to be submitted to the arbitration of the count of Guelders and the margrave of Juliers after Edward's arrival in the Low Countries.[75] Thus the duke was able to pursue a very devious course. He began to get ready his troops and kept them on the border of the *Pays de Liège.*[76] In this way he sought to give the impression to Philip that they were to be used solely in his quarrels with the chapter of St. Lambert and to Edward that he would be ready to come to his sup-

[73] M. J. Wolters, *Codex Diplomaticus Lossensis*, pp. 277–280; I. A. Nijhoff, *Gedenkwaardigheden uit de Geschiedenis van Gelderland*, I, 371–374. A. Wauters, *Table Chronologique*, I, 643, gives February 24 as the date of the document.

[74] See the declarations of the magistrates of Tirlemont, Aerschot, and Brussels of February 7, 8, and 10, respectively. A. Verkooren, *Inventaire, Brabant*, I, 326–327.

[75] *Ibid.*, p. 325, Cf. J. Williams, *Codex Diplomaticus*, I, 811.

[76] Le Bel, I, 136.

port in an attack upon France, and succeeded withal in serving his own purposes first.

Obviously it would now be Philip's care to assuage the passions of the duke and establish peace between him and the chapter. During the closing days of 1337 the bishops of Noyon and Arras made a determined effort to bring the two antagonists to an understanding. That they were acting at Philip's instigation can scarcely admit of doubt. For three weeks they labored, but in vain, and were finally forced to return to France.[77]

A pitched conflict between Bishop Adolph and Duke John and his ally, Thierry, count of Loon, seemed inevitable in January, 1338. It is perhaps at this time that John again sought to secure the erection of a separate diocese for his lands through an appeal to Lewis the Bavarian.[78] The emperor at about this time also ordered the bishop and church of Liège to meet with the electors and other princes of the empire at Cologne a week after Easter to discuss matters of serious import to himself and his *imperium*. Failure to appear would involve legal proceedings. But the bishop and his chapter, allied with Philip and desperately hating the duke, who was allied with the king of England and apparently hoping for support from the heretical and excommunicate emperor, did not even deign to reply to this summons.[79]

Nor could Pope Benedict succeed in bringing the irate duke to terms. On February 11 John had left the question regarding his rights at Hervé to be decided by the bishop of Laon, the abbot of St. Jacques of Liège, and the dean of the church of Rheims.[80] Of their activities no report has come to us. The news of Lewis the Bavarian's summons to the bishop and chapter of Liège frightened Benedict who wrote on March 30 to the scabini and councillors of Liège and other corporations in the *Pays de Liège* and to the nobility as well, urging them to give their full support to the bishop against the "manifest enemy of God and mother church." He also urged Walram, archbishop of Cologne, in whose jurisdiction the proposed diet was to be held, to remain steadfast in his policy and not to allow any harm to come

---

[77] Hocsemius, p. 438.
[78] R. W. Nitzsch, "Heinrich IV und der Gottes und Landfrieden," *Forschungen zur Deutschen Geschichte*, XXI (1881), 295.
[79] Hocsemius, pp. 438–439.
[80] A. Fierens, *Lettres de Benoît XII (1334–1342)*, Nos. 453–454.

to the bishop of Liège. In similar vein he also exhorted the duke of Brabant.[81]

With the aid of the money which Edward had given him, and relying upon help from the emperor, Duke John collected all his available military resources early in April at Heylissem for a blow against the bishop, Adolph de la Marck.[82] The episcopal forces were also mobilized and among them is mentioned the old enemy of the duke, John, king of Bohemia, who, it was said, had gathered from every possible source 1,800 knights. On the 3d Bishop Adolph led forth his troops and was soon confronting the forces of the duke drawn up in three divisions. Among the latter were Thierry, seignior of Valkenburg, Thierry, count of Loon, Reginald, count of Guelders, a number of Englishmen, and some others from Germany. There were present also William, count of Hainault, Holland, and Zeeland, Walram, archbishop of Cologne, and his brother, William, margrave of Juliers, who professed to be interested only in peace, which was naturally enough accepted with scepticism. "Thierry of Heinsberg," as Hocsem, the *scholasticus* of the chapter of Liège, persisted in calling the count of Loon, had brought together the fighting forces of his country, and his son, Godefroid, led a raid against the properties of the chapter and burned five villas.[83]

But the leaders were not to come to blows. The nepotist bishop did not shrink from an encounter with Duke John and his superior forces, but was extremely reluctant to do anything to endanger Thierry's possession of Loon. Negotiations could accordingly be opened wherein Count William, the archbishop, and apparently also his brother, the margrave of Juliers, displayed some zeal. The duke for his part was willing, and on April 8, Count William, the archbishop, John, king of Bohemia, and John of Hainault met at Montenaeken. On the 9th it was determined that satisfaction was to be rendered to the kin of the men beheaded by the duke's officials for bringing the ban of excom-

---

[81] *Ibid.,* nos. 465–467.

[82] Hocsemius: "Deinde Dux confisens in adiutorio Bavari futuro, et stipendiis regis Angliae communitus, exercitum contra Episcopum congregat, et contra ipsum Episcopus e converso." Cf. also Levold de Northof, p. 402.

[83] Hocsemius, pp. 439–440. The Englishmen were, it would seem, members of the various deputations sent by the king to the Low Countries.

munication to Tirlemont at the order of the bishop. The duke and his subjects were henceforth to avoid carefully any further encroachment upon the rights of the church of Liège, to reimburse fully all losses it had incurred up to the sum of 20,000 gold florins, and the extent of the damage was to be settled by the judgment of two persons delegated for the purpose. Melin was to be restored to the church of St. Denis, and the interdict over the duke's land in the diocese was to be lifted. All fiefs and possessions were to be returned as if nothing had happened, prisoners were to be freed and their expenses paid, and Bishop Adolph was to make good all wrongs committed against the seigniors of Cuyk and Stein, William van Duivenvoorde, Thierry van Stralen, and Rase de Grez. In the future Duke John was to be required to respect those clauses of the Treaty of Amiens in 1334 which dealt with his relations with the bishopric. And, finally, all remaining points were left to the arbitration of four men who were to meet at Maastricht, which town they were not to leave until they had reached a settlement.[84] On the same day Adolph accepted these terms without reserve.[85]

While peace was thus being restored between the duke of Brabant and the bishop of Liège, an effort was also made to settle the question of the succession to the county of Loon. This in fact had formed part of the negotiations at Montenaeken. The opposition of the chapter to any proposal granting the county to Thierry of Heinsberg compelled the bishop to treat covertly, and accordingly the stipulations were not divulged. The terms of this " dark peace," as Hocsem calls it, were of course speedily guessed.[86] It was generally believed that the king of Bohemia and the nobles of the *Pays de Liège*, who were present in full force, had decided to grant possession to Thierry; that the chapter was to purchase the castlery of Montenaeken, the *advocatia* of Liège, and certain incomes of about two hundred measures

---

[84] S. Bormans et E. Schoolmeesters, *Cartulaire de l'Église Saint-Lambert à Liège,* III, 1332–1334; Hocsemius, pp. 441–442; Levold de Northof, p. 402.

[85] A. Verkooren, *Inventaire, Brabant,* I, 329. The duke's acceptance has apparently been lost.

[86] Hocsemius, p. 440: "Deinde per dictos Archiepiscopum et comitem Hannoniae, quedam pax involuta tractatur, quae qualis fuerit mensem postea tractatur, non est scitum."

of wheat for 34,000 gold pieces of Mechelen; and that Thierry was to be free to redeem these within twenty-five years by repayment of this sum. Determined opposition to these purported terms, as well as to the others made with the duke of Brabant, developed among the canons who were led by Hocsem. But the bishop was able to overcome their objections.[87]

As the date set for the final decision approached, efforts were made to ensure the peace. On April 20 William, count of Hainault, Holland, and Zeeland,[88] and John of Hainault promised to pay before June 24 in the duke's behalf 20,000 gold florins for the damages wrought by the duke, for which the archbishop of Cologne and seven notables from the *Pays de Liège* acted as guarantors.[89] Count William, the archbishop, John, king of Bohemia, Thierry de Haneffe, Otto, seignior of Cuyk, and Louis, seignior of Diepenbeek, substituted Hasselt for Maastricht and bound themselves to go there on *Misericordia* Sunday (April 26) and not to depart until they had settled all differences between the duke and bishop in accordance with the agreement of April 8.[90] Then it was decided that Thierry of Heinsberg was to have the county of Loon, for which he was to do homage to the bishop of Liège. All prisoners still in captivity were to be liberated and financial compensation was extended to those who had suffered losses during the late clash between the duke and the bishop. The former was required to pay the bishop 16,666 florins, the unpaid remainder of the 30,000 florins fine imposed by King Philip in 1334 at Amiens. The remaining questions were to be settled by eight arbiters, four chosen by each party, who were to meet at Maastricht.[91]

Investigation of the damages which the duke had inflicted upon the churches of Liège was next conducted by William, count of Hainault, Holland, and Zeeland, and John of Hainault who announced their decision at Brussels on June 22. Their report

---

[87] The names of these men are given in the document of April 8.
[88] Hocsemius, pp. 441, 442. Cf. Levold de Northof, p. 402.
[89] S. Bormans, " Notice des Cartulaires de la Collégiale Saint-Denis à Liège," *BCRH*, 3d Ser., XIV (1872), 111.
[90] Hocsemius, p. 442.
[91] *Ibid.*, pp. 443–444; A. Verkooren, *Inventaire, Brabant*, I, 330–333; S. Bormans et E. Schoolmeesters, *Cartulaire de l'Église Saint-Lambert à Liège*, III, 535–544.

contains a long list of names to whom restitution was to be made.[92]   Whether these terms were all faithfully carried out we have no means of knowing, but it is known that a year later, on July 20, 1339, Bishop Adolph gave the duke a receipt for 3,000 florins which had been paid in accordance with these recommendations.[93]

While the trouble with the duke of Brabant was thus temporarily stilled, the real reason for antagonism nevertheless persisted.   Quarrels over Mechelen or over one of many conflicting claims of jurisdiction might break out at any moment.   Under these conditions the truce established in the spring and summer of 1338 had no noticeable influence upon the political policies of the bishop and the duke and they remained as hostile as before.   Indeed it could hardly be otherwise when on April 23 the emperor ordered the provost, dean, and chapter of Liège to send representatives to Frankfurt to treat with him.[94]

King Edward for his part had to continue his efforts to conciliate Duke John.   When in March he took the export of wool into his own hands and received the grant of a moiety of the wool of the realm, he was careful to except the quota which the merchants of Brabant had already collected by the close of July, 1337.   By the end of the month he came to an agreement with Duke John that his merchants dwelling in England should be free to go to Brabant with their merchandise until Easter.   The 2,200 sacks of wool, which the duke's men had secured, were to be collected at Ipswich, whence an English fleet would convoy the same to Brabant.[95]   Commands were thereupon frequently issued urging officials to hasten the collection.[96]   Thus for nineteen months after the embargo had been put into effect the looms in Brabant had been forced to remain practically idle, and Edward's efforts

---

[92] A. Verkooren, *Inventaire, Brabant,* I, 339–343.   Adolph ordered his official to receive the declarations prepared by the churches of Liège.   See S. Bormans, " Notice des Cartulaires de la Collégiale Saint-Denis," *BCRH,* 3d. Ser., XIV (1872), 112.

[93] A. Verkooren, *Inventaire, Brabant,* II, 64–65.

[94] Hocsemius, p. 443.

[95] *Foedera,* II (2), 1031–1032; *CPR* (1338–40), pp. 43, 45, *CFR* (1337–47), pp. 72–73; *CCR* (1337–9), pp. 364, 417–418 (where mention is made of 300 additional sacks).

[96] *CCR* (1337–9), pp. 338, 345, 348, 354, 358; *CPR* (1338–40), p. 48; *CFR* (1337–47), p. 73.

to conciliate the duke were up to this moment futile. The king could ill afford to alienate so potent a prince and was careful on May 8 to thank him for the zeal shown in his cause, and,[97] feeling the need of closer coöperation, on the 12th ordered the earl of Northampton to negotiate a marriage alliance between Edward, duke of Cornwall, and Marguerite, the duke's daughter.[98]

These steps, however, could not counteract the uneasiness created by Edward's delay in coming to the Low Countries in the spring as the bishop of Lincoln advised him to do in April.[99] More serious was the delay in the shipment of wool after Easter. The vessels which the admiral, Walter de Manny, had been ordered to collect had taken to sea before he could act, and it was impossible to bring enough craft together to convey the merchants who had now collected most of their wool at Orwell and were ready with other merchants to return to Brabant. On June 9 Edward impatiently and peremptorily ordered the admiral to speed the matter.[100] But even at this moment we read of the arrest of eight hundred sacks of wool at Boston and of sixty sarplars in London as late as June 25,[101] which must have still further prejudiced the duke's confidence in Edward's extensive promises.

III. The Emergence of van Artevelde (December, 1337)

There was no abatement in the severity of the great social and industrial crisis in Flanders, for the English persisted in their policy of isolating the Flemings from the rest of the world. Since the autumn of 1336 their ships had been seized wherever they could be found and their goods were often confiscated.[102] So rigid was Edward's watchfulness that even the goods of the merchants of Brabant were also seized.[103] Trade in food-stuffs and all other articles was encouraged with Hainault, Brabant, Zeeland, Hol-

---

[97] *Foedera*, II (2), p. 1035.

[98] *Ibid.*, 1036.

[99] E. Déprez, *Les Préliminaires de la Guerre de Cent Ans*, p. 190.

[100] *Foedera*, II (2), 1041; *CCR* (1337-9), p. 364.

[101] *CCR* (1337-9), pp. 412, 417-418.

[102] *Ibid.*, pp. 172, 198, 227-228; *CPR* (1334-8), p. 538.

[103] *CPR* (1334-8), pp. 576-581. The English at Middelburg refused to allow wood intended for the town's use to proceed to Ghent. See N. de Pauw and J. Vuylsteke, *Rekeningen der Stad Gent*, I, 197.

land, and Friesland, places which are usually described in the documents as " in the friendship of the king." Guarantees were usually demanded that the goods would go only to the destination stated and merchants were required to present letters from scabini, bailiffs, the duke, or count, that the goods for which permission had been granted had actually reached their intended destination.[104]

Similar favors were shown the merchants of Almain,[105] and those of Lombardy and Florence were encouraged to trade with Brabant or Zeeland,[106] while the Bardi, from whom Edward had borrowed considerable sums,[107] were authorized to carry wool to Italy.[108] Merchants from Portugal, Castile, Aragon, and Majorca were given every encouragement to trade with the neighbors of Flanders and protection was freely granted and security was always required that goods would not reach the enemy.[109] Spanish ships were frequently seized, as also those of Bayonne,[110] and taken to English ports such as Southampton, Sandwich, and Dover, for they were often found to carry Flemish goods.[111] Edward was eager to accord Spanish merchants every possible favor[112] and showed alacrity in ordering their release.[113]

Complaints of this treatment in violation of safe-conduct and protection were plentiful, and on February 15 Edward felt obliged to issue commissions of oyer and terminer in Norfolk, Suffolk, Essex, Southampton, Devonshire, and Cornwall to in-

[104] *CCR* (1337–9), pp. 90, 229–230, 517, 536–537, 542–3, 546, 557.

[105] *CPR* (1338–40), pp. 20, 46, 51; *CPR* (1334–8), pp. 240, 333, 335, 337, 339, 345, 349, 351, 535–537, 558; *CFR* (1337–47), pp. 5, 13.

[106] *CPR* (1334–8), p. 538; *CPR* (1339–40), pp. 27, 60; *CCR* (1337–9), p. 315; *CFR* (1337–47), pp. 71–72.

[107] *CPR* (1334–8), pp. 345, 349, 556; *CPR* (1338–40), pp. 25, 19; *CCR* (1337–9), p. 187; *CFR* (1337–47), p. 25. Edward had borrowed 62,000*l.* on October 18, 1337. Cf. *CPR* (1334–8), pp. 541–542.

[108] *CPR* (1334–8), p. 537; *CCR* (1337–9), p. 177; *CFR* (1337–47), pp. 48–49.

[109] *CCR* (1333–7), pp. 643–644; *CCR* (1337–9), pp. 85–86, 346; *CPR* (1334–8), pp. 349, 463, 520, 546, 554, 556, 571–572; *CPR* (1338–40), p. 5; *CFR* (1337–47), p. 5.

[110] *CCR* (1337–9), p. 275; *CFR* (1337–47), p. 44.

[111] *CPR* (1334–8), pp. 578–580; *CCR* (1337–9), pp. 181, 206, 207, 229.

[112] See Edward's letter to the mayor and sheriffs of London, November 10, 1337. *CCR* (1337–9), p. 284.

[113] *Ibid.*, pp. 204, 206–207, 228, 303–304.

vestigate all such seizure of ships, merchandise, and goods.[114] Alfonso, king of Castile, asserted in his reply to Edward's request to prevent his subjects from trading with the Flemings that third parties should not be interfered with and asked that his subjects should not be harassed. On January 8 Edward disclaimed all wish to make himself obnoxious and explained that all intercourse with Flanders was unsafe and rendered the merchants of a third party liable to seizure in which case, however, he stood ready to apply proper remedy.[115]

Thus deprived of trade in all ordinary goods and food-stuffs, and especially of the all-important wool which Edward sought to use as a diplomatic weapon, the situation must have appeared utterly hopeless. The promises made by Philip in August could accomplish little, inasmuch as the production of wool in France was negligible as compared with that in England. The Flemings continued their hostility toward Edward and kept sending all manner of aid and supplies to the Scots. The Channel, North Sea, and especially the inlets of Zeeland and Flanders, and the mouths of the Schelde swarmed with French craft, among which doubtless were also those sent out by Flemings, lying in wait for English shipping.[116] They often eluded the activities of English mariners whose failure to apprehend them led Edward on September 10 to order John Datlie and Hugh de Hetham of Newcastle-on-Tyne and Richard de Haseldon of Hartlepool to equip craft of forty tons burden and attack such Flemings as were seeking to aid the party of Robert Bruce by destroying English commerce and bringing victuals and munitions into Scotland. The effect was slight and the order was repeated on November 1.[117]

When news came of the concentration of ships under Walter de Manny at Orwell, it was feared in Flanders that an attempt upon the country was being meditated. All important personages, in fact the whole country, united to resist them.[118] The seignior of Pouke, a staunch supporter of the count, was one of the

---

[114] *Ibid.*, pp. 206–207; *CPR* (1338–40), pp. 68–69.
[115] *Foedera*, II(2), 1010; *CCR* (1337–9), p. 282.
[116] Kervyn, *Oeuvres de Froissart*, XVIII, 52.
[117] *Rotuli Scotiae*, I, 488, 513.
[118] Le Muisit, p. 112: " . . . comes Flandriae et tota patria coadunati eis resisterunt."

commanders of the militia of Ghent; [119] Count Louis went to Sluis in person,[120] and perfect loyalty seemed to exist. Panic was rather general, for a second attack was expected after the enemy had withdrawn from Cadzand. Deputies of the three towns met at Bruges from November 17 to 22 to discuss the problem, and messengers were sent to Paris on the 21st, apparently to request naval aid [121] as the French fleet at this moment was absent from the Flemish coast.[122]

Thus the Flemings were for the time being committed to support Philip and his loyal vassal, Count Louis, in spite of the desperate industrial and social situation in the towns. After the visit of the bishop of Tournai, discussion concerning the payments still due the king in accordance with the Treaty of Athis-sur-Orge was transferred to Tournai where royal commissioners met the deputies of the towns from September 2 to 8. The negotiations were tedious, and a delegation from the towns twice repaired to Paris.[123] A deputation was sent to Brabant to seek out witnesses who could testify in connection with the intricate problem of the past relations of Flanders and the crown.[124] On September 12 Gilles vanden Houtte was sent to Paris by the scabini of Ghent, accompanied by representatives of the other towns. In accordance with agreements reached in the discussions at Tournai and Paris, Philip granted to Ghent a reduction of 48,000*l.* Parisian of its debt and cancelled two sums of 30,000 and 20,000*l.* Parisian which Flanders still owed as penance.[125] Bruges was relieved of 40,000*l.* Parisian still due from the penalties imposed by the Treaty of Arques and also another sum of 3,000*l.*, the unpaid portion of the dowry for the countess.[126]

[119] N. de Pauw en J. Vuylsteke, *Rekeningen der Stad Gent*, I, 230.

[120] *Ibid.*, pp. 174, 195. He was in Sluis on the 11th.

[121] *Ibid.*: " . . . om raet ende beleet te ebbene op dorloghe dat doe was jeghen dIngelsce. . . ."

[122] *Chronographia*, II, 46.

[123] N. de Pauw en J. Vuylsteke, *Rekeningen der Stad Gent*, I, 169–170.

[124] *Ibid.*, pp. 170–171.

[125] See L. Gilliodts van Severen, *Inventaire des Archives de la Ville de Bruges*, I, 482; I. L. A. Diegerick, *Inventaire Analytique et Chronologique des Chartes et Documents appartenant aux Archives de la Ville d'Ypres*, I, 99–100.

[126] L. Gilliodts van Severen, *Inventaire des Archives de la Ville de Bruges*, I, 479.

These concessions [127] could hardly allay the bitter feeling of the men of Ghent who had charged Gilles vanden Houtte to negotiate when in Paris for the release of Sohier de Courtrai.[128]   Their temper was naturally exacerbated when the persistent appeals on his behalf throughout the last months of the year to Count Louis, King Philip, and John, duke of Brabant, proved futile.[129] Besides this invasion of their rights and the serious social crisis within the walls there were additional factors which may have influenced the men of Ghent to assume an independent attitude toward the policy of Philip and their count.   During the crisis before 1328 they had remained loyal to Louis.   The subversive element in Ghent had taken refuge in the lands of William, count of Hainault, Holland, and Zeeland, and on July 12, 1330, the magistrates and the count jointly requested him to arrest 626 men who had taken part in the disturbances.[130]   Whether this was successful is not known, but the few refugees at Mechelen and Louvain, who were apparently involved in the rebellion, were executed in May, 1333.[131]

Since 1333 there had developed a good deal of antagonism against the count.   The latter insisted that Ghent and Ypres should contribute their share of the money needed to commute into a cash payment the pilgrimage of 3,000 men which Bruges had incurred by the Treaty of Arques in 1328.   The case was brought before the Parlement of Paris, and Philip on December 16 of that year condemned the magistrates to contribute their share.[132]   They also complained of other matters.   They had, for example, evaded the terms of the Treaty of Arques by retaining their captains and deans, making illegal assessments, opposing the count's bailiff, and arrogating to themselves much of the criminal jurisdiction of the Quatuor Officia and Waasland.[133]   There were also many contested matters of which the abbot of St.

[127] *Ibid.,* pp. 480–481.
[128] N. de Pauw en J. Vuylsteke, *Rekeningen der Stad Gent,* I, 170.
[129] *Ibid.,* pp. 170–176.
[130] P. van Duyse, et E. de Busscher, *Inventaire Analytique des Chartes et Documents appartenant aux Archives de la Ville de Gand,* pp. 118–126.
[131] J. Vuylsteke, *Gentsche Stads- en Baljuwsrekeningen, 1280–1336,* II, 848.
[132] F. de Potter, *Petit Cartulaire de Gand,* pp. 323–326.
[133] N. de Pauw, *Cartulaire Historique et Généalogique des Artevelde,* pp. 101–103 (memoir of October 27, 1333).

Peter complained most bitterly.[134]   There was no abatement
of the dispute in the following year,[135] and when the scabini were
to be replaced in the middle of August, 1335, Count Louis demanded the surrender of the financial account of their administration, which was refused.[136]   The matter was finally referred for
arbitration to Andrew, bishop of Tournai, and, on October
26, the scabini sent a delegation to the abbey of Eekhout at
Bruges [137] where, on the 28th, the bishop rendered a decision
quite in harmony with the claims of the count. Then on November 3 the matter came to a formal conclusion when the deputies
from Ghent, of whom a number were to play a significant rôle
under van Artevelde, such as John uten Hove, John van Lovene,
the brothers Thomas and William van Vaernewijc, Everdey de
Grutere, and Peter Zoetart, appeared before Count Louis at
Courtrai, begged pardon for their acts, and promised to abide
by the bishop's decision.[138]

Edward apparently understood the situation in Flanders,
for on October 7 he recommended John de Thrandeston to the
scabini of Ghent, and, it appears, to them alone, since similar
letters to Bruges and Ypres are not to be found. Thrandeston
had left Nottingham on September 14 and tarried at Middelburg
during the greater part of October and November. He was thus
in a position to keep in close contact with the situation in Flanders.[139]   On December 13 the magistrates of Ghent sent the
scabinus, Sanders Rijm, and the clerk, John vanden Bossche, to
Hainault to interview William, count of Hainault, Holland, and
Zeeland, who had just come from the conference at Mechelen,
with the duke of Brabant, the count of Guelders, the margrave of
Juliers, the bishop of Lincoln, and the earls and their party.
The two men undoubtedly discussed the economic situation in
Flanders with Count William. This is apparent from the fact that

[134] N. de Potter, *Petit Cartulaire Historique et Généaloquique des
Arteveld*, pp. 104–105.   [135] *Ibid.*, pp. 105–111.
[136] F. de Potter, *Petit Cartulaire de Gand*, pp. 326–328.
[137] J. Vuylsteke, *Gentsche Stads- en Baljuwsrekeningen, 1280–1336*, II,
998.
[138] *Ibid.*, pp. 998–999; N. de Pauw, *Cartulaire Historique et Généalogique des Artevelde*, pp. 111–117.
[139] E. Déprez et L. Mirot, " Les Ambassades Anglaises pendant la
Guerre de Cent Ans," *BEC*, LIX (1898), 564; Kervyn, *Oeuvres de Froissart*,
XVIII, 158–159; *CCR* (1337–9), p. 272.

on the very day of their return, the 23d, a delegation composed of Baldwin de Coke and Henry de Grutere of the scabini, John uten Hove, the clerk, John Breetbaard, John Spelliard, and John de Pape of the fullers, and Lievin Abelin, William Yoons, and Gossin Rebbe of the lesser guilds was dispatched to Bruges to discuss the problem of the crafts with Count Louis and the representatives of King Philip.[140]

On Saturday, the 27th, the envoys returned with the usual news that nothing could be done. On the following day the scabini, just as dissatisfied as the crafts, assembled the public in the open space in front of the Bijloke.[141] It is difficult, if not impossible, to ascertain exactly what happened on that day. It is not necessary here to consider the accounts written much later which contain the French version and in which the events of the day are treated in the light of later struggles between the patricians and the plebeians.[142]

Regarding the fact and nature of the armed demonstration in front of the Bijloke and on the Friday Market Place on the 28th there can be no question. It was an orderly affair and a violent commotion cannot be proved by the testimony of any documents of weight. Such an upheaval would most likely have left some traces in the communal accounts which on the contrary merely show that a few extra guards were stationed during these days. Between September 6 and November 16 apparently no special precautions were taken. On the latter date a small force of eighteen men under the command of a bailiff's lieutenant, a page of the scabini, and a military official, was appointed to patrol the streets and they remained on duty until January 11.[143] There was of course considerable excitement on December 28 [144] and naturally more guards were required. Eighty-seven bowmen with ten captains and their dean, John uten Hove, their standard bearer, John van Everghen, and five others, representing the five

[140] N. de Pauw en J. Vuylsteke, *Rekeningen der Stad Gent,* I, 175–176.
[141] *Breve Chronicon Flandriae,* pp. 6–7.
[142] *Chronographia,* II, 49–50, where two varying accounts are given. Cf. also H. Pirenne, " L'ancienne Chronique de Flandre et la Chronographia Regum Francorum," *BCRH,* 5th Ser., V (1898), 8.
[143] N. de Pauw en J. Vuylsteke, *Rekeningen der Stad Gent,* I, 219–220.
[144] *Ibid.,* p. 220: " . . . sondages voer niewedach, doe men ghewapent was ter maerct. . . ." See also p. 216 (note): " It. van de vridachmarct scoene te makene doe men daer te gadre was, 53s. 4d."

parishes of the town, were appointed to watch on the nights of the 28th, 29th, and 30th. To these, fifty-four guards were added on the 28th, of whom thirty-eight were set to patrol the streets while the others were stationed at the gates. But the excitement speedily subsided, and some of these guards were on duty only one or two nights. The thirty-eight continued to operate throughout the week and twenty-four were disbanded after the fourth day, January 2.[145] These numbers would scarcely be sufficient in a violent commotion which the traditional accounts often represent as having taken place. On the contrary they were possibly strong enough to control a rather abnormal amount of excitement which undoubtedly developed during these days.[146]

A closer view of the events occurring on Saturday, January 3,[147] must dispel the traditional interpretation. Five captains (*hooftmans*), Jacob van Artevelde from St. John's parish, William van Vaernewijc from St. Jacques', Gelnoot van Lens from St. Nicholas', and William van Huse and Peter vanden Hovene from St. Michael's were peaceably chosen to assume the guidance of the town. Supreme direction (*'tbeleet van der steede*) was entrusted to van Artevelde. The first three belonged to the wealthy patriciate,[148] while the others were drawn from the crafts. John Breetbaard and William Yoons were associated with them as deans and captains (*dekenen ende beleeders van den ambachten*) of the fullers and the lesser guilds.[149] The political functions of the weavers' guild were now resuscitated under its new dean, Jacob van Wiendeke.[150] Thus the personnel of the new government was drawn from the patrician as well as from the lower classes. It is evident, therefore, that there can be no question of a popular movement against the aristocratic *maiores*.

The solidarity of all classes in the town is further made apparent if the activities of the scabini before and after the events

[145] N. de Pauw en J. Vuylsteke, *Rekeningen der Stad Gent*, I, p. 219: " . . . ende doe was dat aweit afghedaen."

[146] Cf. le Muisit, p. 113, who makes the same observation: " . . . Jacobus de Artevelde assumptus concorditer ab illis de Gandavo eorum capitaneus. . . ."

[147] *Ibid.*, pp. 157–158. According to le Muisit, p. 113, this took place " intrante quadragesimo."

[148] Van Vaernewijc was scabinus in 1336–1337. See N. de Pauw en J. Vuylsteke, *Rekeningen der Stad Gent*, I, 1–40.

[149] *Ibid.*, p. 157.   [150] *Ibid.*, p. 158.

of the week ending on January 3 are scrutinized. Of the thirteen scabini (*van der keure*) the three who had not gone on any mission now became quite active — Thomas van Vaernewijc,[151] Hugh van Lembeke,[152] and Philip van Audenaerde.[153] Three who did perform duties as deputies, Gilles de Tolnere,[154] Sanders Rijm,[155] and Tonis Bette,[156] now ceased to act in this capacity. Two were inactive throughout the entire official year, and the other five were sent as often as before. Essentially the same may be said of the other thirteen scabini, the councillors (*van ghedeele*). Nor was there any change in the membership of these two bodies. The receivers, Jacob Deynoot and Claes de Keyser, were removed on January 3 and replaced six days later by Gelnoot van Lens and William van Huse.[157]

That van Artevelde was the leader of this movement is the testimony of all the chronicles.[158] This character, later to become so famous in Flemish historical literature, belonged to a family which had become wealthy in the cloth trade,[159] and was then closely associated with the patriciate.[160] According to John le Bel[161] and Froissart[162] he was a brewer of mead, and the chroniclers and the historians have continued this tradition.[163] The his-

[151] *Ibid.*, pp. 180–183, 185–186, 188, 191–192.
[152] *Ibid.*, p. 181.
[153] *Ibid.*, pp. 178, 182, 187–188.
[154] *Ibid.*, pp. 174–175.
[155] *Ibid.*, p. 169–171, 175.
[156] *Ibid.*, p. 170.
[157] *Ibid.*, p. 108, and notes 1 and 2.
[158] Le Muisit, p. 113; Boendale, *Brabantsche Yeesten*, I, 562; Boendale, *Van den derden Eduwaert*, p. 334; le Bel, I, pp. 128–131; Hocsemius, p. 450; *Grandes Chroniques*, V, 371–372; de Nangis, II, 162; *Chronographia*, II, 50; *Istore et Croniques*, I, 363–364; *Chronicon Comitum Flandrensium*, p. 211; *Breve Chronicon Flandriae*, pp. 6–7; Froissart, I, 129–133.
[159] See, for example, N. de Pauw en J. Vuylsteke, *Rekeningen der Stad Gent*, I, 41.
[160] Hocsemius, p. 450, calls him "armiger quidem."
[161] Le Bel, I, 128.
[162] Froissart, I, 127. It became a tradition among later chroniclers and these in turn have generally dominated the scholarship of the past century. The chronicles in question are *Chronique des Quatre Premiers Valois*, p. 7; *Istore et Croniques*, I, 363; *Chronographia*, II, 151; *Grandes Chroniques*, V, 372, where it is stated that his wife was a brewer.
[163] N. de Pauw, "Artevelde Brasseur?" *BCRH*, 5th Ser., XVI (1896), pp. 332–336.

torical writings of the royal Valois tradition and also Froissart were pleased to point out his lowly status. Modern writers have gloried in the rise of a common man who became the savior of his country. But no trustworthy evidence can be adduced to support this contention and the lists of brewers of the time make no mention of him.[164] He was wealthy, for, besides being engaged in the cloth business, he owned valuable lands at Bassevelde.[165] One of the members of the family, John van Artevelde, who also lived in St. John's parish, is listed along with the Borluuts, the vander Sickelens, and others of the wealthier class from whom the town borrowed money in 1327.[166]

Van Artevelde's ability would appear to be well established.[167] Identifying himself with the crafts as well as with the upper bourgeoisie, toward the close of 1337 he was able to gain a hearing. In the concourse in front of the Bijloke on December 28 he emerged as spokesman for the economic interests of the town and championed neutrality in the struggle between Philip and Edward, arguing that only in this way could the Flemings secure the wool necessary for the crafts. His ascendancy is obscured by the fact that, although he had the supreme guidance of the town's affairs, all the official acts were performed by the scabini. But these as well as the crafts had also fallen under the spell of his personality and they undoubtedly coöperated in carrying out the policies suggested by him. That he was first among his colleagues, the *hooftmans* or captains, is indicated by the fact that to him were assigned on January 3 a body guard of twenty-one men-at-arms, while van Vaernewijc was to have twenty, van Huse fourteen, van Lens fifteen, vanden Hovene sixteen, Breetbaard eighteen, and Yoons and van Wiendeke, fifteen each.[168] Financial reward offers a better index of his

---

[164] See the critical note by H. Pirenne, *Histoire de Belgique,* II (2d ed.), 112.

[165] Despite the testimony of Boendale, *Brabantsche Yeesten,* I, 562. See Kervyn, *Oeuvres de Froissart,* III, 186. For the activities of Lievin van Artevelde as cloth merchant, see C. Piot, *Inventaire des Chartes des Comtes de Namur,* p. 131.

[166] F. de Potter, *Petit Cartulaire de Gand,* pp. 321–323.

[167] Boendale, *Brabantsche Yeesten,* I, 562.

[168] N. de Pauw en J. Vuylsteke, *Rekeningen der Stad Gent,* I, 223. The testimony of le Bel, I, 129, is accurate enough in describing the general situation: "Il avoit toudis alans aprez luy par la ville lx ou lxxx arméz

relative importance. Van Artevelde received 1,100*l.* for the remaining thirty-two weeks of the official year, but van Vaernewijc only 480*l.* and the other three 295*l.* 6*s.* 8*d.* each.[169]

An important ordinance was issued on the 5th which aimed to regulate the food-supply of the town and to preserve the peace.[170] The first six articles fixed the maximum price of corn and regulated its sale under heavy penalties. No one might indulge in any game of chance (art. 11). People could appear on the streets only singly and were not to look back or dance under a penalty of ten pounds (art. 10 and 14). All outlaws (*ballinghe*) who had sought exile in the churches of Ghent or in those of the neighborhood were to leave or else be seized and subjected to justice (art. 7). Those who had fled the other towns of Flanders were ordered to leave Ghent by sunrise and the country within three days (art. 9). No one, except the guards and people on errands of mercy, such as priests, surgeons, and midwives, might appear in the streets with or without light after curfew (art. 22). Article 12 announced a general truce until February 23, during which all quarrels were to be forgotten. This was done in the name of the count and at his request and also with the consent of the towns of Flanders, i.e. Bruges, and Ypres. It is apparent that this step was forced upon the count who had no means to resist. On December 29 John vanden Bossche returned from Male where he had been in conference with him. John van Lovene returned on the following day from a similar mission. On the 30th a delegation composed of Claes van Berleghem and Henry de Grutere of the scabini, and John uten Hove, Henry vander Hoyen, John van Ponteraven, and Lievin Gardyser of the crafts went to Bruges to discuss the interests of the guilds and the liberties of the town, and returned on January 1.[171] Perhaps

---

entre lesquelz el y en avoit iii ou iiii qui sçavoient aucuns de ses secrets; et quant il rencontroit ung homme qu'il hayoit ou qu'il avoit pour suspect, cil estoit tantost tué, car il avoit commandé à ses varles: 'Si tost que je rencontre ung homme je faiz ung tel signe, tantost le tuez sans deport, combien grand qu'il soit, sans attendre aultre parolle.'"

[169] N. de Pauw en J. Vuylsteke, *Rekeningen der Stad Gent*, I, 157–158.

[170] N. de Pauw, *De Voorgeboden der Stad Gent in de XIVe Eeuw (1337–1382)*, pp. 7–10. For the refugees in the churches, see N. de Pauw en J. Vuylsteke, *Rekeningen der Stad Gent*, I, 223.

[171] N. de Pauw en J. Vuylsteke, *Rekeningen der Stad Gent*, I, 176.

it was on this occasion that the measure mentioned above was agreed upon.

All extant sources seem to prove conclusively that Bruges and Ypres freely followed the suggestions of van Artevelde. The accounts of Ypres have unfortunately been lost. Those of Bruges are exceedingly laconic and give but the scantiest information. But what can be gleaned points unmistakably to the leadership of Ghent. The magistrates of Bruges sent a deputy, Ghiselin van Roeslare, to Ghent on December 27, who returned on the 29th. Then on January 1, Gilles van Coudebrouc, the burgomaster, went to Ghent where he tarried until the evening of the 3rd.[172] He was thus present when the captains were named, but nothing is known of his activities. These facts would seem to indicate that the magistrates of Bruges and Ypres naturally accepted van Artevelde's policy, which was based upon the simple fact of Flanders' economic dependence on England and feudal dependence on France.

IV. The Neutrality of Flanders (Winter–Summer, 1338)

As the year drew to a close the English agents and their supporters knew that an important crisis was at hand in Flanders and kept a vigilant eye upon the situation. John de Woume had left Reginald, count of Guelders, the bishop of Lincoln, the earls, and the rest of the dignitaries who had gathered at Mechelen early in December, and about the 11th proceeded to Rupelmonde where he tarried two days.[173] He then passed to Flushing where he remained until the 19th in close contact with what was happening.[174] Thrandeston had left these parts on the 6th when he went to Cologne where he tarried as a hostage for thirty-two days in accordance with a private arrangement with the magistrates.[175] De Woume stayed at Dordrecht from the

---

[172] *Ms. Rekeningen*, Bruges, *1336–1337*, folio 98 recto.

[173] Kervyn, *Oeuvres de Froissart*, XVIII, 53–54: " De Durdreght vers Malynes au parlement par comandement l'evesque iii jours, et demourai en la ville viii jours, et de la alez à Rypelmonde à un homme de Peruche qui fust pris par la comte de Fflaundres. . . ."

[174] *Ibid.*, p. 54: " De Rypelmonde a Flyssynge iii jours, et demorai la pour attendre novelles de Fflaundres. . . ."

[175] *Ibid.*, p. 160.

19th to January 2, when he appears to have received news of the demonstration before the Bijloke and on the Friday Market Place in Ghent on December 28.

De Woume hastened to Nijmegen to consult with the bishop and the earls and possibly also Reginald, count of Guelders.[176] The demands of van Artevelde and his supporters unmistakably meant a change of policy toward England, and it was hoped that the Flemings might now be won to aid Edward's designs. Relying upon the prestige of Count Reginald, the bishop and earls on January 7 gave him full powers as proctor of the king, his brother-in-law, to arrange alliances on the continent in his name.[177] In order that he might be well counselled in the impending negotiations with the Flemings, they desired the presence of Thrandeston and begged the magistrates of Cologne to permit him to return to them and to the king.[178]

The scabini of Ghent at once sought to open negotiations with Edward's allies. It is interesting to note that this was done apparently under color of the alliance between Brabant, Hainault, Holland, and Zeeland, and Flanders made at Dendermonde on March 31, 1336. On January 9 they dispatched John vanden Bossche to Duke John and Count William to discuss the dire situation among the crafts of the towns.[179] He was back in seven days and on the 17th was ordered to interview Count Reginald.[180] This was, it appears, in accordance with the news of a meeting which was to be held at Louvain with the count, who was very probably either accompanied by the bishop of Lincoln and the earls or in close consultation with them. John de Woume appeared at Louvain from the 13th to the 18th.[181] Vanden Bossche returned on the 20th and was at once sent back to resume discussions on the 22d. He spent about eighteen days discussing

---

[176] *Ibid.*, p. 54.

[177] I. A. Nijhoff, *Gedenkwaardigheden uit de Geschiedenis van Gelderland*, I, 370–371.

[178] Kervyn, *Oeuvres de Froissart*, XVIII, 158.

[179] N. de Pauw en J. Vuylsteke, *Rekeningen der Stad Gent*, I, 176.

[180] *Ibid.*, p. 177: "Item Jan vanden Bossce, die voer saterdages daer naer (Jan. 17) anden grave van Ghelre omme der stede groten orbare te sprekene. . . ."

[181] Kervyn, *Oeuvres de Froissart*, XVIII, 54: "De Neumaghe vers Louvyn iii jours, et demourai en la ville ii jours sur la parlaunce de Fflaundres, et tournay arrere a Neumaghe iii jours. . . ."

with the count ways and means of securing wool.[182]   He was followed on February 1 by the scabini, Jacob Masch and John Willade, who conducted the negotiations to a happy conclusion and brought the terms under seal back with them.[183]

While Ghent was thus asserting herself in an alarming manner and assuming the leadership of all Flanders, Count Louis sought to retain the affection of his subjects in Bruges. On January 6 he granted them a privilege providing that the goods of homicides should henceforth not be forfeited and no burgher should be imprisoned or have his property seized for violations of the law of the town without first having been condemned by the scabini.[184]   On the 19th he announced further privileges in criminal jurisdiction in view of the aid which the town had rendered him in 1334 in the war against the duke of Brabant.[185]   On the day before, he reconfirmed the privileges of Aardenburg originally granted in 1279.[186]

King Philip could not be pleased with a course which to him seemed like open revolt.[187]   The hideous memories of the slaughter at Courtrai in 1302 were now recalled, and the frightened king on January 12 ordered his vassals to be at Amiens at Mid-Lent.[188]   The royal governor in Tournai had arrested the goods of the burghers of Ghent and an envoy had to be sent by the scabini to negotiate their release.[189]   In view of Edward's impending expedition Philip deemed it best to negotiate with Flanders, and William d'Auxonne, bishop of Cambrai, was sent to Eecloo where he conferred with delegates from Bruges, Ghent, and

---

[182] N. de Pauw en J. Vuylsteke, *Rekeningen der Stad Gent,* I, 177: " Item Jan vanden Bossce, die voer in S. Vincentis daghe toten grave van Gelre te sprekene hoe men te neringhen commen mochte. . . ."

[183] *Ibid.,* p. 178: " Item scep. Jacob Masch ende Jan Willade, die voeren sondages voer lichtmesse te Lovene anden grave van Ghelre omme traitiet ti houdene, hoe men nering ebben soude, dwelke traitiet sij doe brochten gheacordert. . . ."

[184] L. Gilliodts, van Severen, *Inventaire des Archives de la Ville de Bruges,* I, 483.

[185] *Ibid.,* pp. 483–485; Kervyn, *Histoire de Flandre,* III, 192–193.

[186] A. Kluit, *Historia Critica Comitatus Hollandiae et Zeelandiae,* II, 822 (note).

[187] For the impression it gave the French court, see le Bel, I, 131, and *Grandes Chroniques,* V, 372.

[188] Kervyn, *Histoire de Flandre,* III, 188–189.

[189] N. de Pauw en J. Vuylsteke, *Rekeningen der Stad Gent,* I, 179.

Ypres on January 15 and 16 regarding the question of the crafts and communal liberties. The scabini of Ghent sent John van Lovene to Male to discuss with Count Louis the economic situation and undoubtedly also the proposed agreements negotiated with Count Reginald at Louvain, for on that same day, the 22d, vanden Bossche was sent back to resume discussions with the English party.[190] On the 27th John van Lovene was sent to Bruges to meet the towns of Flanders in conference over the proposed step.[191] He returned in three days, and on the 30th the scabini of Ghent sent a delegation composed of their colleagues, Sanders Rijm and Lievin Bevelant, the two clerks, John uten Hove and John van Lovene, and four burghers to meet the bishop of Cambrai and the royal admiral at Eecloo on January 30. In three days Philip's deputies, making of necessity a virtue, consented to the agreement already made between Flanders and England whereby the economic pressure might be relieved.[192] The terms became final when after February 5 the delegates of the other towns of Flanders met at Bruges, and the whole country accepted them.[193] The first step of van Artevelde's policy thus received its official sanction.

The scabini of Ghent were now legally enabled to make concluding arrangements with Count Reginald and the English deputies. On February 11 they dispatched their colleague Jacob Masch with William de Jonchere and John van Steenbeke to secure wool from the immense stores at Dordrecht.[194] Bruges sent John Walkier and John van Coukelaere to Count Reginald who apparently was at Dordrecht at that moment.[195] Five days later were sent the premier scabinus of Ghent, Thomas van Vaernewijc, and his colleague, John Willade, with John vanden

---

[190] *Ibid.*, p. 177.

[191] *Ibid.*, p. 178: "Item meester Jan van Lovene voer te Brugghewaert sdicendaghes daer naer (Jan. 27), ten parlemente daer alt lant was van Vlaendren omme traytiet te houdene, tlant te neringhen ende vriheden te settene. . . ."

[192] *Ibid.*, p. 178: ". . . voeren svridages voer lichtmesse tEkelo, daer de bisscoppe ende sconincx amirael waren van sconinx alven omme te acorderne de goede pointe daer men te neringhen mede comen soude ende te vryeden. . . ."

[193] *Ibid.*, pp. 178–179.

[194] *Ibid.*, p. 179.

[195] *Ms. Rekeningen*, Bruges, *1336–1337*, folio 96 verso.

Bossche and one other to confirm with the delegates of Bruges and Ypres the terms previously agreed upon.[196]   Meanwhile the wool apparently began to arrive when Masch and his companions returned from Dordrecht in the first week of March.   Thus after an embargo of eighteen months the crafts were ready to resume work.   Undoubtedly van Artevelde's position was greatly strengthened by the success of this policy in the spring of 1338.

Philip was far from satisfied with the progress of events and resolved to employ force.   Thomas van Vaernewijc and his associates had returned from Louvain with the representatives of Bruges and Ypres after an absence of twenty-four days.[197]   On March 14 there was a meeting of the deputies of the three towns of Flanders accompanied by members of the crafts to discuss with Philip's representative, John, king of Bohemia, the arrangements made with the count of Guelders at Louvain.[198]   The deputies from Ghent returned on the same day, and on the 16th Thomas van Vaernewijc, John Willade, John van Lovene, and John Moye went to Bruges to resume discussions with the rest of the deputies for Flanders and with Count Louis.   These were back on the 18th, and the first three were at once dispatched again to Bruges to beg the king of Bohemia to come to Ghent.[199]   It appears that this was to convince him of their loyalty to their lawful suzerain and to dispel suspicions, for grave rumors of treason were rife.[200]   On the 14th the scabini had sent to Philip at Paris John uten Hove and Simon Parijs to explain the seriousness of the situation among the crafts, and to allay the king's uneasiness.   Philip received them graciously, apparently accepted their explanations, and promised to preserve the industry

[196] N. de Pauw en J. Vuylsteke, *Rekeningen der Stad Gent*, I, 180; *Chronographia*, II, 47.

[197] N. de Pauw en J. Vuylsteke, *Rekeningen der Stad Gent*, I, 180.

[198] *Ibid.*, p. 180: "Item scep. Maes van Varnewijc, Lievin Bevelant, Gherem uten Zwane, ende met hem meester Jan van Lovene, meester Maechelem, Jacop Rugginstul, Jacop van Wackine, Jan vanden Wallekine, Heinric Goethals, Jan van Dronghine, Willem de Jonghe, Gerard de Neut ende Heinric van Allendriesch, die voeren saterdages voer alf marthe tEkelo dar tlant van Vlaendren was vor den coninc van Beem, om traitiet vanden accorde to makene tusschen minen heere van Vlaendren ende der stede. . . ." See also *Ms. Rekeningen*, Bruges, *1337–1338*, folio 98 verso.

[199] N. de Pauw en J. Vuylsteke, *Rekeningen der Stad Gent*, I, 181.

[200] Cf. *Chronographia*, II, 47.

of the towns.[201] But the royal suspicions could naturally enough
not be wholly removed, and early in April Philip strengthened
the garrison at Tournai and sent a constable with a force to
guard the place.[202] While on their way to Paris, uten Hove
and Parijs had been arrested at Tournai and could return only
with a special safe-conduct.[203]

Philip was confident of his power, and, even while the delegation from Ghent was discussing the matter with him, Sohier
de Courtrai, in spite of all efforts to secure his release, was beheaded in the count's castle at Rupelmonde. It was Saturday,
the day before Palm Sunday when the great fair in Ghent was
held,[204] and naturally the public was profoundly moved by this
mark of Philip's disapproval.[205] At the same moment the bishop
of Senlis and the abbot of St. Denis at Tournai[206] excommunicated the people of Ghent and this inevitably added to the already
intense excitement. The king's deep suspicions were revealed
by the order from Vincennes on March 10 to his constable,
Raoul d'Eu, and his marshal, Robert de Bertrand, to instruct
Count Louis to have the walls of Ghent demolished. These
orders were transmitted to the town on the 23d and recited how
by command of Philip IV the walls of all fortified towns were
to have been torn down by St. John the Baptist's Day of 1307 and
never to be rebuilt, and that by the king's special favor this had
not been exacted in the case of Ghent, but that the walls and
fortifications should remain as they were until such time as the
king might wish to have them razed. In accordance with this
document Philip now demanded his rights and instructed his constable and marshal to employ force should the people refuse.[207]
But at the same moment Bruges was favored by request of the

[201] N. de Pauw en J. Vuylsteke, *Rekeningen der Stad Gent,* I, 180.
[202] Le Muisit, pp. 43–44.
[203] N. de Pauw en J. Vuylsteke, *Rekeningen der Stad Gent,* I, 180.
[204] Cf. Kervyn, *Histoire de Flandre,* III, 182.
[205] Le Muisit, pp. 110–111; de Budt, p. 325; le Bel, 1, 133; *Chronicon
Tronchiniense,* pp. 616–617; *Chronographia,* II, 43–44; *Grandes Chroniques,* V, 362; *Istore et Croniques,* I, 362. *Chronique Normande,* p. 39;
Froissart, I, 129–130, 396–397. Philip discontinued his pension, J. Viard,
Les Journaux de Philippe VI, pp. 879, 904.
[206] Le Muisit, p. 113; de Nangis, II, 159; *Grandes Chroniques,* V, 372.
For the date, see N. de Pauw en J. Vuylsteke, *Rekeningen der Stad Gent,*
I, 181.
[207] Kervyn, *Oeuvres de Froissart,* XXI, 209–211.

count who from the first apparently had sought to divide the Flemings by showing favor to that town. In March Philip allowed the scabini to restore the walls to the condition in which they had been before Philip IV had ordered them to be torn down, and guaranteed them this privilege so long as they should remain loyal to him and his successors.[208]

The scabini of Ghent were in a quandary. On the 21st they sent to Lille, where Raoul d'Eu and Robert de Bertrand were stationed, a representation of the clergy consisting of an ecclesiastical dean, two Dominicans, two Carmelites, two Austin canons, and a man named Lievin vander Leylen who returned on the 24th without accomplishing anything.[209] Equally futile were the discussions at Deinze with the king's deputies on April 3, at Lille on the 6th, and at Tournai from the 10th to the 31st whither Thomas van Vaernewijc, Lievin Bevelant, and John uten Hove had gone. John vanden Bossche was then sent to Liège to seek counsel in appealing the sentence. But the bishop, who had quarreled with the duke of Brabant and viewed Edward's friends with great suspicions, would of course not help. Intercourse with the count of Guelders was in the meantime continued.[210]

Only a comparatively small part of the population of Flanders — a few nobles and their retainers — were really opposed to the new policy championed by van Artevelde, but they were anxious to resist it with arms.[211] They needed little encouragement to raise their heads when Count Louis showed himself hostile and finally, in obedience to orders from his suzerain, executed Sohier de Courtrai. Thus we read of the arrest of a Peter de Amman in Ghent on March 7 [212] who was placed in the Gerard Duivelhuis whence he was speedily transferred to the count's castle, from which, however, he escaped on April 11. His castle at Everghem was watched from March 28 to May 30 by Gilles den Abt and John van Bost and a number of men-at-arms.[213] In March there was an inquest conducted, and a

---

[208] L. Gilliodts van Severen, *Inventaire des Archives de la Ville de Bruges,* I, 486–487.

[209] N. de Pauw en J. Vuylsteke, *Rekeningen der Stad Gent,* I, 181.

[210] *Ibid.,* pp. 182–183.   [211] *Chronicon Comitum Flandrensium,* p. 210

[212] N. de Pauw en J. Vuylsteke, *Rekeningen der Stad Gent,* I, 201.

[213] *Ibid.,* pp. 225–226 and note.

considerable number were no doubt investigated, among them Portegalen, John vander Morstraten, and Peter vander Mersch. These men were brought to the count's castle, but a few others gave considerable trouble. Gilles Bafs, Gilles vander Carren, and John van Mendonc were pursued.[214] In April Henry de Wickere and two other men were set to watch ser Braem's castle outside the town and in the week before Easter another guard was placed at Huges Jonghen's castle at Wondelgem.[215]

These supporters of the count and of the king's rights had active sympathizers outside the walls of Ghent. A number of them came from Bruges and the Frank of Bruges,[216] appeared before the walls on Easter Eve (April 11), and made preparations to stay. The dean of the bowmen, John uten Hove, led out a hundred and sixty-eight men with their captains and a number of white-hoods to oppose them. The dykes were opened and the ground flooded so that the enemy was constrained to withdraw. On the 13th there was another alarm, an extra watch was set, and three days later a large force, accompanied by sailors and carpenters, went up the Lys and tore down a bridge to prevent any possible attack from that quarter.[217] But the opponents of the new policy did not choose to fight, and ensconced themselves in Biervliet whence they could menace the people of Ghent. Van Artevelde determined to dislodge them and on the 23d drew up the communal militia on the Kouter (*Place d'Armes*) in Ghent. On the following day he marched out with a large number of white-hoods, bowmen, and carpenters, and much warlike equipment toward Biervliet by way of Assenede. Nine of the scabini, the other four captains, and the deans of the weavers, fullers, and the lesser guilds, were with the army " to pacify the land and restore to it its peace, order, liberties, and its industry for the honor of the count," as it was euphemistically phrased. After two days' fighting the opposition was suppressed with some bloodshed.[218]

---

[214] *Ibid.*, pp. 216, 225.   [215] *Ibid.*, pp. 226–227.

[216] Count Louis was quite friendly toward the people of the Frank. On April 25 he confirmed old privileges and added some new clauses. See L. Gilliodts van Severen, *Inventaire des Archives de la Ville de Bruges*, II, 106.

[217] N. de Pauw en J. Vuylsteke, *Rekeningen der Stad Gent*, I, 238–240.

[218] *Ibid.*, pp. 224, 240–243. Cf. *Chronographia*, II, 52.

Philip had overreached himself and now became anxious to prevent a wholesale desertion of the Flemings to Edward. Nothing further is heard of the command to tear down the walls of Ghent. The day van Artevelde went to Biervliet two messengers from the king arrived and another from John, king of Bohemia.[219] The count became conciliatory at once. Apparently there was some opposition to the new policy in Bruges, but no authentic data have been preserved.[220] Van Artevelde and his force moved to Bruges before the close of the month.[221] On the 29th a hundred and eight men, magistrates, and others of Bruges were sent to Count Louis at Male to reinforce the men of Ghent to whom the scabini of Bruges sent a large quantity of Rhenish wine on the 30th.[222] An agreement was at once arrived at, for the men of Bruges returned on the following day. On May 5 Thomas van Vaernewijc appeared at Oostcamp and at Bruges to discuss the terms of peace with Louis and the towns. A document setting forth its provisions was received in Ghent on May 9, which most certainly has not survived.[223] When van Artevelde returned on the 8th [224] Count Louis either accompanied him or followed closely and there was apparently the best of understanding.[225]

Meanwhile at Ghent there was little trouble. The efforts of the scabini had everywhere resulted in preventing any successful opposition; in fact, it was not deemed necessary to set a heavy guard during van Artevelde's absence at Biervliet. The regular guards were in his army so that the town must have been very quiet.[226] Later in May some excitement developed, but this too was of no serious nature. On the 27th and 28th either Gilles Bafs or Gilles vander Carren was placed in the pillory, an event appar-

---

[219] N. de Pauw en J. Vuylsteke, *Rekeningen der Stad Gent*, I, 183–205.

[220] See, for example, the excerpts of a chronicle published by N. de Pauw, "Jacques van Artevelde 'Le sage Homme,' Bourgeois de Gand. Notice biographique et Chronique inédite," *BCRH*, LXXXII (1913), 325.

[221] N. de Pauw en J. Vuylsteke, *Rekeningen der Stad Gent*, I, 183; *Grandes Chroniques*, V, 372; *Istore et Croniques*, II, 363.

[222] *Ms. Rekeningen*, Bruges, *1337–1338*, folios 101 verso and 132 verso.

[223] N. de Pauw en J. Vuylsteke, *Rekeningen der Stad Gent*, I, 183–184.

[224] *Ibid.*, pp. 242–243. The militia arrived on the 13th. Cf. also le Muisit, pp. 115–116.

[225] N. de Pauw en J. Vuylsteke, *Rekeningen der Stad Gent*, I, 240. A quantity of wine valued at 150*l*. 13*s*. 4*d*. was presented to him.

[226] *Ibid.*, pp. 223–224 (note 2).

ently connected with some trouble which the captains had had at
the house of the wealthy patrician, John vander Sickelen.[227]
These riotous manifestations were sporadic and indicated that
the hostile movement had only a limited following, while van
Artevelde and his policy had the hearty support of nearly all
the public.

Van Artevelde's next step was to secure the adherence of all
the opponents of his policy. From the 9th to the 20th of May
he headed a delegation composed of two scabini and the captain,
William van Vaernewijc, with John Breetbaard, Henry Goethels,
and William Yoons as representatives of the guilds, which went
into West Flanders to cause the people to confirm by oath the
agreements just made at Bruges.[228] Immediately upon their return the premier scabinus, Thomas van Vaernewijc, went with
members of the crafts to Courtrai to seek the count's confirmation
of what had been done; this was readily enough given.[229]

In June Oudenaarde, Aardenburg, Grammont, Alost, Dendermonde, and the inhabitants of Waasland and the Quatuor Officia
indicated their acceptance by oath.[230] Final accord with the
count had in the meantime been secured in a meeting at Bruges
from May 27 to 31 whither Thomas van Vaernewijc and Lievin
Bevelant, two of the captains, and two heads of the guilds had
been sent.[231] At this time the count once more showed himself
favorable to Bruges by reconfirming the privileges which the
burghers had enjoyed under Count Robert.[232]

Van Artevelde's policy was now to receive the official sanction
of King Philip. Soon after their return to Ghent, Thomas van
Vaernewijc and John uten Hove proceeded to Paris with the
deputies of Bruges and undoubtedly also those of Ypres. They
explained to the king the nature of the accord between the towns
and Count Louis, the agreements and negotiations with Reg-

---

[227] *Ibid.*, pp. 216, 226.

[228] *Ibid.*, p. 184.

[229] *Ibid.*, p. 85. When van Artevelde was in West Flanders, Matthew de
Puur went into Waasland, the Quatuor Officia, and to Nevelle for the same
purpose. See *ibid.*, p. 206, and J. Despars, *Cronycke van den Lande ende
Graefscepe van Vlaenderen*, II, 325.

[230] N. de Pauw en J. Vuylsteke, *Rekeningen der Stad Gent*, I, 187–188.

[231] *Ibid.*, pp. 185–186.

[232] L. Gilliodts van Severen, *Inventaire des Archives de la Ville de
Bruges*, I, 487.

inald, count of Guelders, and the English envoys, and showed that they were in no wise prejudicial to the interests of the crown.[233] Confronted with Edward's hostility and fearful of the enmity of Flanders in case of conflict, Philip had no choice but to submit.

On June 13 he formally approved what had been done. The document set forth that at the earnest request of the count of Flanders in behalf of his towns, the king had listened to the pleas of Ghent and its adherents — which also clearly reveals the leadership of Ghent — pardoned all excesses, promised that the sentence of excommunication should be lifted, and permitted them as neutrals to trade with the English.[234] To the scabini of Ghent he showed special favor. Their request that a sum of 30,000*l.* Tournois paid in 1307 by way of fine for their misdeeds should be deducted from debts they still owed the crown was granted and on the 17th the officials were instructed to make proper entry in the accounts.[235] Philip kept his word, and on July 19 the bishop of Senlis appeared in Ghent to grant absolution.[236] On the following day Count Louis surrendered all claims upon Bruges for compensation in connection with past revolts.[237]

During April, when open rupture threatened between van Artevelde's supporters and those of Count Louis, Edward entertained great hope that the Flemings might be induced to support him without reserve. On May 8 he thanked the men of the three towns for the favor shown him and requested them to negotiate with his emissaries in Brabant. He also promised to provide the son of Sohier de Courtrai with due compensation for losses incurred by his father in his behalf.[238] But a political alliance was out of the question and economic matters alone were discussed during the negotiations. Early in June Reginald, count

---

[233] N. de Pauw en J. Vuylsteke, *Rekeningen der Stad Gent,* I, 197. For the deputies from Bruges, see *Ms. Rekeningen,* Bruges, *1336–1337,* folios 104 recto and verso, 105 verso, 140 verso.

[234] Kervyn, *Oeuvres de Froissart,* XVIII, 62–63; Kervyn, *Histoire de Flandre,* III, 204–206.

[235] I. L. A. Diegerick, *Inventaire Analytique et Chronologique des Chartes et Documents appartenant aux Archives de la Ville d'Ypres,* II, 160–161.

[236] N. de Pauw en J. Vuylsteke, *Rekeningen der Stad Gent,* I, 190.

[237] L. Gilliodts van Severen, "Jacques van Artevelde," *La Flandre,* IX (1878), 441–442.   [238] *Foedera,* II (2), 1035.

of Guelders, was in Rupelmonde where he met Count Louis and the delegates of the towns. Those from Ghent returned on the 8th, and on the following day the scabini dispatched their colleagues, Jacob Masch, John Willade, and John vanden Bossche to Antwerp to close the negotiations.[239]

A long document was at once drawn up setting forth the points hitherto agreed upon. The Flemings were to maintain a purely neutral policy and not support Philip. The English were not to enter the county or cross it, armed or otherwise, nor inflict any damage. Within the boundaries of Flanders the peace was to be maintained so that no subject of the French crown might injure any Englishman. Should Edward invade the county, the Flemings might support their count. If his fleet came into the Zwin and to Sluis or other harbors it should not tarry save in case of tempest. Count Louis was to be free to do as he might wish outside Flanders, but the towns were not to aid him. In return Edward promised them freedom to purchase wool and all manner of goods which had hitherto been freely imported into Holland, Zeeland, or Brabant. Flemish merchants were guaranteed safety for themselves and their goods in England and the cocket seal was to be ample evidence entitling them to protection, but all who were apprehended dealing with the Scots were to be prosecuted.[240] Confirmation of these clauses was received at Antwerp by Thomas van Vaernewijc, William van Huse, and John de Coster who had left Ghent on July 11.[241]

V. Edward's Arrival in Brabant (July, 1338)

The conduct of the wool monopoly in the autumn of 1337 had not brought the anticipated resources into the royal treasury and, as more money would be needed during the coming campaign, Edward was forced to take matters into his own hands. The Parliament held at Westminster in February granted him a moiety of the wool of the realm which was estimated at as much as 20,000 or 25,000 sacks. This was to be loaned by the growers on

[239] N. de Pauw en J. Vuylsteke, *Rekeningen der Stad Gent*, I, 187.

[240] *Foedera*, II (2), pp. 1042–1043, 1045; I. L. A. Diegerick, *Inventaire Analytique et Chronologique des Chartes et Documents appartenant aux Archives de la Ville d'Ypres*, II, 101–102.

[241] N. de Pauw en J. Vuylsteke, *Rekeningen der Stad Gent*, I, p. 190.

good security. No wool save the 3,700 sacks promised to the merchants of Almain and Brabant was to leave the realm until this amount had actually passed into the royal hands.[242]

The same Parliament agreed that active war should be levied upon Philip. Consequently it was an urgent matter to secure money at once. In March the Bardi and the Peruzzi agreed to finance the undertaking which Edward planned. The wool was to be delivered to them in the Low Countries and the profits were to be applied to repay the loans which they were to advance to the king for his passage to the Low Countries, which was planned for a fortnight after Easter.[243] It was decided to pass 4,000 sacks at once for which the Florentines were to lend 15,000*l*.[244] Edward was sanguine enough to believe that this could be accomplished in spite of the very general popular reluctance on the part of the growers and on March 26 instructed the purveyors and takers of wool in all the counties of the realm to have their quotas at certain designated parts ready for the passage.[245] On the 10th proclamation had gone forth that no merchant should take any wool to foreign parts without the king's special order.[246]

Edward also planned to take over the stock of wool which was still unsold at Dordrecht. There were in all 11,497 sacks, 1 quarter, 2 cloves, and 1 pound. Instructions were issued to William de la Pole and Reginald de Conductu to deliver the entire lot into the hands of Paul de Monte Florum and John de Charneles. From this source was derived something like 85,000*l*.,[247] which the king undertook to repay to the merchants from the receipts of the customs.[248] The Bardi and the Peruzzi promised on May 7 to advance 20,000*l*. in addition to their previous contract as soon as Edward should arrive in the Low Countries.[249]

Edward thus revealed determination to fight Philip in spite

[242] *CCR* (1337–9), p. 393; Murimuth, p. 82; *Melsa*, II, 383.

[243] *CCR* (1337–9), pp. 400, 412; E. Russel, " The Societies of the Bardi and the Peruzzi and their Dealings with Edward III (1327–1345)," *Finance and Trade under Edward III*, pp. 110–120.

[244] *CCR* (1337–9), pp. 400, 412.

[245] *Ibid.*, p. 401.

[246] *Ibid.*, p. 393.

[247] S. B. Terry, *The Financing of the Hundred Years' War (1337–1360)*, pp. 21–22. According to *Melsa*, II, 384, this amounted to 150,000*l*. of which one half would of course be the royal share.

[248] *CCR* (1337–9), pp. 424–425.   [249] *Ibid.*, p. 412.

of the protracted sojourn of the papal nuncios in England.[250] But it proved impossible to sail at the date originally set. The concentration of ships at Orwell and Great Yarmouth proceeded but slowly as large numbers of ships of the requisite burden, which the king had ordered arrested, succeeded in putting out to sea and evading the admirals. As the day set for the departure approached Edward perceived that it was necessary to postpone the voyage, and on April 15 issued impatient orders to his officers to have enough ships ready by May 12 at the latest.[251] It was even impossible to get enough craft together to transport and convoy the wool collected by the merchants of Brabant.[252] The arraying of troops, however, appears to have progressed normally.[253]

The country was deeply stirred by the various exactions and purveyance, and Edward thought it necessary as early as March 28 to instruct the archbishop of Canterbury to intercede with the people.[254] In London the populace was disaffected and special precautions were taken in May to allay its discontent.[255] On May 4 all unstamped tin in Devonshire and Cornwall was ordered to be stamped at once and carried to Southampton for exportation to the Low Countries, whereupon the miners refused to stay at their tasks.[256] No one, clergyman, pilgrim, or merchant, was allowed to carry any precious metal out of the realm.[257] Property of foreign ecclesiastical persons was now confiscated, aid was forced from the public, and the clergy were induced to grant large sums; even their vestments and costly vessels were taken.[258] The clergy and nobles of Kent and Sussex who had land near the coast were required to hold their forces in readiness to resist any attack which the French were, it was rumored, contemplating and did make.[259] Evasion of the royal orders became common. As an instance of this may be mentioned the smuggling of live

[250] *Annales Paulini*, p. 367.
[251] *Foedera*, II (2), 1027; *Auctor Bridlingtoniensis*, p. 137.
[252] *Foedera*, II (2), 1041.
[253] *Ibid.*, 1016–1018, 1024, 1034.
[254] *Ibid.*, p. 1025; Knighton, II, 3.
[255] *Foedera*, II (2), 1036–1037.
[256] *Ibid.*, pp. 1035–1036; *CCR* (1337–9), pp. 414–517.
[257] *CCR* (1337–9), p. 414.
[258] Knighton, II, 2–3.
[259] *CCR* (1337–9), pp. 413–414; Knighton, II, 3.

rams from Boston which greatly affected, it was said, the price of wool.[260]

The fond hope of having the royal share of the wool ready for export by about Easter was therefore doomed to failure even greater than that of the previous autumn, and it was necessary again to delay the passage until July. Having put off his expedition, Edward planned to have in his hands all the wool granted him by August 1,[261] and, hopeful that this could be accomplished, proceeded with his preparations. But no progress could be made, and when the king was at Orwell ready to cross over to Brabant he knew that in spite of the advancing summer only about 3,000 sacks had actually arrived at Antwerp. On July 27 peremptory orders were issued by Edward, duke of Cornwall, then acting as regent, that all wool at London, Sandwich, Ipswich, Lynn, Boston, Kingston-upon-Hull, and Newcastle in the hands of collectors should be brought to Great Yarmouth at once by St. Bartholomew's Day or sooner for transportation under safe-conduct to the Low Countries. The royal officials were commanded to arrest enough vessels in these ports and appoint responsible persons to take the matter in hand. Robert Howell and Robert de Watford were appointed to survey all wool collected in the ports named and to expedite shipment.[262]

Edward's position was thus a very difficult one. At home there was a widely diffused disaffection which deprived him of adequate financial support, and in the Low Countries many of his allies who had been secured at vast expense, were eagerly awaiting payment for their efforts in his behalf. The duke of Brabant was wavering, the Flemings were uncertain, and his continued absence and inability to meet his obligations might materially weaken his prestige. Nevertheless Edward was hopeful that the wool could be at Antwerp upon his arrival and prepared for the passage. He left the royal manor of Walton at 3 o'clock on July 12 after he had entrusted the affairs of the realm to his son who was to act as regent. On the 14th he was aboard his ship, the *Christopher*, the pride of the English navy,[263] which

[260] *Foedera*, II (2), 1034.
[261] *CCR* (1337–9), p. 424.
[262] *Foedera*, II (2), 1051.
[263] *Ibid.*, p. 1050.

had been fitted out at great expense and carried the new fire weapons.[264] Until the 16th he lay at anchor in the harbor of Orwell,[265] where the fleet to be collected from the ports west of the Thames had been concentrating.[266] At half past six in the morning he put out to sea [267] and Walter de Manny's fleet, which had been preparing at Great Yarmouth, now hove into sight and the two, variously estimated at from three to five hundred craft,[268] proceeded on their way to Antwerp. The clergy had been requested to pray for a voyage without incident,[269] and by evening the fleet was off the mouth of the Zwin.[270] Its appearance in the waters leading to Bruges caused no commotion in Flanders which was secure in its treaty of neutrality. The king sailed up the Honte past Middelburg,[271] and on the feast of St. Mary Magdalene (July 22) sailed up the broad Schelde before Antwerp.[272] A great crowd had assembled to witness the unusual spectacle. Edward at once disembarked with his household, among whom were Philippa, his two sons, and his daughter, Johanna, followed by his soldiers and archers. The house where the royal pair were lodged during the first night caught fire and the inmates escaped scantily clad,[273] which gave rise in England to a vague rumor of misfortune to the king, soon afterward quieted, however, by the assurance of the chancellor.[274]

[264] N. H. Nicolas, *History of the Royal Navy,* I (*Documents*), 475–476: ". . . iii canons de ferr ove v chambres, un handgone. . . ."

[265] Murimuth, p. 83; Hemingburgh, II, 316.

[266] *Foedera,* II(2), 1050; *Auctor Bridlingtoniensis,* p. 137; *Chronographia,* II, 60.

[267] *Foedera,* II(2), 1050.

[268] Baker, p. 61; Murimuth, p. 83; Villani, col. 817; Boendale, *Van den derden Eduwaert,* p. 312; Boendale, *Brabantsche Yeesten,* I, 553.

[269] *CCR* (1337–9), p. 520.   [270] Hemingburgh, II, 316.

[271] See le Muisit, p. 116, who confuses the two events. A messenger was sent with the news from Sluis to Ghent on July 17. See N. de Pauw en J. Vuylsteke, *Rekeningen der Stad Gent,* I, 209. The *Chronographia,* II, 60, states that Edward disembarked at Middelburg.

[272] For other references, see Avesbury, p. 302; *Lanercost,* p. 304; Knighton, II, 4; *Scalacronica,* p. 618; *Melsa,* II, 385; *French Chronicle of London,* p. 71; *Bourgeois de Valenciennes,* p. 161; le Bel, I, 137; Hocsemius, p. 448; *Gesta Abbatum Sancti Trudonis,* p. 423; E. Dynter, *Chronicon Ducum Brabantiae,* II, 618; *Grandes Chroniques,* V, 371; *Chroniques des Quatre Premiers Valois,* p. 9.

[273] Boendale, *Van den derden Eduwaert,* p. 312; *Auctor Bridlingtoniensis,* p. 140.

[274] E. Déprez, *Les Préliminaires de la Guerre de Cent Ans,* p. 194.

CHAPTER IX

EDWARD'S YEAR OF ENFORCED IDLENESS
(SUMMER, 1338 — SUMMER, 1339)

i. Edward's Difficulties in Brabant (Summer, 1338)   ii. Edward's Diplomacy as Imperial Vicar (Autumn, 1338 — Spring, 1339)   iii. Edward's Financial Difficulties (Spring–Summer, 1339)   iv. The Neutrality of Flanders (Summer, 1338 — Summer, 1339)

I. EDWARD'S DIFFICULTIES IN BRABANT (SUMMER, 1338)

UPON his arrival at Antwerp, Edward was met by the bishop of Lincoln, the earls, and the other English emissaries as well as by numerous princes of the Low Countries, including Reginald, count of Guelders, William, margrave of Juliers, William, count of Hainault, Holland, and Zeeland, John of Hainault, and others of less degree.[1] The scabini of Ghent sent their trusted envoy, John de Coster.[2] But Edward was disappointed; the reception was none too warm, and prospects for an immediate campaign were far from encouraging. He had left England with a light heart, believing that the wool would speedily arrive in Antwerp, but only a tenth of the total levy was on hand and scarcely a sack appears to have crossed during July.[3]

In his relentless opposition to the emperor, Benedict XII had on July 15 ordered the bishop, dean, provost, and chapter of the church of Cambrai, and the scabini and corporation of that town to repel Lewis the Bavarian, should he attempt any invasion of the Cambrésis.[4] King Philip was ready for the expected blow and had taken pains to be able to defend his borders from inva-

---

[1] Le Bel, I, 137; Avesbury, p. 84; Baker, pp. 61–62; *Bourgeois de Valenciennes*, p. 161.

[2] N. de Pauw en J. Vuylsteke, *Rekeningen der Stad Gent*, I, 191.

[3] On July 27 there were said to be 3,000 sacks, on August 7, 2,000, and on the 20th, 2,500. See *Foedera*, II (2), 1051, 1054, 1057–1058.

[4] G. Daumet, *Benoît XII (1334–1342). Lettres Closes, Patentes et Curiales se rapportant à la France*, Nos. 464, 65, 466. He also informed Philip of these orders, *ibid.*, No. 467.

sion.[5] At the beginning of July he summoned his vassals to assemble at Amiens.[6] Since spring his troops had been stationed in Tournai.[7] At Cambrai the bishop, William d'Auxonne, cooperated with him in fortifying the city,[8] and toward the close of August Philip himself appeared at Amiens.[9] Thus all the castles and strongholds on the confines of Hainault and Flanders were ready to resist any attempt by Edward, while all Hainault could be invaded by the French, should they choose to do so.[10]

Edward's presence could arouse no enthusiasm among the princes whose adherence had been purchased at great price and who could be retained only by prompt payment of all instalments soon due. Caught between the hostile forces of France and England, they could see but scant advantage in supporting Edward whose position at this moment must have appeared quite unsatisfactory. It can cause no surprise that the duke of Brabant, who did not relish a return of the hectic days of 1332–1334, should beg Philip not to interpret his apparent friendship for Edward as unfavorable to France.[11] The strategic significance of the duchy, due to its central location, its military power, and its great wealth, gave the duke exceptional prestige with all parties and enabled him now to assume a very independent rôle. His policy was especially unfortunate for Edward's interests, inasmuch as his son-in-law William, count of Hainault, Holland, and Zeeland, although the brother of Queen Philippa, was bound to follow in his steps. Hainault's exposed position in the extreme western point of the empire and the fact that the county of Ostrevant was a fief of the French crown forced William to consider well his interests. For this reason he abandoned the active efforts of his father to recover Arleux and Crèvecoeur from Philip and his rights in the

  [5] P. Varin, *Archives Administratives de la Ville de Reims*, II (2), 786, 791–792; Lescot (*Appendice*), pp. 215–217.

  [6] E. Déprez, *Les Préliminaires de la Guerre de Cent Ans*, pp. 198–199. Cf. A. Longnon, *Documents Inédits de Comté de Champagne et de Brie*, III, 236–237. The bailiff of Arras was ordered to destroy all the bridges which the enemy might use. See E. Petit, *Histoire des Ducs de Bourgogne*, VII (*Pièces Justificatives*), 220, note 2.

  [7] Le Muisit, pp. 113–114.

  [8] Cf. H. Dubrulle, *Cambrai à la Fin du Moyen Âge* (*XIIIe–XVIe Siècle*), pp. 282–283.

  [9] J. Viard, "Itinéraire de Philippe de Valois," *BEC*, LXXIV (1913), 528.
  [10] *Chronographia*, II, 60–64.
  [11] Le Bel, I, 139.

Cambrésis. At the beginning of summer the bishop of Cambrai excommunicated some of his subjects implicated in the murder of a clerk, and also the church at Binche for maltreatment of two priests and placed under the interdict the church of Soignies because a person had been murdered in its churchyard. This was of course a purely spiritual matter in which the bishop was acting entirely within his proper province. But had William been inclined to insist upon his rights in the Cambrésis, these incidents might very well have led to open rupture. Instead, however, he appealed to the episcopal court of Rheims in July and in the litigation which followed appears to have undertaken nothing against the bishop.[12]

There was much discussion between Edward and his allies. The king eagerly pressed them to fulfil their engagements now that his forces were ready for a campaign.[13] But few really cared to precipitate a crisis with Philip even though there was much dissatisfaction with his policy. Only the count of Guelders and the margrave of Juliers, it appears, revealed any inclination to advance Edward's interests.[14] What made his position especially humiliating was the fact that he was forced to rely upon his friends for financial assistance in his great need, since no food, equipment, or money was on hand as had been planned. Bitter were the complaints he made before the bishop of Lincoln, to whom he declared that he had been ill advised.[15] In a letter of August 4 to the regent Edward in England he wrote: " We would have been dishonored forever and our realm imperilled had it not been for the chance loan of money by a friend upon the promise that he should receive some wool." [16] It has been supposed that this friend was none other than van Artevelde; [17] but this is rather unlikely inasmuch as van Artevelde's policy of steering a middle course between Edward and Philip would have been greatly endangered by such a show of sympathy in Flanders, where he had many enemies, as well as in France. Undoubtedly it was none

---

[12] Le Devillers, *Cartulaire,* I, 51–55, 59, 61–66, 68.
[13] Le Bel, I, 137–138.
[14] I. A. Nijhoff, *Gedenkwaardigheden uit de Geschiedenis van Gelderland,* I, 389.
[15] Knighton, II, 5.
[16] Kervyn, *Oeuvres de Froissart,* XVIII, 64–65.
[17] *CCR* (1337–9), pp. 506–507.

other than the king's friend, William de la Pole, who made the necessary loans.[18]

The command of the regent and council from Northampton, whither the clergy, barons, knights, and four merchants from each shire had been summoned,[19] to hasten the collection of the wool, had as yet slight if any effect. On August 4 the impatient king dispatched fourteen ships under the command of Nicholas Pykart, Thomas de Suetesham, and Richard Fill to Boston and Kingston-upon-Hull to secure wool, victuals, and other things needed by the army. He charged the officials in these ports to pay the wages and expenses of the mariners and to send to Sandwich additional money and victuals which the ships should bring with them on their return to Antwerp.[20] Realizing the gravity of the king's predicament, the clergy, barons, and knights had already decreed on August 1 that the collectors appointed in each shire to supervise the collection of wool should take it to the ports ordained by the king with all possible speed by September 1.[21]

On August 6 Edward issued another order to hasten shipment,[22] and on the 7th the mayors and bailiffs of Kingston-upon-Hull and Boston were instructed to arrest all ships necessary to convey the wool to Great Yarmouth as had been commanded on July 27. They had taken no action because they had failed to understand the royal letters of protection which had been issued to certain parties and had assumed that no ships were to be arrested.[23] Edward remained in close contact with the regent in England [24] who on August 14 issued a peremptory command that no wool, woolfells, or hides were to leave the realm until the grant of 20,000 sacks had been fully satisfied, and then only for Antwerp.[25] The king was very uneasy, and on the 7th appointed John Wawayn,

[18] E. Varenburg, *Histoire des Relations Diplomatiques entre le Comté de Flandre et l'Angleterre au Moyen Âge*, p. 321. There were other loans, as, for example, by Henry Sudermann and his associates on August 11. See *CPR* (1338–40), p. 190.

[19] *CPR* (1337–9), pp. 511–512, 517.

[20] Kervyn, *Oeuvres de Froissart*, XVIII, 64–65. See the order to enroll mariners necessary to man the ships, *CPR* (1338–40), p. 197.

[21] *CPR* (1337–9), p. 457.

[22] *Ibid.*, p. 453.

[23] *Ibid.*, pp. 456–457.

[24] See the activities of the envoys, Nicholas de Upton and John de Arches, *ibid.*, p. 454.

[25] *Ibid.*, p. 527.

William de Kingston, and Thomas de Baddeby to superintend in each county the taking of wool and, if necessary, to seize with the aid of the bailiffs and sheriffs the remainder needed to fill the quota.[26] There was, however, no improvement, and on the 20th the king's clerk, Robert de Chickewell, was impatiently hurried to England to supervise the collection and urge them to send wool to Antwerp with the utmost dispatch.[27]

The lack of finances placed Edward at the mercy of his allies of whom a number professed a desire to attend upon his will, if only they would be paid for their pains.[28] None sought to take advantage of his plight more than John, duke of Brabant. Primarily interested in advantages to be won for the industrial and commercial welfare of his subjects, he could not be enthusiastic when English wool did not come to the staple at Antwerp. He demanded what was his due,[29] and Edward was constrained to yield on all points. Cloths belonging to merchants of Louvain which had been seized under the terms of the ordinance of September 29, 1337, were ordered to be returned.[30] He showed special anxiety for the staple.[31] In order to silence the duke's doubts that he would fulfil his obligations, Edward on August 10 confirmed the agreements which the bishop of Lincoln and his colleagues had been negotiating since the previous November.[32] The privileges which had been granted to the burghers of Louvain on May 23, 1331, were reconfirmed on the 18th. Ten days later he granted the merchants of Diest, Brussels, Tirlemont, Mechelen, and Leeuw very favorable conditions to trade and travel in his realm.[33] But such was the duke's independence that he remained stubbornly non-committal.

Accordingly nothing could be accomplished at Antwerp. The princes professed reluctance to serve at once. They declared that they had come to welcome the king and preferred to return to

---

26 *Foedera,* II (2), 1054.

27 *Ibid.,* pp. 1057–1058.

28 Murimuth, p. 84; Baker, p. 62, *Lanercost,* p. 304.

29 Murimuth, p. 84.

30 *CCR* (1337–9), p. 453.

31 *Ibid.,* p. 527; *CPR* (1338–40), p. 189.

32 J. F. Willems, *Codex Diplomaticus,* I, 811 (wrongly dated August 12).

33 *Foedera,* II (2), 1056, 1058; Ch. Stallaert, "Inventaire Analytique de Chartes concernant les Seigneurs de la Ville de Diest," *BCRH,* 4th Ser., III (1876), 220.

their homes and take council after which they would return to Antwerp and answer " so plainly that no blame could attach to them." Edward complained of the vast expense of his army and court and declared that he would never leave until they should have fulfilled their engagements. When the time set to give their decision arrived, they evaded the issue by stating that they could not move without the duke of Brabant. This wily prince now wished to consult his nobles before taking this step, and Edward was forced to agree to a conference.[34] When it was held, the princes sought to excuse themselves on the ground that they did not have proper reason to break with Philip and could move only at the emperor's command. This new subterfuge was very likely hatched in the brain of the circumspect and wily duke of Brabant, and Edward, in the height of his chagrin, unerringly attributed it to him. But to yield to anger at this time would be quite futile; he suavely announced that he would consider the matter and forthwith made plans to secure the emperor's aid [35] by public and official confirmation of his capacity as vicar of the empire.

Philip also sought to render Edward's position difficult by harassing his connections on the sea.[36] After the disembarkation at Antwerp the fleet made its way back to England [37] apparently without incident, save for the plundering of a ship belonging to a subject of the count of Guelders.[38] Piratical craft of French origin swarmed the narrow seas in August and September, and around Michaelmas Southampton was seized and occupied for one night by a fleet of fifty galleys.[39] Later a number of Genoese ships under Carlo Grimaldi appeared off the west mouth of the Schelde (the Honte) and discovered a number of English craft near St. Anna ter Muiden and Sluis, among which were the splendid ships of the king's fleet, the *Christopher* and the *Edward*.[40] Caught off their guard, they nevertheless offered a spirited resistance, but after much bloodshed were forced to

---

[34] According to le Bel, I, 140, at Hal on August 5.
[35] *Ibid.*, pp. 139–143.
[36] *Foedera*, II (2), 1060.
[37] *Chronographia*, II, 60.
[38] *Foedera*, II (2), 1055–1056; *CPR* (1338–40), p. 143.
[39] Murimuth, p. 87.
[40] *Political Poems and Songs Relating to English History*, II, 64–65.

yield.[41]   The ships were taken to Hugh Quieret and henceforth graced the French fleet, while the crews were beheaded, a gruesome procedure that was to have its apposite reward later.[42]   These events led Edward to issue orders on September 27 to Peter Barde, who had succeeded Walter de Manny on July 28 as rear-admiral of the fleet north of the Thames, to collect all ships that could be found, prepare them for war, and destroy the marauders.[43]

II. Edward's Diplomacy as Imperial Vicar
(Autumn, 1338 — Spring, 1339)

Edward made due preparations to meet the emperor at Coblenz.   The royal baggage was sent by the Rhine and with it a large entourage of notables, among whom were the queen and the Princess Johanna.   The king marched out of Antwerp on August 18.[44]   The first night was spent at Herenthals [45] and, passing through Breda on the 20th, Sittard on the 21st, and Juliers on the 22d, where he put up at the house of Juliana von Werth and was met by the margrave, he arrived at Cologne on Sunday the 23d.[46] Here he was greeted with the most enthusiastic manifestations by the people of a city that had long maintained intimate commercial connections with his realm.   He stayed with the wealthy burgher, Henry Scherfgin, who had been granted in August fifty marks annually when he visited Edward at Antwerp.[47]   This presented ample opportunity for devotions at shrines — a matter to which he was not a stranger — and splendid sums were given to the monastic foundations, shrines, altars, and to the cathedral itself, the choir of which had just been finished.

In the metropolitan's palace at Bonn he was welcomed amid popular rejoicing by Walram, the archbishop of Cologne, brother of William, margrave of Juliers.   The next stop was Sinzig on

41 *Scalacronica*, p. 169; Murimuth, p. 87.

42 *Chronique Parisienne Anonyme*, p. 178; *Grandes Chroniques*, V, 375; Outremeuse, VI, 374; Lescot, p. 47; de Nangis, II, 161; Froissart, I, 188–189, and II, 34–36.

43 *CPR* (1338–40), p. 189; *Foedera*, II (2), 1060.

44 *Foedera*, II (2), 1057.

45 *Ibid.*, pp. 1057–1058.

46 For the details of the journey, see R. Pauli, *Pictures of Old England*, pp. 151–163.   47 *CPR* (1338–40), p. 189.

the left bank of the Rhine on the 26th, where entertainment was
furnished by a knight, Wolfram von Diest. Thereupon he proceeded to Niederwerth, where he tarried until the 29th, next to
Andernach, and on the 31st to Coblenz. Memorable scenes which
impressed the chroniclers of the time followed.[48] The nobles of
the empire were in session and, driven by a tide of public sentiment which may be called national and which had already expressed itself in the famous *Declaration of Rense* and the *Licet
Juris*, readily acquiesced in the desires of Edward and the
emperor.[49]

On the 5th occurred the judicial session in the market place
of St. Florian. There were present the archbishops of Mainz and
Trier, the count of the Rhenish Palatinate, and the duke of Sax-
ony; the elector of Brandenburg was absent, and the archbishop
of Cologne, as supporter of the policy of the pope, could not par-
ticipate in these events. Clad in the gleaming regalia customarily
worn on such occasions the emperor was seated on a throne surrounded by the princes of the empire. In his right hand he bore
a golden globe surmounted by a cross, in his left the sceptre.
Above his head, Otto, seignior of Cuyk, as representative of the
duke of Brabant, brandished a naked sword. Below the emperor
sat Edward crowned, while the margrave of Meissen stood at his
right and the margrave of Juliers at his left.[50]

It was decided that the emperor or his vicar should recover
the rights of the empire and repair the wrongs done to it. All
feudatories were bound to lend military support. In the name
of the electors the archbishop of Trier declared that the imperial
vicar should exercise the same powers as the emperor. The electors then named Edward imperial vicar throughout the empire
with power over its vassals.[51] Mass was celebrated in the church,
formal documents were given, and each swore to carry out the

---

[48] Knighton, II, 5.

[49] M. Lucas, *Der Nationale Gedanke und die Kaiseridee in der Historischen Literatur Deutschelands zur Zeit Kaiser Ludwigs des Bayern,*
pp. 23–24. The decree *Licet Juris* was proclaimed in Edward's presence.
See F. G. Boehmer, *Regesten Kaiser Ludwigs des Baiern und seiner Zeit,
Additamentum Tertium,* pp. 370–371.

[50] Murimuth, p. 84.

[51] Cf. Kervyn, *Oeuvres de Froissart,* II, 548–549.

terms to the letter.⁵² On the following day, Archbishop Baldwin
of Trier, who had long been in negotiation with Reginald, count of
Guelders, now bound himself to serve Edward with five hundred
men-at-arms for 100,000 gold Florentine florins, besides wages
for his soldiers.⁵³ On this day also Edward promised to pay the
emperor the sum which he had long owed him. This amounted to
a grand total of 400,000 florins. According to the agreement of
July 23, 1337, Lewis was to have received at Dordrecht 100,000
florins on September 29, 1337, and an equal amount on February
2, 1338. A third instalment of 100,000 florins would be due on
September 29. Of this vast sum only 80,000 florins had been
paid. Edward promised to pay the remainder in two instalments
of 200,000 florins at the coming Feast of the Circumcision (January 1) and 120,000 florins on Palm Sunday (March 21, 1339).⁵⁴
Having thus arrived at an understanding with the emperor and
feeling confident that the advantages gained would materially assist him in prosecuting the war upon France, Edward hastened
back to Brabant by the same route over which he had come.
Passing through Bonn on the 8th, he arrived in Antwerp on the
13th.⁵⁵

Edward now hoped to command his allies and at Mechelen on
September 18 issued summonses to Count Louis of Flanders, Count
William of Hainault, Holland, and Zeeland, Count Reginald of
Guelders, William, margrave of Juliers, and John of Hainault to
appear at Herck, a town in Loon, on October 12 to receive his
orders.⁵⁶ The duke of Brabant, it is said, refused to have this

---

⁵² Knighton, II, 5–6; Murimuth, p. 85; *Scalacronica,* pp. 168–169. Hemingburgh, II, 316; *Lanercost,* p. 304; Boendale, *Van den derden Eduwaert,*
p. 313; *Gesta Abbatum Sancti Trudonis,* p. 423; *Bourgeois de Valenciennes,*
pp. 164–165; *Chronographia,* II, 65–66; Johannes Victoriensis, pp. 432–433;
Grandes Chroniques, V, 374; le Bel, I, 140–142; Villani, col. 817. Cf. K.
Werunsky, *Geschichte des Kaiser Karls IV,* I, 234.

⁵³ W. Günther, *Codex Diplomaticus Rheno-Mosellanus,* III (1), 280.

⁵⁴ J. Schwalm, " Reiseberichte, 1894–1896. Mit Beilagen," *Neues Archiv
der Gesellschaft für Aeltere Deutsche Geschichtskunde,* XXII (1897),
350–352.

⁵⁵ Murimuth, p. 85.

⁵⁶ E. Déprez, *Les Préliminaires de la Guerre de Cent Ans,* p. 197. On
September 18 and 19 Edward was at Mechelen. See *CPR* (1338–40), pp.
190–191. Cf. also J. Schwalm, " Reise nach Holland, Belgien, Nord Frankreich, und dem Niederrhein im Sommer, 1894," *Neues Archiv der Gesellschaft für Aeltere Deutsche Geschichtskunde,* XX (1895), 433.

assembly on his soil as he apparently still wished to disarm the suspicion of Philip.[57] He was, however, present at Herck, where he and others performed homage in a large building used as a granary.[58] On the same day, from Diest, Edward summoned under threat of forfeiture all concerned, the ecclesiastical princes of Cambrai, Utrecht, and Liège, the counts of Virneburg, Loon, Berg, Cleves, Namur, and Marck, the seignior of Cuyk, Henry of Flanders, and others to appear at Mechelen on October 26 to receive his pronouncements as vicar in regard to the rights of the empire.[59] The duke of Brabant, the counts of Hainault, Holland, and Zeeland, and Guelders, Thierry of Valkenburg, and many others responded, but the bishop of Liège was naturally absent.[60] Louis, count of Flanders, sent delegates who declared that he was ready to discharge his obligations toward the empire.[61] Bruges, Ghent, and Ypres also sent delegations charged to discuss their lord's obligation to the empire as well as other matters.[62] The princes all promised to obey Edward as vicar in accordance with their feudal contracts.[63]

It is now necessary to ascertain the state of the royal finances during the closing months of 1338. Little wool arrived in the Low Countries by St. Bartholomew's Day, as Edward had urgently ordered, although shipments became more frequent during October and November.[64] The effort to collect the 20,000 sacks is an interesting story. The clergy were especially difficult to deal with as they claimed that, not having been present at Westminster when the grant was made, its terms did not apply to them. The bishop of St. Albans refused point-blank to surrender any wool.[65] As late as January 16, 1339, no wool had yet been

---

[57] Le Bel, I, 148.

[58] *Gesta Abbatum Sancti Trudonis,* p. 423; Boendale, *Van den derden Eduwaert,* p. 315; le Bel, I, 148 (*sub* 1339); Knighton, II, 7.

[59] I. A. Nijhoff, *Gedenkwaardigheden uit de Geschiedenis van Gelderland,* I, 383–384; Hocsemius, p. 449. Edward was at Louvain on October 10, see *CPR* (1338–40), p. 190.

[60] Knighton, II, 6–7.

[61] Kervyn, *Oeuvres de Froissart,* II, 548–549.

[62] N. de Pauw en J. Vuylsteke, *Rekeningen der Stad Gent,* I, 290.

[63] Knighton, II, 6–7.

[64] *CCR* (1337–9), pp. 506–507, 544–559, 561–562, 564–571. On September 13 the Bardi had secured only eight hundred of the 5,000 sacks for which they had permission to export. See *CPR* (1338–40), pp. 129, 154.

[65] *CCR* (1337–9), pp. 539–540.

collected from the clergy of the province of Canterbury because, as the bishops explained, they had not been "informed of the names of the abbots, priors, and others who were summoned." Orders then went out from the council to collect the quotas with all possible speed.[66]

The laity also failed to collect the quotas assessed upon the shires. In Westmoreland the wool already collected could not be transported for lack of funds.[67] Failure to provide materials for packing in Cambridge and Middlesex prevented all export from these shires and special orders were repeatedly issued to purvey canvas.[68] In Salop and Staffordshire no wool, although collected, was forwarded.[69] Delivery was especially slow in the great wool-producing center of York,[70] as well as in Gloucester[71] and Southampton.[72] In Bedford the sheriffs and bailiffs were negligent and on November 12 were ordered to speed collection under pain of the royal displeasure,[73] and in Suffolk and Norfolk two men were appointed to accelerate the collection and shipment.[74]

Indisposition to coöperate with the royal officials, if these were not also opposed to the king's high-handed measures, appears to have been well-nigh universal. Thus we read of victuals being smuggled[75] and of wool being concealed in casks intended for Flanders.[76] So alarming was the amount of wool that reached the markets of the Low Countries through unlawful channels that on November 12 Edward complained that large quantities were taken out of the realm by private hands from Kingston-upon-Hull, Newcastle, Chichester, Bristol, Ipswich, Hartlepool, London, and Boston contrary to his order of August 14.[77] Owners at the Cinque Ports defied the government, declaring that they did not want to "lend their wool."[78] Some of the collectors, exasperated perhaps by the resistance of the owners, were harsh in their methods and stirred up so much opposition that the crown was forced to intervene.[79] Some communities did not wish to part

[66] *CCR* (1337–9), pp. 663–664.
[67] *Ibid.*, p. 594.
[68] *Ibid.*, pp. 550, 554, 563, 565, 566.
[69] *Ibid.*, p. 554.
[70] *Ibid.*, p. 587.
[71] *Ibid.*, p. 565.
[72] *Ibid.*, p. 564.
[73] *Ibid.*, p. 625.
[74] *Ibid.*, p. 578.
[75] *CPR* (1338–40), pp. 149–187.
[76] *Ibid.*, p. 175.
[77] *CFR* (1337–9), pp. 106–107.
[78] *CCR* (1337–9), p. 539.
[79] See, for example, the case of William de Dunstaple, *ibid.*, p. 449

with their wool but preferred to pay a sum of money instead, as in the case of London.[80] Such compounding was common in October as is shown by the order of November 2 commanding the sheriffs and receivers of wool to forward all sums thus received to the treasurers and chamberlain, who would endeavor to secure wool with it.[81]

There was almost open defiance of the impotent efforts of the regent's government. Thus the collectors of the customs at Newcastle were ordered to prevent Robert de Angerton from taking the king's wool out of the realm because of the suspicion that he intended to send it abroad himself.[82] Such was the indisposition to carry out the royal commands that the regent finally on November 9 summoned a number of merchants from Wiltshire, Northampton, Leicester, London, Norfolk, Gloucester, Lincoln, Nottingham, Salop, Worcester, and Warwick to appear before him and his council at Westminster at various times within the following fortnight after St. Martin's Day " to learn what punishment the king wished to inflict upon them because of the refusal to obey his orders." [83] The sheriffs of the counties mentioned were to bring them to Westminster.[84] But these orders were quite futile, and on November 28 others were issued to the merchants of the same counties and to those of York, Oxford, Derby, Southampton, Northumberland, Hereford, and Cambridge in addition, commanding them to be at London before the council on December 22 " and listen to the exemplary punishment for their disobedience and rebellion." [85]

Edward was thus placed in an extremely embarrassing situation. The extent of his difficulties is revealed by the order of September 8 to the treasurers and barons of the Exchequer to cease payment of the yearly fees of all crown ministers at the Exchequer unless they were " so needy that they could not do without them." [86] In thus depriving his servants he may have added to the general tendency to disregard his orders. The king was forced to borrow from every possible source. Thus Thran-

---

[80] *CPR* (1338–40), pp. 244–245.
[81] *CCR* (1337–9), p. 555. Cf. also p. 545.
[82] *Ibid.,* p. 564.   [83] *Ibid.,* pp. 614–615.   [84] *Ibid.,* pp. 615–616.
[85] *Ibid.,* pp. 621–622. See also *ibid.,* p. 578, for the flagrant case of Henry de Belton of York.
[86] *Ibid.,* p. 467.

deston went to Trier to negotiate with a Jew for financing Arch-bishop Baldwin. Later he was in conference with Rufus Vivelin, a Jew of Strassburg,[87] whom he brought to the council in Antwerp in order to discuss with Edward his financial needs.[88] Letters were issued to John de Roos and Reginald de Donington, king's clerks, to contract loans to the sum of 100,000 gold Florentine florins on the security of the goods of the realm.[89] Two merchants of Newark loaned 640l. for which William de Northwell, king's clerk, and John Darcy, steward of the royal household, were forced to advance a bond of double that amount. Similarly 1,200l. were advanced for loans made by Richard de Hakeneye of London and Robert de Beverleye of Barton-upon-Humber.[90] William de la Pole proved himself an invaluable friend in need. In return for his many loans he was commissioned to take for his own use 2,900 sacks of wool to Antwerp, and the collectors of customs at Yarmouth, Lynn, Ipswich, and Newcastle were instructed to further the despatch of this with the utmost celerity.[91] On November 14 he loaned the royal household 11,000l.[92] for which the king and his council granted in return parts of the royal manor of Brustwyck in York.[93] Advances were made by Paul de Monte Florum, who was subsequently repaid by grants of wool, money, and even royal jewelry.[94]

The Bardi and the Peruzzi had stood loyally by the king, but when the wool failed to arrive in Antwerp they began to press for payment. The king ordered John Wawayn and John de Westmancote to arrest ships to bring to Brabant wool for the Bardi " on which the furtherance of matters of extreme urgency depended." [95] Licenses were granted to numerous parties to export wool in spite of the royal monopoly [96] and especially to the Italian merchants.[97] The numerous loans contracted during November enabled the king to satisfy some of their demands when he delivered to the Bardi 30,000l. and to the Peruzzi 20,000l. and promised speedy settlement of the rest of his debts and presented

[87] *CPR* (1338–40), p. 371.
[88] Kervyn, *Oeuvres de Froissart*, XVIII, 161.
[89] *CPR* (1338–40), pp. 181, 194.
[90] *Ibid.*, p. 191.
[91] *CCR* (1337–9), pp. 567, 568.
[92] *Foedera*, II (2), 1056.
[93] *CPR* (1338–40), pp. 193–194.
[94] *Ibid.*, pp. 194–195.
[95] *CPR* (1338–40), p. 158.
[96] *CFR* (1337–47), pp. 104, 109.
[97] *CPR* (1338–40), p. 154.

handsome gifts to the members of these firms and their wives.[98]
Consequently orders went out on December 11 to the treasurers
and chamberlains that all sums due the king for wool arising
from the practice of compounding in London, Kent, Somerset,
Dorset, Cornwall, Devon, Hereford, Warwick, Wiltshire, Bedford,
Buckingham, Cambridge, and Essex should be given to them.[99]
Equal difficulty was experienced in satisfying William Dunort and
his associates of Mechelen. Impatient orders went out to the collectors at Kingston-upon-Hull and Boston to speed the shipment
of 500 sacks of the 2,500 granted to them,[100] and Wawayn and
Westmancote were commanded to secure ships to convey their
wool to Antwerp.[101] Two weeks later another order was necessary.[102] Some progress, however, was made in December and
January as is shown by orders to collectors to pay the freight on
some of their wool,[103] and to the sheriffs of Norfolk and Suffolk
to buy enough canvas for packing.[104]

Besides these difficulties Edward had to contend with French
privateers in the lanes of commerce between England and the
Low Countries. The passage of wool remained highly uncertain,[105] and Edward was forced to issue instructions to his admirals to stop their activities.[106] The depredations continued and
on October 15 the order was repeated when it was rumored that
a fresh attack from Normandy was meditated.[107] Fearing an attack upon London, the regent on October 23 ordered the officials
to place the customary obstructions in the Thames to stop the
galleys.[108] The panic of the government is strikingly illustrated
by the order of November 20 to all sheriffs of the counties along
the coast to arrange that only one bell should be rung in places
by the sea within a radius of seven miles, so that when the enemy
came a general alarm could be sounded.[109] Nothing, however,
came of the threatened attack as the season was late, and the
state of the weather itself did not permit the passage of wool in
any considerable quantities.[110]

[98] *Ibid.*, p. 195.
[99] *CCR* (1337–9), pp. 545, 555, 575.
[100] *Ibid.*, pp. 507, 560, 568.
[101] *Ibid.*, p. 563.
[102] *Ibid.*, p. 578.
[103] *Ibid.*, p. 575.
[104] *Ibid.*, p. 587.
[105] *CCR* (1337–9), pp. 545, 563, 566.
[106] *Foedera*, II (2), 1060.
[107] *Ibid.*, p. 1061.
[108] *Ibid.*, p. 1062.
[109] *Ibid.*, p. 1066.
[110] Murimuth, p. 88.

Reginald, count of Guelders, and William, margrave of Juliers, revealed a whole-hearted devotion to the English cause at this time. Edward could not meet his obligations to Reginald and was constrained on November 14 to borrow 7,500*l.* from William de la Pole on the promise of repayment by June 24, 1339.[111] On November 6 he promised Reginald that he would not return to England without his consent nor until he had paid all his debts.[112] This satisfied the count who on the 9th advanced to John of Valkenburg, seignior of Borne and Sittard, 9,000 florins in his behalf.[113] Edward also agreed at the suggestion of both Count Reginald and Margrave William to appoint certain parties, in whom they appear to have had especial confidence, to act as royal councillors in the prosecution of the war against Philip.[114] In February Edward borrowed from Reginald 600 marks which the latter had obtained from Simon van Halen of Ghent [115] with promise to repay before May.[116]

In spite of his financial difficulties Edward actively pursued his schemes. He issued orders on November 10 to the duke of Brabant, the counts of Hainault, Holland, and Zeeland and of Guelders, the margrave of Juliers, Otto, seignior of Cuyk, the bishop of Liège, Conrad de la Marck, seignior of Hurde,[117] Thierry of Valkenburg, and John of Hainault to present themselves with their levies between Binche and Mons in Hainault on December 25 in order to consider the usurpations of Philip in the Low Countries and in Burgundy.[118] The French king remained vigilant during the autumn months and ordered his vassals to be with his son John, duke of Normandy, at Péronne on December

[111] *Foedera,* II (2), 1065.

[112] I. A. Nijhoff, *Gedenkwaardigheden uit de Geschiedenis van Gelderland,* I, 387–388.

[113] *Ibid.,* p. 388.

[114] *Ibid.,* pp. 388–391. They were the bishop of Lincoln, his brother Bartholomew, John Darcy, the earl of Salisbury, Galfridus le Scrope, and William de Keldesby.

[115] *Foedera,* II (2), 1069.

[116] I. A. Nijhoff, *Gedenkwaardigheden uit de Geschiedenis van Gelderland,* I, 296; *CPR* (1338–40), p. 196.

[117] He had bound himself at Antwerp to serve Edward with fifty men-at-arms. See *CPR* (1338–40), p. 189.

[118] I. A. Nijhoff, *Gedenkwaardigheden uit de Geschiedenis van Gelderland,* I, 395–396; J. F. Willems, *Codex Diplomaticus,* I, 813–814.

13.[119] Benedict XII was unwearied in his efforts to prevent the clergy from giving any aid or comfort to Edward or acquiescing in any demand for homage or any other right to which he might pretend to be entitled as imperial vicar.[120] On November 13 he reprimanded Edward for assuming this title at the hands of a heretic and begged the archbishop of Canterbury and the bishop of Durham to help in preventing hostilities.[121] The nuncios, Peter and Bertrand, were instructed at the same time to labor for a truce of two years between Edward and Philip,[122] and to prevent any ecclesiastical personages from hearkening to Edward.[123] He urged them to move cautiously before proceeding with rigor.[124] So vitally was the repose of Christendom affected that on the 17th he informed the cardinals that he intended to take up negotiations himself.[125] His uneasiness is revealed by his letter of November 21 to the chapter of Liège and the towns of the *Pays de Liège*, including Liège, Huy, Dinant, St. Trond, and Tongres which urged them all to remain strictly loyal to the bishop.[126] The latter was, however, too closely identified with Philip's interests to warrant the pope's uneasiness.[127] The duke of Brabant and William, count of Hainault, Holland, and Zeeland, evinced no desire to do anything [128] and the meeting between Mons and Binche was barren of results.

[119] E. Petit, *Histoire des Ducs de Bourgogne*, VII, 223. See P. Varin, *Archives Administratives de la Ville de Reims*, I (2), 793–794; le Muisit, pp. 117–118, and especially Lescot (*Appendice*), p. 319.

[120] G. Daumet, *Benoît XII (1334–1342). Lettres Closes, Patentes, et Curiales se rapportant à la France*, Nos. 518–524, 526; A. Fierens, *Lettres de Benoît XII (1334–1342)*, Nos. 525, 526; W. H. Bliss, *Calendar of Entries in the Papal Registers*, III, 750. Edward demanded homage from the princes. For an example, the count of Flanders, see Kervyn, *Oeuvres de Froissart*, II, 548, 549.

[121] G. Daumet, *Benoît XII (1334–1342). Lettres Closes, Patentes, et Curiales se rapportant à la France*, Nos. 515–517.

[122] *Ibid.*, No. 525. [124] *Ibid.*, No. 527.

[123] *Ibid.*, No. 526. [125] *Ibid.*, No. 528.

[126] A. Fierens, *Lettres de Benoît XII (1334–1342)*, Nos. 529–534; W. H. Bliss, *Calendar on Entries in the Papal Registers*, III, 571.

[127] Knighton, II, 7.

[128] Hocsemius, p. 449.

III. EDWARD'S FINANCIAL DIFFICULTIES (SPRING–SUMMER, 1339)

AFTER the unsuccessful attempt to secure the coöperation of his allies for an attack upon Philip in December, Edward retired to Antwerp where he spent the next half year in enforced and fretful idleness.[129] This must have been most galling for a prince upon whom the eyes of all Europe were fixed.[130]

Although John, duke of Brabant, was regarded as an enemy by Philip, he would not, in spite of numerous concessions, show himself inclined to coöperate with Edward. The precarious financial condition of the English king made his success very uncertain and his sojourn in the Low Countries might accordingly be terminated at any moment. On the other hand the interests of his subjects made it imperative for the duke to remain on friendly terms. This explains from beginning to end his dissembling policy which proved highly advantageous for his subjects. During the winter of 1338–1339 the collection and shipment of wool was so successfully prosecuted that by the middle of March the quota of 20,000 sacks allowed by the Westminster Parliament was reached. On the 20th Edward therefore ordered the collectors of the various ports to permit all those who wanted to take wool, hides, and woolfells overseas to do so freely, provided that they should pay the regular customs due and give security that their cargoes should be taken to Antwerp.[131] A glance at the Close Rolls of these months shows that there was a steady export of wool to Brabant.[132]

These shipments were made in spite of the fact that Philip sought to interfere as much as possible and kept the narrow seas swarming with craft ready to pounce upon the cargoes. These ships sailed from the French harbors in the Channel such as Calais, and even operated from Sluis in spite of the neutrality of Flanders. On March 23 Edward ordered the bishop of London to warn the seamen to exercise great caution in venturing forth upon the sea. In February it was learned that Philip's subjects from Calais sought to secure wool by pretending that they were

---

[129] Le Bel, I, 149–150, states that he spent the winter at Louvain.
[130] *Scalacronica*, p. 168.
[131] *CCR* (1339–41), p. 42.
[132] *Ibid.*, pp. 1–41; *CFR* (1337–47), pp. 108–109, 118, 120.

Flemings, Zeelanders, or Brabanters. To put an end to this nuisance Edward, Duke John, and William, count of Hainault, Holland, and Zeeland, agreed on the 26th that every captain should carry letters patent from the English chancery. Order was at once issued by the regent to forbid every person from crossing over to the continent unless armed with such letters provided with the great seal, and Duke John and Count William did the same.[133]

Besides ordering that all wool be exported to Antwerp, Edward further favored the duke's subjects. On February 1 he allowed them to import it at the export rate of 43s. 4d. for each sack, while other foreigners were required to pay 60s., and also reconfirmed all privileges hitherto granted to merchants of Brabant.[134] The scabini and men of Antwerp were shown every possible consideration.[135] On March 3 he released Duke John of all debts and obligations in which he was bound to the crown.[136] The wealthy Duc family of Brussels was not forgotten. On the 5th Katherine, a daughter, and Henry Esto, a son of William Duc, were granted 100l. annually out of the customs of London.[137] He was also careful in his treatment of the men of Middelburg in Zeeland. In full satisfaction of all claims for damages inflicted by his subjects, Edward granted the scabini on February 4 a sum of eight hundred Florentine florins.[138] Safe-conduct was given to them and to the count's other subjects of the county of Zeeland to trade freely in England.[139]

In spite of all these efforts Edward's finances remained very unsatisfactory and his position in the Low Countries was correspondingly precarious. His protracted idleness at Antwerp, where he had to maintain an expensive court and support his soldiers, and the numerous unsatisfied obligations toward his allies sadly impaired his credit. The income from the quota of 20,000 sacks would probably have sufficed to pay the expenses of a campaign in the autumn of 1338, but by the following spring

---

[133] E. Déprez, *Les Préliminaires de la Guerre de Cent Ans,* pp. 247–248 (notes).

[134] J. F. Willems, "Boendale's van den Derden Eduwaert," *Belgisch Museum,* Vol. IV, p. 368 (document 1 and note); *CPR* (1338–40), p. 379.

[135] *CPR* (1338–40), pp. 377, 380.

[136] *Ibid.,* p. 379.   [138] *Foedera,* II (2), 1069.

[137] *Ibid.,* p. 370.   [139] *CPR* (1338–40), p. 379.

he stood in need of even greater sums. He was thus forced to borrow a large amount of money in order to maintain himself in the Low Countries until he could deliver a blow against Philip. He turned for aid to his brother-in-law Reginald, count of Guelders. On January 14 six hundred marks were loaned by Simon van Halen, payment of which was guaranteed on May 1 by Reginald.[140] On the 13th Edward had already granted Simon an annuity of two hundred marks. On the 10th the bishop of Lincoln, Count Reginald, William, margrave of Juliers, and Bartholomew de Burghersh had been given letters patent authorizing them to contract a loan of 300,000 gold Florentine florins.[141]

Money was borrowed from every possible source. From some burghers of Cologne 5,000 small gold Florentine florins were secured, to be repaid by June 24, for which also Count Reginald acted as guarantor.[142] The negotiations which Thrandeston had begun in the previous September with Rufus Vivelin, a Jew of Strassburg,[143] now came to a satisfactory conclusion and two loans were arranged on February 29 and March 18 of 61,000 and 50,000 Florentine florins each, which were to aid the archbishop of Trier in supporting Edward as imperial vicar. So seriously had Edward's credit declined that he had to pledge his crown for payments which had to be made on Palm Sunday and June 24.[144] On April 9 Edward granted the Jew another bond of indebtedness of 340,000 florins to be repaid at Cologne on September 29. In case of default Edward was to pay 5,000 florins a month and, at the end of three months, 10,000 florins a month until the principal should be repaid. As guarantors appeared Count Reginald, the archbishop of Canterbury, the bishops of Lincoln and Durham, the earls of Derby, Salisbury, Suffolk, and Northampton, and from the royal household, John Darcy, the steward, Henry de Ferrariis, the chamberlain, Galfridus le Scrope, and Paul de Monte Florum.[145]

---

[140] *CPR* (1338–40), p. 196; I. A. Nijhoff, *Gedenkwaardigheden uit de Geschiedenis van Gelderland,* I, 396.

[141] *CPR* (1338–40), p. 196.

[142] I. A. Nijhoff, *Gedenkwaardigheden uit de Geschiedenis van Gelderland,* I, 396–397.

[143] Kervyn, *Oeuvres de Froissart,* XVIII, 161.

[144] *CPR* (1338–40), p. 371; *Foedera,* II (2), 1073–1074, 1077.

[145] *CPR* (1338–40), p. 371.

Count Reginald now received a fitting reward for his zeal in promoting the interests of Edward and the emperor. On March 19 Lewis the Bavarian granted him the ducal title and elevated him to the dignity of an imperial prince with the privilege of putting the imperial raiment on the emperor at the occasion of his coronation whether at Aix-la-Chapelle, Milan, or Rome. He was to have also the right to coin money of the same standard as that of the archbishop of Cologne, the count of Hainault, and the duke of Brabant.[146] Two days later East Friesland, exclusive of the rights and lands belonging to William, count of Hainault, Holland, and Zeeland, as seignior of Friesland, were pawned to him by the emperor for 40,000 silver marks.[147]

In spite of the fact that the duke of Guelders and the margrave of Juliers were ready at any moment to advance against Philip,[148] no military effort could be made during the spring months. Edward's financial embarrassments were carefully noted by John, duke of Brabant. The duke still evinced little desire for an attack, collected his troops very slowly,[149] and remained as much of an obstacle as he had been in the previous summer and autumn. For these reasons no invasion from the Low Countries was possible at that moment and nothing came of the plans which were made during the winter for a supporting attack upon Burgundy. In February John de Thrandeston was sent on a mission to the emperor at Frankfurt and in April to the archbishop of Trier. Although this visit was obviously for the purpose of borrowing some money for which the royal crown was to be pawned, it was undoubtedly also concerned with warlike plans.[150] The emperor was loath to move because Edward had not yet paid him the 200,000 gold Florentine florins on the Feast of the Circumcision (January 1) and it was apparently expected that the remaining 100,000 florins would not be paid on Palm Sunday (March 21). Edward's envoys, Reginald, duke of Guelders, and William, mar-

[146] F. van Mieris, *Groot Charterboek*, II, 616.

[147] *Ibid.*, p. 617; J. Pontanus, *Historiae Gelricae Libri XIV*, p. 229. For the privilege concerning the Jews, see I. A. Nijhoff, *Gedenkwaardigheden uit de Geschiedenis van Gelderland*, I, 397–398.

[148] Le Bel, I, 151.

[149] A. Verkooren, *Inventaire, Brabant*, II, 31, 33–67.

[150] Kervyn, *Oeuvres de Froissart*, XVIII, 162; *Foedera*, II (2), 1073–1074, 1077.

grave of Juliers, issued a document at Frankfurt on March 12, and in behalf of the English king promised that the 200,000 florins would be paid before the close of the fifth week after Easter or at the latest within eight days thereafter. Eight weeks after the deposit of this sum should be indicated to the emperor, the latter was to be with his army of 2,000 men-at-arms on the right bank of the Rhine three leagues from Cologne. If he could not appear in person he might be represented by the archbishops of Trier and Mainz and the master of the Teutonic Order, or by any one of them. In this case the army was to be at Frankfurt at the appointed time. The remaining 100,000 florins, deposited with the Teutonic Order in Cologne, would then be paid. In case the emperor failed to advance, he was bound to restore this sum, but at a later moment he might claim it if he should appear between Binche and Mons in Hainault within eight days after making payment. As for the other sums due the emperor from Edward, the two envoys promised to secure full satisfaction.[151] John de Thrandeston also visited Ruprecht, count palatine of the Rhine. On April 27 a sum of 16,000 gold Florentine florins, payable on September 27 at Dordrecht, was granted to him over and above the amount stipulated in the document of July 31, 1337.[152] On February 16 Edward had arranged with Otto and Albert, the dukes of Austria, an invasion of Burgundy.[153] All these plans were, however, destined to fail.

Throughout the entire spring little could be accomplished as the duke of Brabant was loath to move. Yet Edward's pressure could not well be evaded. Toward the close of June a charter was drawn up which seemed to indicate John's full adherence to Edward's cause. On the 22d it was agreed that Edward's eldest son Edward and John's daughter Marguerite were to be married within one year after the youth should be old enough; Marguerite was to have a marriage portion as large as that of Edward's mother Isabella; and should the youth die before his father and leave a son by Marguerite, the son was to be regarded as the heir

[151] J. Schwalm, " Reiseberichte, 1894–1896. Mit Beilagen," *Neues Archiv der Gesellschaft für Aeltere Deutsche Geschichtskunde,* XXIII (1897), 352–354.

[152] *CPR* (1338–40), pp. 371–372; *Foedera,* II (2), 1079.

[153] *Foedera,* II (2), 1072–1073.

apparent. In this case Marguerite was to enjoy an allowance usually accorded to princesses. If the duke should fail in fulfilling these terms, he promised 50,000*l.* sterling, and Edward agreed, should he fail to carry out the contract, to pay twice this sum at Mechelen. Furthermore, the latter also bound himself to secure the necessary papal dispensation and pay all the costs of securing it.[154] Especially interesting is the long list of guarantors named in the document for Edward, while for the duke there were apparently none. Possibly John regarded the treaty as a mere diplomatic maneuver, for he undoubtedly knew that the pope would never sanction a marriage within the prohibited degrees between such parties. On August 2 Benedict XII notified King Philip that the dispensation would not be granted.[155] Yet, in spite of the pessimistic outlook, Edward appeared quite hopeful. Toward the close of June he moved his troops to Vilvoorde where they were obliged to camp in the open fields.[156]

The situation must have been especially trying for Edward during the closing months of the summer. His allies were all waiting for the duke to move. He had more than exhausted his resources, and was forced to borrow money from every possible quarter. The delay was perilous, for, as in the previous year, it might again be impossible to strike a blow at his enemy. The greatest efforts were made to borrow vast sums. In May William de la Pole advanced 32,000 gold Florentine florins,[157] and on June 30 Edward gave him a bond for 76,180*l.* payable on September 29. Another bond payable on November 1 was delivered on July 6 to three merchants of Mechelen, John Richier, William Kerman, and Walter Compsor.[158] Other bonds were given as follows: on June 19 for a sum of 1,035*l.* 5*s.* 4*d.*; on July 25 to the German merchants, Tideman de Revele and Hertwin de Bek, for money loaned to the Bardi and Peruzzi for the king's use; on June 20 to John and Hildebrand Sudermann for 859*l.* 8*s.* 4*d.* payable on August 1; and to John Bochorn, Albert Sobbere, John de Osne-

---

[154] *Ibid.,* pp. 1083–1084. John of Hainault appears to have been Edward's chief agent in his dealings with the duke.

[155] A. Fierens, *Lettres de Benoît XII (1334–1342)*, No. 595.

[156] Le Bel, I, 151.

[157] *CPR* (1338–40), pp. 385, 388.

[158] *Ibid.,* p. 372.

brugge, and others for 1,163*l.* 11*s.* 3*d.* large Tournois.[159] Antwerp merchants, including John Clypping and others, also made loans in return for which Edward granted them the privilege of exporting from Kingston-upon-Hull 1,900 sacks of wool.[160] Authorization was granted important individuals to negotiate loans from whatever source possible. Thus on June 27 Anthony Bache and Thomas de Berwico were instructed to secure 20,000*l.* sterling; [161] on May 30, John de Molyns, William de Northwell, and Nicholas de Falleye, members of the king's household, 100,000*l.*; [162] on August 12 Alan de Kyllum and Henry de Langeton, king's clerks, 40,000*l.*; [163] and two days later, Henry de Ferrariis, the royal chamberlain, 40,000*l.*[164]

Under these circumstances the Italian merchants rendered very great services which Edward was bound to reward in fitting manner. Thus on May 10 Edward gave his bond to Nicholas Bartholomei, merchant of Lucca, for 140,000 gold Florentine florins.[165] On the next day the Bardi and Peruzzi advanced respectively 6,000 and 4,000 florins.[166] On the 13th Nicholas Bartholomei loaned 8,600 small florins more, payable out of the income from the first wool to be shipped out of England; and on the 17th the society of the Busdrak of Lucca received a gift of 1,000 marks for signal services rendered in the royal interests and for possible losses incurred.[167] Gifts were also made to the Bardi and the Peruzzi on June 28, of 30,000*l.* each " in remembrance of their timely subsidies for the king's service and their losses, labours, and expenses endured for him "; [168] and as proof of his gratitude noble presents were given to individuals of these companies on the 30th.[169] On August 12 bonds were issued to the Bardi for 9,600 Florentine florins for which the royal jewels had to be pawned at Bruges, and to the Peruzzi for 9,400 florins.[170] The promises made to the burghers of Cologne on January 29 had been due since June 24, and not until August 12 could they be satisfied when the Bardi advanced another loan.[171] It can cause no won-

[159] *CPR* (1338–40), pp. 387, 388.   [166] *Ibid.,* p. 384.
[160] *Ibid.,* p. 392.   [163] *Ibid.,* p. 391.   [167] *Ibid.,* p. 385.
[161] *Ibid.,* p. 389.   [164] *Ibid.,* p. 392.   [168] *Ibid.,* p. 388.
[162] *Ibid.,* p. 386.   [165] *Ibid.,* p. 372.   [169] *Ibid.,* p. 392.
[170] *CPR* (1338–40), p. 391; *Foedera,* II (2), 1088.
[171] *CPR* (1338–40), p. 390; I. A. Nijhoff, *Gedenkwaardigheden uit de Geschiedenis van Gelderland,* I, 396–397.

der that the royal credit had sadly declined so that the king's military and diplomatic prestige, especially with the wary duke of Brabant, was slight.

Edward was grateful to Reginald, duke of Guelders, for his cooperation in contracting many of these loans and for the zeal shown in his cause, and on August 2 assigned him an annual pension of 1,000*l.* sterling.[172] He now owed him 52,750 Florentine florins for expenses incurred in his service, arrears due him for homage, and efforts to raise his quota of troops. On the next day he promised to pay this sum in two instalments at Nijmegen on June 24, 1340, and February 2, 1341. In case of failure Edward promised to send five knights who were to tarry at that place at his expense until the principal should be paid.[173]

Only slight progress was made in July and August. Duke John remained disinclined, and William, count of Hainault, Holland, and Zeeland, was equally reluctant to break with Philip, with whom he remained on good terms. Philip requested him on June 23 to prevent his subjects from harming the inhabitants of Vermandois and other places.[174] When William complained that Philip's officials had encroached upon his rights outside the limits of France, the king at once, on August 24, named commissioners to investigate.[175] This was of course no more effective than the numerous similar appointments made in the days of William's father, but the youthful count by his delicate position was constrained to remain neutral. Hence all of Edward's concessions were in vain; William would help him only against the bishop of Cambrai, which, as vassal of the empire, he was legally bound to do.[176] On August 13 Edward promised not to commit any hostile act while passing through his lands.[177] On the 20th he declared that all service rendered to him as vicar should never be construed as in any way increasing the imperial power over him;[178] and that his troops would not enter any fortification in

[172] J. Pontanus, *Historiae Gelricae Libri XIV*, p. 227.

[173] I. A. Nijhoff, *Gedenkwaardigheden uit de Geschiedenis van Gelderland*, I, 399–402.

[174] L. Devillers, *Cartulaire*, I, 81.   [175] *Ibid.*, pp. 85–86.

[176] L. P. van den Bergh, *Oorkondenboek van Holland en Zeeland* II, 245.

[177] *Foedera*, II (2), 1088–1089.

[178] *Ibid.*, p. 1089; J. Schwalm, "Reise nach Holland, Belgien, Nord

Hainault without the count's consent or that of his subjects, or commit any depredations, or take anything without payment.[179]

Thus was Edward baffled in his plans by the adroit policy of the duke of Brabant who was naturally very reluctant to surrender the great advantage which a neutral position gave him. This served Philip's interests most acceptably, for the troops which had on July 11 been ordered by the king at Conflans to be ready at Compiègne on the 22d were ordered to meet him on September 8.[180] There was an unconfirmed rumor that Edward and the emperor were in disagreement and that the plans for the recovery of imperial rights in the Low Countries were not to be carried out. To quiet this report Edward and the representatives of Lewis the Bavarian, John of Virneburg, provost of Xanten, John, dean of the church at Mainz, Henry de Zippelingen, commander of the Teutonic Knights at Ulm and Werde, and Dippold of Lipham, knight, made a declaration at Brussels on August 2 which unequivocally asserted the harmony between the king and the emperor.[181] The duke of Brabant could not evade fulfilling his obligations to Edward much longer because he did not want to risk losing the solid advantages which his friendship offered, so finally yielded to his pressing pleas.[182] Possibly John of Hainault, who had represented Edward's interests in the negotiations with Duke John for a matrimonial alliance, proved himself useful during these weeks.[183] Yet Edward had, in spite of a possible campaign against Philip, little reason to congratulate himself. After having been forced to lie idle in the Low Countries for a whole

---

Frankreich, und dem Niederrhein in Sommer, 1894," *Neues Archiv der Gesellschaft für Aeltere Deutsche Geschichtskunde,* XX (1895), 432–433.

[179] L. Devillers, *Cartulaire,* I, 87–88. On June 26 Edward promised to compensate the men of Dordrecht for damages inflicted by his own subjects. See *CPR* (1338–40), p. 388.

[180] Lescot (*Appendice*), pp. 220, 223.

[181] J. Schwalm, " Reiseberichte, 1894–1896, Mit Beilagen," *Neues Archiv der Gesellschaft für Aeltere Deutsche Geschichtskunde,* XXIII (1897), 358–359.

[182] According to le Bel, I, 151, there was a meeting in Mechelen on September 1. Although Edward was in Brussels at this time, the chronicler's statement of what was done there is apparently accurate as a general statement of the duke's change of policy.

[183] *Foedera,* II (2), 1083–1084. For his zeal in Edward's behalf, see the interesting testimony in the *Chronique Parisienne Anonyme,* pp. 177–178.

year, he could only enter upon a campaign late in September when a telling blow was rather improbable because of the advancing autumn.

IV. THE NEUTRALITY OF FLANDERS (SUMMER, 1338 — SUMMER, 1339)

NECESSITY had constrained King Philip to sanction van Artevelde's policy of neutrality in the war and economic *rapprochement* with England. In no other way could the Flemish crafts, and a large part of the patriciate with them, be kept from deserting to the English. But the memory of numerous acts of insubordination by the Flemish townsmen, especially during the reigns of his predecessors and at the opening of his own, made it impossible for Philip to view the Flemings with any but the gravest suspicions.

Under these circumstances the approval of Philip's loyal vassal, Count Louis, was dictated by pure expediency. The feudal elements of Ghent were, it appears, for the most part ever ready to resist by force of arms. Within the walls an important part of the patriciate which had intimate connections with the feudality maintained a sullen resistance which might at any moment imperil the success of the new policy. Public temper was embittered, suspicion was rife, and there was much recrimination. An instance of this is the death of Volker uten Rosen who was slain in an altercation with van Artevelde on August 2 after the latter had returned from the expedition to pacify the castleries in West Flanders. This person, one of the count's entourage, was struck down before Louis' eyes. Rumor had it that a large number of armed men had been collected in the count's castle. Suspicious of some plot, van Artevelde appeared before its walls and effected a breach, but upon entering found only a small number of unarmed men within.[184]

---

[184] For the burial of Volker, which fixes the date, see N. de Pauw, *Cartulaire Historique et Généalogique des Artevelde,* p. 682; N. de Pauw en J. Vuylsteke, *Rekeningen der Stad Gent,* III, 410. For the repair of damage to the castle wall which may have been caused by this event, see *ibid.,* II, 72, 90.

In the face of this opposition, van Artevelde and the scabini were constrained to draw closer to the crafts. They had from the beginning acted in accordance with the needs of the town as a whole, and when the official year came to an end on August 15 the personnel of the thirteen scabini underwent a decided change. The new scabini were all supporters of van Artevelde's policy. Among them appeared William van Artevelde, the captain's brother, and the brewer, Henry Goethals. Others were John van Steenbeke, Jacob vander Hoyen, Gerard de Neut, and John Spelliard, who now became premier scabinus of the college and who had shown a keen interest in the plight of the crafts prior to the events in front of the Bijloke on December 28.[185]

The thirteen councillors, also called scabini (*van den ghedeele* or *des parchons*), were of the same spirit. Most of their names appear in the communal accounts before August of this year, but particularly often is mention made of William de Merseman, Segher uten Dale, John Minneman, Simon de Necker, and William Molenyser.[186] The office of the burgomasters was filled by the captains themselves, van Artevelde and Gelnoot van Lens; that of receiver of imposts by Peter vanden Hovene; and that of receivers of the duty by William van Vaernewijc and William van Huse.[187] As dean of the fullers appears John van Dessele; of the weavers, John vander Vloet, who had succeeded Jacob van Wackinne before the end of the official year;[188] and of the lesser guilds, William Yoons.[189]

The relations of Ghent, Bruges, and Ypres with the other towns of Flanders are difficult to describe in detail as almost all the documents of the innumerable transactions have been lost. The only sources left for the investigator are the meager statements of the chronicles, the laconic entries in the communal accounts of Ghent and Bruges, and a few very precious documents which concern the events in Courtrai. It appears that after the oath to support the treaties with Philip and Edward had been exacted, men were appointed in the towns to associate with the

---

[185] N. de Pauw en J. Vuylsteke, *Rekeningen der Stad Gent,* I, 176.
[186] For their names, see *ibid.,* p. 253.
[187] *Ibid.,* pp. 253–254.
[188] *Ibid.,* p. 158.
[189] *Ibid.,* pp. 275–276.

officials of these corporations. Thus John van Abbinsvoorde, a scion of an old patrician family in Ghent, and Gerard Toen, of an old family in Courtrai who had served as *scultetus* of the count at Bruges in 1320, had been sent to Courtrai to act as captains and to direct the general policy of the town in accordance with the treaties.[190] To guarantee the proper execution of the promises, hostages were often required. Peter vander Asselt was sent by Ghent on August 30 to choose them from among the populace of Hulst and Axel. Two days later the scabinus, Henry Barledonc, and the captain, William van Huse, were dispatched to Assenede where the men of the Quatuor Officia had promised to deliver their hostages. On September 6 John uten Hove and Jacob uter Moerstraten went to Hulst and Axel to conduct the selected persons to Ghent.[191] Hostages were also taken from Courtrai and lodged at Ghent.[192]

The captains exercised extensive powers in the various towns and were in constant communication with the scabini and captains in Ghent. Thus one Langhe Willekine, who had been banished from Courtrai, was seized by Gerard Toen at Ypres and entrusted at the command of the authorities of Ghent to those of Menin to be brought to Courtrai. Toen and van Abbinsvoorde were speedily entangled in the treacherous relations of the guilds. They promised to prevent an increase of more than fifteen pence (*deniers*) in the wages of the fullers, a matter over which the scabini of Ghent assumed control. They also made new regulations for the drapers which proved quite oppressive, so that the prosperity of the guild was threatened. As captains they went on numerous missions in the interests of the town and were regularly reimbursed by the communal treasury. By June 12, 1339, van Abbinsvoorde had gone on fifty-one such expeditions. In fact, all questions of importance were referred to Ghent, Bruges, and Ypres before action could be taken in Courtrai.[193]

This control of the lesser towns of Flanders by Ghent was made effective by the despatch of deputies whenever necessary. The

[190] N. de Pauw, " L'Enquête sur les Capitaines de Courtrai sous Artevelde," *BCRH*, 79 (1910), pp. 243–246.

[191] N. de Pauw en J. Vuylsteke, *Rekeningen der Stad Gent*, I, 285–286.

[192] N. de Pauw, " L'Enquête sur les Capitaines de Courtrai sous Artevelde," *BCRH*, 79 (1910), 243–246.

[193] *Ibid.*, pp. 259, 260–261, 263–264.

decidedly popular changes in the college of the scabini of Ghent in August had its echoes in other towns. The crafts at Bruges and Ypres were more outspoken in their demands, and dissensions arose. Deputies from the three towns met at Ypres between August 21 and 26 to discuss means of preserving the peace, and on the 30th the deans of the fullers, weavers, and lesser guilds, and the captain, Gelnoot van Lens, were sent to Ypres for the same purpose by the scabini of Ghent.[194]

These facts are sufficient to reveal the character of van Artevelde's regime. The demand for an understanding with England had placed Ghent in the ascendancy, and, with the support of Bruges and Ypres, van Artevelde dominated the entire county. The Valois historiographical tradition states that the Flemings regarded him as a god who alone could save them, and that he appointed scabini and councillors to execute judgment at his bidding.[195] The contemporary John le Bel believed that no duke, count, or prince had ever in any country exercised such unlimited authority.[196]

It was not long, however, before van Artevelde's policy began to meet with some active resistance. Before his appointment as captain in Courtrai, Gerard Toen had shown himself a rash and violent man,[197] and with van Abbinsvoorde was soon accused of extortion. While their expenses were paid by the communal treasury of Ghent it appears that special gratuities were necessary to defray all their expenditures. Toen was excessively efficient in securing such gifts by questionable methods which were subsequently repudiated at the conclusion of an inquest.[198] Connected apparently with their activities was the disturbance which appears to have occurred on September 25 or 26. At the request of the provost, scabini, and councillors of Courtrai, Count Louis consented on the 25th to repeal the sentence of banishment against thirty-four burghers who had been guilty of treasonable actions at the time of the battle of Cassel.[199] Among these was William

[194] N. de Pauw en J. Vuylsteke, *Rekeningen der Stad Gent*, I, 284, 285–286.   [195] *Chronographia*, II, 54.   [196] Le Bel, I, 130.

[197] N. de Pauw, " L'Enquête sur les Capitaines de Courtrai sous Artevelde," *BCRH*, 79 (1910), 245.

[198] See the complaint by the burghers, *ibid.*, pp. 256–274.

[199] *Ibid.*, p. 283; C. Mussely, *Inventaire des Archives de la Ville de Courtrai (1190–1792)*, p. 117.

de Pape who returned at once with five others from the Frank of Bruges and was slain in an obscure quarrel which apparently arose among the crafts. Suspicion settled upon Oste 'tKint and his brother John. The scabini of Ghent took prompt notice of these events and at once, on September 27, dispatched three of their colleagues, Peter vanden Hovene, the captain, and another person to investigate the murder. These men were back in Ghent on October 1 and two days later Simon Parijs and two others went to interview Count Louis, who spent most of the autumn and early winter in his castle in Courtrai.[200] On the 4th he authorized the scabini and councillors of Ghent to institute an inquest to determine the guilt of the suspected brothers without prejudice to the privileges of either Courtrai or Ghent.[201]

The feudal seigniors in West Flanders would not willingly accept the ascendancy of Ghent and van Artevelde. On August 20 deputies had been sent into many of the rural parishes west of Ypres to cause the people to accept on oath the treaties with England and France. But there was much restlessness in most of the castleries and on September 21 William van Vaernewijc and Henry de Keyser were dispatched to establish peace and order among the dissatisfied elements. The former was engaged in this work until October 6.[202] There was apparently some difficulty at Oudenaarde whither Gelnoot van Lens and William Yoons were sent on September 29.[203] At Bruges and Ypres also the weavers were greatly agitated, and the Frank of Bruges, which was much more agricultural and seigniorial, was dissatisfied.[204]

Strenuous efforts were deemed necessary to maintain order, and plans were made for another demonstration of force. The scabini of Ghent sent John uten Hove on September 29 to Waasland, the Quatuor Officia, Alost, Grammont, Oudenaarde, Bruges, and Ypres to cause the contingents to be mustered for the expedition.[205] On October 1 a powerful force left Ghent " to preserve peace, order, and the law, to punish the offenders for the honor and profit of our lord of Flanders and the common land." It was composed of eleven of the scabini and councillors, five captains,

[200] N. de Pauw en J. Vuylsteke, *Rekeningen der Stad Gent*, I, 288–289.
[201] N. de Pauw, " L'Enquête sur les Capitaines de Courtrai sous Artevelde," *BCRH*, 79 (1910), 284–285.
[202] N. de Pauw en J. Vuylsteke, *Rekeningen der Stad Gent*, I, 284, 288.
[203] *Ibid.*, pp. 288–289.   [204] *Ibid.*, pp. 295–296.   [205] *Ibid.*, p. 313.

the three deans of the guilds, and seventy-five horses for themselves and servants. Behind them were a hundred white-hoods with ten captains, ninety bowmen with ten captains, fifty-five shieldbearers, a hundred men-at-arms, carpenters to keep the siege machines in order, tents, ships for transportation, and all manner of equipment with the necessary attendants.[206] They proceeded to Courtrai and thence to Ypres and returned to Ghent on the 11th. On the following day a hundred men-at-arms with some of the scabini and captains,[207] accompanied by a number of the count's men and deputies of Bruges and Ypres, rode westward. Toward the close of the month they were at Bruges, whither on the 27th the corporation of Ghent sent the deans of the guilds and two of the scabini, and on the 31st William van Vaernewijc, in order to pacify the guilds of Bruges.[208] The soldiery returned home by November 15, but John van Steenbeke, Gelnoot van Lens, and Henry de Keyser had been detailed to proceed with fifteen men into the Frank, the Quatuor Officia, where they were on the 16th,[209] Oudenaarde, and Alost.[210] In this way order was established and inquests were instituted in the Quatuor Officia, at Ypres, and at Bruges to search for those guilty of causing disturbances. Meanwhile, there was also progress in the investigations in Courtrai.[211] Deputies were sent out from time to time to supervise these activities. Thus on November 18 the scabinus, Lievin van Veurne, went to Bruges, and his colleague, Thierry Hueseldonc, to Ypres. On the 27th Jacob vander Hoyen went into the Quatuor Officia, and on the 24th Hueseldonc and William van Huse went to Courtrai and Ypres.[212]

While van Artevelde was thus silencing all opposition and enforcing his régime of neutrality, an attempt was made to secure reparations from the English for all losses inflicted upon the Flemish merchants during the previous years. The matter, it appears, was the subject of discussion in a meeting of the deputies of the three towns at Bruges from August 25 to 29.[213] On Sep-

[206] N. de Pauw en J. Vuylsteke, *Rekeningen der Stad Gent*, I, pp. 246–249.

[207] *Ibid.*, p. 290.

[208] *Ibid.*, pp. 291, 295.

[209] *Ibid.*, p. 293.

[210] *Ibid.*, pp. 349–350.

[211] *Ibid.*, pp. 293–295, 297.

[212] *Ibid.*, pp. 293–295.

[213] *Ibid.*, p. 285: " Item scep. Jan van Steenbeke, Segre uten Dale, ende met hen Will. van Huse, ende der Willem de Bomere, scepenen clerc, die

tember 9 the scabinus, Lievin van Veurne, and two others were sent to Brabant to confer with Reginald, count of Guelders, and conclude the negotiations which had been in progress for some time, possibly ever since the early spring. This matter was further discussed in the presence of Edward himself at Mechelen, whither deputies from the three towns had gone on the 16th. Discussion dragged on until at least the 26th.[214] Edward had no choice but to entertain their proposals favorably and hoped that the Flemings would sooner or later join him. He had already shown favor to several burghers of Ghent. On August 17 he granted John de la Mote twenty pounds annually at the Exchequer, and in the following month special protection to trade in his realm was given to Gerelin Sirenolker, James de Sabloun, and James de Zeistes.[215]

There were further discussions at Rupelmonde with Reginald, count of Guelders, from September 28 to October 3, and on the 4th, when the deputies had returned, the scabinus John Minneman and two others were sent to Antwerp to carry on the discussions with Edward until the 16th. From the 18th to the 23d John de Coster, who had been associated with Minneman, was in conference with Reginald at Antwerp.[216] By this time it appears that a substantial agreement had been reached.

During these negotiations Edward had given sure indication of his purpose to secure the support of Flanders and also of Count Louis, if possible. As imperial vicar he could command every feudatory of the empire. In obedience to the summons to all such vassals to appear at Mechelen, a delegation was sent by the three towns in behalf of the count. The discussion lasted from October 26 to November 2.[217] The deputies declared that Louis was ready to discharge his obligations and Edward requested him to present himself to do homage.[218] Discussion was put off until the close of November, when the matter was again postponed.[219]

---

voeren (August 25) . . . te Brucghe ten parlemente voer minen heere van Vlaendren metten ghemenen lande omme sorloghen wille dat es van den Ingelscen. . . ."

[214] *Ibid.*, pp. 286–287.   [215] *CPR* (1338–40), pp. 189, 192.
[216] N. de Pauw en J. Vuylsteke, *Rekeningen der Stad Gent*, I, 288–290.
[217] *Ibid.*, p. 290.
[218] Kervyn, *Oeuvres de Froissart*, II, 549.
[219] N. de Pauw en J. Vuylsteke, *Rekeningen der Stad Gent*, I, 292.

On the 10th and 12th Edward invested Count Reginald with full powers to treat with Count Louis and the towns of Flanders. In virtue of his capacity as vicar of the empire, he instructed him to treat on behalf of the emperor for support in the war to recover his rights on the border. At the same time, probably because Edward thought that the friendship of the Flemings meant a readiness on the part of Count Louis to desert his suzerain, Reginald was ordered to broach once more a matrimonial connection between the count's eldest son and one of his daughters.[220] And on November 21 Edward ordered by letters patent William Daubery, John de Sturmy, and Gaman Corder to proceed to Flanders and investigate all claims against his subjects for damages inflicted upon Flemish merchants and to render satisfaction.[221]

With these events Count Louis can have had no sympathy whatever. The ascendancy of Ghent under the leadership of van Artevelde in the affairs of Flanders had reduced his own authority to utter impotence. At the grand annual procession in honor of Our Lady of Tournai on September 15 he appeared among the scabini and captains from Ghent, dressed in the usual manner of the Ghent delegation, and marched in the procession with them.[222] In numerous matters of state he was constrained to accept the authority of the three towns led by Ghent and van Artevelde. His troops accompanied theirs to West Flanders; he was constrained to reply to Edward's command to appear as vassal of the empire at Mechelen, and, as in the case of Courtrai on October 4, to approve the suggestion of the scabini and councillors of Ghent that an inquest be instituted in the western castleries of Flanders.

Nor could these negotiations with Edward please Count Louis' suzerain, Philip. Representatives of the three towns and of Count Louis were in conference with him at Amiens between August 18 and September 2 when problems of general policy appear to have been discussed. These negotiations were resumed from the 5th to the 7th. Royal deputies met those of the three

---

[220] I. A. Nijhoff, *Gedenkwaardigheden uit de Geschiedenis van Gelderland,* I, 392–394.

[221] *CPR* (1338–40), p. 194.

[222] N. de Pauw en J. Vuylsteke, *Rekeningen der Stad Gent,* I, 271–273; le Muisit, p. 116.

towns at Courtrai from September 21 to 25 and again on the 27th.[223] The general policies of Flanders including the negotiations with the English both in regard to reparations and economic matters were undoubtedly discussed on these occasions. Evidence of their desire to maintain a neutral attitude may be seen in the demand of the three towns that Guy, brother of Count Louis, who had been taken prisoner in the attack upon Cadzand, should be restored. On October 8 William van Vaernewijc had been sent to Guy, for it appears that he was in Edward's company at this time, quite probably for diplomatic reasons. A definite request for his release was made to Reginald, count of Guelders, by William van Huse between November 26 and 29.[224] Evil rumors could hardly be avoided in this atmosphere surcharged with suspicion, especially after the summons by Edward in his capacity as imperial vicar to his vassals in the empire west of Cologne, and it was necessary to send John uten Hove to Paris from November 3 to 20. Powerless to resist and fearful of a desertion to the side of Edward, the king accepted his representations.[225]

Reginald, count of Guelders, was at Dendermonde immediately after these negotiations were entrusted to him and on November 15 the scabini of Ghent dispatched two of their colleagues, Baldwin ute Meram and John Rugginstul, and the captain, William van Huse, to conduct him to Ghent. There were further active negotiations at Dendermonde, for another deputation of similar character was again sent on the 21st. On the 26th William van Huse was sent to request once more the surrender of Guy of Flanders. The character of these discussions is not wholly certain. They undoubtedly concerned the general policy of the county, but it may perhaps also be taken for granted that Count Reginald suggested an intimate alliance to Louis. From the 26th to the 29th deputies of the three towns met at Courtrai at the count's command, and this matter may very well have been discussed on this occasion and again at Courtrai and Messines from December 5 to 12. On the following day two scabini were sent by Ghent

[223] N. de Pauw en J. Vuylsteke, *Rekeningen der Stad Gent,* I, 284, 286, 288.

[224] *Ibid.,* pp. 289, 294.

[225] *Ibid.,* p. 292.

to discuss the interests of the town with Count Reginald at Dendermonde.[226]

Van Artevelde's policy had won for Flanders substantial advantages. The industries of the towns had been preserved and Edward had agreed to reimburse the merchants for losses on the seas. It was now resolved to secure from Philip a surrender of the remaining obligations and payments due under the old Treaty of Athis-sur-Orge (1305) and subsequent agreements. On November 7 a delegation was sent by the three towns to Arras to discuss the payments due on account of Douai and Lille.[227] The remission of these debts involved the interests of Count Louis and required his sanction. Frightened by Edward's suggestions, he approved on the 17th the action of Bruges in recalling a number of individuals who had been banished from Flanders,[228] and men were authorized to go to Dendermonde under safe-conduct in order to investigate Louis' accounts which apparently were kept at that place.[229] There were further discussions at Messines with the king's men from December 5 to 12 and from the 19th to the 24th of the same month. On the 27th the scabini of Ghent sent their colleague, Baldwin ute Meram, accompanied by envoys from Bruges and Ypres, to seek the royal favor for the policy of neutrality and cancellation of all the odious obligations.[230]

Confronted with an invasion by Edward, who was bending every effort in Brabant to unite all the military resources of the Low Countries under his command, and realizing the supreme importance of Flemish neutrality at this juncture, Philip swallowed his wrath and made a virtue of necessity. In accordance with the request of Count Louis, he cancelled all sums demanded by the treaties save such as were due the count himself, surrendered the right to demand a force of six hundred men-at-arms in case

[226] N. de Pauw en J. Vuylsteke, *Rekeningen der Stad Gent,* I, 293–295. [227] *Ibid.,* p. 292.

[228] L. Gilliodts van Severen, *Inventaire des Archives de la Ville de Bruges,* I, 487–488.

[229] N. de Pauw en J. Vuylsteke, *Rekeningen der Stad Gent,* I, 296. Cf. *Chronographia,* II, 51–52.

[230] L. Gilliodts van Severen, *Inventaire des Archives de la Ville de Bruges,* I, 487–488; I. L. A. Diegerick, *Inventaire des Chartes et Documents appartenant aux Archives de la Ville d'Ypres,* I, 306. Cf. H. Pirenne, *Histoire de Belgique,* I (2d ed.), 117.

of war, and promised in addition to forgive all misdeeds of which the magistrates of the three towns may have been guilty. The language of this document reveals the royal displeasure with amazing frankness and unprecedented language. The king spoke of the Flemings as " rude, simple, and ignorant folk " who were to be led back to the path of duty by mildness, which was really a euphemistic equivalent to calling them " rebels "; he was at great pains to insist upon his princely " liberality " and dwelt with emphasis upon his numerous " great favors and benefits such as had never been granted by any of his ancestors "; he declared that he did not intend to " enrich himself by sacrificing their wealth but desired only to retain their friendship and loyal bearing." No words could better indicate the prestige of van Artevelde and the uneasiness with which the situation was viewed in France. Meanwhile the Flemings were permitted to carry wine from La Rochelle and St. Jean d'Angely to Flanders according to an order of January 6 which was also issued at the request of Count Louis.[231] Philip's complete surrender of all rights under the treaties of Athis-sur-Orge and Arques and Edward's eagerness to indemnify the Flemish merchants thus marked a new high point of success in van Artevelde's policy.

But as the negotiations with Reginald, count of Guelders, continued and the inquest in the castlery of Ypres progressed,[232] members of the seignioral class began to show more resistance. The count's castle at Oudenaarde was taken over by the scabini on December 22 when they posted two men to guard it " for the lord, the country, and for the town of Ghent." [233] On the 30th the scabini dispatched Gelnoot van Lens with a force of fifty whitehoods and fifteen bowmen to station themselves at Schendelbeke and secure the castle of the seignior of Liedekerke, which was accomplished by February 9.[234] Many of the opponents of the policy of the three towns sought safety in flight while others were banished. Most of these congregated in West Flanders and especially at St. Omer in Artois and were supported by members of

---

[231] I. L. A. Diegerick, *Inventaire des Chartes et Documents appartenant aux Archives de la Ville d'Ypres,* II, 104–105.

[232] N. de Pauw en J. Vuylsteke, *Rekeningen der Stad Gent,* I, 290, 293.

[233] *Ibid.,* p. 343.

[234] *Ibid.,* pp. 351–353.

the feudality. Half of the property of these refugees was said to
have been confiscated by the towns and the rest reserved for the
support of their families.[235] In their extreme bitterness they were
ready to show resistance to the authority of the three towns.[236]
Acts of violence were common, which were, it appears, supported
by the bailiffs of Vermandois, Amiens, and Lille, and their provosts
in such towns and castleries as Veurne, Nieuwpoort, Bergen, Dunkirk, Bourbourg, Cassel, Gravelines, Bailleul, Poperingen, and
Warneton, greatly to the injury of the justice of the count of
Flanders and his vassals, among whom was the lady of Cassel.
Complaints were formulated by Louis at the suggestion of the
three towns, and King Philip, at the moment when he was at the
Bois de Vincennes, released the Flemings from all obligations and
ordered his bailiffs and their officials to cease their judicial activities in these parts except in a limited number of cases which
were to be adjudicated by four sergeants especially deputed for
the task.[237]

A determined effort was made to break this irksome régime of
the three towns, and toward the close of January the enemy began to plan the seizure of Bergen. In this they were successful
after a slight struggle in the market place. They expelled the
officers appointed by the three towns. They next seized Veurne
and Dixmuide. Then they requested Count Louis, who was at
Courtrai, to come to them, as it seemed that all West Flanders
was now in the hands of his friends. But the enthusiasm with
which they received him was soon dampened by the efforts of
the burghers of Dixmuide who plotted against him with the scabini of Bruges. A force was at once sent from Bruges and reached
the hamlet of Beest near Dixmuide without the slightest warning.
When the alarm was raised Louis ordered his partisans to arm
and withdraw, but the gate was already closed and the guards
of the town were ready to offer resistance. Finally they forced
their way out just as the militia from Bruges was pouring through
another gate in eager pursuit. Some of the count's men were

---

[235] Le Bel, I, 170.

[236] N. de Pauw en J. Vuylsteke, *Rekeningen der Stad Gent*, I, 357:
" . . . fugitive die altoes uploep doen wilden. . . ."

[237] I. L. A. Diegerick, *Inventaire des Chartes et Documents appartenant
aux Archives de la Ville d'Ypres*, II, 105–106; E. vanden Bussche, *Inventaire
des Archives de l'État à Bruges, Ire Section, Franc de Bruges*, I, 65.

seized and summarily executed, while the nobles were held for
ransom. Louis fled but scantily clothed, leaving his seal behind
him, and did not stop until he reached St. Omer with only a small
band at his back.[238] He at once issued a statement declaring all
recent acts, which he asserted had been made under duress, null
and void.[239]

Van Artevelde and his colleagues and the scabini, supported
by those of Bruges and Ypres, took up the challenge. On February 13 the scabini, John van Steenbeke and Henry Huenich,
with the captains, William van Vaernewijc and Gelnoot van Lens,
marched from Ghent toward Dixmuide with a formidable force
of fifty bowmen and eleven hundred sergeants (*serianten*) chosen
from the guilds. There had been some disorder at Courtrai,
caused, perhaps, by members of the count's entourage, and the
scabinus, Gerard de Neut, and Peter vanden Hovene were ordered to garrison the town with fifty white-hoods, fifty bowmen,
and a hundred sergeants. On the 17th a delegation composed of
twelve of the scabini and the four captains, van Artevelde, van
Vaernewijc, van Huse, and Peter vanden Hovene, who had returned from his mission to Courtrai, with John vander Vloet and
Martin de Crane as representatives of the weavers, John van Dessele and Josse Apre of the fullers, and Simon Thomaes of the lesser
guilds, was sent to the scene of the uprising. These returned to
Ghent on the 27th and the archers, who had accompanied them, on
the 28th. At Ypres it was decided to destroy once for all the partisans of the count. On the 23d John van Steenbeke and Gelnoot
van Lens were instructed to proceed to Bergen with twenty-six
white-hoods, twenty bowmen, and ninety-two sergeants. With
them were contingents from Bruges and Ypres. Van Steenbeke
was back in Ghent on April 13. These expeditions cost the town
in all 18,091*l*. 14*s*.[240]

The problems confronting the scabini of the three towns were
thus greatly aggravated during the winter months of 1338–1339.
The inquests at Bruges had come to an end by January 20;[241] at

---

[238] *Chronographia*, II, 57–58; *Grandes Chroniques*, V, 375; *Istore et
Croniques*, I, 368–369.

[239] G. Espinas et H. Pirenne, *Recueil des Documents relatifs à l'Histoire et l'Industrie Drapière en Flandre*, III, 214.

[240] N. de Pauw en J. Vuylsteke, *Rekeningen der Stad Gent*, I, 353–359.

[241] *Ibid.*, pp. 293, 295, 297.

Ypres efforts had to be made to quiet the weavers as at Bruges; [242] in the Quatuor Officia progress was made in the inquest; Biervliet was finally ordered to raze its walls which was done between March 14 and 19 under supervision of the captain, Peter vanden Hovene; [243] and at Courtrai efforts to determine the guilty parties in the uproar of September were in full progress.[244]

But new troubles had risen at Dendermonde in November, and on January 13 a deputation had to be sent thither by Ghent to induce the burghers to coöperate with the three towns. There were fresh difficulties at Alost, so that John van Steenbeke, Gelnoot van Lens, and William Molenyser were sent on the 27th to induce the people to obey. A demonstration of force was necessary in the case of Alost whither Simon Godenvalen was sent on February 10 with twenty-four white-hoods. Two days before this the burghers of Dendermonde had taken the oath.[245] In February John vanden Hoyen was stationed at Oudenaarde for a fortnight to preserve the peace.[246] Deputies of the three towns met at Bruges in the first week of February, exactly at the moment of Count Louis' futile effort at Dixmuide.[247] The same policy was maintained after the danger was averted and a series of inquests was at once instituted on a great scale in the castleries of West Flanders which did not come to an end until May. In June confiscation of all the lands of the lady of Cassel was ordered.[248]

Edward and his advisers carefully watched these events and zealously sought to extend the king's influence. Orders to officials in England to permit Flemings to carry on their own affairs in his realm had been violated and on February 20 the king was constrained to demand the greatest kindness of his subjects toward them.[249] To Simon van Halen, who had visited him at Mechelen in company with the delegates from Count Louis and the three towns at the close of October,[250] and who had married a nat-

[242] N. de Pauw en J. Vuylsteke, *Rekeningen der Stad Gent,* I, pp. 295, 298.

[243] *Ibid.,* pp. 294–295, 300.

[244] *Ibid.,* p. 295.

[245] *Ibid.,* pp. 293–294, 297–298, 358.   [248] *Ibid.,* pp. 299–300, 305.

[246] *Ibid.,* p. 299.   [249] *Foedera,* II (2), 1073.

[247] *Ibid.,* p. 298.

[250] N. de Pauw en J. Vuylsteke, *Rekeningen der Stad Gent,* I, p. 290.

ural sister of the count, he assigned on January 14 a life annuity of 200*l.*[251]

In February Henry of Flanders performed homage and promised to aid the king with men-at-arms for a consideration of 1,000 Florentine florins yearly for life. Furthermore, Edward promised to defend him against Philip and pay him 500*l.* Parisian in compensation for income from lands confiscated in France, another 500*l.* for incomes from other sources, and, until such sources should be restored, 1,000*l.* Parisian annually out of the customs receipts of London. Two days later on the 28th, he was promised 3,000 Florentine florins for arrears due from lands in France. These and the 15,000 florins to be paid for furnishing himself and his troops were to be paid in two instalments, 10,000 at once and 8,000 on June 24.[252] John van Coukelaere of Bruges was assigned 300 Florentine florins yearly for life, and James de Bets, bailiff of Poperingen, 20*l.* also at the Exchequer.[253]

There were meetings of the delegates from Flanders and the king at Antwerp from March 5 to 14 and from March 21 to 23. These discussions undoubtedly dealt with economic matters, for at this moment William de la Pole was stationed at Bruges to supervise the distribution of wool where he was constantly interviewed by van Artevelde, William van Vaernewijc, and others from Ghent. At Dendermonde deputies from the towns of Brabant met those of Flanders, also to discuss economic matters from April 18 to 24 and May 10 to 13.[254]

But these negotiations failed to bring Edward much nearer to an alliance with the Flemings or even to secure their coöperation. The emperor, undoubtedly at the suggestion of his vicar Edward, at this juncture stepped in to exercise his *imperium;* on March 13 he ordered the towns to hearken to Edward as imperial vicar.[255] He charged Louis, count of Flanders, to coöperate in the reconquest of Béthune, Lille, and Douai, and appear before Edward to perform homage for his imperial fiefs, urged the people of Flan-

[251] *CPR* (1338–40), p. 196.

[252] *Ibid.,* p. 370.

[253] *Ibid.,* p. 371.

[254] N. de Pauw en J. Vuylsteke, *Rekeningen der Stad Gent,* I, 299–303.

[255] Kervyn, *Oeuvres de Froissart,* II, 551–552; I. A. L. Diegerick, *Inventaire des Chartes et Documents appartenant aux Archives de la Ville d'Ypres,* II, 107.

ders to counsel him to do so, and sought to strengthen Edward's rights by refuting Philip's claims. Should these commands be received loyally, Reginald, count of Guelders, would promise the following points in behalf of Edward: to coin money at all times of the same excellence as that of St. Louis, should God give him the crown of France; to revive all lawful customs and good usages of previous times; to establish the staple of wool in the county; to aid in recovering the castleries of Béthune, Lille, and Douai; to revoke forever all pains, penalties, and sentences illegally imposed by previous kings; to check all brigandage in the county; and to enter into no treaty in the future without the consent of the count and county of Flanders and to grant all such liberties as might be in the royal power to bestow.[256]

This document is highly instructive. Edward was not satisfied with the neutrality of Flanders in his struggle with Philip. As king of France he sought to gain the support of Count Louis by returning to him and his heirs the lands taken from Count Guy by the Treaty of Athis-sur-Orge and later agreements. This would have been an irresistible inducement to many a prince. But so firmly was Louis devoted to his suzerain that he refused to entertain these proposals for a moment. Never would he be disloyal to King Philip. Toward the close of January he had listened to the suggestions of his advisers who were eager to overturn the régime of the three towns. His participation in the uprising of the feudatories in the castleries of West Flanders had made it clear that this hope of the emperor and Edward could never be realized.

In spite of Louis' and Philip's disapproval of their policies and the desire of Edward for an alliance with them, the Flemings persisted for a while in steering a middle course between the two fighting powers. From April 2 to 5 deputies from the three towns met with Philip's men at Messines.[257] The fact that their count was with Philip at this time made a resumption of friendship more difficult.[258] But the absence of the legitimate prince was a grievous obstacle to public peace, and persistent efforts were made to induce him to return. The cantor of St. John's church

[256] Kervyn, *Oeuvres de Froissart,* II, 549–551.
[257] N. de Pauw en J. Vuylsteke, *Rekeningen der Stad Gent,* I, 301.
[258] *Chronographia,* II, 58; *Chronicon Comitum Flandrensium,* p. 211.

in Ghent and deputies from Bruges and Ypres were dispatched on April 19 to beg Louis to come back. Upon their return the cantor was again sent on the 29th. He was back in Flanders on May 5, and on the 9th John vander Vloet, dean of the weavers, the cantor of Lille, and deputies from Bruges and Ypres again went to Louis "to beseech him to return to his country and institute order and peace." [259]

Philip's suspicions were quite patent. Movements of French troops on the borders of West Flanders at this moment produced a delicate situation, for the parties displeased with the policy of the three towns might unite with them and rise at any time. On April 24 Thomas van Vaernewijc, Simon Parijs, and Henry de Keyser were dispatched by Ghent to provide for the defense of that region.[260] But Louis, influenced by Philip's wrath toward the Flemings, did not trust himself in Flanders and convoked deputies to Armentières where efforts were made between June 13 and 18 to arrange a peace. Evil reports at the court were more common than ever and on the 13th a delegation was sent to Paris to dispel if possible the illusion from the royal mind. Philip could do nothing but accept their explanations as he could not afford to drive them into the enemy's camp on the eve of a dangerous invasion.[261]

During the spring and summer the internal situation in Flanders appeared more and more trying. The utmost diligence had to be exercised in arbitrating the differences of the crafts and in restraining the upper bourgeoisie. At Oudenaarde dissensions arose among the crafts, and on April 12 and again on May 9 a delegation headed by William van Huse proceeded thither to make peace.[262] Disputes between Bruges, the Frank, and Sluis developed in May, and Gelnoot van Lens was sent with William van Vaernewijc and two scabini on the 14th, 26th, and 31st to quiet the malcontents.[263] A demonstration of force was necessary in July when the captains and deans of the guilds of Ghent went out with some white-hoods, a hundred and forty-six bowmen, and eighty-seven shield-bearers.[264] Bruges also had dis-

[259] N. de Pauw en J. Vuylsteke, *Rekeningen der Stad Gent*, I, 302–304.
[260] *Ibid.*, p. 303.
[261] *Ibid.*, p. 306.
[262] *Ibid.*, pp. 301–302, 304.
[263] *Ibid.*, pp. 304–305.
[264] *Ibid.*, p. 359.

putes with Eecloo, and efforts were made by John van Steenbeke, Henry Huenich, and the deans, John van Dessele and John vander Vloet, to bring about an accord.[265]   At Axel there was some factional strife which was pacified in June by a delegation from Ghent,[266] and at Houthem there were incipient hostile movements which the magistrates sought to prevent by sending thither Gelnoot van Lens and Lievin van Veurne.[267]   In July there was a violent quarrel between Ypres and Poperingen about privileges concerning the weavers.[268]   This was to remain a serious problem for a long time.   Eecloo still opposed Bruges and on August 1 John van Steenbeke, the scabinus, Henry Huenich, and the deans were sent thither to arrange peace.[269]

At this time the inquests which had been started by William Daubery, John de Sturmy, and Gaman Corder by the royal mandate of November 21 [270] were coming to an end.   The personnel of the group had changed somewhat, for on June 8 when at Diest Edward appointed William de Sturmy and his brother John to take the places of Henry de Ferrariis and Reginald de Donington.[271]   The negotiations were conducted at Ghent on July 20 and their recommendations were embodied in a number of bonds granted by the king.   These covered the amount of the damages inflicted upon Flemish merchants and were delivered as follows: 895*l.* 7*s.* 8*d.* large Tournois, payable on All Saints' Day and on Whitsunday for the claims of the men of Bruges, Aardenburg, Sluis, Ostende, Blankenberg, Monkereede, St. Cateline, Knocke, Wenduine, Heist, and Hugovliet, to John Broad and Jakemin FitzDean, burgesses of Sluis; 42*l.* 7*s.* 9*d.* large Tournois for the claims of various parties at Ypres, Nieuwpoort, Bergen, Poperingen, Dunkirk, Gravelines, and Lombardzijde to Daniel le Stir, Jacques Godaerd, and Jacques Serviour of Dunkirk; 104*l.* 10*s.* 6*d.* large Tournois for the claims at Ghent, Assenede, and Axel to William van Vaernewijc of Ghent.[272]

In May Spanish merchants were illtreated by English mariners and driven from the Zwin with great losses to themselves as well as to the Flemings.   On June 5 the scabini of Ghent dispatched

[265] N. de Pauw en J. Vuylsteke, *Rekeningen der Stad Gent,* I, 308–309.
[266] *Ibid.,* p. 305.
[267] *Ibid.,* p. 307.
[268] *Ibid.,* pp. 308–309.
[269] *Ibid.,* p. 309.
[270] *CPR* (1338–40), p. 194.
[271] *Ibid.,* p. 387.
[272] *Ibid.,* p. 372.

their colleague, Lievin van Veurne, to Diest to secure redress.[273] Edward responded with alacrity. He ordered John and William de Sturmy, John de Molyns, William de la Pole, who was well acquainted with the situation in Flanders, Nicholas de Tynghall, and Gaman Corder to receive information about the alleged violence. When at Vilvoorde on June 27 he appointed John and William de Sturmy, Gaman Corder, and some others to settle what reimbursement should be made.[274] By the close of July this business was completed, and on the 30th the three towns sent delegates to King Edward at Vilvoorde.[275] At Brussels on August 2 a series of bonds was issued, in accordance with the decision of John de Sturmy and his colleagues as follows: 566*l.* 13*s.* to Peter Fonso of Santander; 266*l.* 9*s.* 7*d.* to Bernard de Artryke, John de Peron of Bruges, and John van Vaernewijc; 539*l.* 14*s.* 3*d.* to Martyn Durant and Peter Fonso; 2,173*l.* 6*s.* to Reymund Leuces of Barcelona and Bartholomew de Spyn of Majorca; 474*l.* 11*d.* to William de Paono; 174*l.* 18*s.* 10*d.* to John Gerard du Chastel; 340*l.* 12*s.* to Sancho Sanccis and others of Spain; 148*l.* 7*s.* to Henry Benentendi of Florence; and 775*l.* 4*s.* 2*d.* to John de Houtkerk. These sums were to be paid at Bruges at Easter and Michaelmas of 1340 and distributed by these parties to all those who had sustained losses.[276] Thus by the opening of July van Artevelde's policy of neutrality had attained its greatest success. But while all demands made upon Edward had been granted, the antagonism of Philip became more and more certain and it was problematical just how long aloofness from the struggle could be maintained by the Flemings.

[273] N. de Pauw en J. Vuylsteke, *Rekeningen der Stad Gent,* I, 305.
[274] *CPR* (1338–40), p. 387.
[275] N. de Pauw en J. Vuylsteke, *Rekeningen der Stad Gent,* I, 309.
[276] *CPR* (1338–40), pp. 372–374.

CHAPTER X

THE ANGLO–FLEMISH ALLIANCE (AUTUMN, 1339 — WINTER, 1340)

i. The Invasion of the Cambrésis (September, 1339) ii. The Campaign in Thiérache (October, 1339) iii. Van Artevelde's new Policy (Autumn, 1339) iv. The Treaty between Flanders and Brabant (December 3, 1339) v. Edward's Financial Difficulties at Antwerp (November, 1339 — January, 1340) vi. The Anglo-Flemish Alliance (January, 1340) vii. Internal Problems in Flanders (Spring, 1340)

I. The Invasion of the Cambrésis (September, 1339)

AFTER the interminable discussions in Brabant which had consumed the entire summer Edward's army, now composed of the forces of the margrave of Juliers, the counts of Loon, Namur, Marck, Berg, and Virneburg, John of Valkenburg, seignior of Borne and Sittard, and other lesser figures in large numbers, was finally ready to march toward the Cambrésis.[1] The forces of John, duke of Brabant, were to start last because the astute duke did not wish to reveal any particular alacrity in Edward's service even though he had apparently broken with Philip.[2] The fact that Edward still owed him 100,000 Florentine florins undoubtedly had something to do with his dilatory policy.[3] The margrave of Meissen and elector of Brandenburg, son of Lewis the Bavarian, was known to be on the way.[4] John of Hainault had constantly been in Edward's presence and was marshal of the motley host [5] composed of Germans, Welsh bowmen,[6] and Nether-

---

[1] Boendale, *Brabantsche Yeesten*, I, 557; Knighton, II, 11. Boendale states that the count of Catsenellenbogen was with them. He was with John, king of Bohemia, in the French army. See J. F. Boehmer, *Regesten Kaiser Ludwigs des Baiern und seiner Zeit*, p. 207.

[2] Le Bel, I, 156. Hocsemius, p. 453, however, states that the duke accompanied Edward.

[3] A. Verkooren, *Inventaire, Brabant*, II, 69–70.

[4] *Vita Karoli*, p. 260; Johannes Victoriensis, p. 433.

[5] Froissart, I, 441; le Muisit, p. 119.

[6] *Melsa*, II, 40.

landers, which was estimated by the English chroniclers at about twelve thousand men.[7] These now broke camp in the first week of September and proceeded toward Hainault through which they had to pass to reach the frontiers of the Cambrésis, the first object of their hostile endeavors.

Edward was at Brussels and at Anderlecht during these days.[8] On the 7th he proceeded toward Hainault and on the same day arrived at Braine-le-Comte.[9] Thence by easy stages he went to Mons where he tarried from the 12th to the 16th and lodged in the monastery of Épinlieu.[10] The reluctant duke of Brabant now also arrived, and Edward did his best to secure his heartiest co-operation by promising on the 13th to pay him in three instalments the 100,000 Florentine florins still due him, for the prompt payment of which the archbishop of Canterbury, the bishops of Lincoln and Durham, the earls of Derby, Northampton, Salisbury, and Suffolk, and Henry de Ferrariis and John Darcy, members of the royal household, were named guarantors.[11] Some of the duke's forces now arrived,[12] and the advance could be resumed. On the 16th Edward reached Quiévrain. On the 18th he was at Valénciennes where he halted until the 20th.[13] It had been

[7] Baker, p. 64; Murimuth, p. 102. See also de Nangis, II, 163; le Bel, I, 154; Lescot, p. 46; and Villani, cols. 817–818, who estimates the total force at more than 60,000.

[8] Le Bel, I, 153–154, states that he left after St. Lambert's Day (September 17). See also Avesbury, p. 303. For the itinerary, see the documents in *CPR* (1338–40), pp. 392–393, where "Oudenaarde" is obviously a paleographical error for "Anderlecht." Le Bel, I, 156, states that Edward passed through Nivelles.

[9] Boendale, *Van den derden Eduwaert*, p. 370.

[10] *CPR* (1338–40), p. 393; *Chronographia*, II, 69–70. Edward summoned William, count of Hainault, Holland, and Zeeland, to have his army ready to assist him. The document has apparently been lost, and the date is uncertain. See J. Schwalm, "Reise nach Holland, Belgien Nord Frankreich, und dem Niederrhein im Sommer, 1894," *Neues Archiv der Gesellschaft für Aeltere Deutsche Geschichtskunde*, XX (1895), 432–433: "Item monitio facta domino comiti per regem Anglie ad habendum exercitum suum et ad assistendum eidem in adventu regis."

[11] A. Verkooren, *Inventaire, Brabant*, II, 69–70. Duke John was still in Brussels on the 10th when Tiel, Zandwijk, and Heerewaarden were exchanged for Oud Heusden, Vlijmen, Hedikhuizen, and Engelen in accordance with the arbitral decision of Philip VI at Amiens in 1334. See *ibid.*, pp. 68–69; I. A. Nijhoff, *Gedenkwaardigheden uit de Geschiedenis van Gelderland*, I, 403. [12] Le Bel, I, 156.

[13] *CPR* (1338–40), pp. 393, 395. Cf. *Chronographia*, II, 71; Knighton, II, 9–10.

previously agreed upon that this place should serve as a rendezvous.[14]

As vicar of the empire, Edward now summoned the bishop of Cambrai to open the gates of his city. His friends within the walls were active in securing recognition for him as imperial vicar. One of these was the canon, Étienne Mallion, who was later, on March 8, 1340, deprived of his dignities by Pope Benedict for having carried letters to the bishop from Edward as vicar. Another canon, Henry de Jodoigne, had been active in inducing some of the burghers to admit the emperor's representative within the walls.[15] Froissart has embellished his account at this point with a dramatic touch: the bishop of Lincoln appeared on the steps before the count's castle in Valenciennes and proclaimed the order, and, when no response was made, turning to William, count of Hainault, Holland, and Zeeland, who was now with his royal brother-in-law, ordered him to aid in reducing the recalcitrant vassal of the empire.[16] If this scene was really enacted it was done to make it appear that Count William was acting as a faithful subject of the empire. But the bishop was a bitter enemy of the count and, in obedience to the papal order of July 15 of the previous year not to admit any of the supporters of Lewis the Bavarian,[17] prepared to resist.

Then began the invasion of the Cambrésis. The army, which in the meanwhile had been stationed near Haspres in Hainault,[18] reinforced by the troops of Count William, crossed the border on the 20th and at once began plundering the countryside, destroying crops, cattle, and everything.[19] These activities were accompanied by the greatest violence and brutality, and women and children were often horribly mutilated.[20] This continued for the

---

[14] Avesbury, p. 304.

[15] S. Riezler, *Vatikanische Akten*, Nos. 2064, 2071; A. Fierens, *Lettres de Benoît XII (1334–1342)*, No. 628.

[16] Froissart, I, 450; Boendale, *Brabantsche Yeesten*, I, 558–559.

[17] A. Fierens, *Lettres de Benoît XII (1334–1342)*, No. 499. Cf. *Chronographia*, II, 69.

[18] Boendale, *Brabantsche Yeesten*, I, 558.

[19] Baker, p. 65; *Lanercost*, p. 318; Avesbury, p. 304; *Chronographia*, II, 73; Hemingburgh, II, 340; *Chronicon Tielense*, p. 333; Levold de Northof, pp. 402–403.

[20] H. Dubrulle, *Cambrai à la Fin du Moyen Âge (XIIIe–XVIe Siècle)*, p. 285 (note I). Cf. le Muisit, p. 118.

space of a whole week, until the 27th.[21] The air was thick with
the pall of smoke which rose from the burning homesteads.[22]
This melancholy scene of desolation filled the cardinal, Bertrand
of Montefavence, with sorrow when he was taken to a high tower
by Galfridus le Scrope, chief justice of the King's Bench.[23] On the
24th the troops arrived before Cambrai and surrounded it on the
25th when a siege began which lasted until October 8.[24] The city
had been carefully reinforced by Philip since the summer of 1338
and was in excellent condition to resist a protracted investment.[25]
Success could not be expected except by starvation. The English
apparently took no part in the operations.[26] According to Froissart an assault was delivered on Saturday, September 26, led by
William, count of Hainault, Holland, and Zeeland, and John of
Valkenburg, but was beaten off with comparative ease.[27] The arrival of the duke of Brabant [28] on the 30th and of the margrave of
Meissen on October 6 [29] made no difference in these activities.

While the attack upon Cambrai was thus in full progress, and
even before it had begun, detached groups of Edward's followers were riding through the country inflicting the greatest destruction. In these forays John of Hainault and John of Valkenburg
were especially active.[30] But aside from the ruin of the land and
the villages no significant success had yet been gained by the invaders save the capture through surprise of Thun-l'Évêque by
Walter de Manny.[31] He had, it was said, made a vow in London
to be the first to set fire to the homesteads of France. He had
left the army at Valenciennes and had hastened toward Condé,
then to Rouillon, and finally to Mortagne where in the early

[21] Knighton, II, 10.
[22] Boendale, *Van den derden Eduwaert*, p. 323.
[23] Baker, p. 65. The cardinals Bertrand and Peter, who had been sent
by the pope to urge peace, were granted protection by Edward at Valenciennes on September 19. See *Foedera*, II (2), 1090.
[24] Kervyn, *Oeuvres de Froissart*, XVIII, 85.
[25] For the strength of Cambrai, see H. Dubrulle, *Cambrai à la Fin du
Moyen Âge (XIIIe–XVIe Siècle)*, pp. 283–284; Kervyn, *Oeuvres de Froissart*, XVIII, 85; *Chronographia*, II, 62–63.
[26] Kervyn, *Oeuvres de Froissart*, XVIII, 307.
[27] Froissart, I, 162–163; *Chronique Normande*, p. 41.
[28] Le Bel, I, 157–158, who states that he had 1,200 men with him.
[29] Kervyn, *Oeuvres de Froissart*, XVIII, 85.
[30] Froissart, I, 162.
[31] Kervyn, *Oeuvres de Froissart*, XVIII, 84.

morning the gates were found ajar. The town was hurriedly plundered and some of the inhabitants were slain. Then followed the fall of Thun-l'Évêque. Treachery played a part here, for the commander sold it to the enemy. It was at once garrisoned by English soldiers. Relenghes next fell and was treated in the same manner. William, count of Hainault, Holland, and Zeeland, reinforced the English with some of his own men at these places and at Escaudoeuvre and Bouchain. Selles, near Cambrai, was taken and sold to John of Valkenburg by a friend of the commander of Thun-l'Évêque.[32]

John, duke of Brabant, remained a most wavering reed during the course of these events. Edward had frequently urged him to break definitely with Philip and a declaration to this effect was actually sent to the French king.[33] But John apparently still doubted the advisability of supporting Edward wholeheartedly. Should the English return to England — and this might be expected at any moment because of Edward's financial distress — the Low Countries would be placed at the mercy of Philip's military power. Duke John had very lively memories of the straits to which the French king's diplomacy had reduced him in 1332 and 1334. He accordingly still sought to cultivate some understanding with Philip and even went so far as to seek to mediate between the royal opponents! Edward could not well afford to antagonize him at this moment and was careful to restrict his activities in such a way as to give him but scant chance of success. On October 4, when not far from Marcoing, he authorized the duke to issue a safe-conduct to his envoys for only four days and stipulated that the negotiations were to take place within two or three leagues from Marcoing.[34] It was folly to hope for any success in the present state of things, and nothing further is heard of the matter.

Edward was eager to invade France, but the strength of Cambrai was such that a speedy reduction was impossible. As the autumn was advancing and the weather becoming colder, he de-

[32] *Chronographia,* II, 70–72, 75; *Istore et Croniques,* I, 443–444; Froissart, I, 155–156; *Chronique Normande,* p. 44.

[33] Le Bel, I, 159; Boendale, *Brabantsche Yeesten,* I, 559; Boendale, *Van den derden Eduwaert,* pp. 319–323; Froissart, I, 161, 453. See also Lescot (*Appendice*), pp. 225–226.

[34] *Foedera,* II (2), 1092.

cided to abandon the attempt. On the 25th he had already proceeded toward Marcoing on the borders of France and the Cambrésis, and raids into Philip's territory had actually begun at that moment.[35] Meanwhile the papal nuncios, the cardinals of St. Praxed and St. Mary in Aquiro, had kept the pope informed of the course of events. On October 10 Benedict upbraided Edward for his alliance with the schismatic, heretical, and excommunicate Lewis the Bavarian and begged him to desist from his plan against Cambrai and the Cambrésis.[36] Two days later he again wrote, solemnly calling upon him to consider the penalties which might be visited upon him for acting as vicar of Lewis the Bavarian and begging him to retrace his steps before it would be necessary for the Holy See to inflict the severest penalties. John, the archbishop of Canterbury, and Richard, bishop of Durham, were urged to induce the king to yield. A copy of these letters was transmitted to the nuncios who in a special missive of the same date had been instructed, if it should appear expedient, to declare Edward excommunicated by reason of his persistent refusal to hearken to the advice of the church.[37]

II. The Campaign in Thiérache (October, 1339)

King Philip had taken great pains during the summer to get together his forces [38] which at this moment were scattered between Noyon, St. Quentin, and Péronne.[39] He had acted as much perhaps from motives of policy as from deference to the pope, for he followed Benedict's advice of October 8 not to succor the bishop of Cambrai, but rather to hold himself on the defensive in his own territory.[40] Edward tarried a fortnight at Marcoing on the Schelde while the siege of Cambrai was in progress and after the arrival of the troops, when it was raised on the 8th, crossed into French territory on the 9th.[41]

[35] Avesbury, pp. 304–305; Baker, p. 65; le Bel, I, 158.

[36] G. Daumet, *Benoît XII (1334–1342). Lettres Close, Patentes et Curiales se rapportant à la France*, No. 649.

[37] A. Fierens, *Lettres de Benoît XII (1334–1342)*, Nos. 601–605.

[38] For the army of Philip VI, see E. Déprez, *Les Préliminaires de la Guerre de Cent Ans*, pp. 259–271.   [39] Avesbury, p. 305.

[40] A. Fierens, *Lettres de Benoît XII (1334–1342)*, No. 600.

[41] *CPR* (1338–40), pp. 393–395, where "Marcoign" is spelled "Marquion"; Kervyn, *Oeuvres de Froissart*, XVIII, 85.

William, count of Hainault, Holland, and Zeeland, now asserted that he had discharged all that could lawfully be required of him as vassal of the empire. The county of Hainault occupied a peculiarly exposed position in the extreme western point of the empire and could easily be attacked by Philip. As vassal of the French crown for Ostrevant he feared Philip's vengeance. In accordance with the advice of his councillors he was determined not to share in the raids into France, made plans to hearken to the suzerain's demands for feudal service, and at once made off with his troops to join those of Philip, who was at Péronne.[42] John of Hainault, however, stayed with Edward, and, it would seem, with some of Count William's troops, for we find that some of the latter's horses were lost at Buironfosse and elsewhere in France.[43] Philip, however, refused to receive him because he had allowed the enemy to pass unopposed through Hainault, had permitted John of Hainault to serve as marshal in Edward's army, and because he had participated in the pillaging of the Cambrésis.[44] The king of Navarre, it is reported, sought to mollify Philip's wrath by showing that Count William could not have acted otherwise. He had merely discharged his duties as vassal of the emperor, while the war upon the bishop of Cambrai was really caused by the encroachment of the episcopal power upon his sovereign rights. As proof of his friendliness toward Philip, Count William did not return to Edward, but for the rest of the campaign kept aloof from the war.[45]

Edward and his host advanced, plundering and burning the countryside over a width of twelve or fourteen leagues, exactly in the same manner as in the Cambrésis. Proceeding westward along the Schelde, he arrived at Mont St. Martin and took lodging in the abbey at Vaucelles.[46] Edward plundered everything in his

[42] Le Bel, I, 157, 162; Froissart, I, 457–458; *Chronographia*, II, 76. For Philip's itinerary, see J. Viard "Itinéraire de Philippe VI de Valois," *BEC*, LXXIV (1913), 533–534.

[43] On March 26, 1341, Edward granted him 25,000 Florentine florins for these losses. See *Foedera*, II (2), 1154.

[44] Le Muisit, pp. 118–119; le Bel, I, 157.

[45] *Chronographia*, II, 80. This was Count William's official view of the matter. See his letter to Philip on April 2, 1340, Kervyn, *Oeuvres de Froissart*, XVIII, 137.

[46] Kervyn, *Oeuvres de Froissart*, XVIII, 85; le Bel, I, 159; Froissart, I, 159; Lescot (*Appendice*), pp. 226–227; *Lanercost*, p. 318.

line of ,advance until the 14th.[47] On the 10th John of Hainault
made a lively assault upon Honnecourt, a fortified place which
he carried with some loss of life and gave over to plunder.[48]
Philip and his army were before them at Péronne and St. Quentin,
and Edward now turned southward into the direction of Thiérache, thus keeping close to the lands of the count of Hainault
and John of Hainault's possessions, Beaumont and Chimay. In
this way he would be able to take refuge in friendly territory,
should it at any moment become necessary.[49]

Edward soon arrived at Rue-Sainte-Benoîte, close to St. Quentin, and the bishop of Lincoln and the earls of Salisbury, Derby,
and Northampton were visiting the country and villages up to the
very gates of Laon with fire and sword.[50] On the 15th Edward arrived at Origny on the Oise, where the Benedictine sisters and
their abbess were most grossly maltreated.[51] On the next day
he crossed the Oise, tarried on its banks on the 17th,[52] and on the
18th moved to Origny-Sainte-Benoîte near by.[53] Meanwhile
Philip, finding that Edward did not seek an immediate encounter,
was obliged to change his headquarters from Péronne to St. Quentin [54] and then proceeded to follow Edward in a leisurely manner,[55] thus showing that he too did not care to meet his antagonist
in a test of strength.

Cold weather, the first harbinger of winter, now began to interfere with the spirit of the invaders. On the banks of the Oise
on Sunday, the 17th, Edward's allies declared that it was impossible to advance further because of the chilly weather and the
dwindling food-supply. Thinking that Philip would offer battle
soon after they should enter French territory, they had not taken

[47] *CPR* (1338–40), p. 395; *Foedera*, II (2), 1092–1093; Avesbury, p. 305;
le Bel, I, 159; Levold de Northof, pp. 402–403; *Chronicon Tielense*, p. 333.
[48] S. A. Waller Zeper, *Jan van Henegouwen, Heer van Beaumont*,
pp. 152–154; *Scalacronica*, p. 169.
[49] According to the *Chronographia*, II, 80–81, this was done at the advice of John of Hainault.
[50] Kervyn, *Oeuvres de Froissart*, XVIII, 85–86; de Nangis, II, 64.
[51] Le Bel, I, 158; *Chronographia*, II, 82; R. P. H. Denifle, *La Désolation des Églises, Monastères, et Hôpitaux en France pendant la Guerre de
Cent Ans*, II, 14.
[52] *CPR* (1338–40), p. 395; Avesbury, p. 305.
[53] Kervyn, *Oeuvres de Froissart*, XVIII, 86.
[54] *Chronographia*, II, p. 81; Baker, p. 65; de Nangis, II, p. 163.
[55] Le Muisit, p. 119.

enough provisions with them.[56]   At this juncture the duke of Brabant, who apparently acted as spokesman for the rest, revealed what little desire he had for the enterprise.[57]   But Edward was in no mood to halt the invasion at this point and urged his reluctant ally to continue. He claimed that he had sufficient provisions in his baggage train for all, and that " God would aid them at all times." Eager to inflict as much damage upon his enemy as possible, he now suggested that the vehicles should be abandoned and all men afoot be mounted. By foraging through the country they would be able to secure what they might need. Duke John and the other princes who apparently followed his example were loath to advance much further and professed to believe it unprofitable; but Edward was able to overcome their objections and on Tuesday, the 19th, the plundering was vigorously resumed.[58]

On Monday morning letters which had been written by Philip on the previous evening came into Edward's camp. A battle was suggested, and Edward was challenged to choose ground unencumbered with wood, stream, or marsh so that they might meet by Thursday, the 21st, at the latest.[59] On the following day Edward advanced two leagues further into Thiérache. Letters from John, king of Bohemia, and Raoul, duke of Lorraine, were received by Hugh de Geneva, who was in Edward's army. These declared that Philip fully intended to keep his word and planned to meet Edward on Thursday. But no enemy appeared on that day, and on Friday Edward marched six leagues farther in the direction of La Flamengerie. The men had been kept on the alert on the 22d, and in the evening three spies were brought in who stated in the course of their examination that Philip was planning battle on the 23d in accordance with a request he had made on the previous day.[60]

Council was now held and the army thereupon took up a position before break of day on land belonging to the abbey of Claire-

[56] Knighton, II, 11; Melsa, III, 42–43; Murimuth, p. 102; Avesbury, p. 305; Boendale *Van den derden Eduwaert*, p. 322.

[57] Murimuth, p. 102; Avesbury, p. 304; Baker, pp. 65–66; Kervyn, *Oeuvres de Froissart*, XVIII, 86.

[58] Kervyn, *Oeuvres de Froissart*, XVIII, 86.

[59] *Ibid.*, pp. 87–88; Avesbury, p. 305; Knighton, II, 12.

[60] Kervyn, *Oeuvres de Froissart*, XVIII, 88–89; Avesbury, p. 305.

fontaine, distant about a league from La Flamengerie. Walter
de Manny and Wulfard de Ghistelles were sent out to recon-
noitre. They killed some of Philip's troops and descried the
French forces in the distance hard by Buironfosse. At daybreak
Edward ordered his knights and horsemen to descend and make
ready for the battle.[61] The rear of his army was composed of
the troops of the duke of Brabant, placed there probably because
Edward did not have any too great confidence in them. Duke
John now rose to the occasion, if we may believe Boendale. He
was eager to share in the excitement of battle and sought to
stimulate the enthusiasm of his men to a high pitch. He announced that whoever should bring to him a piece of the oriflamme
of France, even if it were as small as the palm of his hand, would
receive a thousand florins.[62] Immediately in front of the duke's
men Edward placed the troops of his allies the Germans under
the margrave of Meissen, the margrave of Juliers, and the count
of Berg, and the Netherlanders under Reginald, duke of Guelders, John of Hainault, and others. In the front line were placed
the English with the right wing under the command of the earls
of Derby and Suffolk and others, and the left under that of the
earls of Northampton, Salisbury, and Pembroke. On each flank
were stationed groups of archers of whom there were a plentiful
number.[63]

These details are sufficient to indicate Edward's tactics on this
day and during the entire campaign. The arrangement of the
troops was practically, certainly in its essential characteristics,
a repetition of that at Dupplin Moor in 1332 and Halidon Hill
in 1333. Edward fully realized the fact, gleaned from the military experiences of the wars with the Scots ever since the battle
of Falkirk in 1298, that his best chance of victory lay with his
archers. He accordingly so arranged his troops that they would
disorganize the French chivalry in its mad rush upon the English front. The English horsemen would thus be able to receive the impact and soon destroy them. This explains Edward's

[61] Avesbury, p. 305; *Chronographia,* II, 83; le Bel, I, 163; Kervyn,
Oeuvres de Froissart, XVIII, 90.

[62] Kervyn, *Oeuvres de Froissart,* XVIII, 92; Boendale, *Van den derden
Eduwaert,* p. 336.

[63] Kervyn, *Oeuvres de Froissart,* XVIII, 92. For the arraying of the
archers, see *Feodera,* II (2), 1070–1072.

reluctance to act on the offensive when he would be unable to use the archers to the fullest advantage. He apparently hoped to arouse the fury of the French and Philip by the most wanton destruction of the countryside and induce them to assault with the impetuosity characteristic of chivalry. Thus they would be destroyed as were the Scots six years before.[64]

Philip, however, was equally reluctant to come to blows. Did he understand his enemy's tactics? It is possible that he had some inkling of what fearful reception was in store for him if he attacked the English on ground chosen by them. Perhaps he deemed it prudent to avoid an engagement and trusted to the unfavorable weather to put an end to the campaign. But it is certain that he feared the English. One of the German scouts in Edward's army who was captured, revealed to Philip the disposition of the army. Philip at once ordered his vanguard to retreat, encamp, dig trenches, and cut down the large trees in order to prevent any surprise attack. All day Saturday both armies remained in this position, each equally unwilling to take the offensive. At vespers Edward's allies thought that they had waited long enough and the king reluctantly ordered his men to take to their mounts. This movement was observed by Philip who, at the last moment, ordered his men to take a stronger position, in the execution of which many of his horses were caught in a treacherous bog. On the 24th Edward was at Avesnes and informed Philip that he would give battle.[65] But on that day the latter retired to St. Quentin, and Edward gave up all hope of battle on Monday.[66]

The patriotic Boendale states that Philip, who had formed the idea that Duke John had left Edward's army and gone home — probably we are to see in this another proof of his double dealing — was disconcerted when he heard that the troops of Brabant were drawn up in Edward's lines ready to receive him, and

[64] See H. B. George, "The Archers of Crécy," *English Historical Review*, X (1895), 733–738; J. E. Morris, "The Archers at Crécy," *ibid.*, XII (1897), 427–436; T. F. Tout, "The Tactics of the Battles of Boroughbridge and Morlaix," *ibid.*, XIX (1904), 711–713; C. Oman, *A History of the Art of War*, pp. 591–598.

[65] Avesbury, p. 306; le Bel, I, 163; Knighton, II, 13; *Chronographia*, II, 84.

[66] J. Viard, "Itinéraire de Philippe VI de Valois," *BEC*, LXXIV (1913), 533; Avesbury, p. 306; Kervyn, *Oeuvres de Froissart*, XVIII, 92.

decided not to risk his crown in a few hours' combat.[67] But in the light of the strategic situation, the strength of Philip's forces, and the duke's weakness in comparison, Boendale's statement need not be accepted.

Edward's army now began to break up. Duke John and the German nobles at once turned home,[68] Edward proceeded toward Brabant by way of Chimay and Fontaine-l'Évêque in Hainault,[69] disbanded some of his troops, and announced that a tournament would be held at Brussels.[70] There he arrived on the 29th and stayed as late as November 6.[71]

III. Van Artevelde's New Policy (Autumn, 1339)

It is now necessary to trace the course of events in Flanders until January, 1340, when van Artevelde deliberately abandoned the king of France. The great captain of Ghent had found that Philip's hearty acquiescence in his policy of neutrality could never be obtained. This was natural, for, as suzerain of Flanders, the king of France was entitled to certain feudal services which he so sorely needed in the present crisis. Neutrality therefore appeared to him almost equivalent to treason, for what chance would Edward have in the Low Countries if the might of Flanders were actively enlisted on the French king's side? [72] Philip had yielded only through fear of driving Flanders, forced by the industrial necessities and the social problems of her towns to adopt a position of neutrality, into the camp of Edward's supporters and thus solidifying English power in the Low Countries. Count Louis with most of the feudality and some of the patriciate was of the same mind. There was continued hostility in West Flanders. The presence of the count and some of the nobility in the entourage of the king made it apparent that, as soon as opportunity presented itself, hostile measures might be expected from Philip.

[67] Boendale, *Van den derden Eduwaert,* pp. 326–327. According to the *Grandes Chroniques,* V, 378, Edward dared not attack Philip and consequently withdrew.   [68] Le Bel, I, 120; Knighton, II, 13.

[69] Le Muisit, p. 120; Baker, p. 66; Murimuth, p. 103.

[70] *Chronographia,* II, 84–85.

[71] *CPR* (1338–40), pp. 395–396; Boendale, *Van den derden Eduwaert,* p. 32.

[72] See the words of le Bel, I, 168: " . . . Flamens, qui plus luy (i.e. Edward) pouvoient aidier à son besongne que tout le remanant du monde."

But in spite of all resistance, van Artevelde was able to establish his unquestioned authority in the country and in the towns during the summer of 1339. The negotiations conducted by the three towns with the recalcitrant upholders of the count's rights in the castleries of West Flanders now apparently came to an end. The inquests were still in progress as late as September 18 at Bergen and at Dixmuide.[73] On the 19th Peter vander Asselt was dispatched by the scabini of Ghent to bring back the militia which was finally discharged on October 13.[74] The prisoners taken in the disturbances had been brought to Ghent and were later, after August 15, exchanged at Gravelines, on the extreme western border of the county of Flanders, for some of the supporters of van Artevelde and Ghent.[75]

Infractions of the public peace were promptly repressed; on August 18 William van Huse was sent to Deinze to bring to Ghent some persons who had been accused of counterfeiting.[76] Walter van Voorhout, a subject of the duke of Brabant, who possessed some lands in Flanders or had connections there, and his followers had raided and burned sections in the neighborhood of Grammont. The scabinus, Baldwin vanden Walle, was sent on September 5 to Brabant to secure justice from the duke and his towns. He returned on the 10th and, although the request was granted, it was deemed necessary to send William van Vaernewijc with some mounted men-at-arms to request the seignior of Enghien, who apparently was hostile to the policy of Ghent, not to tolerate van Voorhout's using his lands as a base for his destructive forays.[77]

Opposition was thus generally repressed and van Artevelde's control over the towns was considerably extended. To maintain the policy of neutrality against the opposition of King Philip, Count Louis, and their partisans among the feudality and the patriciate necessitated a *rapprochement* with the crafts. This was evident in August of 1338 when Henry Goethals, a member of the brewer's guild, was named one of the scabini. At Easter John vander Vloet was succeeded by John van Steenbeke who, as dean of the weavers, had shown himself zealous in prosecuting

---

[73] N. de Pauw en J. Vuylsteke, *Rekeningen der Stad Gent,* I, 400.
[74] *Ibid.,* pp. 402, 466–469.   [76] *Ibid.,* pp. 348, 452.
[75] *Ibid.,* pp. 424.   [77] *Ibid.,* pp. 400–401, 417.

van Artevelde's designs.[78] He appears to have been a man of much greater ability than vander Vloet and later in the year was to play an especially significant rôle as member of the Council of Flanders which was created as an advisory body for Count Louis upon his return to Ghent.[79]

In August a still more remarkable change was effected. The new lists of the scabini contained more names of less note than previous ones. Two were now drawn from the crafts: John van Lens, fuller, as scabinus, and Roger de Smet, cordwainer, as councillor.[80] The difficulties in the Frank of Bruges, which developed during the early summer because of the opposition of the local seigniorial group, were to be obviated, it was hoped, by the appointment of captains favorable to the policy of neutrality. These were sworn into office between August 16 and 19 in the presence of a deputation from Ghent, composed of the premier scabinus, Simon Parijs, his colleague, Baldwin vanden Walle, the premier councillor, Gilles Rijnvisch, Thomas van Vaernewijc, and William de Bomere. To ensure full adherence to the policy of the three towns and the maintenance of peace, hostages were often taken. For this purpose Brant de Huntere, apparently of the nobility, was chosen and brought with a number of companions to Ghent.[81]

The exact reasons for local disturbances and opposition are usually impossible to ascertain. These varied from place to place as this or that factor became prominent. There were discordant crafts, private feuds, jealous resentment of interference in internal communal affairs which threatened to blaze forth in violent opposition, and the sullen dissatisfaction of the nobility which, as in the case of the Frank of Bruges, sought to stir up trouble.

At Courtrai the captains appointed by the scabini of Ghent were accused of extortion and undue interference in the management of guild life, and, apparently in October, an inquest was ordered by the scabini.[82] In July the presence of men from other

---

[78] *Ibid.*, p. 388.
[79] *Ibid.*, p. 404.
[80] *Ibid.*, p. 395.
[81] *Ibid.*, p. 398 (notes).
[82] N. de Pauw, " L'Enquête sur les Capitaines de Courtrai sous Artevelde (1338–1340)," *BCRH*, 79 (1910), 259. The last dated item in the list of complaints is of September 30.

parts of Flanders had grown so distasteful to the people of Courtrai that an open feud developed in which a number of men from Moerkerke in the Frank of Bruges were slain. An effort was at once made to arrange satisfaction; on August 2 and 3 Henry Goethals and Peter vanden Hovene were sent to Moerkerke, followed by the premier scabinus of Ghent, Simon Parijs, and deputies from Bruges and Ypres to discuss the basis of an accord with the families of the slain.[83] William de Bomere went to Bruges on the 20th and thence to Moerkerke to make final arrangements while the scabinus, Baldwin vanden Walle, proceeded with a mounted party from Bruges to take hostages at Courtrai. On the 21st Peter vanden Hovene arrived at the head of some men-at-arms and twenty-five white-hoods in order to reinforce them. These had all returned to Ghent on the 22d and on the next day another deputation was sent thither in order to put into practice arrangements which proved quite difficult to enforce, for the matter again caused a good deal of trouble in the following January.[84]

There were similar activities in other places. It was necessary to send the scabinus, Simon van Merelbeke, to arbitrate between two factions of the Stroekine family at Aardenburg.[85] Peter vanden Hovene was sent to Teemseke and into Waasland on August 24 and William van Vaernewijc followed him on the 27th.[86] On September 19 they were dispatched to Assenede,[87] and, ten days later, the scabinus, John de Bake, was ordered to go to Grammont.[88] From Dendermonde hostages were taken on August 26 and 27.[89] Captains were appointed to see to it that the will of van Artevelde and the three towns was enforced in Eecloo,[90] the Frank of Bruges, Courtrai, Dendermonde,[91] in the castleries of West Flanders,[92] Oudenaarde,[93] and undoubtedly also in many other places. These captains constantly consulted the scabini of Ghent, Bruges, and Ypres, enforced their decisions, and thereby

[83] N. de Pauw en J. Vuylsteke, *Rekeningen der Stad Gent,* I, 309–310.

[84] *Ibid.,* pp. 309–310, 398–399, 407–408.

[85] *Ibid.,* p. 398.   [89] *Ibid.,* p. 399.

[86] *Ibid.,* pp. 399–400.   [90] *Ibid.,* pp. 401–402.

[87] *Ibid.,* p. 400.   [91] *Ibid.,* p. 426.

[88] *Ibid.,* p. 402.   [92] *Ibid.,* p. 311.

[93] N. de Pauw, *La Conspiration d'Audenaerde sous Jacques van Artevelde (1342),* p. XXXIV.

subordinated nearly all Flanders to the will of Ghent and to the commands of her captain.

Particularly difficult and dangerous were the problems presented by the discordant guilds. At Courtrai the captains established by the scabini of Ghent had been forced to interfere in the relations between the fullers and weavers.[94] The weavers of Bruges complained that those of Eecloo were infringing their rights, and so serious was the quarrel that the three towns intervened. From Ghent the scabini, John van Steenbeke and Henry Huenich, and the deans, John van Dessele and John vander Vloet, were sent thither on July 26 to aid in the settlement which was effected on August 2. A meeting had been arranged to be held at Courtrai on the 1st when these deputies appeared with those of the other towns.[95] It was decided that the weavers of Eecloo might manufacture cloths of certain kinds (*derdelinghe* and *dickedinne*) measuring no more than four quarters in width and thirty-eight ells in length. The weavers of Bruges might at any moment investigate the work of the weavers, violations were to be punished by a fine of three pounds Parisian, and the cloth was to be confiscated. The proceeds from such penalties were to be divided equally among the count, the corporation of Bruges, and the weavers of Bruges.[96]

In October difficulties again became acute at Courtrai whither the scabini of Ghent found it necessary to send some of their militia.[97] Especially serious was the strife in Ypres.[98] On January 3 the scabinus, Michael de Witte, and the captain, Peter vanden Hovene, were dispatched to arrange an agreement with the representatives of the other towns and with the weavers and fullers.[99] At Ypres on January 8, 1340, some preliminary arrangement was effected regarding the members of these corporations.[100] On the 10th settlement was effected at Courtrai. Depu-

---

[94] N. de Pauw, " L'Enquête sur les Capitaines de Courtrai sous Artevelde (1338–1340)," *BCRH,* 79 (1910), 240–242.

[95] N. de Pauw en J. Vuylsteke, *Rekeningen der Stad Gent,* I, 309.

[96] G. Espinas et H. Pirenne, *Recueil des Documents relatifs à l'Histoire et l'Industrie Drapière en Flandre,* II, 349–350.

[97] N. de Pauw en J. Vuylsteke, *Rekeningen der Stad Gent,* I, 403.

[98] *Ibid.,* pp. 400–401, 404.

[99] *Ibid.,* p. 406.

[100] P. van Duyse et E. de Busscher, *Inventaire Analytique des Chartes et Documents appartenant aux Archives de la Ville de Gand,* p. 141.

ties from the three towns, Michael de Witte, a scabinus of Ghent, Peter vanden Hovene, captain of Ghent, John de Wert, a scabinus of Bruges, and John vanden Meustre, Simon van Loe, and John van Inghelant, councillors of Ypres, met and came to agreement with the weavers and fullers. The weavers were to work as many hours each day as the weavers of Ghent, the scabini of Courtrai were to designate two of the officials (*jurati, ghezworenen*) of the weavers to ring the bell as at Ghent, and all dissatisfied elements were banished from the town for one year.[101] Similar difficulties developed at Oostburg, and from Ghent on January 7, the scabini, John de Bake and Simon van Merelbeke, were dispatched, together with deputies from Bruges, to establish harmony.[102]

These facts clearly reveal the gravity of the problems confronting van Artevelde and the three towns. Medieval communes were ever jealous of their privileges and strenuously resisted any infringement of them. The domination of Flanders by Ghent, Bruges, and Ypres had its rise in the dire needs of industry and commerce, yet could soon pass into a systematic effort to curtail the manufacturing of cloth in the smaller competing towns. The interference at Eecloo and Courtrai and at Poperingen in the following year indicated that such was the trend. In the castlery of Ghent a large deputation composed of men from the crafts and scabini went about at the close of November to confiscate the implements used in making cloth contrary to the franchises of Ghent.[103] This spirit would of course sooner or later evoke opposition. In the absence of the legitimate authority of the count this situation might at any moment assume a graver aspect; disgruntled nobles and patricians, together with dissatisfied guildsmen and communes, might jeopardize the ascendancy of Ghent in the affairs of Flanders and destroy the neutral position of the county.

On the other hand, there was an unmistakably rising tide of Flemish feeling against the French, nurtured no doubt in part by the memories of the battle of the Spurs at Groeninghe or Courtrai in 1302. Perhaps the common talk of thirty years ago, when the

---

[101] G. Espinas et H. Pirenne, *Recueil des Documents relatifs à l'Histoire et l'Industrie Drapière en Flandre*, I, 653–654.

[102] N. de Pauw en J. Vuylsteke, *Rekeningen der Stad Gent*, I, 406.

[103] *Ibid.*, p. 405.

Flemings were confronted by the hostility of the king of France,[104] was revived. It was a general feeling that a vast war against the French by all who spoke the Netherlandish tongue was imminent. This was perhaps stimulated by the emperor's demand for Flemish support in his efforts to recover the lands taken by the kings of France, their own enemies.[105] The manner in which King Philip had repeatedly been forced to yield may well have made him appear impotent in their eyes; his lack of sympathy certainly antagonized all who wished to preserve the commerce and industry of Flanders. An expression of this sentiment has been preserved by the poet Boendale who wrote that the news of the victory over the French at Sluis in June of the following year was greeted with intense pleasure by all folk who spoke the Netherlandish (*Dietsch*) language.[106]

The return of Count Louis to Flanders would greatly stabilize the new régime which was quite naturally forced into many acts of doubtful legality. Efforts to induce him to come back during the spring and summer failed. But in September Louis consented, influenced undoubtedly by Philip's desire to allay the rising feeling of hostility in the county against him at the moment when Edward was preparing to invade France.[107] On September 29 the scabinus, Simon van Merelbeke, and Thomas van Vaernewijc proceeded to France, and on October 5 returned with the count.[108] The reception was loyal and splendid enough. Louis was escorted to the town by a guard.[109] Persemiere and his men, the official trumpeters of Ghent, were on duty,[110] the three deans were attended by six men-at-arms commanded by a bailiff who were set as a watch until the 10th,[111] and van Artevelde

---

[104] See *Chronicon Comitum Flandrensium*, p. 183 (*sub* 1313): "Quod proverbium commune est in Teutonia quod Flamingi destruent Franciam et regem eorum adnihilabunt et dominabuntur super Francos."

[105] I. L. A. Diegerick, *Inventaire des Chartes et Documents appartenant aux Archives de la Ville d'Ypres*, II, 107.

[106] Boendale, *Van den derden Eduwaert*, p. 344.

[107] *Chronographia*, II, 85–86.

[108] N. de Pauw en J. Vuylsteke, *Rekeningen der Stad Gent*, I, 402; Philip was at Noyon from November 1 to 9. See J. Viard, "Itinéraire de Philippe VI de Valois," *BEC*, LXXIV (1913), 533.

[109] N. de Pauw en J. Vuylsteke, *Rekeningen der Stad Gent*, I, 428.

[110] *Ibid.*, p. 402 (note 2).

[111] *Ibid.*, note 1.

presented the count with two oxen and a bear for which he was allowed 250*l.* in the accounts of the scabini.[112] Gifts in money were given the count's cook and the bailiff who had kept watch, and later, on All Souls' Day, two more oxen were presented.[113]

But the scabini and van Artevelde were determined to control the actions of the count. Louis was required to renew his oath, which was done, it appears, in the church of St. John.[114] They carefully restricted his liberty.[115] All his former retainers had fled with him to France after the ill-fated effort at Dixmuide and Bergen. A new council, the Council of Flanders (*Raad van Vlaenderen*), became active in November. Its membership is instructive: John van Steenbeke, dean of the weavers, which cannot have pleased Louis, Thomas van Vaernewijc, Jacob vander Hoyen, Master Maechelien van St. Baefs, and Henry de Keyser.[116] It is of course obvious that these men were in whole-hearted harmony with the scabini and van Artevelde who had carefully formulated the count's policy. This council would therefore give their acts a certain appearance of legality. At Rupelmonde some recalcitrant defenders of the count's rights were holding out in the castle against the three towns and it was determined to reduce them at once. On October 10 the scabinus, Baldwin vanden Walle, the councillor, Gilles Rijnvisch, and the captains, William van Vaernewijc and William van Huse, set out, accompanied by Count Louis and twenty bowmen. The castle was delivered and Rijnvisch was named castellan. Floris de Brugdam (or van Brugghendamme), the commander, was compensated by Count Louis with the payment of 2,000*l.* which was loaned by the scabini of Ghent.[117] A more complete subjection could hardly be imagined.

With Count Louis in their midst and apparently supporting them in their efforts, the scabini now sought to secure further advantages. The presence of the legitimate prince would disarm efforts to resist van Artevelde. As for Philip they had little to fear now, except for the papal censures which he could invoke

[112] N. de Pauw en J. Vuylsteke, *Rekeningen der Stad Gent,* I, 383.

[113] *Ibid.,* p. 396.

[114] *Ibid.,* p. 455.   [115] See de Budt, p. 326.

[116] N. de Pauw en J. Vuylsteke, *Rekeningen der Stad Gent,* I, 404–405, 407, 411.

[117] *Ibid.,* pp. 403, 476–477.

in accordance with the Treaty of Athis-sur-Orge. Philip's necessity was their opportunity, and they determined to support with a show of force their demand that these clauses should be rescinded at exactly the time when Edward was invading France. At this moment appears for the first time, at least as far as Flemish official sources are concerned, the proposal of getting back the ancient frontiers of Flanders (*die palen van Vlaenderen*) which would certainly seem to include Artois, Lille, Douai, Tournai, Béthune, and Orchies, taken from the county of Flanders by the French kings, especially during the reign of Philip the Fair. The object is at once plain. Van Artevelde and the three towns were after all interested mainly in their economic security and cared little for the return of these parts. But to secure the cordial approval of their policy by the count nothing, it was fondly hoped, could be better calculated. We shall not be far wrong in ascribing this new policy to the insinuations of Edward and his friends. On March 13 Reginald, duke of Guelders, had been instructed by the emperor to promise the Flemings the return of Béthune, Lille, and Douai if their count would coöperate with Edward as legitimate king of France. The certainty of Philip's opposition to their neutrality in the struggle, the necessity of securing some legal basis for the unusual authority of the three towns, the belief that Count Louis' actions could be fully controlled by the Council of Flanders, and the growing animosity toward Philip now induced van Artevelde and his supporters to win the count for their cause. This step meant of course that Count Louis and Flanders would be forced to join Edward and his alliances.[118]

These measures were debated at once upon Louis' arrival in Ghent on October 5, for on the 7th a messenger was sent to Philip at Noyon " to ascertain the state of affairs " and on the next day another was dispatched to Edward.[119] On October 21, when Edward was at La Flamengerie hoping that Philip would attack him, the scabini, Simon Parijs and Baldwin vanden Walle, ac-

[118] Edward's first recorded suggestion of this proposal is dated January 4, 1340. See *Foedera*, II (2), 1106. The document in *CPR* (1338–40), pp. 377–378, should be assigned to 1340. Edward of course inspired the letter issued by Lewis the Bavarian on March 13. See Kervyn, *Oeuvres de Froissart*, II, 551–552.

[119] N. de Pauw en J. Vuylsteke, *Rekeningen der Stad Gent*, I, 42.

companied by William de Bomere and Count Louis, set out to Philip to request the surrender of these possessions.[120]   A large force was gotten together and equipped from the military stores in the Gerard Duivelhuis.   Horses were shod, and materials were collected and brought up the Schelde toward Courtrai by boat. On the day that Count Louis and the deputies departed for France these also set out.   There were a hundred and thirty-five bowmen, eighty shield-bearers, and a number of white-hoods, accompanied by eleven of the scabini and councillors, the three deans of the guilds, van Artevelde, and the captains.[121]   They were at Courtrai when news of Edward's retreat came to them. Thus deprived of a diplomatic advantage, they at once fell back and were in Ghent on the 28th, followed by the deputies and by Count Louis on the 30th.[122]   The kind of reception they received from Philip has not been reported, but it certainly was unfavorable.   The royal refusal now became a very important matter; it was followed by a definite *rapprochement* of van Artevelde, the duke of Brabant, and the English king.

IV. The Treaty between Flanders and Brabant
(December 3, 1339)

When van Artevelde's diplomatic maneuver between October 21 and 30 failed, the antagonism between the Flemings and the French was noticeably increased.   There was much piratical activity in the narrow waters between England and the mainland during 1339.   French mariners made attempts upon Rye, Sandwich, Hastings, and Harwich,[123] and the English retaliated early in the following year by burning Boulogne and numerous towns in Normandy.[124]   When Edward was on the way to Thiérache

---

[120] N. de Pauw en J. Vuylsteke, *Rekeningen der Stad Gent*, I, 403: "It. scep. Symoen Pariis, Boyd. vanden Walle, ende met hemlieden der Willem de Bomere, die voeren . . . met miin heere van Vlaenderen anden coninc van Vrankerike omme versouke to doene vander sententien quite te ebbene ende andre versouke die sij daden. . . ."

[121] *Ibid.*, pp. 471–475.   The expedition cost Ghent 6,188*l.* 6*s.* 8*d.*

[122] *Ibid.*, p. 403.

[123] Knighton, II, 9; Murimuth, p. 88; Baker, p. 63.

[124] Knighton, II, 10; *Grandes Chroniques*, V, 379; *Chronographia*, II, 94.   For the date, see Baker, p. 67.

at the close of September, a powerful fleet of French galleys appeared in the Zwin and the Honte to prey upon English shipping. The French swore, it was said, that they would not return until they had destroyed a hundred ships and burned fifty more towns in England. The advancing season and the storm on Sunday after Michaelmas, however, apparently interfered with the realization of their plans.[125]

At Calais there was a nest of pirates who were continually robbing and slaying the merchants of Flanders and England. Among the more notorious of these were the desperate Flemish pirate, Lanisius Spoudevisch, whom Boendale described as an " enemy of God and man," [126] and the equally pitiless Henry Pijl, also a Fleming, who, with Spoudevisch, sailed along the coasts of England and Flanders, capturing and plundering ships at will and retreating safely with their loot to Calais.[127] The losses sustained by the men of the three towns exasperated the magistrates, and van Artevelde was reported as having declared his intention of going thither to destroy this nest of marauders. Philip's bailiff at Calais was greatly concerned about this reported expedition and sent spies to keep him informed about the movements of the captain.[128] There was great relief at Calais when it was learned

[125] Knighton, II, 14.

[126] Boendale, *Van den derden Eduwaert*, p. 338

[127] *CCR* (1339–41), pp. 321–323, 355, 369. It is probable that similar activities were carried on at Wissant, for some of the men of that place were held at Ghent and exchanged later by the scabini for some men at Ghent. See N. de Pauw and J. Vuylsteke, *Rekeningen der Stad Gent*, I, 454.

[128] See the reports in the account of the bailiff of Calais published by A. Guesnon, *Documents Inédits sur l'Invasion Anglaise et les États au Temps de Philippe VI et de Jean le Bon*, pp. 18–19 (notes): " A Perrekin Pasquin pour porter lettres à Arras pour faire savoir monsgr le gouverneur de Jaque d'Artevelde nouvelles, qui avoient tué les couletiers de Bruges, vis.

" A une espie pour aler à Bruges et à Gant pour savoir l'estat et le couvine des Flamens, de leur moete et paroles qu'il disoient, xiiiis.

" A Hanne Lellinc pour porter lettres à monsgr le gouverneur à Arras et revint par Béthune, pour faire savoir que Jaques d'Artevelde estoit repariés, et pour autres nouvelles, vis.

" A une espie pour aler à Bruges et à Gant pour ce que on rapportoit de jour en jour que Jaques d'Artevelde avait fait serement qu'il verrait vir Callais et osteroit le mais ni, ce disoit, de chiaus qui roboient les marchans et mettoient à mort, xvs." These activities took place before All Saints' Day. For the robbers of Calais, see *CPR* (1338–40), pp. 373–374; *CCR* (1339–41), pp. 560, 629, 642–643.

that the Flemings had returned to Flanders after the demonstration between October 21 and 30.

This antagonism was also shared by Philip's agents who were sent to Lille to meet from November 3 to 6 the delegation sent by the scabini of Ghent. This was composed of Baldwin vanden Walle and Peter Mabenzone, to whom were added on the 4th the members of the Council of Flanders, John van Steenbeke, Jacob vander Hoyen, and Henry de Keyser. These continued the negotiations at Menin, but apparently without result.[129] Confronted by the hostility of Philip and his officials, van Artevelde keenly felt his weakness in the isolation forced upon him by the policy of neutrality. The alliance of 1336 between Brabant, Hainault, Holland, and Zeeland, and Flanders had been formed to provide protection against all enemies save the emperor and the king of France. In the new crisis these allies might be relied upon for assistance. The duke of Brabant had definitely broken with Philip, and his lands and subjects were now exposed to the king's hostility. Count William, in spite of his friendly bearing toward the French since Edward's arrival in the Low Countries and his desertion of the invading forces at the moment they passed from the Cambrésis into French territory, had been repelled by his uncle who might soon begin to invade his lands. It was only natural that van Artevelde should now turn to the duke of Brabant for help.

It is significant therefore that John de Coster, who had been sent to Brabant by the scabini of Ghent to visit Edward from October 22 to 28, was sent to interview Duke John from the 31st to November 5. Thereupon on the 11th John van Steenbeke and Jacob vander Hoyen, who had returned from the unsuccessful negotiations at Lille on the 8th, and Thomas van Vaernewijc, all three members of the Council of Flanders, accompanied by Count Louis, went to Dendermonde to discuss with Duke John the bases of an offensive and defensive alliance which was obviously directed against the king of France. They returned on the 13th, and a second delegation was sent of which the premier scabinus, Simon Parijs, the captains, Gelnoot van Lens and William van Huse, and Count Louis were the chief members. They returned on the 18th, and on the 27th Count Louis, accompanied by Thomas

129 N. de Pauw en J. Vuylsteke, *Rekeningen der Stad Gent*, I, 404.

. van Vaernewijc, was again sent to the duke and the matter was settled by December 1 when they returned.[130]

Final arrangements were now made at Ghent. Soon a vast number of deputies began to arrive from all parts of Flanders and Brabant. There were magistrates from the towns of Louvain, Brussels, Antwerp, 's-Hertogenbosch, Tirlemont, Leeuw, and Nivelles. There appeared many nobles, the more important of whom were Otto, seignior of Cuyk, William van Duivenvoorde, seignior of Oosterhout, John, seignior of Rotselaer, and William, seignior of Hoorne and Gaasbeek. There were also Flemish notables: Henry of Flanders, seignior of Ninove, Simon de Mirabel (or van Halen), Gossuin vanden Moue, Wulfard de Ghistelles, Eustachius Pascharis, Roger van Vaernewijc, and Raes van Zepe, most of whom were pensioners of King Edward. There were magistrates from Ghent, Bruges, Ypres, Courtrai, Oudenaarde, Alost, and Grammont.

The duke of Brabant came with his household and was splendidly received. Negotiations took place in the hall of the scabini,[131] the duke's minstrels entertained the burghers as well as the nobles, and his cook was given a handsome gift.[132] Count Louis must have appeared a sorry figure. Dominated by the Council of Flanders, van Artevelde, and the scabini of Ghent, he could exercise no initiative and apparently mechanically affixed his seal to the important charters which were now drawn up. These documents were splendid examples of medieval calligraphic art as can be seen from the numerous copies still preserved in the archives. They have an extraordinarily large number of seals and much wax and silk were needed.[133] The expense for Ghent in this connection alone amounted to thirty-six pounds.[134]

The preamble of this significant charter strikes the note of the situation. It declared that the alliance was formed in the interests of commerce and industry which were the only means of livelihood for many of the people of both Flanders and Brabant. The allies promised to aid each other against all parties with-

---

[130] *Ibid.*, pp. 403, 405.
[131] *Ibid.*, p. 458.
[132] See *ibid.*, p. 396: " It. serthoghen menestreelen van Brabant, 20*lb.*"
[133] *Ibid.*, p. 396.   [134] *Ibid.*, pp. 456–457.

out exception and not to undertake any offensive war without
the consent of the other; they declared that the merchants of each
country should be entirely free in the lands of the other, that a
common coinage should be established, which would be legal
tender everywhere in the possessions of each contracting party,
that it was to be struck in Louvain and Ghent subject to the
supervision of two deputies (*wardains*) appointed by the count
and the scabini of Ghent, Bruges, and Ypres, and by the duke
and the scabini of Louvain, Brussels, and Antwerp, that all differences between the two parties or their subjects were to be settled by the arbitration of ten men, of whom four were to be taken
from among the councillors of the duke and of the count, and one
from each of the six towns of Ghent, Bruges, Ypres, Louvain,
Brussels, and Antwerp, and that the deputies and their princes
were to meet three times each year, a fortnight after Candlemas
at Ghent, a fortnight after St. John the Baptist's Day at Brussels,
and a fortnight after All Saints' Day at Alost.[135]

Confirmation followed in due course. On the 11th the deputies
of the duke, accompanied by the scabinus, John de Bake, the captain, William van Huse, the dean, John vander Vloet, and Thomas
van Vaernewijc passed until the 31st from town to town in Flanders and in Brabant to secure formal acceptance from all. From
January 21 to February 3, 1340, another delegation composed of
Simon Parijs, Lievin van Wettere, Segher Seghers, and Thomas
van Vaernewijc was sent to Vilvoorde to secure the final approval
of the nobility and towns of Brabant.[136]

V. Edward's Financial Difficulties at Antwerp
(November, 1339 — January, 1340)

When Edward returned to Antwerp to meet his allies in conference on the day after St. Martin's,[137] two serious problems confronted him: a satisfactory settlement of the debts contracted
with most of the important princes in the Low Countries, and provision for defense of these parts, especially Brabant and Hainault,

---

[135] See A. Verkooren, *Inventaire, Brabant,* II, 71–85, for an analysis,
description, and references to the printed document.

[136] N. de Pauw en J. Vuylsteke, *Rekeningen der Stad Gent,* I, 406, 407,
410, 411, 412, 414, 415; Boendale, *Van den derden Eduwaert,* p. 335.

[137] Avesbury, p. 306; Knighton, II, 9, 13; Murimuth, p. 116.

against the vindictive spite of Philip. Until these could be settled it would be rash to return to England, and efforts were accordingly made to give at least temporary satisfaction.

Edward was especially obligated to the duke of Brabant. At Épinlieu-lez-Mons on September 13 he had given him letters promising payment of 100,000 Florentine florins in three instalments, for which were named as pledges the archbishop of Canterbury, the bishops of Lincoln and Durham, the earls of Derby, Northampton, Salisbury, and Suffolk, Henry de Ferrariis, and John Darcy.[138] Before the end of the year Edward was owing the duke a still larger additional debt of 207,000 Florentine florins which he had promised to pay at the following Easter.[139] That Edward should seek to treat Duke John with the greatest circumspection was only natural. Brabant was still important as a base of operations against France, especially because Count William of Hainault, Holland, and Zeeland could not be relied upon to give any effectual aid. But more than this factor must have weighed the fact that when van Artevelde failed in his maneuvers with Philip and a rupture was imminent, Flanders could rely only upon Duke John and the English for assistance in warding off a blow by the king of France.

Duke John keenly felt the dangers to which he was exposed. On December 4 Edward authorized him to raise and equip at his expense for the space of one year a force of a thousand men-at-arms, and, in case of need, a second thousand. Edward allayed the duke's fear for his security during his absence by promising to return to Brabant or Guelders by the Day of St. John the Baptist and remain in the Low Countries until all promises in the matter of alliance, debts, and other matters had been fully carried out. The earls of Derby and Salisbury were to be left in the Low Countries as pledges and the earls of Suffolk and Northampton were to join them by Laetare Sunday.[140] Meanwhile Edward gave proof of his gratitude toward the abbey of St. Michael at Antwerp where Philippa had found hospitality and where his son Lionel was born in October, 1339, and baptized.[141] On December

---

[138] A. Verkooren, *Inventaire, Brabant,* II, 69–70.
[139] *Ibid.,* pp. 88–89.
[140] *Ibid.,* pp. 86–87.
[141] *Auctor Bridlingtoniensis,* p. 140; *Annales Paulini,* p. 369.

19 he granted the abbot the advowson of the church at Thyngden in the diocese of Lincoln and ordered his officials to provide prompt execution of this order.[142]

On December 28 Duke John finally performed homage and swore fealty as Edward's vassal and received a life annuity of 1,500*l*. sterling, payable in equal amounts at Easter and Michaelmas.[143]   Six days before this, Otto, seignior of Cuyk and Heverle, chief councillor of the duke,[144] was given a similar annuity of 250*l*. sterling payable in the same manner, and an additional annual sum of 3,000 Florentine florins in compensation for his wife's loss of properties in France until restoration could be effected.[145] A difference of opinion arose regarding some claim upon the king which the duke now presented.   It amounted to 70,000*l*. sterling and the royal representatives were willing to allow only 60,000*l*. The matter was left to the decision of the earl of Salisbury and Otto, seignior of Cuyk.   On December 28 this case also came to an end, but only 50,000*l*. were now assigned to the duke, payable in three equal instalments at Michaelmas, 1340, Easter, and Michaelmas of the following year.   At the same time Henry Berthout, seignior of Duffel and Geyle, became his vassal for a consideration of twenty-four pounds annually.[146]   On January 1, Philip Mereward, a burgess of Brussels, referred to as the king's yeoman, was promised five sacks of wool of the first of the year's clipping.[147]

Edward's faithful coadjutor, his brother-in-law, William, margrave of Juliers, also received consideration.   On November 28, Edward issued a document reciting the manifold services which he had rendered.   It promised him an earldom in the English peerage and an annuity of a thousand pounds sterling.   The margrave of Juliers was about to visit the emperor in Edward's behalf for which along with other diplomatic endeavors he was to receive eight pounds sterling daily and an additional sum for his

[142] *Foedera*, II (2), 1102; *CPR* (1338–40), pp. 141–145.

[143] *Foedera*, II (2), 1103.

[144] He was styled " summus domini ducis Brabantiae conciliarius " in a papal document of July, 1343. See U. Berlière, *Suppliques de Clément VI (1342–1352)*, p. 99.

[145] *Foedera*, II (2), 1102.

[146] *Ibid.*, pp. 1103–1104.

[147] *CPR* (1338–40), p. 407.

attendants.[148] On December 8 the king promised to pay him 7,000 Florentine florins with the shield by the beginning of Lent for services in the late campaign and 20,000 small gold florins for losses of horses, followers, and equipment.[149] The margrave's household servant, Tilman de Werda, referred to as king's clerk, was granted ten pounds yearly at the Exchequer on the 19th.[150]

Not less deserving was his other brother-in-law, Reginald, duke of Guelders. When he complained that goods belonging to his subjects had been stolen by some of Edward's men, the king on October 26 started immediate investigation and ordered his officials to render prompt satisfaction.[151] On December 3, James de Lijven, a domestic of Reginald's household, was named sergeant of the king's arms and declared entitled to the pension usually granted holders of this rank. At Reginald's request Edward on December 16 granted the burgesses of Harderwijk while sojourning in England immunity from arrest of their goods for the debts of any other persons.[152]

In August Edward owed Reginald 52,750 Florentine florins for expenses incurred in his services; but payment was out of the question, and on the 21st he promised to pay this sum in two instalments at Candlemas and at St. John the Baptist's Day of 1341. Edward promised to send to Nijmegen as pledges his chief councillors, the archbishop of Canterbury, the bishops of Lincoln and Durham, the earls of Derby, Northampton, Salisbury, and Suffolk, Henry de Ferrariis, John Darcy, John de Tybcost, and John of Hainault and John of Valkenburg. But it appears that Reginald did not insist upon this and the parties never left Edward's presence.[153] This situation may well have caused some financial embarrassment, for Reginald borrowed 157*l.* old Tournois from burgesses of Louvain, Brussels, and Antwerp for which he pledged incomes from Nijmegen, the Rijk van Nijmegen, the tolls at Venloo, the tolls and fisheries at Zutfen, and the tolls at Lobith

[148] *Foedera,* II (2), 1099.

[149] *Ibid.,* p. 1101.

[150] *CPR* (1338–40), p. 374.

[151] I. A. Nijhoff, *Gedenkwaardigheden uit de Geschiedenis van Gelderland,* I, 408–410; *CCR* (1339–41), pp. 401–402.

[152] *CPR* (1338–40), pp. 401–402.

[153] I. A. Nijhoff, *Gedenkwaardigheden uit de Geschiedenis van Gelderland,* I, 399–402.

and Doesburg, and bound himself to indemnify his towns which had affixed their seals to the documents. These were Guelders, Zutfen, Roermond, Nijmegen, Arnhem, Harderwijk, Emmerich, Zaltbommel, Goch, and Venloo.[154] Apparently he even guaranteed a loan of money made by John van Arkel and three money changers of Mechelen for the use of John, duke of Brabant, who on November 1 promised to indemnify him for all losses which he might incur.[155]

Nor had Edward paid the 5,000 Florentine florins to the burgesses of Cologne as he had promised to do on St. John the Baptist's Day, 1339, for which Duke Reginald had acted as guarantor. On January 4 he bound himself to pay this sum at the following Day of St. John the Baptist.[156] All other debts incurred in advancing Edward's interests since his arrival in the Low Countries until Easter following were also to be paid at that time.[157] On February 6 an itemized account was drawn up at Ghent, totalling about 62,900 Florentine florins which covered expenses incurred by the invasion of Thiérache. This was to be paid on the Day of St. John the Baptist or on the octave thereof.[158] That Reginald was reduced to sore financial straits would appear from the fact that in March he requested his councillor, the seignior of Meurs, to act as surety for loans advanced to him by some Lombards.[159] In these transactions Duke Reginald revealed a splendid loyalty toward his brother-in-law, for it was probable that Edward would fail to meet all these obligations on June 24. On May 31 Duke Reginald and John of Hainault promised to coöperate in securing satisfaction for these debts.[160]

To Thierry of Valkenburg, whose losses in the Cambrésis and Thiérache also had to be settled, Edward delivered a bond on December 31 promising payment of 30,000 gold Florentine florins on June 24 and October 1.[161] On November 17 Ruprecht, count of

---

[154] I. A. Nijhoff, *Gedenkwaardigheden uit de Geschiedenis van Gelderland,* I, 404–406.   [155] *Ibid.,* p. 410.

[156] *Ibid.,* pp. 396–397, 411; *Foedera,* II (2), 151–152.

[157] I. A. Nijhoff, *Gedenkwaardigheden uit de Geschiedenis van Gelderland,* I, 412; *Foedera,* II (2), 152.

[158] I. A. Nijhoff, *Gedenkwaardigheden uit de Geschiedenis van Gelderland,* I, 413–414; *Foedera,* II (2), 1108.

[159] I. A. Nijhoff, *Gedenkwaardigheden uit de Geschiedenis van Gelderland,* I, 416.

[160] *Ibid.,* pp. 418–419.   [161] *CPR* (1338–40), p. 404.

Virneburg, was promised 1,500 Florentine florins on the following Feast of the Purification (February 2).[162] But these sums, long overdue, were in most cases entirely in payment of past services. To raise money to continue his stay in the Low Countries and extend his power through diplomatic endeavors with the Flemings required additional sums and Edward and his councillors cudgeled their wits to raise sufficient funds to meet their most pressing obligations until their return to England.

It was agreed during the conferences at Antwerp that at least 40,000*l.* sterling should be raised by contracting loans from the king's subjects. On the 22d Bartholomew de Burghersh, William de Keldesby, William de Cusancia, and Robert Askeby were commissioned to secure this sum.[163] They were successful, for a large number of bonds, some of which were as high as a thousand pounds, were given to his merchants with promise of speedy repayment, mostly at Purification.[164] The Almain merchants, the Clyppings, the de Woldes (de Silva), and Spissenaghel, who had been favored by Edward in the export of wool, also loaned money.[165] John, son of Simon de Gandavo, Lambert del Corve, and John Borky, burgesses of Ghent, loaned a thousand pounds.[166]

But it would be useless to catalogue all these transactions with the Hansa merchants and the Lombards. Evidently the king was fairly well satisfied with the amount thus secured, for on December 14 he instructed his chancellor and treasurer to provide prompt payment at Candlemas.[167] But these measures were hardly sufficient; the Bardi and Peruzzi had to be satisfied as well. Edward arranged these matters before leaving Antwerp for Ghent on January 26. William de la Pole offered to back the king with his own money and secure credit for the royal needs. The great and petty customs at Newcastle, Hartlepool, Kingston, Boston, Lynn, Yarmouth, Ipswich, Sandwich, London, Southampton, Chichester, Exeter, Winchelsea, and Bristol were given him until complete repayment should be effected. With Reginald de Conductu he was commissioned to treat with the Bardi and Pe-

---

[162] *Foedera,* II (2), 1098.
[163] *CPR* (1338–40), p. 398.
[164] *Ibid.,* pp. 375–376, 401–403, 405–406.
[165] *Ibid.,* pp. 400–401; *CCR* (1339–41), p. 313.
[166] *CPR* (1338–40), p. 408.
[167] E. Déprez, *Les Préliminaires de la Guerre de Cent Ans,* p. 285 (note).

ruzzi and the creditors of Mechelen, offering the money to be derived from the sale of the wool brought from England for the king's use.[168]

VI. The Anglo–Flemish Alliance (January, 1340)

The situation in Flanders during the closing months of 1339 was such as to make necessary the presence of Edward in the Low Countries, even if his financial difficulties had not prevented his return to England. Philip's continued antagonism to van Artevelde's activities and the failure to secure Count Louis' support by the prospect of getting back Lille, Douai, Orchies, Béthune, and Artois made it impossible to continue the old policy. This was clearly perceived when van Artevelde advanced the proposal for the return of the lost territories and even supported it by threat of force. When this failed a closer understanding with Edward and his allies was inevitable. The alliance of December 3 with the duke of Brabant was equivalent to an agreement with the English king. It is instructive to note at this point that the chronicler, Gilles le Muisit, speaks of this treaty and of those made with the Flemings early in 1340 in the same passage and as if they were framed at the same time.[169] Dire necessity of maintaining the economic interests of the towns of Flanders now urged van Artevelde to enter into an alliance with Edward.

The scabini of Ghent and Bruges were in constant communication with Edward. John de Coster had returned from his presence in Brabant on the 28th and was sent to Antwerp on November 11 and returned on the 13th,[170] the day after Edward had opened his conferences with his allies. It is a striking fact that on this very day the earl of Salisbury, Henry de Ferrariis, Galfridus le Scrope, and Mauritius de Berkele, were authorized to offer a matrimonial connection between the count's oldest son and Edward's daughter

[168] *CPR* (1338–40), p. 408.

[169] Le Muisit, pp. 120–121: " Anno m° trecentesimo nono, in festo Purificationis beate Marie erat comes Flandriae in Gandavo et tres ville, et tota patria Flandrensis, et obediebat omnes Jacobo de Artevelde. Et tunc dux Brabantie et comes Hannonie, et consilium tocius patrie, pepigerunt fedus ad invicem et juraverunt omnes ferre auxilium regi Anglie contra regem Francie, quem vocabunt Philippum de Valois."

[170] Avesbury, p. 306; N. de Pauw en J. Vuylsteke, *Rekeningen der Stad Gent*, I, 403–404; *Ms. Rekeningen*, Bruges, *1338–1339* folio 108 verso.

Isabella, settle all matters in respect to dowry etc., propose an alliance which would restore to the count the possessions taken from his predecessors by the kings of France, and terminate the right to invoke the sentence of excommunication and interdict at the instance of the king of France.[171] In accordance with the request of Ghent, Bruges, and Ypres, he granted protection to all merchants coming to Flanders from Castile and Majorca.[172]

These facts reveal the situation clearly. The scabini of Ghent, van Artevelde, and the Council of Flanders were still hoping to secure the adherence of Count Louis to the interests of Flanders. The latter had taken part in the negotiations with the duke of Brabant at Dendermonde. He was carefully watched,[173] and all his acts were dictated by the Council of Flanders, dominated of course by the genius of van Artevelde. Externally it appeared that he approved these policies, and it was apparently for this reason that Edward on the 15th issued other letters whereby John, duke of Brabant, and the earl of Suffolk were entrusted with the same task as Salisbury and his associates had been on the 13th. One new clause was added to these instructions; they were to arrange for compensation for the losses inflicted by the English on Cadzand in November, 1337.[174]

The suggestion that Edward who already claimed the crown of France should assume its title was made, it appears, by van Artevelde and his followers.[175] The example of William de Deken in 1328 may well have suggested the idea.[176] Van Artevelde apparently expected the full support of Count Louis as late as the middle of January and evidently thought that Edward's title of King of France would give Louis the necessary legal basis for accepting the lost territories. Thus would be solved the great problem of

---

[171] *Foedera*, II (2), 1097. [172] *CPR* (1338–40), pp. 396–397.

[173] For his impotence at this moment, see *Chronicon Comitum Flandrensium*, p. 211; de Budt, p. 397.

[174] *Foedera*, II (2), 1097; *CPR* (1338–40), p. 397.

[175] G. Gorrini, " Lettere inedite degli Ambasciatori Fiorenini alla Corte dei Papi in Avignone (Anno 1340)," *Archivio Storico Italiano*, 4th Ser., XIV (1884), 164–165: " Volunt etiam Flandrenses ipsi quod idem rex Anglie rex Francie nuncupetur et ejus portet insignia, que ut fertur rex Anglie jam fieri fecit, videlicet pro medietate ad sua insignia, et pro alia dimidietate ad insignia regis Francorum."

[176] H. Pirenne, " La premier Tentative faite pour Reconnaître Édouard III d'Angleterre comme Roi de France," *Annales de la Société d'Histoire et d'Archéologie de Gand*, V (1902), 5–11.

Philip's hostility which would secure for the towns continued prosperity and the abrogation of the right to excommunicate the Flemings and place the county under the interdict. These matters were discussed with Edward at the moment when the negotiations with Philip's men at Lille and Menin failed. Exactly at the moment of the conference at Antwerp, which began on the 12th, Edward issued his instructions whereby he suggested to Count Louis the return of the lost territories.[176a]

Rather than desert his suzerain to whom he had promised lifelong fidelity, Count Louis preferred to lose forever the lands taken by Philip the Fair. As negotiations with the duke of Brabant progressed he meditated escape. But only by a ruse could this be effected. He was submissive in all things and appears to have inspired the feeling that his loyalty was quite genuine. He asked the countess who was staying at Mézières on the Meuse to feign illness and request him to come to her. This was done before he affixed his seal to the document drawn up in Ghent on December 3. On the 4th Edward authorized the duke to equip at his expense a thousand men-at-arms to be used against the French in case of need. Only flight could save his honor, and when the countess' letters came, he had them read in the presence of the Flemings. He begged to be allowed to go to her bedside and promised to return to Flanders at once. He had so ingratiated himself with the scabini and the councillors that they consented, but he betook himself to Paris.[177]

When it was learned that Count Louis did not intend to return as he had promised, Simon van Halen was named guardian (*ruwaard*) of Flanders. This cannot have been before the 21st when the messenger sent to Count Louis in Paris returned.[178] Influential because of his vast wealth and esteemed for his excellent character, van Halen enjoyed the respect of all Flemings.[179]

[176a] *Foedera*, II (2), 1097.

[177] *Chronicon Comitum Flandrensium*, p. 211; de Budt, p. 326; *Chronographia*, II, 88–89. This chronology is based upon the fact that a messenger, sent by the scabini from Ghent to Count Louis in Paris, returned to them on December 21. See N. de Pauw en J. Vuylsteke, *Rekeningen der Stad Gent*, I, 431.

[178] The first mention of this title occurs on February 13. See N. de Pauw en J. Vuylsteke, *Rekeningen der Stad Gent*, I, 402 (note 2).

[179] See the words of le Muisit, p. 172: " . . . homo potentissimus in auro et argento, et in quo Flamingi summopere confidebant."

He was of course well known to Edward whom he had visited in behalf of the interests of Ghent. In January, 1339, he had received a pension from him, and had loaned him in his great need at Antwerp 1,500*l.* sterling.[180] He had affixed his seal to the treaty with Brabant,[181] and, accompanied by the premier scabinus, Simon Parijs, at once went to Antwerp to confer with Edward.[182]

The duke of Brabant played a prominent rôle in the negotiations which now took place. He appeared in Ghent on about the 18th of January at the request of the scabini.[183] For the first time during the war he was active in Edward's behalf. His cultivation of the Flemings and his efforts in behalf of King Edward's assumption of the French crown had an ulterior purpose. As king of France Edward would not harm him seriously, for his lands were situated within the confines of the empire. The economic arrangements would be of vast benefit to his subjects, and a solution of the divided control over Mechelen, undertaken with Count Louis but never sanctioned by Philip, might now be secured.

It is impossible to trace the progress of the negotiations with any detail. On January 4 Edward issued new letters [184] to the earl of Salisbury, Henry de Ferrariis, and Galfridus le Scrope, ordering them to arrange the marriage of his daughter to Count Louis' son, negotiate an alliance with the Flemings, secure the reversion of the lost territories and the abolition of the right of enforcing the royal will through interdict and excommunication, and settle certain financial matters.[185] He also notified the scabini of the three towns that he wished to leave to their judgment the proper settlement of the losses inflicted by his subjects on the island of Cadzand.[186] It appears that Edward's title to the crown was discussed at Bruges on the 9th.[187] Only in the documents as finally drawn up

---

[180] *CPR* (1338–40), pp. 375–376.

[181] A. Verkooren, *Inventaire, Brabant,* II, 74.

[182] N. de Pauw en J. Vuylsteke, *Rekeningen der Stad Gent,* I, 405–406.

[183] *Ibid.,* p. 407.

[184] *CPR* (1338–40), pp. 377–378.

[185] *Foedera,* II (2), 1105–1106.

[186] *CPR* (1338–40), p. 406.

[187] Kervyn, *Oeuvres de Froissart,* III, 221 (note), quoting from the *Rekeningen* of Bruges, 1340, folio 2. Kervyn assumed that the *Protestatio Flandrensium quod illustri rege Francorum defuncto sine liberis Eduardo regis Anglorum tanquam legitimo successori adherere intendebant* (*Pièces*

can the chief points in these discussions be traced. Of these there were three, each containing a separate group of agreements.

The first dealt with economic matters which concerned both Flanders and Brabant. Edward promised that the staple of wool would be maintained in one or the other; striped and other cloth of each would be allowed to enter his realms freely; that all manner of merchandise or products could be exported or imported after Pentecost at the old accustomed rates, and until that date at the rates which subjects of each were now paying; instruments and means of credit were to be carefully maintained and enforced; privileges formerly granted to Flemings were to be confirmed; no separate peace, truce, or negotiations were to be undertaken without the knowledge of the Flemings; Flemings and Brabançons were to be given the king's special protection; prompt aid would be given if at any time the Flemings should be threatened with punishment for their acts against Philip; in case of his own death before the termination of the war, his heir would cross over and take up the defense; and, finally, that no individual Flemings should ever be punished for the debts of any corporation in Flanders.[188]

The second document set forth the points which Edward as king of France conceded to the Flemings. All ecclesiastical processes instituted against them by the Holy See at the instance of the kings of France were declared annulled and no fortifications were to be erected; Lille, Douai, Béthune, Orchies, and Tournai, with their castleries and appertaining rights, and also the county of Artois, were to be returned to them; the privileges in force at the time of Count Robert (1305–1322) and since were to be retained; no obligation, financial or otherwise, was to be imposed in Flanders by the king of France, nor were Flemings to be prosecuted in any court in France outside the county; Brabant and Flanders were to be free to make regulations as they might wish touching the importation of wool from England; there was to be struck a common coinage with varying legends for each country, which was to be legal tender in Brabant, Flanders, and

---

Justificatives), pp. 596–602, was drawn up at this time. But this document must be dated after the interdict and excommunication had been declared.

[188] Kervyn, *Histoire de Flandre*, III (*Pièces Justificatives*), **603–610**; *CPR* (1338–40), pp. 512–516.

France; the subjects of the county and duchy were to have the king's special protection; there was to be prompt settlement in case merchants dwelling outside Brabant and Flanders in France should fail to make payment; and, finally, no Fleming was to be arrested in France for the debts of any town, castlery, or other corporation in Flanders.[189]

In the third document were promised the payments to be made to the Flemings. Edward agreed to give 140,000*l.* sterling to the three towns of Ghent, Bruges, and Ypres, two sums of 30,000*l.* each at Mid-Lent and Pentecost of 1340, and two sums of 40,000*l.* each at Pentecost of 1341 and 1342. To protect the commerce and shipping in the narrow seas, a navy was to be provided at Edward's expense, equipped with a sufficient number of men, one third to be English, two thirds Brabançons and Flemings, or all Flemings. Finally, the staple of English wool and merchandise was to be established for fifteen years at Bruges where it was then located.[190] There undoubtedly was prolonged discussion, but the details have not been preserved.

The die was already cast before Count Louis arrived in Paris, which, as we saw, must have been early in December. The earnest appeal of Benedict XII to the corporations of Ghent, Bruges, and Ypres, which was made at the frightened request of King Philip, could have no effect. On January 8 he wrote to the scabini and councillors of the three towns begging them to bear well in mind that Flanders, a land so populous and filled with so many great towns, stood in great need of the king's grace and that without it its commerce and industry would be at an end, its food-stuffs fail, and prosperity cease. He begged them to remember the severe penalties which had been imposed upon the people for their previous rebellions.[191] But security of their economic life weighed more with the Flemings than the idea of loyalty to their natural lord. Benedict also wrote to the clergy of Flanders requesting them to induce the people to remain loyal.[192] He also besought

---

[189] Kervyn, *Histoire de Flandre,* III (*Pièces Justificatives*), 613–618; *CPR* (1338–40), pp. 511–512. Cf. le Bel, I, 166.

[190] Kervyn, *Histoire de Flandre,* III (*Pièces Justificatives*), 610–612. See also Boendale, *Brabantsche Yeesten,* I, 562; *Breve Chronicon,* p. 8; le Bel, I, 167–168; *Grandes Chroniques,* V, 378–379; Baker, p. 6.

[191] A. Fierens, *Lettres de Benoît XII (1334–1342),* Nos. 614–616.

[192] *Ibid.,* No. 617.

the rival kings to arrange a truce.   On December 12 he urged the
queen of France to labor for peace, and on the 23d begged both
Edward and Philip to hearken to his earnest solicitations.[193]
Three days before this, Edward had given safe-conduct to the cardinals, Peter and Bertrand, who were going to Valenciennes to discuss the matter of peace, and, on January 2, appointed the bishop
of Lincoln, the earls of Derby and Salisbury, William de Exonia,
professor of theology, and Alexander de Oneby, professor of civil
law, to meet them.[194]   But, as so often before, these endeavors
were doomed to failure.

Meanwhile plans were being perfected to receive Edward in
Ghent when solemn ratification of what had been negotiated
would take place.   On January 26 Edward, accompanied by
Philippa and her two sons, Reginald, duke of Guelders, John,
duke of Brabant, his council and household, and many others, arrived and were accorded a most splendid reception.[195]   The royal
family took up its abode in the abbey of St. Bavo and special
guard was posted for them.[196]   Two vats of wine, valued at 250*l.*,
three choice cloths, one red striped, one brown, and one clipped,
valued at 272*l.*, were presented to the king by the scabini.[197]   Van
Artevelde with his colleagues and deans of the guilds went about
the town, attended by seventy-three special men-at-arms taken
from the guilds.[198]   On this same day Edward issued letters
giving Guy, bastard brother of Count Louis, his liberty without
demanding ransom.[199]

On the day of the king's arrival occurred the brilliant scene

---

[193] G. Daumet, *Benoît XII (1334–1342). Lettres Closes, Patentes et
Curiales se rapportant à la France*, Nos. 669–671.

[194] *Foedera*, II (2), 1104; *CPR* (1338–40), pp. 402, 407. See E. Déprez,
Les Préliminaires de la Guerre de Cent Ans, pp. 274–277; G. Gorrini, " Let-
tere inedite delle Ambasciatori Fiorentini alla Corte dei Papi in Avignone
(Anno 1340)," *Archivio Storico Italiano*, 4th Ser., XIV (1884), 116.

[195] For documents issued at Antwerp and Ghent on January 26, see
CPR (1338–40), p. 408, and *Foedera*, II (2), 1107. For the literary references,
see *Chronographia*, II, 89–90; Avesbury, pp. 308–309; Murimuth, p. 103;
Knighton, II, 14; *Lanercost*, p. 332; Froissart, I, 186–187. See N. de Pauw
en J. Vuylsteke, *Rekeningen der Stad Gent*, I, 433, for the services of
Persemiere, the official trumpeter.

[196] N. de Pauw en J. Vuylsteke, *Rekeningen der Stad Gent*, I, 463.

[197] *Ibid.*, p. 384; Froissart, I, 481.

[198] N. de Pauw en J. Vuylsteke, *Rekeningen der Stad Gent*, I, 463.

[199] *Foedera*, II (2), 1107. On May 7 Walter de Manny was indemnified
by a royal grant of 8,000*l.* See *ibid.*, p. 1123.

on the Friday Market Place. The square had been cleared and specially prepared for the occasion.[200] Of what happened and the order of events we have a very excellent description which is based upon the reports of eye-witnesses.[201] Edward with his councillors and barons appeared with van Artevelde and the captains, the deans of the guilds, the scabini of Ghent, Bruges,[202] and Ypres, and undoubtedly also the Council of Flanders, and the public of Ghent, which the square could perhaps accommodate in large part. Edward then asked whether they all recognized him as king of France and England and would swear to do what they had hitherto been wont to do for the king of France. There was some solemn and formal discussion, and then Guy of Flanders, now in full possession of his freedom, did homage as well as all the scabini and the public standing about.[203] As king of France, their suzerain Edward swore with hand resting upon the Scriptures to maintain their privileges and protect them from their enemies.

The terms of the three treaties were then read and proclaimed. The lands taken from Flanders (*residuum Flandriae*) were declared " restored." These were Lille, Douai, Béthune, Tournai, and other places, which expression must be taken to mean their castleries and the county of Artois. In spite of the fact that Count Louis' son was in Paris beyond reach of the Flemings, it was hoped that his marriage to Edward's daughter might yet be consummated. The title of these recovered possessions was to be vested in the count's son.[204] On this occasion also Edward solemnly quartered the lilies of France with the leopards of England. A tailor, according to Froissart, made a tunic provided with this device for the king's use.[205]

---

[200] N. de Pauw en J. Vuylsteke, *Rekeningen der Stad Gent,* I, 452, 461.

[201] G. Gorrini, " Lettere inedite degli Ambasciatori Fiorentini alla Corte dei Papi in Avignone (Anno 1340)," *Archivio Storico Italiano,* 4th Ser., XIV (1884), 116; H. Pirenne, " Documents relatifs à l'Histoire de Flandre pendant la première Moitié du XIVᵉ Siècle," *BCRH,* 5th Ser., VII (1897), 30.

[202] *Ms. Rekeningen,* Bruges, *1338–1339,* folio 113 recto.

[203] Le Muisit, pp. 120–121.

[204] G. Gorrini, " Lettere inedite degli Ambasciatori Fiorentini alla Corte dei Papi in Avignone," *Archivio Storico Italiano,* 4th Ser., XIV (1884), 162–163.

[205] Le Bel, I, 164; de Nangis, II, 165–184; *Chronographia,* II, p. 80; *Chronique des Quatre Valois,* p. 7; Froissart, I, 186–187; Murimuth, p. 103; Knighton, II, 14; *Lanercost,* p. 332; *Scalacronica,* p. 170.

The next step was to confirm the treaties in similar fashion in the other towns of Flanders. But Edward did not care to take this trouble, and resolved to delegate this task to Reginald, duke of Guelders, who was probably proclaimed *gubernator totius Flandriae* and empowered to act in his behalf. Associated with him were the earl of Northampton and Otto, seignior of Cuyk.[206] This was put into immediate execution; on January 29, the scabinus, Baldwin vanden Walle, Segher Seghers, John van Lovene, and Edward's representatives set out for Bruges where on the 31st was enacted a scene much like that on the Friday Market Place on the 26th. This was also done at Ypres before the 3d of February, for by that day the deputies from Ghent had already returned home. The less important places were required to confirm by oath the treaties with England. From February 6 to 8 William van Vaernewijc, John de Visch, and Peter vanden Hovene were sent for this purpose into the Quatuor Officia and a few days later into Waasland.[207]

Since his arrival in Ghent, Edward had been forced to give attention to the pope's earnest entreaties for peace. The two cardinals appeared before him shortly after his assumption of the French crown and prospects of success appeared scant.[208] On January 30 Edward drew up for the pope a statement of his rights which, he declared, he did not purpose to abandon in the least.[209] This was followed on February 8 by a solemn declaration again setting forth his rights, complaining of the unjust bearing of Philip in keeping from him his titles, preventing him from going on the crusade, supporting the rebel Scots, and inflicting severe injuries upon the coast towns of his realm and of Aquitaine.[210]

---

[206] *Foedera*, II (2), 1107; E. Déprez, *Les Préliminaires de la Guerre de Cent Ans*, p. 281. Cf. *Chronographia*, II, 90, which errs here.

[207] N. de Pauw en J. Vuylsteke, *Rekeningen der Stad Gent*, I, 408–409; G. Gorrini, " Lettere inedite degli Ambasciatori Fiorentini alla Corte dei Papi in Avignone (Anno 1340)," *Archivio Storico Italiano*, 4th Ser., XIV (1884), 162–163; H. Pirenne, " Documents relatifs à l'Histoire de Flandre pendant la première Moitié du XIVe Siècle," *BCRH*, 5th Ser., VII (1897), XII (1897), 30, 32.

[208] G. Gorrini, " Lettere inedite degli Ambasciatori Fiorentini alla Corte dei Papi in Avignone (Anno 1340)," *Archivio Storico Italiano*, 4th Ser., XIV (1884), 163; H. Pirenne, " Documents relatifs à l'Histoire de Flandre pendant la première Moitié du XIII e Siècle," *BCRH*, 5th Ser., VII (1897), 33.

[209] *Foedera*, II (2), 1107–1108.   [210] *Ibid.*, pp. 1109–1110.

The inhabitants of France were invited to follow the example of the Flemings in receiving their true suzerain.[211] All who obeyed were guaranteed the king's special protection. Letters requesting their adherence were addressed to the communes of Flanders which had just been returned to the count. These included Lille, Douai, Béthune, Tournai, Arras, Aire, St. Omer, and others.[212] But all of French Flanders remained firm; even Flemish St. Omer, where the adherents of the count were well intrenched, made no response.

John, duke of Brabant, was in a position to profit at once from the rupture of the Flemings with Philip. The three towns now needed his support and could not oppose him in the matter of Mechelen. On March 30 the duke issued letters declaring that he had taken into his hands full control over the town for the duration of the war with the king of France. Nothing was said in them of the rights of the count of Flanders. The duke obviously intended to force Philip to permit these titles to pass into his hands when negotiations for peace or possible alliance should be opened. The fact that he referred in the document to Philip as king of France when he was allied with the Flemings and Edward who claimed the throne of France clearly revealed his intention to seek a *rapprochement* with him when the opportune moment should arrive.[212a]

VII. Internal Problems in Flanders (Spring, 1340)

THE alliance with the duke of Brabant who had invaded France, the repudiation of Philip as legitimate sovereign, and the economic and military treaties with Edward greatly displeased a large part of the Flemish nobility and their adherents.[213] Antagonisms at once became more acute and the scabini of Ghent were forced to take active measures. Even some of the scabini at Bruges ob-

---

[211] *Ibid.*, p. 1111; *Istore et Croniques*, I, 377, 575, 615.

[212] *Istore et Croniques*, I, 377–378; A. Wauters, *Table Chronologique*, X, 8.

[212a] J. David, *Geschiedenis van de Stad en de Heerlykheid van Mechelen*, pp. 513–514 (*Bylagen*).

[213] G. Gorrini, " Lettere inedite degli Ambasciatori Fiorentini alla Corte dei Papi in Avignone (Anno 1340)," *Archivio Storico Italiano*, 4th Ser., XIV (1884), 163: " Tamen predicta displicent bonis hominibus Flandrie, et videtur eis quod ista sunt puerilia."

jected to this radical step, and on February 13, which marked the
end of the official year, the captain William van Huse, accompanied by Peter vander Asselt, was sent thither armed with commissions from Simon van Halen, the *ruwaard* of Flanders, to aid
in appointing the new scabini.[214]   There was similar opposition
at Grammont whither van Huse and Peter vanden Hovene went
on the 28th for the same purpose.[215]   Inclination to resist seemed
to increase as the scabini of Ghent everywhere actively sought to
induce all the towns to ratify the accord with the duke of Brabant.   From February 22 to 28 John van Lovene proceeded to
Bruges, Ypres, and other places for this purpose,[216] and special
messengers were sent to the castlery of Courtrai and to Alost,
Damme, Dendermonde, the Quatuor Officia, and the Frank of
Bruges, to cause representatives to come to Ghent and affix the
seals of their towns to the documents.[217]   Early in March van
Lovene was at Oudenaarde.[218]   Then from March 4 to 16 the
scabinus, Simon Parijs, and the clerk, John uten Hove, accompanied by representatives from Bruges and Ypres, went to Brussels to settle some further formalities regarding the treaty.[219]
On the 18th the clerk, Jacob Bette, went to Bruges, Ypres, and
other towns, and early in April, John van Lovene and John Wal-
raven went to Alost with the final documents.[220]

There was active opposition in various quarters.   Members of
the family of Beveren had for some time made themselves especially obnoxious, and, when some of them were incarcerated at
Ath, a delegation from the scabini of Ghent at the close of February besought William, count of Hainault, Holland, and Zeeland,
to exact justice.   Hard pressed by the French in March and April,
and forced to look to the Flemings and the duke of Brabant for
aid, he ordered them beheaded.[221]   In May the scabini again requested Count William to apply remedy in the case of John
Sceede who had harmed some people from the castlery of Ghent.[222]
Just before this John van Lovene had been sent to the seignior of
Enghien apparently for a similar reason.[223]   Early in March Peter

[214] N. de Pauw en J. Vuylsteke, *Rekeningen der Stad Gent*, I, 409.

[215] *Ibid.,* p. 411.

[216] *Ibid.,* p. 410.

[217] *Ibid.,* pp. 435–436.

[218] *Ibid.,* p. 411.

[219] *Ibid.,* p. 412.

[220] *Ibid.,* pp. 414, 415.

[221] *Ibid.,* pp. 410, 437.

[222] *Ibid.,* p. 410.

[223] *Ibid.,* p. 417.

vander Asselt and Staas d'Amer caught an important fugitive at Blankenberg and brought him to Ghent,[224] and on the 14th Peter vanden Velde and four men were sent into Waasland to catch an outlaw.[225]   An exile, Wulf de Riddere, was apprehended at Merelbeke,[226] and others were seized at Assenede.[227]   Early in February Baldwin Wenemaar and five white-hoods were sent to Eecloo to confiscate the property of another culprit.[228]   There were special inquests at Baudeloo between March 13 and 17,[229] and at Axel concerning a priest accused of homicide who finally sought refuge in a church whence he could be taken only by a large force under Baldwin Wenemaar and twenty-one white-hoods.[230]

Antagonisms were especially grave in the towns.   At Oostburg there were difficulties at the close of 1339, and in January John de Bake and Simon van Merelbeke, accompanied by men from Bruges, proceeded thither to establish peace.   These efforts were not wholly successful, for on March 21 the scabini of Ghent dispatched Peter vanden Hovene with sixty-two men-at-arms to seize those who refused to go to Ghent as hostages in accordance with a previous agreement.[231]   Poperingen was still engaged in its perennial dispute with Ypres regarding the right to manufacture certain kinds of cloth, and on February 23 the scabini of Ghent sent Baldwin de Puur to bring the contestants to an agreement.[232]   At Bruges there were difficulties among the guilds,[233] and some burghers of Ghent had been killed at Deinze.[234] There was serious difficulty in Sluis at the close of January and Thomas van Vaernewijc was sent there on the 27th, followed by the scabinus, John de Bake, and Peter vanden Hovene to establish peace.[235]   The excesses at Courtrai, which had evoked an inquest, were still unsettled.   On January 29 Simon van Merelbeke and John van Lovene were sent to amend the privileges of the town.[236]   Thus in the country and in the towns there were abundant opposition and difficulty which in many cases may

[224] *Ibid.*, p. 412.
[225] *Ibid.*, p. 413.
[226] *Ibid.*, p. 456.
[227] *Ibid.*, pp. 420, 456.
[228] *Ibid.*, p. 434.
[229] *Ibid.*, p. 413.
[230] *Ibid.*, pp. 413–414.

[231] *Ibid.*, pp. 406, 412–413.
[232] *Ibid.*, p. 411.
[233] *Ibid.*, p. 409.
[234] *Ibid.*, p. 395.
[235] *Ibid.*, p. 408.
[236] *Ibid.*, pp. 411–412.

well have been abetted by the adherents of Count Louis. It is accordingly not strange that the scabini of Saeftingen on March 14 decided that it was impossible to carry out the plans, already of several years' standing, of draining the submerged lands because of the troubled state of the country.[237]

Two closely related problems now confronted the Flemings: the attitude of the pope and the measures which Philip would be sure to take. By the close of January all trade between the French and the Flemings had ceased,[238] and when smuggling developed an order was issued by Philip that all such activity on the border should stop at once.[239] This had of course been foreseen. It was believed by some that the recognition of Edward as king of France would cause a complete cessation of trade in Flanders.[240] But van Artevelde and his party apparently placed the greatest confidence in the treaties with England, which, if carried out, could only give the Flemings greater industrial and commercial prosperity than ever. They at once began to employ force, intrigue, and persuasion when Edward sent his letters to the people of Orchies, Douai, Lille, Béthune, Tournai, and the county of Artois in the hope of inducing them to recognize the English king as their lawful suzerain.[241] At this time, it appears, took place the treasonable conversation between Stephen Canard of Lille and some of van Artevelde's party and members of King Edward's followers who had been left in Flanders.[242]

[237] C. Mussely et E. Molitor, *Cartulaire de l'Ancienne Église Collégiale de Notre Dame à Courtrai*, pp. 244–245, 246.

[238] G. Gorrini, " Lettere inedite degli Ambasciatori Fiorentini alla Corte dei Papi in Avignone (Anno 1340)," *Archivio Storico Italiano*, 4th Ser., XIV (1894), 163: " Nulle autem mercature possunt portari in Franciam, nec reportari in Francia et etiam creditur de personis."

[239] E. Petit, *Histoire des Ducs de Bourgogne*, VII (*Pièces Justificatives*), 282: " A i vallet envolez à Henin porter lettres du roy es esquevinz de Hennin de par mons. de Troynel pour deffense que nul ne passassent en Flandre, et que on ne marcandast point es Flamens. . . ."

[240] G. Gorrini, " Lettere inedite degli Ambasciatori Fiorentini alla Corte dei Papi in Avignone (Anno 1340)," *Archivio Storico Italiano*, 4th Ser., XIV (1884), 163: " Et erunt interdicti ex quo creditur quod multa mala procedant, et quando mercatores et draperii non poterunt huc venire nec alli facient pannos et alia ministeria, isti qui vivunt de lanis et aliis ministeriis non habebunt, unde vivunt et multa inconvenientia commictentur nec talis materia poterit durare."

[241] A. Guesnon, *Documents Inédits sur l'Invasion Anglaise et les États au Temps de Philippe VI et de Jean le Bon,* pp. 11–13.

[242] Kervyn, *Oeuvres de Froissart,* XVII, 130–136.

Benedict's opposition was expected with certainty. The pope's letter of January 8 to the towns and the clergy [243] came too late to influence the Flemings even if they would have been open to his suggestion. Very likely it did not arrive before the dramatic scenes took place on the Friday Market Place in Ghent. On January 30 Edward sent a letter to Benedict once more setting forth his arguments in support of his claim to the French throne. The bearer of this missive was Nicholas de Flisco who was taken into the king's service and was granted for himself, his son, and servant 14s. 3d. daily.[244] Baldwin de Lisseweghe was sent by Bruges [245] and Peter van Orchies by Ghent [246] to request the annulment of the clauses in virtue of which the king could excommunicate the people of Flanders or lay the county under interdict.

The documents which they carried on their persons have apparently been lost, but the argument may perhaps be discovered in an undated document containing no names and apparently used as a form. Philip was not *de jure* king and therefore any ecclesiastical censures pronounced at his instance would of course be null and void.[247] Meanwhile a reply to the pope's letters of January 8 was planned. John de Visch was sent by the scabini of Ghent to Bruges on March 1 to draw up the necessary documents.[248] The scabini of the three towns asked for a safe-conduct from the pope to explain their position in recognizing Edward as their king. But Benedict was hostile and on March 19 informed Philip that the Flemings were not acting in good faith and that in consequence he was loath to grant them their request.[249] On the 5th he had written to Edward urging him not to persist in this step. He begged him to consider the weakness of a title derived through female descent and to ponder well the

[243] A. Fierens, *Lettres de Benoît XII (1334–1342)*, No. 617.

[244] *Foedera*, II(2), 1107. On February 8 he was also charged to hire Genoese galleys. Cf. *ibid.*, p. 111.

[245] *Ms. Rekeningen*, Bruges, *1339–1340*, folio 88.

[246] N. de Pauw en J. Vuylsteke, *Rekeningen der Stad Gent*, I, 436.

[247] Kervyn, *Histoire de Flandre*, III (*Pièces Justificatives*), 596–602. This document is not a declaration on the part of the communes recognizing Edward as true king of France, as Kervyn supposed, but rather a form of an appeal against the ecclesiastical censures later imposed.

[248] N. de Pauw en J. Vuylsteke, *Rekeningen der Stad Gent*, I, 411.

[249] G. Daumet, *Benoît XII (1334–1342). Lettres Closes, Patentes, et Curiales se rapportant à la France*, No. 707; A. Fierens, *Lettres Benoît XII (1334–1342)*, No. 634.

difficulty of overcoming the long and uncontested possession of the French crown by Philip. Furthermore, not much confidence could be placed in the Flemings who had so often been at variance with their natural lords.[250] Under these circumstances the envoys were not shown the least courtesy. Of Baldwin de Lisseweghe nothing further is known, but Peter van Orchies was robbed,[251] and Nicholas de Flisco was arrested near Avignon by the pope's men and thrown into prison.[252]

Meanwhile the clergy of Flanders met at Harelbeke to discuss the situation. On March 16 the scabinus, Simon ser Thomaes, the captain, William van Huse, and John van Lovene were sent by Ghent to request their support in the excommunication and the interdict which were expected and also their adherence to the appeal which would be made.[253] On the 22d these three, with the scabinus, Gilles Rijnvisch, and the clerk, John van Dessele, were sent to Harelbeke for the same purpose.[254] Philip had not been slow to act. On February 17 he sent Étienne de Molinis, professor of civil and canon law, with a complaint to the pope stating that the Flemings had risen in rebellion and that, in consequence of the articles in the Treaty of Athis-sur-Orge, they should receive the stated ecclesiastical penalties. William Clavelli and Thomas Sellarius, apostolic notaries of Lyons and Bayonne respectively, appeared in Tournai and, on April 4, in presence of Robert, bishop of Senlis, Guy, abbot of St. Denis, the archbishop of Rheims, a number of canons of the cathedrals, the official of Tournai, and others, ordered the bishops of Tournai, Thérouanne, Arras, and Cambrai, and all the clergy of their dioceses to declare Flanders under the interdict. On the 5th this was formally carried out.[255]

---

[250] G. Daumet, *Benoît XII (1334–1342), Lettres Closes, Patentes et Curiales se rapportant à la France*, No. 624. Cf. *Foedera*, II (2), 1117.

[251] N. de Pauw en J. Vuylsteke, *Rekeningen der Stad Gent*, I, 436.

[252] G. Daumet, *Benoît XII (1334–1342). Lettres Closes, Patentes et Curiales se rapportant à la France*, Nos. 721, 122. For the case of the imprisonment of Nicholas de Flisco, see *ibid., Introduction, Benoît XII et la Liberté du Saint Siège*, pp. xxxvii–xliii.

[253] N. de Pauw en J. Vuylsteke, *Rekeningen der Stad Gent*, I, 413.

[254] *Ibid.*, p. 415.

[255] P. van Duyse et E. de Busscher, *Inventaire Analytique des Chartes et Documents appartenant aux Archives de la Ville de Gand*, pp. 138–139. It was not to take effect until Easter to give those, who might wish to retract, opportunity to do so. Cf. le Muisit, p. 122, and also de Budt, p. 326; *Chronique des Quatres Premiers, Valois*, pp. 7–8.

But these measures were not universally successful, at least in the towns. At Ghent a priest continued to celebrate mass in St. Nicholas' church for which the scabini granted him a gift of eight pounds.[256] A document in justification of their conduct was at once projected by the Flemings.[257] For this purpose the scabini of Ghent sent Josse Rase to Tournai on April 11,[258] and John van Lovene to Bruges on the 25th.[259] On May 11 Peter van Merelbeke was sent around the ecclesiastical divisions (*dekenien*) of Ghent to bring together the clergy who apparently had to be consulted.[260]

Since December the French had carried fire and sword into Hainault [261] and hostilities were extended along the Flemish border during February and March. Philip planned a general attack against Flanders, Brabant, and Hainault,[262] and on March 20 wrote to the pope from Poissy that he intended to invade Brabant.[263] A very large number of the Flemish nobility, including the castellans of Bergen and Dixmuide, were in Philip's army.[264] As count of Artois, Eudes, duke of Burgundy, provided for the defense of St. Omer, which refused to listen to Edward's summons. The garrison was strengthened on May 1 and his officials were ordered to exclude all strangers from the town as there were rumors of an attempt to seize it.[265] In anticipation of Edward's return, Philip strengthened all his fortifications along the border.[266] There were rumors of an attempt by Lewis the Bavarian against Philip through the Moselle valley,[267] and the Flemings had some hope of aid from him, for on April 25 the sca-

---

[256] N. de Pauw en J. Vuylsteke, *Rekeningen der Stad Gent*, I, 454.

[257] Kervyn, *Histoire de Flandres*, III (*Pièces Justificatives*), 596–602.

[258] N. de Pauw en J. Vuylsteke, *Rekeningen der Stad Gent*, I, 416.

[259] *Ibid.*, p. 417.

[260] *Ibid.*, p. 444. For the activities of John de Visch during May in this connection, see *ibid.*, p. 418.

[261] *Bourgeois de Valenciennes*, p. 171.

[262] G. Gorrini, " Lettere inedite degli Ambasciatori Fiorentini alla Corte dei Papi in Avignone (Anno 1340)," *Archivio Storico Italiano*, 4th Ser., XIV (1884), 169, pp. 169–170.

[263] A. Fierens, *Lettres de Benoît XII (1334–1340)*, No. 946.

[264] Kervyn, *Oeuvres de Froissart*, XXI, 211–247.

[265] E. Petit, *Histoire des Ducs de Bourgogne*, VIII (*Pièces Justificatives*), 392.

[266] G. Gorrini, " Lettere inedite degli Ambasciatori Fiorentini alla Corte dei Papi in Avignone (Anno 1340)," *Archivio Storico Italiano*, 4th Ser., XIV (1884), 330.   [267] *Ibid.*, pp. 169, 335.

bini of Ghent sent their messenger John, cantor of St. John's, to Cologne in response to a summons of the emperor to the three towns.[268]   But the Bavarian who had as late as January 25 declared the bishop, chapter, and city of Cambrai rebels, and had ordered Edward, the duke of Brabant, the duke of Guelders, the margrave of Juliers, the count of Hainault, and others to reduce them,[269] was a most uncertain quantity, and these conversations and rumors were without result.

The Flemings took fitting measures to withstand the hostile attempts of the French.   As early as March 1, the scabini of Ghent sent out a force of twenty bowmen and forty men-at-arms to protect the border near Bergen.   These were replaced on the 17th by a small force of bowmen under John van Roosebeke, but one month later, on April 17, a much larger force of about a hundred men-at-arms was dispatched.   On March 19 John van Steenbeke and Jacob vander Hoyen were sent to take up a position at Cassel with a force of twenty bowmen and eighty-one men-at-arms.   On April 4 they were reinforced by twenty white-hoods.[270]

---

[268] N. de Pauw en J. Vuylsteke, *Rekeningen der Stad Gent,* I, 417.

[269] L. Devillers, *Cartulaire,* II, 649.

[270] N. de Pauw en J. Vuylsteke, *Rekeningen der Stad Gent,* I, 477–482.

CHAPTER XI

THE ACME OF EDWARD'S INFLUENCE (1340)

i. Edward's Return to England (February–June, 1340) ii. Philip's Attack upon Hainault (October, 1339 — June, 1340) iii. The Battle of Sluis (June 24, 1340) iv. The Fiasco at St. Omer (August, 1340) v. The Siege of Tournai (August–September, 1340) vi. The Truce of Esplechin (Autumn, 1340)

I. Edward's Return to England (February–June, 1340)

WHILE the final formalities or negotiations between the Flemings and Edward were being concluded during the early days of February, the English king was eager to return to his realm. The Commons had met in Parliament at Westminster on October 13 and petitioned for a special session. On November 16 writs were issued ordering the knights of the shire and the burgesses to appear at Westminster on January 20.[1] Edward was eager to have sufficient funds to pay the pressing debts, amounting to 30,000*l.*, which he had promised to discharge between Candlemas and St. John the Baptist's Day; to which must be added the loans made by the merchants of England, the Italian bankers, the Hansa merchants, and a number of Netherlanders. But only 2,500 sacks were granted as a loan, the Commons insisted upon a redress of grievances, and the demand was made that the merchants of the realm should be invited to consult with the king at Mid-Lent to consider granting the remainder of the 30,000 sacks.[2] Before leaving Ghent, Edward was obliged to borrow 2,803*l.* 2*s.* 8*d.* large Tournois from some money lenders in Brussels on February 18. This sum was to be repaid at Easter and as guarantors appeared, at the special request of the king, John of Hainault, John, duke of Brabant, and his councillors, Otto, seignior of Cuyk, Gilles van Quaderebbe, seignior of Berg, Herman van Oss, John van Meldert, and Reginald, duke of Guelders.

---

[1] *CCR* (1339–41), p. 277.
[2] *Rotuli Parliamentorum*, II, 108.

Should he fail to pay at the appointed time, Edward promised to appear in person in Brussels and not depart until the debt should be discharged.[3]

During Edward's absence from the Low Countries until St. John the Baptist's Day, Flanders might become the object of Philip's hostility and plans had to be made for its defense. This was done in counsel with the Flemings and the duke of Brabant and undoubtedly also with others. Edward had determined to leave his men-at-arms in the Low Countries during his absence,[4] and a special force was given to the earls of Suffolk and Salisbury to aid in the defense of the border toward Douai, Lille, and Armentières.[5] On February 6 he made arrangements with Reginald, duke of Guelders, for the payment of the troops which were actually in arms and were to be kept in his service in Flanders.[6] He also left a sum of money with the provost and *advocatus* of Ypres which was to be used, it appears, to protect those parts of Flanders exposed to the enemy at Lille, Armentières, and elsewhere.[7]

Edward left Ghent on February 20,[8] but did not take with him Philippa, who with her son, Lionel, stayed at the abbey of St. Bavo,[9] According to some chroniclers she and the two earls[10] were retained as informal hostages or pledges. While this is not impossible, it is more likely that her condition made it inadvisable for her to cross the sea as she was in advanced pregnancy. In March was born a son, John, later famous as John of Gaunt.[11] According to a later account, van Artevelde acted

[3] A. Verkooren, *Inventaire, Brabant*, II, 91–93; Kervyn, *Oeuvres de Froissart*, XX, 57–58; I. A. Nijhoff, *Gedenkwaardigheden uit de Geschiedenis van Gelderland*, I, 415–416.

[4] G. Gorrini, "Lettere inedite degli Ambasciatori Fiorentini alla Corte dei Papi in Avignone (Anno 1340)," *Archivio Storico Italiano*, 4th Ser., XIV (1884), 168.

[5] Le Bel, I, 168; Knighton, II, 17; *Melsa*, III, 43; *Lanercost*, p. 332; *Scalacronica*, p. 170; *French Chronicle of London*, p. 73, which also includes Philippa.

[6] I. A. Nijhoff, *Gedenkwaardigheden uit de Geschiedenis van Gelderland*, I, 413–414.   [7] Kervyn, *Oeuvres de Froissart*, III, 480–481.

[8] Lescot (Appendice), p. 207.

[9] Froissart, I, 481, states that it was St. Peter's. See *Grandes Chroniques*, X, 380–381.

[10] *French Chronicle of London*, p. 73; *Melsa*, III, 43.

[11] Murimuth, p. 104; *Lanercost*, p. 332; *Scalacronica*, p. 170; Lescot,

as godfather at his baptism.[12] Philippa was treated with fitting honor, and the scabini presented her when she went to her first mass with three choice cloths, one brown, another red, and the third parti-colored (*ghemincden*) valued at 514*l.*, and a cup worth 52*l.*[13]

When Edward left Ghent for Sluis he was accompanied by the captain, William van Vaernewijc, and the scabinus, Lievin Wavel.[14] The scabinus, Baldwin vanden Walle, and William de Bomere were sent on the day before to accompany him to England in order to secure the ratification of the treaties as had been done in the towns of Flanders during the preceding weeks.[15] There were also delegations from other towns; from Ypres came John Berenger and John Stykerape, and from Bruges, the scabinus, John Hoost, and Nicholas van Scotelaere.[16] Among his own entourage the most noteworthy were the bishop of Lincoln, the earls of Derby and Northampton, and Henry de Ferrariis. A violent storm was raging, but this did not deter him from putting out to sea.[17] A convoy of Flemish ships accompanied him.[18] In spite of the perilous passage, the voyage was performed in record time, for at three o'clock in the afternoon of February 21 Edward arrived at Orwell.[19]

The king at once proceeded to business. Already on the 20th he had drawn up summonses for Reginald de Conductu and a hundred and fifty-three others to appear at Westminster on the Monday after Sunday in Mid-Lent.[20] At Harwich similar sum-

---

pp. 50–51; de Nangis, II, 166–167; Boendale, *Brabantsche Yeesten*, I, p. 562; Boendale, *Van den derden Eduwaert*, p. 336; le Bel, I, 168.

[12] *Chronographia*, II, 93. Froissart, I, 483, states that it was the duke of Brabant.

[13] N. de Pauw en J. Vuylsteke, *Rekeningen der Stad Gent*, I, 384.

[14] *Ibid.*, p. 411.

[15] *Ibid.*, p. 410.

[16] *CPR* (1338–40), pp. 416–480; Kervyn, *Oeuvres de Froissart*, III, 481.

[17] *Scalacronica*, p. 170.

[18] E. Déprez, *Les Préliminaires de la Guerre de Cent Ans*, pp. 283–284. Cf. *Chronographia*, II, 94.

[19] *Foedera*, II(2), 1115. Cf. Knighton, II, 14–15; Murimuth, p. 104; *Lanercost*, p. 332; *Melsa*, III, 43; *French Chronicle of London*, p. 73; Villani, col. 836; Boendale, *Van den derden Eduwaert*, p. 336; le Bel, I, 168; de Nangis, II, p. 165.

[20] *CCR* (1339–41), p. 453; *Report on the Dignity of a Peer*, IV, 153; *Foedera*, II(2), 1114–1115; *French Chronicle of London*, p. 74.

monses were issued for the clergy, peers, knights, and burgesses to appear two days later. In styling himself " King of France " he was apprehensive of possible opposition, and in his summonses begged the members not to marvel at the new title which he had assumed of necessity and added that it would not prejudice the interests of England and that he would ordain what they in Parliament might deem necessary in order to maintain the security of the realm.[21]

At the time designated, March 29, Parliament met, and before it Edward made his earnest plea for money. He told the members how he was in honor bound to return to Brussels as hostage for his numerous debts, how he stood in great danger of losing his allies in the Low Countries and of imperiling his lands.[22] To this plea the magnates, knights, and burgesses responded by granting for two years every ninth fleece, lamb, and sheaf, a ninth of all movable goods, and a fifteenth of all others.[23] The clergy of the province of York already had agreed on the octave of Purification to pay the tenth previously voted for the king's use.[24] There was much dissatisfaction with the royal finances, and the king was forced to recognize anew the liberties of the church and declare expressly that the realm of England would never in any way be subjected to France, that the two crowns would never be joined, and that the privileges granted to the subjects of Brabant and Flanders would be kept separate from those of the English forever.[25] Thereupon the treaties already ratified with the allies in the Low Countries could receive the proper seals in the presence of the delegates of Bruges, Ghent, and Ypres.[26] But even then it was difficult to secure the assent of all the towns, and on May 8 the king was forced to ask Norwich, Lincoln, and York to make

[21] *CCR* (1339–41), pp. 456–457; *Report on the Dignity of a Peer,* IV, 515; *Foedera,* II (2), 1115.

[22] *CCR* (1339–41), p. 468; *Rotuli Parliamentorum,* III, 112, No. 5.

[23] *Rotuli Parliamentorum,* III, 112; *CFR* (1337–47), p. 178; Knighton, II, 15; *Melsa,* III, 44; *Lanercost,* p. 104; Hemingburgh, II, 356. See also G. Gorrini, " Lettere inedite degli Ambasciatori Fiorentini alla Corte dei Papi in Avignone (Anno 1340)," *Archivio Storico Italiano,* 4th Ser., XIV (1884), 170.

[24] *CFR* (1337–47), pp. 173–174; *CPR* (1338–40), p. 499; Hemingburgh, II, 354; Murimuth, p. 104.

[25] *CPR* (1338–40), pp. 570–571; Kervyn, *Oeuvres de Froissart,* XVIII, 128–130; *Foedera,* II (2), 115, 1121; *Lanercost,* p. 333.

[26] *Rotuli Parliamentorum,* II, 112–113; *CPR* (1338–40), pp. 510–516.

no trouble in this matter, promising that their approval would never prejudice them.[27]   Before their return to Flanders the Flemish envoys were retained as members of the king's household for life.   William de Bomere and John Hoost received an annual pension of 40*l.* at the Exchequer and two robes out of the royal wardrobe; Nicholas van Scotelaere, 10*l.*; John Berenger, John Stykerape, and Baldwin vanden Walle, 20*l.* each in addition to robes.[28]

During the spring months Edward clearly showed himself eager to favor the Flemings as much as possible.   Fearing that obstacles in the way of safe commercial intercourse between Flanders and England might affect their attitude toward himself,[29] he diligently sought to remedy the injustice inflicted by English seamen while restricting piracy or destroying French craft on the narrow seas. Upon testimony of the scabini of Bruges he ordered the release of three merchants imprisoned at Norwich because of suspected connections with the pirates, Henry Pijl and Lanisius Spoudevisch.[30]   Other merchants from Sluis and Bruges had been seized near Boulogne and taken to Winchelsea, undoubtedly upon suspicion that they were pirates from Calais or other French ports. A cargo of wine belonging to a merchant of Sluis had been seized, a ship belonging to Kayard of Aardenburg had been captured, and a quantity of cloth owned by a merchant from Ghent had been taken.[31]   The Spanish merchants had also been intercepted, and Edward felt it necessary on March 15 to issue rigid orders to the sheriffs of London, Norfolk, and Suffolk, and to William de Clinton, constable of Dover Castle and warden of the Cinque Ports, to cause proclamation to be made that they should in no way be hindered in trading with Flanders and Brabant.[32]   Upon the suggestion of Bruges, Ghent, and Ypres, Edward on April

[27] *CPR* (1338–40), p. 507. For a similar promise to the corporation of London, see *Calendar of the Letter Books of London, Letter Book E,* pp. 50–51.

[28] *CPR* (1338–40), pp. 416, 480, 544; *Foedera,* II (2), 1124; Kervyn, *Oeuvres de Froissart,* III, 481. On May 1, William de Bomere of Dixmuide, apparently the same person, was granted the prebend of Northmuskham in St. Mary's at Southwell. See *CPR* (1338–40), p. 468.

[29] *CPR* (1338–40), pp. 557–558.

[30] *Ibid.*, p. 433.

[31] *Ibid.*, pp. 381, 463, 467, 494.

[32] *Ibid.*, p. 459.

12 granted his protection to the merchants of Spain, Catalonia, and Majorca in all their commercial activities with the Flemings.[33]

With the new credits approved by Parliament, Edward now sought to relieve his sadly deranged finances. On April 20 commissions were issued to supervisors and other men named in each shire to ascertain the value of the grant of the ninth in the cities and the boroughs, to collect and sell it, and render account to the Exchequer with all speed.[34] But this money could not be collected in time for Edward's return to the Low Countries before St. John the Baptist's Day. The king was forced to resort to loans and on March 1 gave commissions to contract loans to a group of twelve men including the bishop of Lincoln, the earl of Derby, members of the royal household, and others.[35] He asked the aldermen and the mayor of London to appear before him and his council on April 13. A loan of 20,000*l.* was requested, which was roundly declared impossible, but after much discussion and many threats it was finally agreed to lend 5,000*l.* in return for sufficient security of repayment.[36] The inquests in the shires in the meantime had been actively prosecuted, and on May 6 the commissioners were ordered to keep the goods that had been received. The king's clerk, William de Edyngton, was appointed receiver of the ninth and the fifteenth south of the Trent on the 12th.[37]

A large number of assignments were made on the 17th to meet the most pressing obligations of the king. Thus 11,720*l.* 2*s.* were granted to Anthony Bache out of the income from Berkshire, Buckingham, and Rutland in partial payment of the sum of 24,000 gold Florentine florins loaned to the king in Flanders. To the archbishop of Trier were assigned 25,000 florins which had been received by pledging the king's gold crown, 55,000 florins with the shield for which Philippa's gold crown had been pledged, and 4,256 florins for which the small crown had been pawned. Otto, seignior of Cuyk, received 3,000 florins, Walter

[33] *CPR* (1338–40), p. 464.

[34] *Ibid.*, pp. 494–505.

[35] *Foedera*, II (2), 1116.

[36] H. Riley, *Memorials of London and London Life in the XIIIth, XIVth, and XVth Centuries*, pp. 208–210; *CCR* (1339–41), p. 372.

[37] *CFR* (1337–47), pp. 178–180.

de Changeour and Colus Coluche secured 64,781 florins out of the income from Sussex, Surrey, and Middlesex, and Nicholas Bartholomew of Lucca was given 30,000*l*. out of the income from Wiltshire, Dorset, Southampton, and Somerset.[38] Assignments upon the ninth and fifteenth were made for the payment of the king's trusted advisers. On May 30 the king's butler, Raymond Seguyn, received 3,800*l*. sterling from the ninth of Essex and Oxford; the bishop of Lincoln 7,300*l*. from the ninth and fifteenth of the archdeaconry of York; Walter de Manny 4,000*l*. from Essex; and on June 21 the archbishop of Canterbury 3,337*l*. 6*s*. 8*d*. from Kent.[39]

Although Edward's financial situation was much improved by these measures, it still appeared very uncertain to his allies in the Low Countries. Reginald, duke of Guelders, was in great financial straits and was constrained to borrow heavily from the Lombards. He was uneasy about the solvency of his royal brother-in-law. On May 31 he and the duke of Brabant agreed to coöperate in their efforts to secure what was due them.[40] They had had enough experience of the king's collection of wool in the past three years and with justifiable skepticism did not expect any more success in the coming summer. Yet Edward did his best to bind his allies to himself. On April 6 he arranged the betrothal of Reginald's daughter Marguerite to the heir of William de Burgo, earl of Ulster.[41] On May 12 he created William, margrave of Juliers, earl of Cambridge, and granted him and his heirs an annual pension of 1,000*l*. sterling.[42]

II. Philip's Attack upon Hainault
(October, 1339 — June, 1340)

Having abandoned his brother-in-law Edward, and having been rejected by his uncle Philip, William, count of Hainault, Holland, and Zeeland, betook himself to Le Quesnoy [43] and had no further part in the campaign. He soon learned that the bishop of Cambrai, William d'Auxonne, had excommunicated a number

---

[38] *CPR* (1338–40), pp. 532–534.   [39] *Ibid.*, pp. 544–546.

[40] I. A. Nijhoff, *Gedenkwaardigheden uit de Geschiedenis van Gelderland,* I, 416, 418–419.

[41] *Ibid.*, pp. 416–417; *CPR* (1338–40), p. 455.   [42] *Foedera*, II (2), 1124.

[43] The *Chronographia*, II, 80, assumes that Count William first went

of his officials and put his land of Hainault under the interdict.[44] To prepare for the litigation certain to follow he named on October 8 as his proctors, Stephen Malion, canon of Soignies, James de Noulins, canon of Condé, John, a curé of Escaupont, Gilles le Clerk of Ittre, provost of Valenciennes, and a clerk, John de Revin.[45]

The provost ordered John d'Olivier to draw up an appeal to the pope against the conduct of the bishop on the 13th, the substance of which had been publicly proclaimed in the abbey of Crêpins and in three churches in Valenciennes on the 16th.[46] It recited how the count and John, duke of Brabant, had repeatedly urged the bishop to allow them to pass through the Cambrésis and the city of Cambrai in obedience to imperial command, promising that no harm would be inflicted upon him, the chapter, or any person whatever, and that no property would be damaged; that the invasion had been made in obedience to the vicar's demand that the bishop, as count of the Cambrésis, be forced to submit to the empire; that great damage had been occasioned in the execution of this command which Count William could in no way have resisted; that if any goods had been taken it had been done of necessity in the protection of his country and in the execution of the imperial command; that Count William was bound to obey the emperor for his temporalities rather than adhere to the bishop; that the demand had been made in the usual manner and in accordance with the command of a superior; that it was an old imperial custom that after three summonses had been issued other princes or barons of the empire could seize the goods and subjects of a disobedient vassal; and that in addition the bishop had inflicted damage to the extent of 200,000*l.* upon the county of Hainault when he refused to receive the army of the vicar in Cambrai, which was in consequence forced to take provisions from Hainault.[47]

to Le Quesnoy and then presented himself before Philip in Thiérache. See also le Bel, I, 157; le Muisit, p. 118.

[44] Cf. the letter of absolution of December 29, 1341, in Kervyn, *Oeuvres de Froissart*, XVIII, 193–195.

[45] L. Devillers, *Cartulaire*, I, 89–90.

[46] Kervyn, *Oeuvres de Froissart*, XVIII, 79.

[47] *Ibid.*, pp. 75–76; Devillers, *Cartulaire*, I, 91–92, 96–100; de Budt, pp. 326–327.

Thereupon began a series of border raids which soon degenerated into a regular feudal war. Men-at-arms issued forth from Cambrai where the count of Armagnac was in charge of French soldiers, proceeded to Count William's stronghold at Escaudoeuvre, and burned the town. A fruitless appeal was made to Philip, so Jeanne of Valois, dowager countess of Hainault, bestirred herself to arrange a truce in which she was successful.[48] It was violated, however, for on December 17 French soldiers marched out to Relenghes, besieged it with their engines, burned the buildings near it, and finally forced the defenders, Simon, bastard of Hainault, and eighteen crossbowmen, to retire at midnight toward Escaudoeuvre after setting fire to the fortress.[49]

Philip justified the actions of the soldiers and their commander, Thibaut de Moreuil, probably because William's men at Relenghes, Escaudoeuvre, and Thun-l'Évêque had, it was said, sought to prevent the passage of victuals into Cambrai.[50] William's protest that the bishop was the aggressor failed to impress his royal uncle, and the offer to submit the dispute to the decision of John, king of Bohemia, and the count of Alençon was not accepted. At about Christmas, after some further raids into Hainault, the count of Armagnac, Galesius de Bauma, and others left Cambrai with about five hundred men-at-arms and proceeded toward Thiérache whence they raided the lands of John of Hainault,[51] and burned a large number of places such as Chimay, Baileux, Salles, Robechies, Villers-la-Tour, and Froidchapelle. John was absent at this moment, for he was with Edward in Antwerp where he was active in advancing the king's interests.[52] There were other raids in Hainault; people were slain, one of Count William's subjects was beheaded before the eyes of the garrison in Escaudoeuvre, and malefactors were punished in com-

---

[48] See Count William's letter of April 2 to Philip, Kervyn, *Oeuvres de Froissart,* XVIII, 138; Boendale, *Van den derden Eduwaert,* p. 339; *Chronographia,* II, 86–87.   [49] *Bourgeois de Valenciennes,* p. 171.

[50] *Chronographia,* II, 86.

[51] The bishop of Cambrai excommunicated John of Hainault early in March. See G. Gorrini, "Lettere inedite degli Ambasciatori Fiorentini alla Corte dei Papi in Avignone (Anno 1340)," *Archivio Storico Italiano,* 4th Ser., XIV (1884), 164.

[52] S. A. Waller Zeper, *Jan van Henegouwen, Heer van Beaumont,* p. 161. See also Kervyn, *Oeuvres de Froissart,* XVIII, 138.

plete contempt of the count's jurisdiction.[53]   These vengeful incursions continued until Sunday after Mid-Lent (April 1) when a body of the king's men burned and plundered Haspres where they seized some of Count William's men and held them for ransom.[54]

This was more than the pacific William could endure. He at once countermanded an effort which his friends were about to make at Senlis to arrange an understanding with Philip, and refused to appear as he had promised.   On April 2 he drew up a long letter setting forth his complaints.   His father had performed many invaluable services in Philip's behalf and especially in the battle of Cassel.   Far from showing any gratitude, the king had persisted in the encroachments begun by Philip the Fair upon the borders of Ostrevant and Hainault, at St. Amand-en-Pévèle, on the borders of the castleries of Ath and Lens, where a settlement of the boundary had ever been impossible, on the border of the empire and the kingdom of France, at Crèvecoeur, Arleux, and other points, which land his father had purchased and paid for in part, but which Philip had unlawfully seized in 1337.   And now Philip had rejected his proffer of service because he had discharged his oath-bound duty toward the empire, attacked Escaudoeuvre and Relenghes, supported the bishop of Cambrai in his unjust attacks upon Hainault, and, finally, refused to leave the matter to arbitration.   The abbot of Crêpins was sent to deliver the document.[55]   Philip, it is reported, accepted the challenge with a light heart: fifteen princes, besides the Flemings, had levied war upon him; a sixteenth could not make matters much worse! [56]

It was now war in good earnest.   Count William collected a

[53] See Count William's letter of April 2 to Philip, Kervyn, *Oeuvres de Froissart*, XVIII, 138; *Chronographia*, II, 87–88; Lescot, p. 50; *Grandes Chroniques*, V, 379; le Bel, I, 171; *Bourgeois de Valenciennes*, p. 172; Outremeuse, VI, 621.

[54] G. Gorrini, " Lettere inedite degli Ambasciatori Fiorentini alla Corte dei Papi in Avignone (Anno 1340)," *Archivio Storico Italiano*, 4th Ser., XIV (1884), 169–170; *Bourgeois de Valenciennes*, p. 173; *Chronographia*, II, 95.

[55] *Bourgeois de Valenciennes*, p. 173; le Bel, I, 171–172. See Count William's letter of April 2 to Philip, Kervyn, *Oeuvres de Froissart*, XVIII, 136–140.

[56] *Chronographia*, II, 106–107. For the seignior of Valkenburg's letter of April 20, see F. van Mieris, *Groot Charterboek*, II, 635.

large force in which John of Hainault, who especially desired
revenge, and the seignior of Cuyk, the representative of the duke
of Brabant, were present. They marched into Thiérache toward
Aubenton, a town with a thriving cloth industry and a comfort-
able bourgeoisie, which was defended by the seignior of Vervins
and the vidâme of Chalons who were in charge of some French
troops. A determined assault was delivered which broke down
the powerful defense amid the cry of frightened women and
children that rose above the din of battle. When the assailants
burst into the town they began to burn, plunder, slay, and seize
such as could be held for ransom. The church, in which large
numbers had sought refuge, was burned. Many soldiers had
fled when the defense gave way, but John of Hainault gave
chase, followed them toward Vervins and slew large numbers of them. Vengeance was next visited upon the exposed
countryside and about forty towns and hamlets were laid in
ashes.[57]

Meanwhile the Flemings were forced to watch Philip's garrisons at Lille and Armentières which were harrying the border.
Therefore the plan of an expedition against Calais was abandoned. The French undoubtedly watched travelers carefully
and apprehended some Flemings. An interesting case is that of
the most important members of the Austin Canons who were
incarcerated at St. Omer and for whom the three towns gave
180*l.* for their comfort.[58] Later in August one of these was sent
to Bruges as an envoy by the bailiff of St. Omer.[59] It is probably
at about this time that the attempt to deliver Lille into van
Artevelde's hands took place. A certain Stephen Canard discussed the matter with his agents and the English, for which he
was seized and executed.[60] The magistrates of Ypres and the
earls of Salisbury and Suffolk, who were stationed with some
English soldiers in their town, kept a close watch upon the defenders of Lille and Armentières. The burghers of Ypres were

[57] *Bourgeois de Valenciennes,* pp. 173–174; le Bel, I, 171–172; *Chronographia,* II, 105–106; *Grandes Chroniques,* V, 379; Lescot, p. 50; Villani,
col. 836; Outremeuse, VI, 621–622.

[58] N. de Pauw en J. Vuylsteke, *Rekeningen der Stad Gent,* II, 71.

[59] E. Petit, *Histoire des Ducs de Bourgogne,* VIII (*Pièces Justificatives*),
396.

[60] Kervyn, *Oeuvres de Froissart,* XVIII, 131–136. The documents
which are dated 1349 and 1351 do not enable us to give a precise date.

particularly eager to be rid of the obnoxious Genoese crossbow-men in Armentières, and the earls with some of their own troops and the militia of Ypres commanded by their scabini, Jacob de Vroede and Nicholas de Dickebie, and the castellan, Gerard d'Oultre, marched against them. The Genoese offered a sharp resistance, but were beaten on April 6, whereupon the town was plundered and burned.[61]

The militia of Ypres, accompanied by the earls of Suffolk and Salisbury, thereupon turned southward with the intention of joining the forces of van Artevelde who had left Ghent on the 5th with a large number of men and was marching in the direction of Tournai.[62] The captors of Armentières conceived the idea of seizing Lille and wreaking vengeance upon the garrison for their repeated incursions.[63] They were marching up the Deule on which Lille was situated, and were at Le Quesnoy when the governor, learning of their design, forthwith ordered the buildings outside the walls to be burned and prepared for an immediate attack.[64] In spite of the warm reception obviously in store for them, the earls and their party were sanguine enough to expect victory over an enemy much superior in number and having the advantage of a walled town. While studying the fortifications of the place, they were suddenly surrounded and scattered near Marquette by the seignior of Roubaix. The earls and one of the scabini were seized and some of the scabini and a number of the soldiers were slain while the rest fled homeward in confusion.[65] Philip was gratified to have as hostages these two diplomats who had done so much to help build up the solid bulwark of alliances against him in the Low Countries, and incarcerated them in the Châtelet in Paris.[66]

Meanwhile the commander of the French garrison in Tournai,

[61] De Budt, p. 327; *Chronographia*, II, 98; *Grandes Chroniques*, V, 381; Froissart, II, 46. For the date, see E. Petit, *Histoire des Ducs de Bourgogne*, VII (*Pièces Justificatives*), 244.

[62] N. de Pauw en J. Vuylsteke, *Rekeningen der Stad Gent*, I, 486.

[63] Boendale, *Van den derden Eduwaert*, p. 339.

[64] Le Bel, II, 168 (note 2).

[65] Boendale, *Van den derden Eduwaert*, p. 337; le Bel, I, 168–169; de Budt, p. 327; le Muisit, p. 122; Murimuth, pp. 104–105; Knighton, II, 17; *Scalacronica*, p. 170; *Chronographia*, II, 99–104; *Grandes Chroniques*, V, 380–382; de Nangis, II, 167; Villani, col. 836; Outremeuse, VI, 622; Froissart, II, 508.

[66] Murimuth, p. 105, states that Philip wished to kill the earls, but

Gondemar de Fay, had led a band of marauders, which may be estimated at about twelve hundred, northward down the Schelde into Flanders. Crossing the border at Roosbrugge, they passed through Bierne, burning and destroying everything as far as Oudenaarde.[67] The scabini of Ghent at once took measures to protect the country and on the 4th sent out thirty white-hoods under the command of Peter vanden Hovene. On the following day 1,086 sergeants (*serianten*) and twenty-seven bowmen were dispatched, and were reinforced on the 8th by 1,454 sergeants and sixty-eight bowmen. Eight of the scabini and councillors, van Artevelde, the captains, and the three deans of the guilds were with them. This effort " to withstand the great wrong which the king of France and his abettors were seeking to inflict upon Flanders " cost Ghent 18,623*l.* 9*s.*[68] Meanwhile, the burghers of Oudenaarde had gone forth to oppose the invaders,[69] who cared little to meet a superior force of Flemings and retired with their loot behind the walls of Tournai.

It was now van Artevelde's turn to plunder and burn in the Tournaisis. The Flemings pitched their tents at Chin and Ramignies on the 7th and burned and plundered everything in the adjacent country. When the news of what had happened at Marquette was received by them on the 12th, van Artevelde and the captains began to draw back. But they seized the episcopal stronghold at Helchin and placed a guard in it in order to defend the surrounding territory of Flanders and to annoy the defenders of Tournai. The entire force had returned on the 15th.[70] On the 16th twenty-one sergeants and, on May 1, ten white-hoods were sent to Cambrai. With them were the sergeants of the Quatuor Officia and Waasland, commanded by Peter vanden Hovene and Simon Godenvalen.[71]

---

was deterred by John, king of Bohemia. See also *French Chronicle of London,* pp. 73–74; *Melsa,* III, 43; *Lanercost,* p. 332.

[67] De Budt, p. 327; *Chronographia,* II, 96; Villani, col. 836; *Chronique Normande,* p. 43; *Chronique des Pays-Bas,* p. 150. See also Kervyn, *Histoire de Flandre,* III, 241, who assigns this to the evening of the 4th.

[68] N. de Pauw en J. Vuylsteke, *Rekeningen der Stad Gent,* I, 482–487.

[69] *Chronographia,* II, 96–97.

[70] Le Muisit, pp. 121–122; N. de Pauw en J. Vuylsteke, *Rekeningen der Stad Gent,* I, 416, 487–489; Villani, col. 836; *Chronographia,* II, 103, which also states on pp. 97–98 that the cold weather was in part responsible.

[71] N. de Pauw en J. Vuylsteke, *Rekeningen der Stad Gent,* I, 489–490.

At this time Count William was called upon to prepare for a determined attack by Philip. The king had summoned his forces to appear at Cambrai under the command of his eldest son John, duke of Normandy,[72] and he himself prepared to go toward the borders of Hainault and Flanders in May.[73] William was now constrained to turn to his allies who were willing enough to help in the face of a possible invasion. Accompanied by his uncle, John of Hainault, he went to Brabant to consult with Duke John and on April 23 appeared in Ghent.[74] The scabini appointed one of their own number, Gilles Rijnvisch, to accompany them to Bruges and to Ypres and back again to Ghent on the 26th.[75] To Edward also he sent a messenger who undoubtedly apprised him of the gravity of the situation.[76]

Count William next turned to the bishop of Liège. Nearly three years had now passed since his father had died, and he had not yet performed homage for Hainault. He deemed it politic to have this attended to inasmuch as the bishop, his suzerain, was in alliance with Philip. In May, when the siege of Thun-l'Évêque was in progress, he appeared before the chapter in Liège, performed his duties, and then asked the bishop to protect him. This, in the opinion of the chronicler Outremeuse, was a most ridiculous request, but what could be expected from the " count of Hainault who was so young both in years and wisdom " ?[77]

The French were ready to invade Hainault by the close of April. The duke of Burgundy proceeded from Artois and passed through Tournai where he halted for a brief space. On the borders of Ostrevant and the Cambrésis his forces united with those of the duke of Normandy, the count of Armagnac, the king

---

[72] *Bourgeois de Valenciennes*, p. 175; le Bel, I, 172; de Nangis, II, p. 190; *Grandes Chroniques*, V, 182. The royal carriage was to be ready on May 6. See Lescot (*Appendice*), p. 228.

[73] See the itinerary in J. Viard, " Itinéraire de Philippe VI de Valois," *BEC*, LXXIV (1913), 536–537.

[74] For Count William's oath given on the Kouter (*Place d'Armes*) in Ghent and the wine given on this occasion, see N. de Pauw en J. Vuylsteke, *Rekeningen der Stad Gent*, I, 384.

[75] *Bourgeois de Valenciennes*, p. 175, states that a conference was held at Dendermonde, but N. de Pauw en J. Vuylsteke, *Rekeningen der Stad Gent*, I, 417, make no reference to this. For the messengers sent by Count William, see *ibid.*, pp. 442–443. Cf. also *Chronographia*, II, 95–96 and 112.

[76] *CPR* (1338–40), p. 519; *Chronicon Comitum Flandrensium*, p. 213.

[77] Le Bel, I, 175–176; Outremeuse, VI, 623, 662–663.

of Navarre, the count of Alençon, and the captains, Gondemar de Fay and Thibaut de Moreuil.[78] On May 2 the dukes of Normandy and Burgundy were at Douai. They hoped to paralyze Count William's resistance by securing Valenciennes whence they could plunder any part of Hainault at will. From Douai the duke of Burgundy sent a messenger to the provost, scabini, and councillors with command to conduct themselves in accordance with the treaty of alliance of August, 1292, made by them and Philip the Fair, but the burghers remained loyal and offered no response.[79]

Little was done during the next ten or twelve days; but on the 14th with no less than eight thousand men-at-arms they began to burn and plunder everything.[80] After destroying thirty-two towns and laying the countryside waste, a large part of them halted at Montay-sur-Salle. One of the places ravaged was Werchin, a possession of Simon of Werchin, seneschal of Hainault. Furious because of the deed, he at once marched out at night with only forty men and at break of day, accompanied by Thierry of Walcourt, marshal of Hainault, entered their camp, which was commanded by the seignior of Bailleul in Flanders and William de Bréauté, and at once began to lay about them with their swords. Before the surprised forces could move to the defense, the assailants withdrew without loss.[81]

The invaders next moved toward Valenciennes. The duke of Burgundy was at Le Quesnoy on the 22d and at Valenciennes on the 23d.[82] The country around Eurgies, Riesel, Sautain, Ausnois, Famars, and Beauvoir was ruthlessly destroyed, and a few of these towns were burned.[83] Even Fontenelles near Denain was laid in ashes in spite of the fact that Jeanne, dowager countess

[78] Le Muisit, p. 123. For the itinerary of the duke of Burgundy, see E. Petit, *Histoire des Ducs de Bourgogne,* VII, 279.

[79] Kervyn, *Oeuvres de Froissart,* XVIII, 149–152, and the summons repeated on June 3, *ibid.,* pp. 152–153.

[80] *Bourgeois le Valenciennes,* p. 175. For the date, see *Chronographia,* II, 111 (note 4). Villani, col. 836, states that the raid began on May 4 and continued for three weeks.

[81] *Bourgeois de Valenciennes,* pp. 175–176. The *Chronographia,* II, 111–112, states that the duke's men were overcome with wine and that their host betrayed them.

[82] E. Petit, *Histoire des Ducs de Bourgogne,* VII, 267. Le Quesnoy was held by Thierry of Valkenburg. See le Bel, I, 174.

[83] *Bourgeois de Valenciennes,* p. 177.

of Hainault and King Philip's sister, was living there as a religious.[84]　Having destroyed everything up to the faubourgs of Valenciennes, which also were burned, the invaders began to feel the pinch of hunger.　Their supply of wine had been seized by a force led by Gerard of Trazegnies, the commander of the fortress of Escaudoeuvre.　The burghers of Valenciennes now threatened attack; on the evening of the 23d the tocsin sounded, and the invaders apparently deemed it best to withdraw, so retreated toward Cambrai.[85]

Unable to cope with his assailants, Count William was forced to bide his time while Philip exercised his will upon the defenseless lands.　A number of the king's vassals who also owed service to him formally renounced their obligations.[86]　On May 9 the status of the castles of Crèvecoeur, Arleux, St. Supplet, the castlery of Cambrai, and the rights of Rumilly were definitely settled. Engergier, seignior of Amboise and Néelle, as *advocatus* and guardian of his wife, Mary of Flanders, had surrendered possession into the hands of the bishop of Cambrai in accordance with custom, whereupon John, duke of Normandy, was recognized legal possessor on the condition that these fiefs should never be united with the crown of France, and, in case of inheritance, should be regranted within one year.[87]　Philip also secured an important alliance with the corporation of Cambrai.　On May 13 the scabini and councillors issued a document setting forth the terms: Philip bound himself to provide three hundred men-at-arms and as many crossbowmen in time of need and at his own expense against all parties save the emperor or the king of Germany; food-stuffs and other necessaries would be allowed to pass freely from France into the city by paying only the accustomed duties; and the men of the king of France would ever be received in the city in accordance with these terms.[88]

Count William sought the aid of the duke of Brabant and the

[84] *Chronicon Comitum Flandrensium*, pp. 212–213.

[85] *Bourgeois de Valenciennes*, pp. 177–178; le Muisit, p. 124; *Chronographia*, II, 112–113; *Grandes Chroniques*, V, 190; de Nangis, II, 190. Hasnon in Ostrevant had in the meantime been burned.

[86] Kervyn, *Oeuvres de Froissart*, XVIII, 140–144; *Chronographia*, II, 110–111.

[87] Kervyn, *Oeuvres de Froissart*, XVIII, 144–146.

[88] *Ibid.*, pp. 147–148; H. Dubrulle, *Cambrai à la Fin du Moyen Âge (XIIIᵉ–XVIᵉ Siècle)*, *Pièces Justificatives*, No. 27.

Flemings in order to strengthen his defense. The scabini of
Ghent had received numerous messengers from him during April
and a small number of sergeants at Grammont was actually
making plans to go to his aid.[89] Simon van Halen, *ruwaard*
of Flanders, was in Brussels at the close of the month and in the
early days of May. A conference was held there between the 3d
and the 7th at which Count William, Duke John, the deputies
from Ghent, Simon Parijs, Segher Boele, and Thomas van Vaernewijc of the Council of Flanders, and possibly also deputies from
the other towns participated. On the 8th van Vaernewijc proceeded to Hainault, apparently by way of Grammont, and returned to Ghent on the 11th.[90]

A force of men-at-arms was made ready in accordance with
a decision reached at Brussels. These soldiers were drawn from
various parts of Flanders, Bruges, the Frank of Bruges, Oudenaarde, Dendermonde, Alost, and Waasland. They proceeded
toward Bouchain with a small contingent of seventeen men from
Ghent, accompanied by Peter vanden Hovene, and Simon Godenvalen.[91] Besides giving some aid in the fight at Mortagne,[92]
they helped in making the burghers of Cambrai and the people
on the frontier uncomfortable.[93] Just after the invasion of
Hainault from Cateau Cambrésis, another meeting was held at
Brussels on the 20th. Besides the duke of Brabant and Count
William, there were present Simon Parijs and Gilles Rijnvisch
from Ghent, Thomas van Vaernewijc and John vander Vloet,
members of the Council of Flanders, Henry of Flanders, and
undoubtedly also deputies from Bruges and Ypres. The men
of Ghent were back on the 23d, and Count William was either
with them at this moment or followed at once. The scabini
had arranged a conference at Bruges and Ypres whither the
scabini, Simon ser Thomaes and Gilles Rijnvisch, the captain,
William van Huse, John van Steenbeke, John van Dessele, and

---

[89] N. de Pauw en J. Vuylsteke, *Rekeningen der Stad Gent,* I, 442–443.
[90] *Ibid.*, p. 418.
[91] *Ibid.*, pp. 490–491.
[92] *Ibid.*, pp. 454, 491. On May 8 according to le Muisit, p. 123. See
E. Déprez, *Préliminaires de la Guerre de Cent Ans,* p. 300, who identifies
it with Thun St. Martin.
[93] Le Muisit, p. 123; le Bel, I, 174; *Chronographia,* II, 86; *Grandes
Chroniques,* V, 383–384.

Peter vander Asselt accompanied the count.[94] Preparations were
at once hurried, and on the 25th a force of twenty-seven bowmen,
fifty white-hoods, and two hundred and seventy sergeants (*serianten*) was led out by Guy of Flanders and William van Vaernewijc. But they returned after eight days, apparently because the
French had ceased their raids and were confining themselves
to the task of reducing Escaudoeuvre.[95]

After withdrawing from before Valenciennes toward Cambrai,
the duke of Normandy advanced upon Escaudoeuvre, a stronghold of Count William's, situated on the borders of Hainault. It
was commanded by Gerard of Trazegnies and twenty-three men,
and the duke made a determined effort to take it.[96] The siege was
begun and stones were hurled into the fortress by the machines,
but treason was to deliver it into the hand of the enemy. Gondemar de Fay, who knew Trazegnies personally, induced him
to surrender after a number of consultations with the duke of
Normandy. It was agreed that after eight days the stronghold
was to be surrendered and the goods within to be sent to Cambrai
under guard. A price was set; ten thousand florins were paid,[97]
and on the night of Pentecost (June 3–4) the garrison abandoned the place [98] which the French thereupon razed to the
ground. But Trazegnies received fitting reward for his dastardly act; his companions seized him and two guilty esquires as
they were approaching Cambrai, bound them, and brought them
to Mons before John of Hainault, who proceeded to pronounce
justice over them, as Count William was still absent in Brussels or
Flanders. Trazegnies was placed on the wheel, tortured, and
beheaded, and the esquires were executed.[99]

Thun-l'Évêque, a stronghold belonging to Count William,

---

[94] N. de Pauw en J. Vuylsteke, *Rekeningen der Stad Gent,* I, 419–420.

[95] *Ibid.,* pp. 492–493.

[96] *Bourgeois de Valenciennes,* p. 179; le Muisit, p. 124; le Bel, I, 173,
who states that the castle belonged to John of Hainault, and that there
was a second in command, named Robert Marmion. The duke of Normandy was before Escaudoeuvre on the 24th. See E. Petit, *Histoire des
Ducs de Bourgogne,* VII, 277.

[97] *Bourgeois de Valenciennes,* p. 173; *Chronographia,* II, 114–115; le
Bel, I, 173.

[98] E. Petit, *Histoire des Ducs de Bourgogne,* VII, 248.

[99] *Bourgeois de Valenciennes,* p. 179; le Bel, I, 173; le Muisit, p. 129;
N. de Pauw en J. Vuylsteke, *Rekeningen der Stad Gent,* I, 420.

situated where the Scarpe joins the Schelde, was the next object of attack and was invested at once.[100] Count William had been greatly strengthened by the troops sent by the duke of Brabant.[101] Presently he returned from Brussels. With him came, it appears, Duke John, Reginald, duke of Guelders, William, margrave of Juliers, and the seignior of Valkenburg, who were speedily followed by their own levies and some German troops.[102] Some men-at-arms also arrived from Holland and Zeeland,[103] and a large number of Flemings was on the way. A force of 4,269 men was sent out from Ghent with a vast amount of equipment. With them were van Artevelde and the captains, three deans of the guilds, and eight of the scabini and councillors.[104] The soldiers of the French garrison at Tournai were impotent to halt their march up the Schelde from Condé toward St. Amand.[105]

A general engagement was, however, impossible. The relieving forces were stationed on the right bank of the Schelde which they could not cross, and a bridge at this point was totally inadequate in the face of the enemy. The defense, led by Richard de Lymosin, was maintained vigorously although the assailants, as at Escaudoeuvre, threw showers of stones and missiles into the stronghold day and night.[106] There was of course plenty of challenging back and forth in characteristic chivalric fashion, but the duke of Burgundy refused to accept any proffer of combat. Only desultory skirmishing relieved the monotony.[107] The impossibility of crossing the river, the declining food-supply, and the certainty of the capture of the stronghold now induced Count William and his allies to consider the advisability of aban-

---

[100] The duke of Burgundy was before Thun-l'Évêque on June 4. See E. Petit, *Histoire des Ducs de Bourgogne,* VII, 277.

[101] John was at Valenciennes as early as May 12. See A. Verkooren, *Inventaires, Brabant,* II, 95.

[102] *Bourgeois de Valenciennes,* p. 180; le Bel, I, 176; Boendale, *Van den derden Eduwaert,* p. 339; Boendale, *Brabantsche Yeesten,* I, 563; de Budt, p. 327; *Chronicon Comitum Flandrensium,* p. 212; *Chronographia,* II, 117; Froissart, II, 27–28.

[103] S. A. Waller Zeper, *Jan van Henegouwen, Heer van Beaumont,* p. 173 (note).

[104] N. de Pauw en J. Vuylsteke, *Rekeningen der Stad Gent,* I, 495–501; *Bourgeois de Valenciennes,* p. 180; *Grandes Chroniques,* V, 384. This expedition cost Ghent 5,476*l.* 14*s.* 5*d.*

[105] Le Muisit, p. 124; *Chronographia,* II, 117.

[106] Boendale, *Van den derden Eduwaert,* p. 339; *Bourgeois de Valenciennes,* p. 180; le Bel, I, 176–177. [107] *Chronographia,* II, 117.

doning Thun-l'Évêque.[108]   This was agreed upon, probably because of the fact that Edward was due to arrive in the Low Countries by St. John the Baptist's Day.   William ordered its evacuation.   A force of bowmen was brought up from Valenciennes who united with the allied forces and on the evening of the 23d actively engaged the French on the opposite side of the Schelde, thus distracting their attention from the fortification. The defenders set fire to the structure, escaped through a secret gate, and in the early morning were safe with the count and the allied leaders.[109]

Philip had come to his son's army before Thun-l'Évêque on the 18th,[110] and, after razing the place to the ground, made ready to lay siege to Bouchain.[111]   But on the 24th a bloody defeat was inflicted upon the French fleet on the Zwin, and Edward's army might soon be on its way to invade France.   He accordingly withdrew at once in the direction of Arras [112] where the duke of Burgundy had preceded him as early as the 18th.[113] From this place he could advantageously watch Edward's maneuvers and defend such parts of Flanders as he might seek to reconquer in accordance with the promises made in the treaties with the Flemings.   Philip contented himself with sending a small force of bowmen under Thibaut de Moreuil into Hainault who raided and burned Bavay and neighboring places in July.   The garrisons at Tournai, St. Omer, Lille, and Douai were strengthened.[114]   The allied force at once drew back when the besieged had effected their escape, and was in Valenciennes on the evening of the 24th.[115]   Van Artevelde and his colleagues returned to Ghent on the 28th.[116]

[108] Le Bel, I, 177; Froissart, II, 31, states that the duke of Brabant made this suggestion.

[109] *Bourgeois de Valenciennes,* p. 180; le Bel, I, 177; le Muisit, p. 125; *Grandes Chroniques,* V, 383–384; *Chronographia,* II, 118–120; E. Petit, *Histoire des Ducs de Bourgogne,* VII, 251 (note).

[110] J. Viard, "Itinéraire de Philippe VI de Valois," *BEC,* LXXIV (1913), 527.   [111] *Chronographia,* II, 119.

[112] J. Viard, "Itinéraire de Philippe VI de Valois," *BEC,* LXXIV (1913), 527.   [113] E. Petit, *Histoire des Ducs de Bourgogne,* VII, 277.

[114] Le Bel, I, 172 (note); *Chronographia,* II, 119, 120.

[115] *Bourgeois de Valenciennes,* p. 180; *Chronographia,* I, 120. According to Froissart, II, 228, van Artevelde addressed the people in the market place of Valenciennes justifying Edward's claim to the crown of France.

[116] N. de Pauw en J. Vuylsteke, *Rekeningen der Stad Gent,* I, 495–501.

III. The Battle of Sluis (June 24, 1340)

The immediate plan of Philip had been to prevent, if possible, the arrival of Edward in the Low Countries.[117] He exerted himself to collect a large fleet from Picardy and Normandy. The ships, numbering more than two hundred, were of all sizes and descriptions and to them were added the galleys of the Genoese sea rover, Barbaveria.[118] On May 26 [119] the French commanders, Hugh Quieret and John Béhuchet, put out to sea from Honfleur in Normandy, and sailed toward the coast of Flanders. With them were more than twenty thousand men-at-arms and bowmen.[120]

The arrival of this formidable fleet off the Schelde mouths created the greatest consternation among the people dwelling along its banks. The entrance to the Zwin was closed at once, and all ingress and egress were impossible. Cadzand was harried and burned. On the Honte, the west arm of the Schelde mouth, numerous ships were seized and their crews and merchants summarily put to death. At Antwerp the report was current that the French intended to sail up the estuary and lay siege to that town, and preparations were made to meet them. The large tower at the Fish Market was constructed on this occasion. Undoubtedly the presence of the Flemish pirates, Lanisius Spoudevisch and van Eyle, and perhaps also other Flemings hostile to the policies of van Artevelde and the three towns, increased the general uneasiness.[121] Efforts were made at once to prevent a successful landing. On June 11 the scabini of Ghent began to fortify the Quatuor Officia. On the 13th the scabinus, Lievin van Ghent, and John van Dessele went to Aardenburg, and a

[117] Knighton, II, 16; *Melsa*, III, 44; *French Chronicle of London*, p. 74; *Grandes Chroniques*, V, 384–385; de Nangis, II, 168.

[118] *Bourgeois de Valenciennes*, p. 181; Villani, col. 837.

[119] C. de la Roncière, *Histoire de la Marine Française*, I, 443 (note 4).

[120] See C. Dufourmantelle, " La Marine militaire en France au Commencement de la Guerre de Cent Ans," *Spectateur Militaire* (Paris, 1878); S. Luce, *La France pendant la Guerre de Cent Ans. Épisodes Historiques et Vie Privée au XIVe et XVe Siècles* (Paris, 1890), pp. 6–21. See also *Melsa*, III, 44; Knighton, II, p. 16; *Breve Chronicon*, p. 8; Froissart, II, 34.

[121] Boendale, *Van den derden Eduwaert*, p. 338; Boendale, *Brabantsche Yeesten*, I, 564–565; *French Chronicle of London*, p. 77; Villani, col. 837; Froissart, II, p. 219; *Grandes Chroniques*, V, 385.

large force of a hundred bowmen, four hundred sergeants (*ser-ianten*), and others went out to guard Sluis.[122] The situation in the Low Countries was now very precarious because Philip's army was pressing hard upon Hainault and his fleet triumphantly sailing upon the Schelde. Under these circumstances it was not strange that the Flemings should eagerly await the arrival of Edward.[123]

It was the original intention of the English king to cross over to Flanders with a small fleet of about forty ships. The date set was about June 14, which would be comfortably within the limits fixed by Edward in his agreements with the Flemings.[124] But the extensive preparations of Philip could not be kept secret and rumors of the activities in the Norman ports were speedily rife in England.[125] It appeared rash to cross under such circumstances, and the archbishop of Canterbury warned Edward of the dangers to which he would be exposed. Robert de Morley and John Crabbe supported the prelate, but Edward angrily rejected their counsel.[126] At Westminster Edward appointed, on May 27, his son Edward, duke of Cornwall and earl of Chester, keeper of the realm and his lieutenant during his absence, to be attended by the archbishop of Canterbury, the earl of Huntingdon, Henry de Percy, and others.[127] The king had gone to Ipswich with the intention of embarking, but changed his mind and suddenly sent out orders to adjacent ports to provide sailors, men-at-arms, ships, and provisions with great haste. All ships were forbidden to leave London for foreign parts.[128] Within an incredibly short time the fleet was greatly augmented so that the chronicles could speak of as many as several hundred ships.[129]

[122] N. de Pauw en J. Vuylsteke, *Rekeningen der Stad Gent*, I, 420–421, 493–494.
[123] Knighton, II, 17.
[124] Avesbury, p. 310; Murimuth, p. 105.
[125] Baker, p. 68; Murimuth, p. 105; Hemingburgh, III, 355; *Chronographia*, II, 355. [126] Avesbury, p. 311.
[127] *CPR* (1338–40), p. 528; *Foedera*, II(2), 1125. *Report on the Dignity of a Peer*, IV, 521.
[128] Knighton, II, 17; Baker, p. 68; Hemingburgh, II, 355; *French Chronicle of London*, p. 76, where the delay is ascribed to an unfavorable wind. See orders of June 11, 12, and 13 issued to London in *Calendar of the Letter Books of London, Letter Book F*, p. 51, and to Lynn in *CCR* (1339–41), p. 422.
[129] Baker, p. 68; Hemingburgh, II, 355; *Melsa*, III, 44.

Finally, early in the morning of June 22 everything was in readiness for departure from the harbor of Orwell. The king was aboard his ship, the *Thomas,* accompanied by the earls of Gloucester, Derby, Northampton, and Huntingdon, the bishop of Lincoln, and Robert of Artois. At six o'clock the fleet stood out to sea. The regent requested the archbishop, bishops, and the rest of the clergy to pray for victory.[130] Among the crew were a large number of archers as well as men-at-arms and sailors.[131] Before a favoring breeze they sailed all day and night, and on Friday, the 23d, they drew near the Flemish coast. On the way they had been informed that the French fleet was in the mouth of the Zwin, thus blocking the approach to Bruges.[132] The bearers of this intelligence were without doubt Conrad Clypping and Peter de Gildesburgh, king's merchants.[133] About mid-day they passed Blankenberg and drew near Heist, a village in the dunes. The bishop of Lincoln and Reginald de Cobham went ashore, entered the village, and sought to arouse the Flemings to attack the enemy at the favorable moment. Riding toward Sluis, they could descry the entire French fleet lying at anchor with the fair *Christopher* and other captured English craft in its midst. They carefully noted their number and disposition.[134] When this news was received, a consultation at once followed. It was now too late to make the estuary of the Zwin at high tide [135] when they wished to deliver the attack, and it was accordingly decided to wait until the following day.[136]

[130] *Foedera,* II (2), 1129; *CCR* (1339–41), p. 482.

[131] Murimuth, p. 105; Baker, p. 68; Knighton, II, 17; *French Chronicle of London,* p. 76; *Lanercost,* p. 333; *Scalacronica,* p. 170; Walsingham, *Historia Anglicana,* I, 227; *Chronographia,* II, 121; Froissart, II, 219.

[132] See Edward's letter to the regent, July 9, 1340, in Kervyn, *Oeuvres de Froissart,* XVIII, 168. See also *Rotuli Parliamentorum,* II, 118; Murimuth, p. 105; Baker, p. 68; Hemingburgh, II, 358; *Scalacronica,* p. 170; *Chronicon Comitum Flandrensium,* p. 213. [133] *CPR* (1340–43), p. 39.

[134] Knighton, II, 18; Hemingburgh, II, 355–356; *Lanercost,* p. 333.

[135] According to the calculation of the astronomer royal, high tide in the Schelde on June 23, 1340, occurred at 10:35 A.M. and 10:59 P.M., and on the following day at 11:23 A.M. See N. H. Nicolas, *History of the Royal Navy,* II, 51 (note). All the chroniclers, a number of whom are independent witnesses of the battle, state that the attack took place at three o'clock in the afternoon at the moment of high tide.

[136] See Edward's letter to the regent, July 9, 1340, Kervyn, *Oeuvres de Froissart,* XVIII, 168; Murimuth, p. 106; Baker, p. 68; Hocsemius, p. 455.

At the ninth hour, three o'clock in the afternoon, and exactly at high tide, the English were in the channel of the estuary.[137] The wind was at their backs and the beams of the sun fell full upon the faces of the French. The English fleet was divided into three lines and was ready to bear down with great force upon the French before Sluis.[138] The French now made ready to receive them. Their fleet, like that of the English, was divided into three lines. The ships of the foremost line were chained together so that they could not drift apart and thus render less effective resistance to the enemy.[139] It is difficult to determine the relative strength of the two fleets; but it is certain that the French had more than two hundred craft as is conclusively shown by the statistics adduced by Dufourmantelle.[140] John le Bel states that the French had one and one half times as many craft as the English, which agrees very well with the testimony of the *Chronicle of Lanercost* which is, however, none too reliable.[141] When it is borne in mind that many of the French craft had been leisurely equipped and that the English had hastily impressed merchant ships, the relative strength would appear to be entirely in favor of the French.[142] The number of men, however, cannot be determined so accurately. There is a remarkable agreement among the chronicles that thirty thousand Frenchmen were killed, a figure most certainly too high. Edward himself declared that thirty-five thousand were dead and that five thousand had escaped.[143] The figures established by Dufourmantelle make it

[137] For a map of the estuary, see A. Beekman, "De Heidensee," *Tijdschrift van het Koninglijke Nederlandsch Aardrijkskundig Genootschap*, 3d Ser., XLI (1924), 359–368.

[138] Avesbury, p. 312; Baker, p. 68; Hemingburgh, II, 356; *Lanercost,* p. 333; Boendale, *Van den derden Eduwaert*, p. 341; *Breve Chronicon*, p. 8.

[139] Avesbury, p. 312; *Melsa,* III, 45; *French Chronicle of London*, p. 76; Hemingburgh, II, 356, who states that there were four lines; Froissart, II, 36.

[140] On July 9 Edward wrote to the regent that one hundred and ninety ships and barges were captured and that only twenty-four escaped, some of which were taken later. See Kervyn, *Oeuvres de Froissart*, XVIII, 167.

[141] Le Bel, I, 179; *Lanercost*, p. 333.

[142] See Boendale, *Van den derden Eduwaert*, pp. 338, 341; Baker, p. 69; Murimuth, p. 109; *Melsa,* III, 44–45; Hemingburgh, II, 356; Villani, col. 837; Froissart, II, 34, 219; Walsingham, I, 227.

[143] Letter to the regent, July 9, 1340, Kervyn, *Oeuvres de Froissart*, XVIII, 167.

certain that there were at least a good many more than 20,000
men.[144] The number of English dead must have been much
smaller, but accurate statistics cannot be adduced.

All advantage of weight and numbers on the side of the French
was, however, lost. Commanded by inexperienced men, they
allowed themselves to be caught in a narrow body of water
which made it impossible to maneuver properly. On the other
hand, the English had the advantage of the tide and the breeze,
while the rays of the sun fell directly upon the faces of the French
bowmen who accordingly could not aim with precision. The
English were thus able to use the archers with the most terrible
effectiveness in a position which on land would have been most
ideal for this new method of attack. As they approached they
resorted to a trick. The sails were hung at half-mast, and the
anchors thrown out so as to give the impression that they wished
to turn and flee. The French at once unfastened the chains which
held their ships together and began to move toward the English.[145]
Seeing the success of their ruse, the English bore down upon the
enemy. As they advanced upon the foremost line, long before
the French bowmen could shoot their arrows among the English,
the archers wrought fearful execution upon the crowded decks
of the enemy's ships.[146]

This stage of the struggle seems to have been far more important than is generally supposed.[147] The archers played a rôle
in accordance with the methods developed in the Scotch wars
which were later to be employed with similarly fatal conse-

[144] C. Dufourmantelle, *Le Marine militaire en France au Commencement de la Guerre de Cent Ans*, pp. 60–65, notwithstanding the opinion of
S. Luce, *La France pendant la Guerre de Cent Ans. Études Historiques
et Vie Privée aux XIVe et XVe Siècles* (Paris 1840), p. 18, who believes
that there were less than twenty thousand. See *Annales de Bermundeseia*,
p. 474; Murimuth, p. 109; *Melsa*, III, 44–45; Baker, p. 69, who gives two
hundred and twenty thousand as the figure; *Lanercost*, p. 333; Walsingham, I, 227; le Bel, I, 179; *Chronographia*, II, 122; Froissart, II, 219;
Outremeuse, p. 376.

[145] *French Chronicle of London*, p. 76; *Melsa*, III, 45; Avesbury, p. 312;
Froissart, II, 35–36. According to Baker, p. 68, and Murimuth, p. 106, they
advanced about a mile.

[146] According to Froissart, II, 219, Edward alternated each ship of
men-at-arms with two of bowmen of which there were twelve thousand.

[147] For the work of the archers, see *French Chronicle of London*, p. 77;
Avesbury, p. 312; *Melsa*, III, 44; Walsingham, I, 227; Villani, col. 837;
Chronographia, II, 121; Froissart, II, 35–36, 219, 221, 223.

quences on the fields of Crécy, Poitiers, and Agincourt. This fact is perhaps sufficient to account for such a disproportionate number of French slain. When the ships met, the men-at-arms dashed upon each other and a hand-to-hand struggle ensued. Decimated by arrows aimed at short range at the exposed arm-pits, the men were slaughtered in terrific fashion, and the French of the first line could not hold their own.[148] Many who sought to escape the terrible butchery by swimming were drowned.[149] The entire first line of ships was thus soon taken, and the *Chris-topher*, the *St. Denys*, the *St. George*, the *Black Cogg*, and others, some of which had been seized in the Schelde in the fall of 1338, now again were in English possession.[150]

The second line was much more easily destroyed than the first because a panic appears to have seized the men. Many of the sailors apparently from the beginning of the fight had leaped into the water in order to escape. Little has been recorded of this part of the struggle, simply because, it would seem, of the comparatively slight resistance, which was nearly over when darkness came on.[151] The English were exhausted from the long struggle when the attack on the third line began and night soon prevented all progress.[152] The fighting was resumed with re-newed vigor at daybreak and was of but short duration as some twenty-five or thirty ships from this line, under the command of the pirate Spoudevisch, had succeeded at about midnight in eluding the English and escaping to the high seas.[153] In their flight one of their largest ships, the *Jacques de Dieppe*, sought to make away with a ship from Sandwich provided by the prior of Christchurch. The struggle lasted all night, and the vic-torious English found, it is said, four hundred dead in the hull.

[148] *French Chronicle of London*, p. 77; Baker, p. 68.

[149] Boendale, *Van den derden Eduwaert*, p. 342; Hemingburgh, II, 357.

[150] Baker, p. 69; Murimuth, p. 106; Hemingburgh, II, 336–357.

[151] Baker, p. 69, who writes as if the ships of the first line were still chained together, and that this impeded the attack upon the second line; Murimuth, pp. 106–107.

[152] Baker, p. 69; Murimuth, p. 107; *Melsa*, III, 45; Hemingburgh, II, 357.

[153] Boendale, *Van den derden Eduwaert*, p. 342; *French Chronicle of London*, p. 77; Edward's letter to the regent of July 9, 1340, in Kervyn, *Oeuvres de Froissart*, XVIII, 167; Knighton, II, 18; Hemingburgh, II, p. 357; Hocsemius, p. 455.

The flight was discovered at dawn and Edward dispatched forty vessels in pursuit under the command of John Crabbe who overtook some of Spoudevisch's craft in spite of several hours' advantage.[154]

The official French explanation of the defeat is that the two commanders, Béhuchet and Quieret, were in disagreement with the Genoese Barbaveria. The latter was a skilled seaman and advised his colleague Quieret who "knew more about accounts than fighting" to stand out to sea and not await the English in the narrow channel of the Zwin where they would be unable to maneuver and help each other effectively. But his counsel was rejected, whereupon the Genoese threatened to withdraw his galleys. At this moment the English were approaching the French ships. The four galleys of Barbaveria were, it appears, in the front line and promptly withdrew.[155] The English chronicles strangely enough omit all mention of this fact and it is certainly not possible to identify the flight of these ships with those of Spoudevisch.[156] But the story is true in its essential points, for orders were issued by Philip to his officials in the ports on the Channel to arrest the Genoese and Barbaveria "for the treason of which he is guilty." [157]

During the course of the battle the Flemings had hastened to the dykes along the Zwin to witness the struggle upon which so much depended for them. They cut off all hope of escape for the French who sought to swim to the shore. The notice given them by the bishop of Lincoln on the previous day had undoubtedly aroused many. But there can hardly have been enough time to send out sufficient craft from Bruges to render much assistance.[158] As soon as they reached the dykes the Frenchmen were killed.[159] One of the Flemings, John van Eyle of Sluis, an émigré nobleman, who had followed the example of other

[154] Baker, p. 69; Murimuth, p. 107; *Melsa*, III, 45; Hemingburgh, II, 357; *French Chronicle of London*, p. 77.

[155] *Grandes Chroniques*, V, 385–387; de Nangis, II, 169–170; *Chronographia*, II, 122.

[156] As is done by the *Bourgeois de Valenciennes*, p. 181.

[157] C. de la Roncière, *Histoire de la Marine Française*, I, 455 (note 2).

[158] Edward wrote to the regent on July 9 that the Flemings "estoient de bone volentè d'avoir venuz à no ala bataille du commencement tanqe ala fin. . . ." See Kervyn, *Oeuvres de Froissart*, XVIII, 167. Also *Melsa*, III, 45; le Bel, I, 178; *Chronographia*, II, 123.

[159] Hemingburgh, II, 356; *Melsa*, III, 45; Villani, col. 837; Froissart,

nobles and left Flanders with Count Louis, was seized by the English and surrendered to the authorities of Bruges who had him promptly executed on the great square before the belfry.[160]

Thus was the battle won with enormous losses for the French, whose ships were either taken or destroyed, whose men were for the most part slain, and with only very slight losses for the English whose dead perhaps numbered little more than four thousand.[161] Béhuchet and Quieret were both killed, and numerous bodies, cast up in the next few days by the tide, lay upon the banks of the Zwin and the Schelde.[162] Curiously enough, on the morrow of the contest a report was current in London that a great victory had been won, but it was not generally credited until officially confirmed.[163]

Edward was now master of the sea. The battle of Sluis saved his allies in the Low Countries for a while by strengthening them against Philip. Piratical activities by the French were for a time at an end. " May the memory of this battle in the mouth of the Zwin be kept ever green! " wrote the patriotic and enthusiastic poet Boendale who may well have shared in the exultation of the people of Antwerp. All those who spoke *Dietsch,* or Netherlandish, in Flanders, Brabant, and elsewhere were delighted.[164] And among the French who had not yet forgotten the fatal battle of Courtrai the defeat must have been correspondingly depressing. It even became a theme of the songs of Norman peasants.[165] The English were pleased. The abbot of Melsa

II, 38, 222–223; *Chronographia,* II, 123; de Nangis, II, 169, 183; Lescot, p. 52.

[160] Boendale, *Van den derden Eduwaert,* p. 344; *Chronicon Comitum Flandrensium,* p. 212. According to Despars, *Cronijcke van den Lande ende Graefscepe van Vlaenderen,* II, 348, van Eyle was captain of the *Christopher.* He was captured by an Englishman from Sandwich and promptly surrendered, and Edward on July 7 paid the ransom demanded. See *CPR* (1340–43), p. 18; *CCR* (1341–43), p. 68.

[161] Hemingburgh, II, 357–358; *Melsa,* III, 45; Murimuth, p. 109; *Lanercost,* p. 333. The *Chronographia,* II, 123–125, and *Chronique des Quatre premiers Valois,* p. 10, state that the English lost 10,000. The figures are not reliable.

[162] Edward to the regent, July 7, in Kervyn, *Oeuvres de Froissart,* XVIII, 167; see le Bel, I, 179.

[163] Avesbury, p. 312.

[164] Boendale, *Van den derden Eduwaert,* p. 344.

[165] S. Luce, " Le Soufflet de l'Écluse et la Chanson des Pastoureaux Normands," *La France pendant la Guerre de Cent Ans. Épisodes His-*

declared that it was humorously said that had the Lord granted
the fishes speech they would have to speak French after feasting
on so many French bodies![166] On the 28th the regent ordered
the clergy to render thanks for the victory.[167] With pride easy
to understand could Laurence Minot write:

> "Sare it tham smerted that ferd out of France,
> Thare lered Inglis men tham a new daunce." [168]

The troops disembarked, but Edward stayed aboard the
Thomas for several days. He had taken an active part in the
struggle and was wounded in the thigh. Meanwhile plans for
the coming campaign were considered, and for several days there
were conversations in the king's ship.[169] The scabini and captains
of Ghent had been apprised of his arrival and of the glorious
victory on the 24th. Simon van Merelbeke, Thomas van Vaernewijc, and John uten Hove at once left Ghent to welcome Edward.
On Tuesday, the 27th, deputies were sent to confer with him.
Van Artevelde himself, accompanied by his colleague William
van Vaernewijc, the scabinus, Simon ser Thomaes, and William
de Bomere went to Sluis on the 30th and returned on July 5.[170]
The enthusiastic public crowded toward Sluis, and Philippa
also hastened thither from Ghent to be near her husband.[171] Edward was still on board the *Thomas* on July 6.[172] He disembarked when the wound was sufficiently healed and went on pilgrimage to Our Lady of Aardenburg to render thanks for his safe
voyage.[173] His troops and military equipment, it appears, were
sent directly to Ghent.[174]

---

toriques et Vie Privée aux XIVe et XVe Siècles (2d Ser.), Paris, 1893. Cf.
le Bel, I, 180.   [166] *Melsa*, III, 45.   [167] *Foedera*, II (2), 1129.

[168] *Political Poems and Songs relating to English History*, I, 70.

[169] *Grandes Chroniques*, V, 387; *Chronographia*, II, 124; *French Chronicle of London*, p. 77; *Lanercost*, pp. 333–334; Edward's letter to the regent,
June 29, Kervyn, *Oeuvres de Froissart*, XVIII, 168.

[170] N. de Pauw en J. Vuylsteke, *Rekeningen der Stad Gent*, I, 421–422,
448. Cf. Villani, col. 837.

[171] Edward's letter to the regent, July 29, Kervyn, *Oeuvres de Froissart*,
XVIII, 168; *Chronographia*, II, 124; *Grandes Chroniques*, V, 387–388;
French Chronicle of London, p. 77; *Lanercost*, pp. 333–334.

[172] *CFR* (1337–47), p. 202.

[173] Le Bel, I, 180; *Grandes Chroniques*, V, 388; *Chronographia*, II, 124;
Froissart, II, 39; Outremeuse, VI, 376.

[174] Kervyn, *Oeuvres de Froissart*, XVIII, 167–179; *Foedera*, II (2),
1130; Murimuth, p. 107.

IV. The Fiasco at St. Omer (August, 1340)

When King Edward had finished his devotions at Aardenburg he proceeded with his entourage to Bruges [175] where he tarried from July 8 to 10.[176] On board the *Thomas* the Flemings and others had fully revealed to him the situation on the borders of Flanders and Hainault and begged him to take immediate measures to drive back the French.[177] This undoubtedly was the counsel of van Artevelde who had gone with his colleague, William van Vaernewijc, the scabinus, Simon ser Thomaes, and William de Bomere to Sluis on the 30th and returned to Ghent on July 4.[178] Tournai and Artois were to be seized so that they might serve as a base for future hostile activities against Lille and Douai and for incursions as far west as Compiègne.[179] The Flemish demand for the " restoration " of their ancient territories would thus be partially satisfied. John le Bel states that all this was arranged at Vilvoorde whither went many notables such as William, count of Hainault, Holland, and Zeeland, John, duke of Brabant, Reginald, duke of Guelders, William, margrave of Juliers, John of Hainault, the seignior of Valkenburg, van Artevelde, and a great number of advisers from the towns of Flanders.[180] The accounts of Bruges and Ghent, however, make no mention of such a delegation. Nor was there time for such a meeting before the 9th when Edward wrote to his subjects about the coming campaign.[181]

Edward's finances were in a most precarious condition. The money which was to be realized from the grants of the recent Parliament at Westminster was to have been sent to him by ship

[175] *Grandes Chroniques,* V, 388; *Chronographia,* II, 124–125; *French Chronicle of London,* p. 77.

[176] Lescot (*Appendice*), p. 207.

[177] See Edward's letter to his subjects on July 9, in *Foedera,* II (2), 1130.

[178] N. de Pauw en J. Vuylsteke, *Rekeningen der Stad Gent,* I, 422.

[179] Le Bel, pp. 181–182.

[180] *Ibid.,* p. 180. No other chronicler mentions this meeting at Vilvoorde.

[181] *Foedera,* II (2), 1130. The mission of the scabinus Gilles Rijnvisch, William van Vaernewijc, and William de Bomere to the duke at Brussels from the 7th to the 9th may nevertheless have had something to do with these plans. See N. de Pauw en J. Vuylsteke, *Rekeningen der Stad Gent,* I, 422.

on St. John the Baptist's Day, and Edward who had embarked in time to arrive in Flanders at the appointed day had apparently no money with him and waited vainly at Sluis for the promised resources. This as well as his wound may have protracted his convalescence. The Flemings, pressed for money to pay the extraordinary expenses which the alliance had occasioned their towns, were eager to be paid. Edward borrowed such sums as he could from private parties in order to pay current expenses.[182] With great difficulty a small sum was paid to the towns at this time.[183] On the 9th he addressed a most urgent request to the Lords, lay and spiritual, and the Commons who were to assemble in Parliament on July 12 to send money as quickly as possible. He dispatched the earls of Arundel, Huntingdon, and Gloucester, and William Trussel, who had full information of what sums were due, at what time they were to be paid, and to whom. If he did not receive the necessary resources at once, Edward declared that his prestige and honor would be seriously jeopardized. He also wrote about the great victory which he had won at Sluis and of the grandiose plans according to which he intended to lead 100,000 men-at-arms against Tournai, and Robert of Artois would lead 50,000 against St. Omer.[184]

From Bruges Edward went to Ghent where he tarried until the 18th.[185] He was received with open-hearted hospitality; the people, according to John le Bel, greeted him as a god and some, it is said, sought relief from disease by touching the royal garments.[186] The scabini presented him with two vats of wine worth 268*l.* and van Artevelde gave him two oxen valued at 180*l.*[187] In Ghent, as elsewhere, there was much activity in preparation for the coming campaign. On the 12th the scabini sent three of their colleagues, with Gilles Rijnvisch and Michael

---

[182] See the loans of 329*l.* 6*s.* 8*d.* by John de Molyns and 200*l.* by the earl of Warwick. *CPR* (1340–43), pp. 114, 219.

[183] N. de Pauw en J. Vuylsteke, *Rekeningen der Stad Gent*, I, 423.

[184] *Foedera*, II (2), 1130.

[185] Lescot (*Appendice*), p. 207.

[186] *Grandes Chroniques*, V, 388; *Chronographia*, II, 125; *Scalacronica*, p. 170; *Bourgeois de Valenciennes*, p. 182; Outremeuse, VI, 376–377; le Bel, I, 180; *Lanercost*, p. 334. See Villani, col. 838: " . . . e venne a Bruggia e poi a Guanto, e da' Fiamminghi gli fu fatto honore, come a loro signore, facendogli omaggio, come al re di Francia."

[187] N. de Pauw en J. Vuylsteke, *Rekeningen der Stad Gent*, I, 385.

de Witte, to accompany Robert of Artois and the contingents from Bruges and Ypres.[188] At the same moment messengers went back and forth between Ghent and Brussels apparently to secure the duke's full coöperation in the siege against Tournai.[189] On the 12th the bailiffs of the Quatuor Officia and Waasland were ordered to raise their quotas of men-at-arms, and, on August 6, the scabini, François Slove and Segher Seghers, were sent thither.[190] Something of the feeling in the hearts of Flemings at the time when the communal militia marched forth from Ghent on July 16 is preserved for us in the laconic expense accounts of this expedition: "to withstand the King of France in behalf of the lord count for the profit and preservation of the crafts and the peace, for the wives and children of all Flanders." [191]

At Cassel meanwhile were concentrating the contingents from Dixmuide, Ypres, Poperingen, Cassel, Bailleul, Veurne, Bergen, Bourbourg, Bruges, and the Frank of Bruges, which were all under the command of Robert of Artois who intended to invest St. Omer [192] with this force, which was probably not larger than 10,000 men and which included a number of English archers.[193] They marched westward, crossed the Neuf Fosse on July 24, and at once began to burn everything they met. The town of Arques went up in flames. There is some report of a disinclination among the levies of Bergen and Veurne to cross the borders of Artois, which may not have been without significance in connection with the fiasco on the 25th.[194] King Philip had taken proper precautions to defend St. Omer, and within its walls was a strong force with a good number of French and fugitive Flemish notables, the most important of whom were the count of Armagnac, the castellans of Bergen and Dixmuide, and Eudes, duke of Burgundy, who must have been especially eager as count of Artois

[188] N. de Pauw en J. Vuylsteke, *Rekeningen der Stad Gent,* I, p. 422.

[189] *Ibid.,* pp. 339, 422, 450.

[190] *Ibid.,* p. 449. There was apparently some reluctance in these quarters to respond promptly.   [191] *Ibid.,* pp. 503–505.

[192] Boendale, *Van den derden Eduwaert,* pp. 351–353; *Scalacronica,* p. 171. *Grandes Chroniques,* V, 388; *Chronographia,* II, 125; de Budt, pp. 327–328.

[193] Villani, col. 837. See also *Melsa,* III, 46; *Chronique Normande,* p. 46.

[194] *Grandes Chroniques,* V, 390–391.

to defend the disputed country against his rival Robert.[195]
Moved by the sight of burning villages and homesteads, the count
of Armagnac and the duke of Burgundy marched out of St. Omer
toward the Flemings.

The invaders had taken up a position along the great road
which led from Arques to St. Omer. At the extreme right was
stationed Robert of Artois with his English archers and the levies
from Bruges. On the opposite side were the men from Ypres,
and between them those from Veurne, Bergen, and the Frank of
Bruges. The troops from Poperingen, Cassel, and Bailleul were
set to guard the tents. The men on the left had intrenched themselves behind a ditch reinforced by stakes, and were difficult
to approach. The count of Armagnac's forces drew near the
Flemish left, but, seeing their well-nigh impregnable position,
turned and began to retreat. The men of the center, those from
Bergen, Veurne, and the Frank of Bruges, advanced in pursuit,
and after them followed the extreme left. When the followers
of the count of Armagnac saw this, they again turned and hurled
themselves upon the center which was soon driven back. Thereupon the men from Ypres, no longer protected by the ditch and
the stakes, were attacked and forced to leave the field in head-
long flight toward Arques.[196]

Meanwhile, Robert advanced toward the walls of St. Omer,
and the duke of Burgundy drew back. The Flemings rushed at
the gates, which, however, were closed just in time. It was
evening, and the count of Armagnac was returning from his pursuit of the Flemish left and suddenly came upon their right. The
English archers conducted themselves well, and in the fight a
number of the enemy were killed. The French withdrew and
Robert of Artois retired to the tents at Arques which to his great
astonishment had been abandoned, for the guards had followed
the example of the militia from Ypres. Under these circumstances nothing could be done but to withdraw toward Cassel
where there was much indignation.[197] Robert of Artois did not

---

[195] *Ibid.*, p. 389; de Budt, p. 328; Villani, col. 837; *Scalacronica*, p. 171.

[196] *Chronographia*, II, 131–132; Boendale, *Van den derden Eduwaert*,
p. 351.

[197] *Chronographia*, II, 132–134; de Budt, p. 328; Murimuth, p. 108;
Melsa, III, 46; *Grandes Chroniques*, V, 391–392; Villani col. 837; *Chronique Normande*, p. 46.

know how to use the English archers effectively, and the panic of the levies of Ypres proved his undoing. Nothing was accomplished; he could only lead his remaining troops to Tournai and support Edward's efforts.[198]

V. The Siege of Tournai (August–September, 1340)

WHILE Robert of Artois was getting ready to advance upon St. Omer, Edward moved on toward Tournai. With the king, who left Philippa at Ghent, were the archbishop of Canterbury, the bishop of Chichester, the earls of Derby, Northampton, Arundel, Warwick, and Huntingdon, archers numbering possibly 4,000, and many horses.[199] On July 16 van Artevelde and his associates, the captains, the deans of the guilds, and some of the scabini, led out a formidable number of men — 1,800 from the weavers, 1,200 from the fullers, 2,139 from the lesser crafts, 65 bowmen, 32 shield-bearers (*taerghedraeghers*), and 100 white-hoods commanded by Goessine Alipe. The total expenses of this expedition clearly reveal its magnitude. For the remainder of the financial year (until the middle of August) it cost 22,433*l.* 16*s.* 8*d.*, and for the rest of the campaign, 25,510*l.* 3*s.* 4*d.*[200] They passed by way of Oudenaarde and Courtrai and appeared with Edward at Espierre on the 21st. Their tents, which were spread out as far as Estambourc, could be descried from the walls of Tournai. Some of the English were lodged at Helchin, a possession of the bishop of Tournai now held by the Flemings, who had placed it under the guard of Goessine Alipe with ten white-hoods and twenty bowmen. Two days later, on the 23d Edward advanced to Chin, where he stayed nine days.[201]

The English king sent a challenge to Philip on the 26th. He invited him either to a personal combat or to entrust the decision to a conflict of a hundred men from each side, or to a pitched

[198] De Budt, p. 328. See E. Petit, *Histoire des Ducs de Bourgogne,* VII (*Pièces Justificatives*), 395.

[199] *Foedera,* II(2), 1130; *Melsa,* III, 45–46; Boendale, *Van den derden Eduwaert,* p. 364.

[200] N. de Pauw en J. Vuylsteke, *Rekeningen der Stad Gent,* I, 502–505, and II, 87–88.

[201] *Ibid.,* II, 84–85; le Muisit, p. 127; *Chronographia,* II, 125; *Grandes Chroniques,* V, 397–400; *Chronique de Tournai,* p. 344.

battle of all the forces in each camp. But Philip was determined, as in the previous year, to remain strictly on the defensive, for he undoubtedly realized that time would very likely break up the motley array now advancing against him. His answer on the 30th from St. Andrew's priory was characteristic of chivalric bombast. He declared that he had seen Edward's letter addressed to "Philip of Valois," but stated that it was clearly evident from the contents that the missive was not intended for him and so he could not reply. He complained of Edward's violation of his oath of homage, expressed the hope that the Flemings would remain loyal, and declared his intention to drive the invaders from his realm.[202] These formalities meant nothing, and fighting had already begun. Baldwin d'Aubercourt, seignior of Estambourc, sallied forth from Tournai when evening fell and slew a number of Englishmen and Flemings.[203]

Edward halted nine days at Chin, and with the Flemings advanced upon Tournai immediately. His other allies, William, margrave of Juliers, Reginald, duke of Guelders, John of Hainault,[204] and William, count of Hainault, Holland, and Zeeland, with a considerable company of Hollanders and Zeelanders now also appeared.[205] The Flemings who had been sent out with Robert of Artois had arrived on the 27th or 28th after their discomfiture at St. Omer and undoubtedly greatly increased the host under van Artevelde.[206]

Edward and the Flemings folded their tents on the 31st, moved upon Tournai, and began the investment on the following day. They burned the outlying houses, a lazar-house at Val, and other objects.[207] The English took up a position to the southwest of the city with their right wing opposite the gate of St. Martin which

---

[202] *Foedera*, II (2), 1131–1132; Baker, p. 71; *Melsa*, III, 46; Murimuth, pp. 109–110; *Chronographia*, II.

[203] *Chronique de Tournai*, p. 344.

[204] *Melsa*, III, 47; Baker, pp. 70–71; *Chronographia*, II, 125.

[205] *French Chronicle of London*, p. 78; H. G. Hamaker, *Rekeningen der Grafelijkheid van het Graafschap Holland onder het Henegouwsche Huis*, III, 52, 68; Froissart, II, 45, 232; S. A. Waller Zeper, *Jan van Henegouwen, Heer van Beaumont*, p. 178. Some of the Zeelanders passed through Ghent. See N. de Pauw en J. Vuylsteke, *Rekeningen der Stad Gent*, I, 465.

[206] Le Bel, I, 187; de Budt, p. 328; *Melsa*, III, 46; *Scalacronica*, p. 171.

[207] *Chronique de Tournai*, p. 347.

stood on the road to Lille and Douai. Robert of Artois was with him — the Flemings had by this time left his command — and halted at a rivulet called the Ries.[208] This arrangement, it should be noted, placed the English between the city and Philip's army, if it should approach. It is possible that Edward deliberately planned this, for if Philip chose to relieve the place, he would be obliged to attack Edward's archers. Van Artevelde, whom the Flemings regarded as a king according to the anonymous author of the Tournai chronicle, stationed himself below the city on both banks of the Schelde over which was constructed a bridge to maintain communications between the two wings. His forces stretched from the monastery of Notre Dame du Conseil, situated on land popularly known as the Pres-as-Nonnains, northward as far as Maire on the east and Orcq on the west between the gate of Ste. Fontaine on the left bank and that of the Arches on the other side of the river.[209] William, count of Hainault, Holland, and Zeeland, and John of Hainault, now also appeared and drew up their forces above the city so that the count's left was in close contact with Edward's right. The whole section known as the Marvis on the right bank of the Schelde was occupied by the men of Hainault, and the count himself took up his abode in the monastery of Sauchoit.[210] Between his right and the Flemish left were stationed the duke of Guelders, the margrave of Juliers, the counts of Berg and Salm, the seignior of Valkenburg, and other German troops.[211] As in the previous year, the duke of Brabant arrived late, on August 11, and took up a position in the street and suburb of the Marvis on the southeast side of the city. He thus had the count of Hainault, whose troops apparently lay on both banks of the Schelde, on his left, and the mass of Germans and others on his right.[212]

For some time Philip had taken great pains to strengthen the fortifications of the city and the accounts of his treasurer, Barthé-

---

[208] Le Muisit, p. 128; Froissart, II, 44–45; *Chronique de Tournai*, p. 346.

[209] Le Muisit, p. 128; *Chronique de Tournai*, pp. 346–347, 348, 349; le Bel, I, 183.

[210] *Bourgeois de Valenciennes*, p. 347; *Chronique de Tournai*, p. 347; Froissart, II, 45; le Muisit, pp. 127–128.

[211] Le Bel, I, 187; Froissart, II, 45; Baker, pp. 70–77.

[212] *Chronique de Tournai*, pp. 350, 358; le Muisit, p. 128; *Grandes Chroniques*, V, 78; *French Chronicle of London*, p. 78; *Melsa*, III, 45–47.

lemy du Drach, contain numerous items of expense incurred.[213] On the 23d, when Edward was at Chin, Gondemar de Fay entered by the gate of St. Martin. With him arrived 1,500 horse and men-at-arms, and 1,000 foot with forty banners to augment the garrison under the command of Raoul, count of Eu, constable of France, who was attended by his son, the count of Ghines, and others. There were about 2,500 horse and a large number of foot totalling about 5,100 men.[214] All plans had been made to offer a stubborn defense. When an assault threatened or the enemy approached, the two bells, the *bancloche* and the *Wingerons*, were to be rung, and the defenders were to hurry to the places assigned to them on the walls and towers. Special guards of the communal militia, as well as of the soldiery sent by Philip, were placed to guard the gates. The people who could not aid in the defense and who might become a burden upon the defenders were sent out of the city. So vigilant was the watch of Edward and his allies that none could leave the town except at very great peril. The constable rode about the streets and open spaces attended by horsemen, and all manner of siege instruments were erected which began to hurl stones in response to those cast into the city by the enemy.[215]

There were numerous manifestations of loyalty to the king of France on the part of the inhabitants. Gilles le Muisit, the abbot of St. Martin, wrote: " Mention must be made of the great harmony between the king's men and the inhabitants so that there was never heard any discord or strife, but they were at peace like brothers." [216] On the evening of the annual procession of Our Lady, the scabini of Ghent, as was their custom, sent four Dominicans to the gate of Ste. Fontaine with the clothes and other things for the image. They had been at considerable trouble to provide a suitable cap which cost in all, including work and carriage, 512*l.* 7*s.* 9*d.* But they were denied entrance because they were excommunicate. On the following day, September 14, the procession took place. The petticoat of Our

<hr>

[213] Le Bel, I, 182, 183 (notes).

[214] Le Muisit, pp. 126–127; *Chronique de Tournai*, pp. 344–345, 347; le Bel, I, 182–183.

[215] Le Muisit, pp. 130–131; le Bel, I, 192; *Chronique de Tournai*, pp. 353–355; *Grandes Chronique*, V, 389; *Chronographia*, II, 125–126; *Melsa*, III, 47.   [216] Le Muisit, p. 131.

Lady and the shrine were decked out with the arms of the king of France.[217]   Realizing the importance of Tournai, Philip had adopted a more lenient attitude toward the inhabitants and since February had restored to the commune its rights, high and low justice and incomes of various kinds, and regulated in a manner very favorable to the burghers the government and administration of the commune.[218]

During August William, count of Hainault, Holland, and Zeeland, had an opportunity to retaliate for the ravaging of his lands in the previous spring by Philip's soldiers. On August 1 he left the besiegers, and, accompanied by Englishmen and Flemings, soon appeared before St. Amand which they assaulted and carried. They plundered the town and the monastery, slaughtered the townsmen, and took a great quantity of booty and cattle. Orchies came next on the 4th, and, as the annual market was being held at the moment, a great amount of booty was taken. The levies from Valenciennes, who had seen the enemy burn the hamlets and houses around their own walls, were especially active in plundering the countryside and burned as many as seventeen places large enough to have towers with bells.[219] Later, on the 10th, Seclin was burned, and serious damage was inflicted upon many other villages and hamlets. On the 12th and 13th Marchiennes was taken with much slaughter and destruction.[220] There were numerous raids into this region so that soon most of the country west of the Schelde from St. Amand to Douai, Seclin, and Lille was severely pillaged.[221] Serious losses were inflicted upon the properties of the monastery of St. Martin of Tournai.[222]

[217] *Chronique de Tournai*, p. 360; N. de Pauw en J. Vuylsteke, *Rekeningen der Stad Gent*, II, 18.

[218] H. Vanderbroek, *Extraits Analytiques des Anciens Registres des Consaux de la Ville Tournai*, I, 286–287. In December Philip ceded to the corporation the entire royal domain at Tournai, reserving only his rights as suzerain. See Poutrain, *Histoire de la Ville et Cité de Tournai*, II (*Preuves*), 35.

[219] *Bourgeois de Valenciennes*, p. 184; *Chronique de Tournai*, pp. 347–349; Boendale, *Van den derden Eduwaert*, p. 352; le Muisit, pp. 128–130; Murimuth, p. 115; *Chronicon Tielense*, p. 333; N. de Pauw en J. Vuylsteke, *Rekeningen der Stad Gent*, I, 451.

[220] *Chronique de Tournai*, p. 352.

[221] Le Bel, I, 183–184; *Chronicon Comitum Flandrensium*, p. 213; *Melsa*, III, 47; Baker, p. 71; Avesbury, p. 316.   [222] Le Muisit, pp. 129–130.

The siege had in the meantime been prosecuted with vigor. The Flemings were especially active, but as the defense was equal to the energies of the assailants, it was soon evident that the city could be reduced only by a long investment. Philip, not daring to risk an engagement with Edward, kept on the defensive and accordingly could not hope to relieve the besieged. He had stationed his troops between Lens and Arras. As soon as the allied forces had begun to collect around Tournai, he received reinforcements from the bishop of Liège, John, king of Bohemia, Louis, count of Flanders, and others.[223] Philip had slowly advanced eastward; he was at Béthune on August 4 and 6, at Lens on the 13th, near Douai from the 20th to the 26th, at La Bassée on September 4, and only two leagues from Tournai on the 7th when he pitched his tents at Bouvines.[224] The duke of Brabant now moved his troops over to the left bank of the Schelde so that his left wing was stationed on the road to Valenciennes, probably as far as the present Rue Fontenoy or the Rue de la Montagne.[225] Count William's troops thereupon moved nearer the gate of St. Martin.[226] But Philip halted on the banks of the Marcq where he was safe behind the marshes.

Within the city there was great want by the close of August. The investing forces had cut off all supply of fresh water.[227] The large number of horses and cattle consumed all reserve supplies of hay and oats so that these articles soon soared to the most unusual prices. All food-stuffs became increasingly scarcer and a lucrative smuggling trade in cheese, herring, and fruit developed.[228]

But while the situation within the walls was so desperate that further resistance was possible for only a few weeks at the longest, the confidence of the besiegers was seriously undermined. In spite of the fact that the allied forces were constantly being

[223] Le Bel, I, 192–194; *Chronographia,* III, 148–149.

[224] J. Viard, " Itinéraire de Philippe VI de Valois," *BEC,* LXXIV (1913), 537–538; le Muisit, p. 133; le Bel, I, 197; *Chronicon Comitum Flandrensium,* p. 213; Boendale, *Van den derden Eduwaert,* pp. 354–355.

[225] *Chronique de Tournai,* p. 358; Froissart, II, 45; *Chronographia,* II, 139–140.

[226] Le Muisit, pp. 132–133; *Chronique de Tournai,* pp. 358, 360.

[227] *French Chronicle of London,* p. 79.

[228] Le Muisit, pp. 131–132; *Chronique de Tournai,* p. 364; le Bel, I, 191–192; Knighton, II, 19; *Melsa,* III, 47.

supplied with all necessary food by boats and wagons which came from Brabant and Flanders,[229] the militia of the duke of Brabant were very eager to return home. They were not in the least conscious of historic grievances suffered at the hands of the French kings as were the Flemings and had therefore little desire to press the attack; in fact, there is no information that Duke John participated actively in the operations. They were thus easily influenced by the efforts of Philip at this time to stir up trouble in the communes of Brabant. Walter Egloy, his son, Regnier, and Claes Zuaure, patricians of Brussels, conspired with Philip, who gave them large sums of money to induce the militia from the various towns to return home, thus hoping to make impossible the continuance of the siege.

John le Bel states that the patricians were dissatisfied with the position Brussels occupied among the towns of Brabant, which was next to that of Louvain.[230] This feeling had led to difficulties at the moment when Duke John was expected to appear before Tournai. The levies of Brussels demanded the right to occupy the position nearest the duke's right. The matter was left to the decision of the duke who on August 4 decreed that for the future, whenever he led any expedition northward or westward toward Flanders or Hainault, his marshal should place the levies of Louvain, who were to leave before those of Brussels, in the position of honor, and whenever he led them toward the Meuse or Liège or Namur, to the east or the northeast, the quota from Brussels should start first and accordingly be placed at the duke's right.[231] Philip's representatives were successful in stirring up trouble [232] which was undoubtedly communicated to the troops before the walls of Tournai. The levies from Brussels, who appear to have led in the demand, as well as those of Louvain, Antwerp, Nivelles, Jodoigne, Lier, and Mechelen, demanded leave to return home *par congiet ou sans*

---

229 Le Bel, I, 191; Baker, pp. 70–71.

230 Le Bel, I, 210–211.

231 E. Dynter, *Chronicon Ducum Brabantiae,* II, 633–637; J. B. Ansems, *Den Luyster ende Glorie van het Hertogdom van Brabant,* Part I, pp. 116–118.

232 See Philip's letters of December 9, 1341, to the corporations of Brussels, Mechelen, and Antwerp concerning this matter in A. Verkooren, *Inventaire Brabant,* II, 113–114.

congiet. Duke John thereupon held council with the duke of Guelders, the margrave of Juliers, the seignior of Blankenberg, and some English noblemen. The demand was refused, but the men-at-arms were given permission to leave.[233]

Philip's diplomatic activity was also felt in Flanders, where it was supported by the disaffected elements in the Frank of Bruges. When the contingents were sent to Cambrai to reinforce the efforts of William, count of Hainault, Holland, and Zeeland, and aid him against the incursions of Philip, some parties refused to obey. On July 11 the scabini of Ghent sent eleven bowmen and twenty white-hoods at a cost of 1,897*l*. 8*s*. 11*d*. to the Frank of Bruges, accompanied by some troops from the town of Bruges in order to punish the offenders.[234] When the siege began, the enemies of van Artevelde's policy in these districts sought to approach Philip. The king received definite offer of surrender from these people who were apparently sanguine enough to believe that the three towns could also be brought to yield. He discussed the matter at length with the representatives of the Flemings at Béthune where he halted from August 4 to 6.[235]

Even among the troops under the command of the captains from Ghent there apparently was disaffection. The contingents from Waasland and the Quatuor Officia had not moved when the militia of Ghent left for Tournai. On August 6 the scabini sent two representatives to these parts in order to induce them to march. When in April troops had been sent to the border near Cambrai, Peter vanden Hovene and Simon Godenvalen were appointed to watch the leaders of the men who had been sent from these parts.[236] Under these circumstances negotiations were very promising and it was even reported in the curia in Avignon that the Flemings had approached the king in secrecy, asked mercy for

[233] Froissart, II, 250–251; le Bel, I, 207.

[234] N. de Pauw en J. Vuylsteke, *Rekeningen der Stad Gent,* I, 502.

[235] J. Viard, "Itinéraire de Philippe VI de Valois," *BEC,* LXXIV (1913), 538; le Bel, I, 207 (note 2).

[236] N. de Pauw en J. Vuylsteke, *Rekeningen der Stad Gent,* I, 423. See also p. 490: "It. ghaven sij Pietere vanden Hovene ende Symoene Ghodevolen, die waren ghesent te Curterike metten serganten van vierambachten ende vanden landen van Waes, omme haerlieder beleeders te sine, ende adde elc 3*s*. gr. sdaghes, dat comt dat Pieter vanden Hovene metten vors. serganten te Curterike lach 36 daghe, ende Symoen Ghodevolen 34 daghe, 10*l*. 10*s*. gr., maken 420*l*."

all the excesses they had committed, and requested the speedy return of Count Louis.[237]

The coherence of the allied army was further jeopardized by the personal hostility between van Artevelde and the duke of Brabant.[238] John may possibly have disliked the agreement between Edward and the Flemings whereby the wool staple would be transferred from Antwerp, where it had been for several years, to Bruges. Nor could he have had much sympathy with van Artevelde's methods which were based on the principle of communal independence and tended to be popular in character. Furthermore, he had accepted Edward's policy largely because it was expedient for the economic development of his towns and because it seemed to promise political advantages, not to mention substantial sums in hard cash. All the coveted rights in Mechelen were now in his possession. And, finally, Edward's financial position was exceedingly difficult. Inability to pay his many debts would certainly entail a decline of his prestige in the Low Countries. Nor would he be able to protect the Flemings and their neighbors against Philip's attacks. French diplomacy would then have an opportunity to undo much that Edward had gained. The duke with characteristic circumspection accordingly had little desire to advance Edward's interests further.

The Flemings had much at stake and were eager to gain Tournai and the lost parts of Flanders. They pushed the siege with vigor,[239] and were annoyed by the inactivity of the duke of Brabant. They accused the men of Brabant of allowing food to pass into the city and the destitute poor to leave the gates.[240]

---

[237] G. Canestrini, " Di alcuni Documenti risguardanti le Relazioni politiche dei Papi d'Avignone coi Comuni d'Italia avanti e dopo il Tribunato di Cola di Rienzo et de Calata di Carlo IV," *Archivio Storico Italiano,* 1st Ser., VII (Appendice, 1849), 358: " Hodie autem fertur de novo in Curia ista per licteras, ut audio, aliquorum mercatorum, quod Flandrenses occulte miserant ad Regem Francie aliquos ex suis misericordiam postulantes de commissis, et supplicantes eidem, quod eis dignetur concedere quod comes Flandrie, qui fuit et est cum Rege Francie, ad partes Flandrie redeat et secure; quorum supplicationi Rex Francie, habito consilio suo, adsensisse videtur. . . ."

[238] Knighton, II, 19.

[239] *Chronique de Tournai,* pp. 349–350.

[240] Froissart, I, 54, 71.

Nor were they alone in sharing these suspicions, for the chronicler Knighton states that the duke pretended friendship for Edward, but that he was really inclined to favor Philip.[241] At a discussion in Edward's tent, van Artevelde bitterly complained to Duke John that he was making less of an effort than any of the other leaders. A Brabançon knight who had a characteristic contempt for one of van Artevelde's social position angrily replied, it is said, that he should keep his peace and return to Ghent, and that so much power should never belong to one of his rank! Van Artevelde, overcome with wrath, at once killed him. Thereupon Duke John left the tent, but Edward restrained him and was finally able to restore apparent harmony.[242]

Another incident occurred which reveals fully the extent of the animosity which had developed between Duke John and van Artevelde. Herman de Broughere, a piper who was with the duke's forces under the command of William van Duivenvoorde, seignior of Oosterhout, had left his companions on the south side of the city to see the engines cast projectiles over the walls. As he approached a piper from within invited him to come nearer and began a conversation with him. He was at once seized by three English soldiers and questioned. They took him to the head of the English forces where he was further examined, but being unable to discover any guilty purpose, they proposed to force a confession from him. Herman was then delivered to three Flemings who had been sent by the suspicious van Artevelde to ask for his surrender. He was brought before the scabini of Ghent, immediately put to torture, and compelled to declare that William van Duivenvoorde had sent him to the city. The torture was repeated, apparently to the point of death, and at van Artevelde's command, and the unfortunate victim was forced to repeat his statement under oath. Van Artevelde intended to have him repeat this before the estates of Flanders. Herman, however, fled and came to van Duivenvoorde who was just then in consultation with the duke of Brabant.[243] No wonder that distrust was quite general.

[241] Knighton, II, 19; Baker, pp. 71–72.
[242] *Chronographia,* II, pp. 152–153.
[243] G. des Marez, " Un Document Inédit Relatif à Jacques van Artevelde," *BCRH*, 5th Ser., VIII (1898), 307–310. Cf. N. de Pauw, " Rapport," *ibid.*, pp. 311–312.

VI. The Truce of Esplechin (Autumn, 1340)

Desperate as was the situation within the walls of Tournai, that of Edward and his allies was quite as unsatisfactory. The motley character of the allied host made it impossible to hold out long enough to compel the capitulation of the starving city.[244] Edward's own financial difficulties, which made him unable to discharge his obligations in spite of the insistent demands of his allies,[245] must have seriously hurt his influence with the princes upon whose support he had to rely chiefly in defeating Philip.[246] Even his brothers-in-law, the duke of Guelders and the margrave of Juliers, who had for years shown themselves zealous supporters of his claims, seemed to waver. It was reported to the pope that they were now looking out for their own interests.[247] John, duke of Brabant, could not be ambitious in a cause which would profit him but little in the future. Only Edward and the Flemings under van Artevelde were eager to continue the siege, but their forces were too weak in the face of those of the besieged and of Philip's army to disregard the demands of the militia of the duke of Brabant that they be allowed to return home at the earliest possible moment. Philip's emissaries had succeeded in arousing opposition in the towns of Brabant, which led to some extravagant rumors among the credulous soldiery of the duke that a new era was at hand.[248]

Meanwhile, Edward and Philip maintained their positions. For the moment a battle seemed possible, and John, king of Bohemia, on September 9 thought it advisable to make his testament providing for his sepulture in the abbey of Sept Fontaines near Arlon and apportioning his dominions among his sons, of whom Wenceslaus was to have Luxemburg.[249] But Philip apparently relied upon the intrigues of his emissaries to stimulate

[244] Le Bel, I, 205.

[245] *CCR* (1341–43), p. 112.

[246] Murimuth, p. 116; Avesbury, p. 317; *French Chronicle of London,* p. 81. According to Baker, p. 71, this payment was not made for a fortnight.

[247] W. H. Bliss, *Calendar of Entries in the Papal Registers,* II, 582.

[248] This appears to be the meaning of the words quoted by John le Bel, I, 207: " Je voy ung nouveau siècle! "

[249] J. Berthelot, *Histoire du Duché de Luxembourg,* VI (*Pièces Justificatives*), xxxix–xlii.

disaffection among the troops of the duke of Brabant and upon the possibility that the motley group of soldiers would present less and less coherence as the siege wore on. It is under these circumstances that negotiations were to be opened.

The pope had watched with anxious solicitude the return of Edward to the Low Countries and his invasion of the Tournaisis, but had deemed it inopportune to try mediation until the forces of the two kings stood opposed to each other. On August 26 he sent William Amicus and William of Norwich to reason with them. Benedict begged Philip to weigh the dangers of a battle and the evils which might befall his country in the event that his death would bring about a dynastic change. Furthermore, the Flemings — who were fickle and might change their policy — were so situated geographically that their hostility to him, as also that of the people of Aquitaine, must be taken into account. Philip was urged to exert efforts for peace in the interests of a united Christendom which would be able to resist the attacks of the infidel. He suggested the restitution to Edward of the duchy of Guienne, saving all Philip's rights as suzerain. If he should think that this could not be done he was requested to send envoys to Avignon, and, if this would be impossible, the pope would send his own nuncios.

He begged Edward to place little faith in the professions of the Flemings, who, as he could learn from past instances, were fickle in keeping their allegiance. He stated that the duke of Guelders and the margrave of Juliers were not to be trusted, and that the Germans had ever been unstable. He urged the fact that, as he was compelled to attack Philip through the Low Countries, he was at a natural disadvantage which placed him at the mercy of hirelings. In alliance with the excommunicate Lewis the Bavarian he had incurred grave ecclesiastical penalties and was regarded as a heretic. In view of all these difficulties Benedict urged him to consider the advisability of making peace and suggested that these matters should be left to papal arbitration, promising that the cardinals, who were for the most part Frenchmen, would not be consulted.[250]

Edward was in no mood to listen to these pacific counsels, and the Flemings under van Artevelde were eager to gain some advan-

[250] E. Déprez, *Les Préliminaires de la Guerre de Cent Ans,* pp. 338–342.

tage over Philip. But negotiations could not well be refused when the unity of the army seemed to vanish. It was Jeanne, dowager countess of Hainault, whose intervention was to lead to a truce.[251] She now was abbess at Fontenelles, and sought to still the conflict between her brother Philip and her son-in-law Edward in whose army there were many princes bound to her by the tenderest ties. With the fine maternal solicitude which ever characterized her, this "good and godly woman," as the poet Boendale calls her,[252] suggested to Philip when he proposed to advance upon Edward, probably on September 8, that he order several men to open negotiations with Edward. But Philip ignored her tearful pleading.[253] Nevertheless, she persisted and passed to and fro between the hostile forces. Her son, Count William, was apparently influenced by her urging. He may also have asked what would become of him in his exposed position if the bankrupt English king should leave the Low Countries.[254] Reginald, duke of Guelders, and William, margrave of Juliers, were also sympathetic, and the duke of Brabant zealously supported her efforts.[255]

Van Artevelde and the Flemings for a moment refused to listen.[256] But when Jeanne's activities were more and more favorably received by others in the allied host, there was a marked change in their attitude. It is likely that there were individuals in the Flemish army in contact with those of the Frank of Bruges who had held conversations with Philip early in August. There were discussions in which the count of Flanders and Jeanne also had a part.[257] Jeanne asked for some very substantial rights

---

[251] G. Canestrini, "Di alcuni Documenti risguardanti le Relazioni politiche dei Papi d'Avignone coi Comuni d'Italia avanti e dopo il Tribunato di Cola di Rienzo et de Calata di Carlo IV," *Archivio Storico Italiano*, 1st Ser., VII (Appendice, 1849), 358.

[252] Boendale, *Van den derden Eduwaert*, p. 356: " Een goeden godelike vrouwe."

[253] Boendale's patriotism leads him to represent the duke as acting only from disinterested motives. See *ibid.*, p. 356.

[254] Le Bel, I, 204.

[255] Boendale, *Van den derden Eduwaert*, p. 356.

[256] *Grandes Chroniques*, V, 403.

[257] G. Canestrini, "Di alcuni Documenti risguardanti le Relazioni politiche dei Papi d'Avignone coi Comuni d'Italia avanti e dopo il Tribunato di Cola di Rienzo et de Calata di Carlo IV," *Archivio Storico Italiano*, 1st Ser., VII (1849), 358.

—the annulment of those clauses of the Treaty of Athis-sur-Orge whereby the king had the right to excommunicate the Flemings and place them under the interdict — and Count Louis joined her in requesting Philip to surrender this important privilege.[258] Philip finally yielded to their urgent pleas and asked the advice of his councillors; John, king of Bohemia, and Adolph, bishop of Liège, were finally named to negotiate with Edward.[259] Much against his will the latter now also consented, and discussions were opened apparently on the 23d.[260] On the 24th the French representatives, the duke of Lorraine, the counts of Savoy and Armagnac, John, king of Bohemia, and the bishop of Liège met the English delegates, John, duke of Brabant, Reginald, duke of Guelders, William, margrave of Juliers, William, count of Hainault, Holland, and Zeeland, and John of Hainault.[261] These met at Esplechin, not far southwest from Tournai, and came to substantial agreement. Documents were drawn up, and the formalities of affixing the seals were to take place on the 25th.[262]

The truce was to last until sunrise of the day after St. John the Baptist, 1341, and was to take immediate effect. In Gascony, Guienne, and Jersey all hostilities were to cease on the twentieth day and such places as should still be invested were to be held for the duration of the truce by fourteen men, seven to be chosen by each side. Neither side was to accept any intervention of the Holy See nor seek any advantage at the curia. The subjects of all the parties to the truce were to be free to pursue their customary activities and the merchants were to be at liberty to resume their affairs. Those banished from Flanders were not to return to the country under pain of forfeiting all their possessions within its limits. All financial and other levies upon secular and spiritual property were to remain levied. Captives and prisoners were to be freed upon their oath that they would

[258] Boendale, *Van den derden Eduwaert,* p. 363.

[259] Le Bel, I, 202–204.

[260] Baker, p. 71; Avesbury, p. 317; Murimuth, pp. 115–116.

[261] A. Verkooren, *Inventaire, Brabant,* III, 97.

[262] G. Canestrini, "Di alcuni Documenti risguardanti le Relazione politiche dei Papi d'Avignone coi Comuni d'Italia avanti e dopo il Tribunato di Cola di Rienzo et de Calata di Carlo IV," *Archivio Storico Italiano,* 1st Ser., VII (Appendice, 1849), 358; *Bourgeois de Valenciennes,* p. 184; le Muisit, p. 135; le Bel, I, 204–205; *Chronographia,* II, 160,

return, unless ransomed, at the close of the last day of the truce. A similar arrangement was to be negotiated with the Scots, the bishop of Cambrai and his chapter, the city of Cambrai, the castlery and all its inhabitants, the Spaniards, Catalans, Genoese, Provençals, and others.[263]

On the same day Philip issued a document covering the points agreed upon in the negotiations with the Flemings. He declared that at the request of Count Louis and Countess Jeanne he renounced for himself and his heirs all right to excommunicate the Flemings and lay their country under the interdict. All documents upon which these rights rested were to be surrendered to the three towns at Tournai within a week from the following Sunday, or before October 8, and steps were to be taken to secure such annulment by the Holy See before the fourth Sunday in Lent. The interdict was to be raised on the following Sunday, October 1. Finally, King Philip promised to provide each of the three towns with a copy of the letters ratifying this convention.[264]

Thus came to an end the siege which had cost Edward such great effort and expense. The fact that nothing had been gained greatly embittered the leaders of the English forces,[265] especially since it was realized that the allied princes had made their own profit from Edward's difficulties. It was indeed a " useless peace," for the allies who had lost castles and other possessions to Philip now recovered them and would therefore be less eager to take up arms anew.[266] This was especially the case with William, count of Hainault, Holland, and Zeeland, who had lost a number of important strongholds to his uncle, Philip. Disappointed, and filled with bitterness toward his ministers in

---

[263] *Foedera*, II (2), 1135–1137. The text is also to be found in Avesbury, pp. 317–323; Knighton, II, 19–22; *Scalacronica*, 172; de Nangis, II, 172–178. Publication of the truce was ordered by the regent on October 6. See *Foedera*, II (2), 1137.

[264] Kervyn, *Oeuvres de Froissart*, XVIII, 176–177; Kervyn, *Histoire de Flandre*, III, 268–269; C. Diericx, *Appendice aux Mémoires sur la Ville de Gand*, pp. 109–110 (notes); L. Gilliodts van Severin, *Inventaire des Archives de la Ville de Bruges*, I, 492–493; E. vanden Bussche, *Inventaire des Archives du Franc de Bruges*, I, 67–68. See also *Chronicon Comitum Flandrensium*, p. 214; de Budt, p. 328; *Grandes Chroniques*, V, 404–405.

[265] Baker, pp. 71–72; *French Chronicle of London*, p. 82.

[266] Murimuth, pp. 115–116.

England, Edward left Tournai on the 27th [267] and betook himself to Ghent.

The levies of the duke of Brabant made no secret of their
desire to abandon the siege, and hastened homeward. The
actions of the traitors at Brussels and the other towns were now
fully revealed. The duke, who at first was quite unaware of what
had been going on, was greatly enraged when John of Hainault
informed him of the intrigues. The latter had arranged to secure
the names of some of the culprits and had even apprehended
one of their messengers near Anor and Mondrepuis. His name
was Everard tSerclaes. As soon as his arrest was known Walter
Egloy, Regnier Egloy, and Claes Zuaure fled to Namur. The
latter sought to escape his pursuers by crossing the Meuse at
Dinant, with the intention perhaps of seeking refuge in the jurisdiction of the bishop of Liège. He was, however, taken and
brought back to the irate duke, who, after a feast " had him beheaded before all his estates and the councils of his good towns."
Count William in the meantime ordered tSerclaes hanged at
Mons. The other conspirators were forced to remain beyond the
limits of Brabant for a long time, but finally returned quietly and
bought off the duke's anger.[268]

Meanwhile the duke had directed his attention toward those
of Brussels who had opposed the upper group of the bourgeoisie.
On November 6 a large number of persons was compelled to
present themselves before the scabini and declare that in the future they would support the patricians of the town, and, if need
be, aid them with their persons and their goods against all those
who were opposed to the established order.[269] At Louvain an
inquest was apparently held and a large number of culprits was
discovered. On April 1 of the following year the scabini and
other officials pronounced a decree of banishment, which was
confirmed by the duke, against a large number of the inhabitants who apparently belonged to the crafts and had taken up
weapons against the patricians.[270] All officials were to aid in
executing this decree, and should anyone who had been banished

---

[267] *Ibid.*, p. 116; Baker, p. 71; *Chronique de Tournai*, p. 347.
[268] Le Bel, I, 210–212; Boendale, *Brabantsche Yeesten*, I, 841.
[269] A. Wauters, *Table Chronologique*, IX, xvi–xviii (notes).
[270] A. Verkooren, *Inventaire, Brabant*, II, 106–109.

be found lurking within the borders of Brabant, he was to be delivered forthwith to the duke. A reward of ten pounds was promised for every person thus apprehended.[271]

Some were placed in prison, if we may judge from the case of one John vander Calkeren who a year later presented himself before the scabini seeking reconciliation for some acts against the duke.[272] Duke John also sought to bring to justice certain men of Mechelen for dealing with French delegates. On December 9 Philip wrote to the corporation of Mechelen that these activities had not been treasonable, but, as could be proved from the exchanges themselves, were intended solely to bring about peace between himself and Duke John. At the same moment he wrote in like vein to the corporations of Antwerp, Brussels, and Mechelen that the men of Louvain had acted from the same motives, and that they had received no money from him.[273]

[271] J. Molanus, *Rerum Lovaniensium libri XIV*, II (*Codex Diplomaticus*) 1254–1255.

[272] J. F. Willems, *Codex Diplomaticus*, I, 839.

[273] A. Verkooren, *Inventaire, Brabant*, II, 113–114.

CHAPTER XII

THE DECLINE OF ENGLISH PRESTIGE (1340-1343)

i. Edward's Bankruptcy (1340-1343)   ii. Internal Developments in Flanders (1340-1342)   iii. The Tumult at Oudenaarde (September, 1342)   iv. The Papacy and the Low Countries (1340-1343)   v. The Extension of the Truce of Esplechin (1341-1342)   vi. The Breton Campaign and the Truce of Malestroit (1342-1343)

I. EDWARD'S BANKRUPTCY (1340-1343)

THE Parliament which assembled on March 29, 1340, had voted a tax in kind of the ninth sheep, fleece, and lamb, a ninth of the goods of towns and boroughs, and a fifteenth of the rest of the realm.[1] So great, however, were the needs of the king in financing his return to the Low Countries before St. John the Baptist's Day that the total possible income from these sources had been more than exhausted by assignments made to numerous parties before his departure.[2] Unfortunately, the collection of commodities on so vast a scale was a difficult task, and the public, exasperated by the king's repeated extortions, was inclined to show resistance. Furthermore, the magnitude of Edward's debts made further taxation necessary, so that the provisions of the grant of the March Parliament were soon to be modified.

On May 30 the king had convoked a Parliament for July 9.[3] While it was engaged in discussing the many difficulties attending the collection of the goods in kind and the vending of the ninths, the king's messengers, the earls of Arundel and Gloucester, and William Trussel, arrived bearing the letter written by Edward at Ghent on July 9 which told of the brilliant defeat inflicted upon the French on the Zwin, and set forth the plans of the campaign in which he would seize Artois and Tournai.[4] Much

---

[1] *Rotuli Parliamenti*, II, 112.

[2] See S. B. Terry, *The Financing of the Hundred Years' War, 1337–1360*, pp. 53–54; G. Unwin, " The Estate of Merchants, 1336–1365," *Finance and Trade under Edward III*, p. 203.   [3] *CCR* (1339–41), p. 472.

[4] *Foedera*, II (2), 1130; *Rotuli Parliamenti*, II, 118.

money would be needed for this " as well as for paying his numerous allies upon whose coöperation so much depended and who were still waiting to be paid some of their instalments." In spite of the burdensome taxation the magnates and the commons fully understood that the ninth which had been granted for two years was not enough and decided to raise 20,000 sacks of wool at once. These were to be purchased by the merchants who should pay the subsidy, the custom, and the price of the wool, and deliver it in the Low Countries for the benefit of the king. The merchants were then to be reimbursed by the ninth of the second year while the ninth of the first year was to be paid into the treasury to meet the claims of the assignments made by the king in May and June.[5]

Unfortunately, the royal needs were most urgent. Immediately after Parliament dissolved the regent's government began to make contracts with English merchants who agreed to collect a large number of sacks from specified parts of the realm, pay the subsidy and custom, and deposit the price of the wool with the wardrobe at Bruges or other towns in the Low Countries to be designated by the king. Other contracts were made with the Italian companies, the Bardi, the Peruzzi, and the Leopardi, and also with a number of individual foreigners, among whom appear Anthony Bache, Matthew Dast, Simon van Halen, some merchants of the Hansa, Louvain, Mechelen, and elsewhere. Heavy loans were arranged: 10,000*l.* by William de la Pole, 11,-720*l.* by Anthony Bache, 5,032*l.* 3*s.* by Pancius de Contorone, and 9,987*l.* 6*s.* by Matthew Carnaceon. These contracts and loans were to be realized as early as September 1, but most of them were due at Michaelmas.[6] It is obvious that these credits could hardly be available for the campaign which began with the battle of Sluis and ended with the Truce of Esplechin on September 25. And in the light of the vast difficulties attending the collection of the wool during the three previous years and of the determined opposition of the country it was most certain that Edward could not draw upon these credits for a long time.

[5] *Rotuli Parliamenti,* II, 118; *CRR* (1340–3), p. 30.
[6] S. B. Terry, *The Financing of the Hundred Years' War, 1337–1360,* pp. 57–61; G. Unwin, " The Estate of Merchants, 1336–1365," *Finance and Trade under Edward III,* pp. 204–205.

The king was consequently bound to be disappointed. The country was everywhere hostile to his methods, and efforts to collect the ninths and the fifteenths and the wool were quite generally thwarted. Great quantities of wool were locked up in houses in Boston and their owners had left so that the royal mandate apparently could not be executed. In April the king was forced to order his officials to break into the houses and seize it.[7] In Lincoln there was violence, in Nottingham collection was resisted by armed force, and wool which had been stored in a house by a royal official was carried off.[8] In London the better grades of wool were packed as of inferior quality and shipped out of the realm.[9] In Westmoreland, Cumberland, and the bishopric of Durham poor wool was collected which was not even forwarded promptly and hence rotted and depreciated in value until it was scarcely worth 50s. a sack.[10]

Royal officials often dealt fraudulently and were guilty of violent conduct so that the people complained, and the king on January 13 was forced to issue commissions to investigate their actions.[11] Smuggling was most common. In the July Parliament there had been complaint of this, and on the 28th orders were issued to the collectors of the subsidy and custom at the great ports to prevent all such illegal export and to be diligent in their duties, since the king would investigate all violations.[12] If this was a common practice before the loan of 20,000 sacks was made, it would surely be most difficult to check further evasions after August. Uncocketed wool continued to leave York, Kent, Essex, Suffolk, Norfolk, the Cinque Ports, Dover, and London whence it was shipped under cover of the night.[13] At the close of winter the king commissioned Roger Power to search these ports and also the high seas and seize all such wool.[14] On April 16 Benedict de Burgo Sancti Petri was instructed to search all places and all ships in England and in foreign ports where merchants and

---

[7] *CPR* (1340–3), pp. 211–213. For arrest of wool in East Riding, see *CCR* (1339–41), pp. 589–655.

[8] *CPR* (1340–3), pp. 103–104, 110, 112.

[9] *Ibid.*, pp. 212, 386.

[10] *Ibid.*, p. 195.　　　　[12] *CCR* (1339–41), p. 628.

[11] *Ibid.*, pp. 110–111.

[13] *Ibid.*, p. 137; *CPR* (1340–3), pp. 210–211, 213, 214.

[14] *CPR* (1340–3), pp. 208,210, 214, 216; *CCR* (1339–41), p. 655.

mariners with wool and woolfells were wont to ply.[15]   It is not
strange that Edward should complain on April 1 that not half of
the 20,000 sacks had yet been collected.[16]   The temper of the
country is well revealed by the letters of July 30 and August 13
sent by the council to Edward, begging him to name new officials in the counties to manage his assignments, since the feeling toward the old ones was so bitter that they could accomplish
nothing.[17]   For these reasons the king received nothing in
July and while he lay before Tournai only two merchants fulfilled
their obligations in part, for they were so hampered by the
failure of collectors that of the 600 sacks for which they
had contracted only 31 sacks and 10 stones came into their
hands.[18]

Edward was loud in his complaints.   His allies pressed him
persistently for payment during the siege of Tournai and threatened to withdraw from his service unless he would deal rigorously
with those officials who had thwarted his will.[19]   It would be an
exaggeration to state that the financial plight of the king was the
sole cause of his failure in the siege, for we hear a good deal of
Duke John's disinclination, of his antagonism to van Artevelde,
and of Philip's intrigues in Brussels and Louvain.   But it certainly
contributed to stir up dissension in the incoherent forces under
his command, and possibly just robbed him of victory as Tournai
was at the point of yielding through starvation.   The chroniclers
declare that the lack of money was the sole cause,[20] and this is
also the king's version in his letter of February 10, 1341, in which
he declared that he had been forced to conclude a truce with
Philip at the moment when Tournai was ready to yield.   He
complained bitterly of the conduct of his officials and especially
of Stratford, the archbishop of Canterbury, to whom he had
looked for success in his financial plans and whom he therefore
held responsible for the miscarriage of his schemes.[21]   In conse-

---

[15] *CPR* (1340–3), p. 213; cf. *Foedera,* II (2), 1172–1173.

[16] *CPR* (1341–3), pp. 123–124; *Foedera,* II (2), 1155.

[17] *Rotuli Parliamenti,* II, 122.

[18] *CPR* (1340–3), pp. 258–259.   [19] *CCR* (1341–3), p. 112.

[20] Knighton, II, 19; Baker, p. 72.

[21] *CCR* (1341–3), pp. 102–103; *CPR* (1340–3), pp. 151–153; *Foedera,*
II (2), 1147–1148; see also letters to Bernadot d'Albret, November 12,
1340, Kervyn, *Oeuvres de Froissart,* XXV, 343.

quence his credit was impaired and he had to borrow money at ruinous terms. Thus Conrad Clypping paid the debt due the money lenders of Brussels for which Duke John, Reginald, duke of Guelders, Otto, seignior of Cuyk, and Simon van Halen were hostages.[22] The king's embarrassment can be imagined, for a story was current in the Low Countries that in England there was a plot to depose him in favor of his son [23] and that these intrigues were the cause of his failure.[24]

Edward arrived at Ghent by way of Alost [25] at Michaelmas.[26] Here he spent eight most uncomfortable weeks for he was constantly besieged by his numerous creditors. Thierry, seignior of Valkenburg, sent him a letter couched in the most acrid terms of which Edward complained bitterly to the chancellor, the bishop of Chichester, a brother of Stratford.[27] He owed Bernadot d'Albret 10,834*l*. 15*s*. 1*d*. by bills of the seneschal of Gascony and the constable of Bordeaux, and 1,764*l*. 10*s*. 10½*d*. for his annual fee.[28] Edward's reply to his pressing solicitations laid the blame wholly upon his disloyal servants in England.[29]

A vast sum was due his faithful brother-in-law, Reginald, duke of Guelders. This amounted to 1,030 sacks of wool and 110,000 gold Florentine florins. Settlement of this last sum could not be made for a long time because in October of the following year the king arranged to pay it in three instalments of 40,000, 35,000, and 35,000 florins each at Christmas, 1341, Midsummer, 1342, and Midsummer, 1343.[30] The 1,030 sacks represented some transaction with Simon van Halen and were assigned to Reginald's attorneys, Matthew de Cassel and Hildebrand Sudermann, before the close of the year, and a number of mandates was issued

---

[22] *CPR* (1340–3), p. 39.

[23] Boendale, *Van den derden Eduwaert*, p. 365.

[24] *French Chronicle of London*, pp. 82–83.

[25] *CPR* (1340–3), p. 71.

[26] Murimuth, p. 116; *French Chronicle of London*, p. 82; *Chronicon Comitum Flandrensium*, p. 328.

[27] Text in E. Déprez, *Les Préliminaires de la Guerre de Cent Ans*, pp. 355–357.

[28] *CPR* (1340–3), pp. 261, 263, 268. These were the figures in June 1341.

[29] Kervyn, *Oeuvres de Froissart*, XXV, 343–344.

[30] I. A. Nijhoff, *Gedenkwaardigheden uit de Geschiedenis van Gelderland*, I, 427; *CPR* (1340–3), p. 295–296.

to parties to surrender various amounts to them.[31]   To John,
duke of Brabant, he owed a vast sum which was to be liquidated
in part in July of the following year by a large assignment of
3,300 sacks of wool.[32]   The merchants of Mechelen and of Louvain
demanded 42,000 Florentine florins and 580 sacks of wool respectively.   This was paid by an assignment of wool made to the
Bardi and the Peruzzi by the council on October 28.   The wool
was to be delivered within fifteen days at Sluis whereupon the
hostage, the earl of Northampton, would be released of his responsibility.[33]   The king's indebtedness to his brother-in-law, the
margrave of Juliers, amounted to 30,000*l*.   This was to be paid
in the following year by a levy of wool.[34]   The promises made to
the men of Cologne were still unpaid.[35]   To William, count of
Hainault, Holland, and Zeeland, he was 7,555 Florentine florins
in arrears,[36] and still owed most, if not all, of the 25,000 florins
due for the loss of horses and equipment at Buironfosse, in the
Cambrésis, and in subsequent campaigns.[37]

Especially annoying must have been the demand of Edward's
Flemish allies.   To the three towns he owed 35,000 marks.[38]
Their unusual military efforts were a heavy burden and they
were undoubtedly all running into debt.[39]   The deficit in the accounts of Ghent for the financial year ending with mid-August,
1341, was 15,213*l*. 3*s*. 5*d*. in spite of the fact that the confiscation
of the properties of the émigrés amounted to the very large sum
of 25,561*l*. 8*s*. 4*d*.[40]   The scabini who were chosen before the walls
at Tournai were unable to pay the militia, possibly because the
financial year had come to an end with a deficit of 10,087*l*. 11*s*.
2*d*.[41]   It is interesting to note that, while the scabini were all duly

---

[31] *CCR* (1341–3), pp. 8, 9, 54, 155; *CPR* (1340–3), pp. 81, 160, 164,
219–220, 262.
[32] *CPR* (1340–3), pp. 259, 290; Kervyn, *Oeuvres de Froissart*, XX, 431.
[33] *CCR* (1339–41), pp. 639–640.
[34] *CCR* (1341–3), p. 174; *CPR* (1340–3), pp. 314, 414.
[35] *CCR* (1341–3), pp. 104, 478, 479.
[36] *CPR* (1340–3), p. 297.
[37] *CCR* (1341–3), pp. 44, 163; *Foedera*, II (2), 1154.
[38] K. Höhlbaum, *Hansisches Urkundenbuch*, II, 321; *CPR* (1340–3),
pp. 114–115, 257, 258.
[39] For Bruges, see L. Gilliodts van Severen, " Jacques van Artevelde,"
La Flandre, IX (1878), 396.
[40] N. de Pauw en J. Vuylsteke, *Rekeningen der Stad Gent*, II, 13, 92.
[41] *Ibid.*, I, 507.

appointed, no receivers were chosen, and the direction of the town was left to the three deans of the guilds. The reason for this irregularity is difficult to ascertain. But apparently it was expected that Edward would pay his debts as he undoubtedly had promised after the battle of Sluis. In this the scabini, as well as the rest of the allies, were disappointed, and the disgruntled soldiers halted at Oudenaarde, declaring that they would not return to their homes until satisfaction should be made. Accordingly, on September 29 a delegation composed of three of the scabini, one councillor, William Yoons, dean of the lesser guilds, and John de Merseman, a member of the Council of Flanders, was sent to negotiate some plan whereby payment should be made at once. Fifteen persons were chosen to collect the duty (*erfelyke renten*) in Ghent for this purpose. The delegation returned on the 30th, and the fifteen were occupied in their tasks for four days. Meanwhile the militia returned, pleased that they would finally be paid. On October 7 were chosen three receivers of the imposts (*zoengelde*) and two of the duty (*renten*).[42] Edward owed considerable sums to the burghers of Oudenaarde,[43] to his intimate friend and ally, Jacob van Artevelde, and to others.[44]

Edward was therefore reduced to the humiliating necessity of borrowing money at the most usurious rates. His embarrassment was especially keen, for Edward knew that his influence with the duke of Brabant was at stake. On October 30 he again appealed to the pope to grant the necessary dispensation for the projected marriage of his son to the duke's daughter.[45] The duke cared mostly for such economic advantages as he might draw from Edward who was eager to coöperate with him as, for example, when on November 23 he abolished certain prests — 40*d.* per sack of wool, 2*s.* per cloth of scarlet, 2*s.* on each cloth mixed in the grain, 18*d.* on each cloth with part of the grain mixed, and 12*d.* on each cloth without grain, until Sunday in Mid-Lent of

---

[42] *Ibid.,* II, 34, 70–71. They returned on or before Saturday before St. Denis, or October 7, 1340. See *ibid.,* pp. 1–2.

[43] *CCR* (1341–3), pp. 25–26; N. de Pauw, *Cartulaire Historique et Généalogique des Artevelde,* pp. 637–643.

[44] N. de Pauw, *Cartulaire Historique et Généalogique des Artevelde,* p. 184; *CPR* (1340–3), p. 116; *CCR* (1341–3), pp. 102–103.

[45] *Foedera,* II (2), 1140.

1341.[46]   Meanwhile the allies, the dukes of Brabant and Guelders, John of Hainault, who was in Ghent in October,[47] and the Flemings pressed him to reimburse them for their expenses.   On October 31 Edward wrote to the regent about his negotiations with them and announced that he was assigning about 12,000 sacks of wool to them.[48]   He found that he could not buy provender for his horses, and was obliged to send them to England early in October.   Only with the greatest difficulty could he lay hands on enough money to keep his archers from imminent starvation.[49]

Uneasy because he heard rumors of the intrigues of his councillors, the king conceived the plan of returning to England suddenly and secretly in order to settle accounts with them.[50]   To be able to do this he had to make promises.   To the duke of Brabant he bound himself to return to Brabant within four days after Candlemas and at once enter with his pledges a certain house to be designated at Brussels and stay there until full satisfaction should be rendered by November 14, 1341.[51]   On the 21st he informed Bernadot d'Albret of his intention to return to England.[52]   Then, on the 27th, he gave receipt to Leo de Mirabello, seignior of Perwez, for 44,000 Florentine florins.   The duke of Guelders, the earl of Northampton, William de Keldesby, keeper of the privy seal, Henry de Ferrariis, chamberlain, Galfridus le Scrope, William de Cusancia, keeper of the wardrobe, Dinus Forcetti and Chonet de Jony for the Bardi, and James Gherard and Richard de Feigne for the Peruzzi swore on the Gospels that this sum would be repaid on the octave of Easter at Dendermonde or Ghent.   Four knights were to be sent four days before the date of payment and remain as hostages and, in case of default, the merchants were to present themselves as hostages, paying all the ex-

[46] F. J. Willems, *Codex Diplomaticus,* I, 828; *CCR* (1339–41), pp. 600, 659.
[47] N. de Pauw en J. Vuylsteke, *Rekeningen der Stad Gent,* II, 19. The scabini appropriated 72*l.* for Rhenish wine which they presented to him.
[48] E. Déprez, *Les Préliminaires de la Guerre de Cent Ans,* pp. 354–355 (note).
[49] *Ibid.,* p. 355, note 2.
[50] *French Chronicle of London,* p. 82.
[51] Kervyn, *Oeuvres de Froissart,* XX, 56–57.
[52] *Ibid.,* XXV, 343–345.

penses and damages incurred.[53]   Edward also borrowed 2,100*l.*
from certain men at Ghent for which Henry, the earl of Lancaster,
pledged his jewels.[54]

After this loan had been arranged, Edward was ready to depart.
Accompanied by the queen, the earl of Northampton, and a few
members of his household, he covertly stole out of Ghent and
hurried off to Sluis on the 27th and, after spending three days
and three nights on the sea, arrived on the Thames at the Tower
of London before daybreak of the 30th.[55]   The men of Ghent,
it appears, were not aware of his departure.   Chagrined by the
king's flight, they sent John de Coster and John de Lokerne after
him on December 5.[56]   Edward sought to soothe their wounded
feelings in a letter written on the sea on the 28th in which he expressed his gratitude for their favors and their confidence and
explained his unceremonious departure as due to the disloyal actions of his lieges to which he had to put a speedy end or else his
covenants could not be honored.[57]

Soon after Edward's arrival in England began the famous
struggle with the royal ministers and the impeachment of Stratford which, with attempts to realize his revenue from the grants
of the two Parliaments of 1340, kept him more than engaged until
the following spring.[58]   On December 10 commissions of oyer
and terminer were issued to investigate " alleged oppressions
and extortions by justices and any other ministers of the king "
in all the counties.   On January 13 order was given to arrest and
arraign at the king's suit a number of the prominent merchants
of the realm, among whom were named William de la Pole, John
Pulteney, and others, accused, in response to the popular clamor
and petitions, of fraudulent conduct.[59]   On the 26th mandates

---

[53] *CCR* (1339–41), p. 649.   For the duke of Guelders as surety, see
Grandes Chroniques, V, 405.

[54] *CCR* (1341–3), p. 225, 231, 286–287.   See also *Foedera,* II (2), 1176.

[55] Baker, p. 72; Murimuth, pp. 116–117; *French Chronicle of London,*
pp. 82–83; Avesbury, p. 323; Boendale, *Van den derden Eduwaert,* pp.
364–365; *CCR* (1339–41), p. 653; *Foedera,* II (2), 1141.

[56] N. de Pauw en J. Vuylsteke, *Rekeningen der Stad Gent,* II, 37.

[57] E. Varenbergh, *Histoire des Relations diplomatiques entre le Comté
de Flandre et l'Angleterre,* p. 346; Kervyn, *Histoire de Flandre,* III, 272.

[58] G. Lapsley, " Archbishop Stratford and the Parliamentary Crisis of
1341," *English Historical Review,* XXX (1915), 6–18, 193–215.

[59] *CPR* (1340–3), pp. 110–113.

went forth to the collectors of the ninths and the fifteenths that, as a half of the grants had not yet been realized, they were commanded under threat of heavy forfeiture to levy the subsidy in all haste so that the proceeds would be in the hands of the receiver at the Tower by Sunday of Mid-Lent.[60] Numerous commissions were issued in the following months to investigate irregularities such as smuggling, theft, fraud, violence, and negligence.[61]

As the Truce of Esplechin would come to an end on St. John the Baptist's Day, Edward was forced to consider ways and means to continue the struggle with his enemy, as well as to meet his old obligations in the Low Countries. Writs for a new Parliament had been issued on March 3.[62] When it met on April 23 he complained to it that even the ninth and the fifteenth of the first year were still partly uncollected and that of the loan of 20,-000 sacks not one half had yet come into his hands. Seeing the necessity of the situation, the magnates and commons decided that a tax in wool should be levied, 20,000 sacks in 1341 and 10,000 in 1342, and that the grant for 1341 should take the place of the ninth and the fifteenth of the second year and hence also the loan of 20,000 sacks which had been arranged by the Parliament of July, 1340. The remainder of the 20,000 sacks was to be exported by the king by Michaelmas and to be collected for that purpose by August 1 until which time no subject might export any wool on his own account.[63]

Efforts to collect this grant were as unpopular in 1341 as similar activities had been in previous years. During the winter months Edward had from time to time made assignments upon William de Edyngton, receiver of the ninth and the fifteenth in the counties south of the Trent. On March 12 a large number of assignments, for the most part small sums, was made.[64] Disgusted with the tardiness of his officials, he named new collectors of the

---

[60] *CPR* (1340–3), pp. 124–126; *CCR* (1341–3), p. 1.

[61] *CPR* (1340–3), pp. 110–111, 155, 208, 210–214, 216; *CCR* (1341–3), p. 137.

[62] *CCR* (1341–3), pp. 113–114.

[63] *Rotuli Parliamenti,* II, 127, 131, 133; *CPR* (1340–3) p. 261; *CCR* (1341–3), p. 142.

[64] *CCR* (1341–3), pp. 7, 13, 18, 19, 21, 23, 32, 39, 44, 47, 49–50, 53, 55, 61, 62, 68, 82–85.

ninth and the fifteenth of the grant of the second year in all the counties.[65] These were hardly more successful as the meager list of assignments of May 4 would seem to show.[66] Soon, however, the collection of the ninth and the fifteenth was discontinued because of the substitution made by the recent Parliament.[67] The bishop of Chester, the lord of Wake, and Robert de Sadyngton were appointed to determine on the basis of their assessment for the ninths and the fifteenths the amount of wool each county was to furnish. This of course meant that they and their helpers would be required to determine a vast number of petty assessments which consumed much time. The temper of the country was inflamed. There was so much disorder in certain counties that sergeants-at-arms had to be appointed. Smuggling, fraud, graft, and all manner of methods were employed to evade the levy.[68]

It was accordingly impossible to export the wool by Michaelmas. Edward was greatly embarrassed in his diplomatic relations with the princes of the Low Countries. He had made assignments upon the wool of Lincoln, Kent, Buckingham, and Northampton to satisfy Simon van Halen of Ghent for the 1,030 sacks for which Reginald, duke of Guelders, and others were sureties. The receiver of wool for Lincoln refused to carry out the royal orders, and on September 20 the king bitterly accused him of " lightly regarding the mandate contemptuously, and of having refused to deliver the wool although the greater part was then in his custody, to the king's disgrace, the heavy loss of the duke, and the retarding of important business very near the king's heart, whereat he is very greatly distrusted and not without reason." [69] Edward was chagrined by administrative impediments in collection of the quota assigned to Buckingham, and by the plundering of a ship belonging to the duke's subjects off the Isle of Wight in the late winter.[70]

Greater success attended Edward's efforts to redeem his prom-

[65] *CPR* (1340–3), pp. 151–155.

[66] *CCR* (1341–3), pp. 85–87.

[67] *CPR* (1340–3), p. 261; *Rotuli Parliamenti*, II, 133.

[68] F. R. Barnes, " The Taxation of Wool, 1327–1348," *Finance and Trade under Edward III*, pp. 158–160.

[69] *CPR* (1340–3), pp. 284, 295–296.

[70] *Ibid.*, pp. 303, 441, 444, 451–452, 495.

ises to pay his brother-in-law the debt of 110,000 gold Florentine florins. On October 9 he ordered Hugh de Ulseby and four merchants to declare before the merchants of Bruges and a public notary that they would pay the first instalment of 40,000 florins by Christmas out of the royal funds derived from the sale of wool at the staple.[71] Settlement of the claim of 20,000*l.* of William, margrave of Juliers, was equally slow. Edward met this obligation by making assignments of the ninth and the fifteenth to be levied in Cambridge, Huntingdon, and Bedford, which on June 15 were changed to the equivalent in wool.[72] In September the receivers in Bedford had not yet surrendered the wool to the margrave's representatives so that Edward complained on the 8th that they had " contemptuously refused to deliver the wool to such attorney to the king's damage and ill fame." To accelerate collection Henry de Baa was commissioned on the 20th to supervise the collectors and do all that might be necessary to hasten payment.[73] But in June of the following year a part of the debt was still unredeemed.[74]

In July, 1341, 3,300 sacks were ordered to be collected for the duke of Brabant in Nottingham, Warwick, Kent, Norfolk, and Suffolk, but the duke's attorneys were, in spite of all diligence in their suit, quite unable to get any of it. On October 5 Edward ordered his officials to accelerate the collection " which lies very near his heart," and appointed a sergeant-at-arms to supervise it in Norfolk and " attach the bodies of all those found contrary or rebellious herein and bring them before the council for their contempt." [75] But in spite of these vigorous orders the transaction was not yet fully carried out in December of 1343.[76]

In other quarters also Edward's financial straits seriously diminished his prestige. On April 24, 1341, Gerlach, count of Nassau, refused to be considered his vassal any longer, as his pension had not been paid.[77] On May 3 the king confessed in humiliating manner that he could not pay, but begged him to wait

---

[71] *CCR* (1341–3), p. 296, and for the payment of Midsummer, 1342, see *ibid.*, p. 458; *CPR* (1340–3), p. 471.

[72] *CPR* (1340–3), p. 263.

[73] *Ibid.*, p. 280.   [75] *Ibid.*, p. 290.

[74] *Ibid.*, p. 414.   [76] *CCR* (1343–6), p. 207.

[77] *Ibid.*, p. 182; L. Gilliodts van Severen, *Le Cotton Manuscript Galba B I*, p. 1.

until a fortnight after the Day of St. John the Baptist when he would satisfy his claims at Brussels. Nor could he repay the men of Cologne and on February 14, 1342, he replied to their envoys sent to him in England that the matter caused him to blush with shame, and he at once ordered his merchants of the staple at Bruges to pay them.[78]

His inconstant brother-in-law, the emperor, also deserted him. Anxious for reconciliation with the church, Lewis hoped to secure Philip's aid at the curia by revoking Edward's title of imperial vicar. On March 15 Philip swore to use his influence with the pope and act as a friend and ally of the emperor for life. On June 24 Lewis wrote Edward informing him that he was no longer vicar of the empire. He even stated that he was charged by Philip to act as intermediary.[79] Edward's bitterness was undoubtedly sharpened by Lewis' statement that he was displeased because the truce had been made with Philip without his advice and against his will.[80] This was followed by treaties of alliance and friendship between Philip and Baldwin, archbishop of Trier, on July 30 and September 17,[81] and Henry, archbishop of Mainz, in September.[82] It was therefore not strange that Edward's prestige should decline even though he did make some payments, for example, 7,555 Florentine florins to William, count of Hainault, Holland, and Zeeland, on October 16,[83] and to the seignior of Valkenburg on November 15.[84] His allies in the empire outside the Low Countries had virtually all abandoned him. On June 12 he was forced to postpone the marriage of his daughter Joan to Frederick, son of Albert, duke of Austria, at the latter's request.[85]

---

[78] *Foedera*, II (2), 1158.

[79] *Ibid.*, p. 1186; *CCR* (1341–5), p. 478, and for the payment of Henry Scherfgin, *ibid.*, p. 164.

[80] H. Schrohe, " Kleinere Beiträge zu den Regesten der Könige Rudolf bis Karl IV," *Mitteilungen des Instituts für Oesterreichische Geschichtsforschung*, XXVI (1906), 486–489; *Foedera*, II (2), 1166. For Edward's reply, see *Foedera*, II (2), 1167–1168.

[81] Hontheim, *Historia Treverensis Diplomata*, II, 146–147.

[82] H. Schrohe, " Kleinere Beiträge zu den Regesten der Könige Rudolf bis Karl IV," *Mitteilungen des Instituts für Oesterreichische Geschichtsforschung*, XXVI (1906), 488–489.

[83] *CPR* (1340–3), p. 297.

[84] *Foedera*, II (2), 1181.   [85] *Ibid.*, p. 1164; *CCR* (1341–3), p. 245.

II. Internal Developments in Flanders (1340–1342)

A few days after Edward and his allies broke camp before Tournai, Count Louis went to Flanders in accordance with the agreement made between Philip and the Flemings. He halted at Courtrai, and was met on the 5th by representatives of the three towns.[86] Here the affairs of the county were regulated. Louis declared that at the request of his subjects he forgave all illegal acts that had been committed either by the *ruwaard*, Simon van Halen, or by other public officials after he had left in the previous December. He also declared his intention of submitting to the advice of the three towns in all matters.[87] Thereupon he passed directly to his family castle at Male, where on the 12th and 13th he was interviewed by an important delegation from Ghent and undoubtedly also from the other towns of Flanders.[88] The Council of Flanders, which had been constituted in the previous year when Louis returned from France, now resumed its survèillance over the count's activities. Important members of this body at this time were Simon ser Thomaes, Thomas van Vaernewijc, and William de Merseman, three staunch supporters of van Artevelde's policy and burghers of Ghent.[89] Relations between Count Louis and Simon van Halen, who had taken as his wife the count's natural sister Isabella, appear to have been amicable, for in March, 1341, he approved van Halen's project to found a convent in Ghent.[90]

The count's activities were entirely controlled by the Council of Flanders and the envoys of the scabini of the three towns. The close alliance with Brabant and Hainault and especially the question of Edward's debts and the importation of English wool demanded constant attention and there were as a result numerous conferences to which Louis was forced to submit. The haughty

---

[86] N. de Pauw en J. Vuylsteke, *Rekeningen der Stad Gent,* II, 34.

[87] I. L. A., Diegerick, *Inventaire des Chartes et Documents Appartenant aux Archives de la Ville d'Ypres,* II, 121. See le Muisit, p. 137; Boendale, *Van den derden Eduwaert,* p. 364; *Chronicon Comitum Flandrensium,* p. 214.

[88] N. de Pauw en J. Vuylsteke, *Rekeningen der Stad Gent,* II, 35.

[89] *Ibid.,* pp. 35, 36, 38, 39, 40, 41, 44, 45, 46.

[90] V. vander Haeghen, *Het Klooster te Walle en de Abdij van den Groenen Briel,* p. 34.

attitude of van Artevelde toward the page of William van Duivenvoorde at Tournai came up for discussion on October 4 at a meeting of the estates of Brabant at Brussels when the document to
which we owe our knowledge of the episode was drawn up. Copies
were apparently sent to the three towns of Flanders with a request that justice should be done.[91] The matter undoubtedly was
discussed at a meeting held at Alost on the 9th whither King
Edward, William van Vaernewijc, and two scabini had gone.
Some adjustment was made, for on the 12th the scabini sent Josse
Rase to the duke of Brabant and his towns to make fitting
amends.[92]

With these matters Count Louis was apparently not much concerned, but between the 3d and the 7th of November an important
delegation from the three towns went to Male. The envoys of
Ghent were the scabini, John vander Vloet and John van Dessele, John van Steenbeeke, dean of the weavers, and William
Yoons of the lesser guilds. On the 8th four of the scabini of
Ghent and two members of the Council of Flanders, Thomas
van Vaernewijc and Simon ser Thomaes, accompanied by similar
delegations from the other towns, it appears, proceeded to Dendermonde with Count Louis, and from the 9th to the 11th were
engaged in discussions with many important persons from Brabant and Hainault.[93] On the 12th Louis came to Ghent, which
he had not seen for eleven months, and was brought into the town
by the official trumpeter Persemiere and four associates. The
scabini presented him with wine and a bear for which 290*l.* and
50*l.* were allowed in the accounts.[94] He was now thrown into
close contact with Edward who was in Ghent, and also with
other allied princes, among whom was William, count of
Hainault, Holland, and Zeeland.[95] But Louis soon proceeded to
Male whither on the 6th of December the scabini of Ghent sent
Thomas van Vaernewijc, Simon ser Thomaes, and their colleague,

[91] G. Des Marez, "Un Document relatif à Jacques van Artevelde,"
BCRH, 5th Ser., VIII (1898), 310.

[92] N. de Pauw en J. Vuylsteke, *Rekeningen der Stad Gent*, II, 35.

[93] *Ibid.*, pp. 36–37. For the date of the meeting at Dendermonde, see
ibid., p. 55. Whether Edward was present cannot be ascertained.

[94] *Ibid.*, pp. 70, 19.

[95] *Ibid.*, p. 19. Rhenish wine valued at 128*l.* 17*s.* 9*d.* was given him.
At the close of October he was reported to be very ill, see *ibid.*, p. 36.
John of Hainault was in Ghent on October 4, cf. *ibid.*, p. 19.

the premier scabinus, John vander Vloet. These returned on the 9th and on the next day Simon ser Thomaes with John uten Hove, John van Lovene, and Count Louis went once more to Dendermonde whereupon Thomaes and uten Hove went to Brabant.[96] Other important meetings took place at Male from December 20 to 26 and January 13 to 20, and on the 27th Ghent sent two scabini with John uten Hove to Courtrai to welcome the countess.[97] Between January 29 and February 1 Thomas van Vaernewijc, Simon ser Thomaes, and a scabinus were at Rupelmonde with Count Louis in conference with the duke of Brabant and the count of Hainault.[98] On another occasion, between February 23 and 26, these three princes were again in conference with delegates from the towns subject to each.[99]

The presence of Count Louis whose relations with the Council of Flanders, the captains, and the scabini were apparently harmonious was a great advantage for the three towns under the leadership of van Artevelde. One of the clauses in the Truce of Esplechin specified that all refugees and banished persons, hostile to the new régime, were not to return to Flanders, and that their goods were to be confiscated.[100] The opposition of certain elements had become more pronounced when the towns broke with Philip. True to their feudal conceptions of loyalty to a suzerain, they refused to submit and were accordingly forced to leave the country. Their properties were thereupon confiscated and the proceeds used to aliment the communal treasuries. At Ghent, for example, these forfeited properties brought 4,829*l*. 9*s*. 5*d*. by the close of the financial year in August, 1340. During the next year this sum mounted to 25,561*l*. 8*s*. 4*d*.[101] From the bishops and chapters of Cambrai and Tournai 560*l*. were received, and from the abbey of St. Nicholas-en-Bois near Laon [102] 822*l*. 3*s*. 4*d*. Secular persons paid large sums: William of Mortagne, seignior of Oudenaarde, 800*l*.; Walter Vilain, 29*l*. 15*s*.; the wife of Daniel

[96] N. de Pauw en J. Vuylsteke, *Rekeningen der Stad Gent*, II, 38.

[97] *Ibid.*, pp. 39, 40.   [38] *Ibid.*, p. 41.

[99] *Ibid.*, p. 42.   [100] *Foedera*, II (2), 1135–1137.

[101] N. de Pauw en J. Vuylsteke, *Rekeningen der Stad Gent*, I, 376–377, and II, 12–13.

[102] *Ibid.*, II, 13: ". . . van den goede sabbes van sente Niclaus ten Bossche. . . ." See Kervyn, "Jacques van Artevelde," *Messager des Sciences et Arts Historiques* (1856), p. 251.

of Drongen (Tronchiennes), 2000*l.*; Nicholas Guidouche, whose properties lay near Rupelmonde, 333*l.* 6*s.* 8*d.*; and the Lady of Gavere at Meerendre, to whom the scabini early in June sent a delegation of five men led by the captain Gelnoot van Lens, 280*l.*[103] Large sums were taken from the countess of Namur because of the debt of the count whose name for some reason was placed in the list of *fugitieven*. William van Vaernewijc visited her in March and April and returned with 50*l.*, but his absence of nine days cost the town 36*l.*[104] The total amount paid by the countess during the year was 10,880*l.* One large item was received from the clerk, Matthew 'sPuurs, who as the bailiff's official scoured the castlery and took possession of the properties of the exiles.[105]

Enough facts can be found to give some idea of the methods used to render these people impotent. Some of the exiles (*ballinghen*) had sought refuge in the churches. On June 5 the scabini of Ghent sent a colleague, Thomas van Olsene, and the captain, Peter vanden Hovene, with the bailiff and his men to Denterghem to remove a number of them who had taken refuge in the church.[106] There was similar activity at Bruges where the scabini and captains maintained a vigorous pursuit. The accounts of the town make mention of a John Bisscop who was apprehended on suspicion of being an exile, but was exonerated and released after some inconveniences for which he was given 18*l.* as compensation. A sharp lookout was maintained for persons who sold goods to these people or bought things from them. Such goods, of course, could be seized, and people who dealt with these outlaws were naturally viewed with suspicion. In September the burgomasters and scabini went to Moerbeke and Tanekine with an armed force to seize a number of the exiles who had congregated at those places and who apparently were inclined to show resistance. They were taken and brought back to Bruges in wagons.[107]

[103] N. de Pauw en J. Vuylsteke, *Rekeningen der Stad Gent,* II, 47.

[104] *Ibid.,* pp. 43–44.

[105] *Ibid.,* p. 13: "... van der hant Matheeus sPuurs, cleerc ende beridere van der ghere goede die buten ghetrocken sijn die men heet fugitive, bi vele parcheelen die hij ontfaen heeft. ..."

[106] *Ibid.,* p. 47: "... metten bailliu ende sinen gheselscepe te Denterghem omme ballinghe te doen rumene uter kerken daer. ..."

[107] L. Gilliodts van Severen, "Jacques van Artevelde," *La Flandre.* IX (1878), 404–405.

In the castleries of the western part of the country, where the feudality was especially strong and consequently opposition more determined, numerous inquests were conducted. The delegates of the three towns met at Ypres between December 19 and 24 to consider the problem of the émigrés, and in January, 1341, they again assembled to receive the judicial decisions which had been reached.[108] An interesting bit of detail is recorded in the accounts of Bruges where seven clerks were kept busy for nine days until midnight in making four copies with duplicates of the inquest.[109] In the Quatuor Officia and in Waasland there was a constant recurrence of difficulties. An inquest was held at Baudeloo in March, 1340.[110] On February 13 and 14, 1341, Peter vanden Hovene and a company of white-hoods were sent to Hulst,[111] and in January of the following year another group of eighteen soldiers under Baldwin Wenemaar was dispatched thither to apprehend some miscreants, Wolfard and his son, Gilles van Molensteden.[112] Difficulties at Assenede came to a head in June, 1341, whither two scabini were sent on the 1st to settle the quarrel, and in a few days Thomas van Vaernewijc and Simon ser Thomaes were instructed to name a new group of scabini.[113] In July one of the scabini was again sent thither.[114] But the situation remained unsatisfactory in these parts. Watch was also kept over those who had left the country. On June 26 the scabini of Ghent sent their clerk, John vanden Bossche, to Utrecht to ascertain which exiles were staying there.[115]

[108] N. de Pauw en J. Vuylsteke, *Rekeningen der Stad Gent,* II, 39: " It. scepenen Jan Buuc, Jan Coelins sone, ende met hem Matheeus de Puur, die voeren in nieuwe daghe tYprewaerd omme daer orconscepe te horne met gaders den andren steden up de fugitive van den westlande, thaerre there van 8 daghen, 80*lb.*"

[109] L. Gilliodts van Severen, " Jacques van Artevelde," *La Flandre,* IX (1878), 412: " Bi Clais van Scotelaere, verteerd met vij cleerken scriuvende vpt ghiselhuus binnen ix daghen dat zij screven alle daghe toter minnacht die enqueste die ghehort waren jnt Westland metten iij steden, ende ghedobbleerd vier vout, ende j garsoen die hemlieden diende, vj*lb.* vijs." Cf. also *ibid.,* p. 413.

[110] N. de Pauw en J. Vuylsteke, *Rekeningen der Stad Gent,* I, 413.

[111] *Ibid.,* II, 42.   [113] *Ibid.,* p. 48.

[112] *Ibid.,* p. 131.   [114] *Ibid.,* p. 46.

[115] *Ibid.,* p. 48: " It. Janne van den Bossce, scepenen cleerc, die voer tHutrechtwaerd sdisendaechs naer sente Jans dach omme te vernemene wie de fugitive waren die daer incomen waren sint dat de roup ghedaen

While the exiles and the banished element were thus treated with rigor and effectually suppressed, the policy of van Artevelde and his followers was challenged in other ways by forces really far more dangerous than those which desired Flanders to submit to the authority of Philip and the count regardless of the manifest social and economic needs of the bourgeoisie. Van Artevelde and his supporters in Bruges and Ypres had to exercise constant vigilance in order to subordinate the rivalries of the crafts to their policy. This meant that the three towns were repeatedly called upon to invade strictly local rights. Thus the scabini of Ghent often assumed unheard of authority in controlling the appointment of scabini in other towns, as for example, Assenede and Biervliet in June,[116] Veurne in October, 1341,[117] Aardenburg in February, 1342,[118] and Courtrai in January, 1343.[119] At Houthem there was great danger of violence on the occasion of the annual fair at the close of June, and the scabini of Ghent sent a delegation thither to preserve order in 1341, 1342, and again in 1343.[120] Resentment of the rights arrogated by the authorities of Ghent led to a fight with the men of Ghent at Nevele, and on May 29, 1341, a delegation was sent under the captain, Gelnoot van Lens, and upon his return two other captains, William van Huse and Peter vanden Hovene, were charged to arrange a reconciliation.[121] In June of the next year the scabini were again forced to send out representatives to Nevele in order to prevent a fresh outburst.[122]

More details have been preserved in the case of Bruges. One important factor was the discord between the guilds, for which the exact reasons cannot be learned. There was trouble in May, 1341, when the scabini sent a delegation to aid the local scabini in pacifying the dissatisfied elements.[122a] Similar difficulties undoubtedly existed in Sluis, Damme, and Aardenburg. Furthermore, Bruges insisted upon its chartered rights, and the policy of economic restriction and the prosecution of the supporters of

---

was van daer te treckene, tsiere there van 7 daghen, 28*lb*." When the exiles were ordered away from Utrecht and by whom this was done is not clear.

[116] *Ibid.*, p. 48.
[117] *Ibid.*, p. 114.
[118] *Ibid.*, p. 117.
[119] *Ibid.*, p. 212.
[120] *Ibid.*, I, 421–422, I, 48, 218.
[121] *Ibid.*, II, 46.
[122] *Ibid.*, p. 122.
[122a] *Ibid.*, p. 45.

the authority of Philip drove the crafts of the Frank of Bruges and towns near Bruges to unite in opposing the policy of the three towns. In Aardenburg, Damme, and Oostburg there was opposition to the alliance with Edward. On April 23, 1340, a delegation was sent to these towns to secure evidence against those who labored to stir up resistance.[123]   On July 2 a force of white-hoods and also, undoubtedly, another of red-hoods rode about the castlery of the Frank of Bruges. It was at this time, as has been shown above, that the militia from these sections refused to march out for the siege of Tournai.[124]

This sullen resistance continued until trouble finally burst forth at Aardenburg, and in March, 1341, a number of burghers were banished. An imposing delegation was sent to establish harmony. From Ghent went one of the scabini, the dean of the fullers, and five representatives of the crafts.[125]   This, however, did not end the matter, for in June and July envoys had to be sent again.[126]   At this moment dissensions broke forth at Sluis which demanded attention. The scabini of Ghent sent William van Vaernewijc and Peter vanden Hovene at the close of July.[127] But order thus established was again broken in the following spring at the close of April when there were acts of violence and murder, and William van Vaernewijc was sent to Clusen with twenty-five bowmen.[128]   At the close of June there was much trouble at Aardenburg and Sluis, which required the presence of soldiers.[129]   Two scabini from Ghent were sent there on June 25 and immediately after their return were ordered to Bruges in order to share in the formalities when the people of the Frank of Bruges were to take oath. The soldiers left Aardenburg on July 16 when the scabini sent their colleagues, Peter Bollard and

---

[123] N. de Pauw en J. Vuylsteke, *Rekeningen der Stad Gent*, I, 417: "It. scep. Symoen ser Thomaes ende Pieter Mabenzone, ende met hemlieden Jan Tolviin, die voeren up den zelven dagh tErdenboerch, ten Damme, ende tHoestboerch omme oerconscepe te hoerne van den ghenen die hem ghepiint adden int vrie werringhe te makene, thare theere dat sij ute waren 5 daghe, 60*lb*."

[124] *Ibid.*, p. 502, and II, 49.   [125] *Ibid.*, II, 24, 42–43.
[126] *Ibid.*, p. 49.   [127] *Ibid.*, pp. 49–50.
[128] *Ibid.*, p. 120: "Item Willem van Varnewijc vor sdicend. up meyavont ter Clusen met 25 archiers [. . . . .] geslegen adden Jan Modden binnen verde, van enen dage, 20*lb*."
[129] *Ibid.*, pp. 148–149.

John vanden Bossche, to bring them back.[130]   Bollard returned to
Bruges to take hostages for the peace which had been disturbed
by so many feuds.[131]

In the castleries of the west a similar situation prevailed.   There
were serious disturbances among the guilds at Ypres which resented the influence of Ghent and Bruges.   But particularly bitter was the antagonism between Poperingen and Ypres which
was caused by the claim of the latter that their neighbors were
encroaching upon their privileges in the manufacture of cloth.[132]
In February, 1340, the debate was acute, and the scabini of Ghent
dispatched their colleague, Baldwin de Puur, to establish harmony.[133]   The keen rivalry between these two towns was especially dangerous at the moment when van Artevelde and his
associates decided to abandon their policy of neutrality and throw
their support to Edward in his claims to the throne of France.

In April there were disputes between the weavers and the fullers
in Ypres, which compelled the scabini of Ghent to send one of
their own number with representatives of the crafts to maintain the peace.[134]   For a while there was quiet, but in May of the
next year dissensions once more broke out between the weavers
and the fullers.[135]   Early in June the scabini of Ghent sent their
colleague, Thomas van Olsene, Peter Mabenzone, dean of the
weavers, John de Bake, dean of the fullers, and Peter Zoetard,
dean of the lesser guilds.   This delegation was charged to aid in
appointing new deans and *jurati* of the crafts of Ypres and reconcile the factions.[136]   From July 11 to 15 another delegation was
sent to settle the trouble which had again broken out and to punish the offenders.[137]   In September there was a serious conspiracy

[130] *Ibid.*, pp. 122, 123: ". . . omme tFrie te doen swerne."

[131] *Ibid.*, p. 124: ". . . om ghisele te nemen van vele veeten die
[. . . . .] en ellere int lant van Vlaen. . . ."

[132] Cf. N. de Pauw, *Ypre jeghen Poperinghe angaende den Verbonden,*
pp. v–XLVI.

[133] N. de Pauw en J. Vuylsteke, *Rekeningen der Stad Gent,* I, 411.

[134] *Ibid.*, pp. 415–416.

[135] *Ibid.*, II, 45.

[136] *Ibid.*, p. 46: ". . . omme daer te helpen makene dekene, gheswoerne
van den ambachten daer van der stede, ten meesten paise ende rusten van
der stede. . . ."

[137] *Ibid.*, p. 49: ". . . tYpre omme discord dat daer was af te doen
legghene ende corrextie te doen doene up eneghe malfaiteurs. . . ."

and the captain, Gelnoot van Lens, and a number of the scabini from Ghent appeared in Ypres to repress violence.[138]　Feeling ran high, and on one occasion violent language was used before the scabini of Bruges who had come in the interests of the three towns to labor for peace.　This again called forth delegations from Ghent and Bruges at the close of January, 1342.[139]　An inquest was subsequently held and as a result justice was executed in March.[140]　Further violence occurred in May when the malcontents laid hands upon the scabini of Ypres and struck them. The delegates from Ghent, among whom were the captain, William van Vaernewijc, the deans of the guilds, and others, labored from the 16th to the 20th to administer justice.[141]　Meanwhile in October there also was discontent at Poperingen which was caused, it appears, by the antagonisms of the guilds.

A similar situation existed in the castleries of the southwest.[142] In Courtrai, however, there was little or no trouble and the measures taken by the three towns in 1338 and 1339 [143] appear to have been effective because no further difficulty is reported until February, 1342, when there was serious discord between the fullers and the weavers.[144]　At Eename in September, 1341, there were similar troubles which were also followed by measures to bring the culprits to justice.[145]　But at Oudenaarde the situation was more acute.　Efforts in May, 1340, to compose these antagonisms [146] were only temporarily successful.　In December there was fighting between the crafts, and on the 8th a delegation was sent from Ghent to reconcile the weavers and the fullers of Oudenaarde and Pamele, a separate jurisdiction within its walls.[147] There was renewed discord in April, 1341, which led the scabini

138 N. de Pauw en J. Vuylsteke, *Rekeningen der Stad Gent*, II, 113.

139 *Ibid.*, pp. 116–117: " Item scep. Pieter Bollard ende Jan van Bost voeren swonsd. ante Pauli tYpre wart [. . . . .] siere ter correxien die men daer doen soude op de ghene die scepenen van Br. [. . . . .] adden ende blamerlike toegesproken adden, daer si waren in slants bederve. . . ."

140 *Ibid.*, p. 118.

141 *Ibid.*, p. 120: " . . . tYpre wart omme wet te doen doene over de ghene die geslegen adden up de wet [. . . . .] doot ende ghewont. . . ."

142 *Ibid.*, p. 114.

143 N. de Pauw, " Enquête sur les Capitaines de Courtrai sous Artevelde," *BCRH*, 79 (1910), 256–274.

144 N. de Pauw en J. Vuylsteke, *Rekeningen der Stad Gent*, II, 117–118.

145 *Ibid.*, pp. 91, 113.

146 *Ibid.*, I, 417–418.　　　　　　147 *Ibid.*, II, 38.

of Ghent to send Thomas van Vaernewijc and Simon ser Thomaes thither early in June to help in appointing new scabini.[148] In October Gelnoot van Lens and William van Huse were sent to establish order,[149] and in the following February the deans of the crafts at Ghent and some of the scabini were ordered to appease the fighting fullers and weavers.[150]

This chronic discontent embittered the men of the crafts, and envoys had to be sent from Ghent in May, June, and July.[151] The three towns of Flanders were represented in the government of the town and the castlery by the *ruwaard*, Lambert Mondekin, upon whom fell the very difficult task of keeping the thirteen scabini, the thirteen councillors, the bailiff of the town of Oudenaarde, the bailiff of Pamele, and the discordant guilds in harmony with the rest of the country.[152] There was a dispute between Oudenaarde and Ronse where the crafts were infringing the rights of the burghers in the manufacture of cloth, and, as in the case of Bruges and the Frank of Bruges, and later of Ypres and Poperingen, van Artevelde and his associates sought to maintain the rights of the aggrieved party. On May 20 a delegation composed of the heads of the guilds left Ghent and, accompanied by the men of Oudenaarde, rode about the country around Ronse destroying everywhere the vats used by the fullers.[153] The scabini of Ghent also found it necessary to intervene at Grammont. In June, 1341, they had sent two of their colleagues to settle disorders which appear to have arisen between the crafts.[154]

At this time the crafts of Dendermonde were involved in bitter fighting. The scabini of Ghent sent Thomas van Vaernewijc and the scabinus, Peter vander Asselt, thither on February 5, 1341.[155] In the following month another deputation with representatives from the guilds was instructed to establish the

---

[148] *Ibid.*, pp. 44, 46.
[149] *Ibid.*, p. 114.
[150] *Ibid.*, pp. 117–118.
[151] *Ibid.*, pp. 122, 123.
[152] N. de Pauw, *La Conspiration d'Audenaerde sous Jacques van Artevelde (1342). Critique Historique avec Pièces Inédits du Procès*, pp. XXXVII–XXXVIII.
[153] N. de Pauw en J. Vuylsteke, *Rekeningen der Stad Gent*, II, 135: "... met die van Houdenaerde te Ronse en daer omtrent om [. . . . .] tauwen ende commen te slane ontwe die daer stonden jeghen de vriede van Audenaerde. . . ."
[154] *Ibid.*, p. 48.
[155] *Ibid.*, pp. 39–40.

peace,[156] and in March the scabinus Peter vanden Velde and the captain, Peter vanden Hovene were sent to confer as to the satisfaction to be made by a certain Nase Kerstinmanne.[157] This person certainly did not belong to either the weavers or the fullers, as may be inferred from the fact that the accounts of Ghent refer to him as *her* and hence most likely he was a member of the patriciate. The movement in Dendermonde was not merely an instance of guild bickerings, but was apparently due to a chronic resentment of external control. In December the *ruwaard* was in the town,[158] undoubtedly in connection with some fresh violence, for on February 4 two scabini were sent thither to aid in establishing harmony.[159] Soon there was renewed difficulty and when in March some of the men of Dendermonde were imprisoned in Brussels it was found necessary to hold an inquest.[160]

This catalogue of dreary and scanty details clearly shows that the chief difficulty confronting van Artevelde and his party was the internecine strife of the guilds and their opposition to a régime which violated the sense of independence so strong in medieval towns. It is also clear that the general distemper became much worse in the autumn of 1341 and in the first months of the following year. This was undoubtedly due in part at least to the absence of Count Louis, which deprived the three towns of a legal sanction they so much needed in their domination over the others. Louis had left Flanders after submitting to the galling control of the scabini and delegates of the towns and the Council of Flanders.[161] This took place apparently just before the Truce of Esplechin was about to end on June 24, 1341, for the last mentioned delegation from Ghent to Bruges, where he was staying, returned on June 15.[162]

While the exiles apparently offered no serious problem, the three towns found the dissensions a grave embarrassment and

---

[156] N. de Pauw en J. Vuylsteke, *Rekeningen der Stad Gent,* II, 42.

[157] *Ibid.,* p. 44.   [158] *Ibid.,* p. 129.   [159] *Ibid.,* p. 117.

[160] *Ibid.,* p. 119: " . . . omme te horne orconscepen [. . . . .] dat gheweest adde tusscen der ghementen ende den heere ende rewart. . . ."

[161] Le Muisit, p. 137: " . . . sed diu ibi non remansit, nam recessit propter metum vite sue." The abbot was not always well informed.

[162] N. de Pauw en J. Vuylsteke, *Rekeningen der Stad Gent,* II, 47. There was in progress an inquest of exiles in the western castleries at the close of the year. Cf. *ibid.,* p. 39.

the opposition to their authority a positive danger. In the following spring, negotiations were opened with Count Louis for his return.[163] On March 25 a delegation composed of Thomas van Vaernewijc, Simon ser Thomaes, Peter Zoetard, and others was sent to Erkenghem to present with the men from Bruges and Ypres their requests for his return.[164] Louis was willing, but only under certain conditions, the nature of which cannot, for lack of information, be ascertained. This is apparent from the fact that on April 8 the scabini of Ghent sent Gelnoot van Lens and the clerk John vanden Bossche to Courtrai, Oudenaarde, Alost, Grammont, and, on the 15th, Peter vanden Hovene and vanden Bossche to Hulst and Axel to state his demands.[165] In May the scabini of Ghent requested the countess, who was at Bapaume, to return.[166] At this moment Louis was at Halewin near the border whither the envoys of the three towns went to present their solicitations.[167] In July there were further discussions at Halewin.[168] Louis thereupon reappeared in Flanders and went to Male whither on August 4 Ghent sent a delegation.[169] The Council of Flanders again became important. On August 26 Thomas van Vaernewijc and John vander Vloet, now mentioned for the first time as members of the Council of Flanders, were sent to the count to aid him with their advice.[170]

III. The Tumult at Oudenaarde (September, 1342)

Shortly after Count Louis' return to Flanders occurred the uprising at Oudenaarde. This has been regarded as an insurrection fomented chiefly by the disgruntled exiles and their

---

[163] It is exceedingly unfortunate that the accounts for the year 1341–1342, *ibid.*, pp. 93–154, are so fragmentary.

[164] *Ibid.*, pp. 118–119: " . . . tErkenghen ward dar mijn heere [. . . . .] om meminen heere te biddene ende te versouken metsgaders den lande dat hi in sijn lant. . . ."

[165] *Ibid.*, p. 119.

[166] *Ibid.*, p. 121.

[167] *Ibid.*, p. 212: L. Gilliodts van Severen, "Jacques van Artevelde," *La Flandre,* IX (1878), 410.

[168] L. Gilliodts van Severen, "Jacques van Artevelde," *La Flandre,* IX (1878), 410. The accounts of Ghent make no reference to this.

[169] N. de Pauw en J. Vuylsteke, *Rekeningen der Stad Gent,* II, 124.

[170] *Ibid.*, pp. 205, 207, 212.

friends.[171] A careful study of the available documents, however, makes it clear that the trouble originated from the antagonisms of fullers and weavers and the sullen dissatisfaction on the part of the patricians, as well as the craftsmen, with the domination of Ghent in the affairs of the commune. The immediate cause of the trouble was, it seems, the irresponsible and ill-considered action of Gilles Craenhals, the head of the weavers, who believed that some violence was being plotted, and the failure of the *ruwaard*, Lambert Mondekin, to take a decisive step at the critical moment. Any direct responsibility of the count cannot be proved from the extant documents. Nor did the exiles have a serious part in the matter. The Truce of Esplechin, after having been prolonged three times, did not come to an end until September 14, 1342. The scabini of the three towns had a firm grip on the county at the moment. Large forces of at least 8,000 men were placed in Gravelines, Bergen, and Cassel to prevent any hostile incursions.[172] Hence during July and August no effort was made by the exiles to return and stir up trouble, if we may judge from the fact that nowhere in the accounts of Ghent for these months is any mention made of activities on the part of returning outlaws.

Like Craenhals, Mondekin also was fearful of a plot and requested of the scabini a permanent guard of twenty men. Consideration was deferred until the meeting of the council, but the scabini did delegate three of their colleagues to keep watch with those regularly appointed to patrol the streets. The council, however, refused Mondekin's request on the ground that the town was already too heavily burdened by debts incurred in building the town hall. Mondekin was thus forced to be content with men appointed by himself. Craenhals, who was present at the meeting, with his friend, John Stamerard, left the hall in high dudgeon, exclaiming in irate sarcasm, " Lambert, since you are so well guarded we will guard ourselves too! " In the evening Mondekin collected a large number of friends, relatives,

---

[171] N. de Pauw, *La Conspiration d'Audenarde sous Jacques van Arte-velde (1342). Critique Historique avec les Pièces Inédits du Procès* (Gand, 1878) ; " Audenarde sous Artevelde avec une de ses Lettres Inédites," *Annales du Cercle Archéologique et Historique d'Audenarde* (1916), pp. 2–3.

[172] N. de Pauw en J. Vuylsteke, *Rekeningen der Stad Gent*, II, 149–151.

and members of his own guild — he was originally from Oude-naarde, although appointed *ruwaard* on behalf of the three towns, and belonged to the guild of the butchers — and kept guard all night. He also secured possession of all the keys of the town. In the morning he sent Stamerard and John van Abbinsvoorde, the count's bailiff, to Ghent to request help. The scabini at once sent the captains, William van Huse and Peter vanden Hovene, with a force of English archers and other troops, which caused some uneasiness among the townsmen. These were then sum-moned to assemble at the convent of the Franciscans, and, at the order of the delegates from Ghent, the scabini authorized Mon-dekin to choose for his guard twenty men from the guilds, whose expenses were to be paid out of the income from the properties of the exiles, and twenty from the suburban bourgeoisie, who were to pay their own expenses.[173]

On Thursday evening, the 12th, Craenhals and a large body of weavers from Pamele were on guard and were soon joined by Mondekin. Each operated entirely on his own initiative and independently of the legally constituted guard of the town. Armed with weapons, they began to visit the homes of patricians and fullers, but found only a very few men who might be con-sidered dangerous, certainly hardly enough to justify the fears entertained. On the following day there were many complaints of these domiciliary visits, and the scabini decided to convoke the council on the 14th and in the meanwhile strengthen the legal watch. When this guard began its duties on Friday evening a member of the tailors' (*parmentiers*) guild reported that in the house of one of the patricians, Oliver Cabillau, a great number of armed men was being kept in hiding. But a search failed to reveal any such persons; in fact, these activities were as futile as those of the previous night and failed to reveal the presence of any conspirators.[174]

The meeting in the town hall on Saturday morning ended in tumultuous scenes which seriously threatened to develop into bloodshed. There were present Mondekin, the scabini and the councillors, the heads of the guilds, many of the patriciate, and a

[173] N. de Pauw, *La Conspiration d'Audenarde sous Jacques van Arte-velde (1342)*, pp. 1–13, LXXXV–LXXXVII.

[174] *Ibid.*, pp. LXXXVII–LXXXIX.

crowd of armed men who had no right to be there. The question of the visits of the previous nights came up. Mondekin was accused of various irregularities, especially the extra-legal search and the possession of the keys of the town. He was accused of designs to assassinate members of the patriciate by means of the English archers and other troops brought from Ghent. The demand why the extra-legal guard had been instituted evoked a wrathful reply from Craenhals to the effect that he concerned himself only with his own matters and requested others to do likewise.

Words of anger were heard and Craenhals placed his hand on the hilt of his sword. In the confusion which followed he ordered his henchmen to hasten to Pamele and call out his partisans and he himself rushed to the window and shouted to the crowd on the market place " To arms! Behold how they seek to kill me! " Thereupon he rushed out of the hall in spite of all efforts to restrain him. With a group of partisans he hastened to Pamele, ever calling the people to arms. A large number was soon assembled in the market place. Here they found a group of fullers and patricians already drawn up with banners unfurled, shouting *Here ende Wet!* The weavers and their adherents replied, *Ghemeente ende Vrient!* Thus the fullers and wealthy elements of the town demanded the autonomy of the scabini (the *Wet*) and the authority of the prince (the *Here*) as against the control of Ghent. The weavers and their partisans, who supported the *ruwaard*, Mondekin, and the policy of the three towns, saw, or thought they saw, evidences of the machinations of the exiled opponents of van Artevelde's policy. The inquests made after the event fail to reveal any definite facts regarding the connivance of the exiles at Tournai. The few witnesses to testify on this point could report only vague rumors,[175] which may in large part have been born of the suspicions of the weavers and of such men as Craenhals and Mondekin. There is no evidence that the exiles made any active effort to return; at the most, and this is not impossible, their attempts aimed to stir up discontent. In any case, it appears that these events were mainly manifestations of the hostility of the fullers and the weavers. To designate

[175] N. de Pauw, *La Conspiration d'Audenarde sous Jacques van Artevelde (1342)*, pp. 11, 14, 33, 52, 56.

the opponents simply as *Leliaerts* and *Clauwaerts* would therefore not fit the facts which de Pauw did not realize until forty years after publishing the extant documents dealing with these events.[176]

After a good deal of difficulty the scabini succeeded in reestablishing order in both Oudenaarde and Pamele. The truce was accepted and Craenhals promised not to leave the town, while the scabini ordered a general disarmament and threatened all those who sought to break the peace with severe penalties and at once sent a messenger to Ghent. But Craenhals broke his word and was off to Ghent with one of his companions and refused to return at the entreaties of the *ruwaard's* messengers. Meanwhile, report of what had occurred reached the scabini of Ghent. The annual delegation from Ghent to honor the Virgin at Tournai on September 14 was in Oudenaarde on the 12th, waited in vain for the escort from Tournai, and returned home on the 14th.[177] They were already apprised, it appears, of the crisis by the 13th, for it is likely that this was the reason why the scabini on that day sent two of their colleagues and John vander Vloet, a member of the Council of Flanders, to consult with Count Louis at Bruges.[178] At the same time [179] a large force was prepared and the scabini of Oudenaarde were alarmed. They sent Mondekin with a letter to Ghent in the hope of preventing the dispatch of the troops and in the meanwhile made preparations for defense.[180] They also sent a letter to Count Louis declaring that the tumult had subsided and that all parties had accepted arbitration by the scabini, the count's bailiff, and Mondekin.[181]

On Sunday, the 15th, or possibly Monday, the force arrived before Oudenaarde and invested the gate on the road leading to

---

[176] "Audenarde sous van Artevelde, avec une de ses Lettres Inédites et autres Pièces authentiques," *Annales du Cercle Archéologique et Historique de Courtrai* (1916), pp. 2–3. See also Gilliodts van Severen, "Jacques van Artevelde," *La Flandre*, IX (1878), 407.

[177] N. de Pauw en J. Vuylsteke, *Rekeningen der Stad Gent*, II, 186–187, 285–287.

[178] *Ibid.*, p. 207.

[179] *Ibid.*, p. 246 (note): "It. doe scep. waecten in der heleger crusen avonde doe men tHoudenaerde trac. . . ."

[180] N. de Pauw, *La Conspiration d'Audenaerde sous Jacques van Artevelde (1342)*, pp. CXXXII–CXXXVI.

[181] *Ibid.*, pp. 8–9, and XCIII–XCIV.

Ghent. It was under the command of four of the captains, Coudenhove, commander of the militia from Bruges, William van Vaernewijc, Josse Apre, and Gelnoot van Lens, each accompanied by seven aides. Four of the scabini were with them, and also the three deans of the guilds: Gilles van Ghavere with thirty-five weavers, Segher Boele with thirty fullers, and Peter Zoetard with thirty-five from the lesser guilds. There was also a group of bowmen, clerks, sergeants, and a few others.[182] Bruges, and perhaps also Ypres, sent a force.[183] There was but slight resistance and the scabini and captains of the three towns soon were in possession.[184] Thereupon an inquest was instituted. The scabini and captains of Ghent remained in the town for ten days, and their leader, Nicasis vander Haghe, twelve. They were assisted by two envoys from Bruges who were sent on the 16th to Oudenaarde where they stayed sixteen days,[185] and by two scabini and a clerk from Ypres who were allowed expenses for fifteen days.[186] The scabini of Oudenaarde drew up a statement of the events.[187] The delegates of the three towns conducted the investigation by the use of a list of thirty-two questions,[188] which they apparently asked of each one of the six hundred and sixty-three persons taken for the purpose.[189] Fully one month's time was necessary to formulate a decision, and on October 21 two of the scabini of Ghent and others from Bruges and Ypres went to Oudenaarde to pronounce their penalties.[190] Unfortunately, the details of this decree have been lost, but it is certain that the town was heavily fined, for the accounts of Ghent of this year mention receipt of 2,000*l.*[191] In December the scabini of Oudenaarde were required to declare on oath their intention to remain faithful.[192]

Meanwhile, the three towns used their power to check the

---

[182] N. de Pauw en J. Vuylsteke, *Rekeningen der Stad Gent,* II, 256–257. The total cost of this expedition amounted to 1,744*l.* 16*s.* 8*d.*

[183] L. Gilliodts van Severen, " Jacques van Artevelde," *La Flandre,* IX (1878), 407.

[184] N. de Pauw, *La Conspiration d'Audenarde sous Jacques van Artevelde (1342),* pp. cxlii–cxliii.

[185] *Ibid.,* pp. 81–83 (excerpts from the accounts of Bruges).

[186] *Ibid.,* p. cxlv (note).   [188] *Ibid.,* pp. 10–13.

[187] *Ibid.,* pp. 1–9.   [189] *Ibid.,* pp. 13–74.

[190] N. de Pauw en J. Vuylsteke, *Rekeningen der Stad Gent,* II, 209.

[191] *Ibid.,* p. 162.   [192] *Ibid.,* p. 211.

manufacturing of all cloth which in any way infringed their privileges. On October 3, 1342, Count Louis was at Dixmuide and
issued an order to the bailiff of Ypres to stop within eight days
all such illegal activity at Langemaark and other places in the
castlery of Ypres within three leagues of the town of Ypres. This
order, which gave him full power to do everything necessary to
accomplish this task, was given in response to the eager solicitations of the men of Ypres and reveals how the count was dominated
by the power of the three towns.[193] At the close of the month
there was discord among the crafts at Bruges, which demanded
the attention of Ghent, and perhaps also Ypres, and the captain,
Gelnoot van Lens, one of the scabini, and the deans of the fullers
and weavers were sent to establish peace.[194] This apparently
was successful, for no further difficulty is recorded.

The relations between Bruges and the Frank of Bruges were
also regulated at this time. The count was at Damme in the
middle of October when on the 20th he issued his decision concerning the contentions between the two, which was also inspired
by the wishes of the three towns. Henceforth no more cloth
was to be offered for sale in the Frank of Bruges either in large
quantities or in small pieces. A penalty of 50*l.* Parisian was to be
imposed for each offence. The burgomasters were to have the
right to request the bailiff and his men to ride about the Frank
whenever they should deem it necessary. Denizens of the Frank,
however, were allowed to maintain one set of instruments necessary for the fabrication of cloth from their own wool and only
for their own use. It was absolutely forbidden in the future for
anyone to shout *Bruges, Bruges!* or *Frank, Frank!* If anyone
should violate this order and strife result and people be killed,
he was to be beheaded, whether he be burgher or freedman, and
if he could not be seized he was to be banished from Flanders
for a hundred years. If, however, no one should be killed, his
hand should be struck off, and, if he could not be caught, he
should be banished for ten years. No bells of any sort might be
sounded to call the people together to resist the men of Bruges

---

[193] G. Espinas et H. Pirenne, *Recueil des Documents relatifs à
l'Histoire de l'Industrie Drapière en Flandre,* III, 13.

[194] N. de Pauw en J. Vuylsteke, *Rekeningen der Stad Gent,* II, 209–
210.

under penalty of banishment for ten years from the country. The scabini of Bruges were to have the right to take horses and wagons for military purposes in case of need. The names of the owners were to be put in writing so that they could be promptly returned, and, in case of any damage, compensation was to be rendered in accordance with the " good old customs and usages." [195]

Thereupon, from December 2 to 7, a large delegation composed of two of the scabini and representatives from each of the three guilds with thirty-one horses was sent from Ghent to Bruges.[196] There they exhibited the privileges of their town concerning the manufacture of cloth which was forbidden to all who dwelt within five miles of the walls of Ghent. Then they rode out into the castlery of Bruges, accompanied by the men of Bruges, and went about destroying on every hand all instruments used in the making of cloth and forbade all such activity in the future under threat of burning the cloth.[197]

IV. The Papacy and the Low Countries (1340–1343)

In October, 1340, the Flemings were to send delegates to receive from Philip at Tournai the documents touching the right to inflict the ecclesiastical penalties and to grant absolution which had been promised at the time that the truce was made at Esplechin.[198] On the 7th the scabini of Ghent sent their colleagues, Jacob Coelins and Jacob vander Linden, with John uten Hove and two other clerks. They returned on the 13th, and the documents were cancelled before the eyes of the townsmen.[199] On the 10th the bishop of Senlis and the official of Tournai lifted the sentence of excommunication at the royal order.[200]

[195] N. de Pauw en J. Vuylsteke, *Rekeningen der Stad Gent,* II, 209; G. Espinas et H. Pirenne, *Recueil des Documents relatifs à l'Histoire de l'Industrie Drapière en Flandre,* I, 571–575.

[196] N. de Pauw en J. Vuylsteke, *Rekeningen der Stad Gent,* II, 210. 211.   [197] *Ibid.,* p. 211.

[198] G. Daumet, *Benoît XII (1334–1342). Lettres Closes, Patentes, et Curiales se rapportant à la France,* No. 830.

[199] N. de Pauw en J. Vuylsteke, *Rekeningen der Stad Gent,* II, 34–35.

[200] L. Gilliodts van Severen, " Jacques van Artevelde," *La Flandre,* IX (1878), 442–443; E. van den Bussche, *Inventaire des Archives du Frank de Bruges,* I, 68; Kervyn, *Oeuvres de Froissart,* XXI, 472.

Thereupon preparations were begun to make the proper representations at the curia in Avignon. In January, 1341, Philip sent to Flanders a sergeant-at-arms, Baldwin de Créqui,[201] who undoubtedly had something to do with Philip's plans. The matter of appeal was discussed with the duke of Brabant, and on February 1 the clerk, John de Visch, was sent by the scabini of Ghent for the necessary documents.[202] He returned on the 5th.[203] Thereupon a delegation was sent by the three towns to Antoing to secure the removal of the documents from the papal registers and to get the official letters promised by Philip.[204] The king had solemnly sworn to secure from the pope a surrender of his rights before the fourth Sunday in Lent (*Laetare* Sunday), and at St. Germain-en-Laye on March 5 communicated his desires to Benedict XII [205] through his envoy, Raymond de Salgues, canon of the church of Paris. For the Flemings appeared John de Escuria, John Meyre,[206] and Paul de Utkerke, clerks from the dioceses of Tournai, Cambrai, and Thérouanne respectively.[207]

Benedict XII desired above all things to preserve for the *Respublica Christiana* its position and influence in the life of the world. Like his predecessor, John XXII, he had labored to secure harmony between Edward and Philip. Like him also he was

[201] J. Viard, " Lettres d'État enregistrés au Parlement sous le Règne de Philippe VI de Valois, 1328–1350," *Bulletin, Société de l'Histoire de la France;* XXXIV (1897), 232, No. 144.

[202] N. de Pauw en J. Vuylsteke, *Rekeningen der Stad Gent*, II, 41: ". . . anden hertoghe van Brabant omme lettren van beden gaende an onsen vader den paefs van Rome ende an cardinale. . . ."

[203] He was paid 20*l.* for his services at the usual rate of 4*l.* per day. Cf. *ibid.*, p. 41.

[204] *Ibid.:* ". . . tAntoengienwart omme daer te sine ende te vermaenne met gaders den ghenen die daer ghesent waren vanden andren steden omme de bederve van der sententien te doene uten registre daer, ende daere up te ghecrighene sulke instrumente alse de coninc gheloeft hadde te leverne den lande van Vlaendren. . . ." Uten Hove was at Paris soon after this, *ibid.*, p. 60.

[205] G. Daumet, *Benoît XII (1334–42). Lettres Closes, Patentes, et Curiales se rapportant à la France*, No. 817.

[206] John uten Hove was with them, see N. de Pauw en J. Vuylsteke, *Rekeningen der Stad Gent*, II, 60. He borrowed 75*l.* 13*s.* 4*d.* from a merchant of Avignon on the credit of Ghent, *cf. ibid.*, pp. 74–75.

[207] G. Daumet, *Benoît XII (1334–42). Lettres Closes, Patentes, et Curiales se rapportant à la France*, No. 830; P. van Isacker et U. Berlière, *Lettres de Clément VI (1342–1352)*, No. 112.

keenly aware of the great importance of the princes of the Low Countries in the contest between them. His attitude toward the matrimonial alliance between the Plantagenet house and that of Brabant was wholly dictated by these considerations. The marriage could in no way contribute to the repose of Christendom of which he was the universal shepherd and it would solidify the relations already intimate between Brabant, Flanders, and Zeeland, steady the policy of the duke of Brabant as an ally of England, and vastly enhance Edward's power in that quarter. Accordingly, the English king's request of October 30,[208] 1340, for a dispensation could not be entertained. On July 15, 1341, Pope Benedict once more refused to grant it.[209]   Clearly this was not due to Philip's influence, as the poet Boendale thought.[210]

A similar purpose dominated Benedict in his policy toward the reconciliation of Philip and Lewis the Bavarian. The emperor desired more than anything else to be freed from the penalties of the church, and thought that an agreement with Philip would enlist the latter's influence to bring this about. This was a splendid opportunity, for the French king naturally would be only too glad to remove the empire from the struggle. If Edward's title of vicar should be revoked, his prestige in the Low Countries, so far as it rested upon imperial support, would lose its legal sanction. Negotiations between Lewis and the curia had been in progress during the autumn of 1340,[211] and discussions were soon opened with Philip which speedily led to an agreement. On January 24, 1341, at Vilshofen in Bavaria Lewis promised to be henceforth the faithful friend and ally of Philip regardless of any future conditions — even a papal dispensation — which might induce him to act in a contrary manner.[212]   Four days later Lewis further promised to abandon all claim upon those parts of the empire which had fallen into Philip's hands, to revoke Edward's title of imperial vicar, and even prohibit

---

[208] *Foedera*, II (2), 1140.

[209] G. Daumet, *Benoît XII (1334–42). Lettres Closes, Patentes, et Curiales, se rapportant à la France*, No. 857.

[210] *Brabantsche Yeesten*, I, 579–580.

[211] S. Riezler, *Vatikanische Akten*, No. 2082.

[212] Kervyn, *Oeuvres de Froissart*, XVIII, 186; J. F. Boehmer, *Die Urkunden Kaiser Ludwigs des Baiern*, p. 134.

subjects of the empire in the future from aiding Philip's numerous enemies.[213]

This *rapprochement* of course meant that the questions touching the Cambrésis, Crèvecoeur, and Arleux were allowed to remain *in statu quo*, wholly in Philip's favor. After mutual approval of all the points agreed upon in these negotiations had been effected, Philip swore on March 15 to bring about his reconciliation with the curia and act toward Lewis as a faithful friend and ally.[214] But his influence with the pope was far from decisive, especially in matters of papal policy. Thus while on March 1 Benedict had at his request authorized him to retain the biennial papal tenths collected in France, he flatly refused to accede to his request on April 2 to be allowed to use them for his struggle against Edward.[215] The pope was guided by the spirit of John XXII in his policy toward the empire and insisted upon a deferential treatment at the hands of temporal authorities. Accordingly, he could not be enthusiastic over the proposition which Philip sent him from St. Germain-en-Laye on March 2.[216] One month later, on April 23, he expressed his disapproval of the manner in which Philip, a scion of the ancient and Christian ruling house of a faithful people, made arrangements with a pestiferous heretic and schismatic.[217]

While Benedict sought to execute the high calling of the church in dealing with the matrimonial proposals of Edward and the duke of Brabant and to subordinate the relations of Philip and the Bavarian to the wishes of the papacy, he showed himself favorable to William, count of Hainault, Holland, and Zeeland, who desired to become reconciled with the church. This young and restless prince was fond of the tournament and hence by nature unfitted to bear the inconveniences pronounced against him at the time when he had invaded the Cambrésis with Edward. He was soon willing to yield his important claims in the Cambrésis and those touching Arleux and Crèvecoeur. Count Wil-

[213] Kervyn, *Oeuvres de Froissart*, XVIII, 189; J. F. Boehmer, *Die Urkunden Kaiser Ludwigs des Baiern*, p. 287.

[214] J. F. Boehmer, *Die Urkunden Kaiser Ludwigs des Baiern*, pp. 338, 374, and *Fontes Rerum Germanicurum*, I, 223, and IV, 35.

[215] Baronius, *Annales Ecclesiastici*, XVI, 115–117.

[216] S. Riezler, *Vatikanische Akten*, No. 2097.

[217] G. Daumet, *Benoît XII (1334–1342). Lettres Closes, Patentes, et Curiales se rapportant à la France*, No. 857.

liam had appealed against the ecclesiastical censures in 1340,[218] but on April 1, 1341, Benedict instructed the bishops of Liège, Utrecht, and Tournai to disregard his appeal and proceed with rigor.[219] On the 24th he instructed the bishops of Laon, Noyon, and Nola to use force against Count William, John, duke of Brabant, Thierry, seignior of Valkenburg, and their abettors, the corporations and individuals of the counties of Flanders and Alost.[220] But on April 2 William charged Annibal and Peter de Pratis, cardinal bishops of Frascati and Praeneste, to negotiate a settlement with the bishop of Cambrai and his chapter,[221] and at the same moment named five delegates to represent his cause.[222] On May 12 these same commissioners were ordered under penalty of ten thousand gold marks to accept whatever the arbiters might decide.[223] One of these, Stephen Mallion, was directed on June 30 to inform the bishop and chapter that his master had ordered the receiver of Hainault not to use their sequestrated incomes and properties until disposal could be made in accordance with the decision of the cardinals.[224] Two days later he sent three commissioners to Benedict to receive absolution.[225]

Since these were the views of Benedict as revealed in his activities in the spring of 1341, it was certain that, in dealing with Philip's request to surrender the right to excommunicate the rebellious Flemings, he would be guided first of all by the superior interests of the church. He replied on April 2. The first question asked of the Flemings at the curia was whether they would remain faithful subjects of their lawful princes. This condition had not been laid down in the negotiations with Philip and the delegates could not assent. When asked whether they were armed with powers sufficient to discuss this matter, they begged

---

[218] Kervyn, *Oeuvres de Froissart*, XVIII, 74–84.

[219] G. Brom, *Bullarium Trajectense*, Vol. I, No. 979; S. Riezler, *Vatikanische Akten*, No. 2098; A. Fierens, *Lettres de Benoît XII (1334–1342)*, No. 672.

[220] G. Brom, *Bullarium Trajectense*, I, 411; J. M. Vidal, *Benoît XII (1334–1342). Lettres Communes Analysées d'après les Registres dits d'Avignon et du Vatican*, II, 380; S. Riezler, *Vatikanische Akten*, No. 2099.

[221] L. Devillers, *Cartulaire*, I, 129–130.

[222] *Ibid.*, pp. 130–131.

[223] *Ibid.*, pp. 132–138.

[224] *Ibid.*, pp. 142–143.

[225] *Ibid.*, p. 127.

time to consider whether their instructions covered this point and whether they would use them in case they did. The pope gave them time to consider and appointed the cardinal bishops, Peter of Praeneste and Gaucelinus of Albano, to examine their powers, if they were willing to exhibit their credentials, and to ascertain whether they could discuss this point. But they refused, and the pope and cardinals decided unanimously that they could not entertain their request. At the close of the brief respite allowed them the delegates were permitted to appear in the presence of the pope and Raymond de Salgues. They declared that they did not have power to discuss the papal demands, that they could swear or promise nothing in regard to the future nor seek relief from the sentences of the church which, as they asserted, were barred by limitations and were not binding. Just what this argument was cannot be ascertained from the documents. Under these circumstances it would be of no advantage to revoke a right consistently enforced since the Treaty of Athis-sur-Orge of 1305. The general welfare and repose of Christendom would not be advanced in the slightest, and Benedict accordingly refused Philip's request.[226]

This decision placed Philip in the greatest embarrassment. He had made solemn promises which he could not redeem, and on June 24 the truce arranged at Esplechin would expire. The exasperated Flemings [227] would naturally make common cause with his enemy. Philip revealed his nervousness by issuing instructions on May 1 at Montdidier for the bishop of Senlis to hasten and publish the sentence of excommunication against the Flemings.[228] On May 26 Philip wrote two letters from St. Germain-

---

[226] G. Daumet, *Benoît XII (1334–1342). Lettres Closes, Patentes, et Curiales, se rapportant à la France*, No. 830; P. van Isacker et U. Berlière, *Lettres de Clément VI (1342–1352)*, No. 112.

[227] Report of the failure of the negotiations at Avignon was received at Ghent by the 20th at the latest when Lievin van St. Baefs arrived with letters from John uten Hove at Paris, see N. de Pauw en J. Vuylsteke, *Rekeningen der Stad Gent*, II, 62.

[228] He wrote to the queen: "Si voulons quant à la publication des sentences contre les Flamens que tantost et sans délay y envoiés l'evesque de Senlis pour les publier ainsi comme autrefoys vous avons escript, et qu'il ait point de délay; car qui s'en attendroit aux cardinaux, il y pourroit trop d'empeschement et de délays, laquelle chose no vous plairoit point." See Kervyn, *Oeuvres de Froissart*, XXIII, 345.

en-Laye to the curia, stating that he was sending the bishop of Clermont with Raymond de Salgues to plead with the pope. He declared that the Flemings were sorely disappointed and that he appeared remiss in fulfilling his promises to them, that Jeanne, the dowager countess of Hainault, had again appealed to him for a united Christendom in the face of the hostile infidel, and finally, that Alfonso X of Castile needed his aid in resisting the Saracens.[229] Benedict's attitude was not affected by this appeal, and on June 20 he wrote that, as the Flemings had not changed their attitude toward him in the slightest, there was no reason to grant the request.[230] Obviously Philip could not aid Alfonso when the Flemish peril was as acute as ever. In the face of the problems raised by this intransigent attitude, the Flemish clergy were requested to assemble at Thielt.[231] At the meeting on June 28 and 29 John uten Hove of Ghent was present,[232] but what was done must remain unknown.

During the summer and autumn the cardinals occupied themselves with the relations of William, count of Hainault, Holland, and Zeeland, and the bishop and chapter of Cambrai.[233] John of Hainault was represented at the curia by John de Fumone,[234] and toward the close of October Count William determined to proceed to Avignon in person to reinforce his eager pleas.[235] The case of the bishop and chapter was defended by Matthew de Prato, John de Cadzand, and Raynerius de Urbeveteri, canons of Cambrai. These negotiations now came to an end. Count William and his uncle were to restore to the bishop and chapter all the

[229] G. Daumet, *Bénoît XII (1334–1342). Lettres Closes, Patentes, et Curiales se rapportant à la France*, No. 843.

[230] *Ibid.*, No. 844.

[231] N. de Pauw en J. Vuylsteke, *Rekeningen der Stad Gent*, II, 65–66.

[232] *Ibid.*, p. 48.

[233] Three cardinals were appointed. See H. Dubrulle, *Cambrai à la Fin du Moyen Âge (XIIIe–XVIe Siècle)*, pp. 403–404: " Comme par la volónté de nostre saint Pere le Pappe, li évesques de Cambray nostre seigneur d'une part et le comte de Haynaut d'autre, se soient compromis en trois cardinaulx sur les inuires et violences que li dis contes a fait au dit évesque. . . ."

[234] L. Devillers, *Cartulaire*, I, 170–176.

[235] *Ibid.*, p. 170; H. G. Hamaker, *De Rekeningen der Grafelijkheid van Holland onder het Henegouwsche Huis*, III, 69; *De Rekeningen der Grafelijkheid van Zeeland onder het Henegouwsche Huis*, II, 206, 302; E. Déprez, *Les Préliminaires de la Guerre de Cent Ans*, p. 34.

properties which they had seized and still retained. The count was to indemnify the bishop and chapter for all losses inflicted by paying the former 3,000*l.* and the latter 8,000*l.* in four annual instalments of 2,000*l.* each, beginning with All Saints' Day, 1342, and 3,000*l.* for the fifth payment. He was to found two chapels, one in the cathedral of Cambrai, and a second in the abbey of Cambron and endow each with 25*l.* small Tournois. The bishop and chapter were to ratify this arrangement before the Feast of the Purification (February 2), 1342. This of course did not apply to the men of the town of Cambrai who were bitter toward Count William. But the arbiters desired to effect a complete pacification, and suggested that they too should accept the peace now established and negotiate with the count before Easter Sunday. They should, however, be permitted to receive troops within their walls for defense only and not to injure the count in any way.[236] The proctors of the bishop and chapter demanded that these sums should be completely paid before the removal of the ecclesiastical penalties, to which, however, Benedict was opposed, and accordingly on November 9 he instructed the abbot of St. Nicaise of Rheims and the official of Cambrai to lift the interdict from the lands of Count William and his uncle.[237] On December 29 the bishop ordered his vicar general to remove the sentence of excommunication.[238]

The men of Cambrai were little pleased with this decision which involved the return of the important strongholds of Escaudoeuvre and Relenghes which had been taken from the count in

[236] L. Devillers, *Cartulaire,* I, 167–177. It was ratified by the bishop at Dijon on January 24, 1342, *ibid.,* pp. 165–166 and by the chapter on February 1, *ibid.,* pp. 167–177; S. Riezler, *Vatikanische Akten,* No. 763; G. Daumet, *Benoît XII (1334–1342). Lettres Closes, Patentes, et Curiales, se rapportant à la France,* No. 898. For money and chattels, cf. L. Devillers, *Cartulaire,* I, 179–180, and the payment of 2,000*l.* Tournais on November 1, *ibid.,* pp. 182–188.

[237] L. Devillers, *Cartulaire,* I, 154–158; S. Riezler, *Vatikanische Akten,* No. 2114; S. Daumet, *Benoît XII (1334–1342). Lettres Closes, Patentes, et Curiales se rapportant à la France,* No. 899. For special right to celebrate mass, etc., see G. Brom, *Bullarium Trajectense,* Vol. I, No. 986; J. M. Vidal, *Benoît XII (1334–1342). Lettres Communes Analysées d'après les Registres dits d'Avignon et du Vatican,* II, 371; S. Riezler, *Vatikanische Akten,* No. 1341.

[238] L. Devillers, *Cartulaire,* I, 162, 164, 195; Kervyn, *Oeuvres de Froissart,* XVIII, 193–194.

the spring of the previous year.[239]   They wrote to Philip, declaring
that they would not treat with his enemies without his assent and
begged that in the negotiations with Count William he should endeavor to secure fitting compensation for all their losses incurred
in the late wars with their enemy and prevent the restoration of
those two strongholds strategically so dangerous to the safety
of the townsmen.[240]   Philip was also disquieted, for he had heard
a report purporting to have come from Count William himself
that his troops would have to evacuate the town and never return.
He declared that without his garrison in Cambrai his realm
would ever be exposed at that point to hostile incursions from his
enemies in the Low Countries.   To prevent this and at the request
of the bishop, dean, and chapter of Cambrai he had, at the beginning of the present difficulties, placed his soldiers in the town
and undertaken to construct fortifications at great expense.[241]
Benedict replied on January 2, 1342, that there was no question
of removing the French soldiers and that it was only prohibited
to admit troops that would harm the count of Hainault.[242]

V. The Extension of the Truce of Esplechin (1341–1342)

In the spring of 1341 Edward was forced to consider the possibility of a renewal of the war with the expiration of the truce
on St. John the Baptist's Day.   On March 3 he convoked Parliament [243] which convened on April 23.[244]   With the credits it
granted he hoped to pay his clamoring allies in the Low Countries and to reopen the struggle with Philip.   In April he began

---

239 Cf. *supra*, pp. 383.

240 H. Dubrulle, *Cambrai à la Fin du Moyen Âge (XIIIe–XVIe Siècle)*,
pp. 403–404.   The document is undated, but must have been issued soon
after November 9.   The burghers sent no representative, cf. G. Daumet,
*Benoît XII (1334–1342). Lettres Closes, Patentes, et Curiales se rap-
portant à la France*, No. 921.

241 G. Daumet, *Benoît XII (1334–1342). Lettres Closes, Patentes, et
Curiales se rapportant à la France*, No. 917; G. Brom, *Bullarium Trajectense*, I, 407–408; E. Déprez, *Préliminaires de la Guerre de Cent Ans*,
p. 388 (note).

242 G. Daumet, *Benoît XII (1334–1342). Lettres Closes, Patentes, et
Curiales se rapportant à la France*, No. 921.

243 *CCR* (1341–3), p. 113.

244 *Rotuli Parliamenti*, II, 126.

preparations for war;[245] but he needed peace to revive his financial strength and set his house in order, and accordingly chose to negotiate. On April 10 he named Richard de Bury, bishop of Durham, Hugh de Audley, earl of Gloucester, William Fitz-Waryn, Nicolino de Flisco, and William Trussel to treat with Philip's representatives for a peace or truce.[246]

It is not possible to find any trace in English records of the activities of this embassy, and it has been assumed that it never went to the continent.[247] But it is certain that English representatives discussed the matter at Antoing with French delegates who appear to have been the archbishop of Rheims, the bishop of Tournai, and the constable and marshal of France. John, duke of Brabant, William, count of Hainault, Holland, and Zeeland, and John of Hainault were with the party of the bishop of Durham.[248] The Flemish towns sent their delegates. For Ghent appeared the scabini, Peter vander Asselt and Jacob Coelins, and William de Bomere.[249] Of the results of their negotiations nothing can be found, but on May 24 Edward, probably in accordance with the discussions at Antoing, instructed the dukes of Brabant and Guelders, the margrave of Juliers, William, count of Hainault, Holland, and Zeeland, and John of Hainault to confer with Philip's delegates and secure an extension of the truce from the Nativity to the Decollation of St. John the Baptist (August 29).[250]

The possibility that war might be reopened on June 24 now caused the Flemings to take necessary precautions for defense. On May 2 the scabini of Ghent sent their colleagues, Peter van-

---

[245] *CPR* (1341–3), pp. 57, 127.

[246] *Foedera,* II (2), 1156.

[247] E. Déprez, *Les Préliminaires de la Guerre de Cent Ans,* p. 378.

[248] Le Muisit, p. 136: "Anno m⁰ trescentesimo quadragesimo primo, fuit parlamentum apud Anthonium; et fuerunt ex parte regis Franchie archiepiscopus Remensis, episcopus Tornacensis, constabularius et mariscalcus Franchie; pro alia parte fuerunt dux Brabantie, comes Hannonie, dominus de Byaumont, et aliqui milites ex parte regis Anglie et de consilio Flandrensium."

[249] N. de Pauw en J. Vuylsteke, *Rekeningen der Stad Gent,* II, 44: ". . . die voeren up den selven tijt (April 15 or 16) tAntoengien ten paerlemente daer sconincx van Vrankerike boden waren ende sconincx van Inghelant ende vele andre groeter heeren omme te sprekene ende te conformeerne de verste die versproken was vor Dornicke. . . ."

[250] *Foedera,* II (2), 1160–1161.

der Asselt, and William de Bomere to England who during the thirty days of their absence apparently discussed this problem with Edward.[251]   The king now sent William Stury to Flanders to assume charge of a company of archers to aid in the defense of the county.[252]   There also were discussions with the duke of Brabant.   Thus, on May 12 the scabinus, Thomas van Olsene, and the clerks, John uten Hove and John van Lovene, went to Brussels,[253] and on the 31st delegates of the three towns went to Alost to treat with the representatives of Brabant. In the party sent by Ghent were two scabini and the two clerks just mentioned, besides such important persons as the captain, William van Vaernewijc, and two members of the Council of Flanders, Simon ser Thomaes and Thomas van Vaernewijc.[254]

The presence of these men reveals how grave the situation appeared to the Flemings. They soon proceeded to Dendermonde where the delegates of the English king, the duke of Brabant, the duke of Guelders, the margrave of Juliers, and John of Hainault met the representatives of Philip. These were Louis, duke of Bourbonnais, count of Clermont and of La Marche, chamberlain of the king, Eudes, duke of Burgundy, Raoul, count of Eu, and Walter, duke of Athens.[255] They unanimously agreed to extend the period of the truce until the Decollation of St. John the Baptist (August 29). In the successful termination of these negotiations Jeanne, dowager countess of Hainault, Holland, and Zeeland, is said to have played an important part, but the particular facts of her activity have apparently been lost.[256] It was arranged orally, it seems, that conferences were to be opened at Antoing on St. Peter ad Vincula (August 1) to discuss peace. On June 18 Edward accepted the terms arranged at Dendermonde,[257] and three days later King Philip did the same at the Bois de Vincennes.[258]

[251] N. de Pauw en J. Vuylsteke, *Rekeningen der Stad Gent,* II, 44–45.

[252] *CCR* (1341–3), p. 158.

[253] N. de Pauw en J. Vuylsteke, *Rekeningen der Stad Gent,* II, 45.

[254] *Ibid.,* p. 46.

[255] L. Devillers, *Cartulaire,* I, 139–140.

[256] E. Déprez, *Les Préliminaires de la Guerre de Cent Ans,* p. 378 (note 5).

[257] *Foedera,* II (2), 1165–1166; *CCR* (1341–3), p. 245.

[258] L. Devillers, *Cartulaire,* I, 139–141.

The brief space of time left before the expiration of the truce was a great inconvenience, and, because of the tension between Edward and Philip, a dangerous matter. Would the negotiations at Dendermonde be accepted by Philip? This question was not to be settled in England before the 24th and great fear was expressed that the war was about to be reopened. It was rumored that Philip was preparing a huge fleet to invade and attack England, and preparations for defense were continued unabated.[259] This is the reason for the uncertainty in the Low Countries, and the plans for dealing with this emergency appear to have been discussed between the delegates of the three towns of Flanders and of the duke, nobility, and towns of Brabant. On the 18th the scabini of Ghent sent a clerk, John vanden Bossche, to interview the duke of Brabant and Otto, seignior of Cuyk. He returned on the 21st,[260] and on the 22d a small force was sent to guard the frontier at Cassel in case hostilities should be renewed.[261] On the following day William van Vaernewijc and John vanden Bossche were sent to Brabant to confer with the duke and his towns.[262] But the crisis passed the moment news arrived that Philip had on the 21st accepted the extension of the truce until August 29. After fourteen days' service the troops were recalled from Cassel.

Yet the tension remained, for Edward, fearing the reopening of hostilities on August 29, made renewed preparations pending the outcome of the negotiations at Antoing of which he was quite pessimistic.[263] This feeling is also revealed by the actions of the Flemings, it seems, for from July 8 to 12 a delegation from Ghent was in Brussels to discuss important matters touching Flanders, Brabant, and Hainault, which would all be exposed to the attacks of Philip in case war should break out. Later in the month,

---

[259] E. Déprez, *Les Préliminaires de la Guerre de Cent Ans,* p. 380.

[260] N. de Pauw en J. Vuylsteke, *Rekeningen der Stad Gent,* II, p. 47.

[261] *Ibid.,* pp. 88–89: " . . . die ute trocken sfridaechs voer sente Jans dach in middenzomere te Cassele waerd omme daer te ligghene ten cante van den lande jeghen de viande ofts te doene adde gheweest, van haerre saudeien van 14 daghen, ende daerbinnen was de verde verlingt. . . ."

[262] *Ibid.,* p. 48.

[263] On September 2 Edward wrote to the men of Bayonne: "Cum essemus jam parati ad proficiscendum in manu valida supra mare, et ad progrediendum ulterius in Franciam pro juribus nostris hereditariis perquirendis. . . ." See *Foedera,* II (2), 1175.

on the 18th and 19th, there was further discussion between the Flemings and lieges of the duke.[264]

On July 14 Edward appointed William de Clinton, earl of Huntingdon, Bernadot d'Albret, Bartholomew de Burghersh, John de Offord, archdeacon of Ely, and Nicolino de Flisco to undertake the discussions with Philip for the purpose of establishing peace or arranging a truce. Similar powers were given to John, duke of Brabant, Reginald, duke of Guelders, William, count of Hainault, Holland, and Zeeland, and John of Hainault. At least two of each group could make a binding arrangement.[265] On the 20th Edward ordered his English agents to hasten to the continent with all possible speed " so that the dissolution of the treaty may not be imputed to any fault of the king." [266] Philip's representatives John, archbishop of Rheims, Andrew, bishop of Tournai, Aymes, count of Savoy, and Walter, duke of Athens,[267] met the party of the earl of Huntingdon.[268] The delegation of Bruges was composed of Gilles van Coudenbroec, Jacob Wittebolle, Lamsin de Vos, and Peter de Man. They were absent from the town for fifteen days.[269] The scabini of Ghent sent their colleagues, Jacob Coelins, John van Dessele, the receiver, Simon Parijs, John uten Hove, and John vanden Bossche.[270] On St. Lawrence's Day (August 10) the envoys apparently at Antoing agreed that the truce should be extended once more, this time for fifteen days, to Exaltatio Sanctae Crucis (September 14).[271] Two days later the French agents issued letters to this effect,[272] and William, count of Hainault, Holland, and Zeeland,

---

[264] N. de Pauw en J. Vuylsteke, *Rekeningen der Stad Gent,* II, 49.

[265] *Foedera,* II (2), 1168–1169. For John de Offord, see *CCR* (1341–3), p. 195.

[266] L. Mirot et E. Déprez, " Les Ambassades Anglaises pendant la Guerre de Cent Ans," *BEC,* LXXXIV (1898), 565. See *CCR* (1341–3), pp. 200, 268.

[267] L. Devillers, *Cartulaire,* I, 150–151; le Muisit, p. 137.

[268] According to le Muisit, p. 137, the margrave of Juliers, referred to as " Comes de Julers," and Thierry, seignior of Valkenburg, appeared among Edward's agents.

[269] L. Gilliodts van Severen, " Jacques van Artevelde," *La Flandre,* IX (1878), 399.

[270] N. de Pauw en J. Vuylsteke, *Rekeningen der Stad Gent,* II, 50, 67, 111.

[271] Le Muisit, p. 137.

[272] L. Devillers, *Cartulaire,* I, 150–151.

at Antoing did likewise for himself in a special letter,[273] separate from a similar document given by the dukes of Brabant and Guelders and the margrave of Juliers.[274]

These agreements afforded only a very brief respite, but the delegates, it appears, had agreed to come together again at Antoing early in September. Thither the magistrates of Ghent sent one of their scabini, Baldwin ute Meram, and John uten Hove on August 29, and Simon Parijs and another on September 11.[275] For Bruges appeared a similar delegation.[276] The duke of Brabant went thither by way of Tosseniert near Grammont where he was on September 4.[277] The French king's representatives, the same as those who had negotiated the treaty in the previous month, also appeared, and it was agreed to extend the truce from September 14 to St. John the Baptist's Day in the next year.[278] On the 11th at Antoing Edward's allies [279] and, on the following day at Tournai, the French agents issued documents to this effect.[280] On September 27 Edward ordered his sheriffs to proclaim this truce in all parts of their jurisdictions.[281]

VI. THE BRETON CAMPAIGN AND THE TRUCE OF MALESTROIT (1342–1343)

ALTHOUGH the truce had again been extended from Exaltatio Sanctae Crucis (September 14) to St. John the Baptist's Day, 1342, relations between Edward and Philip soon again became strained to the point of breaking. The question of the Breton succession and the proffer of the suzerainty of Brittany [282] by John

[273] *Ibid.*, pp. 148–149.

[274] *Ibid.*, pp. 147–148.

[275] N. de Pauw en J. Vuylsteke, *Rekeningen der Stad Gent*, II, 111–112.

[276] L. Gilliodts van Severen, "Jacques van Artevelde," *La Flandre,* IX (1878), 399.

[277] J. Corday, *Les Comtes de Savoie et les Rois de France pendant la Guerre de Cent Ans (1329–1391)*, p. 296 (*Pièces Justificatives*). He promised the count of Savoy that he would be at Antoing on the 5th.

[278] *Bourgeois de Valenciennes*, p. 186; Murimuth, p. 121.

[279] Kervyn, *Oeuvres de Froissart*. XXIII, 344.

[280] *Ibid.*, p. 344; L. Devillers, *Cartulaire*, I, 152–153.

[281] *Foedera*, I (2), 1177.

[282] Murimuth, p. 121. For the Breton succession, see T. F. Tout, *The History of England from the Accession of Henry III to the Death of Edward III (1216–1377)*, pp. 352–354.

de Montfort who swore fealty and rendered homage to Edward and received from him the earldom of Richmond on September 24,[283] were almost sufficient to break relations between the embittered kings. Edward was active in all manner of warlike activities. His sergeants-at-arms were instructed on October 3 to arrest all ships in the ports of Somerset, Dorset, Devonshire, Cornwall, and those between London and Sandwich and have them ready at Portsmouth before the octave of St. Martin's Day (November 18).[284] Closer relations were sought with Simon Boccanigra, doge of Genoa, the barons of Aragon, the king of Majorca, and the count of Roussillon and Cerdagne.[285] On February 20 Edward again issued orders for ships to be ready at Orwell on Palm Sunday for an expedition against Philip.[286] The latter was successful in securing the alliance of the archbishops of Trier and Mainz and sought an understanding with Robert, king of Sicily.[287]

The outlook for peace was dubious and Pope Benedict XII was too old to exert much statesmanlike influence in this crisis. Accordingly, nothing was done by the curia during the winter to assuage the passions of the kings. A meeting had been arranged between them at Antoing for the morrow of Purification. On January 4 Edward appointed the bishop of St. David's, John de Offord, archdeacon of Ely, Simon de Islip, canon of St. Mary's of Lincoln, and William Trussel to come to London and be ready to proceed to the Low Countries.[288] Delegates from Flanders were dispatched to Condé where, it appears, the envoys of Philip and Edward met. The scabini of Ghent sent two of their own number of whom Baldwin ute Meram was one, and two clerks, John uten Hove and John vanden Bossche, who returned in twelve days. Just before this, delegates from the towns of Flanders, Brabant, and Hainault met at Ninove, but the exact purpose of their deliberations is not recorded.[289] John vanden Bossche and John de Coster were sent with others from Bruges and Ypres to England on March 17 to discuss important interests of Flan-

---

[283] *Foedera*, II (2), 1176.   [285] *Ibid.*, pp. 1179, 1185–1186, 1187.
[284] *Ibid.*, p. 1177.   [286] *Ibid.*, pp. 1187–1188.
[287] E. Déprez, *Les Préliminaires de la Guerre de Cent Ans*, pp. 385–386.
[288] *CCR* (1341–3), p. 368; *Foedera*, II (2), 1185.
[289] N. de Pauw en J. Vuylsteke, *Rekeningen der Stad Gent*, II, 117. Baldwin uten Meeram was sent to Condé at once upon his return from Ninove.

ders,[290] and at about the same time the captain, William van Vaernewijc, went to Valenciennes to interview William, count of Hainault, Holland, and Zeeland.[291] But the negotiations at Condé were totally barren of result, and, as spring drew near, the tension appears to have become greater.

Alfonso X, king of Castile, appealed to the antagonists in the interests of peace. On March 28 Edward replied that he had ever been eager to labor for harmony, but put the blame entirely upon his opponent's unwillingness. Nevertheless he pronounced himself willing to send delegates to meet Philip's lieges a fort-night after Easter at the place already agreed upon.[292] On April 5 he appointed his delegates, Bernadot d'Albret, John de Offord, William FitzWaryn, and Nicolino de Flisco, and from among his Netherlandish allies, John, duke of Brabant, Reginald, duke of Guelders, William, margrave of Juliers, William, count of Hainault, Holland, and Zeeland, and John of Hainault.[293] To Condé went the delegations of Ghent, among whom were the important Thomas van Vaernewijc and Peter Zoetard, dean of the lesser guilds,[294] and of Bruges, under the leadership of the captain, Gilles van Coudenbroec, Jacob Wittebolle, John van Coukelaere, and Lamsin de Vos.[295] Undoubtedly there was also a representation from Ypres. William, count of Hainault, was present,[296] but no mention is found of the other deputies named in the letter of April 5. The negotiations were fruitless. Edward himself had expected nothing else, for on April 10 he issued orders for the arraying of archers. On May 20 he announced his intention to set out against Philip [297] and four days later he ordered the bishop of London, Thomas de Beauchamp, earl of Warwick,

---

[290] *Ibid.,* pp. 118, 125.

[291] *Ibid.,* p. 214.

[292] *Foedera,* II (2), 1190–1191.

[293] *Ibid.,* p. 1191. See L. Mirot et E. Déprez, " Les Ambassades Anglaises pendant la Guerre de Cent Ans," *BEC,* LIX (1898), 565.

[294] *Bourgeois de Valenciennes,* p. 187; N. de Pauw en J. Vuylsteke, *Rekeningen der Stad Gent,* II, 120.

[295] L. Gilliodts van Severen, " Jacques van Artevelde," *La Flandre,* IX (1878), 400, 406. They were sent to Antoing on the 14th, but an item of April 21 states that they were at Condé for eleven days.

[296] L. Devillers, *Cartulaire,* I, 178–179. Count William was at Condé on April 25.

[297] *Foedera,* II (2), 1192; *CCR* (1341–3), p. 520.

Nicholas de Cantelupo, Bartholomew de Burghersh, and John de Offord to go to the Low Countries and arrange plans against Philip with the dukes of Brabant and Guelders, the margrave of Juliers, John of Hainault, and the envoys of the Flemish towns. They were also empowered to meet Philip's delegates and negotiate a truce which would preserve peace while negotiations for a definite peace were pending.[298]

Benedict XII died on April 25, 1342, and on May 7 Peter Roger, formerly bishop of Arras and archbishop of Sens, and now archbishop of Rouen, was chosen to succeed him as Clement VI. Only six weeks remained before St. John the Baptist's Day when the truce would expire. The war seemed certain to begin and the Flemings were dissatisfied because Philip had not been able to fulfil his solemn promises made to them at Tournai. William, count of Hainault, Holland, and Zeeland, was especially fearful of an attack from Philip. The accounts of Zeeland reveal much warlike activity as spring wore on. Troops were sent to Thunl'Évêque early in April, ships were forbidden to leave Zeeland because they were needed to collect the necessary weapons, and efforts were made to purchase herring at Sluis, apparently for provisioning the troops.[299] The count was in constant communication with the captains and scabini of Bruges [300] and Ghent [301] who were of course ready to resist invasion. Count Louis was negotiating with the three towns, but his return,[302] whatever the motives of Philip may have been in this connection, was to have no influence upon the conduct of the Flemings who kept him under rigid control. The English plenipotentiaries under the leadership of the bishop of London met the duke of Brabant and the representatives of the Flemish towns on May 20. A few days later there was a conference of the duke of Brabant, William, count of Hainault, Holland, and Zeeland, and the Flemings at Dendermonde where the means to be taken to defend their lands

---

[298] *Foedera,* II (2), 1195.

[299] H. G. Hamaker, *De Rekeningen der Grafelijkheid van Zeeland, onder het Henegouwsche Huis,* II, 212, 213, 305, 306, 307.

[300] L. Gilliodts van Severen, "Jacques van Artevelde," *La Flandre,* IX (1878), 406, 409.

[301] N. de Pauw en J. Vuylsteke, *Rekeningen der Stad Gent,* II, 134. One of William's messengers arrived from England at Ghent at about May 12. See *ibid.,* p. 135.   [302] *Ibid.,* p. 119.

if war should break out after St. John the Baptist's Day were discussed. In the first week of June these discussions were continued at Brussels.[303]

Even before the election [304] of Clement, the cardinals in the curia had bestirred themselves. On May 2 they wrote to Reginald, duke of Guelders, begging him to labor for peace and to support the efforts of William, bishop of Apt in France, and William of Norwich, dean of Lincoln, whom they were sending to Philip and Edward respectively.[305] William met the bishop of London, who had just disembarked on the continent and was hurrying to Brabant, and informed him that he was bearer of letters from Clement and the cardinals containing suggestions of peace. At Westminster Edward on June 4 named him and John de Offord, who appears not to have accompanied the bishop of London, to negotiate a truce with Philip.[306] On the 16th he ordered Henry, earl of Lancaster, and the earl of Warwick, who had just come from the Low Countries, to return to Hainault.[307] But these efforts, like the preceding ones, were wholly futile, and Edward persistently planned an expedition to Brittany.[308] Thus when St. John the Baptist's Day arrived, the truce came to an end and Christendom was again arrayed in two hostile camps. Hostilities developed along the frontier of Hainault.[309] The duke of Brabant was in consultation with the delegates of the three towns of Flanders at Brussels from July 7 to 12,[310] and all the allies, including Count William of Hainault, Holland, and Zeeland, met at Alost from July 25 to 27.[311]

[303] Le Muisit, p. 137; N. de Pauw en J. Vuylsteke, *Rekeningen der Stad Gent*, II, 121.

[304] L. Gilliodts van Severen, "Jacques van Artevelde," *La Flandre*, IX (1878), 408.

[305] I. A. Nijhoff, *Gedenkwaardigheden uit de Geschiedenis van Gelderland*, I, 441–442.

[306] *Foedera*, II (2), 1198.

[307] E. Déprez, *Les Préliminaires de la Guerre de Cent Ans*, p. 397, (note 3).

[308] See, for example, his letters of June 25 in behalf of Raoul de Stafford, *Foedera*, II (2), 1201.

[309] H. G. Hamaker, *De Rekeningen der Grafelijkheid van Zeeland onder het Henegouwsche Huis*, II, 292, 293, 297.

[310] L. Gilliodts van Severen, "Jacques van Artevelde," *La Flandre*, IX (1878), 401.

[311] N. de Pauw en J. Vuylsteke, *Rekeningen der Stad Gent*, II, 124.

Clement VI now sent Beltraminus, bishop of Bologna, to Flanders. On June 12 he gave him a transcript of the negotiations with the Flemings during the previous year under Benedict XII, and on the 13th instructed him to grant them their requests in regard to the sentence of excommunication and the interdict if they should be willing to submit to the church. Should they still refuse, he was to proclaim the excommunication and place the whole country under the interdict.[312] Not until the close of July can any evidence of his presence in the Low Countries be discovered. On the 29th Ghent sent the clerk of the scabini, John van Lovene, to Tournai where the bishop was staying.[313] On August 1 the scabini of Bruges sent a delegation to Avignon under their captain, Gilles van Coudenbroec, who was accompanied by Jacob Wittebolle, Gilles Hooft, John de Meier, John van Harlebeke, Lamsin de Vos, and Peter de Man.[314] Later in the month the bishop was in Bruges, whither the scabini of Ghent sent John van Lovene on the 23d.[315] There was much discussion, and on September 11 and 12 the clergy of Flanders were assembled to treat with the bishop at Cambrai. The scabini of Ghent were represented by John uten Hove and John van Lovene. The mendicants were present to support the contentions of the towns.[316] So sympathetic were the Dominicans to the interests of the townsmen that Heinekin den Pelsenayere, an enemy of van Artevelde's policy, criticized both the Dominicans and the captains in the same breath, for which he was brought to justice.[317] The bishop, however, could discover much inclination among the Flemings

---

[312] P. van Isacker et U. Berlière, *Lettres de Clément VI (1342–1352)*, Nos. 112, 113.

[313] N. de Pauw en J. Vuylsteke, *Rekeningen der Stad Gent*, II, 124.

[314] L. Gilliodts van Severen, " Jacques van Artevelde," *La Flandre*, IX (1878), 400. The accounts of Ghent contain no reference to this matter.

[315] N. de Pauw en J. Vuylsteke, *Rekeningen der Stad Gent,* II, 205.

[316] *Ibid.,* p. 207.

[317] *Ibid.,* p. 206 (note 2): " Nicasis vander Haghe, Pieter Stocman voeren te Malenwaerd an minen heere van Vlaendren up onser vrouwen avonde in spelmaend ende Sy. ser Thomaes voer naer hem in onser vrouwen daghe omme vele bederven vander stede, ende omme de bederve van Heinekin den Pelsenayere die daer ghevaen was vanden quaden worden die hi seide vanden Jacopinen ende van Jacoppe, etc." See also p. 207. For favors by the magistrates to the Franciscans, Dominicans, and Austin Friars, see *ibid.,* pp. 21–22.

to submit to the wishes of the papacy, and, influenced apparently by the general desire for absolution, asked Clement on October 12 whether his commission permitted him to absolve them *ad cautelam*. But as this could be granted only in doubtful cases, and, as the question of the duty of the Flemings toward their king was entirely clear, this privilege could not be extended to them. Nothing was left for the Flemings but to submit to the discipline of the church or suffer the inevitable censures.[318]

Meanwhile, Clement sent to the Low Countries the cardinals, Peter, bishop of Praeneste, and Annibal, bishop of Frascati, to prevent the outbreak of hostilities. It was none too soon, for actual fighting occurred on the borders of Hainault in August. The French under the constable, Raoul d'Eu, and the duke of Bourbon left St. Quentin and raided Hainault, and Count William invaded Thiérache and made an attempt upon Hirson, but was forced to retreat to Valenciennes.[319] The nuncios had arrived at Tournai in August where they were received by processions and every mark of honor due them and were lodged in the hospice of St. Martin's abbey. Thence they proceeded to Antoing and Valenciennes where they found Count William in the midst of warlike activities.[320] Between the 17th and the 21st John van Lovene, who had been sent by the scabini of Ghent, held discussions with them [321] as did also the duke of Brabant and Count William. The Flemings refused to agree that they would not accept any peace or truce without receiving freedom from the sentence of excommunication.[322] But Duke John and Count William promised on the 19th to remain neutral in case of hostilities and not to seek to inflict any damage upon the king of France or his subjects or upon the Cambrésis. If, however, they should wish to open hostilities, they were to give a month's notice to the king's

---

[318] P. van Isacker et U. Berlière, *Lettres de Clément VI (1342–1352)*, No. 567.

[319] *Chronographia*, II, 200.

[320] Le Muisit, p. 137, states that Count William received them at Mons.

[321] N. de Pauw en J. Vuylsteke, *Rekeningen der Stad Gent*, II. 204.

[322] Lescot, p. 58: "Ad Flamingos denique venientes, responderunt [quod], nisi prius fuissent absoluti, numquam se ad pacem aliquam inclinarent. Cumque ad Brabantinos Hanoniosque venissent, responderunt quod, salva confederatione quam ad regem Anglie habebant bono pacis se voluntarie offerebant."

provost or lieutenant at Tournai. But as they were bound to
defend their allies under the terms of the treaty of 1336 and
that of 1339, a clause was inserted in the documents by the Flemings reserving the right to support them in case Philip should
attack Flanders.[323] Thereupon the cardinals went to Mons, but
discussions with the Flemings continued, for on the 26th the scabini, William van Huse and Peter vanden Hovene, and the clerk,
John uten Hove, were sent to Condé with the envoys of Bruges,
who had left on the 24th.[324] It is possible that the Flemish refusal to accept a truce was made at this time.[325] With this notable
success to their credit, the cardinals proceeded to Paris, and, when
Edward landed in Brittany, hastened to the English camp to continue their efforts to end the strife.[326]

During the summer Edward had vigorously hurried preparations for his passage to Brittany.[327] On August 18 writs were
issued for permitting the loading of wool by parties taking
archers and men-at-arms over seas,[328] and on October 5 his
son Edward, duke of Cornwall, was named keeper of the
realm.[329] On the 8th all subjects of Philip in England were
ordered to be apprehended as spies.[330] But the passage, ordained
to take place on October 23, had to be postponed until the
octave of St. Nicholas (December 13) as ships in sufficient number could not be brought together at Portsmouth.[331] Meanwhile the Flemings greatly strengthened their borders and placed
strong contingents at Bergen and Cassel to prevent any incursions.[332] A delegation from Ghent, represented by Simon

[323] Le Muisit, pp. 137–138; L. Devillers, *Cartulaire*, I, 180–182. See
H. G. Hamaker, *De Rekeningen der Grafelijkheid van Zeeland onder het
Henegouwsche Huis*, II, 214. See also *ibid.*, p. 58.
[324] L. Gillidots van Severen, "Jacques van Artevelde," *La Flandre*,
IX (1878), 406.
[325] N. de Pauw en J. Vuylsteke, *Rekeningen der Stad Gent*, II, 205.
[326] Le Muisit, p. 138. The cardinal bishop of Frascati was in Brussels
on September 6. See A. Wauters, *Table Chronologique*, X, 104.
[327] *CCR* (1340–3), pp. 495, 513–516.
[328] *Ibid.*, pp. 567, 575, 585, 586.
[329] *Ibid.*, p. 527.
[330] *Ibid.*, p. 660; *Foedera*, II (2), 1213.
[331] Murimuth, p. 129.
[332] N. de Pauw en J. Vuylsteke, *Rekeningen der Stad Gent*, II, 152–
153, 204, 207, 254; L. Gilliodts van Severen, "Jacques van Artevelde," *La
Flandre*, IX (1878), p. 401.

Parijs, Bruges, and Ypres was sent to England on September 4 to confer about the situation, but so stormy was the sea off Cadzand and the Flemish coast that they were constrained to land at Dunkirk and return.[333] There was a good deal of activity during the autumn months as is revealed by the town accounts of Ghent and Bruges. Numerous messengers were sent out to all parts of Flanders, and all necessary precautions were taken to provide for the defense of the country. Exchanges with the duke of Brabant and William, count of Hainault, Holland, and Zeeland, are recorded in great number.[334] In October there was a conference between the allies when John uten Hove and two scabini were sent by Ghent on the 21st and four delegates by Bruges on the 20th. But the theatre of the war was not to be in the Low Countries, and no important military enterprises were to occur on the Flemish border. Philip's officers accordingly did little more than seize and detain some Flemings, among whom were a number of Dominicans at Bapaume, for whose liberation the captains and scabini of Ghent showed themselves especially eager.[335]

During the autumn Edward was represented in Flanders by William Trussel. In spite of the firm attitude taken by the Flemings toward the suggestions of the cardinals at Valenciennes and Tournai in August, Edward appears to have had some misgivings of their loyalty. There was some danger that they might yield to the persuasion of the bishop of Bologna whose activities in Flanders were not at an end at the close of October. Clement assumed a less instransigent attitude than his predecessor had shown. He apparently hoped to be successful in winning some advantage from the Flemings who naturally desired relief from the censures of the church. This probably explains the letter of Bishop Beltraminus on October 12 asking for greater freedom in proceeding with the absolution. The whole matter came up for discussion in the meeting at Damme between October 16 and 21.[335a] Count Louis was consulted, but he can hardly have been free to argue against continuing the close rela-

---

[333] N. de Pauw en J. Vuylsteke, *Rekeningen der Stad Gent*, II, 206.

[334] *Ibid.*, pp. 224–230; L. Gilliodts van Severen, "Jacques van Artevelde," *La Flandre,* IX (1878), 406–407.

[335] N. de Pauw en J. Vuylsteke, *Rekeningen der Stad Gent,* II, 209.

[335a] *Ibid.*, p. 209.

tions with Edward. The three towns promised faithful allegiance to him as their rightful sovereign and lord and decided to reaffirm by oath the alliance with him in all the castleries of Flanders. When the three towns were assembled at Ghent on November 29 a document was drawn up to this effect and the seals duly affixed.[336] The king was thus reassured of the devotion of the Flemings who, in any case, never seriously thought of abandoning him.

This could hardly be otherwise in view of the Flemish dependence upon English wool and the debts which Edward was still so slow in discharging. This was a serious problem, for in the three towns the current year would again end in a serious deficit. In Ghent it amounted in August, 1343, to 20,251*l.* 16*s.* 10*d.*[337] To secure financial relief a delegation was sent to England. Among the envoys were Catherine van Artevelde, wife of the captain, John Lenvall from Ypres, Jacob van Scotelaere, provost of Our Lady's at Bruges, Thomas Witlostael, and Peter Ternincmaker from Bruges. Lenvall crossed from Dunkirk to Sandwich in October. Termincmaker was sent by the regent, the duke of Cornwall, to Plymouth with a guard of a sergeant-at-arms and two archers. Van Artevelde's wife also passed over to Brittany, and Lenvall landed at Brest where he was met upon his arrival by a guard sent by the countess of Montfort and conducted to Edward's presence. The cardinals were already endeavoring to secure a truce when Catherine van Artevelde arrived in the English army.[338]

The negotiations for peace were due mainly to papal initiative and owed little or nothing to Catherine's suggestions as has been asserted.[339] The envoys were successful if we may judge from the fact that the men from Bruges packed two hundred and eighty-seven sacks of wool which Edward owed the town.[340]

[336] *Foedera,* II (2), 1215–1216.

[337] N. de Pauw en J. Vuylsteke, *Rekeningen der Stad Gent,* II, 264. The accounts for 1341–1342 are incomplete.

[338] Le Muisit, p. 138.

[339] See N. de Pauw, " Catherine de Coster, Femme d'Artevelde et sa Famille," *BCRH,* 82 (1913), 318: " C'est à Norwell que les députés de Bruges et d'Ypres vont la rejoindre et poursuivre des négociations qui semblant ne pas avoir été étrangères à la conclusion."

[340] L. Gilliodts van Severen, " Jacques van Artevelde," *La Flandre,* IX (1878), 413.

Early in the next year the party returned.[341] John de Coster, brother of Catherine van Artevelde, also went to England, probably in her company, and was absent seventeen weeks. But he returned to Ghent before proceeding on the way to Brittany.[342] Meanwhile the Truce of Malestroit was arranged. On December 8 the pope had extended the mandate given to the cardinals to arrange a peace between Edward and his allies and Philip, which also included William, count of Hainault, Holland, and Zeeland.[343] By the terms of the treaty, which was definitely accepted on January 19, war was to cease for a period of almost four years, until Michaelmas, 1346. It included the bishop and chapter of Cambrai, burghers of Cambrai, all the subjects of the Cambrésis, the subjects of King Philip, the king of Scotland, and all the allies of Edward including the Flemings, the duke of Brabant, the duke of Guelders, the margrave of Juliers, the count of Hainault, Holland, and Zeeland, and John of Hainault. William, count of Hainault, was to send envoys to the curia armed with full power to approve what the pope should ordain in his disputes with Philip. The cardinals were to labor earnestly to bring about the absolution of the Flemings. During the period of the truce, Louis, count of Flanders, was to remain the legitimate prince of his county, and his subjects were to confirm this agreement. The fugitives of Flanders were not to return, and should anyone violate this condition, he was to be brought to justice in France and all his goods in the kingdom were to be forfeited.[344]

---

[341] For the expedition, see Kervyn, "Jacques van Artevelde," *Messager de Sciences et des Arts Historiques,* 1856, p. 248 (note). The *French Chronicle of London,* p. 89, has an interesting passage regarding Catherine's presence in England: "Puisse après un Griffyn de Gales, qe avoit occys le frere et la femme Jacob de Artefelde de Flandres, q'estoit pris et amenez à le tour de Loundres, et mys en fort prisoun, et fiergés de deus fort peire gives et manicles."

[342] N. de Pauw en J. Vuylsteke, *Rekeningen der Stad Gent,* II, 214. His expenses, including the loss of his horses, amounted for the two trips of twelve weeks and seventeen days to 2,780l.

[343] G. Brom, *Bullarium Trajectense,* Vol. I, No. 1050.

[344] A. Verkooren, *Inventaire, Brabant,* II, 122–124; Murimuth, pp. 129–135; le Muisit, pp. 139–145. See also *Bourgeois de Valenciennes,* p. 193.

CHAPTER XIII

THE TOTAL COLLAPSE OF KING EDWARD'S ALLIANCES (1343–1345)

i. The Situation in Flanders (1343–1344)   ii. William, Count of Hainault, Holland, and Zeeland, Abandons Edward (1343)   iii. The Death of Reginald, Duke of Guelders, Deprives Edward of his Chief Ally (October, 1343 — Spring, 1345)   iv. The Friesians and the Death of William, Count of Hainault, Holland, and Zeeland (1344–1345)   v. John, Duke of Brabant, Reconsiders his Policy (Spring, 1345)   vi. The Murder of van Artevelde (July, 1345)

I. The Situation in Flanders (1343–1344)

BY THE terms of the Truce of Malestroit the exiled adherents of Count Louis had been forbidden to return to Flanders. Philip promised to bring them to justice, should they attempt to do so, and it was agreed that their property should be confiscated.[1] During 1343 and 1344 the relations between the Flemings and the king of France were regulated by these clauses, and it is interesting to note that no serious efforts against the régime of the three towns were to be attempted by the enemies sojourning in France until the spring and summer of 1345. For this reason the border was comparatively quiet during these years and very little is recorded of the movements of forces at strategic points guarding the country. The troops, which had been stationed at Cassel, Bergen, and Gravelines when the truce had expired on June 24, 1342, were recalled in the following February.[2] It is impossible to find trace of soldiers in these parts until the close of August when the scabini sent representatives of the weavers, fullers, and lesser guilds to Cassel with some troops. It cannot, however, be ascertained how long they were stationed there. From December 22 to February 9, 1344, a force

---

[1] Le Muisit, pp. 143–144.
[2] N. de Pauw en J. Vuylsteke, *Rekeningen der Stad Gent*, II, 250–256; L. Gilliodts van Severen, "Jacques van Artevelde," *La Flandre*, IX (1878), 415–16.

of fifty sergeants (*serianten*) was sent to Bergen who also, it appears, served at Cassel. After April 6 another force of fifty sergeants was sent to guard these parts.[3]

Nor do the adherents of Count Louis still living in Flanders appear to have put forth much effective opposition. In the castlery of Ghent the income of their confiscated properties, which by the close of July, 1341, had amounted to 25,561*l.* 8*s.* 4*d.*, declined in the year 1343–1344 to 1,200*l.* 1*s.* ½*d.*, and in 1344–1345 rose to 2,901*l.* 3*s.* 4*d.*[4] The captains and scabini watched the activities of the émigrés very attentively. An item in the accounts of Ghent states that 400*l.* was allowed to van Artevelde for a horse and two cloths which were sent in the year 1343–1344 to secret friends in Hainault who had given some information about the enemy.[5] Stringent vigilance was necessary to discourage any effort of these elements to attempt to overthrow the domination of van Artevelde and his party.

The chief problem for the captain and his colleagues in Ghent, Bruges, and Ypres during 1343 and 1344 was, as in the two preceding years, the strife between the guilds and the antagonisms of the lesser towns to the domination of the three great ones. Count Louis could not acquiesce cordially in the unprecedented control which they exercised through their delegates and the Council of Flanders, and accordingly left the county after the meeting of the three towns at Ypres between November 24 and 29, 1342.[6] His absence robbed van Artevelde and his supporters of an apparent authority which could prove valuable in stabilizing their régime amid the violent antagonisms that might at any moment burst forth into serious conflict. In response to Louis' request the three towns sent delegates to Menin between January 14 and 23, 1343, in order to discuss the bases of an agreement which, however, proved little acceptable.[7] These parleys were apparently resumed between March 7 and 14.[8]

---

[3] N. de Pauw en J. Vuylsteke, *Rekeningen der Stad Gent,* II, 339–340.

[4] *Ibid.,* pp. 12–13, 272, 352–353. From the figures of 1344–1345 should be deducted the sums derived from the properties of John van Steenbeke and his accomplices.

[5] *Ibid.,* p. 288. [6] *Ibid.,* p. 210.

[7] *Ibid.,* p. 302: ". . . te Minene an minen here van Vlaendren bi sinen ontbiedene omme te sprekene van acorde. . . ."

[8] *Ibid.,* p. 304.

A serious problem at Ghent was the annual deficit. In the year ending July, 1341, this amounted to 14,213*l*. 3*s*. 5*d*. For the next year the figures cannot be ascertained because of the defective condition of the accounts, but for the year ending July, 1343, it amounted to 20,251*l*. 16*s*. 10*d*., and for the year thereafter declined to 8,303*l*. 3*s*. 9*d*.[9] King Edward was still in arrears and could not pay all his obligations, especially after his return from the campaign in Brittany. John de Coster had been commissioned to negotiate with Edward in April, 1343. With the envoys of Bruges and Ypres he visited the king in England and returned after an absence of thirty days.[10] At the close of May, when the demands upon the communal chest were especially heavy, he went to Bruges to discuss payment with the king's representatives, undoubtedly those connected with the staple.[11] Early in August he was again sent to England and was cordially received by Edward who on the 24th gave him the archdeaconry of the East Riding of Yorkshire.[12] On September 23 the scabini of Ghent sent Peter vander Asselt and William de Bomere to England for the same purpose who returned after forty-five and forty-nine days respectively.[13] During the official year 1343–1344 Edward paid 1,224*l*. 10*s*. and in the following year 6,913*l*.[14] Large sums had to be borrowed, and the scabini approached the *ruwaard*, Simon van Halen, in September, 1343,[15] who loaned 4,000*l*. in this year and in the next 429*l*. 5*s*. 8*d*. and 2,000 shields.[16] In 1342–1343 public-spirited burghers loaned 5,175*l*. 6*s*. 8*d*.[17] and, in

---

[9] N. de Pauw en J. Vuylsteke, *Rekeningen der Stad Gent,* II, 92, 264, 441.   [10] *Ibid.,* p. 215.

[11] *Ibid.,* p. 217: " It. den here Janne den Costere, die voer te Brucgewaert omme te sprekene eneghen van ons heeren sconinx lieden van Yngelant omme gelt ter stede bouf. . . ."

[12] *Ibid.,* p. 219; *CPR* (1343–5), p. 120; N. de Pauw, *Cartulaire Historique et Généalogique des Artevelde,* pp. 655–656. On his return he received from the scabini at the hand of van Artevelde handsome gifts which cost 680*l*. See N. de Pauw en J. Vuylsteke, *Rekeningen der Stad Gent,* II, 288.

[13] N. de Pauw en J. Vuylsteke, *Rekeningen der Stad Gent,* II, 298–299. Apparently because of their efforts Edward resumed payment of the pensions which he had granted on May 12 and 19 to John Stykerape, William de Bomere, and John Berenger. Cf. *CCR* (1343–6), pp. 185–186.

[14] N. de Pauw en J. Vuylsteke, *Rekeningen der Stad Gent,* II, 274–275, 353.   [16] *Ibid.,* pp. 273, 356.

[15] *Ibid.,* p. 298.   [17] *Ibid.,* p. 170.

1344–1345, 33,920*l.* of which 11,733*l.* 6*s.* 8*d.* were advanced by van Halen.[18]

These difficulties were greatly increased by the acute problem of providing the town with corn. It appears that in spite of the truce little corn found its way down the Schelde from the grain-growing sections of northeast France such as Artois, and toward the close of the year there was a serious shortage. On December 5 groups of men were appointed to search for corn in the castlery of Ghent, the Quatuor Officia, Waasland, the county of Alost, and the parishes of Ghent. These men were active for fifty-one days, after which they were busy for eight days within the walls. The corn was stored apparently in space especially provided for it in the belfry. Men were appointed to distribute bread in each parish. There was also some supervision of dairy products.[19] This evidently is the reason why the scabini of Ghent under the influence of van Artevelde insisted that all ships coming down the Schelde should not carry salt, wine, or other articles without carrying a corresponding value of grain.[20] It is evident that this scarcity of corn in Ghent was in part due to the hostility of Philip's officers.

At this time a determined effort was made within Ghent itself by John van Steenbeke and his accomplices to end the career of van Artevelde. According to Despars [20a] and Meyerus,[21] van Artevelde had strongly opposed the return of Count Louis in the summer of 1342, but had been overruled by the three towns who received their legitimate prince joyfully. When Louis supported the claims of the towns in the matter of manufacturing of cloth in smaller places, a good deal of opposition was aroused, and at Aardenburg, a victim of Bruges' monopolistic selfishness, more than fourteen banners were, it is said, kept in hiding ready for the favorable moment to throw off the hateful domination.[22]

---

[18] *Ibid.*, pp. 351–352.   [19] *Ibid.*, pp. 331–333.

[20] Le Muisit, p. 146 (*sub* 1344). The date is not certain, but it is quite possible that these measures were taken at the close of 1343 or at the opening of 1344.

[20a] N. Despars, *Cronijcke van den Lande ende Graefscepe van Vlaenderen (405–1492)*, II, 364–367.

[21] J. Meyerus, *Rerum Flandricarum Libri X*, p. 45 (*sub* 1342).

[22] Kervyn, *Histoire de Flandre*, III, 281–283; N. Despars, *Cronijcke van den Lande ende Graefscepe van Vlaenderen (405–1492)*, II, 364–365.

Van Artevelde acted promptly, and on November 2 three scabini and sergeants were sent to Aardenburg and Damme where they tarried for ten days to establish peace.[23]

Shortly after this, according to the statements of Despars and Meyerus, the storm broke out about the conduct of the inquests in the castleries of West Flanders. Concerning these inquests but little information has been preserved. Between July 2 and 8, 1342, a delegation was sent to Dunkirk to investigate the accounts of the bailiffs.[24] In May of the following year others were sent into the castleries of West Flanders, and in July the accounts of the bailiffs were under official scrutiny.[25] It is possible that the investigations were carried out with great harshness in this section where the towns were small and the feudal elements always under suspicion. The storm broke out when van Steenbeke complained of the conduct of the inquests and demanded that the régime of the captains should be replaced by that of the lawful scabini. Van Steenbeke's friends were assembled in the Friday Market Place and rushed to the hall of the scabini to carry out their demands. The magistrates, however, were able to resist, and van Steenbeke was lodged in the count's castle and van Artevelde in that of Gerard the Devil. Meanwhile, the aid of the other towns was invoked and troops came from Bruges, Ypres, Courtrai, Oudenaarde, Dendermonde, Dixmuide, Alost, and Waasland. The gates of Ghent were opened to let them in whereupon van Artevelde's authority was restored and van Steenbeke and eighty of his supporters were banished.

While this story as told by Despars and Meyerus is not mentioned by chroniclers of the time, it yet appears to be substantially correct as can be shown from the accounts of Ghent. It seems that the four captains, William van Vaernewijc, Gelnoot van Lens, Peter van Coudenhove, and Josse Apre, remained faithful to van Artevelde, for no change was effected in the personnel of the captains as each received the full annual pension

[23] N. de Pauw en J. Vuylsteke, *Rekeningen der Stad Gent,* II, 259; L. Gilliodts van Severen, " Jacques van Artevelde," *La Flandre,* IX (1878), 414.

[24] N. de Pauw en J. Vuylsteke, *Rekeningen der Stad Gent,* II, 123,

[25] *Ibid.,* pp. 216, 218,

of 480*l*.[26] John van Steenbeke, who was one of the receivers of
the duty for the year,[27] was supported by Peter de Amman and
by John Borluut, one of the councillors for the year,[28] and
apparently also by Solomon Borluut. Van Steenbeke and de
Amman had in the past shown themselves devoted friends of
van Artevelde's policy, but for some reason which eludes the
investigator had now grown resentful of his power. John Borluut
was superseded by Hugh Melaus,[29] and in the next two years the
property of van Steenbeke, Solomon Borluut, and de Amman
was attached by the scabini, and regular sums derived from its
sale were entered along with those of the exiles.[30] That troops
were sent to aid van Artevelde is also certain. Those of Bruges,
for example, were stationed before the town on January 8, and
the scabini sent them wine valued at 210*l*.[31] The soldiers of
Ypres arrived on the 11th and received wine which cost 102*l*.
10*s*.[32] Thus passed a crisis which sprang from disagreement with
van Artevelde's policy in the castleries of the west or perhaps
from personal animosities. There is nothing apparently that
can be adduced to show that van Steenbeke and his friends opposed the alliance with England or wished a return of Philip's
authority. ·

Besides these financial difficulties such problems as feeding the
town and meeting the opposition of men who had formerly
supported him, van Artevelde and his colleagues, as in 1341 and
1342, were constantly called upon to settle the disputes between the guilds in the various towns of Flanders and defend the
privileges of the three large towns against encroachments by
the smaller ones. At Courtrai internal dissensions forced the
scabini of Ghent to send their colleague, Peter vanden Hovene,
and the receiver, John vander Vloet, on January 21, 1343, to assist
in appointing new scabini.[33] The trouble was quite acute, for in

[26] *Ibid.*, p. 194.   [27] *Ibid.*, p. 155.

[28] *Ibid.*, p. 163. De Amman's property was confiscated by the scabini.
For Borluut, see *ibid.*, p. 155.   [29] *Ibid.*, p. 194.

[30] *Ibid.*, pp. 352–353, 458. An arrangement was made with the families
of these men in the year 1345–1346. Cf. *ibid.*, III, 15–16.

[31] *Ibid.*, II, 190–191. For the expedition, see L. Gilliodts van Severen,
" Jacques van Artevelde," *La Flandre,* IX (1878), 414.

[32] N. de Pauw en J. Vuylsteke, *Rekeningen der Stad Gent,* II, 191.

[33] *Ibid.*, p. 212. ". . . te Curterikewaerd omme daer scepenen te helpen
maken, van 3 daghen, 24*lb*"

May the captain, Josse Apre, and the three deans were sent
thither to settle the conflict between the guilds.[34]   At the close
of the month another deputation was dispatched to continue
these efforts to arrange a settlement.[35]   On January 28 Thomas
van Vaernewijc and John vander Vloet were sent to Aardenburg
to aid in naming the new scabini,[36] and in June the scabini were
concerned in the violent disputes between Alost and Grammont.[37]
In each of these instances it is evident, as far as the testimony
enables one to judge, that the chief difficulty arose from the
conflict between the guilds.   In the castlery of Courtrai it appears that there were fresh manifestations against the authority
of the three towns, for among the amounts listed in the accounts
of Ghent of the sequestrated properties of those who had fled
the county a sum of 160*l.* is recorded for eighteen parishes of the
castlery.[38]   But, unfortunately, the scanty details do not permit
us to assume any connection between these enemies of van
Artevelde's régime and the industrial disturbances within the
town.   On June 20 the captain, Gelnoot van Lens, and a company of men were sent to Dixmuide to allay the strife between
the fullers and the weavers, and a smaller delegation followed
on July 5 to effect a final settlement.[39]   The magistrates, aided by
those of Bruges, appointed the new scabini in August.[40]

At the same time the guilds in Ypres were in uproar, and on
January 1 the scabini of Ghent sent a number of men under their
captain, Peter van Coudenhove, and Peter vanden Hovene to
quiet the weavers and the fullers.[41]   An inquest was made which
came to an end at the close of the month.[42]   From February 15
to 22 there was a meeting in Ypres to discuss the situation there
as well as that of the county in general.[43]   It was perhaps at this

---

[34] N. de Pauw en J. Vuylsteke, *Rekeningen der Stad Gent*, II, 216:
" It. Jos Aper alse hooftman, ende vanden dekenen Gerard Denijs, Jan de
Bake ende Pieter Zoetard voeren sdicendages voer ascentions dagh te
Curterike omme daer te pointe te settene discord van gescil dat daer rees
onder de ghemeente alse vanden neringhen onderlinghe, thare there dat sij
ute waren 3 daghe, 48*lb.*"

[35] *Ibid.*, p. 217: " It. scep. Pieter vanden Hovene ende met hem Michel
de Witte voeren swonsdages voor tsinxenen te Curterike omme de ghemeente te pointe te settene, thare there van 3 daghen, 24 *lb.*"

[36] *Ibid.*, p. 212.   [39] *Ibid.*, p. 218.   [42] *Ibid.*, p. 212.
[37] *Ibid.*, p. 217.   [40] *Ibid.*, p. 298.   [43] *Ibid.*, p. 213.
[38] *Ibid.*, pp. 162–163.   [41] *Ibid.*, p. 211.

time that the sentence was delivered by the scabini of Ypres against Michael de Pore, who, with his accomplices, was accused of having attacked the bailiff of the town and his agents with stones, sticks, and knives, and of killing one of them.[44]

But especially serious was the violent discord between Ypres and Poperingen which now broke forth in all its fury. This was dangerous because the weaker party sought to strengthen its position by appealing to the authority of the count. On March 1 the scabini of Ghent sent the captain, William van Vaernewijc, and some of the scabini thither to establish harmony.[45] They were again sent on the 20th.[46] These deputies worked in coöperation with the delegates from Bruges. On the 23d both parties agreed to accept the arbitration of the three towns.[47] During the whole of the next month a delegation from Ghent under the captain, Peter van Coudenhove, and another from Bruges were at Courtrai to settle disputes.[48] Another group went to Ypres on April 12.[49] From Ypres were sent to Courtrai thirty-four men of the guilds and a force of twenty red-hoods who also went to Ghent and Bruges.[50] At Deinze there was a meeting on the 22d, and the envoys sent there soon repaired to Courtrai and thence to Ypres to declare their final decision.[51] The men of Poperingen ever after complained that they had been too severe in their judgment and that the delegates empowered to negotiate had exceeded their authority. An appeal to the absent count was of no avail, and hence they were forced to yield to the " violence of the three towns," as they later referred to this decision.[52]

[44] E. Vandenpeereboom, " Recherches sur la Draperie et la Gilde ou Corporation des Drapiers d'Ypres (1282–1545)," *Annales de la Société Historique, Archéologique et Littéraire de la Ville d'Ypres et de l'Ancienne West-Flandre*, VII (1876), 37–38.

[45] N. de Pauw en J. Vuylsteke, *Rekeningen der Stad Gent*, II, 213: ". . . omme discort dat was vanden wullewerke tusscen dien van Ypre ende van Poperinghen te settene in paise ende in rusten. . . ."

[46] *Ibid.,* p. 214.

[47] G. Espinas et H. Pirenne, *Recueil des Documents relatifs à l'Histoire de l'Industrie Drapière en Flandre*, III, 120–121.

[48] N. de Pauw en J. Vuylsteke, *Rekeningen der Stad Gent*, II, 214–215.

[49] *Ibid.,* p. 416.

[50] N. de Pauw, *Ypre jeghen Poperinghe*, p. 270.

[51] N. de Pauw en J. Vuylsteke, *Rekeningen der Stad Gent*, II, 216.

[52] G. Espinas et H. Pirenne, *Recueil des Documents relatifs à l'Histoire de l'Industrie Drapière en Flandre*, III, 172–173.

The document of April 29 is of great interest because it was drawn up at Ghent and by a clerk of Ghent.[53] From this it is evident that the initiative in this matter proceeded from Ghent and thus strikingly reveals the domination of van Artevelde and his associates over the three towns and county of Flanders. It is also important because it illustrates in great detail the antagonism which existed between the large towns and their weaker competing neighbors. The men of Poperingen were not to manufacture any more striped half cloths nor others known as *ghesmoutte*, unless they were twelve ells in length and nine quarters in width and intended only for their own use. No cloths were to be sold in retail except those that had been rejected as imperfect. If in the future they should ever adopt practices deemed by the men of Ypres prejudicial to their interests, they were to submit to the arbitrament of the three towns, two of which could make a decision. In case they should refuse to obey their commands, they were to pay a penalty of 100*l*. Tournois of which twenty were to be paid to the count, twenty to the bishop of Thérouanne and twenty to each of the three towns. They were also to appear before the count in fourteen days after being requested to do so by the three towns and seek his confirmation of these points. Failure to do this would entail a fine of 100*l*. Tournois to be divided in exactly the same manner as the penalty for failure to submit to their will. And, in case they should fail to approach the count, the document would nevertheless have full authority.[54] Threatened with destruction, the men of Poperingen maintained that the privileges granted by the count could not be legally altered in his absence.[55] The industrial antagonism between the small towns and the three great ones forced the former to look to the count for protection in their desire to save themselves.

At Oudenaarde there were fresh troubles in the autumn. Craenhals, whose ill advised actions were partly responsible for the curious uproar of the previous year, now directed his efforts

---

[53] N. de Pauw, *Ypre jeghen Poperinghe*, p. 217: ". . . Item, au clerc de Gand, pour l'escripture de le lettre de l'accord d'Ypre et de Poperinghes, 4*lb*. 8*s*."

[54] G. Espinas et H. Pirenne, *Recueil des Documents relatifs à l'Histoire de l'Industrie Drapière en Flandre*, III, 122–126.

[55] *Ibid.*, p. 173.

against the authority of Ghent. On October 29 the captain, Josse Apre, was sent thither with sixty men chosen from each of the three guilds who were led by their deans. But the effort at treason, as the accounts refer to it, was of short duration, and the men returned in four days. Three representatives of the weavers, the fullers, and the lesser guilds were left in Oudenaarde to assume control in which capacity they served thirty-two days.[56] From November 9 to 12 the captain, Peter van Coudenhove, and one of the receivers, Michael de West, were sent thither to prevent any further treasonable actions on the part of Craenhals' followers.[57]

A rash effort to seize the town at night was nevertheless made soon thereafter by a certain Persemiere with some accomplices who are referred to in the accounts of Ghent as exiles. But the loyal group of the burghers repelled them, slaying some and capturing others. The troops of Ghent were sent forth on the 22d, but returned at once when the news that the attempt had been frustrated reached them at Eecke. Two of the captains, Gelnoot van Lens and William van Vaernewijc, and the deans of the three guilds, however, proceeded to Oudenaarde to investigate the case of the dead and to bring Persemiere to Ghent.[58] It was now decided to post a small force of nine bowmen under Peter vanden Velde in the town to prevent any further disturbance.[59] There was further discussion in December as to how the town and the castlery were to be administered,[60] and the trouble did not completely subside, for at the close of April, 1344, the scabini of Ghent were forced to send their colleague, Gilles vander Pale, thither to aid in the nomination of new scabini.[61] This manifestation of hostility to the control of Ghent was obviously the work of a few men aided by a handful of émigrés or dissatisfied parties still in the country, and had very little support among the men of Oudenaarde.

Less serious disturbances in other towns demanded the atten-

---

[56] N. de Pauw en J. Vuylsteke, *Rekeningen der Stad Gent,* II, 335–336.
[57] *Ibid.,* p. 300.
[58] *Ibid.,* p. 336. Cf. N. de Pauw, "Audenaerde sous Artevelde, avec une de ses Lettres inédits et autres Pièces authentiques," *Annales du Cercle Archéologique et historique de Courtrai,* (1916), p. 33.
[59] N. de Pauw en J. Vuylsteke, *Rekeningen der Stad Gent,* II, 422–423.
[60] *Ibid.,* p. 301.   [61] *Ibid.,* p. 306.

tion of van Artevelde and his colleagues. In October and November there was some disturbance at Bruges in which a certain Peter Man was concerned and which required three successive deputations from Ghent.[62] There was some trouble about the retail sale of cloth which apparently was resumed by those of the Frank of Bruges in violation of the count's orders of October 20, 1342. On February 18, 1344, Peter van Coudenhove and the dean of the fullers, John de Bake, and Gerard Denys, dean of the weavers, were sent to discuss the matter.[63] Another very large group was sent on April 30.[64] In June the matter still occupied the attention of the scabini of Ghent,[65] and in July the fullers were loudly demanding better conditions.[66] In January there were commotions in Dixmuide, and to settle them the scabini sent their colleague, John van Vinct, who was ordered thither a second time on February 16.[67] In March these troubles were discussed at Bruges and were further regulated at Dixmuide by the scabinus, Peter Mabenzone.[68] The disaffection there was particularly serious because of hostile elements in the castleries in the western parts of the county. This led the scabini to send Peter van Coudenhove to these castleries on June 20, eight days after Josse Apre had been sent to aid in appointing new scabini in Dixmuide.[69] In January, 1345, it was again necessary to collaborate in naming new scabini.[70] Gelnoot van Lens and two of the scabini were sent to prevent once more the outbreak of hostilities at the *kermis* at Houthem.[71] In September another scabinus went into the Quatuor Officia to secure the appointment of satisfactory scabini.[72] At Damme there was difficulty with the fullers for which Gelnoot van Lens was sent thither and also to Bruges.[73]

[62] N. de Pauw en J. Vuylsteke, *Rekeningen der Stad Gent,* II, 299–300.

[63] *Ibid.,* p. 304: ". . . te Br. omme der sneden wille die daer af geleit was."

[64] *Ibid.,* p. 306: ". . . te Br. ward omme daer te sprekene voer de maerct van der snede die sij daer af adden ghedaen."

[65] *Ibid.,* p. 307.

[66] *Ibid.,* p. 308: ". . . te Br. waert . . . doede volres daer hare huse gebetert wilden hebben. . . ."

[67] *Ibid.,* pp. 302, 303–304

[68] *Ibid.,* p. 304.

[69] *Ibid.,* p. 307.

[70] *Ibid.,* p. 302.

[71] *Ibid.,* pp. 308, 381.

[72] *Ibid.,* p. 382.

[73] *Ibid.,* p. 309.

In the spring of 1344 the antagonisms between Ypres and Poperingen again became acute. Stoutly maintaining the illegality
of the decision of the three towns, some of the men of Poperingen
began to make the cloths prohibited by the decision of the previous year. Through the good offices of the baron de Stanford,
who appears to have been none other than Raoul de Stafford,
Edward's envoy to the Low Countries in the spring and summer,
a truce was arranged.[74] The bitter controversy required vigorous efforts to settle it, and accordingly on March 22 two
scabini were sent from Ghent to Ypres. One of these, John van
Vinct, was again sent thither on April 1 and was followed by
three scabini and the captain, Josse Apre, who went to Ypres
by way of Bruges where they were in consultation with the
magistrates. Similar discussions followed on April 5 and 11,
and on the 13th a large delegation went forth to labor for peace.
Some of these were back in Ghent on the 25th, and on the
27th another and smaller delegation was dispatched to discuss
the bases of an agreement.[75]

At this time the quarrel became so intense that hostilities
broke out. The militia of Ypres under William de Vos arrived
before Poperingen and killed and arrested a number of people
and burnt some property. Thereupon they placed soldiers in
the fortified place of Reninghelst, east of the town. Early in
May John Outkerke, the captains, and deans of the guilds of
Ypres led forth a large force, and serious fighting developed in
which a hundred men of Poperingen were slain.[76] Serious losses
were also inflicted upon the troops from Ypres, and some were
taken prisoner.[77] Meanwhile, the envoys from Ghent between

[74] G. Espinas et H. Pirenne, *Recueil des Documents relatifs à l'Histoire
de l'Industrie Drapière en Flandre,* III, 173. In March he was in Ghent
when he received red wine valued at 100*l*. See N. de Pauw en J. Vuylsteke,
Rekeningen der Stad Gent, II, 288. For his credentials from Edward, see
Foedera, II (2), 1227.

[75] N. de Pauw en J. Vuylsteke, *Rekeningen der Stad Gent,* II, 304,
305, 306.

[76] G. Espinas et H. Pirenne, *Recueil des Documents relatifs à l'Histoire
de l'Industrie Drapière en Flandre,* III, 173–174. For the references to the
accounts of Ypres, see N. de Pauw, *Ypre jeghen Poperinghe,* pp. 276–278.

[77] G. Espinas et H. Pirenne, *Recueil des Documents relatifs à l'Histoire
de l'Industrie Drapière en Flandre,* III, 143–145.

May 4 and 6 and on the 9th and 10th sought to quiet the contestants and secure an accord.[78]

The men of Poperingen were forced to yield. Reluctantly they charged three knights and twelve of their magistrates and some others to present themselves at Ypres before the captains and scabini and declare under oath their intention of approving whatever they should decide.[79] On the 21st these declared that they had violated the terms laid down in the document of April 19 of the preceding year. They expressed regret, promised never again to manufacture the forbidden cloths or sell in retail, and agreed to submit to such penalties as might be imposed. And to add the greatest possible sanctity to these promises, Allard, provost of St. Martin's of Ypres, and John Berenger, a notary of the diocese of Thérouanne, were requested to affix their seals.[80] The magistrates of Poperingen expressed acceptance of this in a charter of June 1 which also received the seals of the same provost and notary.[81] There were further discussions at Bruges between the delegates early in June, and a large delegation proceeded directly to Ypres at the same time.[82] The men of Poperingen were helpless and yielded from necessity, but did not abate their claims. There was naturally much ill-feeling and violence. This induced the scabini of Ghent to send one of their colleagues and the captain, William van Vaernewijc, with a hundred and fifty sergeants to aid the forces under John van Outkerke.[83]

No information has been preserved of the negotiations which took place in July. Apparently the men of Poperingen were cowed into submission by the superior forces of the three towns. On August 5 the official of the diocese of Thérouanne ordered the dean of Ypres and a clerk, Bernard de Rinc, to go to Ypres and be present when the sentence should be pronounced, testify to the oaths, and draw up in form of a charter a report of all the proceedings.[84] Two days later the magistrates of Ypres pronounced

---

[78] N. de Pauw en J. Vuylsteke, *Rekeningen der Stad Gent,* II, 306.

[79] G. Espinas et H. Pirenne, *Recueil des Documents relatifs à l'Histoire de l'Industrie Drapière en Flandre,* III, 128–130.

[80] *Ibid.,* pp. 130–135.　　　　[81] *Ibid.,* pp. 136–138.

[82] N. de Pauw en J. Vuylsteke, *Rekeningen der Stad Gent,* II, 306.

[83] *Ibid.,* pp. 333–334.

[84] G. Espinas et H. Pirenne, *Recueil des Documents relatifs à l'Histoire de l'Industrie Drapière en Flandre,* III, 138–139.

judgment which was certified by the clerk of the official of the diocese and a notary. It reconfirmed all the provisions of the decision of April 19 of the previous year and, in addition, assessed certain penalties. The men of Poperingen were to pay a fine of 100*l.* Parisian for violating these terms, indemnify Ypres for the plundering and the slaying in time of truce of a leader of the militia of Ypres and some of his men, pay certain sums for killing, burning, and pillaging their properties at Reninghelst, pay annually 20*l.* Parisian for daily masses in the church at Reninghelst for the repose of their souls, and 5*l.* Parisian to the chapel of the Holy Spirit at Ypres, whose properties they had damaged. On August 24 of each year they were to send to Ypres a delegation of their magistrates and burghers to reaffirm by oath their acceptance of this decision. The authorities of Ypres were to have the right to demand at any time, and for as long a period as they might wish, twelve hostages. An inquest was to be held to discover those who were guilty of violating the terms of the settlement and twenty of them were to spend three years in England. The magistrates, who were nominated annually, were to swear to abide by this decision, and, finally, the town was condemned to pay 20,000*l.* Parisian, the amount expended by Ypres when the red-hoods and other troops were sent forth to defend its rights. This fine, however, was to be paid only in case the terms should ever be violated.[85]

II. William, Count of Hainault, Holland, and Zeeland, Abandons Edward (1343)

William, count of Hainault, Holland, and Zeeland, was by nature wholly unreliable as an ally. This youthful character loved the glamor of the crusade and the tournament. The careful, patient, and circumspect statecraft which characterized the reign of his father was now gone. The struggle with the church was irksome, and in 1342 William was willing to abandon the claims for which his father had so stubbornly fought. In 1343 he completely gave up all pretense of remaining the ally of Edward and sought reconciliation with Philip VI. During the

[85] *Ibid.,* pp. 139–153. See also pp. 136–137 for the letters of the official and of Bernard de Rinc.

past few years there had naturally been close contacts with France and it is interesting to note that already in 1341 the king at the hands of Galesius de Bauma compensated him for the provisions found in the fortress of Escaudoeuvre which had been taken from him in full battle.[86]

The Truce of Malestroit had provided that the allies of each of the two kings, among whom Count William was especially named, should send properly accredited envoys to the Holy See to discuss peace.[87]   The cardinals of Praeneste and Tusculum knew that William was in a pliant mood and persisted in their efforts to secure peace.   On June 8 Philip declared that out of respect and love for his sister, the dowager countess of Hainault, he granted a truce to last until Michaelmas of 1346. All subjects of Count William in Hainault were to be reinstated in their possessions in France, which had been confiscated in the recent war, upon the condition that those of Tournai and Douai should be accorded corresponding treatment.   Philip also stated that the subjects of Hainault, Cambrai, and the Cambrésis could do the same.   This clause is interesting because these two jurisdictions which were wholly subject to the empire were thus surrendered to the territorial greed of the French monarchy. Philip also ordered all his officials to proclaim the terms [88] which were at once carried out.[89] Thus Count William abandoned the old claims of his house and removed the last hindrance which kept him in the group of allies of the English king.

Count William was now free to realize his ambition of a glittering career of chivalric activity. He conceived the wish of going to the aid of the Christians beleaguered in Algeciras since the previous year. In February he began his preparations for his trip to Granada.[90]   Large quantities of provisions were gathered at Sluis, beer was brought from Haarlem, wheat and flour were collected, a horse was purchased for the count's use,[91]

[86] H. G. Hamaker, *De Rekeningen der Grafelijkheid van Holland onder het Henegouwsche Huis*, III, 14–15.

[87] Le Muisit, p. 140; L. Devillers, *Cartulaire*, I, 919 (note).

[88] L. Devillers, *Cartulaire*, I, 197–201.

[89] Cf. the documents of June 19 and 20 and July 20, *ibid.*, pp. 202–204.

[90] See J. L. J. ten den Ham, " Is Graaf Willem IV naar Spanje Geweest?," *Bijdragen voor Vaderlandsche Geschiedenis en Oudheidkunde*, 5th Ser., IX, 283–286.

[91] H. G. Hamaker, *De Rekeningen der Grafelijkheid van Holland onder*

and on March 20 John of Hainault was appointed lieutenant in
his lands during his absence.[92] Money was loaned by the town of
Mons and the Lombards of Valenciennes.[93] But this grand project was hastily abandoned in order to go to Munich to deny
a rumor that the electors were inciting him to claim the imperial
title. It was on this expedition that Louis of Hohenloch became
his vassal for some property at Golloch, and Dirk of Havolzheim
for a house at Frickenhausen.[94] On May 3 William was 'at
Nuremburg where he bought a horse.[95] The time spent in Munich
in allaying suspicions [96] was very brief, for he was back at Binche
in Hainault on May 17.[97]

At this moment the antagonisms of John, duke of Brabant,
and the bishop of Liège burst forth once more, and, as the struggle
bade fair to become serious, engaged the attention of Count William. For several years the two enemies had been at peace. On
January 2, 1342, the duke had taken a decided stand in the
matter of tithes and other manorial dues to be paid to the chapter
of St. Lambert and ordered his officers to enforce payment.[98]
And on June 2 the bishop and the duke had concluded a treaty
of arbitration for all questions which might rise between them.[99]
But the antagonism between the two was a fundamental matter,
because the duke naturally persisted in his efforts to strengthen
his position toward the east. Thierry of Heinsberg, count of
Loon, looked to John for support since the chapter of St. Lambert continued to oppose him by secular and ecclesiastical
means. On February 20 Duke John had compensated him for
his losses in the campaign in the Cambrésis and Thiérache when

---

het Henegouwsche Huis, I, 258–259, 286, 287; H. G. Hamaker, *De Rekeningen der Grafelijkheid van Zeeland onder het Henegouwsche Huis,* II,
296, 297.

[92] L. Devillers, *Cartulaire,* I, 192; Kervyn, *Oeuvres de Froissart,* II
(notes), 515.

[93] L. Devillers, *Cartulaire,* I, 190, 193–194.

[94] *Ibid.,* pp. 194–195.

[95] H. G. Hamaker, *De Rekeningen der Grafelijkheid van Zeeland onder
het Henegouwsche Huis,* II, 300–301.

[96] Vitoduranus, "Chronicon," *Thesaurus Historiae Helveticae* (Tiguri,
1735), p. 62.

[97] L. Devillers, *Cartulaire,* I, 195.

[98] S. Bormans et E. Schoolmeesters, *Cartulaire de St. Lambert,* III,
585.

[99] A. Verkooren, *Inventaire, Brabant,* II, 120.

he accompanied the forces of Brabant.[100]   Meanwhile, the duke and William, count of Namur, had come to an agreement regarding the disputed territory of Aiseau.   Since 1334, when Philip VI had essayed to arbitrate this question, the matter had been in abeyance.   But in July, 1340, arbiters to be presided over by Reginald, duke of Guelders, and John of Hainault had been named to compose these tedious questions.   The matter was finally settled in favor of the duke after wearisome inquests and investigations.   On May 22, 1343, the count of Namur yielded his claims to the territory.   This settlement coincided with the struggle of the count and the duke against the bishop of Liège and each agreed to aid the other against their common enemy.[101]

The political situation was favorable for the duke's new maneuver.   The Truce of Malestroit had established peace between Philip and Edward and their allies.   The French king would not endanger this truce by intervening actively in favor of the bishop, even if he had been inclined to do so.   The duke realized that a recurrence of the situation in 1332 and 1334 was impossible, and assumed a bold attitude.   The burghers of Huy were debating with the bishop the value of their money and payment of their dues to the clergy.   When they perceived that they could not gain their point they sent a delegation to the duke which made a treaty with him.   They were to give 40,000 shields and aid in serving against their lord, and the duke was to defend them with a garrison and protect them against aggressions from the bishop.[102]

On May 17 the duke and Thierry, count of Loon, gave still further evidence of their friendship when the latter bound himself and his successors never to sell or pledge in any manner the goods which he held in fee of the church of Liège, and also transferred to him his castle at Dalenbroech and the allodial possessions and village of Herkenbosch, also to be held as a fief.[103] Thus the duke's position was extremely dangerous to the chapter of Liège, as the bishopric was practically surrounded by

---

[100] A. Verkooren, *Inventaire, Brabant,* II, pp. 116–118.

[101] J. de St. Genois, *Monumens Anciens,* I, DCCCCLXXXX; C. Butkens, *Trophées tant Sacrés que Profanes du Duché de Brabant,* I (*Preuves*), 179.

[102] Hocsemius, p. 466.

[103] F. J. Willems, *Codex Diplomaticus,* II, 458.

enemies who were aided and abetted by the men of Huy. The frightened bishop called the representatives of his estates to assemble on May 15, but the knights refused to give aid or counsel unless he should give Loon in fee to the possessor, Count Thierry, to which the chapter would under no circumstances agree. The embarrassed bishop turned to Count William of Namur, which was quite useless, and found himself in an impossible position.[104] Then on June 3 the magistrates of Huy banished a number of their citizens and promised never to permit them to return without the assent of the duke of Brabant.[105]

Thus the affairs of the bishop and chapter were in a very precarious condition. In his struggle with the duke, the bishop was deserted by his estates who demanded a reform of the old reactionary government. A commission was appointed at the meeting of May 15 which began its sessions on June 2 and created a council of twenty-two of which fourteen members were to be drawn from the third estate, four from the nobility, and four from the chapter, whose tenure of office was for life and who were to be appointed by coöptation.[106] This highly·disadvantageous measure was probably arranged in consultation with William, count of Hainault, Holland, and Zeeland, whom the knights called in to serve as arbiter.[107] He now clearly showed that he was chosen to favor the opponents of the bishop. As husband of Johanna, daughter of John, duke of Brabant, with whom he was on friendly terms, he acted wholly in his favor and in that of Thierry, count of Loon. On July 23 he demanded that all the documents touching the succession in Loon should be placed in his hands. Even before this, he and John of Hainault, accompanied by a number of the feudality of Liège, had appeared before the chapter demanding that Count Thierry should

[104] Hocsemius, pp. 466–467.

[105] A. Wauters, "Analectes Diplomatiques," *BCRH*, 4th Ser., X (1882), 101.

[106] S. Bormans, *Recueil des Ordonnances,* 1st Ser., I, 247 (June 6, when the bishop accepted the institution.)

[107] Hocsemius, p. 467. This is the opinion of Waller Zeper, *Jan van Henegouwen,* p. 245 (note 2). The document inaugurating the new institution has been lost, but Waller Zeper assumes that it was drawn up on July 7 (really July 17) when a document of that date was " à Liège sayellet . . . dou grant sayel, de le ordinanche dou pays de Liège, le XVII jour dou moys dou Julet." See L. Devillers, *Cartulaire,* I, 239.

be legally invested.[108]   After much discussion it was decided on
August 3 to submit the question of the succession to the pope
after which the documents were surrendered.   On the next day
Huy formally accepted the arbitration of Count William and
John of Hainault.[109]   Two days later the bishop, with the
approval of the chapter, likewise submitted his differences with
the duke, but expressly reserved the question of the rights of
Thierry of Heinsberg.[110]   This was also done by the bourgeoisie and the princes.[111]   On the 6th Count William was at
Duras in consultation with the interested parties and formulated his judgment on the 8th.[112]

The decision was quite favorable to the bishop's opponents.
The appeals (*vogements*), which by the treaty of Hasselt made
in 1338 were to have been the subject of inquest, the time of
which had elapsed, were now declared a closed matter, and the
duke and his subjects were released from all obligations.   Only
the spiritual jurisdiction in Brabant was to remain.   Debated
points were hastily settled: Herstal was to remain in the duke's
possession, judicial acts by the officials of each party were to be
dropped, restoration of the goods of the seignior of Melin by the
bishop's officials was ordered, all lesser questions were to be
settled at Maastricht by arbitration of six men, three being
chosen for each side, the disputes regarding Marche were to be
settled by inquest, and the duke was to render homage for
fiefs held of the bishop.   Without any regard for the reservations
touching the county of Loon, they proceeded to make pronouncement in favor of the occupant.   Curious is the statement that
the " count of Loon should have the county of Loon," as if no
question existed regarding Thierry's legal claim.   The interdict
was to be lifted by the pope, and the bishop, chapter, and the
land of Liège were to send a request to the Holy See within
fifteen days to secure the annulment of all proceedings against the

---

[108] See the letters of September 4 and 14 from the bishop and chapter
of Liège to the pope, Hocsemius, pp. 472, 473.

[109] L. Devillers, *Cartulaire*, I, 205–206.

[110] S. Bormans, *Recueil des Ordonnances*, 1st Ser., I, 254–256 (note).

[111] L. Devillers, *Cartulaire*, I, 206–207.   For the promise of Count
William, see *ibid.*, pp. 207–208.

[112] H. G. Hamaker, *De Rekeningen der Grafelijkheid van Holland onder
het Henegouwsche Huis*, II, 222, 230, 242–259.

county. And, finally, the bishop was to retain his full spiritual jurisdiction. Among the articles regulating the relations of Huy with the church was one which declared null and void the alliance with the duke. The bishop was to reinstate the count of Namur in all his titles and was to retain his spiritual jurisdiction in the county. Other debated points were to be settled at Fleurus by six men, three to be appointed by each side.[113]

It is obvious that this decision, so disastrous to the interests of chapter and bishop, could not last long. They again renewed the interdict over the county of Loon, requested the pope on September 4 to confirm it, and complained to him of the attitude of Count William. Ten days later they presented their complaints to the college of cardinals and requested its support. The bishop, whose flagrant nepotism was the cause of this difficulty, was perhaps forced by the canons to take this step with them.[114] The curia acted promptly, and its legate excommunicated the magistrates and burghers of Huy and put their territories and those of the duke under the interdict.[115]

While occupied with these affairs in the Liégeois, Count William impatiently awaited the moment to set out on an expedition to the Holy Land. He had petitioned Pope Clement VI to approve this project for himself and the sixty men who were to accompany him. This permission was granted on August 5 on condition that he should carry nothing which might aid the enemies of Christendom.[116] On the very day that Count William pronounced his decision in the quarrel between the bishop of Liège and his enemies, he left Duras and proceeded to Huy, and thence to Venice by way of Marche, Bastogne, Arlon, Thionville, Colmar, Basel, Lausanne, Como, Cremona, and Mantua. On September 1 he took ship at Venice, and passed Pola, Ragusa, Cephalonia, Rhodes, Candia, and, on October 26, was at Famagusta in Cyprus whence he passed over to Syria and on to Jerusalem.[117] Retracing his steps hastily, he was in Venice on No-

---

[113] S. Bormans, *Recueil des Ordonnances,* 1st Ser., I, 254–260; S. Bormans et E. Schoolmeesters, *Cartulaire de l'Église de St. Lambert,* IV, 8–16.

[114] Hocsemius, pp. 472–474.   [115] *Ibid.,* p. 474.

[116] Ph. van Isacker et U. Berlière, *Lettres de Clément VI (1342–1352),* No. 973.

[117] H. G. Hamaker, *De Rekeningen der Grafelijkheid van Holland,*

vember 30 and on December 2 set out for Prussia to take part in the struggles of the Teutonic Knights against the pagan Lithuanians. Passing through Padua, Vienna on the 15th, Znaim on the 19th, and Breslau on January 1, he reached Thorn on the 5th. Little is known of his activities in these parts and he cannot have covered himself with much glory as a crusader. Early in March he was on his way homeward. On the 15th he was in Dantzig, and, passing through Bremen, Osnabrück, Oldenzaal, Deventer, Woerden, Amersfoort, and Utrecht, arrived at The Hague on April 8.[118]

The year 1344 thus saw a serious decline of Edward's influence in the Low Countries. Count William definitely abandoned him and, lightly forgetting the old policy of his house, occupied himself with matters which would be of no profit to himself or to Edward. The duke of Brabant knew how to make use of the situation to advance his own interests against the chapter and bishop of Liège. Edward's financial exhaustion and prolonged absence from the Low Countries undoubtedly contributed to this situation. Yet the English king could not abandon the policy of maintaining alliances in the Low Countries to aid in his claims upon the French monarchy. Peace with Philip was impossible, and the delegation, consisting of Hugh Despenser, Raoul de Stafford, William de Norwich, dean of Lincoln, William Trussel, and Andrew de Offord, sent in accordance with the terms of the Truce of Malestroit to treat with the pope who was represented by the cardinals of Praeneste and Tusculum, could accomplish nothing.[119] It is not strange, therefore, that Edward should on July 1 commission Raoul de Stafford, William Trussel, Philip de Weston, and John Wawayn to treat with the Flemings concerning the numerous questions which continually came up

---

onder het Henegouwsche Huis, III, 80–87, 92–97, 109, 130, 175, 179, 181, 189, 223–226, 230–231, 242. See also *Bourgeois de Valenciennes,* pp. 193, 196, for the companions whom he dubbed knights at the sepulchre.

[118] H. G. Hamaker, *De Rekeningen der Grafelijkheid van Holland onder het Henegouwsche Huis,* III, 74–75, 87–91, 99, 101, 104, 131, 135, 165, 166, 169, 183, 184, 221, 226–229. See also J. G. Frederiks, " Ysebouts Ontfanc ende Wtgheven (1345), eene Bijdrage tot de Geschiedenis van Graaf Willem den Vierde," *Bijdragen voor Vaderlandsche Geschiedenis en Oudheidkunde,* New Ser., VII (1877), 69–71.

[119] *Foedera,* II (2), 1224. They received their credentials on May 20, 1343.

between them and his subjects, and to labor for alliances with the princes and magnates of Germany and elsewhere.[120] During the year John de Offord visited Guelders,[121] but it is impossible to discover any results from these diplomatic efforts.

III. The Death of Reginald, Duke of Guelders, Deprives Edward of his Chief Ally (October, 1343 — Spring, 1345)

A real misfortune for Edward's interests in the Low Countries was the sudden death on October 12, 1343, of his faithful ally and brother-in-law Reginald, duke of Guelders.[122] The duke's eldest son Reginald was but a youth, and the strife which now broke out for the chief control of Guelders and Zutfen made it impossible henceforth to rely upon any assistance from this quarter. Reginald and his brother, Edward, were children of Eleanor, sister of Edward III of England. By his first wife, Sophia Berthout, there were three daughters, Marguerite, betrothed to Gerard, eldest son of William, the margrave of Juliers,[123] Matilda, formerly the wife of Godefroid, seignior of Millen, and Elizabeth, betrothed since March 25, 1337, to Ruprecht, count of the Rhenish Palatinate.[124] By the terms of the marriage agreement between Eleanor and Reginald, these children of his first wife were specifically excluded from the inheritance.[125] The youth of Reginald and the interests of relatives and connections of Sophia's children might make the situation very dangerous. But neither they nor Thierry, count of Cleves, who had married Margaret, the dead duke's sister, apparently ever raised any claim because in the troubles which followed their names are not mentioned. But the descendants of Philippa, sister of Reginald I and wife of Walram, seignior of Valkenburg, were ambitious to advance their interests. These were her

[120] *Ibid.,* p. 1227.

[121] L. Mirot et E. Déprez, "Les Ambassades Anglaises pendant la Guerre de Cent Ans," *BEC,* LIX (1898), 565.

[122] I. A. Nijhoff, *Gedenkwaardigheden uit de Geschiedenis van Gelderland,* II, v–vii, *Introduction.*

[123] For Marguerite, see *Codex Diplomaticus Neerlandicus,* 2d Ser., Part I (Utrecht, 1852), pp. 59–62.

[124] I. A. Nijhoff, *Gedenkwaardigheden uit de Geschiedenis van Gelderland,* I, 357–358.   [125] *Ibid.,* pp. 269–270.

grandsons Thierry, seignior of Valkenburg, and John of Valkenburg, seignior of Sittard and Borne.[126]

While the question of the succession could not be raised in view of the legal objections, the control over the lands of the house and the guardianship of the youthful Reginald were bound to cause much anxiety. There was serious danger of strife between noble factions. There was the eternal problem of the relations with the bishop of Utrecht and the control over his lands beyond the Yssel. Also the legacy of a heavy debt, which Duke Reginald had incurred in the service of King Edward, proved a serious obstacle to pacific government. The bourgeoisie at once moved to maintain order, and on December 1 the magistrates of the towns formed a league to enforce the laws and secure justice under the government of their legal duke.[127] The towns helped in meeting the duke's financial obligations, and Arnhem pledged its credit to the Sudermann brothers of Dortmund to the extent of 34,000 small florins. In similar fashion a number of the important nobles of the land came to the support of the exchequer on January 28 of the following year. The list is headed by John of Valkenburg who apparently from the first was able to exert his influence among them. In a charter of September 12 Eleanor is described as *ruwaard* (*overste meystersche*).[128]

Internal dissensions developed rapidly between John of Valkenburg, who was receiver general of the finances (*rentemeester*), and Thierry of Valkenburg. The latter had established himself in the ducal castle at Nijmegen and is referred to as stadtholder (*overste berechter*). These quarrels were apparently caused by their desire to control the youthful duke, and Eleanor was no longer mentioned as guardian in a document of October 14.[129] This, however, did not put an end to her influence in the affairs of the duchy. Early in November John of Cleves, dean of Cologne, Arend van Arkel, Dirk van Lynde, Claes Tengnagell and William van Gendt, knights, and Wennemaer van Tiel, were sent at her order to William, count of Hainault, Holland, and

[126] A. Stokvis, *Manuel d'Histoire, de Généalogie, et de Chronologie de tous les États du Globe,* III, 485.
[127] I. A. Nijhoff, *Gedenkwaardigheden uit de Geschiedenis van Gelderland,* II, 3–6.
[128] *Ibid.,* pp. 7–13.
[129] *Ibid.,* pp. 15–16.

Zeeland, at Middelburg to discuss the project of marriage between Reginald and William's sister Isabella who had been betrothed to John, son of the duke of Brabant, in 1329. The death of her fiancé [130] had left her free to marry, and once more she was called upon to aid the affairs of the duchy. These envoys conferred with the count and his councillors at Middelburg and agreed to this proposal and also that, should Reginald die before the consummation of the marriage, his brother Edward should take her to wife.[131]

The motives behind this act are not difficult to divine. As sister of Edward, Eleanor was undoubtedly devoted to English interests. The English king had sent Philip de Weston to Flanders, Brabant, Germany, and Guelders on July 24 and his return on November 1 coincides well with the negotiations for the betrothal.[132] That Philippa and Edward were concerned in this matter is certain, for on December 24 messengers were sent to England and also to Avignon. This was undoubtedly to secure, among other things, a dispensation from the pope since Reginald and Isabella were nephew and aunt, inasmuch as Eleanor and Isabella were sisters-in-law.[133] Another messenger was sent to Philippa on January 14, 1345, when Simon van Teilingen and Claes Stuyck were dispatched to negotiate the dispensation with Clement VI.[134] That Eleanor should desire to draw closer the ties with the count of Holland can readily be explained by the precarious internal divisions in Guelders caused by the ambitions of John and Thierry of Valkenburg and the problems which might arise concerning the ducal power and rights in the lands of the bishop of Utrecht. So desirable were Count William's friendship and support that Eleanor did not hesitate to act contrary to the terms of the arrangements made at Amiens in 1334

[130] C. Butkens, *Trophées tant Sacrés que Profanes du Duché de Brabant,* I, 444.

[131] W. A. van Spaen, *Oordeelkundig Inleiding tot de Histoire van Gelderland,* II, 265–266. The original of this document yet unpublished was found in the archives of Hemmen. See P. L. Muller, *Regesta Hannonensia,* p. 295.

[132] L. Mirot and E. Déprez, "Les Ambassades Anglaises pendant la Guerre de Cent Ans," *BEC,* LIX (1898), 566.

[133] H. J. Hamaker, *De Rekeningen der Grafelijkheid van Holland onder het Henegouwsche Huis,* III, 395.

[134] *Ibid.,* pp. 392, 393, 394.

whereby Marie, the daughter of John, duke of Brabant, had been betrothed to Reginald. As late as March 21, 1342, William, count of Hainault, Holland, and Zeeland, had promised not to interfere in the affairs of the lands beyond the Yssel which Duke Reginald regarded as his sphere of influence.[135]

Eleanor was successful in enlisting William's influence in her cause against the Valkenburg factions. The count decided to invite them to a conference in which the strife could be allayed. That in this matter he was himself directly interested is certain because of his own interest in the lands of the bishop of Utrecht. On November 20 or 21 he requested William van Duivenvoorde to come to him at Dordrecht, and ordered his councillors and the representatives of the towns in South Holland and Amstelland and the abbot of Middelburg to meet him at Tiel.[136] There William's advisers came together, and on December 2 a strongly worded letter was sent to Thierry of Valkenburg at Nijmegen ordering him to stop the quarrel with his uncle John.[137] The result of these diplomatic activities was that the two Valkenburgs were constrained to submit to William's arbitration.

At Tiel, perhaps on January 23, 1345, the count decreed that all obligations incurred on the part of Duchess Eleanor toward Thierry of Valkenburg should cease. Thierry was to restore not later than January 30 the duke's castle at Nijmegen and its archives to exactly the same condition in which he had found them. For his pains and expenses he was to receive 30,000*l.* small pennies to be paid at Dordrecht, one half at Pentecost and one half at St. Bavo's Day (October 1), which moneys, it was understood, were to be advanced by William himself. All parties were declared fully reconciled and to have acted entirely in the best interests of Duke Reginald. The specific points in the dispute between John and Thierry, however, were reserved for settlement to be rendered before August 1. Finally, John of Valkenburg was deprived of his control over the ducal finances.

[135] F. van Mieris, *Groot Charterboek,* II, 647.

[136] H. J. Hamaker, *De Rekeningen der Grafelijkheid van Holland onder het Henegouwsche Huis,* III, 389–390.

[137] *Ibid.,* p. 391: ". . . i knecht ghesent van Tiele, bi nachte ende met groter haesten, met mijns heren brieve te Nimaghen an den here van Valkenborch, als om der kijf te beletten, dien hi hadde jeghens sijn oem." On the previous day a letter had been sent, also by night.

Because of Reginald's financial plight, William declared that, as he had to manage his lands as economically as possible, a person of less lofty position should be entrusted with them.[138] These functions were given to John van Groesbeek, apparently on the 21st, when Reginald promised his brother to reimburse him fully for the payment of the 30,000*l.* small pennies.[139]

IV. The Friesians and the Death of William, Count of Hainault, Holland, and Zeeland (1344–1345)

The Friesians had not yet played a rôle in the important events which had actively engaged the attention of their neighbors to the south. Their alliance with King Philip in 1337 was devoid of any noticeable results. In 1338 the youthful William, count of Hainault, Holland, and Zeeland, was accepted at Stavoren as their prince.[139a] This appears to have happened without any opposition, which may possibly be due to the fact that he showed slight zeal at that moment to follow Edward's suggestions against his uncle, the king of France. During the following years little is heard regarding their relations with him. In fact Count William's authority in these parts appears to have dwindled so much that only the town of Stavoren remained faithful. The extant documents of 1342 concern only the men of this place who were eager to remain friendly with the count of Holland because of their close commercial contacts with his subjects. Thus on November 30, Count William granted them freedom from tolls in Holland and Zeeland which facilitated their economic activities with Flanders, Brabant, and the Rhineland.[139b] He was also concerned in the disputes between certain men of the Bisschoping party in Lübeck and those of Stavoren. This undoubtedly was to preserve the peace on the commercial

---

[138] F. van Mieris, *Groot Charterboek*, II, 689. This charter bears no date nor is the place of its origin given. It is apparent, however, that it preceded the document printed by van Mieris which was drawn up at Tiel on January 23, 1345.

[139] *Ibid.,* p. 690. This document, dated Sunday after St. Agnes, or January 23, 1345, was not drawn up in the Easter style as van Mieris thought.

[139a] *Ibid.,* p. 605.

[139b] G. F. thoe Schwartzenberg en Hohenlansberg, *Groot Placaat-boek en Charterboek van Friesland*, I, 199. For other charters, see *ibid.,* p. 198.

routes toward the east — in other words, with the Hansa. A number of Friesians from Stavoren were held as hostages in the count's care at Haarlem. On August 23 William freed them on condition that they return upon his request. He also released the hostages who had been sent to him by their opponents.[140]

Count William was also interested in retrieving his rights, and in December, 1343, the *grietmannen* of Westergoo were in Haarlem in consultation with him and the scabini and consuls of Haarlem, Alkmaar, and Medemblik regarding their mutual relations and the privileges of Stavoren.[141] It is instructive to note that in the declaration of the abbot of Bloemkamp and several other ecclesiastics, made apparently in the following year, the count's rights in Stavoren are stated to be four hundred years old. Once a year he might come to Vroenacher with scabini, sheriffs (*schouten*), and judges (*asegen*) to administer justice in all cases which had not been adjudicated by the magistrates. He had the right to remove all these officials in East Friesland, by which is apparently meant Westergoo, at any time and as often as he wished.[142] On August 22, 1344, when at Geertruidenberg, Count William received the declaration of a certain Andelof Esseling, sheriff (*schout*) of Elsmardorp and Boncherst in East Friesland, that this office was held from him. On the 26th he ordered him to be faithful in his service and commanded the people of his jurisdiction to be loyal.[143] The paucity of documents, unfortunately, makes it impossible to trace the situation very clearly, but from the few that are extant it is apparent that William was bending every effort to define his rights and secure recognition of them.

The Friesians, however, persisted in their traditional opposition, and William proceeded to use force. The monks of the monastery at Mariengaarde had much property situated in the count's domains at Markerhoofd on the island of Marken and at Monnikendam, which could easily be seized. A deputation of monks from Friesland was sent to Holland toward the close of

---

[140] F. van Mieris, *Groot Charterboek*, II, 684–688.
[141] G. F. thoe Schwartzenberg en Hohenlansberg, *Groot Placaat-boek en Charterboek van Friesland*, I, 199.
[142] F. van Mieris, *Groot Charterboek*, II, 683.
[143] *Ibid.*, pp. 683–684.

October. On the 30th a number of the count's officials were sent to conduct them to Geertruidenberg. Their esquires (*knapen*) were brought to Dordrecht on November 5.[144] No satisfaction was obtained from the discussions with them, and on December 3, when Count William was at Tiel and actively concerned in the disputes between Eleanor, the duchess of Guelders, and her advisers, orders were issued for William van Duivenvoorde to repair to the count's side, and for his subjects in Hainault and Zeeland to cease their preparations for an expedition against the Friesians.[145] Apparently this hostile demonstration had been planned for the winter months when the country, intersected by numerous canals and bogs, could more readily be invaded. Messengers were sent to Friesland on December 9 and to Groningen, described as situated "in Friesland" as was common at that time, on the 20th.[146] Later, on February 20 of the following year, Floris, an official of the count, was in conference with the Friesians.[147] At some time during these negotiations, possibly after the recent conference at Alkmaar, the property of the monks was ordered seized, and soldiers were sent out from Amstel, Abcoude, Loenen, Waterland, and the parts around Edam, then called Zeevanc.[148] Three monks were seized, and steps were taken forthwith to dispose of their rich possessions in order to replenish the treasury of the spendthrift count.[149]

Count William postponed his expedition against the Friesians in order to gratify once more his ambition to aid the Christians against the pagan Lithuanians. At Tiel he tarried just long enough to dispose of the dissensions in the duchy of Guelders, and on December 12 hastened eastward by way of Zutfen, Osnabrück, Lüneburg, Lübeck, Rostock, Greifswald, Wolgast, Königsberg, and Marienburg. He appears to have done little more than gratify his desire for empty show, as in his former expeditions, and soon returned by way of Stettin, Brunswick, Lippe, Cologne,

[144] H. J. Hamaker, *De Rekeningen der Grafelijkheid van Holland onder het Henegouwsche Huis*, I, 338.

[145] H. J. Hamaker, *De Rekeningen der Grafelijkheid van Zeeland onder het Henegouwsche Huis*, III, 390–391.

[146] *Ibid.*, pp. 258, 394.

[147] H. J. Hamaker, *De Rekeningen der Grafelijkheid van Holland onder het Henegouwsche Huis*, I, 330, 339, 349–351, 354, 383, 387, 389.

[148] *Ibid.*, pp. 350, 359–372.

[149] *Ibid.*, pp. 330, 348, 350, 351, 354, 359, 371, 372, 383, 387, 389.

and Gemmenich.[150] Shortly after his return, plans to attack
the Friesians were reconsidered, and on May 7, 8, and 9, and
again on June 5 and 6, a group of the nobility of Holland and
intimate councillors of Count William assembled at Medemblik.[151] Meanwhile plans were laid to reduce the town of Utrecht
which resented the count's efforts to extend his power in the
episcopal dominions of Utrecht. William strove to secure the
appointment of his candidate, John van Arkel, as bishop. Since
August the accounts of the count's household reveal the bitter
feeling along the border where hostile acts took place. Early
in June his troops took their positions before Utrecht. The
siege lasted until July 22 when the differences between the town
and William were submitted to the arbitration of John, of
Hainault who pronounced his decision on various points but reserved others to be decided before St. Bavo's Day (October 1).[152]

It is not necessary to treat at length the campaign against the
Friesians.[153] After great preparations which began in March and
were concentrated at Amsterdam, Count William crossed over
the Zuider Zee from Enkhuizen on September 26 and approached
Stavoren. Troops were landed, and William and some of his
followers rushed into the country without taking consideration of
the nature of the boggy land and the great danger his rash
attack invited. His troops were soon assailed from all quarters
as he hastened forward from Laaxum to Warns, his retreat was
cut off and he and nearly all his followers were killed before
they could effect retreat to their ships. Thus perished the last
male scion of the house of Avesnes. The debates which ensued
form an interesting and instructive part of the general political
relations of the Low Countries with the diplomatic and military
struggle between Edward and Philip. The hostility of the townsmen of Utrecht, quieted by the truce which was to last until

[150] H. J. Hamaker, *De Rekeningen der Grafelijkheid van Zeeland onder
het Henegouwsche Huis*, III, 376–388, 400; J. G. Frederiks, " Ysebouts Ontfanc ende Wtgheven (1345), Eene Bijdrage tot de Geschiedenis van Graaf
Willem den Vierde," *Bijdragen voor Vaderlandsche Geschiedenis en Oudheidkunde*, VII (1872), 65–92.

[151] H. J. Hamaker, *De Rekeningen der Grafelijkheid van Holland onder
het Henegouwsche Huis*, II, 413, 529.

[152] S. A. Waller Zeper, *Jan van Henegouwen, Heer van Beaumont*,
pp. 250–258.

[153] *Ibid.*, pp. 260–269, where the tragedy is described in great detail.

November 11, would also become important when Edward should attempt to strengthen himself in the bishopric and seek to secure the recognition of Queen Philippa's alleged rights to some of the territories of the Avesnes house.

V. John, Duke of Brabant, Reconsiders His Policy (Spring, 1345)

The political situation in the Low Countries had undergone a marked change since the Truce of Malestroit in 1343. William, count of Hainault, Holland, and Zeeland, after being reconciled with the church of Cambrai, had abandoned the old claims of his house upon the Cambrésis, Crèvecoeur, and Arleux. He now gave himself over to his chivalric inclinations, visited the Holy Land, went on two crusades to East Prussia, and in the spring of 1345 was preparing an attack upon Utrecht and an invasion of Friesland. Reginald, duke of Guelders, had died, and henceforth it was uncertain just what the policy of his successor would be. In Flanders there was much opposition among the smaller towns to the dictatorial hegemony of Ghent supported by Bruges and Ypres, and among the feudality which in sullen wrath only awaited the moment when the count should return to establish his authority. Under these circumstances it is not strange that the duke of Brabant, whose interests in Mechelen were as keen as ever, should begin to reconsider his political policy.

Until this time Duke John in conjunction with Edward had sought the dispensation necessary for the marriage of his daughter Marguerite to the latter's son, but Benedict XII and Clement VI regarded the project with disfavor as it was not at all apparent that such an alliance would bring about any more peaceful conditions in this part of Europe. Clement, therefore, kept deferring the matter, neither refusing nor granting the much sought permission.[154] On February 23, 1345, Edward once more urgently pressed the pope and repeated his pleas on April 12.[155] At this time Duke John sent his trusted representatives, Henry

---

[154] Ph. van Isacker et U. Berlière, *Lettres de Clément VI (1342-1352)*, Vol. I, No. 1379.

[155] *Foedera*, III (1), 32, 35.

Coke, dean of St. Mary's of Dendermonde, John van Wicvliet, seignior of Blaersveld, and Robert de Otelenden, knight, to the curia for the same purpose. Once more, on May 11, Clement declared that for the time being the dispensation could not, in the opinion of the curia, be granted.[156]

The date at which Duke John actively began to seek a reconciliation with Philip and Louis, count of Flanders, can definitely be set at about April. It had been agreed between the count and Philip, king of Navarre, before his death on September 10, 1343,[157] that the youthful Louis, heir apparent of Flanders, should marry the latter's daughter. Later, when an alliance between Duke John and Count Louis was projected, it was decided that the son should marry Marguerite, Duke John's daughter. This cannot have been broached before April, 1345, for on March 7 the pope replied to a letter from Philip of Valois commending enthusiastically the projected union of young Louis with the daughter of the king of Navarre. On that same date Pope Clement urged the count of Flanders not to delay the marriage any longer but to proceed at once with its execution.[158]

The occasion for Duke John's new friendship with Count Louis was the attempted return of the latter to Flanders and his determined effort to cause his subjects to accept their lawful suzerain, the king of France. Since the close of November, 1342, when Louis was at Ypres,[159] he had not appeared in his county. But shortly after the opening of the new year there was a rumor current according to which Count Louis wished to bring the countess and his sons to England with Edward's consent. It is impossible to trace the origin of this strange report which was so pernicious to English political interests in Flanders that on February 20 [160] Edward begged the men of Ghent, Bruges, and Ypres not to place any faith in the story, and at the same moment warned them that

[156] S. Riezler, *Vatikanische Akten,* No. 2214; P. van Isacker and U. Berlière, *Lettres de Clément VI (1342–1346),* Vol. I, No. 1558.

[157] J. de Mas Latrie, *Trésor de Chronologie d'Histoire, et de Géographie,* Col. 1597.

[158] Ph. van Isacker et U. Berlière, *Lettres de Clément VI (1342–1352),* Vol. I, Nos. 1442, 1443.

[159] N. de Pauw en J. Vuylsteke, *Rekeningen der Stad Gent,* II, 210.

[160] *Foedera,* III (1), 30.

Louis was seeking to come to an arrangement with them and that they should be on their guard against all reports which were hostile to their good relations.[161]

On March 21 Louis' messenger who apparently carried letters requesting a conference at Menin was received at Ghent.[162] On the 28th the scabini of Ghent sent their colleagues, John vander Scatte, Hugh van Lembeke, Peter vanden Hovene, and Peter vanden Velde, together with William de Bomere and Simon Parijs, collector of the duty, to receive the count's request. They were accompanied by delegations from Bruges and Ypres.[163] But the towns were determined not to recognize Philip as their king, which apparently was the condition advanced by Louis for his return. On April 21 the three towns once more sent their representatives to Menin with the demand that the count should recognize Edward as true king of France. But Louis was determined to remain loyal to his sovereign, and the meeting was barren of all result.[164]

Repulsed by the three towns, Count Louis resolved to use force. The opportunity was at hand, for there were enough discontented elements in Flanders, which, supported by the émigrés or " fugitives," could be used to destroy the hegemony of the three towns under the guidance of van Artevelde. Since the previous autumn Dendermonde had been in conflict with

---

[161] It is perhaps needless to point out that if Edward really wished to make the Prince of Wales count of Flanders this rumor could not have risen.

[162] N. de Pauw en J. Vuylsteke, *Rekeningen der Stad Gent,* II, 405.

[163] *Ibid.,* p. 387: " Item Scepenen der Jan van den Scatte, der Hughe van Lembeke, der Pieter van den Hovene ende der Pieter van den Velde, ende met hem der Willem de Boomere ende Symoen Parijs, voeren smaendaechs naer onser vrouwen dach in maerte te Meenine an minen heere van Vlaendren metten steden van Vlaendren die daer ontboden waren omme te hoorne en te verstane mijns heeren versouc van Vlaendren ende dat weder over te bringhene in de steden omme daer up raet te hebbene, thaerre theere van 4 daghen ende van haren paerdehuere, 144*lb.*"

[164] *Ibid.,* p. 388: " Item scepenen der Jan Diedericx, der Gillis van Contelsvoerde, der Pieter van den Velde, ende van den ontfanghers Symoen Parijs, ende met hem Heinric de Mindere, scepenen cleerc, die voeren sdonredaechs den 20ᵉⁿ dagh van Aprille te Meenine waerd metten steden van Vlaendren vore minen heere van Vlaendren die daer was omme te hoorne dantworde die overeenghedreghen was metten ghemeenen lande upt versouc dat mijn heere van Vlaendren ter dachvaerd voren versocht hadde, thaerre theere dat sij ute waren, 4 daghe, 70*lb.*" For the date, see note, *ibid.*

Ghent because it had infringed the rights of the latter in the manufacture of striped cloths. There was a vigorous protest from the scabini and the deans of the guilds of Ghent who, after repeated representations had failed,[165] sent an imposing delegation on January 27 demanding that the method of folding the cloths and other practices should be forthwith abandoned.[166] But this was without effect, and consequently at the close of February another delegation was ordered to secure a definitive compliance.[167] On March 5 the scabini, councillors, and heads of the guilds issued a document in which they expressly declared their intention not to manufacture the striped half cloths (*strijpte half lakene*) and promised that they would prepare the striped cloths (*strijpte lakene*) thirteen ells in length and no more, exactly measured by the ell used at Ghent, and five quarters in width under a penalty of 2,000*l.* Tournois.[168]

But the people of Dendermonde were little disposed to abide by this agreement and appealed to Count Louis at about the time when his request that the Flemings should return to their old allegiance was rejected by the delegates of the three towns at Menin.[169] The men of Dendermonde begged Louis as their lord and prince to give them protection against the claims of Ghent. On April 29 the count was at Hal in Hainault, evidently on the way to Brabant, and there issued a document authorizing them to take all necessary steps to protect themselves against any possible attempt of the scabini of Ghent to force them into obedience. They were given permission to tear down any dykes, change the course of such waters as they might deem expedient, and build fortresses. Two days later the grateful scabini bound themselves to be ever faithful to him and his heirs and to enter

[165] N. de Pauw en J. Vuylsteke, *Rekeningen der Stad Gent,* II, pp. 383–398.

[166] *Ibid.,* p. 384: "Item scepenen der Jan van den Scatte, der Hughe van Lembeke ende der Pieter van den Hovene, Joes Rase, ende uten neeringhen Aernout Abelin, Jan Donter, Seghere Boele, Jan de Scoutheete, Pieter Dulhuus ende Gillis de Tolneere, voeren sdonredaechs vore onser vrouwen dach lichtmesse te Denremonde waert omme den vout van den lakenen te doen verkeerne, te haerre teere van 2 daghen, 80*lb.*"

[167] *Ibid.,* p. 386.

[168] G. Espinas et H. Pirenne, *Recueil des Documents relatifs à l'Histoire de l'Industrie Drapière en Flandre,* III, 363–365.

[169] N. de Pauw en J. Vuylsteke, *Rekeningen der Stad Gent,* II, 388.

into no alliance against him nor even begin any conversations with the men of Ghent or any other enemies.[170]

In the face of this danger van Artevelde and his followers were called upon to maintain a determined policy toward the smaller towns. The scabini of Ghent were forced to collaborate in naming the scabini at Courtrai in the middle of January and at Aardenburg in February.[171] They also intervened at Alost and Grammont when trouble threatened to break out about the appointment of a bailiff.[172] In April deputies were sent to quiet the discord between the fullers and the weavers.[173] But at Oudenaarde the discontent was chronic. The small guard of eight bowmen and four aides had been withdrawn on December 20.[174] In February there was some violence which was caused by John Faloyse of whose connections and motives nothing can be ascertained. The *ruwaard*, Simon Godenvalen, a fuller from Ghent, was murdered, and on February 25 the scabinus, Gilles van Contelsvoorde, and William van Huse were sent thither and were followed on the 26th by four representatives of the weavers, three of the fullers, three of the lesser crafts, and four others, Henry de Grutere, Simon de Amman, Peter van Over d'Water, and John uten Hove who were described as " count's men." Then on the 27th followed the captain, Gelnoot van Lens, a scabinus, and Lievin van Veurne, receiver of the duty. The first two of this group returned on the 28th, but the large delegation remained to carry on the work of pacification.[175] In July another delegation was sent to help choose the new bench of scabini.[176]

This was a propitious moment for the duke of Brabant to change his policy. His son-in-law, William, count of Hainault, Holland, and Zeeland, had once more shown his disinclination to follow in the footsteps of his father. When Bruges, Ghent, and perhaps Ypres, requested the towns of Hainault on April 1 and 4, to renew with their oaths the alliance made with them by their

---

[170] G. Espinas et H. Pirenne, *Recueil des Documents relatifs à l'Histoire de l'Industrie Drapière en Flandre*, III, 363–365.

[171] N. de Pauw en J. Vuylsteke, *Rekeningen der Stad Gent*, II, 384–385.　　　　　　　　　　　　[173] *Ibid.*, pp. 387, 388.

[172] *Ibid.*, p. 386.　　　　　　　　　　[174] *Ibid.*, p. 423.

[175] *Ibid.*, p. 385: ". . . omme daer de poort te settene in rusten ende in pointe ende te verhoedene . . . ende doe was daer seker ghenomen tfait te doen beterne dat daer ghevallen was."

[176] *Ibid.*, p. 393.

count in the spring of 1340,[177] there was no response, for the accounts of Ghent contain no statements of the formalities which would have been necessary in reaffirming the old alliance. At the close of the month Count Louis passed from Hal into Brabant where he was undoubtedly received by the duke. This fact, as well as the presence of the émigrés in his following, made the authorities of Ghent very uneasy. On May 12 they dispatched a force of twenty men to watch the approaches of Flanders from Brabant in the region around Alost.[178] But for the moment no serious attempt was made from that quarter.

The men of Dendermonde now took courage and began to violate their pledge of March 5, and on May 22 the scabini of Ghent sent out a force of seven bowmen, twenty-eight men-at-arms, and thirteen white-hoods, commanded by three captains who halted at Calkin, a castle situated three leagues from the town, in order to restrain the burghers. Within six days they returned to Ghent.[179] More serious were the difficulties at Waasmunster and Hulst, for a considerable force of two hundred and thirty-one men was sent out to those parts on the 29th, who returned on June 1.[180] The scabini revealed their anxiety by sending a clerk, Jacob van Lovelde, to Bruges to beg for assistance.[181] The men of Bruges acted at once and on June 1 sent forth their burgomaster, Gilles van Coudenbroec, three of the scabini and three councillors with their clerks, forty men with one hundred and nine mounts, and three companies of bowmen.[182] The enemies were reduced much sooner than had been expected, and the troops of Bruges were not needed. On June 6 three of the scabini of Ghent went out to confer with them and thanked them for their efforts.[183] A delegation of two scabini

---

[177] L. Devillers, *Cartulaire*, II, 348, 349.

[178] N. de Pauw en J. Vuylsteke, *Rekeningen der Stad Gent*, II, 426–428.

[179] *Ibid.*, pp. 423–424.

[180] *Ibid.*, pp. 390, 424–425.

[181] *Ibid.*, p. 389: " Item den selven Jacoppe voer te Brugghe waerd omme te sprekene ende te vermaenne de goede liede daer, dat sij ute wilden trecken omme te vaerne daers te doene ware onse viande te wederstane, tsiere theere van 2 daghen, 8*lb*."

[182] L. Gilliodts van Severen, " Jacques van Artevelde," *La Flandre*, IX (1878), 423–424.

[183] N. de Pauw en J. Vuylsteke, *Rekeningen der Stad Gent*, II, 390: " Item scepenen der Hughe van Lembeke ende der Lievin van Waes ende

and six men from the guilds was thereupon sent to Waasmunster
and Hulst on June 3 to ascertain the cause of the difficulties and
who the guilty men were.[184] Perhaps the captive who was
brought from Biervliet to Ghent was one of the culprits apprehended.[185] At the same time, on May 30, the magistrates of
Bruges sent a force of twenty men with sixty-one horses to
Assenede.[186] From these facts it is evident that the elements
in these parts which were hostile to the régime of the three towns
were in close sympathy with Count Louis' efforts to return. In
the western castleries no difficulties arose, or, at least, were not
recorded. At Poperingen the authorities of Ypres conducted
an inquest in January,[187] but the events of the previous spring
and summer had apparently so cowed them that they put forth
no armed effort to show their resentment.

Soon the situation at Alost assumed a more threatening aspect,
and on June 11 a large force composed of a hundred and six men
was ordered to reinforce the men who had already been watching the border for a whole month.[188] On the 13th a delegation
was sent from Ghent to arrange with the magistrates of Bruges
the dispatch of troops to support them. Upon their return, after
an absence of three days, an imposing group of fourteen men,
headed by the captain, William van Vaernewijc, three scabini,
and nine men from the guilds, proceeded to Bruges.[189] A force
was at once sent out from Bruges, and Sohier de Courtrai was
put in charge of the defense of Alost and was given the title of
ruwaard.[190]

While John, duke of Brabant, was thus reconsidering his policy
during May and June, he remained on friendly terms with the

Pieter van den Velde voeren smaendages up sente Godewalen dach tEe-
keloo tote den goeden lieden van Brugghe riders die daer laghen omme
hemlieden te dankene dat sij daer commen waren, thare there van 1 daghe,
12*lb*."

[184] *Ibid.*, p. 390.   [185] *Ibid.*, p. 410.
[186] L. Gilliodts van Severen, "Jacques van Artevelde," *La Flandre*,
IX (1878), 422.
[187] N. de Pauw, *Ypre jeghen Poperinghe*, p. 279 (quoting from the accounts of Ypres).
[188] N. de Pauw en J. Vuylsteke, *Rekeningen der Stad Gent*, II, 391.
[189] *Ibid.*, pp. 390–391.
[190] L. Gilliodts van Severen, "Jacques van Artevelde," *La Flandre*,
IX (1878), 425.

Flemish towns. This undoubtedly was in accordance with the economic clauses of the treaty of December 3, 1339. This also appears to be the explanation of the many messengers sent back and forth between Ghent and Bruges and the duke. On May 10, at the moment when the scabini of Ghent feared an attempt by the émigrés at Alost, delegates from the three towns went to consult the duke in Brabant regarding matters of interest to both countries.[191]   Another delegation went to Brussels on the 26th. Whether the presence of Count Louis was discussed at these meetings is impossible to determine from the all too brief accounts of Bruges and of Ghent.[192]   But on June 13, exactly at the moment when the danger of an invasion by the émigrés became more acute, the scabini of the three towns sent deputies to Brussels to discuss the case of the count who had apparently just arrived there. It also appears that this meeting was convoked by the duke.[193]   If so, Duke John for the moment sought to act as intermediary between the count and the three towns.

VI. The Murder of van Artevelde (July, 1345)

THREE factors complicated the relations of Flanders between May and August of 1345. The continued intrigues of Count Louis seriously challenged the domination of the three towns. The antagonisms of the fullers and the weavers in Ghent greatly embittered the guildsmen and led finally to the murder of van Artevelde. And when in the spring the truce between Edward and Philip could no longer be maintained, the English king was forced to take steps to ensure his control over the Flemings. Historians have as a rule been interested mainly in the personal fortunes of van Artevelde and hence have overlooked his relations with the more far-reaching political movements of the day. A proper perspective was thus impossible, and all the events of these months were made to revolve around the sudden

[191] N. de Pauw en J. Vuylsteke, *Rekeningen der Stad Gent,* II, 388.
[192] *Ibid.,* p. 389.
[193] *Ibid.,* p. 390: "Item meester Jan uten Hove ende Joesse Rasen voeren smaendachs daer naer te Bruesele waerd metten goeden lieden van den steden ten paerlemente dat daer was omme de comste van minen heere van Vlaendren, thaerre theere dat sij ute waren 6 daghe, mids dat verleit was omme de siechede van minen heere den hertoghe, 72*lb* "

end of this man. While the references of the chroniclers are unfortunately only too uncertain and those in the accounts of Ghent usually too brief to enable one to reconstruct in a satisfactory manner the events which preceded his death, enough facts are known to enable us to obtain a better conception of the events attending the tragic death of the remarkable bourgeois character who since December, 1337, had wielded a predominant influence in the counsels of the three towns of Flanders.

On May 2 occurred the sanguinary encounter on the Friday Market Place of Ghent between the fullers and the weavers who were led by their deans, John de Bake and Gerard Denys.[194] The occasion of the struggle was the demand of the fullers that they should receive higher wages, which the weavers refused to sanction.[195] In the struggle which ensued as many as three hundred are reported in the chronicles to have been wounded and five hundred slain, among whom was John de Bake himself.[196] It was a serious crisis which endangered the position of van Artevelde who was forced to intervene and espouse the contentions of the weavers.[197] He is said to have appealed for help to the captains and magistrates of Bruges and Ypres.[198] The accounts of Ghent contain entries showing that two messengers were hastily dispatched at night to both towns.[199] Little is known of the final arrangements which cannot have been mild for the vanquished fullers. Gilles van Gavere was chosen dean of the fullers in the place of John de Bake.[200] Some of those who participated in the fight were banished from Flanders, and, although the only case recorded is that of a weaver, it is quite certain that many of the fullers must have suffered a like fate.[201]

[194] For an account of the event, see O. Pyfferoen, *Une Émeute au Moyen Âge. Den Quaden Maendach — Le Mauvais Lundi* (Gand, 1888).

[195] *Chronicon Comitum Flandrensium,* pp. 214–215.

[196] *Ibid.,* le Muisit, p. 145.

[197] De Budt, p. 329; le Muisit, p. 145.

[198] N. Despars, *Cronijcke van den Lande ende Graefscepe van Vlaendren (405–1492),* II, 373; N. de Pauw, *Cartulaire Historique et Généalogique des Artevelde,* p. 247.

[199] N. de Pauw en J. Vuylsteke, *Rekeningen der Stad Gent,* II, 407: " Item de selve Fobrie voer in der helegher crucen avonde bi nachte tYpre, 40s. . . . Item Boudin van den Damme te Br. up den selven nacht, 20s."

[200] *Ibid.,* p. 372.

[201] G. Espinas et H. Pirenne, *Recueil des Documents relatifs à l'Industrie Drapière en Flandre,* II, 477–478.

Meanwhile the agitation in Flanders clearly alarmed Edward who feared that Count Louis' return would deprive him of this most valuable ally. The truce accepted at Malestroit was not well kept between Edward and Philip, and in the autumn of 1344 the English king had begun to get together another army. More active preparations were made in the following spring when on April 24 the earl of Northampton was appointed captain in Brittany with full power to do what was needed for the defense of the land.[202] The earl of Derby was ordered to lead an expedition to Gascony, and in June troops were arrayed and ships of all kinds, capable of crossing the seas, were forbidden to leave port in order to insure passage for the king's forces.[203] On the 15th Edward requested the clergy of the provinces of Canterbury and York to pray for the success of the expedition.[204] As early as February he had appointed Otto, seignior of Cuyk, and Philip de Weston, canon of York, to treat for an alliance with Lewis the Bavarian, on the same day, the 23d, that he again begged Clement VI to grant the dispensation for the marriage of the Prince of Wales and Marguerite, daughter of the duke of Brabant.[205] The son of the Bavarian, Lewis, elector of Brandenburg, replied by sending Master Simon Brenner of Vynstyng to Westminster. On June 6 Edward answered with thanks and dispatched Philip de Weston and John Stury to form an alliance.[206] He thus hoped to use his old allies in the empire and also in the Low Countries, where the duke of Brabant, the margrave of Juliers, and the duke of Guelders, were formally at least still bound to him. It was not strange, therefore, that the insidious agitation of Count Louis should make King Edward apprehensive.

When in June the situation apparently became more serious — the émigrés were threatening Alost and there was trouble in the Quatuor Officia — Edward came to the conclusion that only a personal visit to Flanders could save the county from a return

[202] *Foedera*, III (1), 37.

[203] *CCR* (1343–6), pp. 569–570, 573, 588.

[204] *Foedera*, III (1), 45. For these events, see S. B. Terry, *The Financing of the Hundred Years' War, 1337–1360*, pp. 116–118; T. F. Tout, *The History of England from the Accession of Henry III to the Death of Edward III (1216–1377)*, pp. 355–358.

[205] *Foedera*, III (1), 32.   [206] *Ibid.*, p. 43.

to Philip.[207] Men were arrayed,[208] and a fleet was collected at Sandwich whither Edward went at the close of June. On July 1 he named his son Lionel regent of his realm during his absence.[209] On the 3d he delivered the great seal to the chancellor, Robert de Sadyngton,[210] and at about the ninth hour put out to sea with a fleet, according to report, of a hundred and thirty ships, and 1,030 men-at-arms and archers. On the 5th he arrived on the Zwin and lay before Sluis for a fortnight.[211] The Flemings at once went forth to meet him. On the 6th a large group of officials from Bruges went out under Gilles van Coudenbroec and returned on the 7th.[212] Van Artevelde left Ghent on the 7th and stayed with Edward apparently until the 17th.[213] Then followed the discussions in the course of which Edward presented his demands. To receive them a group composed largely of the same men who had gone out to Sluis on the 6th left Bruges on the 11th. With the exception of a few who did not return until the 14th they were back on the following day.[214] An important delegation also arrived from Ghent and returned on the 11th.[215]

[207] See Edward's words of August 3, *ibid.*, p. 55: " Et, ordinato nuper propter hoc passagio nostro supra mare, propter aliqua nova subita, quae venerunt nobis, super procinctu dicti passagii, de perditione terrae nostrae Flandriae, et quorundam alligatorum nostrorum, nisi illuc statim personaliter veniremus, illuc cum exercitu nostro, sicut necessitas exigebat transivimus, et dictam terram Flandrie (laudetur Deus) stabilivimus, ita quod nunquam fuit in fidelitate nostra magis firma."

[208] *CPR* (1343–5), p. 516.

[209] *Foedera,* III (1), 50.   [210] *CPR* (1343–5), p. 516.

[211] *Chronicon Comitum Flandrensium,* p. 216; Murimuth, p. 168; *Breve Chronicon,* pp. 9–10; cf. *Foedera,* III (1), 50.

[212] L. Gilliodts van Severen, " Jacques van Artevelde," *La Flandre,* IX (1878), 429.

[213] N. de Pauw en J. Vuylsteke, *Rekeningen der Stad Gent,* II, 391: " Item Jacop van Aertevelde voer up den zelven tijt ter Sluus waerd an onsen heere den coninc van Vrankerike ende van Ingelant, die doe int Zwen commen was, omme hem te dankene ende te willecommene dat hij ant land commen was. . . ."

[214] L. Gilliodts van Severen, " Jacques van Artevelde," *La Flandre,* IX (1878), 429–430.

[215] N. de Pauw en J. Vuylsteke, *Rekeningen der Stad Gent,* II, 392: " Item scepenen der Jan van der Vloet, der Lievin van Waes, der Pieter van den Hovene, ende met hem meester Jan uten Hove, der Willem de Boomere,Willem van Vaernewijc, Joes Aper ende Augustijn, der ontfanghers cleerc, voeren smaendages 11 daghe in hoymaend ter Sluus waert daer Jacop van Aertevelde was omme daer te hoorne ons heeren sconincx begheerte, ende waren ute 2 daghe met 21 paerden. . . ."

Edward did not want Count Louis to return to Flanders unless he would recognize him as true king of France and perform his feudal obligations.[216] He requested that the Flemings should have nothing to do with him unless he would comply with this condition.[217] This was accepted with alacrity, for when the deputies of Ghent arrived with the demand on the 12th, an imposing delegation, composed of two scabini, Lievin de Waes and Lievin Everbout, the captain, William van Vaernewijc, the three clerks of the scabini, John uten Hove, William de Bomere, and John van Lovelde, and representatives from the guilds went forth to Sluis for the purpose of affixing the proper seals upon the document.[218] Little is heard of Ypres, but her delegates shared, as well as those of Bruges and Ghent, in the negotiations on the Zwin. This is clear from the fact that the document drawn up on the 19th, of which the only example — that of Bruges — which is known to be extant, bears on its *verso* the statement in contemporary handwriting that a similar charter was delivered to the magistrates of Ypres.[219] In fact, the three towns were fully determined to have nothing to do with Count Louis. On the 16th and 17th deputies from Ghent were at Sluis to discuss a letter which had been received from him.[220] Nothing can be learned of its contents, but it may be assumed that it met with no favor. Philip also sent letters, and the messengers bearing them were apprehended by the men of Bruges.[221]

---

[216] *Chronicon Comitum Flandrensium*, p. 216; Murimuth, p. 170.

[217] N. de Pauw, *L'Assassinat d'Artevelde et l'Instruction de ce Crime* (Gand, 1905), p. 26. The nature of the request can be ascertained from the document of July 19 drawn up at Sluis.

[218] N. de Pauw en J. Vuylsteke, *Rekeningen der Stad Gent*, II, 392: ". . . ende deze voeren omme deselve bederve alse upt last van der bezeghelinghen die onse heere de coninc begheerde, thaerre theere dat dese achterste zome ute waren 2 daghe ende zome 3 daghe met 56 paerden, in minderinghen, 238*lb*. 8*s*. 4*d*."

[219] N. de Pauw, *L'Assassinat d'Artevelde et l'Instruction de ce Crime*, p. 27 (note).

[220] N. de Pauw en J. Vuylsteke, *Rekeningen der Stad Gent*, II, 393: " Item scepenen Seghere van Beghem, Lieven Everbout, ende met hem Jan van Vinct, Jan van der Hoyen, Jan Louf, ende der Heinric de Mindere, scepenen cleerc, voeren . . . omme daer (i.e., at Sluis) te sprekene up de lettere van minen heere van Vlaendren ende omme de eendrachtechede te blivene van den ghemeenen lande, thaerre theere van 2 daghen, 48*lb*."

[221] L. Gilliodts van Severen, "Jacques van Artevelde," *La Flandre*, IX (1878), 430: " Bi Meus Denaerd ygheven den ij knapen die yleet waren

The document drawn up at Sluis on July 19 completely refutes the story found in so many of the chronicles that Edward wished to have his son, the Prince of Wales, recognized as count of Flanders.[222] It is probably impossible to trace the origin of this rumor which was quite commonly believed by van Artevelde's enemies, but it evidently arose from their inability to understand his alliance with Edward which appeared to them nothing less than treason. The Flemings could not well do without their count whose authority they needed so much to keep down the recalcitrant fullers and weavers and especially to maintain the privileges of the manufacture of cloth which the large towns claimed were constantly being infringed by the smaller ones. The policy of van Artevelde had ever been either to secure the favor of the count or to restrict his liberty of action. Louis, however, was not to be reconciled; he was an avowed enemy of the régime which had dominated Flanders now for more than seven years. By means of the new understanding with the three towns Edward hoped to prevent the county from falling into King Philip's hands.

The charter declared that Count Louis had sought to return to Flanders without doing homage to his sovereign lord, the king of France; that the magistrates of the three towns who desired to keep their obligations toward their king had promised not to enter into negotiations with him or his heirs until after he should have appeared before his lord to do homage and swear fealty; that, notwithstanding the fact that the count had borne himself unfavorably toward his king, his lord nevertheless would graciously and readily receive him as his vassal; and that, should he fail to appear, the governance of Flanders should continue as in the past few years in the hands of the present parties and in accordance with the privileges of the county. Furthermore, Edward promised to aid the three towns to maintain their authority against anyone who should seek to oppose them for making

---

ter Sluus met sconinx Philips lettren van Valoys, te haren costen, xxxvjs. Van ij yvanghenen die yvaerd waren van der Sluus tote onsen here den coninc met lettren comende vanden coninc Philips jn contrarie den coninc van Ingheland, vlb. xs.

[222] *Chronicon Comitum Flandrensium*, p. 217; le Muisit, p. 146; *Chronographia*, II, 211; *Istore et Croniques*, II, 14; Froissart, III, 100; Villani, Col. 926.

these promises.[223]   Edward returned to Sandwich on the 26th and on August 3 expressed his satisfaction with these results in letters addressed to his sheriffs. He declared that his power was stabilized in Flanders and that it was much stronger than ever before.[224]

The murder of van Artevelde has been ascribed to the opposition aroused by the suggestion that the Prince of Wales should become count of Flanders.[225]   The error of this need hardly be pointed out. The opposition to van Artevelde's authority in Ghent certainly had nothing to do with his external policy. The real motives will probably never be known fully, but it is certain that they sprang in large part, if not entirely, from the animosities which flourished between the guilds and out of which had come the unfortunate struggle on May 2. This event brought still more to the fore the dean of the weavers, Gerard Denys, a man who was a zealous supporter of van Artevelde's policy toward Edward and Philip. It appears from the accounts of Ghent that he had played an increasingly important rôle since the sanguinary clash on the Friday Market Place.[226]   Personal feelings no doubt also entered into the opposition which came to a head while van Artevelde was in conference with Edward at Sluis. It appears that the scabini themselves were opposed to van Artevelde, for they subsequently confiscated his horses for the communal chest.[227]   The revolt began shortly after van Artevelde left Ghent, possibly because his absence made it safe for his enemies to assert themselves. Efforts were made to bring him back. The names of the men sent in the first deputation to Sluis are not recorded.[228]   The captain John de Scoutheete was hurriedly sent to van Artevelde. This is evident, for he returned on the same

[223] For the best text, see N. de Pauw, *L'Assassinat d'Artevelde et l'Instruction de ce Crime*, pp. 25–27.

[224] *Foedera*, III(1), 55–56 (memorandum), and letter of August 3: ". . . dictam terram Flandrie (laudetur Deus) stabilivimus, ita quod nunquam fuit in fidelitate nostra magis firma."

[225] *Chronographia*, III, 211.

[226] N. de Pauw en J. Vuylsteke, *Rekeningen der Stad Gent,* II, 406, 407, 409, 410, 411, 412, 413.

[227] *Ibid.,* p. 454 (note); N. de Pauw, *Cartulaire Historique et Généalogique des Artevelde,* p. 256.

[228] N. de Pauw en J. Vuylsteke, *Rekeningen der Stad Gent,* II, 391: ". . . de ghene die naer hem ghesent waren te paerde ende te voet ter Sluus van der stede halven omme hem te ghebringhene te Ghentward. . . ."

day.[229] On the 13th the same captain and Josse Apre were sent to him *met neerensten laste,* that is, on the most urgent business.[230] It is possible, but not entirely certain, that these last two carried summons for van Artevelde to return. Unfortunately, the positive guidance of documents stops at this point and the student must rely upon the confused reports of chroniclers who could at best report only what they heard.

John Bernier of Valenciennes appears to have received very accurate information about what took place.[231] According to his account, van Artevelde refused to return at once, but did send his attendants, a hundred in number. The men of Ghent, apparently the mob, went to his house, but found neither his wife and children, nor his gold and silver. Another account states that these had been sent to England before this,[232] which can easily be shown from the accounts of Ghent to be untrue. Catherine van Artevelde was, on the contrary, sent to Edward in England to secure settlement of the king's debts.[233] This must have taken place about the 26th, or later, for on that date Edward arrived at Sandwich. According to John Bernier the magistrates again sent two scabini as deputies to Sluis, and van Artevelde promised to be back in Ghent on Sunday before St. Mary Magdalene's Day, which would be on the 17th. Some echo of the lowering storm is reported by the chronicler Murimuth who undoubtedly received his information from persons who were in Edward's *entourage*. Very probably these had been with the king at Sluis and had some inkling of the uneasiness felt when van Artevelde returned to Ghent. Murimuth states that he was accompanied by " five hundred armed men for his safety." [234]

[229] *Ibid.,* p. 393: "Item hooftman der Jan de Scoutheete die ghesent was jeghen Jacoppe van Aertevelde doe hij eerst voer ter Sluus jeghen onsen heere den coninc, ende voer doe der Jan met 12 paerden, van eenen daghe dat hij ute was. . . ."

[230] *Ibid.,* " Item van den hooftmans Joes Aper ende der Jan de Scoutheete voeren 13 daghe in hoymaend ter Sluus an Jacoppe van Aertevelde met neerensten laste, van 2 daghen die sij ute waren. . . ."

[231] *Bourgeois de Valenciennes,* p. 199. These passages have been reprinted by N. de Pauw; *Cartulaire Historique et Généalogique des Artevelde,* pp. 248–250.

[232] Froissart, III, 101–102.

[233] N. de Pauw en J. Vuylsteke, *Rekeningen der Stad Gent,* II, 393.

[234] Murimuth, p. 170. Bernier states that he was accompanied by a guard of a hundred, see *Bourgeois de Valenciennes,* pp. 199–200.

The question at this point is complicated by the debate which has been waged about the date of van Artevelde's death.[235] A number of chroniclers place it on the evening of the 17th,[236] while the excellent abbot of St. Martin's at Tournai dates it *circa festum beate Marie Magdalene*, or July 22.[237] The passage in the accounts of Ghent hitherto invoked to combat the view that the event occurred on the 17th cannot be appealed to, for, as Napoleon de Pauw has shown, the sum allowed for messengers to and from van Artevelde on the 20th is really for a number of messengers and may very well have been allowed after his death.[238] The large amount mentioned would also convey this impression.[239] Furthermore, a late copy of the obituary of the Hospital of Our Lady of the Bijloke in Ghent relates that an annual service was celebrated for the death of the man on July 17.[240] The event did not in the least change the relations of Flanders with Edward who was on the Zwin until the 19th at the latest, and it is not at all strange that the king should not take any steps. Yet Edward returned to England profoundly moved by the event.[241]

It is not necessary to dwell upon the details which led to the sanguinary climax. When van Artevelde entered the town, he noted the unfavorable bearing of the public. In the evening Gerard Denys and a crowd of people were massed before his house on the Kalanderberg. Many of the weavers were, it appears, from the parish of St. Peter.[242] In the violence that took place van Artevelde's house was broken into, and, in order to escape

---

[235] See H. Pirenne, *Histoire de Belgique*, II (2d ed.), 128 (note).

[236] De Budt, p. 329; *Chronicon Comitum Flandrensium*, p. 216; *Breve Chronicon*, p. 10; *Istore et Croniques*, II, 13; *Bourgeois de Valenciennes*, p. 201. According to Murimuth, p. 170, he returned on the 17th and his men-at-arms were not allowed to enter.

[237] Le Muisit, pp. 146–147.

[238] N. de Pauw en J. Vuylsteke, *Rekeningen der Stad Gent*, II, 413: "Item van boden commende an Jacoppe ende weder ute ghesent, 52*lb*. 13*s*. 4*d*."

[239] N. de Pauw, *L'Assassinat d'Artevelde*, p. 29.

[240] The manuscript has, however, never been carefully studied or printed. The passage in question may be found in N. de Pauw, *Cartulaire Historique et Généalogique des Artevelde*, p. 257.

[241] Murimuth, p. 170: ". . . offensus plurimum et turbatur in Angliam rediit. . . ."

[242] *Chronicon Comitum Flandrensium*, p. 217.

the fury of the mob, he fled and sought to obtain refuge in the church of the Minorites which was situated in the Veld Straat (Rue des Champs) within the Ketel Gate, on the site now occupied by the Palace of Justice. But he was overtaken and slain.[243]

Touched by the melancholy end of this man, one of the most remarkable figures among the burghers of the Middle Ages who engaged in politics, writers have busied themselves with these events. His death has been allowed to overshadow the importance of the general political situation. His successor as captain was Gilles van Gavere,[244] a staunch advocate of his policy and a fitting associate of William van Vaernewijc and the scabini, who were reconstituted on August 15, and made no change in the political policy of the town.[245] Edward could with reason assert on August 3 that his power in Flanders was firmer than ever. He cared for an alliance with Flanders chiefly as a factor in the struggle against the Valois monarchy. The internal situation in the county concerned him but little. In his financial plight he failed to make his payments, and at the close of the official year at Ghent in August, 1345, there was a deficit of 8,303*l*. 3*s*. 9*d*.[246] As the policy of subsidizing the princes of the Low Countries and Germany was abandoned for that of maintaining a native army provided by the grants of Parliament, the former allies were important only for diplomatic purposes. Hence his debts were paid grudgingly. Even the archers stationed in Flanders were left to shift for themselves.[247] In this respect van Artevelde, who had shown such sagacity and resourcefulness in 1337 and 1338, had lately failed to evaluate properly the nature of his alliance with Edward.[248]

[243] *Ibid.*, pp. 216–217; *Bourgeois de Valenciennes*, pp. 199–200; le Muisit, pp. 146–148; de Budt, p. 329; *Chronographia*, II, 211–212; *Breve Chronicon*, p. 10; le Bel, II, 38; *Grandes Chroniques*, V, 439; Murimuth, p. 170. These passages are for the most part printed in N. de Pauw, *Cartulaire Historique et Généalogique des Artevelde*, pp. 246–256. For van Artevelde's house on the Kalanderberg, see G. Des Marez, *Étude sur la Propriété Foncière dans les Villes du Moyen Âge*, p. 387.

[244] N. de Pauw en J. Vuylsteke, *Rekeningen der Stad Gent*, II, 474.

[245] *Ibid.*, pp. 443–444.

[246] *Ibid.*, p. 440.

[247] *Ibid.*, pp. 393–394.

[248] H. Pirenne, "La Seule Lettre Connue de Jacques van Artevelde," *Bulletin de la Société d'Histoire et d'Archéologie de Gand*, XI (1903), 106–108.

Was John, duke of Brabant, in any way implicated in the murder of van Artevelde? It has often been assumed that he was in some degree guilty, but an examination of the sources leaves the matter far from convincing. Assertions of his guilt are not found in any contemporary chronicler whose words carry much authority as, for example, Hocsem, le Bel, Boendale, le Muisit, and Bernier. Nor do the Flemish compilations of de Budt and that known as the *Chronicon Comitum Flandrensium* mention the duke in connection with the murder. The statement of Froissart that the duke inspired the dean of the weavers against van Artevelde appears only in the last version of his chronicle prepared at least a half century after the event. Its worthlessness is clearly revealed by the chronicler's gross inaccuracies in recounting the events of the summer of 1345. He states that the young Count Louis, who really succeeded his father as count after the battle of Crécy, was held in duress by van Artevelde in 1345, an event which took place in the spring of 1347.

Froissart's statement that van Artevelde stood in the way of the marriage of the duke's daughter Marguerite (betrothed since the summer of 1339 to one of King Edward's sons) to Count Louis' heir apparent, Louis, can also be dismissed.[249] The chronicler is evidently thinking of the effort of the Flemish towns to control the youth in the spring of 1347 and to force him to accept Edward's daughter. Definite intimation of the proposed marriage of Marguerite and Louis is not to be found until November 26, 1345, when Count Louis appointed representatives to negotiate the matter with the duke.[250] It is possible that the proposal was first made when the count was at Brussels. On July 15 Louis ordered the seignior of St. Venant, the dean of Bruges, and the seignior of le Vichte to go to King Philip and discuss with him something which his representatives and those of Clement VI had in mind " touching our honor and estate." [251] These words are vague enough, but it is possible and probable that the pope was suggesting a matrimonial connection between Flanders and Brabant, especially in view of the fact that Clement had in the

[249] Froissart, III, 317.
[250] *Archives du Département du Nord,* Lille, No. B416 (7,517).
[251] *Ibid.,* No. 3271 (7,506).

past shown great interest in the proposed marriage of the youthful Louis. From the point of view of the pope such a union would go far to establish quiet in the Low Countries. Even if this supposition is not correct, the proposal was nevertheless most likely made in the summer or autumn of 1345. But this would not leave sufficient time for van Artevelde to interfere in the plans for the marriage. Furthermore, the sources do not make any mention of any such opposition.

Villani states that the duke had agreed to help Count Louis to return to Flanders with armed forces. But this chronicler is not at all certain as to the duke's complicity which is cited as only one of several possible explanations of van Artevelde's death.[252] Perhaps the association of Duke John's name with this event is a slight indication of the fact that he was beginning to seek a reconciliation with Philip or, at least, to give a new direction to his policy. It thus appears that the story of the duke's guilt, which is drawn directly from Froissart's last version, is quite valueless. Furthermore, if the duke induced Gerard Denys or others to murder van Artevelde, it can hardly have been to secure a more favorable attitude in Flanders toward Philip and Count Louis, for the dean of the weavers was himself a most determined advocate of the Plantagenet alliance.

[252] Villani, Col. 926: ". . . e per quello sospetto preso o per l'arroganza del detto Giacomo o per operazione del duca di Brabante, certi della comune di Guante levarono la terre a romore, e corsone e combatterono e assalirono alle case il detto Giacomo d'Artevello. . . ."

CHAPTER XIV

THE ECLIPSE OF ENGLISH DIPLOMACY (1345–1347)

I. John, Duke of Brabant, Allies with Philip, King of France (Autumn, 1345)

WHILE King Edward was at Sluis arranging the treaty with the three towns of Flanders, Louis, count of Flanders, planned aggressive action. He had sent troops against the Flemish border in the west, and the magistrates had since June taken the precaution to strengthen the guard at Cassel.[1] The policy of the duke of Brabant was to extract the greatest possible profit from the needs of King Philip and Count Louis rather than to have the Flemings return to their former allegiance as speedily as possible. He managed to appear a loyal ally in the eyes of the Flemings. Within one month after the murder of van Artevelde he assumed the rôle of mediator in the difficulties which suddenly became worse at the close of July. This would not have been easy if it had been known that he was plotting the destruction of those who were eager adherents to the English alliance.

Opposition to the domination of Bruges in the affairs of Aardenburg led to difficulties there in July, and on August 18 the scabini of Bruges were obliged to send some troops to restore order.[2] There also was opposition at Axel and Hulst, and Count

---

[1] *Istore et Croniques,* II, 9 (note 3); N. de Pauw en J. Vuylsteke, *Rekeningen der Stad Gent,* II, 425–426.

[2] L. Gilliodts van Severen, "Jacques van Artevelde," *La Flandre.* IX (1878), 431–432.

Louis, deeming this a favorable opportunity to undertake an aggressive movement with Dendermonde as a center, sent some of his retainers under Floris de Brugdam and Francis Vilain to strengthen the opponents of Ghent who were still numerous in the Quatuor Officia.[3] The captains and scabini responded with alacrity and sent a force of men to Hulst and Axel. In the latter place they came in contact with the forces of de Brugdam and Vilain, cut them to pieces, and put them to flight.[4] Dendermonde became the vital point of resistance. Count Louis' followers had been received in some numbers within the walls, and the magistrates had placed all manner of obstacles in the Schelde and the Dender in order to stop commercial activity on its waters and especially to ruin the trade of Ghent, since its chief contact with the sea was by means of the river which flowed under the walls of Dendermonde.[5] On August 4 the scabini called forth the fighting forces of Ghent, and on the two following days a large number of them marched out with all the warlike equipment necessary to storm the recalcitrant town. There were no less than 6,996 men from the weavers alone, to whom of course must be added those from the fullers and the lesser crafts, and the more professional white-hoods. The total cost of this expedition and of that against Alost was 56,029*l*. 3*s*. 10*d*. which forced the scabini to borrow money in large sums from money-lenders at Brussels and Bruges.[6] A large force led by Sohier de Courtrai came from Bruges to reinforce their efforts.[7] Another group was sent by Ypres. The combined forces stormed the town. The defenders, although reinforced by the adherents of the count, were far outnumbered and could not, in spite of their very strong defences, withstand the assault, and the town was soon in the hands of the enemy.[8]

[3] *Chronicon Comitum Flandrensium*, p. 217; *Breve Chronicon*, p. 10.

[4] *Chronicon Comitum Flandrensium*, p. 217; N. de Pauw en J. Vuylsteke, *Rekeningen der Stad Gent*, II, 437–438.

[5] G. Espinas et H. Pirenne, *Recueil des Documents relatifs à l'Histoire de l'Industrie Drapière en Flandre*, III, 375.

[6] N. de Pauw en J. Vuylsteke, *Rekeningen der Stad Gent*, II, 438–439, 520–527.

[7] L. Gilliodts van Severen, "Jacques van Artevelde," *La Flandre*, IX (1878), 432–434. The cost of this expedition was 3,596*l*. 18*s*. 4*d*. They were out twenty-seven days during which time they also were required to visit Sluis where there was some resistance.

[8] *Chronicon Comitum Flandrensium*, p. 217; de Budt, p. 239. For

The magistrates thereupon surrendered at the advice of the duke of Brabant who now appeared as mediator.[9] The three towns of Flanders professed great confidence in him,[10] but apparently demanded that all those who had been banished or who had left Flanders of their own accord to aid Dendermonde or who were known as émigrés should henceforth not be allowed to stay in the town or in Brabant and should be regarded as enemies by the duke.[11]   On the 9th Duke John named as arbiters, John van Wicvliet, seignior of Blaersveld, Gilles van Quaderebbe, seignior of Berg, Gerard vander Heyden, his sheriff (*drossart*), John van Meldert, a knight, and John, provost of Arnhem, his councillor.[12] On the 10th the corporation of Dendermonde solemnly declared its readiness to abide by the duke's decision in all the points contested by Ghent and Flanders. As further guarantee of this promise, Engergier, seignior of Amboise and of Dendermonde, and Count Louis also affixed their seals.[13] At the same time the three towns bound themselves to submit to the duke's decision.[14] Thereupon the duke, the towns of Louvain, Brussels, and Antwerp, and the arbiters promised to pronounce decision before the troops should leave their positions in front of Dendermonde and declared that in the future they would treat the émigrés and other adherents of the count as their own enemies.[15]

Then followed the duke's pronouncement. Each party was to surrender its prisoners, and all promises that had been made were to be cancelled. The men of Dendermonde were required to compensate the merchants for all damages inflicted except those losses which had been occasioned by fire or in combat, and

---

this episode, see also M. Heins, " Gand contre Termonde. Épisode de l'Histoire industrielle des Flandres au XIVᵉ Siècle," *Annales du Cercle Archéologique de Termonde,* 2d Ser., VI (1895), 69–108.

[9] *Chronicon Comitum Flandrensium,* p. 217: " Redidit enim se ville de consilio ducis Brabantie qui mediatorem se faciebat in hoc facto sub certis pactionibus et intromissi stipendiarii pacifice recesserunt." See also de Budt, p. 329; *Breve Chronicon,* p. 10.

[10] G. Espinas et H. Pirenne: *Recueil des Documents relatifs à l'Industrie Drapière en Flandre,* III, 369; " . . . aensiende ende merkende de grote jonste, trouwe, ende dueght, die wij vonden hebben ende vinden talre tijt tonswart in eenen wel hoghgen wel edelen ende moghenden prince, here Janne, bi der gracien Ons Heeren, hertoghe van Lottier, van Brabant, ende van Lymborgh. . . ."

[11] *Ibid.,* pp. 370–371.

[12] *Ibid.,* pp. 366–367.

[13] *Ibid.,* pp. 367–369.

[14] *Ibid.,* pp. 369–370.

[15] *Ibid.,* pp. 370–371.

all such compensation was to be approved by the duke and the three towns of Flanders or their deputies. Three great permanent breaches, each forty feet wide, were to be made within a fortnight in the walls which faced the three towns. All obstacles to navigation which the burghers had placed in the Schelde and in the Dender were to be removed at once. The decisions of the scabini and the deans of Ghent, which had been given on March 5, regarding the manufacture of cloth in Dendermonde, were to be fully observed. All émigrés and banished parties and those who had only recently joined the disgruntled followers of the count were to be kept out of Dendermonde and also out of Brabant. One of the most prominent of these persons, and undoubtedly the chief abettor of the resistance, Henry vanden Wijngaarden, was specifically forbidden ever to appear again in Brabant, Flanders, or Dendermonde. As the people of Dendermonde had violated their pledge of loyalty toward the three towns, they were required to promise under oath that they would abide by the terms contained in the document and would give hostages, eight to the duke and eight to each of the three towns, whose expenses were to be paid by the town and who were not to return until each of these provisions should be completely carried out. And, finally, a fine of a thousand pounds Tournois was to be paid to each of the three towns. This decision, pronounced in the cemetery at Herderchem, was thereupon read to the army of Count Louis before the town, and finally also within the town itself to the burghers who had been assembled for the purpose.[16] Thereupon the magistrates bound themselves to respect this pronouncement in the future.[17]

While Duke John was thus emphatically asserting his adherence to the convention of December 3, 1339, and supporting the three towns of Flanders in their efforts to prevent the return of the banished parties and even agreeing to keep them out of Brabant, steps were taken by him to come to an understanding with Philip of Valois. Exactly when the conversations began is impossible to ascertain, but, considering that they came to a definitive conclusion on September 17, it is safe to assume that opinions were exchanged during the entire summer and probably as early as May when Count Louis was getting ready to appear

[16] *Ibid.,* pp. 371–376. [17] *Ibid.,* pp. 375–377.

in Brabant. During the entire month of June Louis appears to have been in Brussels.[18] An unpublished document drawn up by him at that place on July 15 apparently concerns these negotiations. In it Louis appoints his councillors, the seignior of St. Venant, seneschal of Flanders, the dean of Bruges, and the seignior of le Vichte to learn what Philip wished to say to them concerning some conversations which the latter had had with Clement VI *touching our honor and our estate,* to treat with him, and even to consent to the proposals to be made.[19] While the exact nature of these conversations is not indicated, they most likely related to the marriage of Count Louis' son and heir apparent Louis and Marguerite, daughter of John, duke of Brabant. If this is correct, the project was suggested by the pope who undoubtedly thought that a union between Brabant and Flanders would help to establish peace in the Low Countries. This supposition is not entirely ungrounded, for on March 7 Clement had urged the marriage of the youthful Louis and the daughter of the king of Navarre.[20]

The sagacious duke had well calculated the favorable moment. The political needs of Philip and Count Louis were to be the occasion for settling the vexed question regarding Mechelen. William, count of Hainault, Holland, and Zeeland, had abandoned his alliance with Edward. Reginald, duke of Guelders, was too young and too much occupied with the internal difficulties of his duchy to be of any assistance to his uncle. Under these circumstances the alliance of William, margrave of Juliers, with King Edward could not be effective because of that prince's isolation. By accepting an alliance with Philip at this moment the duke of Brabant would be able to drive a sharp bargain. Realizing that such a diplomatic success would weaken Edward most seriously in the Low Countries and give him security from attacks in this quarter, Philip was willing to pay a good price. He wished to bring about a matrimonial connection between the ducal house and important members of the French nobility connected by blood with the royal family. In this way the Flemings

---

[18] N. de Pauw en J. Vuylsteke, *Rekeningen der Stad Gent,* II, 390.

[19] *Archives du Département du Nord,* Lille, No. B1, 271 (7,506).

[20] Ph. van Isacker et U. Berlière, *Lettres de Clément VI (1342–1352),* Nos. 1441–1443.

would be isolated and, with a count who was loyal to his interests, they might soon be forced to return to their allegiance. The duke's envoys, one of whom was the dean of Our Lady's church in Antwerp, met the royal delegates, the secretary, Peter de Verberia, Firmin de Coquerel, and some others at St. Germainen-Laye on September 17, and put in writing the points agreed upon in the previous negotiations.[21]

A definitive alliance was formed. Duke John was to go to France and request pardon of Philip for his hostile acts. The document containing the terms of the alliance was to receive the sanction by seal of the towns of Louvain, Brussels, Antwerp, 's-Hertogenbosch, Tirlemont, Nivelles, Leeuw, and others. In case of peace between France and England, the subjects of Brabant were to be included in its terms and were to share in the privileges extended to the subjects of the contracting parties. The possessions at Mechelen were to be given to the duke who was to invest his son and heir apparent Henry with them and the duchy of Limburg at the time of his marriage. The duke was also to receive the lands of Dendermonde which were to be given as dowry to his daughter Marguerite who had been betrothed to Louis, son of Louis, count of Flanders. The duke's second son Godefroid was to receive as wife a daughter of the duke of Bourbon or of the prince of Tarentum, and his daughter Marie was to become the wife of the eldest son of Philip, king of Navarre, or of the count of Alençon. Henry of Brabant was to receive as wife the eldest daughter of the count. All three were to be sent to France to be brought up with the children of the duke of Normandy. Philip promised Duke John 266,000 Florentine florins, of which 66,000 were given without condition and the remainder was to be used to purchase incomes in land to be held in fee of the French crown. A sum of 6,000*l*. Parisian in land was promised to the daughter of the duke of Normandy, or instead an annual income of 12,000 Florentine florins. Should Henry die before he could marry the daughter of the duke of Normandy, his brother Godefroid should assume this obligation. Since these children were related within the prohibited degrees Philip agreed to pay the expenses of securing the necessary dispensations from the pope. And, finally, those who had been banished

[21] A. Verkooren, *Inventaire, Brabant*, II, 145.

by the king or duke were to return to their homes, and reciprocal commercial advantages were granted.[22]

In regard to the Flemings it was decided that the duke's alliance with them and with Hainault was to remain in force, but only to serve for defensive purposes. But Duke John was to repudiate it as soon as opportunity presented itself and in such a way as would not disgrace him. This was to be formally promised by a document bearing the seals of twenty-four notables of Brabant and of the duke's council and of six men from each of the towns of Louvain, Brussels, and Antwerp. All these were to swear that the duke would break his alliance with the Flemings. Furthermore, Duke John was to aid in reducing these rebels to obedience with a force of a hundred men-at-arms, and a thousand foot at his own expense. These and other points in the document were to be further discussed at St. Quentin on November 1.[23]

It is impossible to ascertain to what extent the Flemings were acquainted with these negotiations. The terms may have been kept secret for the time being. They were willing to have Count Louis return, but only on certain conditions, and probably were not displeased with the prospect of having young Louis take as his wife Marguerite, daughter of their ally, John, duke of Brabant. At any rate there is no hint of any change in the relations between the duke and the three towns during the next year. There was a meeting of the delegates of Flanders and Brabant at Alost on November 10. Apparently the situation in Dendermonde was discussed, for a few days later Josse Rase was sent to the duke in Brabant when at about the same time a large delegation was sent to Dendermonde. On December 15 there was a meeting of the delegates of the three towns and those of Brabant in Brussels.[24] Evidently the duke meant to subserve the interests of his towns and probably never seriously intended to aid Philip in the reduction of the Flemings.

---

[22] A. Verkooren, *Inventaire, Brabant,* II, 143–145.
[23] *Ibid.,* p. 145. The analysis is defective.
[24] N. de Pauw en J. Vuylsteke, *Rekeningen der Stad Gent,* II, 485–486.

II. EDWARD III AND THE SUCCESSION IN HAINAULT, HOLLAND, AND ZEELAND (1345–1346)

THE death of Count William in September, 1345, introduced a serious crisis into the affairs of Hainault, Holland, and Zeeland. The uncertainties of succession in medieval times were always dangerous for the repose of the country, for they gave opportunity for ambitious parties to endeavor to extend their power. Especially grave under these circumstances was the hostility in Utrecht. The truce which had been arranged on July 23, 1345, was to come to an end on November 11, and Bishop John van Arkel was making use of the interim to reduce those who had joined with Count William in the siege of the episcopal city. Warlike preparations were soon made and the castle at Vredeland was strengthened. There was great fear of invasion in Amstelland and in the lands around Ysselstein, and in those of the bishop there was a great deal of trouble with those hostile vassals who had favored the count of Holland. Not until January and February, however, did hostilities break out. The bailiff of Amstelland and the people of Gooiland were forced to take active measures for defence, and Eemsland was ravaged. In March Ysselstein was burned.[25] Not until July 13, 1346, was a two-year truce arranged between the bishop, Countess Margaret, and John of Hainault.[26]

But the peace and unity of the three counties were much more seriously endangered by the debate which now ensued regarding the succession. Count William had left no heirs of his body. The nearest kin were his sisters, Margaret, wife of Lewis the Bavarian, Philippa, wife of Edward, king of England, and Johanna, wife of William, margrave of Juliers. His lands were all fiefs of the empire, and the emperor could claim that Holland and Zeeland had fallen vacant and hence should revert to the sovereign. Female succession in Hainault was a settled matter. On the other hand, it might be urged that the patrimony of the

[25] H. G. Hamaker, *Rekeningen der Grafelijkheid van Holland onder het Henegouwsche Huis*, I, 403, 425, 447, 448, 449; see also W. A. Waller Zeper, *Jan van Henegouwen, Heer van Beaumont*, pp. 273–274.

[26] Cf. W. A. Waller Zeper, *Jan van Henegouwen, Heer van Beaumont*, Bijlage II, p. 419.

house of Avesnes should be partitioned among the three sisters.
This was apparently the view entertained by Edward who on
October 20 gave full powers to John of Hainault, John de Levedale of Brabant, William Stury, and Ivo de Clinton to collect all
incomes, receive the homage and oath of vassals, appoint officials,
and maintain in every way Philippa's rights in the county of
Zeeland " and parts adjacent." Another order was sent to the
clergy, nobility, burgomasters, scabini, and all subjects to co-
operate with them.[27] Ivo de Clinton's account shows that he
left England on the following day and that he was busy with
his associates in securing a recognition of Philippa's claims.[28]

John of Hainault, however, did not care to serve Edward's
interests at any cost, and, as a nobleman interested in the welfare
of Holland and Zeeland where he had extensive possessions,[29]
disregarded the commission. This was the beginning, it appears,
of a different attitude on his part toward Edward. His failure
to act in Philippa's behalf is undoubtedly the reason why Edward omitted his name from the group of plenipotentiaries named
on December 27 to pursue her rights. These were John de Levedale, William Stury, Ivo de Clinton, Otto, seignior of Cuyk, Roger
de Beauchamp, and Wulfard de Ghistelles. The properties were
now described as " lying in Hainault, Holland, Zeeland, Friesland,
and in other places." [30] John de Levedale appears to have been
active in this matter, for on June 1 of the following year Edward
granted him an annuity of a hundred marks payable out of the
issues of the customs at London.[31] The seignior of Cuyk appears
to have done nothing. As councillor of the duke of Brabant, it
was probably best for him not to labor in Edward's behalf at
the moment when his master was negotiating with Philip of Valois
for a solution of the status of Mechelen. Hence, when Edward
perceived that nothing was to be gained from him or from John
of Hainault, new letters were issued on April 20 to Ivo de Clinton
and Adam de Shoreshull to take Philippa's lands into their pos-

[27] *Foedera,* III (1), 61.

[28] L. Mirot et E. Déprez, " Les Ambassades Anglaises pendant la
Guerre de Cent Ans," *BEC,* LIX (1898), 568.

[29] See W. A. Waller Zeper, *Jan van Henegouwen, Heer van Beaumont,*
Ch. XII, for a summary of these payments.

[30] *Foedera,* III (1) 65; *CPR* (1345–18), p. 26.

[31] *CPR* (1345–8), p. 26.

session and to treat for an alliance with the bishop of Utrecht and the nobles and other subjects of the four regions.[32] It is thus apparent that Edward sought to use the bishop, who had reasons enough to be hostile to the count of Holland, and also the disgruntled nobles and other persons against John of Hainault into whose hands had fallen for the moment the supreme direction of the affairs of the four parts of the Avesnes patrimony.

Edward also maintained negotiations with the Wittelsbach family. The emperor was in a very difficult position in the empire where he had to face the perennial hostility of the Luxemburg house. Just at this moment Clement VI was preparing to drive him from his power and put in his place Charles, son of John, king of Bohemia. On January 2 he sent letters to the bishops of Liège, Cambrai, Tournai, and Utrecht urging them to be diligent in publishing the sentence of excommunication against the emperor and his supporters.[33] He dispatched his chaplain Gerald de Magnaco to them and to Jeanne, the old dowager countess of Hainault, and also to Brabant, Hainault, and adjacent parts with the intention of weakening the emperor's power.[34] On April 13 Clement pronounced the ban whereby Lewis was deprived of all legal rights as emperor. His acts were declared null and void; even a Christian burial was to be denied him. Finally, after much preparation, the electors came together at Rense and named Charles king of the Romans.[35] But in spite of all their difficulties, the Wittelsbachs refused to listen to the representations of Edward regarding Philippa's claims. The English king was said to be making some preparations against Zeeland. Countess Margaret's accounts show that a messenger, Baldwin den Lodder, was sent to Flanders from Middelburg on July 2, in order to learn something about these rumored attempts.[36]

[32] *Foedera*, III(1), 80; *CPR* (1345–8), pp. 70, 71.

[33] Ph. van Isacker et U. Berlière, *Lettres de Clément VI (1342–1352)*, No. 1761.

[34] *Ibid.*, Nos. 1762–1765.

[35] T. Lindner, *Deutsche Geschichte unter den Habsburgern und Luxemburgern (1273–1437)*, I, 468–479; K. Werunsky, *Geschichte Kaiser Karls IV*, I, 394–441.

[36] *Ms., Rijksarchief in Zeeland*, Middelburg, *Rekeningen van Jan Symons zoon van Bisanten, rentmeester van Bewesten Schelde*, No. 12, folio 33 recto: "Item, des sondaghes vor Sente Martins dach in den somer (i.e., July 2, 1346) Boudekin den Lodder ghesent in Vlaendren omme te proe-

On the 9th Heynkijn Sijs was sent to The Hague with the news that had been obtained.[37]

It is interesting to note that at this moment Edward exchanged letters with King Charles. On October 12 he replied to the latter's request, which was presented by his secretary, that a truce should be arranged with Philip and declared that it was impossible to do so because troops had already been sent to Gascony and Brittany.[38] Meanwhile, the suspense in Zeeland, so clearly revealed in the countess' accounts for July,[39] continued. In October this had not at all grown less, for it was reported toward the close of the month that a fleet of more than two hundred English ships had arrived on the Zwin in order to attack Zeeland. A messenger was sent to Sluis, Damme, and Bruges to observe their actions, and to Ghent and from there to report the matter to the countess who at that moment was at Ath in Hainault.[40] The rumor was apparently unfounded because no

---

vene omme des coninxs staet van Engheland also als mijn vrouwe die keyserinne den rentmeester bevolen hadde hem ghegheven te terghelde xvi ghesellen die maken xvis. turn."

[37] *Ibid.*: " Item, des sondaghes na Sente Martijns dach in den somer (i.e. July 9, 1346) Heynkijn Sijs ghesend tot miere vrouwen der keyserinne in die Haghe als miere vrouwen den staet te laten weten van den coninc van Engheland hem ghegheven te terghelde: i scilt die maect xxiijs. turn."

[38] J. F. Boehmer, *Die Regesten des Kaiserreichs unter Karl IV (1346–1378)*, p. 525.

[39] *Ms., Rijksarchief in Zeeland,* Middelburg, *Rekeningen van Jan Symons zoon van Bisanten, rentmeester van Bewesten Schelde,* No. 12, folio 33 recto: " Item, up Sente Margrieten dach (July 20) Henric Alaerde den pape ghesend in Vlaendren omme te vernemene van des coninxs state van Engheland ende hi liet den rentemeester weten ende die rentmeester liet vord weten miere vrouwe der keyserinne te coste ende te terghelde ghegheven iiij*l.* turn."

" Item, des dinxendaghes na Sente Margrieten dach (July 25, 1346) Jan Loys ghesend tot miere vrouwen der keyserinne in die Haghe met brieven van den staet van den coninc van Engheland ende van alrehande anderen saken daer tslands orbare anelach hem ghegheven te terghelde enen scild die maect xxiiijs. turn," and *ibid.,* folio 33 verso: " Item des vridaghes na Sente Jacops dach (July 28, 1345) Boudekin den Lodder ghesend ute Vlaendren tot miere vrouwen der keyserinne in die Haghe met alsuulken vernemene als die rentmeester vernomen hadde van des coninxs state van Engheland hem ghegheven te terghelde enen scilt die maket xxiiijs. t."

[40] *Ibid.,* folio 34 recto: " Item des maendaghes vor Sente Symons ende Iuden dach (October 23, 1346) so voer Jan Symoens sone tot mire vrouwen der keyserinnen tot Aet omme miere vrouwen te sprekene vanden parlemente van Duvenee. Daer vereeschede Jan Symons sone te Biervliet dat die Enghelse waren comen int tSwin wel met cc scepen met ghewapende

proof can be found that these ships were ever sent out, and, if they did arrive in the Zwin, they attempted nothing. The rumor undoubtedly reveals the anxiety in the minds of the countess' officials in Zeeland.

William, margrave of Juliers, had perhaps as good a claim to a share of the Avesnes possessions as Philippa, but appears to have made no effort whatever at this moment to claim his portion. This was undoubtedly because he wished to secure definitive possession of the county of Ravensburg and could not afford to antagonize the emperor. On August 10, 1346, Lewis the Bavarian granted the investiture of the fief to Gerard, the margrave's son.[41] Since William of Juliers thus did not oppose the rights of Margaret, Edward had on December 27 of the previous year appointed him with Otto, seignior of Cuyk, Roger de Beauchamp, John de Levedale, William Stury, Wulfard de Ghistelles, and Ivo de Clinton to treat with the emperor for an alliance.[42] Nothing is said in these instructions about the disputed succession, but that they intended to discuss it is quite certain. Edward had a special envoy, Edward Chamberlain, at Düren and Juliers in January who also visited Brussels. Ivo de Clinton's expense account of his journey to Juliers and Bavaria covered the period from December 24 to March 21.[43]

It is interesting to note that while Philip was eager to have a member of the Luxemburg house seated on the imperial throne and helped to bring about Charles' election,[44] he did not hesitate to do what he could to advance the rights of his niece Margaret in Hainault, Holland, and Zeeland.[45] He apparently reasoned

volke omme tlant van Zeeland te bestokene daer hi sende enen bode met enen perde ter Sluus ten Damme ende te Brugghe omme te provene wes die Enghelse wille hadden te doene ende die bode die verbeide Jan Symons sone te Ghent omme miere vrouwen te ondersegghene in die selve reyse tstaen daer af, dat coste ij scilde die maken xlviij*s*. t."

[41] T. Lacomblet, *Urkundenbuch für die Geschichte des Niederrheins,* III, 352. [42] *Foedera,* Vol. III (1), p. 65.

[43] L. Mirot et E. Déprez, " Les Ambassades Anglaises pendant la Guerre de Cent Ans," *BEC,* LIX (1898), 568.

[44] *Bourgeois de Valenciennes,* p. 208; H. Moranvillé, " Extraits de Journaux du Trésor," *BEC,* XLIX (1888), 175; J. Viard, *Journaux du Trésor de Philippe VI de Valois,* p. 69.

[45] Nuwenburg, p. 201: " Promovit autem rex Francie imperatricem, neptem suam, nonforsan amore principis, set quia terras per Anglum timuit occupari."

that this extension of the Wittelsbach *hausmacht* in these lands would be less dangerous for him than to let some of them fall into Edward's hands. John of Hainault and the dowager countess Jeanne were convinced that Margaret's authority alone could prevent disaster.[46] The sentiment of the people of Hainault, Holland, and Zeeland was, however, not very definite. Lewis the Bavarian had sent to the Low Countries a Magister Otto who made an extensive report of what he saw. It was rumored that Edward was preparing a fleet to seize Zeeland where the people were said to be little inclined to defend the county against him in the absence of a prince. Probably Edward counted upon the friendship of the Zeelanders for the English to accomplish his designs. Possibly the winter would prevent him from making the attempt, but the uncertainty produced great uneasiness. The bishop of Utrecht was planning an invasion of Holland. There was no justice in the land, as many spurned the tribunals. Everywhere there was a desire for a prince, and, according to Lewis' representative, Margaret's arrival was expected daily. Otto also suggested that she should be invested with these lands by the emperor before her departure and that she should receive the title of margravine of Hainault, Holland, Zeeland, and Lady of East and West Friesland.[47]

John of Hainault had left the northern countries in November and was in Hainault at Aymeries on the 25th,[48] and in Valenciennes on December 1.[49] One reason for this visit to Hainault undoubtedly was to be present at the final ceremonies in honor of his nephew whose body had been brought from Bloemkamp in Friesland to be interred in the church of the Friars Minor.[50] This solemn occasion, which was certainly as much of a family matter with Philip as with John of Hainault, presented an excellent opportunity to discuss matters with him and others who would be present as a matter of course, and the royal secretary,

---

[46] *Bourgeois de Valenciennes,* p. 205.

[47] L. Ph. C. van den Bergh, *Gedenstukken tot Opheldering der Nederlandsche Geschiedenis,* I, 160–161. The document is not dated, but as the bishop of Utrecht is spoken of as planning to invade Holland it should be dated before he actually did do so in January. Most likely it was written in December, 1345.

[48] L. Devillers, *Cartulaire,* I, 251.

[49] A. Verkooren, *Inventaire, Brabant,* II, 149–159.

[50] L. Devillers, *Cartulaire,* I, 255 (note 7).

Peter de Verberia, was entrusted with the task.[51] It also drew Philip into close contact with the dowager countess and it was apparently at this time that the two, urged on by the king,[52] actively labored to bring the empress to the Low Countries.[53]

In Hainault the sentiment of a very considerable group of the people was also favorable to her. In February a memoir was drawn up apparently at the time when Magister Otto wrote to the emperor and undoubtedly with the knowledge or coöperation of John of Hainault and his nobles. It set forth the reasons why Margaret should return. Representatives of the towns and of the nobility (*li boines gens des pays*) of Hainault, Holland, and Zeeland were to meet on the morrow of Candlemas and it was deemed highly advisable that Margaret should be present. It would then be decided who should by right be entitled to the succession. The memoir declared that the loyal followers of Count William, father of Margaret, desired to remain faithful to her also, and that until her arrival, which, it was hoped, would be soon, they would be greatly troubled. The numerous debts of the late count had to be paid and many of the nobles had pledged themselves heavily. Only her speedy arrival could soothe the troubled state of mind. They were stricken with grief by the loss of many of the more important men of the three counties and were much troubled by the menacing attitude of John van Arkel, bishop of Utrecht, and by the reports that Edward was fitting out a large fleet to vindicate his rights. Since William's death a number of seigniories, as, for example, that

[51] J. Viard, *Journaux du Trésor de Philippe VI de Valois,* p. 49: " Cepimus super Regem sic: Magister Petrus de Verberia, clericus et secretarius domini Regis, pro expensis suis eundo apud Valencenas, mense Novembris ultimo, ad funeralia comitis Hanonie ultimo defuncti, pro loquendo cum plurimis personis, ex parte domini Regis, que ibidem esse debebant, morando ibidem et redeundo, per XV dies cum VII equis, 34*s.* p. per diem ultra vadia sua, 25*l.* 10*s.* p. per cedulam curie (*sub* Dec. 19, 1345).

[52] For the pension which the dowager countess received from Philip, see *ibid.,* p. 42: " Domina Johanna de Vallesio, soror domini Regis et quondam comitissa Hanonie, nuncque monialis apud Fontenelles, pro dono sibi semel facto per dominum Regem de gratia speciali, 100 scut. auri, quodlibet pro 13*s.* 4*d.* p., valent 666*l.* 13*s.* 4*d.,* etc. (*sub* June 30, 1345).

[53] *Bourgeois de Valenciennes,* p. 205. It has been impossible to find a document containing any trace of information concerning the truce which, according to the terms of June 8, 1343, was to last until Michaelmas, 1346. Devillers apparently nowhere makes any reference to this, nor are there any charters in the archives at Mons or Paris relating to a settlement.

of Altena, had reverted to the count and these were not taken care of for fear of starting trouble. Those which William had sold for cash money to nobles could not be taken over by their rightful owners because of the opposition of the families concerned. And, finally, serious contentions were breeding in Holland and Zeeland, and at Zierikzee and Dordrecht there had been actual violence.[54]

The result of these activities was that the emperor paid no attention to Edward's representations and transferred the title to all of these lands to his wife Margaret, eldest heiress of the house of Avesnes. On January 15 at Nuremburg Lewis officially granted to his wife the four lands and promised to make no changes or separate them without her consent.[55] What happened on the morrow of Candlemas and where the delegates from the three counties met is unknown. Most likely it was at Geertruidenberg, the customary place. Margaret and her youngest son left Bavaria and travelled in the depth of winter by way of Lorraine and France. She was accompanied by two German counts and clerks to serve as councillors, besides many knights and esquires.[56] On March 14 she was in Mons where she swore to maintain the privileges of the town.[57] At Valenciennes on the 23d she was received with every mark of courtesy. The officials performed homage for the town before the provost, Alard de Gardin,[58] then swore fealty in the church of St. Jean, after which, as was the custom with her predecessors, she went to the count's hall.[59] On the 30th she was at Lessines,[60] and passed into Brabant on Sunday, April 2,[61] and by way of Brussels and Mechelen, where she halted on the 6th,[62] into Zeeland where she was at Middelburg on the 14th.[63] On the 30th she

[54] L. Devillers, *Cartulaire*, I, 254–256. Devillers assigns this charter to February, and Alphonse Wauters, *Table Chronologique*, X, 202, to February 3 (the morrow of Candlemas). But there is no foundation for this.

[55] *Bourgeois de Valenciennes*, p. 205; Nuwenburg, p. 201; Beka, p. 119.

[56] F. van Mieris, *Groot Charterboek*, II, 702, 703.

[57] Nuwenburg, p. 201; *Bourgeois de Valenciennes*, pp. 206–208, 242.

[58] L. Devillers, *Cartulaire*, I, 257–259.

[59] *Ibid.*, p. 259; *Bourgeois de Valenciennes*, pp. 206, 207.

[60] L. Devillers, *Cartulaire*, I, 260, 261.

[61] *Bourgeois de Valenciennes*, p. 207.

[62] J. C. de Jonge, *Verhandeling over den Oorsprong der Hoeksche en Kabbeljaauwsche Twisten*, p. 56.

[63] Nuwenburg, p. 201: *Bourgeois de Valenciennes*, p. 207; F. van Mieris, *Groot Charterboek*, II, 705, 706.

was at Dordrecht whence she passed to The Hague. At every hand she confirmed privileges or extended old ones evidently with the desire to ingratiate herself with the public and possibly to quiet the murmurs of the opposition.[64]

When the authority of Margaret was thus definitely established Edward's further pretensions were vain. From April 12 to May 18 Ivo de Clinton was in Germany,[65] and on July 25, when he appears to have been thoroughly dissatisfied with the activities of his representatives, Edward turned to Thierry, seignior of Valkenburg, and authorized him to act as arbitrator between Philippa and her sisters.[66] But Margaret's power seemed secure, especially when on June 13 she concluded a truce with the bishop of Utrecht.[67] Thus King Edward was henceforth unable to seek support among the nobility of Holland and Zeeland or from the bishop of Utrecht, the perennial enemy of the counts on the east border of Holland.

III. The Negotiations of John, Duke of Brabant, and Philip, King of France (1346)

Nothing is known about the negotiations which were to take place between the duke of Brabant and King Philip at St. Quentin on November 1, 1345. But it is certain that the king became active in executing the agreements effected at St. Germain-en-Laye. On December 28 Clement acceded to Philip's request and issued letters of dispensation whereby Duke John was released from the promises made under oath at Amiens in 1334 that his children Marie and Godefroid should marry Reginald, son of Reginald, then count of Guelders, and the daughter of the count of Juliers. On the same day other letters granted permission for the marriage of his daughter Marguerite to Louis, the youthful heir apparent of the count of Flanders.[68]

Nothing is heard of further negotiations until February 3 when

[64] F. van Mieris, *Groot Charterboek,* II, 707–718, Beka, p. 119. According to Nuwenburg, p. 201, she was not to receive any income from these lands until the debts of her brother were paid.

[65] L. Mirot et E. Déprez, " Les Ambassades Anglaises pendant la Guerre de Cent Ans," *BEC,* LIX (1898), 569.

[66] *CPR* (1345–8), p. 150; *Foedera,* III (1), 83.

[67] Beka, p. 119.

[68] A. Verkooren, *Inventaire, Brabant,* II, 159–160; Ph. van Isacker et U. Berlière. *Lettres de Clément VI (1342–1352),* Nos. 1752–1755.

Philip's envoys, Berenger de Montaud, archdeacon of Lodève, Simon de Bucey, knight, his *maître de parlement*, Peter des Essars, *maître des comptes* and royal councillor, and Peter de Verberia, the royal secretary, met Duke John's delegates. These were Henry de Jodoigne, canon of Cambrai, Henry Coke, dean of Dendermonde, John, seignior of Blaersveld, Louis, seignior of Diepenbeek, John van Corsslaer, seignior of Witten, and the duke's seneschal, Gerard vander Heyden. The conditions laid down in the Treaty of St. Germain-en-Laye were now formulated in greater detail in regard to Mechelen and Dendermonde. Louis, count of Flanders, was to receive for his rights in Mechelen the sum of 86,500 gold *regales*, to be paid of course ultimately out of Philip's treasury. The duke's son Henry was to receive these titles in fee from the church of Liège. All letters of Count Louis and Duke John regarding Mechelen, especially of course those of March 31, 1336, and March 30, 1340, were to be regarded as null and void. In regard to Dendermonde, which on September 17 had been promised as marriage portion to the duke for his daughter Marguerite, the king was bound to pay 2,000*l.*[69] On the 14th these terms were read before Philip in the hostel of the queen at Notre Dame-des-Champs near Paris and received the royal approval.[70]

Meanwhile Philip had also made his wants known to Clement in regard to Mechelen. The pope was eager to see peace established and was readily won over to Philip's representations that the surrender of these contested rights to the duke of Brabant would greatly aid the cause of peace in the Low Countries. On February 1 he issued a bull setting forth in brief outline the history of the quarrel since 1333 and stating that the whole matter could be settled by revoking the oaths of homage made at the time of the sale and giving the rights in question to Henry, heir apparent of the duke of Brabant, and to his successors, dukes of Brabant, to be held by them in fee of the church and chapter of Liège, provided that just compensation should be given. He appointed Fulco, bishop of Paris, Raymond, bishop of Thérouanne, and Hugo, bishop of Laon, with full powers to call together all the parties concerned, determine whether the dispensa-

[69] A. Verkooren, *Inventaire, Brabant,* II, 163.
[70] *Archives du Département du Nord,* Lille, No. B416 (7,522).

tion should be given, and absolve Count Louis of his oath so that the titles in question could be transferred.[71] Philip, however, preferred to have the dispensation granted without all these formalities, probably because he understood from past experience what interminable difficulties might thus be put in the way. But the pope was firmly decided to proceed only by way of inquest as he explained on March 21.[72] At the same time he begged the bishop of Liège not to oppose the proposed transfer, threatening drastic action, and informed the duke of his efforts.[73] Duke John, as well as King Philip, had sent delegates to the curia, and on the 30th ordered his envoy, the dean of the St. Nicholas' church in Antwerp, back to the curia with letters of reassuring tone.[74]

The bishops forthwith proceeded with their task and cited the bishop, dean, and chapter of Liège to appear in the great church of Laon at a stated time under threat of contumacy should they not respond, in which case they would complete the business of transferring the rights of Mechelen to Henry of Brabant. They dispatched two archdeacons to carry the summons to Liège which was to be answered within ten days.[75] On April 9 the bishop, dean, and chapter drew up an appeal to the pope and protested against the summons of the bishop on the ground that the time allowed to appear was too short, that no copy of the summons had been given them, that violent words had been addressed by the delegates to the clerk who drew up the appeal, and for other reasons.[76] The bishop and chapter then sought to procrastinate; their envoys, three canons and the chaplain, John of Rheims, requested time to consult the bishop, chapter, the dean, the towns subject to the bishop's jurisdiction, the clergy and others of the diocese of Liège, and even King Philip.[77] But the French king was alarmed by this step and sent Philip de

---

[71] J. F. Willems, *Codex Diplomaticus,* II, 461–462; Ph. van Isacker et U. Berlière, *Lettres de Clement VI (1342–1352),* No. 1786.

[72] S. Baluzius, *Vitae Paparum Avenionensium,* Vol. II, col. 692; Ph. van Isacker et U. Berlière, *Lettres de Clément VI (1342–1352),* No. 1808.

[73] Ph. van Isacker et U. Berlière, *Lettres de Clément VI (1342–1352),* Nos. 1806, 1807.

[74] *Ibid.,* No. 1813.

[75] F. J. Willems, *Codex Diplomaticus,* II, 463.

[76] S. Bormans et B. Schoolmeesters, *Cartulaire de l'Église St. Lambert de Liège,* IV, 40–41 (notes).

[77] F. J. Willems, *Codex Diplomaticus,* II, 466–467.

Tallasii and Peter de Verberia to the curia. On May 1 Clement ordered the bishops to disregard the appeal and proceed at once in accordance with his instructions of February 1.[78] Further citation to appear was fruitless, and on June 29 the bishops of Paris and Laon declared that the dispensation should be granted and that the count of Flanders could transfer his rights and titles in Mechelen to Henry of Brabant.

IV. THE RENEWAL OF FRENCH AND ENGLISH HOSTILITIES: THE BATTLE OF CRÉCY (1346–1347)

THE truce arranged at Malestroit on January 19, 1343, was to expire at Michaelmas of 1346. In spite of the pope's ardent desire to establish peace between the two monarchs, the hostility between them had not abated in the least. The truce had been repeatedly broken by both sides and in the spring of 1346 reopening of hostilities appeared certain. In reply to the rumor that Philip intended to invade England, Edward on January 20 ordered the sheriffs south of the Trent to have all men-at-arms between sixteen and sixty at Portsmouth by March 8.[79] He requested loans of considerable sums from many people on February 12. On the 27th he asked the clergy of the province of Canterbury to pray for success, celebrate masses, organize processions, and perform works of piety.[80] An unusually violent storm shattered the ships that had been collected at Portsmouth, and on March 5 the expedition had to be postponed until the first of May. The king ordered the bailiffs of a large number of towns to array troops and send their quota of men-at-arms if they had not already done so, which appears to have been the case.[81] Philip's plans to invade and conquer England, which were fantastic enough,[82] stirred the king who issued orders on April 20 for arraying 3,550 Welsh archers who were to be at Portsmouth at the appointed time.[83]

Edward's allies in the Low Countries had sadly decreased in

[78] F. J. Willems, *Codex Diplomaticus,* II, pp. 464–465; Ph. van Isacker et U. Berlière, *Lettres de Clément VI (1342–1352),* No. 1869.

[79] *Foedera,* III (1), 67.   [80] *Ibid.,* pp. 68–69, 70.

[81] *Ibid.,* pp. 71–72.

[82] See the memoir drawn up at the Bois de Vincennes, March 23, *ibid.,* p. 76.   [83] *Ibid.,* p. 79.

number since the late truce had been arranged. The duke of
Brabant had definitely, though not officially, deserted him, the
duke of Guelders was not in a position to do much, and in
Hainault, Holland, and Zeeland the succession was disputed between Queen Philippa and her eldest sister Margaret, wife of
Lewis the Bavarian. Fortunately, Edward had decided to rely
mostly upon his own troops, and thus the allies were needed not
so much for their military assistance as for their diplomatic significance. The margrave of Juliers made no effort to aid. Only
the Flemings were called upon to assume an active rôle. The
expiration of the truce meant that the war would be resumed
with them, and they began to look for help from Edward who was
eager to retain their support because he needed this country for
military aid in the coming campaign. There was a meeting
of the deputies, scabini, clerks, and representatives of the guilds,
from the three towns of Flanders at Deinze on April 8 when it
appears that the general political situation was under discussion.[84] On November 25 Pope Clement had named Annibal,
cardinal bishop of Tusculum, and Stephen, cardinal priest of
SS. John and Paul, his nuncios to negotiate peace between the
two hostile kings.[85] These ecclesiastics had requested letters of
safe-conduct to treat with the English representatives to which
Edward assented on April 20 on condition that the Flemings
should also be heard. The king named Andrew de Offord and
William de Bomere, now styled canon of Southwell, to convey
his views to them.[86]

Edward had already sent William Stury and Gilbert de Wen-
delynburgh [87] to treat with the magistrates of the three towns
concerning the coining of the so-called noble which was to be
struck in conformance with the treaties of 1340.[88] Stury's powers
were extended when on April 26 he was ordered with Andrew
de Offord [89] and John Mattaness to treat with the Flemings and

---

[84] N. de Pauw en J. Vuylsteke, *Rekeningen der Stad Gent,* II, 490:
" . . . daer de goede liede van Brugghe ende van Ypre waren, omme
raed te gadere te hebbene up vele groeter bederven van den lande. . . ."

[85] *Foedera,* III (1), 64.

[86] *Ibid.,* pp. 80–81. [87] *Ibid.,* p. 77.

[88] For this coin, cf. Pegge," Remarks on the First Noble, coined 18
Edward III, A.D. 1334; wherein a new and more rational Interpretation is
given of the Legend on the Reverse," *Archaeologia,* III (1775), 316–323;
Melsa, III, 45. [89] *Foedera,* III (1), 80.

to proceed to Arras where they were to meet the cardinals.[90]
On the 22d Edward informed the magistrates of the three towns
that at the advice of his councillors he had named William de Bomere, a clerk of Ghent attached to his wardrobe, to appear for
them before the cardinals. If they desired some other person
to represent them they might choose him.[91] On the 29th William
van Vaernewijc was sent to Bruges to speak with Stury to whom
the magistrates presented a valuable scarlet striped broadcloth
valued at 142*l.* 10*s.*[92] Then on May 6 William de Bomere and
John de Visch were sent by the magistrates of Ghent with the
deputies from Bruges and Ypres and the English envoys to take
part in the discussions with the cardinals at Arras. But the
tension between the hostile kings was so great that the meeting
could not take place, and the deputies from Ghent were warned
when they were at Ypres that it was not safe to proceed.[93] They
returned on the 15th and the anxiety caused by the situation led
the three towns to assemble at Bruges between May 27 and 29
to discuss measures for protection and consider the requests of
Edward who was, it appears, demanding coöperation in the coming campaign.[94] In response to their request made at this time,
Edward, on June 20, appointed Hugo de Hastings his lieutenant
and captain of his forces in Flanders.[95] This person arrived at
Sluis in the middle of July, for at that time William Stury notified the magistrates in Ghent of his arrival.[96]

[90] L. Mirot et E. Déprez, " Les Ambassades Anglaises pendant la
Guerre de Cent Ans," *BEC,* LIX (1898), 569. Their account submitted to
the treasury shows that they were engaged on this mission from April 26
to June 1.   [91] *Foedera,* III (1), 80–81.

[92] N. de Pauw en J. Vuylsteke, *Rekeningen der Stad Gent,* II, 472.

[93] *Ibid.,* pp. 491–492: "Item der Willem de Boomere ende Jan de
Visch, die voeren saterdachs na der elegher crucen dach te Atrecht waert
omme te vaerne sprekene ande cardenale die daer laghen, metgaders ons
heeren sconincx boden van Vrankerike ende van Ingeland ende den boden
van Brugghe ende van Ypre, omme te sprekene van vele groeten bederven
van den lande, ende als sij quamen tYpre so vonden sij zulke niemaren
dat sij daer letten moesten ende niet voert en voeren, ende ghedroech hare
raet dat sij weder keerden elc te ziere stede. . . ."

[94] *Ibid.,* p. 492: " . . . ten parlemente dat daer gheleit was omme raet
te hebbene hoe men bestellen soude ende ordineren dlant te zettene in
paise ende in rusten up tversouc dat onse heere de coninc van Vrankerike
ende Inghelant hadde doen versouken an dlant van Vlaendren. . . ."

[95] *Foedera,* III (1), 83.

[96] N. de Pauw en J. Vuylsteke, *Rekeningen der Stad Gent,* II, 510.

The duke of Brabant's tortuous schemes at this moment are revealed by his policy toward the Flemish towns. At the time when the problem of Mechelen was being solved at Philip's instigation and seven months after he had agreed with Philip to abandon the Flemings, his subjects reconfirmed by oath the allegiance of December 3, 1339. From March 11 to 18 delegates from Ghent, two scabini, William van Vaernewijc and John uten Hove, and a corresponding number from Bruges and Ypres went to Brabant to receive the oaths.[97] Thereupon the delegates from the towns of Brabant appeared in Flanders on the 20th, and William van Vaernewijc and one of the scabini accompanied them until the 26th on their visit to the towns for the same purpose.[98] From July 8 to 14 there was a meeting at Brussels where delegates from Brabant and Flanders met, but the subject of the discussions is not recorded.[99] To all appearances the best of relations existed. Peter Toene had been an accessory in the murder of a man of Ghent and had sought to evade justice by fleeing to Mechelen, but the duke willingly helped in bringing him to justice.[100]

It is instructive to note how the duke's double policy was viewed by Clement VI. In the negotiations for the dispensation for the marriage of John's daughter Marguerite to the heir apparent of Flanders, it had been argued that a union between Brabant and Flanders would materially further the prospect of peace in the Low Countries. But the pope came to doubt these arguments and possibly felt that the duke had not abandoned the alliance with the Flemings behind whose rebellion he naturally saw the influence of the king of England. For this reason, apparently, he informed the bishops of Paris, Thérouanne, and Tournai on November 30 that he had suspended the dispensation tem-

---

Hastings went to Ghent within a few weeks when the scabini gave him wine valued at 119*l.* 9*s.*, *ibid.*, p. 473.

[97] *Ibid.*, p. 489: " . . . die voeren . . . in Brabant metten goeden lieden van den steden van Vlaendren omme te vernieuwene in elke stede den eet ende de alianche die beede de lande manlic andren ghedaen ende beloeft hebben. . . ."

[98] *Ibid.*, p. 489: " . . . in de steden van Vlaendren metten goeden lieden van den steden van Brabant, omme denselven eet ende alianche te vernieuwene ghelijc dat in Brabant ghedaen was. . . ."

[99] *Ibid.*, p. 494.

[100] *Ibid.*, pp. 493, 494, 495.

porarily, and instructed them to inquire more fully into the duke's motives.[101]

At this moment John of Hainault abandoned his English friend. Edward's prestige had sadly declined, and it would have been folly to persist in a relationship which might in the future be highly deleterious. Louis, count of Flanders, was in Mons in December, 1345, whither on the 12th Ghent and Bruges sent delegates armed with letters.[102] The Flemings still desired to have him return, and on January 26 Ghent sent to Menin an important delegation of scabini, captains, among whom was William van Vaernewijc, and members of the guilds, who were accompanied by envoys from the other two towns, to discuss the terms on which Count Louis would come back.[103] Whether there was any connection between the count's presence at Mons and John of Hainault's attitude toward the English alliance is difficult to determine. The Flemings apparently thought that as Count William was dead and John of Hainault was temporarily in control of Hainault a reconfirmation of the alliance could be effected. Thus on October 20 the magistrates of Ghent sent their clerk John van Lovelde, to him in Holland.[104] John of Hainault returned to Hainault and was at Aymeries on November 25 [105] and at Valenciennes on December 1.[106] This was the occasion of the funeral of his nephew Count William,[107] when he, as has been shown above, apparently began negotiations with King Philip.[108]

Perhaps it was at this moment that Philip actively began to urge John of Hainault to abandon his old friend Edward. John was more than occupied with the troubled condition of the three counties and could, even if he had been inclined, have taken little interest in Flemish affairs. The mission on March 7, apparently sent to seek reconfirmation of the alliance, was thus futile.[109]

[101] S. Riezler, *Vatikanische Akten,* Nos. 2310, 2311.
[102] N. de Pauw en J. Vuylsteke, *Rekeningen der Stad Gent,* II, 501.
[103] *Ibid.,* pp. 487–488.
[104] *Ibid.,* p. 485.
[105] L. Devillers, *Cartulaire,* I, 251.
[106] A. Verkooren, *Inventaire, Brabant,* II, 149–150.
[107] L. Devillers, *Cartulaire,* I, 255 (note 7).
[108] J. Viard, *Journaux du Trésor de Philippe VI de Valois,* p. 49.
[109] N. de Pauw en J. Vuylsteke, *Rekeningen der Stad Gent,* III, 488.
See the excerpt from the accounts of Mons published by L. Devillers,

Unlike the duke of Brabant, John of Hainault could readily afford to abandon the Flemings. He is said to have complained that Edward did not fulfil his promises [110] which cannot, however, refer to his annuity as Froissart states,[111] because Edward had always been careful to pay this promptly.[112] It is instructive to note that the chronicler John Bernier expressly states that his change of attitude was effected through the influence of Philip, Oudart de Ham, Gondemar de Fay, seignior of Esne, a person named "Madame de Brabant" — apparently Johanna of Brabant, the widowed countess of Hainault — and his own wife, Marguerite de Nesle.[113] According to Froissart the negotiations were carried on by Louis, count of Blois, and the duke of Lorraine, and, finally, on March 21 at Beaulieu near Valenciennes in the presence of Gondemar de Fay and the seigniors of Fagnolles and of Tupigney,[114] a provisional statement was drawn up.[115]

A charter containing the definitive terms was finally drawn up on July 21, also at Beaulieu. King Philip was to pay John of Hainault at the hand of his receiver of Vermandois an annuity of 3,000*l.* Tournois, payable in three instalments, and make a gift of 20,000 gold shields. In return John was to perform homage and swear fealty. He was to receive no one in his towns or fortified places to the prejudice of Philip, serve with a hundred men at a fixed schedule of payment anywhere except in Brittany and Gascony, and even aid in defending Arleux, Crèvecoeur, and Rumilly. This was not to be construed in such a way as to require him to serve against the emperor, the count or countess of Hainault, Holland, and Zeeland, or the duke of Brabant. If, however, the count of Hainault or the duke of Brabant in person should aid the Flemings in the defense of their land, he should

---

Cartulaire, II(*Appendice*), 759: "Pour les frais Jehan Ghillart, Thieri Galon et Pérart dou Parch, à Binch, pour oyr nouvielles dou débat que les gens le conte de Flandre y avoient fait . . . xviijs." This bit of information is unfortunately not dated.

[110] *Bourgeois de Valenciennes,* p. 210.

[111] Froissart, III, 107–108, 282.

[112] *CCR* (1343–6), pp. 161, 163, 175, 210, 273, 289, 306, 309, 421, 518, 622.

[113] *Bourgeois de Valenciennes,* p. 209.

[114] Froissart, III, 107–108.

[115] S. A. Waller Zeper, *Jan van Henegouwen, Heer van Beaumont, Bijlage* II, p. 418 (analysis of B1177:7525,³ *Achives Dép. Nord.* Lille).

not be required to fight against them. Furthermore, he could
still serve the king of England, but not against Philip.[116] Thus
John of Hainault knew how to change sides and yet preserve
much of the advantages gained by his former diplomatic maneuvers. His position in the Low Countries remained as important
as it had been. The reservations regarding the Flemings
are especially instructive, for they show that while Duke John
had promised to abandon them he was still formally allied with
them as they themselves believed. The same is true of Hainault
which could not well act independently of Brabant in this matter.

The campaign of Crécy followed in July and August.[117] In
Philip's army appeared now for the first time since the opening
of the wars with Edward, John of Hainault and Philip, count of
Namur.[118] With him of course were Louis, count of Flanders,
and Adolph, bishop of Liège, who, however, was forced to return
before the battle took place at Crécy because of renewed troubles
in his lands.[119] Edward had landed at La Hogue on July 11 and
12 and hurriedly moved eastward in order to unite with the
Flemings who were kept informed of the king's movements.[120]
On the 29th the magistrates of Ghent sent for Henry of Flanders
to take charge of the communal militia,[121] and on August 2 the
troops of Ghent marched forth.[122] These joined the levies of
Bruges and Ypres, and, accompanied by English archers and
men-at-arms, moved westward toward the borders of Arras and
sought to cross the Lys at Estaires. In an attempt to cross the
bridge which was defended by some of Philip's men they were
beaten back with some loss. They then moved up the left bank

[116] Kervyn, *Oeuvres de Froissart,* XVIII, 274–282; *Bourgeois de Valenciennes,* pp. 209–210.

[117] A. Colville, *Les Premiers Valois et la Guerre de Cent Ans (1328–
1422),* pp. 58–64; W. A. Waller Zeper, *Jan van Henegouwen, Heer van
Beaumont,* pp. 285–300; T. F. Tout, *The History of England from the
Accession of Henry III to the Death of Edward III (1216–1377),* pp.
359–365.

[118] *Bourgeois de Valenciennes* pp. 224, 236.

[119] De Budt, p. 330; le Muisit, p. 164.

[120] N. de Pauw en J. Vuylsteke, *Rekeningen der Stad Gent,* II, 510.
William Stury was stationed at Sluis from whom letters were received on
the 17th.

[121] *Ibid.,* p. 495; le Muisit, p. 151, who states that agreement was made
with the English at Ghent on June 24 to coöperate with the English.

[122] *Ibid.,* pp. 533–537.

and crossed at Marville and attacked St. Venant which they took and burned.[123] Then they moved southward and on the 14th arrived before Béthune and besieged it. They laid waste the country around it. The defence under Godefridus d'Anekins was very capable while the Flemings showed themselves particularly weak. They had lost a large number of their wagons and there were serious dissensions between the militia of Bruges and the levies from the Frank of Bruges who undoubtedly resented the authority of Bruges which had brought them to Arras. A sortie was made and some of the tents of the Flemings were destroyed. Apparently disheartened by this resistance and hearing that Flanders was being invaded at Gravelines by some French troops, they retreated northward over the Lys at Marville.[124] On the 29th, three days after Edward had thoroughly defeated the French at Crécy, the militia of Ghent had returned home.[125]

Two important figures in the political life of the Low Countries lost their lives in the terrible slaughter at Crécy. John, king of Bohemia, met with a fitting close to his restless career, and his son Charles was wounded on the 27th when a group of soldiers with whom he was leaving the field was assailed by English soldiers.[126] Louis, count of Flanders, also perished and his son, the youthful Louis of Male, was slightly hurt.[127] The Flemings were greatly relieved when the report of victory came, for the rumor was current that Edward had been defeated.[128] The king moved northward by way of Montreuil-sur-Mer, unhindered by the French, and took up his position before Calais on September 4.[129] The Flemings determined to march out at once and join forces with the English. At Ghent, according to Gilles le Muisit, all men between sixteen and sixty were ordered out.[130]

[123] Le Muisit, pp. 152–153, 154; *Chronicon Comitum Flandrensium,* p. 219. Menreville in le Muisit is apparently Marville. Cf. *Chronographia,* II, 225.

[124] Le Muisit, pp. 154–155, 159; *Chronicon Comitum Flandrensium,* p. 219; *Istore et Croniques,* II, 21, 25; *Breve Chronicon,* p. 12; le Bel, II, 134; *Chronographia,* II, 225.

[125] N. de Pauw en J. Vuylsteke, *Rekeningen der Stad Gent,* II, 533–537.

[126] E. Werunsky, *Geschichte Kaiser Karls IV and Seiner Zeit,* II (Part I), 64–72.   [127] Le Muisit, p. 164.

[128] *Istore et Croniques,* II, 25.

[129] Le Muisit, p. 165; de Budt, p. 330.   [130] Le Muisit, p. 165.

By this measure more than 3,742 men were drawn from the guilds. The bowmen with their officers and esquires numbered 155. Thus the total levy, including the men to manage the engines, the scabini, and the captains with their assistants, numbered well over 4,000.[131]   On September 3 they marched out and, following the levies of Bruges and Ypres who had set out on the 1st, proceeded toward Calais under the command of Henry of Flanders.[132]

Edward did not want them in his camp before Calais. He feared that it would be impossible to maintain the peace between them and the English, apparently because some of the Flemings, according to Gilles le Muisit, might resent the fact that he was responsible for their count's death.[133] He accordingly counselled them to direct their activities elsewhere. This was agreed upon, and they turned their attention toward Thérouanne. Thus the whole region between St. Omer and Boulogne was fearfully devastated.[134] Accompanied by a body of English soldiers and archers, they moved southward. The bishop of Thérouanne had collected a force and issued forth to give them battle, but he was driven back with heavy losses and forced to retreat to St. Pol. The city and the episcopal establishment were sacked and burned.[135] Then they turned their attention to St. Omer. The Flemings at Gravelines joined them and they took up their positions before the fortified places, Ruhout and Arques. With their siege engines they captured the former. The season was advanced and, as Edward apparently felt that little more could be accomplished by them, he advised them to return to their homes. Those of Ghent were back on October 1.[136]   It is appar-

[131] N. de Pauw en J. Vuylsteke, *Rekeningen der Stad Gent,* III, 121–130. The cost of the expedition was 92,373*l.* 3*s.* 4*d.*

[132] Le Muisit, p. 165.

[133] *Ibid.,* pp. 165–167. On June 28 Edward had empowered Hugo de Hastings to settle all quarrels between Flemings and the English under his command. Cf. *Foedera,* III (2), 84.

[134] *Chronicon Comitum Flandrensium,* p. 219, *Breve Chronicon,* p. 12.

[135] Le Muisit, pp. 166–167, places the bishop's offer of battle around Exaltatio Sanctae Crucis (September 14). According to the *Chronicon Comitum Flandrensium,* pp. 219–220, the sack took place on the 20th. See *Bourgeois de Valenciennes,* p. 240, where the battle is dated the 25th, and *Istore et Croniques,* II, 58.

[136] *Chronicon Comitum Flandrensium,* pp. 219–220; *Breve Chronicon,* p. 12; *Istore et Croniques,* II, 58; N. de Pauw en J. Vuylsteke, *Rekeningen der Stad Gent,* III, 121–130.

ent that Edward's policy had undergone an important change. No longer was as much reliance to be placed upon Netherlandish and German mercenaries as upon the native English soldiery. Instead of Flanders as a *pied à terre* on the continent in his struggle with Philip, he now wished to have Calais. Military considerations no longer influenced Edward's policy in the Low Countries; only the diplomatic and political connections remained vital.

During these months the usual ecclesiastical censures were pronounced in Flanders. While the Truce of Malestroit was in force there had been negotiations with the church [137] which appear to have been quite fruitless. In the spring of 1346 absolution was readily enough secured from the excommunication which had been pronounced for the expedition to Axel in the previous summer.[138] When the war broke out there was a general expectation that excommunication would be pronounced the moment that hostilities should commence. Between August 3 and 5 the clergy of Flanders were assembled at Aardenburg, and on the 8th and 10th at Thourout where delegates from Ghent, and undoubtedly from Bruges and Ypres also, appeared for consultation.[139] The hostility of the bishop of Tournai was real, and the Flemings feared to appear within the walls of the city. They asked him to hold his court at Courtrai which was granted, and from March 5 until sentence was pronounced the business of the county under the bishop's jurisdiction was transacted there.[140] Of course the burghers of Ghent could not pay their customary respects to Our Lady of Tournai in September, and were forced to content themselves with merely making the necessary preparations.[141] As in former years, the Dominicans, Franciscans, and Carmelites, paid little attention to the pronouncements of the church.[142]

[137] N. de Pauw en J. Vuylsteke, *Rekeningen der Stad Gent,* III, 299.
[138] *Ibid.,* p. 490.
[139] *Ibid.,* p. 495.   [140] Le Muisit, p. 172.
[141] N. de Pauw en J. Vuylsteke, *Rekeningen der Stad Gent,* III, 35–36.
[142] *Ibid.,* II, 535.

V. The Position of Hainault, Holland, and Zeeland
(1346–1347)

Edward's diplomatic prestige in the Low Countries had greatly declined in spite of the brilliant victory of Crécy and the investment of Calais. John of Hainault had deserted him. The entire heritage of the house of Avesnes had fallen into the hands of the Wittelsbach house with which relations were seriously strained, and, since the summer of the previous year, the duke of Brabant had come to terms with Philip. The situation was much more serious than it perhaps appeared to him, for the duke remained for the time being the ally of the Flemings. Although it could not well be hidden from Edward and his allies, the Flemings, that Duke John was seeking some understanding with Philip, the fact of the papal dispensation of December and the formal steps taken at Laon to secure for him full title to Mechelen seemed to be offset by his reconfirmation in March, 1346, of the treaty of December 3, 1339. With characteristic astuteness this step was apparently arranged to coincide with the citation of the chapter and bishop of Liège by the bishops at Laon. In the summer, when Edward was moving toward the Flemish border, the duke had sent some troops for the protection of Flanders.[143] But it is evident that he was only awaiting the favorable moment to throw off the mask and reap the fruits of his diplomatic subtlety. The Luxemburg house was bound by tradition and also by the necessity of opposing the Wittelsbach Lewis the Bavarian in the claims upon the imperial title to look to King Philip. Engelbert de la Marck, now the bishop of Liège, was, like his predecessor, a pensioner of the French king,[144] and the count of Namur was in the enemies' ranks at Crécy. Only the Flemings, Guelders, whose duke was too young to exercise any influence, and the margrave of Juliers remained faithful.

The empress Margaret's position was a difficult one in the summer of 1346. Although recognized as legitimate successor

---

[143] E. van Even, " Mengelingen voor de Nederlandsche Geschiedenis," *Vaderlandsche Museum voor Nederduitsche Letterkunde, Oudheid, en Geschiedenis vitgegeven door C. P. Serrure*, II (Gent, 1858), 294–296.

[144] J. Viard, *Les Journaux du Trésor de Philippe VI de Valois*, pp. 764–765.

of her brother, Count William, in Hainault, Holland, and Zeeland, the Friesians were still hostile. Particularly dangerous were Edward's plans. She was very much interested in what the English proposed to do after the expiration of the Truce of Malestroit on June 24. For this reason she dispatched messengers into Flanders on July 2, 9, and 20 to acquaint her with Edward's plans.[145] These obviously were of vital importance to her, for might he not join with the Flemings and attempt to enforce some recognition of his rights? The opposition of the Luxemburgs, on the other hand, could not be effective now that she was in full control of the patrimony of her house. She informed Lewis that she could maintain herself with her own forces, but could not march out to Aix-la-Chapelle [146] to aid the townsmen who were determined to remain faithful to her husband.[147]

Meanwhile, Lewis the Bavarian greatly desired to have his wife with him, and preparations were made in the summer for her return. The nobles of Hainault, Holland, and Zeeland are said to have expressed a desire for the eldest of Margaret's sons. The emperor sent the second son William, disguised as an esquire and accompanied by John, the count of Catzenellenbogen. This was done with the greatest secrecy, for it was feared that he might be seized by sympathizers of the Luxemburg cause.[148] This cannot have been done later than July or the first part of August, for Margaret and John of Hainault on the 15th declared that the youthful William had received the count of Catzenellenbogen as his vassal in return for a grant of a thousand gold shields of which five hundred were yet to be paid.[149] Then on September 7 at Frankfurt the emperor issued a series of documents in which he confirmed all the privileges of Hainault, Holland, Zeeland, and Friesland, promised never to separate the three coun-

[145] J. C. de Jonge, *Verhandeling over den Oorsprong der Hoeksche en Kabeljaauwsche Twisten*, pp. 63–64.

[146] Nuwenburg, p. 201: "Imperatrix autem stans tunc in Hollandia scripsit Ludowico principi, quod per gentem suam posset resistere Karolo, ne posset Aquisgrani venire."

[147] C. Quix, *Codex Diplomaticus Aquensis*, I, 231. Cf. also, A. Werunsky, *Geschichte Kaiser Karls IV und seiner Zeit*, II (Part I), 60–61.

[148] Nuwenburg, p. 201.

[149] J. Laenen, *Les Archives de l'État à Vienne au Point de Vue de l'Histoire de Belgique* (Bruxelles, 1924), p. 49.

ties, stated that his eldest son Lewis, elector of Brandenburg, had abandoned all title to these lands in favor of his brother William, and confirmed Margaret's appointment of him as governor in these lands and also her promise not to interfere in their affairs so long as she should be absent from them.[150]   When Margaret was at Mons on the 24th, she transferred her authority to her son and ordered all her subjects to obey him.[151]

Before leaving the Low Countries Margaret rendered one more service to the Wittelsbach house in those parts.   The hostility of Edward was a very real matter, especially since the investment of Calais in the autumn had brought him and his army to the confines of Flanders.   The anxiety of the administrative officials in Zeeland is revealed by the report of the receiver, John Symonsz van Bisanten, on October 23, that he saw at least two hundred English ships before Biervliet filled with armed men.   To ascertain their purpose he sent a messenger to Sluis, Damme, and Bruges to make enquiries.[152]   Nothing could be more desirable than to come to an arrangement with Philippa, and for this purpose she invited her sister to a conference.   Edward, who was at Calais, did not want to let the queen proceed further than Ypres, but Margaret willingly consented to meet her there.   With Philippa came the earl of Warwick, a large number of knights and esquires, and two hundred archers.   She arrived first and went out of the town to meet her imperial sister whom she had not seen for many years.   The magistrates of Ypres were at great pains to show themselves worthy of the signal honor accorded their town, and deputies — the scabinus, John Willade, and the clerk, John uten Hove — appeared for Ghent, and others undoubtedly also appeared for Bruges.   The negotiations and ceremonies lasted from the 12th to the 17th of October,[153] when the two separated,[154] but not before setting forth in form of a charter an arrangement regarding their rights.   But what was stated in the document cannot be ascertained, for the charter,

---

[150] F. van Mieris, *Groot Charterboek*, II, 726–729. Cf. Beka, p. 119.

[151] L. Ph. C. van den Bergh, *Gedenkstukken tot Opheldering der Vaderlandsche Geschiedensis,* I, 165–168.

[152] Cf. *supra,* p. 538.

[153] N. de Pauw en J. Vuylsteke, *Rekeningen der Stad Gent,* III, 60. The deputies left Ghent on the 11th and returned on the 18th.

[154] *Bourgeois de Valenciennes,* pp. 242–243; le Muisit, p. 168.

which is still to be found in the archives at Mons, is in a sadly decayed state. That it was drawn up at Ypres and was given a seal by Philippa is practically certain because more than a century ago the baron J. de St. Genois and the archivist J. C. de Jonge reported having seen it. Even then it was so seriously damaged that the essential parts of the agreement could not be read.[155] It does not, however, appear from what is left of the text that the two came to any important decision. This is the opinion of Dr. S. A. Waller Zeper, who has made a recent attempt to decipher the charter. Apparently Philippa agreed to suspend all hostile action until she could produce the documents upon which she based her contention which Margaret would for the time being recognize.[156] Any aggressive action by Edward was thereby postponed.

Before leaving the Low Countries, Margaret attended a conference for diplomatic purposes at Ath. Between October 20 and 24 the delegates of Ghent, the scabinus John Louf and the clerk Jacob van Lovelde, were sent to negotiate with her.[157] The object of this meeting is very obscure. According to Gilles le Muisit representatives of the English, Flemings, Brabançons, and of Hainault were present and reconfirmed by oath their alliance.[158] Early in November Margaret was at Oudenaarde whither the scabini of Ghent sent two of their colleagues, but it is not known for what purpose.[159]

VI. The Flemings, Count Louis, and Edward, King of England (1346–1347)

For King Edward the death of Count Louis presented an unforeseen opportunity to suggest once more a matrimonial alliance

[155] J. C. de Jonge, *Verhandelingen over den Oorsprong der Hoeksche en Kabeljaauwsche Twisten,* pp. xxvii–xxviii. For the document, see L. Devillers, *Cartulaire,* I, 278.

[156] S. A. Waller Zeper, *Jan van Henegouwen, Heer van Beaumont,* p. 280 (note 6). The writer's efforts to read the document (February, 1927) were no more successful.

[157] N. de Pauw en J. Vuylsteke, *Rekeningen der Stad Gent,* III, 61.

[158] Le Muisit, p. 168: "Et post fuit parlamentum in villa d'Ath, et ibi Anglici, Hannonienses, Flandrenses, et Brabantini renovaverunt sua juramenta."

[159] N. de Pauw en J. Vuylsteke, *Rekeningen der Stad Gent,* III, 61–62.

with Flanders. And the Flemings, now rid of their old count who
had ever shown himself hostile toward their intimate connections
with Edward, hoped that the youthful successor would be more
pliant in their hands. They were eager to have him return
so that he might be used to strengthen the régime of the three
towns, now, as ever, encumbered with many internal difficulties,
and also to legitimatize their official and illegal acts.[160]

At Ghent the deficit for the year ending August 15, 1346,
amounted to 6,814*l*. 7*s*. 4*d*.,[161] in spite of the very large loans
made by the citizens during the course of the year. The scabini
had great difficulty in paying the soldiers who had gone forth
against Béthune and they were forced to borrow heavily. A
sum of 2,500 shields was received at Brussels of which, however,
six hundred and twenty-five, or twenty-five per cent, were deducted in advance for interest.[162] Undoubtedly the delegation,
which went on August 23 by way of Bruges and Ypres to the
army, had something to do with finances.[163] But it was very
difficult to pay those who had gone out in September to coöperate with Edward at Calais, and when the soldiers returned they
halted at Courtrai and refused to enter the town until they
should be paid. On the 29th William van Vaernewijc, the scabinus Peter vanden Velde, and Josse Rase were sent by them
to discuss the matter with the magistrates.[164] Vanden Velde
returned after the conference on October 7 to explain to them
the difficulties which prevented the scabini from making a prompt
payment.[165] Similar difficulties obtained at Bruges and undoubtedly also at Ypres. At Ghent there was some unrest,
for, while the troops were out for the first time, a special guard
was set to preserve the peace.[166] Then there was the danger of a

[160] Characteristic is the order given to John den Zeghelsnidere to cut
a new count's seal for the use of the scabini. See N. de Pauw en J.
Vuylsteke, *Rekeningen der Stad Gent*, III, 129: ". . . meester Janne den
Zegelsnidere te Brucghe, die mijns heeren van Vlaendren zegele sneet,
omme dat hi hem te bet spoeden soude omme ons te elpen te delivererne
van den bezegelte an onse chaerters. . . ."

[161] *Ibid.*, II, 540.

[162] *Ibid.*, p. 525.   [163] *Ibid.*, III, 58.

[164] *Ibid.*, p. 59: ". . . quamen . . . uten here van Curterike daer onse
liede laghen die niet inne commen en wilden of sine adden soudeye. . . ."

[165] *Ibid.*, pp. 59–60: ". . . te Curterike waerd tote onsen here omme
daer te toghene de zwaerhede van den fine te ghecrighene van der sou-
deyen. . . ."   [166] *Ibid.*, II, 536.

corn famine, for the enemy would certainly prevent exportation of food-stuffs from Artois and the Tournaisis.[167] The church had again excommunicated the Flemings when hostilities re-opened.[168] There was also the perennial problem of the émigrés who were ever eager to make trouble.[169] Thus in May some of them from motives of revenge had killed Simon van Halen, the *ruwaard* of Flanders,[170] whose death, it is stated by a late chron-icler, was expected to hasten the return of the count.[171]

Count Louis was only sixteen when he was wounded at Crécy. He was at once made a knight, and on September 3 he performed homage for his fiefs before Philip at Amiens.[172] The three towns sent delegates to him at about All Saints' Day, and at Halewin and Menin negotiated his return under certain conditions which apparently were not much different from those imposed upon his father after the siege of Tournai.[173] On November 5 an impos-ing delegation left Ghent for Menin and returned on the 7th.[174] Thereupon Count Louis entered the country [175] and was every-where joyfully received.[176] On the 10th he was at Courtrai [176] and on the 12th at Ghent, where every effort was made to accord him a hearty welcome. The scabini presented him with cloths valued at 1,454*l.* 16*s.* 8*d.*, wine at 660*l.* 18*s.* 4*d.*, and the members of his household, the chancellor, the clerk, and ushers with gifts in proportion.[177] On the 18th

[167] For the efforts to conserve the corn supply, see *ibid.*, III, 109–112.

[168] *Ibid.*, p. 113.

[169] For example, in the spring of 1346 at Axel, Hulst, and Lokeren, whither a force of men was sent in March after which these places "granted" 8,740*l.* 13*s.* 4*d.* for the needs of the town. Cf. *ibid.*, II, 454–456, 527–528.

[170] Le Muisit, p. 172.

[171] *Breve Chronicon*, p. 10: ". . . et quia putabant, si mortuus esset, quod comes Flandrie citius ad terram rediret, cum alius vicarius non ex-isteret."

[172] *Chronicon Comitum Flandrensium*, p. 219, 221; *Breve Chronicon*, p. 12; de Budt, p. 330; le Muisit, p. 116.

[173] Le Muisit, p. 169; *Istore et Croniques*, II, 61.

[174] N. de Pauw en J. Vuylsteke, *Rekeningen der Stad Gent*, III, 62.

[175] *Chronographia*, II, 236; *Chronicon Comitum Flandrensium*, p. 221; le Bel, II, 136–137; de Budt, p. 331, who states that he entered Flanders about September 27.

[176] N. de Pauw en J. Vuylsteke, *Rekeningen der Stad Gent*, III, 62; le Muisit, p. 169.

[177] N. de Pauw en J. Vuylsteke, *Rekeningen der Stad Gent*, III, 62, 39–41. Persemiere and eight other trumpeters were paid 18*l.*

a large delegation accompanied him to Bruges. Until the 30th they were occupied with the formalities of reception in the various towns.[178] Everywhere he reconfirmed their privileges and received their homage and oaths, forgave certain crimes, and received vast quantities of gifts, such as jewelry and cloth.[179] On the 25th Louis was at Ypres, and on December 3 at Oudenaarde,[180] when at the request of delegates sent by the magistrates of Poperingen he confirmed the judgment of the three towns which had condemned the manufacture of cloth in their town.[181]

Soon the Flemings began to press him to recognize Edward as legal king of France and perform homage before him for Flanders. It was now also proposed that he marry Isabella, the eldest daughter of the English king.[182] These suggestions were made, it appears, early in December, for on the 11th a delegation was sent from Ghent to confer with Edward's representatives at Bergen.[183] Two of the delegates, the scabinus, Peter vanden Velde, and the clerk, John uten Hove, were back in Ghent on the 18th and 19th, and with others at once proceeded to Male where the envoys of Bruges and Ypres also appeared. Vanden Velde returned on the 30th, but uten Hove went to Edward at Calais and was back in Ghent on January 13.[184] Edward's agents, the earl of Northampton, Bartholomew de Burghersh, and William, margrave of Juliers, thereupon were sent into Flanders and instructed to dissuade Louis from his purpose of taking Marguerite of Brabant as his wife.[185] The date is uncertain, but the fact of their visit to Ghent is beyond doubt, for the scabini presented

[178] N. de Pauw en J. Vuylsteke, *Rekeningen der Stad Gent*, III, p. 62.

[179] *Chronicon Comitum Flandrensium*, p. 221; le Muisit, p. 169; *Bourgeois de Valenciennes*, pp. 244–245.

[180] N. de Pauw en J. Vuylsteke, *Rekeningen der Stad Gent*, III, 63.

[181] G. Espinas et H. Pirenne, *Recueil des Documents relatifs à l'Industrie Drapière en Flandre*, III, 157–158.

[182] *Chronicon Comitum Flandrensium*, pp. 221–222: " . . . secundum sua perversa desideria se regebant, et eum arctabant continue, ut regi Angliae faceret homagium de comitatu Flandriae quod tamen facere semper recusavit." See also *Bourgeois de Valenciennes*, p. 245; le Bel, III, 135; le Muisit, p. 169.

[183] N. de Pauw en J. Vuylsteke, *Rekeningen der Stad Gent*, III, 63. According to one tradition Edward went to Ghent to suggest the marriage. See *Chronographia*, II, 237; *Istore et Croniques*, II, 48.

[184] N. de Pauw en J. Vuylsteke, *Rekeningen der Stad Gent,* III, 64.

[185] Le Bel, II, 137; *Istore et Croniques*, II, 62.

them with wine on that occasion. Most likely it coincided with Louis' visit on February 6.[186] But these very persistent efforts to influence the youth were futile. Louis declared that he could not accept the daughter of the man whose troops had slain his father, nor would he do so without the advice of his mother, friends, and councillors.[187] The magistrates of the three towns kept him under the most minute surveillance.[188] Twenty men, according to John le Bel, accompanied him wherever he went and watched his every action and permitted none of his old councillors save two knights to attend him.[189] These two men were undoubtedly Roland de Pouke and Louis de le Wale.[190]

In this situation Louis revealed something of the mettle which was to distinguish him in the future as a most skilful diplomat. Finding that nothing could be accomplished because of the determination of his guards, he began to dissemble and agreed to discuss the terms.[191] Finally a meeting was arranged and on March 1 the delegation from Ghent went forth to Veurne and thence to Bergen to settle all points and draw up the necessary documents.[192] Louis was forced to accompany the delegates of the three towns and consent to all the arrangements that were made for him. "The young count bowed meekly before the king and the noble king tenderly begged to be pardoned for the death of his father and declared that on the day of battle he did not see his father." [193] Willy-nilly he was forced to accept the terms arranged for him in spite of the ecclesiastical handicap

---

[186] N. de Pauw en J. Vuylsteke, *Rekeningen der Stad Gent*, III, 39, 41.

[187] Le Bel, II, 135; Boendale, *Brabantsche Yeesten*, I, 576; *Istore et Croniques*, II, 49; *Grandes Chroniques*, V, 467.

[188] Thus Boendale, *Brabantsche Yeesten*, I, 576, states:

> "Maer in alsulken kere,
> Als si sinen vader hilden
> Si desen oec houden wilden.
> Hi moest singhen alsulken sanc
> Als si wilden, wast cort of lanc."

According to the *Bourgeois de Valenciennes*, p. 244, he "... fut rechups par ainsy q'il les debvoit tenir et mener aux us et aux costumes du bon conte Guion, son antecesseur."

[189] Le Bel, II, 137–138.   [190] Le Muisit, p. 169.

[191] Boendale, *Brabantsche Yeesten*, I, 577.

[192] N. de Pauw en J. Vuylsteke, *Rekeningen der Stad Gent*, II, p. 67.

[193] Le Bel, II, 138.

that he and Isabella were related in the second degree.[194]   The charter which was drawn up at Dunkirk on March 13 specified that Louis should marry Isabella within a fortnight after Easter and endow her with 10,000*l.* income derived from the lands of Nevers and Réthel, or, in the event that this should be impossible, from other property.   Edward promised 25,000*l.* Parisian annually in compensation for Ponthieu, Montreuil-sur-Mer, and Provost Chastel and in addition 4,000 gold pennies with the shield to be paid in certain instalments.   Louis' chancellor, Gilles van den Houtte,[195] affixed the count's seal and surrendered the instrument at Bergen in the presence of Edward, the margrave of Juliers, the earl of Northampton, Reginald de Cobham, Bartholomew de Burghersh, and John Darcy.[196]

Thereupon the deputies returned home, those of Ghent arriving on the 17th.   On the following day delegates were sent to Alost to confer with those of Brabant.[197]   What was the duke's attitude during these days?   In view of the fact that this meeting came immediately after the return of the delegates from Bergen, one is led to surmise some connection between this and the matrimonial proposals, but the brevity of the town accounts prevents any certainty in the matter.   Duke John was still formally allied with the Flemings in accordance with the terms arranged on December 3, 1339, and it is certain that in July he sent, or allowed to be sent, the communal militia from Louvain to coöperate with the Flemings against Calais.[198]   He was only dissembling and awaiting the favorable moment to throw off the mask in order to draw his profit from the devious course he had so dexterously planned.   Count Louis was resolved not to be dominated by the three towns and determined to escape from Flanders before April 15, the date set for his marriage to Isabella.[199]   He acted

[194] *Chronicon Comitum Flandrensium,* p. 222; le Bel, II, 138; de Budt, p. 331; *Breve Chronicon,* p. 12; le Muisit, p. 169; *Chronographia,* II, 237–238; *Istore et Croniques,* II, 49–50, 62.

[195] N. de Pauw en J. Vuylsteke, *Rekeningen der Stad Gent,* III, 40. The inscription refers to him as " Egidius."

[196] *Foedera,* III(1), 111–112.   The words " marchione de . . . ule . . ." undoubtedly refer to the margrave of Juliers.

[197] N. de Pauw en J. Vuylsteke, *Rekeningen der Stad Gent,* III, 67.

[198] E. van Even, " Mengelingen voor de Nederlandsche Geschiedenis," *Vaderlandsche Museum voor Vaderlandsche Letterkunde, Oudheid, en Geschiedenis, uitgegeven door C. P. Serrure,* II (Gent, 1858), 294–296.

[199] *Bourgeois de Valenciennes,* p. 245; de Budt, p. 331.

and spoke as if he were ready for the ceremony.[200] But when
the time for the spring campaign drew near and Edward demanded that he appear as leader of the Flemish forces in the
attack upon Philip or send a relative as substitute, he had to
decide his course of action. His reply was evasive: he begged
time for counsel which was granted, but only till the morrow.[201]
The duke of Brabant and Philip, it is said, wrote, begging him
to flee.[202]

On the following morning, which was the 28th, Louis was prepared to execute his covert design. He arose at an unusual hour,
pretended illness, and went out into the open with some falcons.
Noticing that his guards were occupied with the preparations of
a great banquet, and that they were lax in their attentions, he
moved rapidly away from them in pursuit of his falcons. Then
putting spurs to his horse he rode off at top speed, accompanied
by Roland de Pouke and Louis de le Wale, and after a long ride
arrived at Lille.[203] Philip was of course greatly pleased with this
signal diplomatic victory over his rival. The count's chamberlain, Marquet du Galliel, who appears to have been of especial
service during his flight, was handsomely rewarded by Philip on
May 1.[204] The Flemings were naturally depressed by this event
and delegations went from Ghent to Bruges on March 30, April 4,
and again on the 7th, and men were at once ordered to ride out
into the castleries of the west in order to protect the country from
any sudden invasion.[205]

VII. The Eclipse of Edward's Prestige
(Summer, 1347)

After the flight of Count Louis from Male, Edward suffered
another serious setback in his diplomatic efforts when his youthful

[200] Boendale, *Brabantsche Yeesten*, I, 577; le Muisit, p. 169.
[201] Le Muisit, p. 170; N. de Pauw en J. Vuylsteke, *Rekeningen der Stad Gent*, III, 133.
[202] *Bourgeois de Valenciennes*, p. 246; *Breve Chronicon*, p. 12.
[203] Le Muisit, p. 170; *Bourgeois de Valenciennes*, p. 246; de Budt, p. 331; *Chronicon Comitum Flandrensium*, p. 222; Boendale, *Brabantsche Yeesten*, I, 577; *Istore et Croniques*, II, 50; *Grandes Chroniques*, V, 467; le Bel, II, 138–139; *Chronographia*, II, 238–239.
[204] Kervyn, *Oeuvres de Froissart*, XXIII, 343.
[205] N. de Pauw en J. Vuylsteke, *Rekeningen der Stad Gent*, III, 68, 69.

nephew, Reginald, duke of Guelders, deserted him in May. He had been brought to Calais by William, margrave of Juliers, and attended the betrothal ceremonies of Count Louis and Isabella of England in the church of the abbey of St. Winoc at Bergen.[206] The margrave had assumed a very prominent rôle during the negotiations of the winter in Flanders and showed himself thoroughly devoted to English interests. Disappointed by the failure of their design to cement Flanders and England by a matrimonial connection and eager to save some vestige of former Plantagenet alliances in the Low Countries, the two brothers-in-law now decided to hasten the marriage of the fourteen-year-old Reginald to the margrave's eldest daughter. In 1343 Reginald's mother Eleanor had negotiated a marriage for him with Isabella, a sister of William, count of Hainault, Holland, and Zeeland, but the arrangements made at Middelburg had not been carried out, apparently because the necessary papal dispensation had not been obtained. The betrothal of Reginald to Marie, daughter of John, duke of Brabant, which had been agreed upon by the Treaty of Amiens in 1334, was therefore still binding. It was certain that the duke would be grievously offended by this step; and in order to quiet Reginald's fears of retaliation at the hands of the duke, Edward and the margrave promised that, should John or his heirs seek satisfaction from Reginald, his heirs, his towns, lands, or subjects, they would reimburse him fully. Should the duke employ violent means, they bound themselves to assist him with all their armed power and never make peace without specifically including him, his lands, and subjects.[207] It was a desperate scheme to stay Edward's waning alliances in the Low Countries, for it could not be doubted that the pope would refuse to grant dispensation between the two cousins.

But this treaty, which was made on May 6 at Calais, little pleased the youth, who appears to have taken to heart the counsel of his father to marry the daughter of the duke.[208] Notwithstanding the fact that a papal dispensation would have to be given for this marriage of the children of two sisters, which the pope and curia could hardly be expected to grant, the ceremonies

---

[206] *Bourgeois de Valenciennes*, p. 245.
[207] *Foedera*, III (1), 119.   [208] Boendale, *Brabantsche Yeesten*, I, 578.

were hastily performed. There was a splendid feast on the Sunday before Pentecost, May 6, and the couple lived together for a fortnight. But Reginald profited from the example of Count Louis and determined to flee. His uncles listened to his request to be allowed to visit Guelders, whereupon the youth and his brother hastily departed. When they arrived almost destitute at Antwerp they entered into discussions with the duke of Brabant and the marriage with his daughter was then duly hastened.[209] Thus a second time in the space of two months Edward and his party were balked in their plans.

Meanwhile the Flemings coöperated with Edward against Philip's subjects along the borders of Artois. According to Gilles le Muisit a force of 5,000 men left Bruges who were followed by the levies of Ypres and Ghent, but returned at the king's orders as nothing could be accomplished.[210] More determined hostilities began in the middle of April when troops from the garrison of St. Omer conducted a raid against the Flemings who in turn pursued them to Arques and burned the town. A large force then left St. Omer and overwhelmed them. The English retaliated and destroyed a considerable number of their assailants who came upon them at night from St. Omer and Arques. Other troops from this garrison harried the country toward Cassel for three days, burned the monastic establishment of Woestine, and even appeared before the defences of the place.[211] It was to resist these dangers that on April 27 the troops from Ghent were hurried to Cassel to fortify this important strategic place.[212] In May another force was sent to Courtrai, Oudenaarde, and Dendermonde in order to strengthen the approaches of the country.[213] On June 8 another attempt was made by the garrison of St. Omer against Cassel which again failed because of the timely reinforcements brought by the son of Sohier de Courtrai who had defended the country at Alost in 1345.[214] To

[209] *Ibid.,* pp. 578–579; *Bourgeois de Valenciennes,* p. 250.

[210] Le Muisit, p. 171. The accounts of Ghent make no reference to this activity.

[211] Le Muisit, pp. 173–174; *Istore et Croniques,* II, 63, 66; *Chronographia,* II, 244; le Bel, II, 152.

[212] N. de Pauw en J. Vuylsteke, *Rekeningen der Stad Gent,* III, 133–136.

[213] *Ibid.,* pp. 136–137.

[214] *Bourgeois de Valenciennes,* p. 251; le Muisit, p. 178.

meet this danger the magistrates of Ghent on the 14th sent out a force of fifty bowmen, fifty white-hoods, and a number of the magistrates to Courtrai and thence to Woestine and Calais.[215] Thus in June and July a considerable number of Flemings was stationed on the borders of Artois ready to engage in petty warfare or coöperate with Edward. At this moment William, margrave of Juliers, was made *ruwaard* of the country at the instigation of the magistrates of Ghent, and from June 17 to 22 William van Vaernewijc, who had been superseded as captain of the parish of St. Jacques on December 29, and the scabinus, John van Meesine, were sent to the border in order to install the margrave in his functions.[216]

During these months there was active diplomatic intercourse between the Flemings and the towns of Brabant and Hainault. The references to the meetings are unfortunately very brief and it is impossible to make a satisfactory statement of what was discussed. From May 1 to 3 the magistrates of Ghent sent delegates to Brussels to meet the negotiants of Brabant. This was followed by a conference with Edward at Calais from May 4 to 10. On June 10 and 11 delegates were at Alost with those of Brabant, and from the 22d to the 25th at Veurne with Edward's men.[217] That these negotiations aimed to secure action in conformity with the treaty of December 3, 1339, is beyond doubt. The towns of Hainault were invited to reconfirm these articles, and from Valenciennes, Mons, Binche, Maubeuge, and Ath letters with a copy of the treaty were sent to Munich to Countess Margaret for advice. After consulting the emperor she replied on June 17 that she desired to have them carry out the terms point by point (*de tenir et d'aemplir de point en point*) in the manner in which her brother, Count William, and the towns had formerly done, and instructed them to append their seals, should the towns of Brabant and Flanders request it.[218] Apparently Margaret did not care to appear hostile to Edward at this juncture

    [215] N. de Pauw en J. Vuylsteke, *Rekeningen der Stad Gent,* III, 138–141, 244–249.

    [216] *Ibid.,* p. 72; Nuwenburg, p. 232.

    [217] N. de Pauw en J. Vuylsteke, *Rekeningen der Stad Gent,* III, 70–73.

    [218] L. Devillers, *Cartulaire,* I, 300. The document was put into Latin apparently for the imperial court. See *ibid.,* p. 759 (extracts from the accounts of Mons).

since the arrangements of October 17 of the previous autumn had for a time placed Edward's demands in abeyance. But Margaret's lieutenant, her son William, influenced of course by the important nobles, was eager to remain neutral. It was known that John of Hainault intended to aid Philip in person and that the seignior of Enghien and others were ready to join Edward. On May 4 Count William forbade any of them to leave the county to take service under alien princes.[219]

It seems likely that the duke of Brabant's influence was of great importance at this juncture when William and his government were not eager to choose any side in the struggle. Between June 26 and 29 John van Lovelde, the clerk of the scabini of Ghent, was at Louvain where the delegates of Brabant were in session, and in July between the 4th and the 11th there was a meeting in Brussels of the representatives of Flanders and Brabant in the duke's presence.[220] But John's daughter had become the wife of Count Louis on the 2d and apparently nothing was accomplished, for no further reference to similar meetings can be found in the accounts of Ghent until November 15.[221] It is therefore quite possible that the towns of Brabant did not join with the Flemings in requesting a reconfirmation. It is certain that John of Hainault was consulted by the towns of Hainault,[222] but as an ally of Philip he cannot have labored zealously to tighten the bonds between Hainault and Flanders. Thus, as in 1345, no steps were taken to carry out the clauses of the treaty. Had there been a reconfirmation the fact would most likely have been recorded in some way in the transactions of the scabini of Ghent. Margaret's letter of June 17 therefore appears to have been without result. Two weeks before the dispatch of her letter, John of Hainault, little heeding the order of William who had lately entrusted the castellan of Mons to enforce it, rode out with sixty knights, and on the 8th passed through Tournai on his way to join King Philip in Artois.[223] Thus Edward's efforts to preserve some vestige of his former

---

[219] *Ibid.,* IV, 681–682.
[220] N. de Pauw en J. Vuylsteke, *Rekeningen der Stad Gent,* III, 73.
[221] *Ibid.,* p. 209.
[222] L. Devillers, *Cartulaire,* I, 759 (extracts from the accounts of Mons).
[223] Le Muisit, p. 177.

alliances in the Low Countries through his domination of Flanders proved a dismal failure.

The siege of Calais continued in the meanwhile. Philip had collected troops and appeared in person at Amiens from April 4 to 7 and at Arras at Pentecost.[224] A large body of Flemings was stationed along the frontier under the command of their new *ruwaard*. A considerable force crossed the Neuf Fosse, seized St. Venant, invaded Artois as far as Béthune, took Lalleu, and entered the castlery of Lille. They plundered and harried the country and returned heavily laden with booty of all kinds.[225] As they retired Philip sent a force in pursuit. The Flemings were surprised at St. Venant on June 13 where they were resting from their strenuous raids. There was much slaughter and the men fled in great confusion.[226]

In July there was but little activity in this region. They led a raid against St. Omer and Aire at the close of the month which Philip thought was the beginning of an investment.[227] The French drew nearer Calais and halted within a league of Edward's forces. But on August 3 and 4 the town surrendered, and, having no desire for another encounter, he drew back two leagues.[228] Soon he retired to Arras and began to discharge his men on the 10th. Then on the 11th the English and the Flemings raided Fauquemberghes. In September there was some further plundering between Calais, Cassel, and Aire.[229]

Negotiations for a truce were now in order, for Edward was sorely pressed for money, his diplomacy in the Low Countries had failed, and the general desire for rest made it necessary to terminate his campaign. In June, Jeanne, dowager countess of Hainault, once more left the cloistered quiet of Fontenelles and went to Montreuil-sur-Mer on a mission of peace. But Edward

---

[224] *Bourgeois de Valenciennes,* p. 249; le Muisit, pp. 180–181; *Grandes Chroniques,* V, 468. For the king's itinerary, see J. Viard, "Itinéraire de Philippe VI de Valois," *BEC,* LXXIV (1913), 575–576.

[225] Le Muisit, pp. 178–180; le Bel, II, 152; *Istore et Croniques,* II, 52–54, 67.

[226] *Bourgeois de Valenciennes,* p. 252; *Istore et Croniques,* II, 54–55, 67.

[227] *Bourgeois de Valenciennes,* p. 261; Nuwenburg, p. 214, le Muisit, p. 187.

[228] Nuwenburg, p. 233. For the siege, see Knighton, II, 52; le Bel, II, 111–173; *Chronographia,* II, 244–245.

[229] Le Muisit, pp. 187–188.

was determined to have Calais which was now suffering acutely from hunger and she could accomplish nothing.[230] The cardinals were ready to take advantage of the opportunity now offered to secure a truce.[231] On October 18 the magistrates of Ghent sent as their representatives William van Artevelde, Peter van Coudenhove, and John uten Hove.[232] Several days were consumed in negotiations, but no difficulty was raised, it appears, on either side, and on the 28th the long document received the necessary seals.[233] The truce was to last from the 28th until a fortnight after St. John the Baptist's Day or the morning of July 9, 1348, and apply to all the allies of each side. Those in the Low Countries specified by Philip were the duke of Brabant, the count of Guelders — for his title of duke was not recognized by the French king — the bishop of Liège, John of Hainault, the countess of Hainault and her subjects, the count of Namur and Louis of Namur, and by Edward the duke of Brabant, the margrave of Juliers (whose title was not admitted in France), Robert of Namur, Henry of Flanders, the county of Flanders and its subjects, and also Lalleu and the county of Hainault and its subjects.

Count Louis was to promise by oath to abide by the terms of the truce and in no way levy war upon the Flemings. All ecclesiastical measures instituted by the officials of the dioceses of Tournai, Thérouanne, Arras,[234] and Cambrai [235] on May 13 were to be annulled for the duration of the truce upon appeal to the pope. None of Philip's men or the count of Flanders might enter Flanders, nor might any diplomatic effort be undertaken to draw the Flemings from their English alliance. All banished parties and émigrés of Flanders and Lalleu were forbidden to re-

---

[230] *Bourgeois de Valenciennes,* pp. 253–254; le Muisit, p. 176.

[231] Le Muisit, pp. 175–176, 181; *Chronicon Comitum Flandrensium,* pp. 219–223.

[232] N. de Pauw en J. Vuylsteke, *Rekeningen der Stad Gent,* III, 207.

[233] For the document, see *Foedera,* III (1), 136–138. See also, le Muisit, p. 189; Nuwenburg, pp. 233–234; Avesbury, pp. 396–402; *Chronicon Comitum Flandrensium,* pp. 396–402.

[234] Cf. N. de Pauw en J. Vuylsteke, *Rekeningen der Stad Gent,* III, 71, 74; le Muisit, p. 176.

[235] Sentence of excommunication was pronounced in Hainault against the Flemings. See L. Devillers, *Cartulaire,* I, 759 (extracts from the accounts of Mons).

turn under pain of forfeiture of all their goods in France. The Flemings could freely visit France in order to carry on their economic activities. This treaty was to be published in Paris and other towns of France. Edward was now eager to return to England. After providing for the government of Calais he embarked and was at London on October 14.[236]

VIII. The Alliance of John, Duke of Brabant, and Philip, King of France (1347)

IN THE spring of 1347 John, duke of Brabant, clearly saw that the moment to break decisively with English connections had arrived. His neighboring states, Hainault, Holland, and Zeeland had by reason of the Wittelsbach succession and internal antagonisms withdrawn from the English alliance. John of Hainault had deserted Edward and was now ready to join Philip. Guelders was certain to play a very passive rôle and the duke was determined to take as his wife Duke John's daughter Marie. Louis, count of Flanders, had fled, and the matrimonial arrangements with the late count, which involved settlement of the vexed question of Mechelen, could now be carried out. Only William, margrave of Juliers, and the Flemings remained faithful to Edward. Furthermore, John knew only too well that after the present campaign Edward's financial condition would make it impossible to dominate the diplomatic relations in the Low Countries. It was, in fact, a foregone conclusion that the duke, able diplomat that he was, would at this moment carry out the arrangements which had been negotiated with the king of France during the past two years.

With the arrival of Count Louis in Philip's camp at the close of March plans were made to bring the long diplomatic exchanges to a formal conclusion. Apparently all or most of the points were by this time agreed upon so that when Duke John, Count Louis, and the official representatives of Philip met, little remained to be done but to draw up the final official charters. At Conflans on May 17 Louis instructed his councillors, Robert de Beauffort or Wingles, his constable, and Philip d'Arbois to be at St. Quentin on the 24th to treat with the delegates of John,

[236] *Foedera,* III (1), 139.

duke of Brabant, and Philip, and settle all points touching the marriage which had been arranged by his father and the king.[237]

By this time Philip and Duke John had come to a decision regarding the matrimonial arrangements between the latter's sons and the daughters of the dukes of Normandy and Bourbon. On May 18 John named as his representatives John van Wicvliet, seignior of Blaersveld, Nicholas du Chastel, dean of Our Lady's in Antwerp, and Henry Coke, dean of Ste. Gudule in Brussels, to draw up the terms of marriage between his son and heir apparent, Henry, and Jeanne, eldest daughter of John, duke of Normandy and Guyenne, and Godefroid his second son and Bonne, daughter of Peter, duke of Bourbon.[238] Philip's delegates were named on the 25th at Arras. They were Peter Andrée, bishop of Clermont, William Flote, seignior of Revel, who was his chancellor, Gilles de Soicourt, Jacques la Vache, and Oliver de Laye, his bailiff of Vermandois.[239]

Philip had been at Arras since May 21. He arrived at St. Quentin on June 5, and returned on the 8th.[240] Duke John appeared a few days before and during the discussions which were already apparently in progress drew up a charter setting forth the points he had promised in regard to the treaty of December 3, 1338.[241] Upon Philip's arrival, a large number of documents was drawn up in the brief space of two days. Among these is the categorical disavowal by Duke John of any alliance with Edward,[242] evidently demanded by Philip who reluctantly consented that the treaty between Brabant, Flanders, and Hainault should remain binding for the time being. John promised to abandon it as soon as he could do so, but in the meantime it was to remain in force notwithstanding the fact that some of

[237] *Archives Nationales,* Paris, J523, No. 16. Cf. A. Verkooren, *Inventaire, Brabant,* II, 182–183.

[238] *Archives Nationales,* Paris, J523, No. 19 (*bis*). A notarial act of June 6 at St. Quention names in addition Henry de Jodoigne. See *ibid.,* J523, No. 19 (*ter*).

[239] *Archives Nationales,* Paris, J523, No. 19. Cf. also *ibid.,* J523, No. 19 (*ter*).

[240] J. Viard, "Itinéraire de Philippe VI de Valois," *BEC,* LXXIV (1913), 575–576.

[241] *Archives Nationales,* Paris, J524ª, No. 29 (*bis*). Cf. A. Verkooren, *Inventaire, Brabant,* II, 184.

[242] A. Wauters, "Analectes Diplomatiques," *BCRH,* 4th Ser., X (1882). 102–103.

the clauses provided for mutual aid against the common enemy. Should John at the moment of breaking the alliance have any complaint against the count and the land of Flanders and appeal to Philip, the latter as sovereign prince promised to arbitrate within two months with the consent of the count and his subjects. Should these refuse he would send a captain with five hundred men on horse and two thousand foot to force them to obey. In such an event the duke would be bound to employ all his resources in coöperation with the king. Similar action was provided for in case the count would be willing but his subjects refuse. Philip was to give this aid within two months after the duke's request.[243]

Relations between the subjects and territories of Philip and Duke John were also regulated. Neither was to hurt the other, give aid or comfort in any manner whatever, nor permit the enemies of the other to pass through any land under his jurisdiction if it was known that they purposed to harm the other. The subjects of each were given safe conduct to visit the lands of the other and pursue their usual activities. The treaty was to be renewed by the heirs of each and within three months after the decease of the duke or king upon the request of the other. The duke, as vassal of the emperor, was to be free to fulfil his obligations even against the king in case of war between the empire and France. The exception made in the case of Hainault and Flanders was only temporary and could not invalidate the duke's general obligation. John promised to abandon all alliances not in harmony with these stipulations and surrender the documents in question, and Philip promised to forget all hostile acts of the duke against himself. In case of truce between England and France the duke and his subjects were to be included in the terms which were also to extend to commercial activity between the two lands and England.[244] John promised to use his influence with his towns of Louvain, Brussels, Antwerp, 's-Hertogenbosch, Tirlemont, Nivelles, and Leeuw in order to carry out the terms of the alliance, and his sons Henry and Godefroid were required to promise over their seals to abide by these terms.[245]

[243] *Archives Nationales,* Paris, J524ᵃ, No. 29.

[244] *Ibid.,* J523, No. 11 (*bis*).

[245] *Archives Nationales,* Paris, J524ᵃ, No. 26. Cf. A. Verkooren, *Inventaire, Brabant,* II, 188.

The subjects of each were to enjoy full liberty of commerce in the lands of the other and be exempt from all special or unusual impositions, and be permitted to carry all manner of coins in passing to and fro. No one was to be seized for any debts save his personal obligations or those of the town of which he was a burgher. All persons convicted of crime were to lose their personal goods but those of the master were not to be attached.[246] And, finally, all those who had been banished, degraded from their positions, or deprived of their goods, were to receive full pardon and restitution.[247]

The double marriage between the families of the king and Duke John was now also definitely arranged. To Henry who was to take as his wife Jeanne, eldest daughter of John, duke of Normandy, John assigned 12,000 small gold florins of Florence or 6,000*l.* Parisian or its equivalent, annual income from land at Nivelles and, if he should die before the marriage could take place, then his brother Godefroid would assume this obligation. Furthermore, Henry should receive the duchy of Limburg and the titles to Mechelen which were to be surrendered by the count of Flanders.[248] Philip in turn promised to settle upon Jeanne within four months after request 12,000 small gold florins of Florence or its equivalent, 6,000*l.* Parisian annually in land at Meaux, Troyes, and in the county of Champagne.[249] In recognition of the services of the duke and of Henry, the latter was to receive the sum of 100,000 florins or its equivalent in land. Of this 5,000*l.* Parisian or 10,000 florins were at once assigned to him at Pierrefons, Béthisi, Chambli, and Chaumont-en-Veuguessin for which Henry at once performed homage and swore fealty.[250]

To his niece, Bonne, daughter of Peter, duke of Bourbon, Philip promised to give within four months after request 6,000 small gold florins of Florence or 3,000*l.* Parisian,[251] and to Godefroid in consideration of the services rendered by the alliance and to be

---

[246] *Archives Nationales,* Paris, J524ᵃ, Nos. 28 and 28 (*bis* B). See A. Verkooren, *Inventaire, Brabant,* p. 192.

[247] *Archives Nationales,* Paris, J523, No. 17 and No. 17 (*bis* A).

[248] *Archives Nationales,* Paris, J523, No. 20 (*bis*). See A. Verkooren, *Inventaire, Brabant,* pp. 187–188.

[249] *Archives Nationales,* Paris, J523, No. 20.

[250] *Ibid.,* J524ᵃ, No. 27 (*bis*).   [251] *Ibid.,* J523, No. 22.

rendered, 100,000 florins or its equivalent in land, of which 10,000 florins were assigned in land at Belleville-sur-Mer in Poitou and for which Godefroid performed his feudal obligations of homage and fealty.[252]   Duke John bound himself to give Bonne 3,000*l.* Parisian in land at Herenthals and Lier in four months after request.   Each party was to forfeit 40,000*l.* Parisian in case he broke this engagement.[253]   Henry and Godefroid were to be at the royal manor at the Bois de Vincennes on June 19, and Philip promised that Jeanne and Bonne would also be there at that time for the marriage.[254]   It appears that Philip was eager to have Henry and Godefroid under his influence at once, for it was agreed that they should go to France and spend some time with the children of the duke of Normandy.[255]   Letters of safe-conduct were at once issued for both.[256]   The duke of Normandy and Philip's second son, Philip, duke of Orléans, solemnly swore to carry out these obligations in good faith.[257]   The delegates of the three negotiants, Philip, John, and Louis, and John Marie and John Dailly, secretaries of Philip, William Clavelli, notary for the duke of Normandy, and Nicholas Grenoul, secretary of the duke of Brabant, solemnly swore before a notary that they would labor for the full execution of all these terms.[258]

At the same time the arrangements between Duke John and Count Louis were put in definite form.   On the 5th Philip declared that Louis at his request was ready to surrender all his rights to his share of the jurisdictions in Mechelen to Henry, son of Duke John, who should perform homage for them before the bishop of Liège and promise for himself and his heirs to safeguard the count and his heirs against all losses and damages he might suffer from the opposition of the bishop, chapter, or church of Liège.[259]   Louis then declared that he would surrender all his rights to Henry of Brabant two months after request should be

[252] *Archives Nationales,* Paris, J523, No. 23; J524ᵃ and No. 27 (*bis*).
[253] *Ibid.,* J523, No. 22 (*bis*). See J524ᵃ, No. 27 (*ter*).
[254] *Ibid.,* J523, No. 19 and J523, No. 18 (*bis*).
[255] *Ibid.,* J523, No. 13; A. Verkooren, *Inventaire, Brabant,* II, 185–186.
[256] A. Verkooren, *Inventaire, Brabant,* II, 186–187.
[257] *Archives Nationales,* Paris, J523, No. 12.
[258] *Ibid.,* p. 523, No. 19 (*ter*).
[259] *Ibid.,* J523, No. 14 (*ter*), printed by S. Baluzius, *Vitae Paparum Avenonensium,* Vol. II, col. 699–700.

made for them, and not require the payment of the 86,500
regales gold which were still due.[260] This was guaranteed by
Philip.[261] The king granted Louis, in consideration of his marriage to Marguerite of Brabant, the 3,000*l.* of land in Nevers
and 2,000*l.* in Réthel which belonged to his aunt, the countess
of Montfort, but which had, because of the trouble attending
the Breton succession, been forfeited to the crown. He also
promised to buy from the countess of Bar land valued at 2,130*l.*
Parisian at Nieuwpoort, Deinze, or Bergen in Flanders and give
them to him. Should this prove impossible, he would purchase the
seigniory of Dendermonde for his wife or some other possession
valued at 2,000*l.* Tournois or would give 40,000 gold florins of
Florence in one sum as the count might wish, besides a cash gift
of 10,000*l.* Parisian.[262]

Count Louis agreed to assign to Marguerite as her dowry
60,000*l.* Tournois from land in the county of Alost, and 2,000*l.* in
addition near it or in the seigniory of Dendermonde, should he
secure possession of it, in which case she should retain it for life.
The child born of this union was to be recognized as legitimate
heir of the count by the three towns of Ghent, Bruges, and Ypres
and by twelve men to be chosen by the duke.[263] The duke promised to help Louis secure the full obedience of his subjects with
all his resources and at his own expense.[264] John's specific
promises in the matter of Marguerite's marriage are unfortunately unknown. Louis bound himself to be at Tervuren
on the 26th for the marriage.[265] Philip also promised that Louis
would do this, and John declared that Marguerite would be present at that time for the ceremony.[266]

Thus did the duke of Brabant reverse his political policy. In
all these negotiations his position had been exceptionally strong.
His desertion from Edward's side, ultimately certain by reason
of the failures of the English king and his change of method in

---

[260] *Archives Nationales,* Paris, J523, No. 14 (*bis*), printed in E. Dynter,
Chronicon Brabantiae, II, 825–826.

[261] E. Dynter, *Chronicon Ducum Brabantiae,* II, 824–825.

[262] *Archives Nationales,* Paris, J523, No. 21.

[263] A. Verkooren, *Inventaire, Brabant,* II, 189; Vredius, *Genealogia
Comitum Flandriae,* II, 198.

[264] *Archives Nationales,* Paris, J523, No. 24. Cf. le Bel, II, 136–138.

[265] *Archives Nationales,* Paris, J523, No. 16 (*bis*).

[266] *Ibid.,* J523, No. 18: J523, No. 18 (*bis*).

prosecuting the war, was a capital stroke of fortune for Philip's diplomacy. It was at the same moment a brilliant instance of the tenacity with which the duke pursued unswervingly the best interests of his subjects so clearly marked out by his predecessors. Mechelen would now soon be added to Brabant, the economic advantages flowing forth from the treaty with Flanders would remain, and he was assured of the coöperation of Philip and his heirs in his difficulties with the Flemings. Louis received no advantage save the promise of John's friendship and assistance to regain the loyalty of his subjects. As in 1332 and 1334, Philip sought to dispose of the local problems in the Low Countries in order to advance his own interest.

The marriage clauses were at once carried out. It was known that Clement's delegates would now validate the dispensation for the marriage of Marguerite and Louis. On the 19th Fulco, bishop of Paris, in the presence of the bishops of Laon and Clermont, John de Semur, and Peter de Forest, professors of canon law, William Tardini, official of Paris, and Nicholas du Chastel and Henry Coke declared that the dispensation granted on December 28, 1345, and suspended pending an inquest on November 30, 1346, could now be put into effect.[267] The ceremonies could not be performed on the 24th, the day planned, and accordingly were postponed to July 1. On the 21st Clement issued a dispensation at the request of Philip for the marriage of Reginald, duke of Guelders, and Duke John's second daughter, Marie.[268] The ceremony took place at the Bois de Vincennes at the appointed time and with much splendor.[269] At Tervuren the double marriage of Louis to Marguerite and Reginald to Marie followed, in accordance with the arrangements that had been made.[270]

---

[267] A. Verkooren, *Inventaire, Brabant,* II, 190–191; S. Riezler, *Vatikanische Akten,* Nos. 2310, 2311.

[268] G. Brom, *Bullarium Trajectense,* Vol. II, No. 1220, where the date given is June 21. Cf. U. Berlière, *Suppliques de Clément VI (1342–1352),* pp. 319–320, and also Boendale, *Brabantsche Yeesten,* I, 581.

[269] Le Muisit, p. 180; *Bourgeois de Valenciennes,* p. 254; de Budt, p. 331; Nuwenburg, p. 232.

[270] Le Muisit, p. 180; *Bourgeois de Valenciennes,* p. 256; Boendale, *Brabantsche Yeesten,* I, 581; le Bel, II, 142; Nuwenburg, p. 232; de Budt, p. 331; *Chronicon Comitum Flandrensium,* p. 222; *Breve Chronicon,* p. 13; *Istore et Croniques,* II, 72.

CHAPTER XV

CONCLUSION

IN SUMMARIZING the varied activities of all the princes involved in the diplomatic, political, and military operations in the Low Countries during the opening years of the Hundred Years' War, no simple *leitmotiv* can be found. Placed between the major secular forces of Christendom, France, England, and Germany, each one acted as best suited his interests and was greatly influenced by the actions of his neighbors. It is of course evident that because of his numerous matrimonial and political relations, William, count of Hainault, Holland, and Zeeland, was bound to play an exceedingly important rôle in the formation of a vast chain of alliances against Philip and in determining Edward's policy during the earlier years of the war. The part of van Artevelde is of much less importance; in fact it was a natural adaptation to the pressure of Edward and his allies. Instead of leading in any major sense, van Artevelde's policy followed in the wake of political influences quite beyond his control. Throughout the entire period the duke of Brabant displayed a most remarkable cunning which has usually been totally misunderstood. In spite of the impossibility of drawing up a clear and succinct yet sufficient summary, a brief résumé may be of some value.

The political relations of William, count of Hainault, Holland, and Zeeland, and seignior of Friesland, are of prime importance for an adequate understanding of the beginnings of the Hundred Years' War. Situated in the extreme western part of the Low Countries and within the borders of the empire, the county of Hainault had long been used by Capetian kings to extend their influence in the lands which formerly were part of the duchy of Lotharingia. Philip the Fair had made it a cardinal point in his political policy to seek the aid of the count of Hainault in reducing the count of Flanders to impotence. This policy which was now of more than thirty years' standing lost its *raison d'être* in the treaty of March 6, 1323, between Count William and Louis, count of Flanders, which definitively closed the long contest between the Avesnes and Dampierre branches of the Hainault-Flemish dynasty. For the moment, however, the traditional intimacy between Count William and Charles IV (1322–1328) continued. Countess Jeanne, daughter of Philip of Valois and aunt of the French king, undoubtedly exercised an important influence in this matter.

In the northern part of the Low Countries Count William ruled over Holland and Zeeland and claimed some rights over Friesland which could not be enforced. These lands were situated on the broad highways of the world's commerce, the Rhine, Meuse, and the Schelde, the Zuider Zee, and the North Sea. Political orientation in these parts was more likely to be toward the German hinterland or England than toward France. William and his father John had fought the counts of Flanders for the county of Zeeland. This struggle had added materially to the bitterness which already existed between the Avesnes and the Dampierre families. When it came to an end in the settlement of March, 1323, and when Count Louis of Flanders yielded in the struggle of his house with the Capetian kings, Count William no longer needed the support of the king of France to maintain his position. A *rapprochement* with the English kings was now possible.

The fact that the lands of the Avesnes patrimony were scattered in irregular manner in the northern and southern Low Countries inevitably brought Count William into intimate political relations with all the princes who ruled in those parts. Especially is this the case with the duke of Brabant and Limburg, whose lands separated Hainault from Holland and Zeeland. By treaty of October 21, 1323, the count's heir apparent William was betrothed to Duke John's eldest daughter Johanna. In 1329 his daughter Isabella was promised to the duke's heir apparent John. This significant harmony between the Avesnes and Louvain families greatly enhanced Count William's prestige which had already become quite striking in 1324 when his eldest daughter Margaret became the wife of Lewis the Bavarian, the king of the Romans, and when another daughter Johanna, married William, heir apparent of Juliers. His lands were so situated as to secure for him an unquestioned ascendancy over the bishops of Cambrai in the south and the bishops of Utrecht in the north where this success was achieved by his sympathetic understanding with the count of Guelders and Zutfen.

In the wider field of European politics these family relations brought Count William into contact with some of the chief phenomena in the political life of his day, such as the long and obstinate struggle between his son-in-law and the papacy and the affairs of the French monarchy and the empire. The marriage of his daughter Philippa to Edward III of England in 1328 gave him the unique opportunity of playing a rôle as mediator between the French king and his recalcitrant vassal, the duke of Aquitaine and king of England. Pope John XXII was keenly alive to this fact, for he feared that the proposed marriage might seriously disturb the peace of Europe. He thought that as father-in-law of Lewis the Bavarian, his own mortal foe, and of Edward III of England, who was the ever-potential enemy of the French king, Count William might possibly bring into one camp the opponents of the church and the French monarchy. This appeared particularly grave because the Flemings had since 1323 been in conflict with their suzerain, the French king, and were inclined to look to England for aid. While the pope was withholding the dispensation, Lewis the Bavarian was invading Italy in league with the Ghibellines and Count William in July threatened to join his son-in-law in person. William's evident reluctance to join Lewis failed to convince the pope who remained adamant. In the meantime the rankling hatred between Reginald, seignior of Valkenburg, and John, duke of Brabant, broke out into violent conflict. This serious matter demanded his immediate attention, for the conflict concerned the counts of Guelders and Juliers and involved the peace of all the princes between the Rhine and the Meuse. Finally, John XXII yielded to the representations of his envoys and to those of John of Hainault and King Edward who promised that the proposed union would not lead to the disastrous consequences which had been imagined.

While the marriage of Philippa of Hainault and Edward III was being celebrated in England, Charles IV of France died and was succeeded by his cousin, Philip of Valois, first as regent and in the spring as king. Count William was his brother-in-law, and for that reason an influential personage in the affairs of the Valois monarchy. Particularly important was this because there was much expectation in Flanders that as father-in-law of Edward who, the Flemings argued, should be king of France because he was the nearest male heir, he would support both his own and their cause. But William could not sympathize with the Flemish position — he had lost a brother in that ill-fated battle at Courtrai or Groeninghe in 1302 — and when Edward did nothing to enforce his claims, William was unencumbered by his connections and supported Philip VI. At the battle of Cassel on August 23, 1328, he was chiefly responsible in saving the day for his brother-in-law.

Count William's intimate connections with the courts of England, France, and Germany thus greatly enhanced his prestige in the affairs of the Low Countries and made him a personage of importance in the political questions of Christendom. He was occupied in arranging a treaty between the seignior of Valkenburg and the duke of Brabant. A definitive agreement was reached with the duke, who had ever sought to keep aloof from his influence, concerning the betrothal of his daughter Isabella and the heir apparent of Brabant and Limburg. In 1330 William went to Avignon to plead for peace between the spiritual and temporal heads of Christendom, but was repulsed by the pope who feared that he might have some ulterior motives because he was accompanied by what appeared to him an unusually large following. This was followed by the conferences with his imperial son-in-law at Speier in June. Meanwhile Edward was constantly looking to him for aid in arranging his differences with Philip. Edward had performed homage at Amiens in 1329; but this was not liege homage, and the negotiations which followed became acute in 1330 so that Edward actually sought to secure alliances with John, duke of Brabant, Reginald, count of Guelders, Louis, count of Flanders, Louis, count of Loon, and others. The treaty of March 9, 1331, was negotiated by Edward's envoys and Count William.

The influence of his brother-in-law apparently made Philip VI uneasy. Disquieted by his intimacy with the duke of Brabant

with whom he had arranged a double marriage, with the count of
Juliers who was his son-in-law, with the count of Guelders who
was so closely in agreement with him in regard to the policy
to be followed toward the bishop of Utrecht, with the emperor,
and especially with the Plantagenet court, the French king became alarmed. The crisis in the relations between himself and
Edward had passed, but he could not help noticing the marriage
of Eleanor Plantagenet to Reginald, count of Guelders, which
to him appeared largely due to Count William's influence. This
seemed especially dangerous because of the experience which
his predecessors had had with the Flemings. Philip could rely
only upon the bishop of Liège and the count of Luxemburg to
support his cause in the Low Countries, for the personal loyalty
of Louis, count of Flanders, might at any moment be made in-
effectual by the opposition of the Flemish craftsmen. He determined to make William impotent by securing an alliance with
the duke of Brabant. Formerly Philip the Fair had sought to
ensure his influence in the Low Countries by an alliance with the
count of Hainault, Holland, and Zeeland; now Philip sought to
secure an ascendancy in these parts by an understanding which
would remove the duke of Brabant from Count William's influence, and, in separating Hainault from Holland and Zeeland
by the neutral territory of Brabant, weaken William's influence.

But the duke of Brabant was determined to remain independent in his political policies and haughtily rejected Philip's
proffer of arbitration in his disputes with Reginald of Valkenburg. An opportunity soon presented itself, however, to interfere in the duke's affairs. John had numerous enemies who were
eager to redress old wrongs, and when Robert of Artois fled
France and found asylum in Brabant, Philip supported the duke's
neighbors in an attack upon his duchy. This was merely a part
of an extensive plan to encroach upon the fiefs of the empire as
was shown by the treaty made between Philip and John, king of
Bohemia and count of Luxemburg, at Fontainebleau early in
1332, whereby King John promised to sanction Philip's encroachments upon the empire, help Philip in any struggle with
a vassal of the empire, and agreed to assist him with an armed
force in Champagne and Vermandois. The war broke out in
April, but a truce was arranged by William, count of Hainault,

Holland, and Zeeland, in accordance with the wishes of King Philip. At Compiègne Philip's decision was given in part of the disputes between the duke of Brabant and his neighbors, but what was particularly significant was the *rapprochement* between the duke and the king. John agreed to banish Robert of Artois from his lands, repudiate his agreement with Count William whereby his son John should marry Isabella, and accept instead Philip's daughter Marie. The king's allies went home highly dissatisfied, for they felt that Philip had abandoned them.

This event certainly marked an important stage in the estrangement of the brothers-in-law. But Count William did not at once openly display any hostility. For the moment his wrath toward the duke of Brabant was so great that he joined the enemies of the duke during 1332–1333. Duke John's efforts to dismember the diocese of Liège, for which he had hoped that Philip's influence at the curia might be valuable, failed in 1333, and Philip's daughter Marie soon died. The sale of the seigniory and the *advocatia* of Mechelen during the same year once more brought into action the coalition of the duke's enemies, to whom were now added Count William and Louis, count of Flanders. Hostilities, which had already broken out on the Dyle in the autumn, became quite general in January of 1334. The papacy, ever solicitous to maintain peace and to enlist a united Christendom against the infidel, sought to intervene, and actually succeeded in arranging a truce on March 16. In the negotiations which followed and which came to a conclusion in the decisions made at Amiens in August, Philip disposed of the disputes among the princes in the Low Countries in unprecedented manner. Only in the matter of Mechelen did he fail, for, while Count Louis was willing to listen to Philip's suggestions to return the properties to the church of Liège, the chapter which wanted to use the moneys received from the sale in contesting the succession of Thierry of Heinsberg to the county of Loon proved intractable.

The triumphant intervention of 1332 and 1334 was to prove very disastrous for King Philip. He did not gain the gratitude of such allies as the counts of Namur, Guelders, and Juliers, for he had shown a disposition to look chiefly to his own advantage during the negotiations at Compiègne. The duke of Brabant's belief that a policy of aloofness was best for him was decidedly strengthened when Philip completely failed to aid him in securing a sympathetic hearing at the curia when he made his request for a separate diocese for Brabant. The French king won the undying hatred of his brother-in-law in inducing Duke John to repudiate the agreement whereby his son and heir apparent was to marry Count William's daughter Isabella. When Philip's daughter Marie died the way was opened for a *rapprochement* between the two princes. In the spring of 1334, while preparations were made for the sessions in which Philip was to give his arbitral decision, many questions were settled between them. Disputes in connection with the marriages were adjusted, boundary difficulties were disposed of, the problem of Heusden came to an end, and on September 5 a treaty of amity, commerce, and defense was made by Count William, the duke of Brabant, the count of Guelders, and the archbishop of Cologne. In 1335 and 1336 Count William proved a valuable friend to Duke John who was confronted with serious financial problems brought on by the settlements made at Amiens. William came to agreement with Louis, count of Flanders, on May 1, 1336, regarding the disputed lands of Flobecq and Lessines. John and Louis settled the status of Mechelen at this time by establishing a sort of *condominium*. On March 31 the three princes met at Dendermonde and drew up a treaty of alliance for defense and arbitration of differences.

King Philip had thus gained nothing from his efforts. On the contrary he had lost the friendship of his brother-in-law William, count of Hainault, Holland, and Zeeland, who now had greatly strengthened his position by his alliance with the duke of Brabant and even with Count Louis of Flanders who was really a faithful satellite of the French king. Count William complained bitterly of Philip's treatment. He had aided him materially during the uncertain days of the regency and had saved the day for him at Cassel. In return Philip had induced the duke of Brabant to repudiate his promise that his son John should marry Isabella; he had failed to hearken to his protests against the aggression of French officials at Crèvecoeur, Arleux, and St. Supplet; and, finally, he had sought to secure possession of the castlery of Cambrai contrary to an express understanding with him.

The baleful consequences of this shortsighted policy were soon apparent. Relations between the English and French courts became strained, Robert of Artois fled to England in the spring of 1334, and the Scotch crisis of 1335 produced a dangerous tension. Edward looked to his connections on the continent to aid him, and Count William's hatred of Philip became a most important matter in forging a vast chain of alliances in the Low Countries and in Germany against France. William sought the support of the empire in resisting the acquisition by Philip of the castlery of Cambrai. On September 18, 1335, Lewis the Bavarian had ordered the abbot of Vicogne to appear before the bishop of Cambrai and in his name protest against the suggested transfer. This solemn declaration was of no avail, for on February 28, 1337, Philip finally acquired title to these rights. Meanwhile the count of Juliers, who had visited Edward in 1335 and had taken part in the campaign against the Scots, had been exceedingly busy as an agent of the English court in the Low Countries and Germany. So active were Edward's emissaries that most princes in these parts were approached with the view of forming alliances.

The chief cause of the Hundred Years' War was political. It grew out of the antagonisms between lord and vassal in Aquitaine. The situation of Flanders illustrates this very well. In order to exert pressure upon the Flemings who, as subjects of the French crown, were inclined to aid the Scots, Edward ordered an embargo upon the export of wool on August 12, 1336. The rupture between England and Flanders came in the autumn and was due solely to political and not to economic matters. Edward could surely rely upon the support of Count William, Reginald, count of Guelders, William, margrave of Juliers, the count of Namur, John, duke of Brabant — who was withal determined to maintain his traditional aloofness and extract the greatest possible benefit from the troubles of his neighbors — the emperor, Lewis the Bavarian, and many other persons of less degree. Philip could depend only upon John, king of Bohemia and count of Luxemburg, the bishop of Liège, the Friesians, and the count of Flanders. But in the case of Flanders the situation was unsatisfactory for the French. The English embargo upon wool, woolfells, hides, and food-stuffs of all kinds produced a serious crisis among craftsmen of Ghent, Bruges, Ypres, and other towns. It was idle to suppose that they would ever support the royal policy which proposed to sacrifice their well-being in the struggle with the English king. Relentless was the pressure exerted by Edward and his allies, the duke of Brabant, whose industrial classes were favored at the expense of the Flemings, and the count of Hainault, Holland, and Zeeland.

By the opening of 1338 there were vast stores of wool collected at Dordrecht. The monopoly of the wool which Parliament had granted Edward in 1336 was intended for both diplomatic and financial purposes. To remain faithful to their suzerain, the king of France, spelled social upheaval, starvation, and misery; to support Edward was impossible because of the determination of Count Louis and the feudality in Flanders to remain loyal to their suzerain in accordance with their oath of homage. Could a middle course be found? To Jacob van Artevelde, a burgher of Ghent, a policy of neutrality seemed to be the only possible solution. This person rose from obscurity at the close of December, 1337, when the scabini of Ghent peaceably chose five captains of whom van Artevelde was the chief. There was an unmistakable greatness about this man as becomes evident the more one reflects upon the laconic statements recorded in the accounts of Ghent. But all his acts and his influence are veiled in great obscurity. The scabini of Ghent continued as before to govern the town even though a marked change in policy was at once evident. Since he occupied a position outside the normal political organs of the day, but few traces of his official career were ever recorded. Just how much influence such men as William and Thomas van Vaernewijc exerted upon him will of course never be known. But it remains true that van Artevelde, by securing control of Ghent, and through Ghent of all Flanders, saved the Flemish crafts from destruction. The situation in Flanders was created by external forces, the policy of the English and French kings. Van Artevelde adopted the simplest and most feasible plan whereby the interests of the bourgeoisie could be saved.

During 1337 Edward's envoys had been active in consolidating the alliances of the other princes in the Low Countries and Germany. Valenciennes was the center of this intrigue which was directed by Count William up until the moment of his death in May. The duke of Brabant proved a most cautious bargainer who was firmly resolved to sell himself as dearly as possible and yet remain free. It had been Edward's original plan to appear in the Low Countries on the borders of the Cambrésis in the early autumn when, supported by the levies of his numerous allies, he hoped to strike a blow for his right to the crown of France. But this plan failed because of his inability to realize sufficient income from the wool monopoly. The expedition was postponed until the following spring, but it was not until July that Edward arrived in Brabant. The wily duke knew how to employ all manner of subterfuge and was actually successful in putting him off until the autumn of 1339! Meanwhile Edward's debts grew to enormous proportions, his credit declined, and his prestige with his allies threatened to become seriously compromised. In the summer of 1339 the duke was forced to adopt a new attitude. He agreed to the betrothal of his daughter Marguerite to Edward's son, and in September was in Edward's army when it advanced upon France. The invasion of the Cambrésis was a brief affair; but the moment the allied forces passed into France the youthful William, count of Hainault, Holland, and Zeeland, who displayed none of the zeal of his father in insisting upon the rights of his house to Crèvecoeur, St. Supplet, Arleux, and the castlery of Cambrai, abandoned his uncle and rode off toward Philip to discharge his feudal obligations to him.

Van Artevelde's policy of neutrality attained its highest success in the summer of 1339 when Edward agreed to compensate the Flemings and even the Spanish merchants for losses incurred since the rupture which came in 1336. But the great weakness in his position was the hostility of Philip who, as suzerain, could be little pleased with a policy of neutrality which robbed him of much-needed assistance in fighting Edward and his allies. Count Louis and the feudality also were hostile. Van Artevelde now sought to gain the support of Louis by proposing that the lands taken from Flanders by the Treaty of Athis-sur-Orge should be returned. In this he relied upon help from Edward; in fact the scabini of Ghent sent a force toward the Cambrésis at the moment when Edward was marching toward Thiérache and made a formal demand of Philip that the lands in question should be returned. After these events Count Louis returned to Flanders, and a Council of Flanders, composed of a number of burghers from Ghent, was appointed to govern his actions. Need for support in the face of Philip's hostility drove van Artevelde into Edward's camp. The English suggestions were now accepted; on December 3 the alliance with Brabant was made, and at the close of January occurred the brilliant scene on the Friday Market Place at Ghent which announced the break with France in most dramatic fashion. Edward was accepted as king of France and a series of treaties was made. In 1337 the exigencies of Flemish industries called forth van Artevelde's policy of neutrality; in 1339 and 1340 the political implications of his position demanded an alliance with Brabant and England.

In the spring of 1340 Philip, who had repulsed Count William's proffer of service, began an attack upon Hainault and threatened invasion of Brabant and Flanders. Count William joined the Flemings and the Brabanters and accepted the alliance of December 3. But the gravity of the situation was brusquely changed by the sanguinary battle on the Zwin before Sluis in which the French fleet was totally destroyed. For the moment Edward's prestige was greater than ever. It soon suffered a serious reverse, however, in the failure of Robert of Artois to take St. Omer and secure control of his patrimony. But far worse than this was Edward's failure to maintain sufficient harmony among his motley troops long enough to capture Tournai. The purpose of this *démarche* was to return it to the Flemings as part of the possessions which had once been taken from them. Edward, as King of France, had returned all lands which his predecessors had taken from the count of Flanders. The failure revealed the fact that van Artevelde's plan of recovering former lands lost to the French monarchy could not be realized. The great captain's prestige sank rapidly and especially as Edward's bankruptcy became more and more apparent. His support and that of Flanders had been virtually necessary for Edward as long as the king remained in the Low Countries, but during the next few years it became more and more apparent that Flanders stood in even greater need of English support. This was the fundamental weakness of van Artevelde's policy. The régime of the three towns in the affairs of Flanders, which was largely inspired by him, was confronted by the determined opposition of certain towns, such as Oudenaarde, Poperingen, and Dendermonde, and by the bitter hatreds of the crafts in nearly every town. Besides, Count Louis and the feudality of Flanders remained firm in their loyalty to the French king.

The Truce of Esplechin, which had closed the siege of Tournai, was repeatedly extended until June 24, 1342. In January, 1341, Edward left Flanders in a most unceremonious fashion. He owed vast sums, he had lost his credit, in England there was serious disaffection in Parliament, and during 1341 and 1342 he could do little more than pay off his most pressing obligations and prepare for a renewal of the war. The slight value that Edward now placed upon his allies in the Low Countries as active supporters of his pretensions to the French crown is shown by the assistance which he gave to John, count of Montfort, who had some claims upon the duchy of Brittany. At the most he cared only for the diplomatic advantages which the alliances with them gave him. The Breton campaign at the close of 1342 was thus planned and executed without expectation of help from the Low Countries. That the diplomatic importance of these alliances and especially the one with Flanders was nevertheless very great is revealed by Philip's state of mind in the spring of 1341 when the pope refused to have expunged from the registers the clauses of the Treaty of Athis-sur-Orge whereby the church was to excommunicate the Flemings and lay them under the interdict for violation of their promises to their suzerain.

The decline of Edward's influence during these years is further illustrated by the desertion of William, count of Hainault, Holland, and Zeeland, and by the death on October 12, 1343, of his most faithful aid, Reginald, duke of Guelders. The duke of Brabant was not the person to sacrifice his advantage and was coolly looking forward to the moment when he could secure legitimate title to Mechelen which he had assumed in the spring of 1340 after Count Louis had fled Flanders. For such a settlement the coöperation of the French king would be necessary, and Duke John was quite right in thinking that Philip would regard this a cheap price for his alliance. His agreement with Philip would completely destroy Edward's influence in the Low Countries and provide an opportunity for a flanking movement against the rebellious Flemings who would be entirely isolated. Between the Truce of Malestroit in January, 1343, which closed the Breton campaign, and the battle of Crécy, Edward's prestige waned steadily. The murder of van Artevelde was an incident of but slight importance in the general diplomatic situation, for it did not effect the position of Flanders in the least.

The death of William, count of Hainault, Holland, and Zeeland, at the hands of the Friesians in September, 1345, was a more important matter, for it raised the question of heirs. Edward demanded a part of the patrimony in the name of Philippa, and English intrigue at once became active. But Lewis the Bavarian certainly had as much right as Edward, and the margrave of Juliers was inclined to antagonize neither of his brothers-in-law because he hoped for the settlement of certain claims nearer home. Covertly supported by the king of France, who did not wish to see Edward's influence in the Low Countries strengthened by the acquisition of any of these territories, the empress Margaret was able to succeed to Hainault, Holland, and Zeeland without serious difficulties. John of Hainault, Edward's faithful friend since the moment he and his mother Isabella had arrived in Hainault in 1326, now also abandoned him. The Flemings had repulsed an effort of Count Louis to return to Flanders by force during the summer of 1345, and hence for the moment remained faithful to their alliance. Under these circumstances the duke of Brabant thought that the moment to open negotiations with Philip had arrived and a definite treaty was agreed upon during the early winter of 1345–1346.

This completely reversed the political alliances of all the states of the Low Countries except Flanders where a change was after all but a question of time. Edward's preparations for the campaign of 1346 apparently caused the duke to proceed more slowly. The battle of Crécy was followed by the siege of Calais, and, while Edward desired an alliance with him, it was obvious that in the future he would not seek to realize his claims upon the French crown by relying upon his Netherlandish allies. Duke John's claim upon Mechelen had been legalized in the negotiations at Laon in June, 1346. The youthful Louis, count of Flanders, whose father had been killed at Crécy, returned to Flanders after the battle. The Flemings sought to induce him to take Edward's daughter Isabella as his wife and thus bind him to their cause. The margrave of Juliers, who had been named *ruwaard*, vigorously supported their endeavors. The youthful Reginald, duke of Guelders, was in Edward's camp before Calais, and a marriage between him and the margrave's daughter was planned. But these schemes were quickly frustrated by the flight of Count Louis to Philip and of Reginald to Antwerp. Philip and John now came to a definitive agreement in June. And in July at the Bois de Vincennes John's sons, Henry and Godefroid, were married to Jeanne, daughter of the duke of Normandy, and to Bonne, daughter of Peter, duke of Bourbon. At Tervuren Louis, count of Flanders, married the duke's daughter Marguerite and Reginald, duke of Guelders, received her sister Marie. Of all the allies whom Edward had won with the expenditure of so much treasure, only the margrave of Juliers and the Flemings remained faithful. But the margrave could effect nothing in his isolation, and the Flemings might, because of their dissensions and because of the policy of the duke of Brabant, sooner or later be forced to modify their policy.

BIBLIOGRAPHY

Abbreviations

BCRH   Bulletin de la Commission Royale d'Histoire
BEC   Bibliothèque de l'École de Chartes
CCB   Collection de Chroniques Belges
CCR   Calendar of Close Rolls
CDI   Collection des Documents Inédits
CFR   Calendar of Fine Rolls
CPR   Calendar of Patent Rolls
Foedera   Rymer, Th., *Foedera, Conventiones, Literae, et Cujuscunque Generis Acta Publica*

I. THE DOCUMENTS

ANSEMS, J. B., Den Luyster ende Glorie van het Hertogdom van Brabant hersteld door de genealogique Beschrijving van desselfs souverreyne Princes, 3 Parts. Brussel, 1699.

BALUZIUS, S., Vitae Paparum Avenionensium, hoc est Historia Pontificum Romanorum qui in Gallia sederunt ab anno Christi MCCCV usque ad annum MCCCXCIV, 2 Vols. Paris, 1693.

BARONIUS, C., Annales Ecclesiastici denuo excusi et ad nostra usque tempora predicti . . . , 37 Vols. Barri Ducis, 1864–1883.

BERGH, L. PH. C. VAN DEN, Gedenkstukken tot Opheldering der Nederlandsche Geschiedenis Opgezamelt uit de Archieven te Rijssel, Vol. I. Utrecht, 1849.

BERLIÈRE, U., Suppliques de Clément VI (1342–1352). Textes et Analyses, Analecta Vaticano Belgica. Rome, 1906.

BLED, O., Registres des Évêques de Thérouanne (500–1553). Saint Omer, 1909.

BLISS, W. H., Papal Letters, Calendar of Entries in the Papal Registers Relating to Great Britain and Ireland, Vols. I and II. London, 1893–1895.

BLOK, P. J., Oorkonden betrekkelijk Friesland in zijne Verhouding tot Frankrijk in de 13e en 14e Eeuw, De Vrije Vries, 4th Ser., Vol. I. Leeuwarden, 1898.

BLOK, P. J., FEITH, J. A., GRATEMA, J., REITSMA, J., EN RUTGERS, C. P. L., Oorkondenboek van Groningen en Drenthe, 2 Vols. Groningen, 1886, 1899.

BOEHMER, J. F., " Briefe Ludwigs des Baiern," Fontes Rerum Germanicarum, I, 192–227.

—— Die Regesten des Kaiserriechs unter Karl IV, 1346–1376, aus dem Nachlasse Böhmers herausgegeben von A. Huber, Innsbruck, 1877, with Additamentum Primum. Innsbruck, 1889.

—— Die Urkunden Kaiser Ludwigs des Baiern, König Friedrich des Schönen und König Johanns von Böhmen nebst einer Auswahl der Briefe und Bullen der Päpste und anderer Urkunden welche für die Geschichte Deutschlands von 1314 bis 1347 vorzüglich wichtig sind. Frankfurth-am-Main, 1834, with Additamentum Primum and Secundum. Frankfurth-am-Main and Leipzig, 1841–1846.

BOND, C. G., " Extracts from the Liberate Rolls, Relative to Loans Supplied by Italian Merchants to Kings of England in the 13th and 14th Centuries with an Introductory Memoir," Archaeologia, or Miscellaneous Tracts Relating to Antiquity, XXVIII (1840), 207–326.

BONGARSIUS, J., Gesta Dei per Francos sive orientalium Expeditionum et Regni Francorum Hierosolimitani Historia, 2 Vols. Hanover, 1612.

BORMANS, S., " Notice des Cartulaires de la Collégiale Saint-Denis à Liège," BCRH, 3d Ser., XIV (1872), 23–190.

—— " Recueil des Ordonnances de la Principauté de Liège," Recueil des Anciennes Ordonnances de la Belgique, 1st Ser. Bruxelles, 1878.

BORMANS, S., ET SCHOOLMEESTERS, E., Cartulaire de l'Église Saint-Martin de Liège, CCB, 4 Vols. Bruxelles, 1893–1900.

BROM, G., Bullarium Trajectense Romanorum Pontificum Diplomata Quotquot olim usque ad Urbanum Papam VI (Anno 1378) in veterem Episcopum Trajectensem destinata, 2 Vols. Haga-Comitis, 1892–1896.

BUTKINS, C., Les Trophées tant Sacrés que Profanes du Duché de Brabant, 2d ed., 2 Vols. La Haye, 1724–1746.

Calendar of Close Rolls Preserved in the Public Record Office, Prepared under the Superintendance of the Deputy Keeper of the Records.

Calendar of Documents Relating to Scotland Preserved in Her Majesty's Public Record Office, London, Edited by Joseph Bain, 4 Vols. Edinburgh, 1881–1888.

Calendar of Fine Rolls Preserved in the Public Record Office, Prepared under the Superintendance of the Deputy Keeper of the Records.

Calendar of Letter Books, Preserved among the Archives of the Corporation of the City of London at the Guildhall. Letter-Book E and F, Edited by Reginald R. Sharpe. London, 1903, 1904.

Calendar of Patent Rolls Preserved in the Public Record Office, Prepared under the Superintendance of the Deputy Keeper of the Records.

CANESTRINI, G., " Di alcuni Documenti risguardanti le Relazionie politiche dei Papi d'Avignone coi Comuni d'Italia, avanti e dopo il Tribunato di Cola di Rienzo e de la Calata di Carlo IV," Archivio Storico Italiano, VII (Appendice, 1849), 349–430.

Codex Diplomaticus Neerlandicus. Verzameling van Oorkonden betrekkelijk de Vaderlandsche Geschiedenis, 8 Vols., published by the Historisch Genootschap gevestigd te Utrecht. Utrecht, 1848–1863.

COULON, A., Lettres Sécretes et Curiales du Pape Jean XXII (1316–1334) relatives à la France extraites des Registres du Vatican, Bibliothèque des Écoles Françaises d'Athènes et de Rome, 3d Ser. (*in progress*).

CUVELIER, J., Les Dénombrements de Foyers en Brabant, XIVᵉ–XVIᵉ Siècles, *CCB*. Bruxelles, 1912.

DAUMET, G., Benoît XII (1334–1342). Lettres Closes, Patentes, et Curiales se rapportant à la France, Bibliothèque des Écoles Françaises d'Athènes et de Rome. Paris, 1920.

DELEPIERRE, O., ET PRIEM, F., Précis analytique des Documents que renferme le Dépôt des Archives de la Flandre Occidentale, 12 Vols. Bruges, 1840–1852.

DELPIT, J., Collection Générale des Documents Françaises qui se trouvent en Angleterre, *CDI*. Paris, 1847.

DÉPREZ, E., Clément VI (1342–1352). Lettres Closes, Patentes, et Curiales se rapportant à la France publiées ou analysées d'après les registres de Vatican, Bibliothèque des Écoles Françaises d'Athènes et de Rome, 3d Ser. (*in progress*).

DES MAREZ, G., " Un Document inédit relatif à Jacques van Artevelde," *BCRH*, 5th Ser., VIII (1898), 305–310.

DEVILLERS, L., Cartulaire des Comtes de Hainaut de l'Avènement de Guillaume II à la Mort de Jacqueline de Bavière (1337–1436), *CCB*, 6 Vols. Bruxelles, 1881–1896.

—— Description analytique de Cartulaire et de Chartriers du Hainaut, 3 Vols. Mons, 1865–1878.

—— (with the Baron de Reiffenberg), Monument pour Servir à l'Histoire des Provinces de Namur, de Hainaut et de Luxembourg, *CCB*, 8 Vols. Bruxelles, 1844–1848.

—— " Notice sur un Cartulaire concernant les Terres dites de débat (Hainaut et Flandre)," *BCRH*, 4th Ser., III (1876), 467–512.

—— " Notice sur un Cartulaire de Guillaume I, Comte de Hainaut, de Hollande, de Zélande, et Seigneur de Frise," *BCRH*, 3d Ser., VII (1865), 351–382.

—— " Notice sur un Cartulaire de la Trésorerie des Comtes de Hainaut 1184–1314)," *BCRH*, 3d Ser., XII (1871), 339–468.

—— " Sur la Mort de Guillaume le Bon, Comte de Hainaut, de Hollande, de Zélande, et Seigneur de Frise," *BCRH*, 5th Ser., V (1878), 409–436.

—— " Sur les Expéditions des Comtes de Hainaut et de Hollande en Prusse," *BCRH*, 4th Ser., V (1878), 127–144.

DEVON, J., Issues of Exchequer, Henry III–Henry VI: Extracts from Pell Issue Rolls. London, 1837.

DIEGERICK, I. L. A., Inventaire Analytique et Chronologique des Chartes et Documents appartenant aux Archives de la Ville d'Ypres, 7 Vols. Bruges, 1853–1868.

DOREN, P. J. VAN, Inventaire des Archives de la Ville de Malines public sous les auspices de l'Administration communale, 2 Vols. Malines, 1859–1862.

DUMONT, J., Corps universel et diplomatique du Droit des Gens contenant un Recueil des Traitéz . . . , 8 Vols. and 5 Vols. Supplement. Amsterdam et la Haye, 1726–1739.

DUYSE, P. VAN, Inventaire Analytique des Chartes et Documents appartenant aux Archives de la Ville de Gand. Gand, 1849.

ENNEN, L., UND ECKERTZ, G., Quellen zur Geschichte der Stadt Köln, 6 Vols. Köln, 1860–1879.

ESPINAS, G., ET PIRENNE, H., Recueil des Documents relatifs à l'Histoire de l'Industrie drapière en Flandre, 1st Part, *CCB*, 4 Vols. Bruxelles, 1906–1924.

EVEN, E. VAN, Inventaire des Registres des trois ci-devant Chambres échevinales de Louvain. Louvain, 1865.

—— "Mengelingen voor de Nederlandsche Geschiedenis," Vaderlandsche Museum voor Nederduitsche Letterkunde, Oudheid, en Geschiedenis, uitgegeven door C. P. Serrure, II (1858), 294–332.

FAYEN, A., Lettres de Jean XXII (1316–1334). Textes et Analyses, Analecta Vaticano-Belgica, 2 Vols. Rome, 1908–1909.

FICKER, J., Urkunden zur Geschichte des Römerzuges Kaiser Ludwigs des Baiern. Innsbruck, 1865.

FIERENS, A., Lettres de Benoît XII (1334–1342). Textes et Analyses, Analecta Vaticano-Belgica. Rome, 1910.

FINKE, H., Acta Aragonensia, Quellen zur Deutschen, Italienischen, Französischen, Spanischen, zur Kirchen- und Kulturgeschichte aus der Diplomatischen Korrespondenz Jaymes II (1291–1327), 3 Vols. Berlin, 1908–1922.

FINOT, J., Inventaire Sommaire des Archives Départmentales antérieures à 1790, Archives civile, Serie B, Vol. VII. Lille, 1892.

FUNCK-BRENTANO, F., "Additions au Codex Diplomaticus Flandriae," *BEC,* LVII (1896), 373–417, 529–572.

—— "Documents relatifs aux Formes diplomatiques aux XIIIe et XIVe Siècles," Revue d'Histoire Diplomatique, Vol. II (1897).

GACHARD, L. P., "Les Archives Royales de Düsseldorf. Notice des Documents qui concernent l'Histoire de Belgique," *BCRH,* 4th Ser., IX (1881), 267–366.

GACHET, E., "Un Cartulaire de Guillaume Ier, Comte de Hainaut, de Hollande, etc.," *BCRH,* 2d Ser., IV (1852), 9–118.

GILLIODTS VAN SEVEREN, L., Inventaire des Archives de la Ville de Bruges, 7 Vols. Bruges, 1871–1878.

—— " Jacques van Artevelde," La Flandre, Revue des Monuments d'His-toire et d'Antiquité, IX (1878), 257–314, 375–443.

GORRINI, G., " Lettere inedite degli Ambasciatori Fiorentini alla Corte dei Papi in Avignone (anno 1340)," Archivio Storico Italiano, 4th Ser., XIV (1884), 153–171.

GUESNON, A., Documents inédits sur l'Invasion Anglaise et les États au Temps de Philippe VI et de Jean le Bon. Paris, 1898 (reprinted from the Bulletin Historique et Philologique, 1897).

GÜNTHER, W., Codex Diplomaticus Rheno-Mosellanus, 5 Vols. Coblentz, 1822–1828.

HABETS, J., " Codex Diplomaticus Mosae-Trajectensis," Publications de la Société Historique et Archéologique dans le Duché de Limbourg, V (1868).

HAMAKER, H. G., De Rekeningen der Grafelijkheid van Holland onder het Henegouwsche Huis, Werken van het Historisch Genootschap gevestigd te Utrecht, New Ser., Nos. 21, 24, and 26, 3 Vols. Utrecht, 1875–1878.

—— De Rekeningen der Grafelijkheid van Zeeland, onder het Henegouwsche Huis, Werken van het Historisch Genootschap Gevestigd te Utrecht, New Ser., Nos. 29 and 30. 2 Vols. Utrecht, 1879–1880.

HARDY, T. D., Syllabus of the Documents Relative to England and other Kingdoms Contained in the Collection known as Rymer's Foedera, 3 Vols. London, 1869–1885.

HEERINGA, K., De Rekeningen en andere Stukken in 1607 uit de Hollandsch Rekenkamer naar de Zeeuwsche overgebracht. 's-Gravenhage, 1913.

HENDRYX, P., Jaarboeken van Veurne en Veurneambacht. Veurne, 1853.

HERMANS, C. R., Analytische Opgave der gedrukte Charters, Diplomas, Handvesten, Plakaten, Keuren, Ordonnantien, Reglementen, en andere Staatsstukken betrekkelijk de Provincie Noord Braband van het Jaar 704 tot en met het Jaar 1648, uitgegeven door het Provinciale Genootschap van Kunsten en Wetenschappen in Noord Braband. 's-Hertogenbosch, 1844.

HÖHLBAUM, K., Hansische Urkundenbuch, herausgegeben vom Verein für Hansische Geschichte, 11 Vols. Halle, 1876–1916.

HONTHEIM, J. N. AB, Historia Treverensis Diplomatica et Pragmatica, 3 Vols. Herbipolis, 1750.

HUILLARD-BRÉHOLLES, Titres de la Maison ducale de Bourbon, 2 Vols. Paris, 1867–1874.

HULSHOF, A., " Oorkonden aangaande de Betrekkingen der Geldersche Vor-sten tot Frankrijk," Werken uitgegeven door de Vereeniging Gelre, No. 8. Armhem, 1912.

—— " Oorkonden in de Archives Nationales te Parijs aangaande de Betrek-kingen der Hollandsche Graven uit het Henegouwsche en het Beieris-che Huis tot Frankrijk," Bijdragen en Mededeelingen van het Historisch Genootschap gevestigd te Utrecht, XXXII, 266–387. Am-sterdam, 1911.

Inventaire chronologique et analytique des Chartes et autres Documents sur Parchemin appartenant aux Archives de la Ville de Louvain, 1164–1793. Louvain, 1873.

ISACKER, PH. VAN, ET BERLIÈRE, U., Lettres de Clément VI (1342–1352), Analecta Vaticano-Belgica, Vol. I. Bruxelles, 1924.

JANSEN, M., Inventaris van het Oud Archief der Gemeente Sittard, 1243–1609. Sittard, 1878.

JONGE, J. DE, Verhandelingen en onuitgegeven Stukken betreffende de Geschiedenis der Nederlanden. Delft, 's-Gravenhage, en Amsterdam, 1825–1827.

JUSSELIN, M., "Comment la France se Préparait à la Guerre de Cent Ans," *BEC*, LXXIII (1912), 209–239.

KERVYN DE LETTENHOVE, Oeuvres de Froissart, 25 Vols. Bruxelles, 1867–1877.

KLUIT, A., Historia Critica Comitatus Hollandiae et Zeelandiae ab Antiquissimis inde deducta, 2 Vols. Medioburgi, 1777–1782.

KRELINGER, A., "Extrait des Pièces relatives à l'Histoire de Belgique qui se trouvent aux Archives de Coblence, *BCRH*, 1st Ser., III (1839), 202–274.

KROM, C. C. N., EN SASSEN, A., Oorkonden betreffende Helmond, Werken van het Provinciaal Genootschap van Kunsten en Wetenschappen in Noord Braband, New Ser., Vol. I. 's-Hertogenbosch, 1884.

LACOMBLET, TH. J., Urkundenbuch für die Geschichte des Niederrheins, 4 Vols. Düsseldorf, 1840–1858.

LAENEN, J., Les Archives de l'État à Vienne au Point de Vue de l'Histoire de Belgique. Bruxelles, 1924.

LIMBURG STIRUM, LE COMTE DE, Cartulaire de Louis de Male, Comte de Flandre. Decreten van den Grave Lodewijck van Vlaenderen (1348–1358), 2 Vols. Bruges, 1898–1901.

—— Codex Diplomaticus Flandriae, 1296–1327. 2 Vols. Bruges, 1879–1889.

LONGNON, A., Documents inédits du Comté de Champagne et de Brie, 1172–1367, *CDI*. Paris, 1924.

LOUVREX, M. G. DE, Recueil contenant les Édits et Règlements fait pour le Pais de Liège et Comté de Loon, 4 Vols. Liège, 1750–1752.

LUDEWIG, J. P. DE, Reliquiae Manuscriptorum omnis aevi Diplomatum ac Monumentorum ineditorum, 12 Vols. Frankfurt et Leipzig, 1720–1731.

LÜNIG, J. CH., Codex Italiae Diplomaticus, 4 Vols. Leipzig, 1726–1735.

MANNIER, E., Les Flamands à la Bataille de Cassel (1328). Noms de Flamands morts dans cette Journée, publiés pour la première Fois d'après le Manuscrit unique de la Bibliothèque Impériale. Paris, 1863.

MANTELUS, J., Historiae Lossensis libri X cui adjuncta sunt Diplomata Lossensia, Privilegia, Paces, Pacta, etc., cum Topographia seu Descriptione Urbium, Pagorum, et Locorum ejusdem Comitatus, Labore et Studio Laur. Robyns. Leodii, 1717.

MARTÈNE, D., ET DURAND, U., Thesaurus novus Anecdotorum complectens Regum ac Principum sanctorum Patrum aliorumque Virorum illustrium Epistolas et Diplomata bene multa, 5 Vols. Parisii, 1717.

—— Veterum Scriptorum et Monumentorum amplissima Collectio, 9 Vols. Parisii, 1724–1733.

MIERIS, F. VAN, Groot Charterboek der Graven van Holland, van Zeeland, Heeren van Friesland, 523–1426, 4 Vols. Leyden, 1753–1756.

MIRAEUS, A., Opera Diplomatica, 4 Vols. Louvanii et Bruxellis, 1723–1748.

MIROT, L., ET DÉPREZ, E., "Les Ambassades Anglaises pendant la Guerre de Cent Ans. Catalogue chronologique (1327–1450)," *BEC,* LIX (1898), 550–577, and LX (1899), 177–214.

MOLANUS, J., Historiae Lovaniensium libri XIV, *CCB,* 2 Vols. Bruxelles, 1861.

MOLLAT, G., Jean XXII (1316–1334). Lettres Communes Analysées d'après les Registres dits d'Avignon et du Vatican, Bibliothèque des Écoles Françaises d'Athènes et de Rome. 3d Ser. (*in progress*).

MORANVILLÉ, H., "Extraits de Journaux du Trésor (1345–1346)," *BEC,* XLIX (1888), 149–214, 368–452.

MULLER, Fz. S., De Registers en Rekeningen van het Bisdom Utrecht, 1325–1336, Werken van het Historisch Genootschap gevestigd te Utrecht, New Ser., Nos. 53 and 54, 2 Vols. 's-Gravenhage, 1889–1891.

MULLER, P. L., Regesta Hannonensia. Lijst van Oorkonden betreffende Holland en Zeeland, 1299–1345, die in het Charterboek van van Mieris ontbreken. 's-Gravenhage, 1882.

MUSSELEY, C., Inventaire des Archives de la Ville de Courtrai, 2 Vols. Courtrai, 1858–1870.

MUSSELY, C., ET MOLITOR, E., Cartulaire de l'ancienne Église Collégiale de Notre Dame à Courtrai. Gand, 1880.

NEELEMANS, E., Geschiedenis der Stad Eecloo, Verzameling van Charters, Kronijken, en andere geschiedkundige Stukken. Gent, Eecloo, 1863.

NIJHOFF, I. A., Gedenkwaardigheden uit de Geschiedenis van Gelderland door onuitgegeven Oorkonden opgehelderd en bevestigd, 7 Vols. Arnhem, 1830–1875.

NIJHOFF, P., Inventaris van het Oud Archief der Gemeente Arnhem. Arnhem, 1864.

NITZSCH, K. W., "Heinrich IV und der Gottes- und Landfrieden," Forschungen zur Deutschen Geschichte, XXI (1881), 269–297.

PAUW, N. DE, Cartulaire Historique et Généalogique des Artevelde, *CCB.* Bruxelles, 1920.

—— De Voorgeboden der Stad Gent, Maatschappij der Vlaamsche Bibliophilen, 4th Ser., No. 5. Gent, 1885.

—— La Conspiration d'Audenarde sous Jacques van Artevelde (1842). Gand, 1879.

—— "La Vie intime en Flandre au Moyen Âge d'après des Documents inédits," *BCRH*, LXXXII (1913), 1–96.

—— "L'Enquête de Bruges après la Bataille de Cassel. Documents inédits publiés," *BCRH*, LXVIII (1899), 665–704.

—— "L'Enquête sur les Capitaines de Courtrai sous Artevelde (1338–1340)," *BCRH*, LXXIX (1910), 219–288.

—— Nécrologie de l'Église de St. Jean à Gand, *CCB*. Bruxelles, 1889.

—— Ypres jeghen Poperinghen angaende den Verbonden. Gedenkstukken der XIVe Eeuw nopens het Laken, Koninklijke Vlaamsche Academie voor Taal en Letterkunde, Afdeeling: Middelnederlandsche Letterkunde, Part XVI. Gent, 1899.

PAUW, N. DE, EN VUYLSTEKE, J., Rekeningen der Stad Gent, Tijdvak van Jacob van Artevelde, 1336–1349, 3 Vols. Gent, 1874–1880.

PIOT, C., Inventaire des Chartes des Comtes de Namur anciennement déposées au Château de cette Ville. Bruxelles, 1890.

PIRENNE, H., "Documents relatifs à l'Histoire de Flandre pendant la première Moitié du XIVe Siècle," *BCRH*, 5th Ser., VII (1897), 15–36.

—— "Documents relatifs à l'Histoire de la Flandre pendant la première Moitié du XIVe Siècle (note supplémentaire)," *BCRH*, 5th Ser., VII (1897), 477–493.

—— Le Soulèvement de la Flandre Maritime de 1323–1328. Documents inédits publiés avec une Introduction. Bruxelles, 1900.

Placaeten ende Ordonnantien van de Hertoghen van Brabant, Princen van dese Neder-landen, Vol. I. 'tHantwerpen, 1648.

POTTER, F. DE, Petit Cartulaire de Gand. Gand, 1885.

—— Second Cartulaire de Gand. Gand, 1888.

POTVIN, CH., "Panégyriques des Comtes de Hainaut et de Hollande, Guillaume I et Guillaume II," Publications de la Société des Bibliophiles Belges séant à Mons, No. 20. Mons, 1863.

Recueil général des anciennes Lois Françaises dépuis l'An 420 jusqu' à la Révolution de 1789, 25 Vols. Paris.

Reports of the Lords Commissioners touching the Dignity of a Peer of the Realm . . . , with Appendices, 4 Vols.

RIEZLER, S., Urkunden zur Bayerischen und Deutschen Geschichte, 1256–1343, Forschungen zur Deutchen Geschichte, Vol. XX (1880).

—— Vatikanische Akten zur Deutschen Geschichte in der Zeit Kaisers Ludwigs des Baiers. Innsbruck, 1881.

RILEY, H. T., Memorials of London and London Life. A Series of Extracts from the Archives of the City of London, 1276–1419. London, 1868.

Rotuli Parliamentorum: ut et Petitiones et Placita in Parliamento (1278–1503), 6 Vols.

Rotuli Scaccarii Regum Scotorum. The Exchequer Rolls of Scotland, Edited by the late John Stuart and George Burnett. Edinburgh, Vol. I, 1878.

Rotuli Scotiae, 1291–1516, 2 Vols. London, 1814–1819.

RYMER, TH., Foedera, Conventiones, Literae, et Cujuscunque Generis Acta publica, 4 Vols. Londinii, 1816–1869.

SAGHER, E. DE, Notice sur les Archives Communales d'Ypres et Documents pour servir à l'Histoire de Flandre du XIIIᵉ au XVIᵉ Siècle. Ypres, 1898.

SAINT GENOIS, J. DE, Inventaire des Chartes des Comtes de Flandre avant l'Avènement des Princes de la Maison de Bourgogne, autrefois déposées au Château de Rupelmonde et conservées aujourd'hui aux Archives de la Flandre Orientale. Gand, 1843–1846.

SAINT GENOIS, J. DE, Monuments anciens essentiellement utiles à la France et aux Provinces de Hainaut, Flandre, Brabant, Namur, Artois, Liège, Hollande, Zélande, Frise, Cologne, et autres Pays limotrophes de l'Empire. Vol. I, 1st Part, also under title: Droits primitifs des anciennes terres et Seigneuries . . . de Hainaut, Paris, without date, and 2d Part, Lille, without date, and Bruxelles. 1806. Vol. II, Tables des Noms de Familles, Villes . . . , Lille, without date.

SANUTO, Marinus, dictus Torsellus, "Epistolae," Bongarsius, Gesta Dei per Francos sive Liber Secretorum Fidelium Crucis, Vol. II. Hanoveriae, 1611.

SASSEN, J. N. G., Charters en Privilegiebrieven berustende in het Archief der Gemeente 's-Hertogenbosch. 's-Hertogenbosch, 1862.

SCHÄFER, K. H., "Deutsche Ritter und Edelknechte in Italien während des 14 Jahrhunderts," Quellen und Forschungen aus den Gebiete der Geschichte, Vol. XV (1911).

SCHMIDT, G., Päpstliche Urkunden und Regesten aus den Jahren 1295–1352, die Gebiete der heutigen Provinz Sachsen und deren umlande betreffend, Geschichtsquellen der Provinz Sachsen, Vol. XXI (1886).

SCHOOLMEESTER, E., "Recueil des Lettres adressées pendant le XIVᵉ Siècle aux Papes et aux Cardinaux pour les Affaires de la Principauté de Liège," Analectes pour Servir à l'Histoire Ecclésiastique de la Belgique, Vol. XV (1878).

SCHOONBROODT, J., Inventaire analytique et chronologique des Chartes du Chapitre de Saint-Lambert à Liège. Liège, 1868.

—— Inventaire analytique et chronologique des Chartes du Chapitre de Saint-Martin à Liège. Liège, 1871.

SCHROHE, H., "Kleinere Beiträge zu den Regesten der Könige Rudolf bis Karl IV," Mitteilungen des Istituts für Oesterreichische Geschichtsforschung, XXIV (1903), 309–312; XXV (1904), 490–494; and XXVI (1905), 482–489.

SCHWALM, J., "Beiträge zur Reichsgeschichte des 14 Jahrhunderts aus dem Vatikanischen Archive," Neues Archiv der Gesellschaft für Aeltere Deutsche Geschichtskunde, XXV (1899), 559–584.

—— " Reise nach Italien in Herbst, 1898," Neues Archiv der Gesellschaft für Aeltere Deutsche Geschichtskunde, XXV (1899), 517–599, and XXVI (1900), 707–741.

—— " Reiseberichte, 1894–1896, Mit Beilagen," Neues Archiv der Gesellschaft für Aeltere Deutsche Geschichtskunde, XXIII (1897), 291–374.

—— " Reise nach Holland, Belgien, Nord Frankreich, und dem Niederrhein im Sommer, 1894," Neues Archiv der Gesellschaft für Aeltere Deutsche Geschichtskunde, XX (1895), 423–433.

—— " Reise nach München und Coblentz im Sommer 1897, Mit Beilagen," Neues Archiv der Gesellschaft für Aeltere Deutsche Geschichtskunde, XXIII (1897), 667–687.

—— " Reise nach Oberitalien und Burgund im Herbst 1901. Mit Beilagen," Neues Archiv der Gesellschaft für Aeltere Deutsche Geschichtskunde, XXVII (1901), 695–733.

SCHWARZENBERG EN HOHENLANSBERG, G. F. THOE, Groot Placaat- en Charterboek van Vriesland, 5 Vols. Leeuwarden, 1768–1793.

SLOET, L. A. J. W., Oorkondenboek der Graafschappen Gelre en Zutfen tot op den Slag van Woeringen, 5 June, 1288. 's-Gravenhage, 1872–1876.

SMIT, H. J., De Rekeningen der Graven en Gravinnen uit het Henegouwsche Huis, Werken uitgegeven door het Historisch Genootschap gevestigd te Utrecht, 3d Ser., No. 46. Amsterdam, 1924.

SOLLERIUS, J., Acta Sancti Rumoldi Episcopi et Martyris Apostoli et Patroni Mechliniensium. Antwerpen, 1718.

Statutes of the Realm, 11 Vols. London, 1810–1828.

STEIN, H., " Les Conséquences de la Bataille de Cassel pour la Ville de Bruges et la Mort de Guillaume de Deken son ancien Bourgmestre (1328)," BCRH, 69 (1899), 647–664.

STELLAERT, CH., ' Inventatire analytique des Chartes concernants les Seigneurs et la Ville de Diest," BCRH, 4th Ser., III (1875), 165–314.

STRAVEN, F., Inventaire analytique et chronologique des Archives de Saint Trond, 6 Vols. Saint Trond, 1886–1899.

VANDENBROEK, H., Extraits analytiques des anciens Registres de Consaux de la Ville de Tournai, 1385–1442, suivis d'une Analyse de Documents concernant le Magistrat de 1211 à 1400, 2 Vols. Tournai, 1861–1865.

VANDERLINDEN, H., " Les Relations politiques de la Flandre avec la France, au XIVᵉ Siècle," BCRH, 5th Ser., III (1893), 469–542.

VARIN, O., Archives administratives de la Ville de Reims, CDI, 4 Vols. Paris, 1843.

VERACHTER, F., Inventaire des anciens Chartes et Privileges et autres Documents conservés aux Archives de la Ville d'Anvers, 1193–1856. Anvers, 1860.

VERKOOREN, A., Inventaire des Chartes et Cartulaires des Duchés de Brabant et de Limbourg et des Pays d'Outremeuse, 5 Vols. Bruxelles, 1910–1913.

—— Inventaire des Chartes et des Cartulaires du Luxembourg (Comté puis Duché), 4 Vols. Bruxelles, 1914–1917.

VIARD, J., Documents Parisiens du Règne de Philippe VI. Extraits des Registres de la Chancellerie de France, Société d'Histoire de Paris, 2 Vols. Paris, 1899–1900.

—— "Itinéraire de Philippe de Valois," *BEC,* LXXIV (1913), 74–128, 524–592, and XXXIV (1923), 166–170.

—— Les Journaux du Trésor de Philippe VI de Valois, suivis de l'Ordinarium Thesauri de 1338–1339, *CDI.* Paris, 1899.

—— "Lettres d'État enregistrées au Parlement sous le Règne de Philippe VI de Valois," Annuaire Bulletin, Société d'Histoire de France, XXXIV (1897), 193–267, and XXXV (1898), 177–249.

VIDAL, J. M., Benoît XII (1334–1342). Lettres communes analysées d'après les Registres dits d'Avignon et du Vatican, Bibliothèque des Écoles Françaises d'Athènes et de Rome. 2 Vols. Paris, 1903–1906.

VISVLIET, P. VAN, Inventaris van het Oud Archief der Provincie Zeeland, 3 Vols. Middelburg, 1874–1881.

VLAMINCK, A. DE, Cartulaire de la Ville de Termonde, Gand, 1876–1877.

—— "Inventaire des Archives de la Ville de Termonde," Annales du Cercle Archéologique de Termonde, Vol. IV (1866).

VUYLSTEKE, J., Cartulaire de la Ville de Gand. Comptes de la Ville et des Baillis de Gand, 1280–1336, 2 Vols. Gand, 1900.

WARNKÖNIG, L. A., Histoire de la Flandre et de ses Institutions civiles et politiques jusqu'à l'Année 1305, translated by A. E. Geldolf, 5 Vols. Bruxelles, 1835–1864.

WAUTERS, A., Table Chronologique des Chartes et Diplômes imprimés concernant l'Histoire de la Belgique, *CCB,* 11 Vols. Bruxelles, 1866–1907.

WILLEM, J. F., Codex Diplomaticus, printed in his edition of Boendale's Brabantsche Yeesten, *CCB,* 3 Vols. Antwerpen, 1839–1869.

WINCKELMANN, E., Acta Imperii Inedita, 2 Vols. Innsbruck, 1880–1869.

WOLTERS, M. J., Codex Diplomaticus Lossensis. Gand, 1849.

WURTH-PAQUET, F. X., Table Chronologique des Chartes et Diplômes relatifs à l'Histoire de l'Ancien Comté de Luxembourg, Règne de Jean, Roi de Bohème, et Comté de Luxembourg, Publications de la Société pour la Recherche et la Conservation des Monuments Historiques de l'Institut Grand-Ducal du Luxembourg, Vol. XVIII (1862), Vol. XIX (1863), and Vol. XX (1864).

II. THE CHRONICLES

*When references are given to separate volumes of a series
the date of publication applies to them alone.*

Annales de Bermundeseia, Annales Monastici, edited by H. R. Luard, Rolls Ser., III, 423–487. London, 1886.

Annales Londonienses, edited by W. Stubbs, Chronicles of the Reigns of Edward I and Edward II, Rolls Ser., Vol. I. London, 1882.

Annales Paulini, edited by W. Stubbs, Chronicles of the Reigns of Edward I and Edward II, Rolls Ser., Vol. I. London, 1882.

Annales Tronchiniense, Corpus Chronicon Flandrensium, *CCB*, I, 591–700.

Auctor Bridlingtoniensis. Gesta Edwardi de Carnarvon auctore canonico Bridlingtoniensi, Chronicles of the Reigns of Edward I and Edward II, Rolls Ser., Vol. II. London, 1883.

AVESBURY. ROBERTUS DE AVESBURY, De Gestis mirabilibus regis Edwardi Tertii, edited by E. M. Thompson, Rolls Ser. London, 1889.

BAKER. Chronicon Galfridi le Baker de Swinbroke, edited by E. M. Thompson. Oxford, 1899.

BEKA. JOHANNIS DE BEKA, Canonicus Ultrajectinus, et Wilhelmus Heda, Praepositus Arnhemensis, De Episcopis Ultrajectinis recogniti et notis illustrati ab Arn. Buchelio. Ultraiectini, 1643.

BOENDALE. De Brabantsche Yeesten of Rymkronyk van Brabant door Jan de Klerk van Antwerpen, *CCB*, 3 Vols. Antwerpen, 1839–1869.

BOENDALE. Van den derden Eduwaert, Coninc van Engelant. Rymkroniek geschreven omtrent het Jaar 1347, door Jan de Clerc van Antwerpen. Belgisch Museum, Vol. IV. Gent, 1840.

Bourgeois de Valenciennes. Récits d'un Bourgeois de Valenciennes, publiés pour la première Fois d'après le Manuscrit de la Bibliothèque de l'Arsenal par Kervyn de Lettenhove. Louvain, 1877.

Breve Chronicon Clerici anonymi, Corpus Chronicorum Flandriae, *CCB*, III, 5–30.

Chronica de D. Alfonso el Onceno de este Nombre de los reyes que reynaron en Castilla y en Leon, 2d ed., Parte I. Madrid, 1787.

Chronicon Angliae ab Anno Domini 1326 usque ad Annum 1388 auctore Monacho quodam Sancti Albani, edited by E. M. Thompson, Rolls Ser. London, 1874.

Chronicon Comitum Flandrensium, Corpus Chronicorum Flandriae, *CCB*, Vol. I. Bruxelles, 1837.

Chronicon Tielense Auctoris incerti, edited by J. D. van Leeuwen. Traiecti ad Rhenum, 1789.

Chronique de London dépuis l'an 44 Henri III jusqu'à l'an 17 Édouard III. Edited from a MS. in the Cottonian Library by G. T. Ainger for the Camden Society. London, 1844.

Chronique des Pays-Bas, de France, d'Angleterre et de Tournai, Corpus Chronicorum Flandriae, *CCB*, III, 111–570.

Chronique des Quatre Premiers Valois (1327–1393), Société d'Histoire de France. Paris, 1862.

Chronique de Tournai, Kervyn de Lettenhove, Oeuvres de Froissart, XXV, 344–365.

Chronique Parisienne Anonyme de 1316 à 1339, précédé d'Additions à la Chronique Française dits de Guillaume de Nangis (1206–1316), publiés par M. A. Hellot, Mémoires de la Société d'Histoire de Paris, Vol. XI. Paris, 1885.

Chronographia Regum Francorum, publiée pour la Société d'Histoire de France par H. Moranvillé, 2 Vols. Paris, 1891–1897.

DE BUDT. Chronicon Flandriae scriptum ab Adriano de Budt, Corpus Chronicorum Flandriae, *CCB*, Vol. I. Bruxelles, 1837.

DE NANGIS. Chronique Latine de Guillaume de Nangis de 1113 à 1300 et les continuations de cette Chronique de 1300 à 1368. Nouvelle Édition revue sur les Manuscripts, Société d'Histoire de France, 2 Vols. Paris, 1843.

Die excellente Cronike van Vlaanderen, Beghinnende van Liederick Buc den eersten Forestier tot . . . desen onsen doorluchtisten . . . Keyser Karolo V. Antwerpen, 1531.

FORDUN. Johannis de Fordum Chronica Gentis Scotorum, edited by W. F. Skene, Historians of Scotland. Edinburgh, 1871.

FROISSART. Chronique de Jean Froissart, publiée pour la Société d'Histoire de France, 11 Vols. Paris, 1859–1899.

Gesta Abbatum Sancti Trudonis. Gesta Abbatum Sancti Trudonensium, Continuatio Tertia (1180–1366), Monumenta Germaniae Scriptores, Vol. X. Hannover, 1851.

Grandes Chroniques de France, ed. par Paulin Paris, 6 Vols. Paris, 1836–1838.

HEMINGBURGH. Chronicon domini Walteri de Hemingburgh, vulgo Hemingfort nuncupati. . . , English History Society, 2 Vols. London, 1848.

HOCSEMIUS. Gesta Pontificium Leodiensium Adolphi et Engelberti a Marcka, Chapeaville, Qui Gesta Pontificum Leodiensium scripserunt Auctores, Vol. II. Leodii, 1613.

Istore et Croniques de Flandres, d'après les Textes de divers Manuscrits par M. le Baron Kervyn de Lettenhove, *CCB*, 2 Vols. Bruxelles, 1879–1880.

KNIGHTON. Chronicon Henrici Knighton vel Cnithton, Monachi Leycestrensis, edited by J. R. Lumby, Rolls Ser., 2 Vols. London, 1889–1895.

Königsaaler Geschichts-Quellen. Chronica Aulae Reginae, 1250–1338 (Verfasst von Otto und Peter von Zittau), herausgegeben von J. Losert, Fontes Rerum Austriacarum, Scriptores, Abtheilung I, Vol. VIII (1875).

LANERCOST. Chronicon de Lanercost MCCI–MCCCXLVI e Codice Cottoniano nunc primum typis mandatum, edited by J. Stevenson. Edinburgh, 1839.

LE BEL. Chronique de Jean le Bel, publiée pour la Société d'Histoire de France par Jules Viand et Eugene Déprez, 2 Vols. Paris, 1904–1905.

LE MUISIT. Chronique et Annales de Gilles le Muisit, Abbé de Saint-Martin de Tournai (1272–1352), publiée pour la Société d'Histoire de France. Paris, 1906.

LESCOT. Chronique de Richard Lescot, religieux de Saint-Denys (1328–1344) suive de la continuation de cette chronique (1344–1364), publiée pour la Société d'Histoire de France par Jean Lemoine. Paris, 1896.

LEVOLD DE NORTHOF. Chronica Levoldi de Northof, Equitis Marcani, Canonici Leodiensis et Origines Marcanae sive Chronicon Comitum de Marca et Altena a qui descendunt Duces Juliacenses, Clivenses et Bergenses . . . , Rerum Germanicarum Tomi III . . . recensuit et edidit Henricus Meibomius, I, 371–424. Helmstadii, 1688.

Liber Pluscardensis, edited by Felix J. Skene, Historians of Scotland. Edinburgh, 1877.

MUEVIN, Chronicon, Corpus Chronicorum Flandriae, II, 449–471.

MURIMUTH. Adae Murimuth Continuatio Chronicorum, edited by E. M. Thompson, Rolls Ser. London, 1899.

NUWENBURG. Chronica Matthias de Nuwenburg, in Monumenta Germaniae Historiae, Scriptores, Nova Ser., Vol. IV. Berlin, 1924.

OUTREMEUSE. Ly Myreur des Histors, Chronique de Jean des Preis dit d'Outremeuse, publiée par Ad. Borgnet et S. Bormans, *CCB,* 6 Vols. Bruxelles, 1864–1880.

Scalacronica, by Sir Thomas Grey of Heton, Knight. A Chronicle of England and Scotland from A.D. MLXVI to A.D. MCCLXII, edited by Joseph Stevenson. Edinburgh, 1836.

VILLANI. Historie Fiorentine, L. A. Muratori Rerum Scriptores Italicarum, Vol. XIII.

Vita Karoli Quarti Imperatoris ab ipso Karolo Conscripta, 1316–1341, Fontes Rerum Germanicarum, Vol. I.

WALSINGHAM. Thomas Walsingham quodam Monachi Sancti Albani Historia Anglicana, edited by H. T. Riley, Rolls Ser., 2 Vols. London, 1863–1864.

WILLELMUS PROCURATOR. Willelmi Capellani in Brederode postea Monachi et Procuratoris Egmundensis Chronicon, uitgegeven door C. Pijnacker Hordijk, Werken van het Historisch Genootschap gevestigd te Utrecht, 3d Ser., No. 20. Amsterdam, 1904.

WYNTOUN. The Orygynale Chronykil of Scotland by Andrew of Wyntoun, Historians of Scotland, 3 Vols. Edinburgh, 1872.

III. BOOKS AND ARTICLES

*Many of these titles contain some documentary materials
to which reference is usually made by citing
only the work itself.*

ALTMANN, W., Der Römerzug Ludwig's des Baiern. Berlin, 1886.

ARMITAGE-SMITH, S., John of Gaunt. Westminster, 1904.

ASHLEY, W. J., James and Philip van Artevelde. London, 1883.

—— "The Early History of the English Woollen Industry," Publications of the American Economic Association, II (1887), 1–85.

BÄCHTOLD, H., "Der Norddeutsche Handel im 12. und beginnenden 13. Jahrhundert," Abhandlungen zur Mittleren und Neueren Geschichte, Heft 21 (1910).

BAHR, K., Handel und Verkehr der Deutschen Hanse in Flandern während des vierzehnten Jahrhunderts. Leipzig, 1911.

BANNIER, W. A. F., De Landgrenzen van Nederland. I (tot aan den Rijn). Leiden, 1900.

BARNES, F. R., "The Taxation of Wool, 1327–1348," Trade and Finance under Edward III. Manchester, 1918, pp. 137–177.

BEEKMAN, "De Heidensee," Tijdschrift van het Koninglijke Nederlandsch Aardrijkundig Genootschap, 2d Ser., XLI (1924), 359–368.

BENSE, J. F., Anglo-Dutch Relations from the Earliest Times to the Death of William the Third. The Hague and London, 1925.

BIGWOOD, G., "Gand et la Circulation des Grains en Flandre," Vierteljahrschrift für Sozial- und Wirtschafts Geschichte, IV (1906), 397–460.

—— "Le Régime juridique et économique du Commerce de l'Argent dans la Belgique du Moyen Âge," Mémoires Couronnés et autres Mémoires, Académie Royale de Belgique, Vol. XIV, Part I (1921).

—— "Les Finances d'Arras. Contribution à l'Étude des Origines du Capitalisme Moderne," Revue Belge de Philologie et d'Histoire, III (1924), 465–508, 769–814, and IV, 109–119, 379–421.

BLANCHARD, R., La Flandre, Étude géographique de la Plaine Flamande en France, Belgique, et Hollande. Paris, 1906.

BLINK, H., "Studien over Nederzettingen in Nederland," Tijdschrift van het Koninglijke Nederlandsche Aardrijkskundig Genootschap, 2d Ser., Vol. XXI (1914).

BLOK, P. J., "De Financien van het Graafschap Holland," Bijdragen voor Vaderlandsche Geschiedenis en Oudheidkunde, 3d Ser., III (1886), 36–130.

—— "Friesland in 1338," Historische Avonden. Bundel uitgegeven door het Historisch Genootschap te Groningen, ter Gelegenheid van zijn tienjarig Bestaan, pp. 291–292. Groningen, 1896.

—— Geschiedenis van het Nederlandsche Volk, 3d ed., 4 Vols. Leiden.

—— "Studien over Friesche Toestanden in de Middeleeuwen," Bijdragen voor Vaderlandsche Geschiedenis en Oudheidkunde, 3d Ser., VI (1892), 1–56.

BOISLISLE, A. DE, "Le Budget et la Population de la France sous Philippe de Valois," Annuaire Bulletin, Société de l'Histoire de France, XII (1875), 86–94, 181–190, 199–207, 232–240.

BONDAM, A., De Ortensche Verwikkelingen. 's–Bosch, 1886.

BOS, P. G., Het Groningensche Gild en Stapelrecht tot de Reductie in 1594. Groningen, 1904.

BOURQUELOT, F., Études sur les Foires de Champagne, Mémoires presentés par divers Savants à l'Académie des Inscriptions et Belles Lettres, 2d Ser., Antiquités de la France, Vol. V (in two parts). Paris, 1865.

BRANDEN DE REETH, F. VANDEN, "Recherches sur l'Origine de la Famille des Berthouts," Mémoires Couronnés et Mémoires des Savants étrangers, Académie Royale de Belgique, Vol. XVII (1845).

BRASSART, F., "Coup d'Oeuil sur quelques anciennes Seigneuries. IV. Arleux, Hamel, et L'Écluse," Souvenirs de la Flandre Wallone, 2d Ser., VII, 79–93. Douai, 1887.

BROSIEN, H., "Heinrich VII als Graf von Luxemburg," Forschungen zur Deutschen Geschichte, XV (1875), 473–511.

BRUGMANS, H., EN PETERS, C. H., Oud-Nederlandsche Steden, 3 Vols. Leiden, 1909–1911.

BRUYSSEL, W. VAN, Histoire du Commerce et de la Marine de Belgique, 3 Vols. Bruxelles, 1861–1865.

BUCHON, A., "Antiquités de Valenciennes et Histoire de Jean Bernier," Archives Historiques et Littéraires du Nord de la France et du Midi de la Belgique, New Ser., I, 238–267. Valenciennes, 1837.

BUITENRUST HETTEMA, E., EN TELTING, Een Bezoek aan eene Nederlandsche Stad in de 14de Eeuw. 's-Gravenhage, 1906.

BUSSCHE, E. VANDEN, Une Complainte ecclésiastique au Duc de Brabant et au Comte de Hainaut. Document inédit du XIVe Siècle, BCRH, 4th Ser., XIII (1886), 109–125.

BUSSCHER, E. DE, "Correspondance," Messager des Sciences et des Arts Historiques (1864), pp. 160–167.

CARLIER, J. J., "Robert de Cassel, Seigneur de Dunkerque, de Cassel, Nieppe, Warneton, Gravelines, Bourbourg," Annales du Comité Flamand de France, X (1870), 17–248.

CAUCHIE, A., "Rapport sur les Chroniques du Brabant," BCRH, 69 (1900), XXXVII–XCII.

CHROUST, A., Beiträge zur Geschichte Ludwigs der Baier und seiner Zeit, Vol. I, Die Römerfahrt (1327–1329). Gotha, 1897.

COLINS, P., Histoire des Choses les plus Mémorables. Tournay, 1643.

CORDAY, J., Les Comtes de Savoie et les Rois de France pendant la Guerre de Cent Ans (1329–1391), Bibliothèque de l'École des Hautes Études, fascicule 189. Paris, 1911.

CORNELISSEN, N., De l'Origine, des Progrès et de la Décadance des Chambres de Rhetorique establis en Flandre, avec une Notice Historique sur Jacques van Artevelde. Gand, 1812.

―― "Discours prononcé le 2 Juillet, 1845, Jour de l'Inauguration sollenelle du Buste colossal en Bronze de J. van Artevelde," Messager des Sciences et des Arts Historiques (1845).

COSTER, H. R., De Kroniek van Johannes de Beka, haar Bronnen en haar eerste Redactie. Utrecht, 1914.

COVILLE, A., "Les prèmiers Valois. La Guerre de Cent Ans (1338 à 1422)," E. Lavisse, Histoire de France, Vol. IV, Part I.

CUNNINGHAM, W., "The Commercial Policy of Edward III," Transactions of the Royal Historical Society, New Ser., Vol. IV (1899).

―― The Growth of English Industry and Commerce during the Early and Middle Ages, 5th ed., 2 Vols. Cambridge, 1910.

DARIS, J., Histoire de l'Éveché et de la Principauté de Liège, 10 Vols. Liège, 1868–1890.

DARMSTETER, M., Froissart. Paris, 1894.

DAUMET, G., Étude sur l'Alliance de la France et de la Castile au XIVe et au XVe Siècles, Bibliothèque de l'École des Hautes Études, fascicule 118. Paris, 1898.

DAVID, J., Geschiedenis der Stad en de Heerlykheid van Mechelen. Leuven 1854.

DELEWARDE, M., Histoire Générale du Hainaut, 6 Vols. Mons, 1718–1722.

DENIFLE, R. P. H., La Désolation des Églises, Monastères, et Hôpitaux en France pendant la Guerre de Cent Ans, 2 Vols. Paris, 1899.

DÉPREZ, E., Études de Diplomatique Anglaise de l'Avènement d'Edward I à Henri VII (1272–1485). Paris, 1908.

―― Les Préliminaires de la Guerre de Cent Ans. La Papauté, la France, et l'Angleterre, 1328–1342, Bibliothèque des Écoles Françaises d'Athènes et de Rome, fascicule 68. Paris, 1902.

DES MAREZ, G., Étude sur la Propriété Foncière dans les Villes du Moyen Âge et Spécialement en Flandre. Gand, 1898.

―― L'Organisation du Travail à Bruxelles au XVe Siècle, Mémoires Couronnés et Autres Mémoires, Académie Royale de Belgique, Vol. LXV. Bruxelles, 1903–1904.

―― "Les Lettres sociales en Flandres au Moyen Âge," Revue de l'Université de Bruxelles, V (1900), 649–663, 781–798.

DESPARS, N., Cronycke van den Lande ende Graefscepe van Vlaenderen, 4 Vols. Brugge, 1837.

DIERICX, C. L., Appendice aux Mémoires sur la Ville de Gand. Gand, 1816.

―― Mémoires sur la Ville de Gand, 2 Vols. Gand, 1814.

DIERCXENS, J. C., Antverpia Christo nascens et crescens seu Acta Ecclesiam Antverpiensem ejusque Apostolos ac Viros Pietate conspicuos concernentia usque ad seculum XVIII. . . . 7 Vols. Antverpia, 1773.

DIFEREE, H. C., De Geschiedenis van de Nederlandschen Handel tot den Val der Republiek. Amsterdam, 1908.

DILLEN, J. G. VAN, Het Economische Karakter der Middeleeuwsche Stad. Amsterdam, 1914.

DOBNER, R., Die Auseinandersetzung zwischen Ludwig IV dem Bayer und Friedrich dem Schönen von Oesterreich im Jahre 1325. Göttingen, 1875.

DOMINICUS, A., Baldwin von Lützelburg, Erzbischof und Kurfürst von Trier. Ein Zeitbilde der ersten Hälfte des vierzehnten Jahrhunderts. Coblentz, 1862.

DUFAYARD, C., "La Réaction féodale sous les Fils de Philippe le Bel," Revue Historique, LIV (1894), 241–272, and LV (1895), 241–290.

DUFOURMANTELLE, CH., La Marine militaire en France au Commencement de la Guerre de Cent Ans. Paris, 1878.

DUNN-PATTISON, P. P., The Black Prince. New York, 1910.

DUREAU DE LA MALLE, "Document statistique inédit du XIVe Siècle," *BEC*, II (1840–1841), 169–176.

DUVIVIER, C., La Querelle des d'Avesnes et des Dampierre jusqu'à la Mort de Jean d'Avesnes (1257), 2 Vols. Bruxelles, 1894.

ERNST, S. P., Histoire du Limbourg, suivie de celles des Comtes de Daelhem et Fauquemont, des Annales de l'Abbaye du Rolduc, 6 Vols. Liège, 1837–1852.

—— Hierarchia Catholica Medii Aevi, 3 Vols. Münster, 1898.

ESPINAS, G., "Jehan Boine Broke, Bourgeois et Drapier Douaisien," Vierteljahrschrift für Social- und Wirtschaftsgeschichte, Vol. II (1904).

—— La Draperie dans la Flandre Française au Moyen Âge, 2 Vols. Paris, 1923.

Esquisse Biographique sur Jacques d'Artevelde. Bruxelles, 1841.

EUBEL, K., "Der vom Grafen Wilhelm von Jülich am 30 Januari, 1332, dem Papste Johann XXII geleistete Treueid," Historisches Jahrbuch, XIX (1898), 568–570.

FABYAN, The New Chronicles of England and France in two Parts named by Himself Concordance of Histories . . . to which are added a Biographical and Literary Preface and an Index. London, 1811.

FAIRON, E., "Un Projet de Démembrement du Diocèse de Liège, proposé par les Brabançons en 1332–1336," *BCRH*, 78 (1909), 142–192.

FELTON, W., Die Bulle Ne Pretereat und die Reconcilations-Verhändlungen Ludwigs des Bayers mit dem Papste Johann XXII, 2 Vols. Trier, 1885–1887.

—— Forschungen zur Geschichte Ludwigs des Bayern. Neuss, 1900.

FINOT, J., Étude historique sur les Relations commerciales entre la France et la Flandre au Moyen Âge. Paris, 1894.

FISCHER, A., Ludwig IV der Baier in den Jahren 1314–1318. Nordhausen, 1852.

FOURNIER, P., " La Bulle ne Pretereat de Jean XXII, est-elle authentique? " Revue des Questions Historiques, Vol. XLV (1889).

—— Le Royaume d'Arles et de Vienne (1138–1378). Paris, 1891.

FRANKE, K., " Beiträge zur Geschichte Johanns II von Hennegau," Westdeutsche Zeitschrift für Geschichte und Kunst, Ergänzungsheft V, pp. 75–164. Trier, 1889.

FRIEDENBURG, W., Ludwig IV der Baier und Friedrich von Oesterreich von dem Vertrage zu Trausnitz bis zur Zusammenkunft in Innsbruck, 1325–1326. Gottingen, 1877.

FRUIN, R., Verspreide Geschriften, met Aanteekeningen, Toevoegsels, en Verbeteringen uit des Schrijvers Nalatenschap. Uitgegeven door P. J. Blok, P. L. Muller, en S. Muller Fzn., 11 Vols. 's-Gravenhage, 1900–1905.

GAILLARD, V., De Ambachten en Neringen van Brugge. Brugge, 1854.

—— " Études sur le Commerce de la Flandre au Moyen Âge. Les Foires," Messager des Sciences et des Arts Historiques (1851), pp. 193–220.

GAULE, J. DE, " Isabelle de Hainaut," Archives Historiques et Littéraires du Nord de la France et du Midi de la Belgique, New Ser., I, 338–355. Valenciennes, 1837.

—— " Ancienne Chronique en Langue vulgaire de Valenciennes," Archives Historiques et Littéraires du Nord de la France et du Midi de la Belgique, IV, 453–461. Valenciennes, 1834.

GÉNARD, F., Anvers à travers les Siècles, 2 Vols. Bruxelles, 1888–1892.

GEORGE, H. B., " The Archers at Crécy," English Historical Review, X (1895), 733–738.

Geschiedkundig Atlas van Nederland uitgegeven door de Commissie van het Geschiedkundig Atlas van Nederland door het Lid der Commissie, Dr. A. A. Beekman. 's-Gravenhage (*in progress*).

GILLIODTS VAN SEVEREN, L., Bruges anciennes et moderne, Notice historique et topographique sur cette Ville à l'Usage des Archéologues et des Touristes. Bruxelles, 1890.

GIMBERG, J., " Handel en Nijverheid te Zutfen in de Middeleeuwen," Bijdragen en Mededeelingen, Gelre, Vereeniging tot Beoeffening van Geldersche Geschiedenis, Oudheidkunde en Recht, XXV (1922), 3–34.

GLASSCHRÖDER, F. X., " Zu den Ausgleichsverhandlungen Ludwigs des Bayern mit Papst Benedict XII im Jahre 1336," Römische Quartalschrift, III (1889), 354–385.

GLAY, E. LE, Cameracensum Christianum. Lille, 1849.

—— Histoire des Comtes de Flandres jusqu' à l'Avènement de la Maison de Bourgogne, 2 Vols. Bruxelles, 1853.

GOETSHOUWERS, L , Les Métiers de Namur sous l'Ancien Régime. Contribution à l'Histoire sociale, Recueil de Travaux publiées par les Membres de Conférence d'Histoire et de Philologie, Universite de Louvain, fascicule 20. Louvain.

GOOR, T. VAN, Beschrijving der Stad en Lande van Breda. 's-Gravenhage, 1744.

GOSSES, I. H., De Vorming van het Graafschap Holland. 's-Gravenhage, 1915.

GRAS, N. S. B., The Early English Customs System. A Documentary Study of the Institutional and Economic History of the Customs from the Thirteenth to the Sixteenth Century. Cambridge (U. S. A.), 1915.

GYSELEER–THYS, O., Additions et Corrections à la Notice sur les Archives de la Ville de Malines de M. L. P. Gachard, Archiviste du Royaume de la Belgique inserée dans son Ouvrage institulée " Collection de Documents inédits concernant l'Histoire de la Belgique," tome second, page 30 et seqq. 3 Vols. Bruxelles, 1834.

—— Tijd-Reken-Kundige Beschrijving der Heerlijkheid van Mechelen, 3 Parts. Mechelen.

HABERKERN, E., " Der Kampf um Sizilien in dem Jahren, 1302–1337," Abhandlungen zur Mittleren und Neueren Geschichte, Heft 67 (1921).

HÄPKE, R., Brügges Entwicklung zum mittelalterlichen Weltmarkt, Abhandlungen zur Verkehrs- und Seegeschichte, Vol. I (1908).

HAERYNCK, H., Jan Boendale, ook geheten Jan de Clerc, zijn Leven, zijne Werken en zijn Tijd. Gent, 1888.

HALL, H., A History of the Customs Revenue in England from the Earliest Times to the Year 1827. Compiled Exclusively from the Original Authorities. London, 1892.

HANSEN, J., " Der Englische Staatskredit unter König Edouard III (1327–1377) und die Hansischen Kaufleute," Hansische Geschichtsblätter, XVI (1910), 323–415.

HARAEUS, F., Annales Ducum seu Principum Brabantiae, totiusque Belgii Tomi Tres. . . . 2 Vols. Antverpiae, 1623.

HARKEMA, H. G., " De Betrekkingen van het Bisdom Munster tot de Nederlanden, inzonderheid tot Gelderland tot aan de Vrede van Kleef, 18 April, 1666," Bijdragen en Mededeelingen, Gelre, Vereeniging tot Beoefening van Geldersche Geschiedenis, Oudheidkunde en Recht, VII (1904), 1–65.

HAUCH, A., Kirchengeschichte Deutschlands, 5 Vols. Leipzig, 1904–1910.

HAUTLE, C., " Beiträge zum Itinerar Kaiser Ludwigs des Bayern," Forschungen zur Deutschen Geschichte, XIII (1873), 507–532.

HEATON, H., The Yorkshire Woollen and Worsted Industries, from the Earliest Times up to the Industrial Revolution. Oxford, 1920.

HEINS, M., Gand contre Termonde. Épisode de l'Histoire industrielle de Flandre au XIVe Siècle, Annales du Cercle Archéologique de Termonde, 2d Ser., VI (1895), 67–108.

—— La Monnai et la Prix des Choses à Gand sous Jacques van Artevelde. Bruxelles, 1886.

HENNE, A., ET WAUTERS, A., Histoire de la Ville de Bruxelles, 3 Vols. Bruxelles, 1845.

HENNEBERT, F., Histoire Générale ecclésiastique et civile de la Ville et du Comté de Namur, 6 Vols. Liège, 1788–1791.

HERBOMEZ, A. D', "Comment le Quartier du Château fut réuni à la Cité de Tournai en 1289," Bulletin de la Société Historique et Littéraire de Tournai, XXIV, 49–88.

—— "Élections d'Evêques à Tournai à Moyen Âge (1274–1489)," Bulletin de la Société Historique et Littéraire de Tournai, XXIV, 17–46.

—— Histoire des Châtellains de Tournai et la Maison de Mortagne, 2 Vols. Tournai, 1895.

—— "Les Constitutions de Tournai sous Philippe de Valois," Nouvelle Revue Historique de Droit Français et Étranger, XXX (1906), 351–381, 453–476.

—— "Notes et Documents pour Servir à l'Histoire des Rois Fils de Philippe le Bel," BEC, LIX (1898), 497–532, 689–711.

—— "Philippe le Bel et les Tournaisiens," BCRH, 5th Ser., III (1893), 19–197.

—— "Un Épisode du Règne de Philippe le Bel, l'Annexion de Mortagne à la Flandre en 1314," Revue des Questions Historiques, LIII (1893), 27–55.

HEERINGA, K., Het oude Staveren. Groningen.

HENTZE, C., England, Frankreich, und König Adolf von Nassau, 1294–1298. Kiel, 1904.

HERENT, J., La Bataille de Mons-en-Pévèle (18 Août, 1304). Lille, 1904.

HIRSCHAUER, Les États d'Artois, 2 Vols. Paris, 1923.

HOFFMAN, K., Die Haltung des Erzbistums Kölns in der Kirchenpolitischen Kämpfen Ludwigs des Baiern. Bonn, 1910.

HOLINSHED, Chronicles of England, Scotland, and Ireland, 6 Vols. London, 1807.

HOUTTE, H., VAN, Essai sur la Civilisation Flamande au Commencement du XIIe Siècle d'après Galbert de Bruges. Louvain, 1898.

HUIZINGA, J., "De Opkomst van Haarlem," Bijdragen voor Vaderlandsche Geschiedenis en Oudheidkunde, 4th Ser., IV, 412–446, and V, 16–175.

—— Herfsttij der Middeleeuwen. Levens- en Gedachtenvormen der XIVe en XVe Eeuw in Frankrijk en de Nederlanden. Haarlem, 1918.

HUTTON, J., James and Philip van Artevelde. Two Episodes in the History of the Fourteenth Century. London, 1882.

HUYTTENS, J. F., Les Recherches sur les Corporations Gantoises, notamment sur celles des Tisserands et des Foulons. Gand, 1861.

JENCKES, A. L., Origin, Organization, and Location of the Staple of England. Philadelphia, 1908.

JOHANNESEN, R. T. H., " Une Princesse Namuroise sur le Trône de Norvège," Revue Belge de Philologie et d'Histoire, IV (1924), 323–325.

JONGE, J. C. DE, Verhandling over den Oorsprong der Hoeksche en Kabeljaauwsche Twisten. Leyden, 1817.

KEMPENEER, A., " Les Aliénations de Malines au XVe Siècle. Étude sur la Situation politique de la Seigneurie (1300–1357)," Bulletin du Cercle Archéologique, Littéraire, et Artistique de Malines, V (1905), 81–104.

KERN, F., Die Anfänge der Französischen Ausdehnungspolitik bis zum Jahr 1308. Tübingen, 1910.

—— " Frankreich und die Friesen," Mitteilungen des Instituts für Oesterreichischen Geschichtsforschung, XXXI (1910), 76–87.

KERVYN DE LETTENHOVE, " Du Jugement que l'Histoire doit porter sur Jacques van Artevelde," Bulletin de l'Académie Royale de Belgique, XXII, Part I (1856), 277–323.

—— " Du Vicariat Impériale conféré à Edouard III, Roi d'Angleterre," Annales de la Société d'Émulation pour l'Histoire et les Antiquités de la Flandre, 2d Ser., Vol. IX.

—— Froissart, Étude Littéraire sur le XIVme Siècle, 2 Vols. Bruxelles, 1857.

—— Histoire de Flandre, 7 Vols. Bruxelles, 1847–1855.

—— " Jacques van Artevelde," Messager des Sciences et des Arts historiques (1856), pp. 242–256.

—— " Le Procès de Robert d'Artois," Bulletin de l'Académie Royale de Sciences, des Arts, et des Beaux Arts de Belgique, 2d Ser., X (1860), 641–668, and XI (1861), 107–125.

—— " Les Relations de l'Angleterre et de la Flandre au XIVe Siècle," Bulletin de l'Académie Royale de Sciences, des Arts, et des Beaux Arts de Belgique, XXVIII (1869), 367–384.

KLAGES, J., Johann von Luxemburg und siene auf Böhmen gerichtete Heiratspolitiek. Prague, 1912.

KLUIT, A., Historia Critica Comitatus Hollandiae et Zeelandie, 4 Vols. Medioburgi, 1777–1782.

KNOTTE, E., Untersuchungen zur Chronologie von Schriften der Minoriten am Hofe Kaiser Ludwigs des Bayern. Wiesbaden, 1903.

KÖHLER, G., Die Entwicklung des Kriegswesens und der Kriegführung in der Ritterzeit, von der Mitte des XIten Jahrhunderts bis zu den Hussitenkriegen, 3 Vols. Breslau, 1886–1889.

KOHT, H., " Magnus Erikssons Giftermal med Blanche av Namur," Historisk Tidsskrift, 5th Ser., V (1924), 566–582.

Kretschmer, K., Historische Geographie von Mitteleuropa. München, 1904.

Krones, F. von, Handbuch der Geschichte Oesterreichs von der ältesten bis zur neuesten Zeit, mit besonderer Rücksicht auf Länder, Völkerkunde, und Kulturgeschichte, 5 Vols. Berlin, 1876–1879.

Kunze, K., Die politische Stellung der Niederrheinischen Fürsten in den Jahren 1314–1334. Göttingen, 1886.

—— "Das erste Jahrhundert der deutschen Hanse in England," Hansische Geschichtsblätter, XVIII (1889), 127–152.

Kurth, G., La Cité de Liège au Moyen Âge, 3 Vols. Bruxelles, 1909–1910.

Kuske, B., "Handel und Handelspolitik am Niederrhein vom 13.–16. Jahrhundert," Hansische Geschichtsblätter, XXXVI (1909), 301–327.

Lacabane, J., "De la Poudre à Canon et son Introduction en France," *BEC*, VI (1844), 28–57.

Laenen, J., "Les Lombards à Malines (1295–1457)," Bulletin du Cercle Archéologique, Littéraire, et Artistique de Malines, XV (1915), 23–47.

Laird Clowes, W., The Royal Navy: a History from the Earliest Times to the Present, 7 Vols. London, 1897–1903.

Lambin, J. J., "Revue succincte de quelques Comptes de la Ville d'Ypres," Messager des Sciences et des Arts Historiques, IV (1836), 181–192.

Lancelot, "Justification de la Conduit de Philippe de Valois dans le Procès de Robert d'Artois," Mémoires de Littérature tiréz des Registres de l'Académie Royale des Inscriptions et Belles Lettres, VIII, 669–681. Paris, 1733.

—— "Mémoires pour servir à l'Histoire de Robert d'Artois," Mémoires de Littérature tiréz des Registres de l'Académie Royale des Inscriptions et Belles Lettres, X, 571–663. Paris, 1736.

Lapsley, G. T., "Archbishop Stratford and the Parliamentary Crisis of 1341," English Historical Review, XXX (1915), 6–18, 193–215.

Lehleiter, A., Die Politik des Königs Johanns von Böhmen, 1330–1334. Bonn, 1908.

Lenz, P. A., Jacques van Artevelde considéré comme Homme politique. Gand, 1863.

—— "Jacques van Artevelde. Histoire des six premiers Mois de son Administration," Nouvelle Archives Historiques, I (1837), 261–310.

—— "Jean l'Aveugle, Roi de Bohème et Comte de Luxembourg, Marquis d'Arlon," Nouvelles Archives Historiques, II (1840), 222–322.

—— "La Bataille de Cassel," Nouvelle Archives Historiques, I (1837), 519–532.

—— "Notice sur l'Invention de la Poudre à Canon et des armes à Feu," Nouvelle Archives Historiques, I (1837), 589–609.

—— "Recherches sur l'État moral de la Flandre au XIVme Siècle," Nouvelles Archives Historiques, I (1837), 95–118.

LERBERGHE, L. VAN, EN RONSSE, J., Audenaerdsche Mengelingen (1201–1794), 4 Vols. Audenaarde, 1845–1852.

LEROUX, A., Recherches critiques sur les Relations politiques de France avec l'Allemagne de 1298–1378, Bibliothèque d'École des Hautes Études, fascicule 50. Paris, 1882.

LEWIS, G. R., The Stanneries. Boston (U. S. A.), 1908.

LINDNER, T., Deutsche Geschichte unter den Hapsburgern und Luxemburgern (1273–1437), 2 Vols. Stuttgart, 1890.

LIPSON, E., The History of the Woollen and Worsted Industries. London, 1921.

LIZERAND, G., "Philippe le Bel et l'Empire au Temps de Rodolphe de Hapsburg (1285–1291)," Revue Historique, CXLII (1923), 161–191.

LONGMAN, W., The Life and Times of Edward III, 2 Vols. London, 1869.

LORENZ, O., Genealogisches Handbuch der Europäischen Staatsgeschichte, 3d ed. Stuttgart, 1908.

LONGNON, A., "Limites de la Flandre et l'Étendue de la Domination Anglaise à l'Époque de la Mission de Jeanne d'Arc," Revue des Questions Historiques, XVIII (1875), 446–546.

LOSERTH, J., Geschichte des späteren Mittelalters von 1197 bis 1492. Munich, 1903.

Low, I. W., "The Considerations which Induced Edward III to Assume the Crown of France," Annual Report of the American Historical Association, I (1900), 537–583.

LUBIMENKO, I., Jean de Bretagne, Comte de Richmond, sa Vie et son Activité en Angleterre en Écosse et en France (1226–1334). Paris, 1908.

LUCAS, M., Der nationale Gedanke und die Kaiseridee in der historischen Literatur Deutschlands zur Zeit Kaiser Ludwigs des Bayern. Breslau, 1910.

LUCE, S., La France pendant la Guerre de Cent Ans, Épisodes historiques et Vie privée aux XIVᵉ et XVᵉ Siècles, 2d ed., 2 Vols. Paris, 1890–1893.

MACKINNON, J., The History of Edward the Third, 1327–1377. London, 1900.

MALDEGHEM, J. VAN, La Bataille de Staveren, 26 Septembre, 1345. Poèmes et Armoires des Chevaliers tués dans cette Journée. Bruxelles, 1869.

MARTIN, E., Histoire financière et économique de l'Angleterre (1066–1902), 2 Vols. Paris, 1912.

MATTHIAS, Beiträge zur Geschichte Ludwigs des Baier während seines Römerzuges. Halle, 1908.

MEERDINK, C. J. A., Roermond in de Middeleeuwen. Roermond, 1909.

MEILINK, P. A., De Nederlandsche Hanzesteden tot het laatste Kwartaal der 14ᵈᵉ Eeuw. 's-Gravenhage, 1912.

MEINSMA, K. O., De Zwarte Dood (1347–1352). Zutfen, 1924.

MERTENS, F. H., EN TORFS, K. L., Geschiedenis van Antwerpen sedert de Stichting der Stad tot onze Tijden, uitgegeven door de Rederijkkamer de Olyftak, 8 Vols. Antwerpen, 1845–1853.

MEYERE, J., Commentarii sive Annales Rerum Flandricarum Libri Septendecim. Antverpia, 1561.

MOELLER, R., Ludwig der Bayer und die Kurie im Kampf um das Reich. Berlin, 1914.

MOLHUYSEN, P. C., EN NANNINGA-UITERDIJK, J., Register van Charters en Bescheiden in het Oude Archief van Kampen (1251–1620), 6 Vols. Kampen, 1862–1887.

MOLLAT, G., Les Papes d'Avignon (1305–1378), 4th ed. Paris, 1924.

MORANVILLÉ, H., " Guillaume du Breuil et Robert d'Artois," *BEC*, XLVIII (1887), 641–650.

—— " La Trahison de Jean de Vervins," *BEC*, LIII (1892), 605–611.

—— " Notes de Statistique douanière sous Philippe VI de Valois," *BEC*, LXIV (1903), 567–576.

—— " Rapporte adressé à Philippe VI sur l'État des Finances," *BEC*, XLIII (1887), 380–395.

MORD, P., Les Lombards dans la Flandre Française et de Hainaut. Lille, 1908.

MOREAU, F. DE, " Un Évêque de Tournai au XIVe Siècle: Philippe d'Arbois," Revue Belge de Philologie et d'Histoire, II (1923), 23–60.

MOREL, O., La Grande Chancellerie Royale et l'Expédition des Lettres Royaux de l'Avènement de Philippe de Valois à la Fin du XIVe Siècle. Paris, 1900.

MORRIS, J. E., "The Archers at Crécy," English Historical Review, XII (1897), 427–436.

MÜLLER, K., Der Kampf Ludwigs des Baiern mit der Romischen Kurie, 2 Vols. Tübingen, 1879–1880.

MULLER, Fz. S., " De Elect Jan van Nassau," Je Maintiendrai, een Boek over Nassau en Oranje, I, 31–59. Leiden, 1906.

MUNCH, P. A., Pavelige Nuntiers Regnskabs- og Dagböger förte under Tiende- Opkraevningen i Norden (1282–1334). Christiania, 1864.

NANNINGA, J., Het Handelsverkeer der Oosterlingen door Holland in de dertiende Eeuw. Bussum, 1921.

NAPIER, H. A., Historical Notices of the Parishes of Swyncombe and Ewelne. Oxford, 1858.

NELIS, H., " L'Origine de Titre: ' Duc de Brabant,'" Revue des Bibliothèques et Archives de la Belgique, VI (1908), 145–161.

NEW, C. W., History of the Alien Priories in England to the Confiscation of Henry VIII. Chicago, 1916.

NICOLAS, N. H., A History of the Royal Navy from the Earliest Times to the Wars of the French Revolution, 2 Vols. London, 1847.

NIFFLE-ANCIAUX, E., " Guy II de Namur," Annales de la Société Archéologique de Namur, XVIII (1889), 231–288.

Noë, A., De Handel van Noord-Nederland op Engeland in de dertiende Eeuw. Amsterdam, 1919.

OMAN, C., History of the Art of War in the Middle Ages. London, 1898.

OUDEGHERST, P., Les Chroniques et Annales de Flandres. . . . Anvers, 1571.

PAULI, R., " Die Beziehungen Edwards III zu Kaiser Ludwig IV, 1338–1339," Quellen und Erörterungen zur Bayerischen und Deutschen Geschichte, Vol. VI (1862).

—— Geschichte Englands, 10 Vols. Hamburg, Gotha, 1834–1897.

—— Pictures of Old England. Cambridge, 1861.

PAUW, N. DE, " Artevelde, Bourgeois de Gand, dit ' le sage Homme,' " Grande Encyclopédie, Inventaire raisonné des Sciences, des Lettres, et des Arts, III, 1183–1187. Paris, 1887. Reprinted, *BCRH,* 82 (1913), 296–315.

—— " Artevelde Brasseur? " *BCRH,* 5th Ser., XVI (1896), 332–336.

—— " Audenaerde sous Artevelde, avec une de ses Lettres inédits et autres Pièces authentiques," Annales du Cercle Archéologique et Historique de Courtrai, 1916 (reprint).

—— " Catherine de Coster, Femme d'Artevelde et sa Famille," Biographie Nationale, V, 1–9. Bruxelles, 1875. Reprinted, *BCRH,* 82 (1913), 315–323.

—— " Note supplémentaire en Rapport sur le Document inédit relatif à Jacques van Artevelde," *BCRH,* 5th Ser., IX (1899), 197–201.

PERUZZI, S., Storia del Commercio e dei Banchieri di Firenze in tutto il Mondo conosciuto del 1200 al 1345. Firenze, 1868.

PETIT, E., Histoire des Ducs de Bourgogne de la Race Capetienne avec des Documents et des Pièces Justificatives, 9 Vols. Dijon, 1885–1905.

PETIT, L., Charles de Valois (1270–1325). Paris, 1900.

PIOT, C., " Une Enquête sur la Conduite des Fonctionnaires sous le Règne de Jean III, Duc de Brabant," *BCRH,* 4th Ser., IX (1881), 49–70.

PIRENNE, H., Belgian Democracy, its Early History. Translated by J. V. Saunders. Manchester, 1915.

—— Histoire de Belgique, Vol. I, 3d ed., and Vol. II, 2d ed. Bruxelles, 1909–1908.

—— " La Hansa flamande de Londres," Bulletin de l'Académie Royale de Belgique, 3d Ser., Vol. XXXVII, 2d Part (1899).

—— " L'ancienne Chronique de Flandre et la Chronographia Regum Francorum," *BCRH,* 5th Ser., VIII (1898), 199–208.

—— " La première Tentative faite pour faire reconnaître Édouard III comme roi de France (1328)," Annales de la Société d'Histoire et d'Archéologie de Gand, V (1902), 5–11.

—— "La Rijmkronijk van Vlaenderen et ses Sources," *BCRH,* 4th Ser., V (1888), 346–364.

—— "La Version Flamande et la Version Française de la Bataille Courtrai," *BCRH,* 4th Ser., XVII (1890), 11–50.

—— "Les Dénombrements de la Population d'Ypres au XVᵉ Siècle," Vierteljahrschrift für Sozial- und Wirtschaftsgeschichte, I (1903), 1–32.

—— "Les Sources de la Chroniques de Flandre jusqu'en 1342," Études d'Histoire du Moyen Âge dediés à Gabriel Monod, pp. 3–13. Paris, 1896.

—— Medieval Cities, their Origin, and the Revival of Trade. Princeton, 1925.

POELMAN, H. A., Geschiedenis van de Handel van Noord-Nederland Gedurende het Merovingische en Karolingische Tijdperk. 's-Gravenhage, 1908.

POLS, M. S., "Graaf Jan I van Holland," Bijdragen voor Vaderlandsche Geschiedenis en Oudheidkunde, 3d Ser., X (1899), 1–60 (second pagination).

PONTANUS, J. I., Historiae Gelricae Libri XIV. Hardervice Gelrorum, 1639.

PÖPPELMANN, L., "Johann von Böhmen in Italien, 1330–1333, Ein Beitrag zur Geschichte des XIV. Jahrhunderts," Archiv für Oesterreichischen Geschichte, XXXV (1866), 247–456.

POSTHUMUS, N. W., De Geschiedenis van de Leidsche Lakenindustrie. I. De Middeleeuwen. 's-Gravenhage, 1908.

POTTER, F. DE, "Geslachtsboom der Van Artevelden van de veertiende Eeuw vermoedilijk opgesteld door Willem, Zoon van Jacob van Artevelde," Mémoires Couronnés, Académie Royale de Belgique, Vol. XXII (1872).

—— Gent in den vroegsten Tijd tot Heden, 8 Vols. Gent, 1883–1901.

—— Jacob van Artevelde. Gent, 1864.

POULET, C., Guelfs et Gibelins, 2 Vols. Bruxelles, 1922.

POUTRAIN, Histoire de la Ville et Cité de Tournai, 2 Vols. La Haye, 1750.

PREGER, W., "Beiträge und Erörterungen zur Geschichte des Deutschen Reichs in den Jahren 1330–1334," Abhandlungen der Historischen Classe der Bayerischen Akademie, Vol. XV (1880).

—— "Der Kirchenpolitische Kampf unter Ludwig dem Baier und sein Einfluss auf die öffentliche Meinung in Deutschland," Abhandlungen der Historischen Classe der Bayerischen Akademie, Vol. XIV (1878).

—— "Die Politik des Papstes Johann XXII in Bezug auf Italien und Deutschland," Abhandlungen der Historischen Classe der Bayerischen Akademie, Vol. XVI (1886).

—— "Die Verträge Ludwigs des Baiern mit Friedrich dem Schönen in den Jahren 1325 und 1326. Mit J. H. Reinkens Auszügen aus Urkunden des Vatikanischen Archive von 1325–1324," Abhandlungen der Historischen Classe der Bayerischen Akademie, Vol. XVII (1886).

—— "Ueber die Anfänge des Kirchenpolitischen Kampfes unter Ludwig dem Baier. Mit Auszügen aus Urkunden des Vatikanischen Archivs von 1315–1324," Abhandlungen der Historischen Classe der Bayerischen Akademie, Vol. XV (1883).

PRIESACH, J., Die Reichspolitik des Erzbischofs Baldwin von Trier in den Jahren 1314 bis 1328. Tübingen, 1894.

PUYMAIGRE, le Comte de, "Une Campaigne de Jean de Luxembourg, Roi de Bohème," Revue des Questions Historiques, XLII (1887), 168–180.

PYFFEROEN, O., Une Émeute au Moyen Âge. Den Quaden Maendach-Le Mauvais Lundi. Conférence donnée le 17 Mars, 1887, à la Société Académique d'Histoire. Gand, 1888.

RAMAER, J. C., "Geographische Geschiedenis van Holland Bezuiden de Lek en Nieuwe Maas in de Middeleeuwen," Verhandelingen der Koninglijke Academie van Wetenschappen, Afdeeling Letterkunde, New Ser., Vol. II (1899), No. 3.

RAMSAY, J., A. History of the Revenues of the Kings of England, 1066–1399, 2 Vols. Oxford, 1925.

—— Genesis of Lancaster or the Three Reigns of Edward II, Edward III, and Richard II, 1307–1399, 2 Vols. Oxford, 1913.

REAL, J., Das ehemahlige Herzogtum Geldern. Seine Entstehung und seine Grenzen. Geldern, 1900.

REES, O. VAN, Geschiedenis der Staathuishoudkunde in Nederland tot het Einde der Achttiende Eeuw, 2 Vols. Utrecht, 1865–1868.

RIEZLER, S., Die literarische Widersacher der Päpste zur Zeit Ludwig des Bayers. Leipzig, 1874.

RIJSWIJK, B. VAN, Geschiedenis van het Dordsche Stapelrecht. 's-Gravenhage, 1900.

ROHRMANN, A., Die Procurationen Ludwigs des Baiern, Nordhausen. 1882.

RONCIÈRE, CH. DE LA, Histoire de la Marine Française, 4 Vols. Paris, 1899–1900.

ROOSEBOOM, M. P., The Scottish Staple in The Netherlands. An Account of the Trade Relations between Scotland and the Low Countries from 1292 till 1676, with a Calendar of Historical Documents. The Hague, 1910.

RUINEN, J., De Oudste Handelsbetrekkingen van Holland en Zeeland met Engeland. Amsterdam, 1919.

RUSSEL, E., "Societies of the Bardi and the Peruzzi and their Dealings with Edward III, 1327–1345," Finance and Trade under Edward III by Members of the History School, pp. 93–135. Manchester, 1918.

SAGHER, H. E. DE, "L'Immigration des Tisserands Flamands et Brabançons en Angleterre sous Édouard III," Mélanges d'Histoire offerts à Henri Pirenne, Vol. I. Bruxelles, 1926.

SANDERUS, A., Flandria Illustrata, 2d ed., 3 Vols. Hagae Comitum, 1732–1735.

SAPORI, A., La Campagne dei Bardi e dei Peruzzi in Inghilterre nei Secoli XIII e XIV. Firenze.

SCARGILL-BIRD, S., A Guide to the Principal Classes of Documents Preserved in the Public Record Office, 2d ed. London, 1896.

SCHANZ, G., Englische Handelspolitik gegen Ende des Mittelalters, 2 Vols. Leipzig, 1880–1881.

SCHEPERS, J. B., Groningen als Hansestad. Groningen, 1891.

SCHEVICHAVEN, H. D., J. VAN, "Bijdrage tot de Geschiedenis van het Handel van Gelre voor 1400 en zijn Verhouding tot de Hanze, Bijdragen en Mededeelingen, Gelre, Vereeniging tot Beoefening van Geldersche Geschiedenis, Oudheidkunde en Recht, XIII (1910), 1–148.

SCHMITZ, J., Sühnewahlfahrten im Mittelalter. Bonn, 1910.

SCHNEIDER, FR., Kaiser Heinrich VII, 3 Parts. Leipzig, 1924–1926.

SCHÖTTER, J., Johann, Graf von Luxemburg und König von Böhmen, 2 Vols. Luxemburg, 1865.

SCHRADER, J., "Isabella von Aragonien, Gemahlin Friedrichs des Schönen in Oesterreich," Abhandlungen zur Mittleren und Neueren Geschichte, Heft 58 (1915).

SCHULZE, F., Die Hanse und England von Eduards III bis auf Heinrichs VIII Zeit. Berlin, 1911.

SCHWALM, J., Die Landsfrieden in Deutschland unter Ludwig dem Baiern. Göttingen, 1889.

SIEVERS, G., Die politischen Beziehungen Kaiser Ludwigs des Baiern zu Frankreich in den Jahren 1314–1337. Berlin, 1896.

SLICHTENHORST, A. VAN, Geldersche Geschiedenissen van 't Begin af, vervolghd tot aen de Afzweeringh des Konincx van Spanien. Arnhem, 1654.

SMET, G., Henri Ier Duc de Brabant. Bruxelles, 1908.

SMIT, H. J., De Opkomst van den Handel van Amsterdam. Onderzoekingen naar de economische Ontwikkelingen der Stad tot 1441. Amsterdam, 1914.

STECHELE, W., "England und der Niederrhein bei Beginn der Regierung König Eduards III (1327–1377)," Westdeutsche Zeitschrift für Geschichte und Kunst, XXVII (1908), 98–151.

STEIN, W., Die Genossenschaft der Deutschen Kaufleute im Brügge in Flandern. Berlin, 1890.

STENZEL, A., Seegeschichte in ihren wichtigsten Abschnitten mit Berüchsicht auf der Seetaktik, 2 Vols. Hannover, 1909.

STORMANN, A., "Studien zur Geschichte des Königreichs Mallorka," Abhandlungen zur Mittlerer und Neueren Geschichte, Heft 66 (1918).

STOKVIS, A., Manuel d'Histoire, de Généalogie et de Chronologie de tous les États du Globe, 3 Vols. Leide, 1888–1893.

TEBBE, H., Kaiser Ludwig der Baier, Erzbischof, Heinrich III von Mainz und die Beschlüsse des Kurfürstentages von Rense im Jahre 1338. Breslau, 1920.

TERPSTRA, J. L. A., Nijmegen in de Middeleeuwen. Amsterdam, 1917.

TERRY, S., The Financing of the Hundred Years' War, 1337–1350. London, 1914.

TESCHENMACHER, W., Annales Cliviae, Juliae, Montium, Marcae, Westphalicae Ravensbergae, Geldriae, et Zutphiae. Frankfurt, 1712.

TESDORPF, W., Der Römerzug Ludwigs des Baiern (1327–1330). Königsberg, 1885.

THEISSEN, J., Centraal Gezag en Friesche Vrijheid. Groningen, 1907.

THEOBALD, T., Beiträge zur Geschichte Ludwigs des Baiern. Mannheim, 1897.

TIJDEMAN, H. W., Verhandelingen over de Hoeksche en Kabeljaauwsche Partijschappen. Leiden, 1805.

TOUT, T. F., France and England in the Middle Ages and Now. Manchester, 1922.

—— The History of England from the Accession of Henry III to the Death of Edward III (1216–1377). London, 1905.

—— The Place of Edward II in English History. Manchester, 1914.

UBAGHS, G. C., Korte Schets der Geschiedenis van het Land van Valkenburg. Leuven, 1858.

UEDING, P., Ludwig der Bayer und die Niederrheinischen Städte. Paderborn, 1904.

UNGER, W. S., Levensmiddelenvoorziening der Hollandsche Steden in de Middeleeuwen. Amsterdam, 1916.

UNWIN, G., "The Estates of Merchants, 1336–1365," Trade and Finance under Edward III, pp. 179–255. Manchester, 1913.

VANDENKINDERE, L., La Formation territorialle des Principautés Belges au Moyen Âge, 2 Vols. Bruxelles, 1902.

—— Le Siècle des Arteveldes. Études sur la Civilisation morale et politique de la Flandre et du Brabant, 2d ed. Bruxelles, 1907.

VANDENPEEREBOOM, A., "Recherches sur la Draperie et la Gilde ou Corporation des Drapiers d'Ypres (1282–1545)," Annales de la Société Historique, Archéologique, et Littéraire de la Ville d'Ypres et de l'ancienne West Flandre, VI (1876), 1–85.

—— Ypriana. Notices, Études, Notes, et Documents sur Ypres, 7 Vols. Bruges, 1878–1883.

VANDERLINDEN, H., Histoire de la Constitution de la Ville de Louvain. Gand, 1892.

—— Les Gildes marchandes dans les Pays Bas au Moyen Âge. Gand, 1896.

VARENBERGH, E., Histoire des Relations Diplomatiques entre le Comté de Flandre et de l'Angleterre au Moyen Âge. Bruxelles, 1874.

VIARD, J., "La France sous Philippe VI de Valois. État géographique et militaire," *BEC,* LIX (1896), 337–402.

—— "La Guerre de Flandre (1328)," *BEC,* LXXXIII (1923), 362–382.

—— "L'Hôtel de Philippe VI de Valois," *BEC,* LV (1894), 465–487, 598–626.

—— "L'Ostrevant. Enquêtes au Sujet de la Frontière Française sous Philippe VI de Valois," *BEC,* LXXXII (1921), 316–329.

—— "Philippe VI de Valois, la Succession au Trône," Le Moyen Âge, 2d Ser., XXIII (1921), 219–222.

—— "Un Chapitre administrative. Les Résources extraordinaires de la Royauté sous Philippe VI de Valois," Revue des Questions Historiques, XLIV (1888), 167–218.

VICKERS, K., England in the Later Middle Ages. London, 1926.

VOGEL, W., "Die Binnenfahrt durch Holland und Stift Utrecht vom 12. bis 14. Jahrhundert," Hansische Geschichtsblätter, XXXVI (1909), 12–36.

VOGT, E., Die Reichspolitik des Erzbischofs Baldwin von Trier in den Jahren 1328–1334. Gotha, 1901.

VOISIN, A., Examen critique des Historiens de Jacques van Artevelde. Gand, 1841.

VUYLSTEKE, J., Eenige Bijzonderheden over de Artevelden in de 14de Eeuw. Gent, 1872.

WALDEYER, K. J., Walram von Jülich, Erzbischof von Köln, und seine Reichspolitik, 2 Parts. Bonn, 1890–1891.

WALLER ZEPER, S., Jan van Henegouwen, Heer van Beaumont. Bijdrage tot de Geschiedenis der Nederlanden in de eerste Helft der veertiende Eeuw. 's-Gravenhage, 1914.

WAP, J., Geschiedenis van het Land en der Heeren van Cuyk. Utrecht, 1858.

WARD, G. F., "The Early History of the Merchant Staplers," English Historical Review, XXXIII (1918), pp. 297–319.

WAUTERS, A., Histoire des Environs de Bruxelles ou Description historique des Localités qui formèrent autrefois l'Ammanie de cette Ville, 3 Vols. Bruxelles, 1855.

—— Le Duc Jean Ier et le Brabant sous le Règne de ce Prince (1267–1294), Mémoires Couronnés et Autres Mémoires, Académie Royale de Belgique, Vol. XIII (1862).

—— "Le Hainaut pendant la Guerre du Comte Jean d'Avesnes contre la Ville de Valenciennes (1290–1297)," *BCRH,* 4th Ser., II (1875), 295–342.

WEBER, F., König Ludwig der Baier in der Lombardei. Heidelberg, 1867.

WECKERLIN, J. B., Le Drap "Escarlate" au Moyen Âge, Essai sur l'Etymologie et le signification du Mot Escarlate et Notes techniques sur la Fabrication de ce Drap de Laine au Moyen Âge. Lyon, 1905.

Werveke, N. van, Kulturgeschichte des Luxemburger Landes, 2 Vols. Luxemburg, 1923–1924.

Zaman, Exposition des Trois États du Pais et Comté de Flandres, scavoir du Clergé, de la Noblesse, et les Communes, 1711.

Zeller, B., Philippe VI et Robert d'Artois. Les Commencements de la Guerre de Cent Ans, 1328–1345. Paris, 1885.

Zeumer, K., " Ludwigs der Bayern Königswahl Gesetz " Licet Juris " vom 6 August, 1338. Mit einer Beilage: das Renser Weisthum vom 16 July, 1338," Neues Archiv der Gesellschaft für Aeltere Deutsche Geschichtskunde, XXX (1905), 85–114.

IV. BIBLIOGRAPHICAL AIDS

Balau, S., " Étude critique des Sources de l'Histoire du Pais de Liège au Moyen Âge," Mémoires Couronnés et Mémoires des Savants Étrangers, Vol. LXI (1901).

Dahlmann-Waitz, Quellenkunde der deutschen Geschichte, 8th ed., Leipzig.

Fris, V., Bibliographie de l'Histoire de Gand dépuis les Origines jusqu'à la Fin du XVᵉ Siècle, Publications Extraordinaires II et III, Société d'Histoire et d'Archéologie de Gand, 2 Vols. Gand, 1907–1921.

Gouda Quint, P., Grondslagen voor de Bibliographie van Gelderland, Werken uitgegeven door de Vereeniging Gelre, Vol. VIII (1910).

Gross, C., The Sources and Literature of English History from the Earliest Times to about 1485. London, 1900.

Hardy, T. D., Descriptive Catalogue Relating to the History of Great Britain and Ireland to the End of the Reign of Henry VIII, 3 Vols. London, 1862–1871.

Laar, A. van, Bibliographie van de Geschiedenis van de Stad Antwerpen, Brussel, 1927.

Molinier, A., Les Sources de l'Histoire de France, 6 Vols. Paris, 1901–1906.

Petit, L. D., Repertorium der Verhandelingen en Bijdragen betreffende de Geschiedenis des Vaderlands in Mengelwerken en Tijdschriften tot op 1900 verschenen. Leiden, 1905.

Pirenne, H., Bibliographie de l'Histoire de Belgique, 2d ed. Bruxelles, 1902.

Wind, S. de, Bibliotheek der Nederlandsche Geschiedschrijvers. Middelburg, 1831.

INDEX

furs, trade in, 2, 3.
Fygas, Alexander, 235.

G

gabellum, in the Cambrésis, 26, 33.
Gales, Griffyn de, 479 *n*.
Galleil, Marquet du, 565.
Galon, Thierry, 551 *n*.
Galoppe, tolls at, 105.
Gandavo, John de, 357.
— Simon de, 357.
Garde, Stephen de la, 191.
Gardin, Alard de, 542.
Gardyser, Lievin, 267.
Garonne, 1, 2.
Gascony, 2, 30, 56, 57, 62, 74, 76, 89, 90, 109, 116, 141, 209, 237, 421, 429, 519, 538, 551.
Gaucelinus, cardinal bishop of Albano, 461.
gavenne, see gabellum.
Gavere, 220.
— Gilles van, 517, 525.
— lady of, 441.
Geertruidenberg, 58 *n*, 59 *n*, 84, 90 *n*, 147, 234, 506, 507, 542.
Gelderland, province in the Netherlands, 24.
Geldrop, 104.
Gembloux, 13.
Gemenaith, Henry de, 208, 208 *n*.
gemincden, 377.
Gemmenich, 508.
Genappe, 13, 68, 162.
Genderen, 104, 162.
Gendt, William van, 502.
Geneva, count of, 209.
— Hugh de, 336.
Genoese, 422; trade with Low Countries, 3; galleys sought for Edward's navy, 271 *n*; crossbowmen at Armentières, 386.
Gent, town in Guelders, 22, 100.
Gerard, count of Juliers (1297–1329), 47, 50, 61, 166; arbitrates between duke of Brabant and count of Holland, 48, 103; influence in Rhineland and policy of, 59; policy toward papacy, 66.
— seignior of Pottes, 71.
— seignior of Roussy, 155, 173.

— seignior of Rasseghem, Lens, and Liedekerke, 148, 165.
— seignior of Voorne, burgrave of Zeeland, 129, 140, 248.
— son of Duke William of Juliers, 539; betrothed to Marguerite, daughter of Count Reginald of Guelders and of Zutfen, 126, 140, 501.
Gerard Duivelhuis, castle in Ghent, 274, 348, 484.
Gerlach, count of Nassau, 436, 437.
Germany, kingdom of, 51, 58, 73, 92, 94, 109, 122, 133, 181, 192, 193 *n*, 194, 195, 197, 223, 229, 230, 239, 253, 501, 503, 525, 542, 579, 586.
Gerulf, count in Friesia, 15.
Gette, 12, 118, 119.
Geule, 69.
Ghavere, Gilles van, 454.
Ghent (Gent, Gand), 5, 6, 8, 11, 32, 77 *n*, 79, 111, 134, 138, 142, 143, 143 *n*, 156, 159, 191, 203, 204, 222, 224, 226, 240, 257 *n*, 260–262, 264 *n*, 268, 270, 277, 283 *n*, 298, 318, 339–341, 348 *n*, 349 *n*, 350, 352, 356, 357, 358 *n*, 360 *n*, 363, 364 *n*, 371 *n*, 375, 376, 379, 386, 387, 394, 405 *n*, 409 *n*, 415, 417, 425, 429, 431, 432, 432 *n*, 433, 435, 438, 439, 439 *n*, 440, 441, 445–448, 450, 451, 453, 454, 456, 457 *n*, 461 *n*, 462, 472 *n*, 474, 478, 479, 481, 487, 488 *n*, 491, 491 *n*, 492, 509, 510, 512, 513, 516, 519, 520, 522, 522 *n*, 527 *n*, 529, 530, 538, 539 *n*, 548, 549 *n*, 550, 552, 552 *n*, 553–555, 558, 558 *n*, 562 *n*, 563–565, 567, 568, 577, 587, 588; rise of, 8; proletarian uprising of 1275, 10; appeals to Philip the Fair against Count Guy, 39; militia opposes rebels of Flanders, 85; sends militia against duke of Brabant, 150, 151 *n*; scabini seize English wool, 190; social and economic crisis (1336–37), 200; violence among craftsmen, 201; money distributed for relief of fullers and other craftsmen, 202; measures to repress violence, 202; seeks to enforce monopoly in manufacturing of cloth, 202; enforces rights upon

jects **of,** in Philippa's household, 94; possessions of King John of Bohemia in, 170; representatives meet at Male with envoys from three towns of Flanders, 221, 222; exposed to French king's hostility, 285, 334; ravaged by French (1339), 373; placed under interdict, 383; raided by subjects of Cambrai, 383; invaded by French (1340), 388, 391, 396; troops take part in siege of Tournai, 410; sends delegates to Dendermonde, 439; receiver of, 460; female succession in, 535; disputed succession in, 537, 547; *see* Hainault, John of, seignior of Beaumont, and William, count of Hainault, Holland and Zeeland, and seignior of Freisland.

Hainault, Isabella of, daughter of William, count of Hainault, Holland, and Zeeland, and seignior of Friesland, 123, 128, 168, 503, 584; betrothal to John of Brabant discussed, 92; betrothal to John of Brabant, 146; marriage to John of Brabant, 160, 582; projected marriage to Count Reginald of Guelders, 566.

Hainault, John of, seignior of Beaumont, 23, 48, 51, 57, 58 *n*, 65, 67 *n*, 70, 71, 72, 79, 80 *n*, 88, 121 *n*, 129, 180, 206, 284, 305 *n*, 308, 335 *n*, 337, 355, 356, 375, 392 *n*, 404, 421, 432, 439, 465 *n*, 466, 471, 479, 495, 497, 535, 536, 556, 557, 569, 571, 572, 581; arbitrates between Count Reginald of Guelders and his son, 49, 50; character of, 52; accompanies Queen Philippa to England, 56; commissioned by Edward to treat with Charles IV, 56; takes part in tournament at Condé, 57; takes part in Stanhope Park campaign, 64; escorts Philippa to England, 71; present at coronation of Philip VI, 80; part in battle of Cassel, 86; witnesses Edward perform homage to Philip, 90; crusade against Moslem in Spain, 98; receives pension from Edward,

110; joins coalition against duke of Brabant, 118; lends money to King John of Bohemia, 121; serves as guarantor for counts of Juliers and Guelders and archbishop of Cologne, 121; visits Paris, 126; guarantees sale of *advocatia* of Mechelen, 140; joins enemies of duke of Brabant, 152; military activity at 's-Hertogenrade, 154; seeks to intervene in quarrel between King Philip and Robert of Artois, 207; meets English negotiants at Mechelen, 246; relations to negotiations between Loon and Brabant, 249; arbitrates between duke of Brabant and bishop of Liège, 255; summoned to appear before Edward at Herck and in Hainault, 292, 298; serves as marshal in Edward's army, 328; conducts raids in the Cambrésis, 331; remains faithful to Edward when Count William deserts, 334; attacks Honnecourt, 335; lands ravaged by King Philip, 383; raid in Thiérache, 385; supports Count William in negotiations with duke of Brabant and scabini of Ghent, 388; orders Trazegnies beheaded, 392; joins Edward before Tournai, 409; position before walls of Tournai, 410; presses Edward to pay debts, 432; negotiates at Antoing as ally of Edward, 465; negotiates truce of Dendermonde in Edward's behalf, 466; sent as envoy by Edward to treat for truce with Philip, 468; serves as arbiter between count of Namur and duke of Brabant, 496; arbitrates between Count William of Hainault and city of Utrecht, 508; fails to support Edward's claim to part of Avesnes' patrimony, 536; supports claim of empress Margaret, 540; *rapprochement* with Philip VI, 540, 541; deserts Edward III, 550, 552, 591; joins army of Philip (1346), 569.

— Nicasius of, usher of Queen Philippa, 94 *n*.

Maaseyck, 211.

Maasland, 15.

Maastricht, 27, 28, 107, 132, 149, 154, 155, 158, 164, 168, 195, 212, 214, 254, 255, 498; importance of, 12; burghers of, 49; relations with Reginald, seignior of Valkenburg, 68, 91; tolls at, 105.

Mabenzone, Peter, 350, 444 *n,* 445, 490.

Maechelen, master, 272 *n.*

Magnaco, Gerald de, 537.

Magnus, king of Norway, 184, 197 *n.*

Mahaut, countess of Artois, 112, 113.

Mainz, see of, 93, 95.

Maire, 410.

Majorca, king of, 470.

— kingdom of, 2, 258, 327, 359, 380.

Malderen, 150.

Male, 221, 222 *n,* 267, 271, 276, 439, 440, 449, 565.

Malestroit, Truce of (1343), 479, 480, 494, 496, 500, 509, 519, 543, 555, 557, 562, 591.

Mallion, Stephen, 382, 470; deprived of dignities by the pope for supporting Edward, 330.

Man, Peter, 490.

Man, Peter de, 468, 474.

Manfred, 29.

Manny, Walter de, 180, 257, 259, 290, 337, 364 *n,* 381; accompanies Philippa to England, 71; appointed admiral of fleet north of the Thames, 236; sails with fleet to Low Countries, 241; attacks Cadzand, 242; conveys wool to Dordrecht, 243; returns to Orwell, 243; escorts Edward to Brabant, 283; surprises Thunl'Évêque, 331.

Mantua, 499.

Marche, 498.

Marchiennes, 412.

Marck, Conrad de la, seignior of Hurde, 298.

— counts of, 211.

— Engelbert de la, 228 *n; see* Engelbert, bishop of Liège.

Marcke, Louis, 155.

Marcoing, 332, 333, 333 *n.*

Marcoville, 170.

Marcq, 413.

Marfontaine, Thomas de, 79.

Margaret, daughter of Count William of Hainault, wife of Lewis the Bavarian, 55, 58, 74, 538 *n,* 547, 559, 591; betrothed to Lewis the Bavarian, 48; birth of son Lewis, 94, 95; claims Hainault, Holland, and Zeeland, 535; fears Edward's attack on Zeeland, 537, 538; supported in Low Countries by Philip VI against Luxemburgers, 539–541; arrival of eagerly awaited in Low Countries, 540; succession desired in Hainault, 541; leaves Bavaria, 542; arrives in Hainault, 542; arrives in Zeeland and Holland, 542, 543, 591; secures truce with bishop of Utrecht, 543; prepares to return to Bavaria, 557; appoints son William governor, 558; confers with Philippa at Ypres regarding titles in Hainault, Holland, Zeeland, 558, 559; attitude toward alliance of towns of Hainault with those of Brabant and Flanders, 568, 569.

— sister of Duke Reginald of Guelders, count of Zutfen, 501.

Marguerite, countess of Flanders (1244–80), 33–35.

— countess of Flanders, daughter of Philip V, 46.

— daughter of Duke Henry of Carinthia, 115.

— daughter of Duke John III of Lotharingia, Brabant, and Limburg, 518, 526, 543, 544, 549, 562, 577, 588; marriage to duke of Cornwall proposed, 257; betrothal to duke of Cornwall, 304, 305; negotiations for dispensation for marriage of, 431, 509; betrothed to Louis of Flanders, 510, 532; to secure Dendermonde as dowry, 533; marries Count Louis of Flanders, 578.

— daughter of Duke Reginald of Guelders, count of Zutfen, heiress of *advocatia* of Mechelen, 140, 149 *n,* ratifies sale of *advocatia,*

UNIVERSITY OF MICHIGAN STUDIES

HUMANISTIC SERIES

General Editors: JOHN G. WINTER AND EUGENE S. McCARTNEY

Size, 22.7 × 15.2 cm. 8°. Bound in Cloth.

VOL. I. ROMAN HISTORICAL SOURCES AND INSTITUTIONS. Edited by Henry A. Sanders. Pp. vii + 402. (*Out of print.*)

VOL. II. WORD FORMATION IN PROVENÇAL. By Edward L. Adams, University of Michigan. Pp. xvii + 607. $4.00. Postage extra.

VOL. III. LATIN PHILOLOGY. Edited by Clarence Linton Meader, University of Michigan. Pp. vii + 290. (*Out of print.*)

Parts Sold Separately in Paper Covers:

Part I. THE USE OF IDEM, IPSE, AND WORDS OF RELATED MEANING. By Clarence L. Meader. Pp. 1–112. $0.75.

Part II. A STUDY IN LATIN ABSTRACT SUBSTANTIVES. By Manson A. Stewart. Pp. 113–178. $0.40.

Part III. THE USE OF THE ADJECTIVE AS A SUBSTANTIVE IN THE DE RERUM NATURA OF LUCRETIUS. By Frederick T. Swan. Pp. 179–214. $0.40.

Part IV. AUTOBIOGRAPHIC ELEMENTS IN LATIN INSCRIPTIONS. By Henry H. Armstrong. Pp. 215–286. $0.40.

VOL. IV. ROMAN HISTORY AND MYTHOLOGY. Edited by Henry A. Sanders. Pp. viii + 427. (*Out of print.*)

Parts Sold Separately in Paper Covers:

Part I. STUDIES IN THE LIFE OF HELIOGABALUS. By Orma Fitch Butler, University of Michigan. Pp. 1–169. $1.25 net.

Part II. THE MYTH OF HERCULES AT ROME. By John G. Winter, University of Michigan. Pp. 171–273. $0.50 net.

Part III. ROMAN LAW STUDIES IN LIVY. By Alvin E. Evans. Pp. 275–354. $0.40 net.

Part IV. REMINISCENCES OF ENNIUS IN SILIUS ITALICUS. By Loura B. Woodruff. Pp. 355–424. $0.40 net.

VOL. V. SOURCES OF THE SYNOPTIC GOSPELS. By Rev. Dr. Carl S. Patton. Pp. xiii + 263. $1.30. Postage extra.

Size, 28 × 18.5 cm. 4to.

VOL. VI. ATHENIAN LEKYTHOI WITH OUTLINE DRAWING IN GLAZE VARNISH ON A WHITE GROUND. By Arthur Fairbanks. With 15 plates, and 57 illustrations in the text. Pp. viii + 371. $4.00. Postage extra.

VOL. VII. ATHENIAN LEKYTHOI WITH OUTLINE DRAWING IN MATT COLOR ON A WHITE GROUND, AND AN APPENDIX: ADDITIONAL LEKYTHOI WITH OUTLINE DRAWING IN GLAZE VARNISH ON A WHITE GROUND. By Arthur Fairbanks. With 41 plates. Pp. x + 275. $3.50. Postage extra.

VOL. VIII. THE OLD TESTAMENT MANUSCRIPTS IN THE FREER COLLECTION. By Henry A. Sanders. With 9 plates showing pages of the Manuscripts in facsimile. Pp. viii + 357. $3.50. Postage extra.

Parts Sold Separately in Paper Covers:

Part I. THE WASHINGTON MANUSCRIPT OF DEUTERONOMY AND JOSHUA. With 3 folding plates. Pp. vi + 104. $1.25. Postage extra.

Part II. THE WASHINGTON MANUSCRIPT OF THE PSALMS. With 1 single plate and 5 folding plates. Pp. viii + 105–349. $2.00. Postage extra.

VOL. IX. THE NEW TESTAMENT MANUSCRIPTS IN THE FREER COLLECTION. By Henry A. Sanders. With 8 plates showing pages of the Manuscripts in facsimile. Pp. x + 323. $3.50. Postage extra.

Parts Sold Separately in Paper Covers:

Part I. THE WASHINGTON MANUSCRIPT OF THE FOUR GOSPELS. With 5 plates. Pp. vii + 247. $2.00. Postage extra.

Part II. THE WASHINGTON MANUSCRIPT OF THE EPISTLES OF PAUL. With 3 plates. Pp. ix + 251–315. $1.25. Postage extra.

VOL. X. THE COPTIC MANUSCRIPTS IN THE FREER COLLECTION. By William H. Worrell. With 12 plates. Pp. xxvi + 396. $4.75. Postage extra.

Parts Sold Separately in Paper Covers:

Part I. THE COPTIC PSALTER. The Coptic text in the Sahidic Dialect, with an Introduction, and with 6 plates showing pages of the Manuscript and Fragments in facsimile. Pp. xxvi + 112. $2.00. Postage extra.

Part II. A HOMILY ON THE ARCHANGEL GABRIEL BY CELESTINUS, BISHOP OF ROME, AND A HOMILY ON THE VIRGIN BY THEOPHILUS, ARCHBISHOP OF ALEXANDRIA, FROM MANUSCRIPT FRAGMENTS IN THE FREER COLLECTION AND THE BRITISH MUSEUM. The Coptic Text with an Introduction and Translation, and with 6 plates showing pages of the Manuscripts in facsimile. Pp. 113–396. $2.50. Postage extra.

VOL. XI. CONTRIBUTIONS TO THE HISTORY OF SCIENCE.

Part I. ROBERT OF CHESTER'S LATIN TRANSLATION OF THE ALGEBRA OF AL-KHOWARIZMI. With an Introduction, Critical Notes, and an English Version. By Louis C. Karpinski, University of Michigan. With 4 plates showing pages of manuscripts in facsimile, and 25 diagrams in the text. Pp. vii + 164. $2.00. Postage extra.

Part II. THE PRODROMUS OF NICOLAUS STENO'S LATIN DISSERTATION CONCERNING A SOLID BODY ENCLOSED BY PROCESS OF NATURE WITHIN A SOLID. Translated into English by John G. Winter, University of Michigan, with a Foreword by Professor William H. Hobbs. With 7 plates. Pp. vii + 169–283. $1.30. Postage extra.

Vol. XII. STUDIES IN EAST CHRISTIAN AND ROMAN ART. By Charles R. Morey and Walter Dennison. With 67 plates (10 colored) and 91 illustrations in the text. Pp. xiii + 175. $4.75. Postage extra.

Parts Sold Separately:

Part I. EAST CHRISTIAN PAINTINGS IN THE FREER COLLECTION. By Charles R. Morey. With 13 plates (10 colored) and 34 illustrations in the text. Pp. xiii + 86. Bound in cloth. $2.50. Postage extra.

Part II. A GOLD TREASURE OF THE LATE ROMAN PERIOD. By Walter Dennison. With 54 plates and 57 illustrations in the text. Pp. 89–175. Bound in cloth. $2.50. Postage extra.

Vol. XIII. FRAGMENTS FROM THE CAIRO GENIZAH IN THE FREER COLLECTION. By Richard Gottheil, Columbia University, and William H. Worrell, University of Michigan. Text, with Translation and an Introduction. With 52 plates showing the different styles of writing in facsimile. Pp. xxxi + 273. Bound in cloth. $4.00. Postage extra.

Vol. XIV. TWO STUDIES IN LATER ROMAN AND BYZANTINE ADMINISTRATION. By Arthur E. R. Boak and James E. Dunlap, University of Michigan. Pp. x + 324. Bound in cloth. $2.25. Postage extra.

Parts Sold Separately in Paper Covers:

Part I. THE MASTER OF THE OFFICES IN THE LATER ROMAN AND BYZANTINE EMPIRES. By Arthur E. R. Boak. Pp. x + 160. $1.00. Postage extra.

Part II. THE OFFICE OF THE GRAND CHAMBERLAIN IN THE LATER ROMAN AND BYZANTINE EMPIRES. By James E. Dunlap. Pp. 164–324. $1.00. Postage extra.

Vol. XV. GREEK THEMES IN MODERN MUSICAL SETTINGS. By Albert A. Stanley, University of Michigan. With 10 plates. Pp. xxii + 385. $4.00. Postage extra.

Parts Sold Separately in Paper Covers:

Part I. INCIDENTAL MUSIC TO PERCY MACKAYE'S DRAMA OF SAPPHO AND PHAON. Pp. 1–68. $0.90 net.

Part II. MUSIC TO THE ALCESTIS OF EURIPIDES WITH ENGLISH TEXT. Pp. 71–120. $0.80 net.

Part III. MUSIC FOR THE IPHIGENIA AMONG THE TAURIANS BY EURIPIDES WITH GREEK TEXT. Pp. 123–214. $0.75 net.

Part IV. TWO FRAGMENTS OF ANCIENT GREEK MUSIC. Pp. 217–225. $0.30 net.

Part V. MUSIC TO CANTICA OF THE MENAECHMI OF PLAUTUS. Pp. 229–263. $0.60 net.

Part VI. ATTIS: A SYMPHONIC POEM. Pp. 265–384. $1.00 net.

Vol. XVI. NICOMACHUS OF GERASA: INTRODUCTION TO ARITHMETIC. Translated into English by Martin Luther D'Ooge, with Studies in Greek Arithmetic by Frank Egleston Robbins and Louis C. Karpinski. Pp. vii + 318. $3.50. Postage extra.

Orders should be addressed to The Librarian, University of Michigan, Ann Arbor, Michigan. Postage extra.

Vols. XVII, XVIII, XIX, XX. Royal Correspondence of the Assyrian Empire. Translated into English, with a transliteration of the text and a Commentary. By Leroy Waterman, University of Michigan. (*In press.*)

Vol. XXI. The Minor Prophets in the Freer Collection and the Berlin Fragment of Genesis. By Henry A. Sanders and Carl Schmidt. With 7 plates. Pp. xiii + 436. $3.50. Postage extra.

Vol. XXII. A Papyrus Codex of the Shepherd of Hermas. By Campbell Bonner, University of Michigan. (*In press.*)

Vol. XXIII. The Complete Commentary of Oecumenius on the Apocalypse: Now printed for the first time from Manuscripts at Messina, Rome, Salonika and Athos. By H. C. Hoskier. Pp. viii + 260. $4.00. Postage extra.

Vol. XXIV. Zenon Papyri in the University of Michigan Collection. By C. C. Edgar. (*In press.*)

FACSIMILES OF MANUSCRIPTS
Size, 40.5 × 35 cm.

Facsimile of the Washington Manuscript of Deuteronomy and Joshua in the Freer Collection. With an Introduction by Henry A. Sanders. Pp. x; 201 heliotype plates. The University of Michigan. Ann Arbor, Michigan, 1910.

Limited edition, distributed only to Libraries, under certain conditions. A list of Libraries containing this Facsimile is printed in *University of Michigan Studies, Humanistic Series*, Volume VIII, pp. 351–353.

Size, 34 × 26 cm.

Facsimile of the Washington Manuscript of the Four Gospels in the Freer Collection. With an Introduction by Henry A. Sanders. Pp. x; 372 heliotype plates and 2 colored plates. The University of Michigan. Ann Arbor, Michigan, 1912.

Limited edition, distributed only to Libraries, under certain conditions. A list of Libraries containing this Facsimile is printed in *University of Michigan Studies, Humanistic Series*, Volume IX, pp. 317–320.

Size, 30.5 × 40.6 cm.

Facsimile of the Washington Manuscript of the Minor Prophets in the Freer Collection and the Berlin Fragment of Genesis. With an Introduction by Henry A. Sanders. With 130 plates. The University of Michigan. Ann Arbor, Michigan, 1927.

Limited edition, distributed only to Libraries, under certain conditions. A list of Libraries containing this Facsimile is printed in *University of Michigan Studies, Humanistic Series*, Volume XXI, pp. 431–434.

SCIENTIFIC SERIES
Size, 28 × 18.5 cm.   4°. Bound in Cloth.

Vol. I. The Circulation and Sleep. By John F. Shepard, University of Michigan. Pp. ix + 83, with an Atlas of 63 plates, bound separately. Text and Atlas, $2.50. Postage extra.

Orders should be addressed to The Librarian, University of Michigan,
Ann Arbor, Michigan. Postage extra.

Vol. II. Studies on Divergent Series and Summability. By Walter B. Ford, University of Michigan. Pp. xi + 194. $2.50. Postage extra. Size, 16 × 23.6 cm.

Vol. III. The Geology of the Netherlands East Indies. By H. A. Brouwer. With 18 plates and 17 text figures. Pp. xii + 160. $3.00. Postage extra.

Vol. IV. The Glacial Anticyclones: The Poles of the Atmospheric Circulation. By William Herbert Hobbs. With 3 plates and 53 figures. Pp. xxiv + 198. $2.75. Postage extra.

MEMOIRS OF THE UNIVERSITY OF MICHIGAN MUSEUMS
Size, 26 × 17 cm. 4°. Bound in Cloth.

Vol. I. The Whip Snakes and Racers: Genera Masticophis and Coluber. By A. I. Ortenburger, University of Oklahoma. With 36 plates and 64 text figures. Pp. xviii. + 247. $6.00. Postage extra.

Vol. II. Description of the Skull of a New Form of Phytosaur, with Notes on the Characters of Described North American Phytosaurs. By E. C. Case, University of Michigan. With 7 plates and 24 text figures. Pp. vi + 56. $2.00. Postage extra.

UNIVERSITY OF MICHIGAN PUBLICATIONS

HUMANISTIC PAPERS

General Editor: EUGENE S. McCARTNEY

Size, 22.7 × 15.2 cm. 8°. Bound in Cloth.

The Life and Work of George Sylvester Morris. A Chapter in the History of American Thought in the Nineteenth Century. By Robert M. Wenley. Pp. xv + 332. $1.50. Postage extra.

Latin and Greek in American Education, with Symposia on the Value of Humanistic Studies, Revised Edition. Edited by Francis W. Kelsey. Pp. xiii + 360. $2.00. Postage extra.

The Menaechmi of Plautus. The Latin Text, with a Translation by Joseph H. Drake, University of Michigan. Pp. xi + 130. Paper covers. $0.60. Postage extra.

LANGUAGE AND LITERATURE

Vol. I. Studies in Shakespeare, Milton and Donne. By Members of the English Department of the University of Michigan. Pp. viii + 232. $2.50. Postage extra.

Vol. II. Elizabethan Proverb Lore in Lyly's 'Euphues' and in Pettie's 'Petite Pallace,' with Parallels from Shakespeare. By Morris P. Tilley. Pp. x + 461. $3.50. Postage extra.

VOL. III. THE SOCIAL MODE OF RESTORATION COMEDY. By Kathleen M. Lynch. Pp. x + 242. $2.50. Postage extra.

VOL. IV. STUART POLITICS IN CHAPMAN'S 'TRAGEDY OF CHABOT.' By Norma D. Solve. Pp. x + 176. Cloth. $2.50. Postage extra.

VOL. V. EL LIBRO DEL CAUALLERO ZIFAR: Part I, Text. By C. P. Wagner, University of Michigan. Pp. xviii + 532, with 9 plates. Cloth. $5.00. Postage extra.

HISTORY AND POLITICAL SCIENCE

(The first three volumes of this series were published as "Historical Studies," under the direction of the Department of History. Volumes IV and V were published without numbers.)

VOL. I. A HISTORY OF THE PRESIDENT'S CABINET. By Mary Louise Hinsdale. Pp. ix + 355. Cloth. $2.00. Postage extra.

VOL. II. ENGLISH RULE IN GASCONY, 1199–1259, WITH SPECIAL REFERENCE TO THE TOWNS. By Frank Burr Marsh. Pp. xi + 178. Cloth. $1.25. Postage extra.

VOL. III. THE COLOR LINE IN OHIO: A HISTORY OF RACE PREJUDICE IN A TYPICAL NORTHERN STATE. By Frank Uriah Quillan. Pp. xvi + 178. Cloth. $1.50. Postage extra.

VOL. IV. THE SENATE AND TREATIES, 1789–1817. THE DEVELOPMENT OF THE TREATY-MAKING FUNCTIONS OF THE UNITED STATES SENATE DURING THEIR FORMATIVE PERIOD. By Ralston Hayden, University of Michigan. Pp. xvi + 237. Cloth. $1.50. Postage extra.

VOL. V. WILLIAM PLUMER'S MEMORANDUM OF PROCEEDINGS IN THE UNITED STATES SENATE, 1803–1807. Edited by Everett Somerville Brown, University of Michigan. Pp. xi + 673. Cloth. $3.50. Postage extra.

VOL. VI. THE GRAIN SUPPLY OF ENGLAND DURING THE NAPOLEONIC PERIOD. By W. F. Galpin, Syracuse University. Pp. xi + 305. Cloth. $3.00. Postage extra.

VOL. VII. EIGHTEENTH CENTURY DOCUMENTS RELATING TO THE ROYAL FORESTS, THE SHERIFFS AND SMUGGLING: SELECTED FROM THE SHELBURNE MANUSCRIPTS IN THE WILLIAM L. CLEMENTS LIBRARY. By Arthur Lyon Cross, University of Michigan. With 4 plates. Pp. xviii + 328. $3.00. Postage extra.

VOL. VIII. THE LOW COUNTRIES AND THE HUNDRED YEARS' WAR, 1326–1347. By Henry S. Lucas, University of Washington. Pp. xviii + 696. Cloth. $4.00. Postage extra.

CONTRIBUTIONS FROM THE MUSEUM OF PALEONTOLOGY

VOL. I. THE STRATIGRAPHY AND FAUNA OF THE HACKBERRY STAGE OF THE UPPER DEVONIAN. By Carroll Lane Fenton and Mildred Adams Fenton. With 45 plates, 9 text figures and 1 map. Pp. xi + 260. Cloth. $2.75. Postage extra.

VOL. II. Consisting of 14 miscellaneous papers, published between July 10, 1924, and August 3, 1927. With 41 plates, 39 text figures and 1 map. Pp. ix + 240. Cloth. $3.00. Postage extra.

Orders should be addressed to The Librarian, University of Michigan,
Ann Arbor, Michigan. Postage extra.

Parts Sold Separately in Paper Covers:

Orders should be addressed to The Librarian, University of Michigan, Ann Arbor, Michigan. Postage extra.

UNIVERSITY OF MICHIGAN COLLECTIONS

CATALOGUE OF THE STEARNS COLLECTION OF MUSICAL INSTRUMENTS (Second edition). By Albert A. Stanley. With 40 plates. Pp. 276. $4.00.

PAPERS OF THE MICHIGAN ACADEMY OF SCIENCE, ARTS AND LETTERS

(Containing Papers submitted at Annual Meetings)

Editors: EUGENE S. McCARTNEY AND PETER OKKELBERG

Size, 24.2 × 16.5 cm. 8°. Bound in Cloth.

VOL. I (1921). With 38 plates, 1 text figure and 5 maps. Pp. xi + 424. $2.00. Postage extra.

VOL. II (1922). With 11 plates and 7 text figures. Pp. xi + 226. $2.00. Postage extra. Bound in paper, $1.50. Postage extra.

VOL. III (1923). With 26 plates, 15 text figures and 3 maps. Pp. xii + 473. $3.00. Bound in paper, $2.25. Postage extra.

VOL. IV (1924), PART I. With 27 plates, 22 text figures and 3 maps. Pp. xii + 631. $3.00. Bound in paper, $2.25. Postage extra.

VOL. IV (1924), PART II. A KEY TO THE SNAKES OF THE UNITED STATES, CANADA AND LOWER CALIFORNIA. By Frank N. Blanchard. With 78 text figures. Pp. xiii + 65. Cloth. $1.75. Postage extra.

VOL. V (1925). With 27 plates, 26 text figures and 1 map. Pp. xii + 479. $3.00. Bound in paper, $2.25. Postage extra.

VOL. VI (1926). (This volume contains papers in botany only.) With 28 plates, 4 text figures and 3 maps. Pp. xii + 406. $3.00. Bound in paper, $2.25. Postage extra.

VOL. VII (1926). (This volume does not contain papers in botany.) With 28 plates, 17 text figures and 7 maps. Pp. xii + 435. $3.00. Bound in paper, $2.25. Postage extra.

VOL. VIII (1927). With 32 plates, 35 text figures and 2 maps. Pp. xiv + 456. $3.00. Bound in paper, $2.25. Postage extra.

VOL. IX (1928). With 99 plates and 29 text figures. Pp. xiv + 597. $4.00. Bound in paper, $2.25. Postage extra.

CONTRIBUTIONS TO A MONOGRAPH ON THE GENUS HELIANTHUS. By E. E. Watson, Michigan State College. Reprinted from Vol. IX, pp. 305–476, with forty plates. Bound in Paper, $2.00.

VOL. X (1928). With 24 plates, 61 text figures and 13 maps. Pp. xvii + 620. $4.00. Bound in paper, $2.25. Postage extra.

Orders should be addressed to The Librarian, University of Michigan, Ann Arbor, Michigan. Postage extra.